# Supply Management

# Supply Management

**Eighth Edition**

**David N. Burt**
*Emeritus Professor of Supply Management*
*University of San Diego*

**Sheila D. Petcavage**
*Assistant Professor and Business Coordinator*
*Cuyahoga Community College*

**Richard L. Pinkerton**
*Emeritus Professor of Marketing and Logistics*
*California State University, Fresno*

McGraw-Hill
Irwin

Boston   Burr Ridge, IL   Dubuque, IA   New York   San Francisco   St. Louis
Bangkok   Bogotá   Caracas   Kuala Lumpur   Lisbon   London   Madrid   Mexico City
Milan   Montreal   New Delhi   Santiago   Seoul   Singapore   Sydney   Taipei   Toronto

McGraw-Hill
Irwin

SUPPLY MANAGEMENT

Published by McGraw-Hill/Irwin, a business unit of The McGraw-Hill Companies, Inc., 1221 Avenue of the Americas, New York, NY, 10020. Copyright © 2010, 2003, 1996, 1990, 1984, 1977, 1971, 1965 by The McGraw-Hill Companies, Inc. All rights reserved. No part of this publication may be reproduced or distributed in any form or by any means, or stored in a database or retrieval system, without the prior written consent of The McGraw-Hill Companies, Inc., including, but not limited to, in any network or other electronic storage or transmission, or broadcast for distance learning.

Some ancillaries, including electronic and print components, may not be available to customers outside the United States.

This book is printed on acid-free paper.

1 2 3 4 5 6 7 8 9 0 DOC/DOC 0 9

ISBN       978-0-07-338145-9
MHID      0-07-338145-4

Vice president and editor-in-chief: *Brent Gordon*
Editorial director: *Stewart Mattson*
Executive editor: *Richard T. Hercher, Jr.*
Editorial coordinator: *Christina Lane*
Project manager: *Kathryn D. Mikulic*
Full service project manager: *Michael Ryder, Macmillan Publishing Solutions*
Senior production supervisor: *Debra R. Sylvester*
Design coordinator: *Joanne Mennemeier*
Senior photo research coordinator: *Jeremy Cheshareck*
Media project manager: *Suresh Babu, Hurix Systems Pvt. Ltd.*
Cover design: *Brittany Skwierczynski*
Typeface: *10/12 Times New Roman*
Compositor: *Macmillan Publishing Solutions*
Printer: *R. R. Donnelley*


**Library of Congress Cataloging-in-Publication Data**

Supply management.—8th ed. / David N. Burt, Sheila D. Petcavage, Richard L. Pinkerton.
    p. cm.
    Includes index.
    Rev. ed. of: Purchasing and supply management. 6th ed., international ed. 1996.
    ISBN-13: 978-0-07-338145-9 (alk. paper)
    ISBN-10: 0-07-338145-4 (alk. paper)
    1. Industrial procurement.   2. Purchasing.   3. Materials management.   I. Burt, David N.
II. Petcavage, Sheila D.   III. Pinkerton, Richard L.   IV. Dobler, Donald W. Purchasing and supply management.
HD39.5.D62 2010
658.7—dc22                                                    2008048602


www.mhhe.com

# DEDICATION

This eighth edition of what originated in 1965 as the textbook *Purchasing and Materials Management: Text and Cases* is dedicated to founding coauthor Donald W. Dobler.

Dr. Dobler was truly one of the "grand old men" of purchasing and supply management.

After graduating from Colorado State University with a B.S. in Mechanical Engineering in 1950, Don began his professional life as an applications engineer with the Westinghouse Electric Corporation. Subsequently, he was Manager of Purchasing and Materials for the FMC Corporation.

Don then enrolled in the doctoral program at Stanford University's School of Business, where he collaborated with the late Lamar Lee, Jr., to create the first three editions of their increasingly popular and impactful textbook. He received a Ph.D. and an M.B.A. in Industrial Management from Stanford University in 1960.

After graduating, Dr. Dobler joined the faculties of Utah State University and then Dartmouth College. In 1966, Dr. Dobler accepted the Deanship of the School of Business at Colorado State University, where he was the school's longest serving Dean. In addition to his duties as Dean, Dr. Dobler found time for his wife, Elaine, and their children and his many civic contributions to the city of Fort Collins and the state of Colorado, consulting to manufacturing and service organizations in both the operations and the educational/training areas. In recognition of his distinguished service to the purchasing profession, Dr. Dobler was awarded the J. Shipman gold medal from the Institute for Supply Management.

Don joined the National Association of Purchasing Management (the forerunner of the Institute for Supply Management) in 1970. He built an impressive record of service: editor of the *Journal of Purchasing and Materials Management*, member of the P.M.A of Denver's Pro-D Committee, contributing author to the *C.P.M. Study Guide*, coeditor of the *Purchasing Handbook,* and Corporate Vice President for the National Association of Purchasing Management, where he was responsible for its certification and educational programs.

Clearly, Dr. Donald W. Dobler has had an incredible impact on his community, academia, corporate America, and the profession of procurement! He is truly a remarkable individual. The dedication of this edition is a modest recognition of Dr. Dobler's role as a thought leader and a gentleman. I am greatly honored to have been Don's coauthor on four editions of this text!

Respectfully,
David N. Burt, Ph. D.

# ABOUT THE AUTHORS

**David N. Burt** is Professor Emeritus of Supply Management at the University of San Diego. In 2008, Dr. Burt completed 50 years in the fields of Procurement, Supply Management and Value Network Management. He was recognized by the National Association of Purchasing Management as a NAPM Professor in 1992.

David created the University of San Diego's undergraduate and graduate programs in procurement during the 1980s. His greatest joy has been in finding meaningful employment for several hundreds of his students. He is founder and Director Emeritus of USD's Supply Chain Management Institute and of the Strategic Supply Management Forum, an annual meeting of innovative supply management professionals from North America, Europe and Australia. Under Dr. Burt's leadership, the University initiated a graduate hybrid resident/Internet program in 2002. This program grants a Master of Science in Supply Chain Management (MS SCM) on successful completion of the two year program. It transfers cutting-edge knowledge and practices to working professionals, while minimizing time away from the participant's workplace, develops leaders in supply chain management, and provides immediate payback to sponsoring firms. USD's MS in SCM is the only program endorsed by the Institute of Supply Management.

David's publications include seven books and numerous articles. His articles have appeared in *The Journal of Purchasing*, *Harvard Business Review*, *Thexis*, MIT's *Sloan Management Review*, *The Journal of Marketing Research* and *The California Management Review*.

David has been a buyer, negotiator, and a CPO (Chief Procurement Officer) of three organizations. He began his career as an Air Force Procurement Officer during the 1950s at a time when the Air Force was one of the few organizations in the world to recognize the critical importance of procurement. As a result, at the tender age of 22, he gained responsibilities and experience which few purchasing people in their thirties and forties enjoyed. His most productive years in the Air Force were as an Associate Professor of Logistics at the Air Force Institute of Technology's Graduate School of Logistics. During this assignment, he was an in-service consultant to the Air Force Director of Procurement and the program directors of the F-15 and B-1 programs. His final assignment in the Air Force found him Chief of Military Sales based in Canberra, Australia. Dr. Burt then began his civilian career as an Associate Professor of Acquisition Management at the Naval Postgraduate School in Monterey, California.

David studied under the great Lamar Lee, Jr. at Stanford and subsequently became co-author with the late Admiral Lee and Dr. Donald W. Dobler of earlier editions of this text (then known as *Purchasing and Materials Management: Text and Cases*).

In addition to his hands-on and academic experience, Dr. Burt has consulted with small, medium and large business including: IBM, Motorola, Lockheed, Avery Dennison, and Southern California Edison with the objective of upgrading their procurement operations to world-class status. Dr. Burt received his B.A. in Economics at the University of Colorado, M.S.I.A. at the University of Michigan and Ph.D. in Logistics from Stanford University.

**Sheila D. Petcavage**  is Assistant Professor and Business Coordinator at Cuyahoga Community College Western Campus in Cleveland, Ohio. She is the Coordinator of Business, Math and Technology Associate Degree Programs. Ms. Petcavage has a B.A. degree in Business administration with honors—Cum Laude and an M.B.A. from Baldwin Wallace College in Cleveland, Ohio.

She has over 15 years of purchasing and operations management experience in both manufacturing and distribution including Corporate Purchasing Manager, Premier Industrial Corporation, Senior buyer at Johnson & Johnson Corporation, Technicare Division and Material Planner/Buyer at the Tappan Corporation, Air Conditioning Division.

She is an active member of The Institute for Supply Management (ISM) and the Purchasing Management Association of Cleveland, Ohio, where she has served on the Board of Directors. She is a board member of the ISM Management Materials Group and serves as Editor of its News Publication. She holds the Lifetime Certified Purchasing Manager (C.P.M.) Designation. In 2003, she received the Ted R. Thompson Award for outstanding leadership in purchasing education from the Columbus, Ohio, Purchasing Management Association.

**Richard L. Pinkerton**  is Professor Emeritus of Marketing and Logistics at California State University, Fresno. He received his B.A. in Economics from the University of Michigan in Ann Arbor, his M.B.A. from Case Western Reserve in Cleveland, Ohio, and a Ph.D. in Marketing and Curriculum Studies from the University of Wisconsin, Madison. His Dissertation "A Curriculum for Purchasing," 1969, was sponsored by the National Association of Purchasing (NAPM) and is regarded as one of the key benchmark studies in the field of purchasing. A past Dean of the Graduate School of Administration at Capital University in Columbus, Ohio, he also served as Chair and Business Center Director of the Craig School of Business, California State University at Fresno, California. He is a Certified Purchasing Manager (C.P.M.) with a lifetime designation.

His industrial experience includes Market Research Analyst for the Harris Corporation of Melbourne, Florida, and Manager of Sales Development at the Webb-Triax Company of Cleveland, Ohio. His consulting experience includes, Pepsi-Cola, Quaker Oats, Perkin Elmer Laser Lamps, Con Edison of New York City, PG&E of San Francisco, IBM and the Oracle Corporation. For almost 40 years he has served The Institute for Supply Management (ISM) (NAPM) in various leadership roles at both the national and local levels, including Chair of the Academic Planning Committee. He was a long-time member of the *Purchasing Today* (now called *Inside Supply Management*) and *Info-Edge* Editorial Review Boards, Chair of the 1992 NAPM Research Symposium and the NAPM representative at the 1992 convention of the Chile Procurement Society in Santiago, Chile. At the local level, Professor Pinkerton was very active in the Columbus, Ohio, Cleveland, Ohio, Fresno, California and Silicon Valley Purchasing Associations and is a life member of the Northern California Purchasing Association.

His research on European Union Procurement Issues, Competitive Intelligence and Supply Chain Management is quoted in eight leading supply chain books. He has taught and consulted in Singapore, United Kingdom, Germany, Slovakia, Chile, Poland and Saudi Arabia.

He is co-author with David N. Burt of *A Purchasing Manager's Guide to Strategic Proactive Procurement*, published by the American Management Association. In 2002, he was given the Ted R. Thompson Purchasing Educator's Award by the NAPM—ISM Columbus, Ohio, Purchasing Association for his outstanding contribution to purchasing education. A retired Lt. Col. in the USAF Ready Reserves, he holds the Meritorious Service Medal for his many years of military service. He is an honorary member of the Purchasing Management Association of Cleveland, Ohio, his hometown, where he now lives.

# BRIEF CONTENTS

Foreword   xxix

Preface   xxxi

**PART** 1
## The Foundation   1

1. The Progression to Professional Supply Management   5
2. Organizational Issues   30
3. Supply Management: An Organization-Spanning Activity   49
4. A Portfolio of Relationships   63

**PART** 2
## The Requirements Process   89

5. New Product Development   93
6. Purchasing Descriptions and Specifications   118
7. Managing for Quality   141
8. The Procurement of Equipment   177
9. Purchasing Services   194

**PART** 3
## Sourcing: Sourcing Perception and Corporate Outsourcing   215

10. Outsourcing   217
11. Sourcing   240
12. Global Supply Management   273

PART 4
**Cost Management** 301

13. Total Cost of Ownership 303

14. Price and Cost Analysis 321

15. Methods of Compensation 352

16. Negotiation 371

PART 5
**Managing Contracts and Relationships** 397

17. Contract Formation and Legal Issues 399

18. Contract and Relationship Management 419

19. Ethics and Social Responsibilities 437

PART 6
**Materials Management** 459

20. Production and Inventory Control 461

21. Demand Management and Logistics 527

PART 7
**Implementing Value Network Management** 541

22. Implementing Value Network Management 543

Name Index 585

Subject Index 590

# CONTENTS

Foreword   xxix

Preface   xxxi

## PART 1
## The Foundation   1

Chapter **1**
## The Progression to Professional Supply Management   5

**Chapter Objectives**   5

**Vignette: Careers in Purchasing and Supply Management**   5

**The Five M's**   7

**Supply Management and the Bottom Line**   9

    *Increased Sales*   10

    *Lower Total Cost of Ownership*   11

**Supply Management and Return on Investment**   13

**The Progression to Strategic Supply Chain Management**   13

    *Supply Chains*   13

    *The Supply and Value Networks: The Next Phase of Supply Chain Management*   15

    *The Extended Enterprise*   17

**Implementing Strategic Supply Chain Management**   17

**The Roles of a Supply Management Professional**   17

**Concluding Remarks**   19

**Discussion Questions**   19

**Internet Exercise: Honda in America**   20

**Suggested Reading**   20

**Appendix: An Overview of the Mechanics of Supply Management**   21

Chapter **2**

# Organizational Issues   30

**Chapter Objectives**   30

**Vignette: A Strategic Shift for Xenia**   30

**Placement of Supply Management Within the Organization**   32

**Other Factors That Affect Organizational Structure**   33

*Classification of Responsibilities and Activities*   33

*Operational versus Strategic Responsibilities*   33

*Organizational Authority*   34

*e-Commerce*   36

**Organizational Structures**   36

*The Materials Management Organization*   36

*The Supply Chain Management Structure*   37

*Organizing with Cross-Functional Teams*   37

**Concluding Remarks**   38

**Discussion Questions**   38

**Internet Exercise: United Technologies: Company Highlights "Supply Management wins** *Purchasing* **medal of excellence"**   38

**Suggested Reading**   39

**Appendix: Benefits Resulting from Cross-Functional Teams**   39

Chapter **3**

# Supply Management: An Organization-Spanning Activity   49

**Chapter Objectives**   49

**Vignette: Troubles at Eagle Manufacturing Company**   49

**Supply Management's Relations with Other Departments**   51

*Supply Management and Engineering*   51

*Supply Management and Manufacturing and Operations*   53

*Supply Management and Quality*   54

*Supply Management and Marketing*   55

*Supply Management and Finance*   56

*Supply Management and Information Technology*   56

*Supply Management and Logistics*   58

*Supply Management and Accounts Payable*   58

*Supply Management and Lawyers*   59

**Supply Management in Nonmanufacturing Organizations**   59

**Supply Management in Government**   60

**Supply Management and the External Environment**   60
  *Business Relationships*   *60*
  *Monitoring the Supply Environment*   *60*
**Completing the Supply Chain Linkage: Supplier Integration with the Customer**   61
**Concluding Remarks**   61
**Discussion Questions**   62
**Internet Exercise: Reverse Auction Sites**   62
**Suggested Reading**   62


Chapter **4**
**A Portfolio of Relationships**   63
**Chapter Objectives**   63
**Vignette: A Supplier Alliance at Quaker Oats**   63
**A Transformation in Relationships**   65
**Three Types of Buyer-Supplier Relationships**   65
  *Transactional Relationships*   *66*
  *Collaborative and Alliance Relationships*   *68*
  *Collaborative Relationships*   *69*
  *Supply Alliances*   *70*
  *Which Relationship Is Appropriate?*   *72*
**The Supplier's Perspective**   73
**Questions to Be Addressed before Proceeding**   74
**Developing and Managing Collaborative and Alliance Relationships**   74
  *Situations in Which Alliances May Not be Appropriate*   *74*
**The Role of Power**   76
**A Portfolio Approach**   77
**New Skills and Attitudes Required**   77
**e-Commerce and the "Right" Type of Relationship**   78
**Relationships of the Future**   79
**Concluding Remarks**   80
**Discussion Questions**   80
**Internet Exercise: TradeAccess, Inc.**   81
**Suggested Reading**   81
**Appendix A: Institutional Trust**   81
**Appendix B: Supply Management in Action**   84

**PART** 2
**The Requirements Process**  89

Chapter **5**
**New Product Development**  93

**Chapter Objectives**  93
**Vignette: An Opportunity at Elite Electronics?**  93
**The Design Process**  97
   *The Investigation or Concept Formation Phase*  100
   *The Development Phase*  104
   *Value Engineering vis-à-vis Value Analysis*  106
   *The Production Phase*  110
**Engineering Change Management**  112
**How to Expand Supply Management's Contributions**  113
   *Design or Project Teams*  113
   *Materials Engineers*  114
   *Colocation*  114
**Supply Management Professionals Who Interface Successfully with Engineers**  114
**Concluding Remarks**  114
**End Notes**  115
**Discussion Questions**  115
**Internet Exercise: New Product Development: WIKIPEDIA**  116
**Suggested Reading**  116

Chapter **6**
**Purchasing Descriptions and Specifications**  118

**Chapter Objectives**  118
**Vignette: The Simple Sandwich**  118
**Specifications and Standardization**  119
**Purposes of Specifications**  120
   *Collaborative Development*  120
**Categories of Specifications**  121
   *Simple Specifications*  122
   *Complex Specifications*  125
   *Combination of Methods*  128
**Development of Specifications**  128
   *Organizational Approaches*  128
   *Supply Management Research*  130

*Writing Specifications    130*

*Common Specifications Problems    130*

**Standardization**    132

*History of Standardization    132*

*Types and Sources of Standards    133*

*Benefits of Standardization    134*

**Simplification**    135

**Developing a Standardization Program**    136

*Standards Team    137*

*Importance of Supply Management    137*

*Materials Catalog    137*

*Electronic Materials Catalogs    138*

**Concluding Remarks**    138

**Discussion Questions**    139

**Internet Exercise: About ANSI**    139

**Suggested Reading**    140

Chapter **7**

**Managing for Quality**    141

**Chapter Objectives**    141

**Vignette: The Quality Walk**    141

**Evolution of Quality Management**    143

**Philosophies of the Gurus**    144

*W. Edwards Deming    144*

*Philip Crosby    145*

*Masaaki Imai    145*

*Genechi Taguchi    145*

*Joseph Juran    146*

**Management Approaches**    146

*Total Quality Management    147*

*Continuous Improvement    148*

*Six Sigma    149*

*DMAIC Cycle    150*

*Quality Management System    152*

**Tools and Methodologies**    153

*Common Tools    153*

*Costs of Quality    155*

*Loss to Society    155*

*Process Capability Analysis    156*

*Statistical Process Control    159*

**Quality Movement Support**  162

*Organizations  162*

*Standards  162*

*Awards  164*

**Supply Management Issues**  165

*Requirements Development  165*

*Supplier Quality Analysis  166*

*Inspection Dependence  168*

*Supplier Development  172*

*Certification  172*

**Concluding Remarks**  174

**Discussion Questions**  174

**Internet Exercise: ISO: Latest News**  175

**Suggested Reading**  175


Chapter **8**

**The Procurement of Equipment**  177

**Chapter Objectives**  177

**Vignette: The Impact of Equipment Acquisition**  177

**The Nuances of Capital Equipment Procurement**  178

*Nonrecurring Purchases  178*

*Nature and Size of Expenditure  178*

**Building the Foundation**  179

*Identify the Need for a Procurement  179*

*Project Management  179*

*Selection of an Equipment Sourcing Team  179*

*Build and Train the Team  181*

**Identify Objectives and Estimate Costs**  181

*Identifying Objectives  181*

*Used Equipment  181*

*Spares  184*

*Estimating Acquisition Costs and the Total Cost of Ownership  184*

**Develop Specifications and Initiate Sourcing, Pricing,
and TCO Analysis**  184

*Develop Specifications  184*

*Sourcing  186*

*Develop Updated Acquisition Cost and TCO Estimates  186*

*Meet Budget and TCO Objectives?  187*

*Top Management Approval  187*

*Negotiation  187*

**Leased Equipment**   187

Types of Leases   187

Factors Favoring Leasing   189

Factors Weighing against Leasing   190

To Lease or to Buy?   190

**Initiate Lease or Contract**   191

**Post-Award Activities**   191

**Concluding Remarks**   191

**End Notes**   192

**Discussion Questions**   192

**Internet Exercise: Overview: Buying and Accounting for Capital Equipment**   192

**Suggested Reading**   193


Chapter **9**

**Purchasing Services**   194

**Chapter Objectives**   194

**Vignette: Lessons Learned**   194

**Hidden Opportunities**   196

**The Statement of Work**   196

Four Formats for Statements of Work   197

Planning the Statement of Work   197

Writing the Statement of Work   199

Artificial Intelligence   200

Tips on Writing an Effective S.O.W.   200

**Selecting Service Contractors**   201

Tips from a Professional   203

The Ideal Services Supplier   204

**Pricing Service Contracts**   204

Professional Services   205

Technical Services   205

Operating Services   206

Third-Party Contracts   206

So Your Services Contact Is about to Expire   206

**Contract Administration**   207

**Services Purchases and the Internet**   207

**Construction Services**   207

Conventional Method   207

Design and Build, Firm Agreed Price Method   209

Design and Build, Cost-Reimbursable Method   209

Building Team   209

*The Owner as a Contractor    209*

*Construction Purchasing Entails Unique Problems    210*

*Performance Contracting    211*

**Concluding Remarks**    211

**Discussion Questions**    212

**Internet Exercise: Procuring Services and Outsourcing Agreements**    212

**Suggested Reading**    213

**PART** 3
# Sourcing: Sourcing Perception and Corporate Outsourcing    215

Chapter **10**
# Outsourcing    217

**Chapter Objectives**    217

**Vignette: Making or Outsourcing Pump Housings**    217

**Outsourcing: A Growth Industry**    218

**Strategic Issues**    219

*Core Competencies    219*

*Supplier Dominance    220*

*The Creation of Strategic Vulnerabilities    220*

*The Dangers of Vertical Integration    220*

**Horizontal Integration**    220

*New Product Development and Outsourcing    221*

*Lean Manufacturing    221*

**Tactical Decisions**    222

**Factors Influencing Make-or-Buy Decisions**    223

*Cost Considerations    223*

*Control of Production and Quality    227*

*Business Process Outsourcing    228*

*Technology Risk and Maturity    229*

*Unreliable Suppliers    230*

*Suppliers' Specialized Knowledge and Research    230*

*Small-Volume Requirements    230*

*Limited Facilities    231*

*Workforce Stability    231*

*Multiple-Source Policy    232*

*Managerial Control Considerations    232*

*Procurement and Inventory Considerations    232*

**Netsourcing**   232

**The Volatile Nature of the Make-or-Buy Decision**   233

*Insourcing   233*

*Dangers of Outsourcing   234*

**Administration of Make-or-Buy Activities**   235

*Chief Resource Officer   235*

*Framework for Outsourcing   236*

*Executive-Level Involvement   236*

*The Special Disadvantages of Outsourcing Business Processes   237*

**Concluding Remarks**   237

**Discussion Questions**   238

**Internet Exercise: Business Process Outsourcing**   238

**Suggested Reading**   239


Chapter **11**

**Sourcing**   240

**Chapter Objectives**   240

**Supply Management and Strategy**   240

**The Strategic Sourcing Plan**   241

**Discovering Potential Suppliers**   241

**Evaluating Potential Suppliers**   244

**Selecting Suppliers**   247

*Bidding versus Negotiation   247*

*Reverse Auctions   249*

*Two-Step Bidding/Negotiation   249*

*The Solicitation   250*

*Weighted-Factor Analysis   250*

*Responsibility for Source Selection   252*

**Developing Suppliers**   252

**Managing Suppliers**   252

**Additional Strategic Issues**   253

*Early Supplier Involvement   253*

*Supply Base Reduction   253*

*Single versus Multiple Sourcing   254*

*Share of Supplier's Capacity   255*

*Local, National, and International Sourcing   256*

*Manufacturer or Distributor?   257*

*"Green" Supply Management   258*

*Minority- and Women-Owned Business Enterprises   258*

*Ethical Considerations   259*

*Reciprocity   259*

*Consortium Purchasing and Group Buying   259*

**Concluding Remarks**   261

**Discussion Questions**   261

**Internet Exercise: The Supplier Selection Process**   262

**Suggested Reading**   262

**Appendix A: Illustrative Plant Survey**   263

**Appendix B: Financial Statement Analysis**   268

**Appendix C: Planning a Facility Visit**   270

Chapter **12**

## Global Supply Management   273

**Chapter Objectives**   273

**Vignette: Sopraffino Goes Global**   273

**Global Management Perspective**   275

*Future of Global Supply Management   275*

*Stages to Global Supply Management   276*

*Reasons for Global Sourcing   276*

*Potential Problems   277*

*Questions before Going Global   279*

**Supply Channels**   279

*Global Trade Intermediaries   280*

*International Procurement Offices   281*

**Direct Suppliers**   282

*Eliminating Intermediaries   282*

*Identifying Direct Suppliers   282*

*Qualifying Direct Suppliers   283*

*Preparing for Direct Relations   284*

*The Initial Meeting   286*

**Currency and Payment Issues**   286

*Exchange Rates   286*

*Payments   287*

**Countertrade**   288

*Supply Management's Role   289*

*Creative Countertrade   290*

**Political and Economic Alliances**   290

*European Union   290*

*North American Free Trade Agreement   293*

*Mercosur   293*

*Association of Southeast Asian Nations  294*
*Asia Pacific Economic Cooperation  294*
**Concluding Remarks**  294
**Discussion Questions**  295
**Internet Exercise: One Red Paper Clip**  295
**Suggested Reading**  296
**Appendix: Currency Risk**  296

# PART 4
# Cost Management  301

Chapter **13**

# Total Cost of Ownership  303

**Chapter Objectives**  303
**Vignette: Purchase Price: Just *One* Component of Cost**  303
**The Three Components of Total Cost**  304
*Acquisition Costs  304*
*Ownership Costs  306*
*Post-Ownership Costs  309*
**TCO, Net Present Value Analysis, and Estimated Costs**  310
**The Importance of Total Cost of Ownership in Supply Management**  312
*Service Providers  313*
*Retail  314*
*Manufacturing  314*
*Supply Chains/Supply Networks  315*
**Concluding Remarks**  315
**Discussion Questions**  316
**Internet Exercise: Total Operating Costs**  316
**Suggested Reading**  317
**Appendix: Supply Management in Action**  317

Chapter **14**

# Price and Cost Analysis  321

**Chapter Objectives**  321
**Vignette: A Problem of Price**  321
**General Economic Considerations**  322
*Conditions of Competition  322*
*Variable-Margin Pricing  324*
*Product Differentiation  325*

*Six Categories of Cost*   *326*

*Regulation by Competition*   *328*

**Price Analysis**   330

*Competitive Price Proposals*   *330*

*Regulated, Catalog, and Market Prices*   *330*

*Internet/e-Commerce II*   *331*

*Historical Prices*   *331*

*Independent Cost Estimates*   *331*

**Cost Analysis**   332

*Cost Analysis Defined*   *332*

*Capabilities of Management*   *332*

*Efficiency of Labor*   *333*

*Amount and Quality of Subcontracting*   *333*

*Plant Capacity*   *333*

**Sources of Cost Data**   334

*Potential Suppliers*   *334*

*Supply Partners*   *334*

*Cost Models*   *334*

**Direct Costs**   334

*Direct Labor*   *336*

*Direct Materials*   *337*

**Tooling Costs**   337

**Learning Curves**   337

*The Cumulative Curve and the Unit Curve*   *337*

*Target Cost Estimation*   *338*

**Indirect Costs**   341

*Engineering Overhead*   *341*

*Material Overhead*   *341*

*Manufacturing Overhead*   *341*

*General and Administrative*   *341*

*Selling*   *341*

*Recovering Indirect Costs*   *342*

**Activity Based Costing**   342

**Target Costing**   343

**Profit**   343

**Concluding Remarks**   345

**Discussion Questions**   345

**Internet Exercise: Defining the New Oligopolies**   346

**Suggested Reading**   346

**Appendix A: Application of Learning Curves**   347

**Appendix B: Discounts**   349

Chapter **15**

# Methods of Compensation 352

**Chapter Objectives** 352
**Vignette: R&D Contract Development at PNS** 352
**Introduction to Compensation Arrangements** 354
    *Observation* 356
**Contract Cost Risk Appraisal** 356
    *Technical Risk* 356
    *Contract Schedule Risk* 357
**General Types of Contract Compensation Arrangements** 357
    *Fixed Price Contracts* 357
    *Incentive Contracts* 357
    *Cost-Type Contracts* 358
**Specific Types of Compensation Arrangements** 358
    *Firm Fixed Price Contracts* 358
    *Fixed Price with Economic Price Adjustment Contracts* 360
    *Fixed Price Redetermination Contracts* 361
    *Incentive Arrangements* 361
    *Fixed Price Incentive Fee* 363
    *Cost Plus Incentive Fee Arrangements* 364
    *Cost Plus Fixed Fee Arrangements* 365
    *Cost Plus Award Fee* 366
    *Cost without Fee* 366
    *Cost Sharing* 367
    *Time and Materials* 367
    *Letter Contracts and Letters of Intent* 367
**Considerations in Selecting the Method of Compensation** 368
**Concluding Remarks** 369
**Discussion Questions** 369
**Internet Exercise: NASA Procurement: Use of Award Fees for Achieving Program Outcomes Should Be Improved** 370
**Suggested Reading** 370

Chapter **16**

# Negotiation 371

**Chapter Objectives** 371
**Vignette: Negotiating for Gold** 371
**Objectives of Negotiation** 373
    *Quality* 373
    *Fair and Reasonable Price* 373
    *On-Time Performance* 373

*Control    373*

*Cooperation    374*

*Supplier Relationship Management    374*

**When to Negotiate**    374

**Supply Management's Role in Negotiation**    375

*The Supply Management Professional Acting Alone    375*

*The Supply Management Professional as the Negotiating Team Leader    376*

**The Negotiation Process**    377

*Preparation    377*

*Establishing Objectives    380*

*Identify the Desired Type of Relationship    381*

**Five Powerful Preparation Activities**    381

**Face-to-Face Discussions**    382

*Fact Finding    382*

*Recess    383*

*Narrowing the Differences    383*

*Hard Bargaining    383*

**Techniques**    384

*Universally Applicable Techniques    384*

*Transactional Techniques    386*

*Collaborative and Alliance Negotiating Techniques    388*

**The Debriefing: An Incredible Learning Opportunity**    389

**Documentation**    390

**Online Negotiation**    390

**Negotiating for Price**    392

*Price Analysis Negotiation    393*

*Cost Analysis Negotiation    394*

**Characteristics of a Successful Negotiator**    394

**Concluding Remarks**    395

**Discussion Questions**    395

**Internet Exercise: Reverse Auction Sites**    396

**Suggested Reading**    396

**PART** 5
## Managing Contracts and Relationships    397

Chapter **17**
## Contract Formation and Legal Issues    399

**Chapter Objectives**    399

**Vignette: Chrysler, LLC, versus Plastech Engineered Products Inc.**    399

**Litigation Prevention**    400

**Dispute Resolution**    401

*Negotiation    401*

*Mediation    401*

*Litigation    402*

*Arbitration    402*

*Courts    402*

**Development of Commercial Law**    402

*Electronic Contract Considerations: Cyberlaw    403*

*Attempts to Revise the UCC    404*

**Basic Legal Considerations**    404

*Status of an Agent    404*

*The Purchase Contract    405*

**Special Legal Considerations**    408

*Inspection Rights    408*

*Rights of Rejection    408*

*Title and Risk of Loss    409*

*Warranties    409*

*Evergreen Contracts    410*

*Order Cancellation and Breach of Contract    411*

*JIT Contracts    412*

*Honest Mistakes    413*

*Patent Infringement    413*

*Restraint of Trade Laws    414*

**International Considerations**    414

*Contracts for the International Sale of Goods    415*

*Foreign Corrupt Practices Act    415*

**Concluding Remarks**    416

**Discussion Questions**    417

**Internet Exercise: U.S. Bankruptcy Courts**    417

**Suggested Reading**    417

Chapter **18**

**Contract and Relationship Management**    419

**Chapter Objectives**    419

**Vignette: Managing Contract Performance**    419

**Need for Better Contract Management**    420

**Pre-Award Conference: The Stage Has Been Set**    420

**Monitoring and Controlling Project Progress**    421

*Operations Progress Reports    422*

*Gantt Charts    422*

*CPM and PERT  423*

*Closed Loop MRP Systems  424*

**Monitoring and Controlling Total Supplier Performance  424**

*Supplier Performance Evaluation  425*

**Motivation  427**

*Punishment  427*

*Rewards  428*

**Assistance  428**

*Transformational Training  428*

*Quality Audits and Supply System Reviews  428*

*Problem Solving  429*

**Collaboration  429**

*Managing the Relationship  429*

**Concluding Remarks  430**

**Discussion Questions  430**

**Internet Exercise: Reforming Project Management  431**

**Suggested Reading  431**

**Appendix A: Supplier Reporting Requirements for Unique Major Projects  431**

**Appendix B: How Critical Path Scheduling Works  432**

**Appendix C: Supplier Questionnaire  436**

Chapter **19**

## Ethics and Social Responsibilities  437

**Chapter Objectives  437**

**Vignette: A Question of Ethics?  437**

**Ethics in the Supply Management Context  439**

**Professional Supply Management Ethics  440**

**Principles and Standards of Ethical Supply Management Conduct  440**

*1. Perceived Impropriety  440*

*2. Conflict of Interest  441*

*3. Issues of Influence  441*

*4. Responsibilities to your Employer  442*

*5. Supplier and Customer Relationships  443*

*6. Sustainability and Social Responsibility  443*

*7. Confidential and Proprietary Information  443*

*8. Reciprocity  444*

*9. Applicable Laws, Regulations and Trade Agreements  445*

*10. Professional Competence  445*

*National and International Supply Management Conduct  446*

**Important Areas Requiring Amplification  447**

*Avoid Sharp Practices  447*

*Competitive Bidding    448*

*Negotiation    449*

*Samples    449*

*Treating Salespeople with Respect    449*

*Substandard Materials and Services    449*

*Gifts and Gratuities    450*

**Management Responsibilities**    452

*Written Standards    452*

*Ethics Training and Education    452*

*Departmental Environment    453*

*Miscellaneous Factors    453*

**Dealing with Gray Areas**    453

*The Four Way Test    454*

**Social Responsibilities**    454

**Concluding Remarks**    455

**Discussion Questions**    456

**Internet Exercise: Corporate Ethics**    456

**Suggested Reading**    456

**PART** 6

**Materials Management**    459

Chapter **20**

**Production and Inventory Control**    461

**Chapter Objectives**    461

**Vignette: Sales Forecasts: Fact or Fiction?**    462

**Part I: The Fundamentals of Production Planning**    462

**Modern Production Planning Systems**    463

*Aggregate Planning and Master Scheduling    464*

*Material Requirements Planning    466*

*Capacity Requirements Planning    470*

*Control of Production Activities    471*

*Two Management Considerations    472*

**Evolution of MRP and MRP II Systems**    473

*Impact on Purchasing and Supply Management    474*

**Just-in-Time Production Planning**    476

*A JIT Illustration    477*

*The Impact of JIT on Purchasing and the Supply Chain    479*

*ERP Systems    480*

*Conclusion    480*

**Part II: The Functions of Inventories** 480

**Definition of Inventories** 482

**Inventory Analysis** 482

    *Inventory Catalog* 482

    *ABC Analysis: The 80-20 Concept* 483

    *Dependent Demand and Independent Demand* 485

**Costs Associated with Inventories** 485

    *Carrying Costs* 485

    *Acquisition Costs* 487

    *Economic Order Quantity Concept* 488

    *Other Uses of the EOQ Concept* 490

    *The Weaknesses of the EOQ Formula* 491

**Types of Inventory Control Systems** 492

    *Cyclical or Fixed Order Interval System* 492

    *The Just-in-Time Approach* 493

    *Material Requirements Planning System* 494

    *Order Point or Fixed Order Quantity System* 495

**Concluding Remarks** 499

**Discussion Questions** 500

**Suggested Reading** 502

**Appendix: The Fundamentals of Inbound Transportation** 502

Chapter **21**

**Demand Management and Logistics** 527

**Chapter Objectives** 527

**Vignette: Circus Tents for MCC Logistics** 527

**The Key to Supply Chain Management** 528

    *The SCM Triangle* 529

    *Evolution to Strategic SCM* 529

**Strategic Demand Management** 530

    *The Bullwhip Effect* 532

    *Evolution of Strategic Demand* 533

    *Forecasting Demand* 534

    *Planning with Time Fences* 535

    *Implications for Supply Management* 536

**Strategic Logistics Management** 536

    *Logistics Defined* 536

    *The Role of Logistics in Supply Chain Management* 536

    *Eliminate the Warehouse, If Possible* 537

**Concluding Remarks** 537

**Discussion Questions**  538

**Internet Exercise: Infor SCM: Transportation and Logistics**  538

**Suggested Reading**  538

**PART** 7

# Implementing Value Network Management  541

Chapter **22**

# Implementing Value Network Management  543

**Chapter Objectives**  543

**Overview**  543

**Megatronics: Background**  544

*Vision Statement*  *544*

*Value Proposition*  *544*

**Leadership**  546

**Transformational Training**  554

**Transformational Planning**  555

*Cost*  *558*

*Quality*  *560*

*Technology*  *561*

*The New Product Development Cycle*  *561*

*Supplier Feedback*  *564*

*Social Responsibilities*  *564*

*Standardization*  *565*

*Value Engineering and Value Analysis*  *565*

*Organization and Staffing*  *565*

**Bringing the Troops Onside**  568

**More Initiatives**  571

**January 2012**  575

**Concluding Remarks**  575

**Discussion Questions**  576

**Suggested Reading**  576

**Appendix A: The Institute for Supply Management's R. Gene Richter Awards for Leadership and Innovation in Supply Management**  577

**Appendix B: At Rolls-Royce North America, an organizational shift is the driving force behind an innovative new journey to engage its supply chain**  580

**Name Index**  585

**Subject Index**  590

# FOREWORD

Great books always present great ideas and motivate the reader to understand, utilize and expand those great ideas to new venues. In this book, the authors create *Value Network Management* to take the dynamic Supply Chain Management process to a new and higher level. In my mind, *Value Network Management* is the appropriate name for the complexities of the new world of supply management, now and into the future.

Value Network Management embraces the new complex idea of collaborative supplier relationships where suppliers make real contributions to overall competitiveness, not only in cost, but also in design, lean manufacturing techniques, and minimal inventory levels throughout the network. We take 100 percent quality and 100 percent just-in-time delivery as accepted standards. Similarly, our major customers depend on us for input from our special areas of knowledge to create new models and new products. In many cases, Value Network Management represents a new collaborative model where core members of one network compete with other total value networks for market share as well as other value networks creating new products.

My experience in Purchasing began in the 1950s. At that time purchasing was totally tactical and nonstrategic. Even worse, the Purchasing function was decentralized plant by plant across the organization. Few, if any, purchasing managers held college degrees, and the purchasing function was seen as a back-room support operation. Purchasing leaders were not a part of senior management. The importance of value and spend analysis compared to revenue was minimized by the high level of vertical integration and the lack of knowledge-generating equipment such as copy machines, electric typewriters, and computers. The purchasing profession was years away from the Internet, cell phones or Blackberrys with global access on a 24/7 basis.

Contrast this to my most recent job where we had 2,324 people in supply management in 185 plants located in 42 countries buying $18 billion of goods and services for six diverse business units and with the spend representing almost 70 percent of revenue. All had at last an undergraduate degree, many had a Masters degree and several held the Ph.D. degree. Many were also specialists and leaders in their particular field. All of them had full access to the company's worldwide sophisticated systems from their personal computers. Today's Chief Procurement Officer (CPO) is a company officer and equal in every way to the other company officers and divisional presidents. The CPO has as much or more impact on the firm's success and survival than does any of his or her fellow executives.

This new idea of moving to Value Network Management takes the supply management network to new levels where all processes at all tiers communicate instantly, not just with items like schedules, quality, delivery and costs, but to a new integrated multi-directional relationship concerning difficult areas such as specifications, flexibility, risk management. Similarly, the complex problems of new designs, new model launches, and many other areas can be identified, evaluated and resolved in minutes compared to days, weeks or months in the past. The Value Network Management concept, as created by the authors in this book, is a great and timely idea to propel supply management into the future. "Supply Management" needs to be read and reflected on by all purchasing, materials and logistics students and managers.

## R. David Nelson

*R. David Nelson is a towering figure in the fields of purchasing/procurement/supply management and value network management. In 1985, he became Worldwide Director of Purchasing at TRW. He became Vice President-Purchasing at Honda America in 1987. His next assignment was as Vice President, Worldwide Supply Management at Deere & Company. In 2002, Mr. Nelson became Vice President-Global Supply Management at Delphi Corporation. He is currently CEO and Chief Supply Chain Officer, Best Windows Company and has served as Chairman of the Board and former President of the Institute of Supply Management (formerly the National Association of Purchasing Management) and serves on the Board of Trustees of CAPS Research. David has been a member of the University of San Diego's Supply Chain Management Institute and its predecessor since their establishment in 1984. In recognition of his distinguished service to the purchasing profession, David Nelson was awarded the J. Shipman gold medal given by the Institute for Supply Management.*

Welcome to the exciting, wonderful world of supply management! During the first portion of the 21st century, more changes are taking place in the areas of supply management, supply chain management, value network management, buyer/supplier alliances, and virtual corporations than in the history of humankind.

Dynamic collaborative and trusting alliance relationships and networks are the keys to survival and success in the 21st century. On the supply side, these relationships are best established and nurtured by supply management professionals. Information technology, engineering, marketing, operations, quality, and finance all play critical, enabling roles in our quest of value-add relationships.

The transformation from clerical and mechanical purchasing through proactive procurement and supply management to value network management parallels the evolution of mankind from caves to visiting the moon. In some ways, this transformation has been mirrored by one of the leading supply management professional organizations. Where we once had the National Association of Purchasing Agents, and then the National Association of Purchasing Management, today we have the Institute for Supply Management.

What is the primary reason for the shift from tactical purchasing roles to strategic supply management and value network roles? Supply management has major impact on the organization's bottom line. It can facilitate or destroy marketing's efforts to increase sales. Supply management has always been a part of the "front line" defense to contain costs. Today supply management and value network management have as much or more impact on the organization's return on assets than does any other business function.

The term "supply chain management" came into vogue during the 1990s. Many information technologists, logisticians, management scientists and industrial engineers have argued that their individual function should be the drivers of the chain. But informed practitioners and academics alike recognize that carefully developed cross-functional supply management teams are the key to successful supply chains and supply networks. All functional areas must collaborate with relevant suppliers to realize the greatest opportunity for success.

Many executives have been brainwashed by aggressive software vendors into believing that e-commerce will eliminate the need for supply professionals. Wrong. Dead wrong!

E-commerce must be viewed for what it is and what it contributes: e-commerce and the Internet are wonderful, powerful enablers. They are slaves, not masters!

The thinking underlying this edition of our text began in the 1950s when I enjoyed my first appointment as a Chief Procurement Officer. Many wonderful people and events have contributed to my knowledge and evolving philosophy during the years subsequent to 1955. My evolving philosophy first saw the power of the press in 1984 with the publication of "Proactive Procurement: The Key to Increased Profits, Productivity, and Quality." In 1984, I was privileged to join Lamar Lee, Jr., my former Professor of Purchasing during my days at Stanford, and his co-author, Donald W. Dobler, as the junior co-author of the 4th edition of *Purchasing and Materials Management: Text and Cases.*

Our new edition has benefited enormously from the invaluable contributions of countless colleagues. Rommy Los (my former student and currently a manager at Henkel KGaA) developed the important material addressing supply management's role in protecting Mother Earth. Tom Olesen, formerly of Nationwide Insurance, assisted with the services chapter. Robert Porter Lynch has contributed to my insight on buyer/supplier alliances. Ray Hummell took my preliminary work on the total cost of owner-ship and carried it forward as a key cornerstone of the cost portion of the last two editions. Ray also provided invaluable assistance in upgrading and updating our material on price and cost. Bill Richardson provided deep insight into Deere & Company's approach to supplier development. Professor Craig Barkacs brought our work on legal and ethical issues into the 21st century. R. David (Dave) Nelson, Chair-man of the Institute of Supply Chain Management$^{TM}$, formerly employed as VP of Worldwide Supply Management at Deere & Company and as VP of Global Purchasing at Delphi Automotive Systems, has provided invaluable insight through the book's evolution. Bob Kemp (former President of NAPM); Emiko Banfield, VP, Shared Services at Southern California Edison; Teresa Metty, VP Motorola; Dr. Dave Lehmann, VP Operations, Solar (ret.); Merle Roberts, Founder and President of Perpetual Frontiers; and Professor Scott Kunkel of USD, all played important contributing roles. Dr. Stephen Starling provided valuable input to the 7th edition. We also want to thank Joseph V. Shannon, President of Po$e in Cleve-land, Ohio for his review of the Transportation Appendix, Tricia Sharp of Minuteman Press in Strongsville, Ohio, for assistance on word processing, and Dr. Ken Killen, ISM Shipman Medalist and Professor Emeritus, of Cuyahoga Community College in Cleveland, Ohio, for his invaluable advice. In addition, special thanks go to Jim Reeds, who played a key role in developing the Graduate Program in Supply Management at the University of San Diego, and former co-authors of Burt, Warren Norquist, Jimmy Anklesaria, Michael Doyle and Stephen Starling for their contributions cited in this edition.

It is with a combination of pleasure and pain that we say adieu and bon voyage to former co-author Donald W. Dobler. Don has played a key role in the success of the previous six editions of our text. Don's contributions to the fields of purchasing and materials management resulted in his selection as a Shipman Medalist by the National Association of Purchasing Management. His accomplishments are listed on the dedication page of this edition.

**David N. Burt**

# Supply Management

# The Foundation

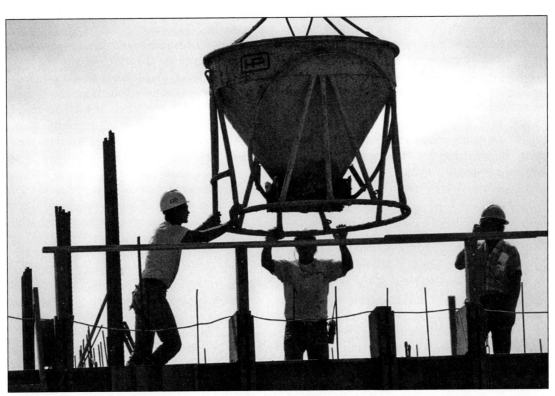

Supply management is the heart and soul of supply chain interaction since "the chain" starts with finding, selecting and managing effective and efficient suppliers of materials, equipment and services. All organizations must design their procurement-purchasing contracting activities to provide the lowest cost of what is now the major cost center in most operations. Part one chapters introduce the reader to the concepts behind Value Network Management, the ultimate goal of supply management.

Purchasing is one of the basic processes that are common to all organizations. It is the process of acquiring goods, services, and equipment from another organization in a legal and ethical manner. Professional purchasing addresses five rights: purchase of the right item or service, in the right quality, in the right quantity, at the right price, and at the right time. Purchasing provides the foundation of supply management, which tends to have a wider scope of activities: The focus shifts from price to the total cost of ownership. Supply management also puts more emphasis on helping a firm increase its profitable sales.

A firm's supply system includes all internal functions plus external suppliers involved in the identification and fulfillment of needs for materials, equipment, and services in an optimized fashion. Supply management lays the foundation for, and is the key to, successful supply chain management.

Supply management can affect a firm's bottom line positively as much as or more than any other business function. Supply management contributes to increases in profitable sales by enhancing the quality of the firm's products, ensuring on-time performance, reducing time to market, enabling the inflow of technologies which are the basis of successful new products, and giving sales and marketing freedom to maximize the firm's net revenue through the application of pricing elasticity. Supply management's focus on the total cost of ownership (defined as the summation of the costs of acquiring and owning or converting an item of material, piece of equipment, or service and post-ownership costs) plays a major role in reducing a firm's expenditures. Through its impact on profitable sales and reduced expenditures, supply management has a major impact on the firm's return on investment and return on assets.

Supply management consists of a five stage process: The generation of requirements, sourcing, pricing, developing an enforceable agreement, and the post-award managing of the relationship. These phases are interdependent. The generation of requirements is the most crucial of these four phases. Approximately 85 percent of the cost of purchased material, services, and equipment is "designed in" during this phase. It is an interesting paradox that supply management is a contributor to, not the "owner" of, this crucial phase. Supply management assumes a greater leadership role in the three remaining phases: sourcing, pricing, and post-award activities.

The Internet and B2B e-commerce are accelerating the transformation of supply management to a core competency. The key to optimizing the power of the Internet as an enabler of supply management is to analyze each critical supply management process systematically and then reengineer the process while incorporating the power of the Internet. Technological integration of processes that span the supply chain requires collaboration among the chain's members. As firms' supply management systems progress, they develop information technology (IT) systems that facilitate strategic planning of this critical process.

Through the process of acquiring goods, services, and equipment from other organizations, a chain of upstream suppliers is formed: a supply chain. A firm's supply chain includes all internal functions (such as operations, engineering, production control and scheduling, inventory management, demand forecasting, and marketing) plus external suppliers involved in meeting the organization's needs for materials, equipment, and services in an efficient manner. The supply chain is the upstream portion of the organization's value chain, responsible for feeding the production or conversion process. Marketing and distribution are the principal components of the downstream portion of the value chain. The value chain, then, is a series of organizations that add value to goods and services that flow from Mother Earth to the end customer, the source of funds for the entire chain. The value chain focuses on the end customer. It must be designed and managed so that one member does not benefit at the expense of another.

An organization's success is driven by its ability to compete effectively as a member of its supply and value chain communities, not as an isolated enterprise. The ability to interact quickly with customers and suppliers is critical to the firm and to its supply and value chains' survival and success.

Chapter 2 shows how supply management departments organize for effectiveness. The placement of the function within the organizational structure significantly affects its influence on corporate strategy. Factors that influence where supply management falls in the structure include the availability of the materials and services being procured, the dollar volume of purchases, and the classification of the responsibilities and activities performed. As materials and services gain importance, various organizational structures have arisen that elevate the importance of the procurement function. Those structures include the materials management organization, the supply chain management structure, and cross-functional teams. Cross-functional teams are being used proactively to address a myriad of issues from design to salvage. The teams are composed of both internal and external (i.e., suppliers) members, reflecting the new interdependencies in today's competitive environment.

Chapter 3 discusses how supply management spans functional boundaries and company borders. At a tactical level, supply management is responsible for the acquisition of required materials, services, and equipment. The supply management department is the hub of a large part of a company's business activity. By its nature, supply management has continuing relationships with all other departments in the firm as well as with the firm's suppliers. Supply management operations cut across virtually all departmental lines.

Supply management has as much impact on the success of nonmanufacturing organizations as it has on that of manufacturing firms. The timely availability of reliable equipment, supplies, and services at the right total cost of ownership affects the ability of organizations to provide timely quality services at a profit or, in the case of nonprofit institutions, while minimizing expenditures.

Supply management has a major impact on the efficient and effective use of tax dollars at all levels of government. Not surprisingly, many advances in the art and science of supply management originated in the federal government. Virtually all the problems present in manufacturing organizations are also present in government procurement.

Supply managers are responsible for protecting their firms from unexpected threats or shocks from their supply world in the form of price increases and supply disruptions. Those threats include material shortages which affect one or more industries that supply the firm. Shortages affect both the price and the availability of purchased materials and supplies. The firm should take actions to minimize the impact of such shortages by monitoring changes in its supply environment.

Chapter 4 describes the three fundamental types of relationships which exist between industrial customers and their suppliers: transactional, collaborative, and alliance. Professional supply managers recognize that there is a time and a place for each type of supplier relationship. They know the strengths and weaknesses of each type and design their "relationship strategy" to maximize the return on the available investment in human resources. There is no question that well-developed and well-managed alliances deliver optimal outcomes in the areas of cost, quality, time to market, technology flow, and continuity of supply. However, those relationships require a significant investment in human resources. Based on anecdotal evidence, we recommend that buyer-supplier relationships evolve through a collaborative phase before blooming into alliances. Unfortunately, most alliances appear to be doomed to failure unless the strategic objectives of the two firms are properly aligned, there is compatibility of corporate cultures, and institutional trust is developed and maintained.

The last section of Chapter 4 addresses the effect of "e-commerce" on relationships. E-commerce goes beyond the transactional capabilities of electronic commerce to fulfill strategic goals across supply chains. It is our belief that electronic commerce is adapting to facilitate long-term collaborative relationships and provide synergistic rewards. As seen throughout this book, e-commerce is an enabler, not a replacement for the essential human aspect of buyer-supplier relationships. And now, on to supply management. ■

# The Progression to Professional Supply Management

## CHAPTER OBJECTIVES

*After reading this chapter, you should be able to:*

1. Describe the impact of effective supply management on the bottom line.

2. Explain the relationship between supply management and return on investment.

3. Appreciate the progression from purchasing to strategic supply chain management.

4. Understand the attractiveness of a career in purchasing and supply management.

5. Understand the terms introduced in this chapter.

## VIGNETTE: CAREERS IN PURCHASING AND SUPPLY MANAGEMENT

Josh Longborne, a second-semester student at Cuyahoga Community College (affectionately known as Tri-C), is talking with a fellow student. "Harry, I've got a pretty good schedule for next semester, but I need one more class. Any ideas about which ones won't require much work?" Harry: "I've got a suggestion. It may help you get a great job on graduation. But you don't get something for nothing. It will be a lot of work, but it will be incredibly profitable. The class is all about purchasing and supply management." Josh: "What in the heck is purchasing? Sounds boring!" Harry: "I thought so too until I took the class. I've completed four courses in the area and have started having interviews with prospective employers. Anyhow, to answer your question, purchasing is one of the core processes of any business or governmental organization. It involves working with engineers, operations, and quality people and suppliers to help the firm obtain necessary supplies, materials, and services. The thing I am so excited about is the prospect for employment. Several recent graduates of Tri-C have gotten starting jobs at $30,000 or higher! And with a four-year degree, starting jobs pay $50,000 or more![1] The people I've talked with have all commented on the awesome authority and responsibility they have gained after only a few months' experience. They are dealing with engineers who have been with the company for several years. They deal with suppliers who are considerably older. They love the responsibility and authority they have every bit as much as the salary." Josh: "Wow, sounds interesting. Maybe I will look into this purchasing class!"

That evening, Josh is talking with his mother about purchasing. She says: "Josh, that's a great idea. Your uncle David teaches procurement at a university in southern California. I remember that when we were talking about his professional life on a recent visit to Cleveland, he said that one of his BBA supply management graduates had received an incredible job offer at a public utility. Her starting salary was $70,000! Sounds to me like you may want to take a concentration in this area!" ∎

## CRITICAL THINKING QUESTIONS

1.  Does purchasing sound like a class (or career) you would be interested in? Why or why not?
2.  Share with your classmates what you know about the function of purchasing.
3.  Can you identify someone who might be a mentor during your early days if you decided to pursue a career in purchasing?

**P**urchasing is one of the basic processes that are common to all organizations. It is the process of acquiring goods, services, and equipment from another organization in a legal and ethical manner. Professional purchasing addresses five rights: purchase of the right item or service, in the right quality, in the right quantity, at the right price, and at the right time. The term "purchasing" frequently is used as the title of a business function. As the process of purchasing has evolved to include broader and more strategic responsibilities, the functional name has evolved to "purchasing and supply management," "supply management," "procurement," "strategic sourcing," and "supply chain management." Purchasing provides the foundation of supply management, which tends to have a wider scope of activities: The focus shifts from price to the total cost of ownership. This shift allows the purchaser to understand all supply chain–related costs of doing business with a particular supplier for a particular good or service. Supply management also puts more emphasis on helping a firm increase its profitable sales. Appendix A provides more detailed insights into the mechanics of purchasing and supply management.

**Supply management** (also known as procurement at many firms and governmental agencies) is a five-stage process which begins with the identification of an item or service required to meet the needs of an organization. During this stage, the need is translated into a statement describing the item or service required to satisfy the need. It is estimated that some 85 percent of the cost of an item or service is determined during this stage. Supply management professionals and, frequently, carefully prequalified suppliers are involved in this stage. The second stage of supply management involves identifying the supplier who will best satisfy the need(s). The third phase involves the process of establishing a fair and reasonable

---

[1]For information on salaries, see the current Institute for Supply Management salary survey results at www.ism.ws.

price for the item or service to be purchased. The fourth phase results in an enforceable agreement for the purchase which meets the needs of both parties. The fifth phase requires management of the relationship to ensure timely delivery of the required item or service, in the quality specified, at the agreed time. During this final stage the supply management organization may work with the supplier in an effort to improve the supplier's efficiency with the objective of improving quality, reducing costs, or both.

Several departments, including marketing, sales, and logistics have begun to lay claim to the term "supply management." Although this can cause confusion, it emphasizes supply management professionals' need to communicate with those groups so that supply chain management can be effective. Throughout this text, the term "supply management" will be limited to the definition contained in this chapter.

**Strategic sourcing** represents increasing responsibility for supply management. Strategic sourcing formalizes three activities: (1) periodic analysis of an organization's spending (what is purchased and from whom), (2) analysis of the supply market (who offers what and what changes are taking place in the relevant component of the supply world), and (3) development of a sourcing strategy which supports the corporate strategy while minimizing risks and costs.

## The Five M's

The basic goal of any industrial or commercial activity is the development and production of products (including services) that can be marketed at a profit. Governmental agencies and not-for-profit organizations are concerned with developing and providing products and services which satisfy the needs of their constituents, normally at the lowest possible cost and without a concern for profit. These goals are accomplished by the appropriate blending of what management authorities historically have called the five M's: machines, manpower, materials, money, and management. Materials are the lifeblood of industry. Materials of the appropriate quality must be available at the right time, in the proper quantity, at the needed location, and at an acceptable total cost. Failure to meet any of these criteria concerning materials adds to company costs and decreases company profits just as surely as do outmoded production methods, inefficient personnel, and ineffective marketing activities. Increasingly, services ranging from landscaping and janitorial services to information technology and even manufacturing are being **outsourced,** that is, provided by external suppliers. For many firms, the procurement of such services is as important as or more important than the procurement of production materials.

Materials have not always been so vital. Throughout the nation's industrial development, the relative importance of the five M's has shifted continually. In the management sense, materials became important around 1900. Before then they were taken for granted because they were simple, readily available, and cheap. The role of the supply function in business can be seen more clearly after one explores the factors that caused the shift in the relative importance of the components of the five M's.

During the first 100 years of the U.S. industrial system, productivity increased very little. The availability of manpower and horsepower exceeded that of machine power by almost 50-fold. That relationship started to change around 1850. Between 1850 and 1950 a remarkable increase in productivity took place. In 1850, productive power was divided as shown in Figure 1.1: 2 percent machine power and 98 percent horsepower and manpower. By 1900 that division of power became approximately equal. In 1950, the 1850 power relationship was reversed: 98 percent machine power and 2 percent horsepower and manpower.

Because manpower was the first source of productive power, the initial industrial emphasis was on the human element; labor costs represented the major operating expense. As machines and technology began to develop, management emphasis shifted toward them. As new products, specialized labor, and materials

**Figure 1.1 I** Power Source Relationships, 1850 to 1950
The gray columns represent machine power, and the blue columns represent horsepower and human labor.

distribution became more complex, emphasis shifted toward scientific management. Still later, as both the complexity of materials and the volume of production skyrocketed, materials became an increasingly important element of cost. Consequently, emphasis naturally shifted toward that element. In fact, one of the nation's first professional associations, the National Association of Purchasing Agents (NAPA), was founded in 1915 to educate buyers about materials procurement. This organization has evolved into today's Institute of Supply Management, headquartered in Tempe, Arizona.

Today, for the vast majority of manufacturers, materials are purchased from outside sources. Thus, the purchasing or supply management function has grown in importance and complexity.

The introduction of better machines, coupled with progressive management to develop and utilize more sophisticated man-machine systems, made the emergence of the factory system possible. That in turn sparked many industrial changes: Inventions such as the steam turbine, the electric motor, and automated controls changed the entire complex of manufacturing. Gradually, materials became more complex, mechanization increased, automation emerged, and labor became more specialized. Those changes inevitably led to specialization in manufacturing and a continuing need for more sophisticated and specialized materials. As these trends accelerated and the volume of production increased, labor costs *per unit* decreased. The reduction of unit labor costs increased the relative cost and importance of materials in the manufacturing process. *Percentagewise, labor costs went down while materials costs went up.* This change in the value of materials relative to total production costs continues to this day. For example, in 1945 materials represented approximately 40 percent of a manufacturer's total cost to produce an airplane. In 1955 the materials proportion of total cost increased to around 50 percent. By 2000 the figure was slightly over 65 percent. The results have been an increased focus on purchasing and supply management in businesses that hope to sustain a competitive edge in this global market.

Increasingly, purchasing and supply management's focus has shifted from the procurement of materials to the procurement of services ranging from legal and marketing services to manufacturing by outside suppliers. (Such procurement commonly is called "outsourcing.") The term "offshoring" is becoming increasingly common. Offshoring is the process of locating and sourcing from international sources of supply for both products and services. The critical importance of such procurements makes today's supply management professional one of the firm's most valued employees at both manufacturing firms and services providers.

# Supply Management and the Bottom Line

Historically, supply management has been considered important because of its impact on costs. At an increasing number of firms today, the procurement process is recognized as having a significant impact on sales and revenues. Supply management has an overwhelming impact on a firm's bottom line. It directly affects the two forces which drive the bottom line: sales and costs. Therefore, it must be a core competency of the firm, an expertise that is highly valued by the organization. For a typical manufacturing firm, purchasing and supply management are responsible for spending over half of every dollar the firm receives as income from sales. More dollars are spent for purchases of materials and services than for all other expense items combined, including wages, depreciation, taxes, and dividends. It is important for management to note that the cost of materials is approximately 2½ times the value of all labor and payroll costs and nearly 1½ times the cost of labor plus all other expenses of running the business.

For the typical services firm, supply management plays an equally important, though more subtle, role. Millions of dollars are spent on marketing and advertising, communications, and information technology. Those services can enhance or degrade any firm's efficiency and effectiveness. Management at both manufacturing and service firms ensures that supply management professionals are involved at all stages of the procurement of such services. Strategic Supply Chain Management enables a company to maximize its bottom line in an ethical manner. Figure 1.2 shows how supply management can drive sales up and costs down. This impact on the firm's net income has a major impact on shareholder value.

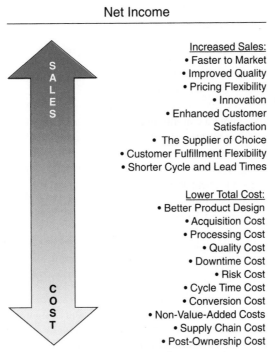

Net Income

S A L E S

Increased Sales:
• Faster to Market
• Improved Quality
• Pricing Flexibility
• Innovation
• Enhanced Customer Satisfaction
• The Supplier of Choice
• Customer Fulfillment Flexibility
• Shorter Cycle and Lead Times

Lower Total Cost:
• Better Product Design
• Acquisition Cost
• Processing Cost
• Quality Cost
• Downtime Cost
• Risk Cost
• Cycle Time Cost
• Conversion Cost
• Non-Value-Added Costs
• Supply Chain Cost
• Post-Ownership Cost

C O S T

**Figure 1.2 |** A Graphic Reproduction of Supply Management's Impact on the Bottom Line

## Increased Sales

Supply management has a significant impact on a firm's sales, principally in the following eight areas.

**Faster to Market or Time-Based Competition**    Thirty years of marketing research has demonstrated the importance of being early to market. In many cases, the first firm to introduce a successful new product or service will hold 40–60 percent of the market after competition enters the picture. This research also demonstrates that the profit margins enjoyed by the first firm to introduce a new product tend to be twice those of its competitor, as first reported in the Profit Impact of Market Strategy (PIMS) approach.[2] Firms that have embraced strategic supply chain management have reduced their new product development cycles by an average of 30 percent as a direct result of taking a cross-functional approach to product development (this also is known as concurrent engineering). Supply management and carefully selected suppliers are key members of these cross-functional teams. (This topic is addressed in greater detail in Chapter 5.)

Time-based competition also includes a firm's ability to meet unexpected surges in demand for its products. In many cases, a firm's ability to ramp up production is constrained by its suppliers' abilities to meet those surges in demand. The development and management of a competent, responsive supply base plays a critical role in a firm's ability to meet unexpected demand.

**Improved Quality**    We are all sensitive to the quality of the products and services we purchase. An automobile with a reputation for transmission problems will drive potential customers to its competitors. Conversely, a firm whose products or lines of products have a reputation for quality gains market share over its competitors and frequently is able to command premium prices. Some 75 percent of many manufacturers' quality problems can be traced back to defects in purchased materials. The percentage of quality problems that can be attributed to defective incoming materials for a service provider is usually less but still significant.

Thus, if a manufacturer or service provider is able to reduce defects in incoming materials, it can improve the quality of its products in the marketplace. Firms that embrace Strategic Supply Chain Management work with their suppliers to design quality into the suppliers' products and maintain quality during production. The result is virtually defect-free incoming materials, improved quality in the marketplace, more sales, and improved profit margins.

**Pricing Flexibility**    Research conducted at the University of San Diego indicates that a strategic approach to supply management will reduce the total cost of ownership[3] associated with purchasing and owning or leasing materials, equipment, and services an average of 25 percent. When the cost of producing an item or service is reduced, marketing receives the gift of pricing elasticity. Through the application of sound economic principles, marketing can estimate whether net income will increase more by (1) holding selling price and sales volume constant and increasing net profit per unit, (2) reducing the sales price and thus increasing sales volume, or (3) using a combination of increasing net profit and reducing sales price.

**Innovation**    The University of San Diego research study cited above indicates that in 240 firms surveyed, approximately 35 percent of all successful new products were the result of technology gained from the supply base.[4] This leveraging of supplier technology is a major source of income for these firms.

---

[2]Robert D. Buzzell and Bradley T. Gaze, *The PIMS Principles: Linking Strategy to Performance* (New York: Free Press, 1987), pp. 183–84.

[3]This research was reported at the 8th International Annual IPSERA Conference, London, U.K., March 1998.

[4]Total cost of ownership is addressed in Chapter 13.

Collaborative and alliance relationships with the firm's supply base play a key role in ensuring and enhancing this technology flow. The development and management of supplier relationships is a key responsibility of supply management.

**Enhanced Customer Satisfaction**   Strategic Supply Chain Management helps achieve shorter fulfillment lead times, consistent on-time delivery, high fill rates, complete orders, quicker responses to customers' requirements, and the ability to meet unique or special requests.

**The Supplier of Choice**   By providing the best value (a combination of quality, service, and price), a firm becomes the supplier of choice to another channel member or to the end customer.

**Customer Fulfillment Flexibility**   Strategic Supply Chain Management provides the supply support which allows a firm to be responsive to customer desires for flexible lead time and changes in product configurations.

**Shorter Cycle and Lead Times**   These benefits result from improved supplier relationships and involvement in supplier product and process improvements.

## Lower Total Cost of Ownership

The total cost of ownership is the summation of the costs of acquiring and owning or converting an item of material, piece of equipment, or service and post-ownership costs, including the disposal of hazardous and other manufacturing waste and the cost of lost sales as a result of a reputation for poor product quality caused by defective materials or purchased services that are incorporated in the end product or service.

**Better Product Design**   We estimate that 70%–80% of the total cost of ownership is built into a requirement—whether for production materials, equipment, services, or Maintenance, Repair and Operation Items—during the requirements development process. Early supply management and supplier involvement can reduce costs significantly during this critical stage.

**Acquisition Cost**   The acquisition cost, or the price paid for an item or service, is normally a major component of the total cost of ownership. As will be seen in many of the following chapters, numerous actions can be taken to reduce the acquisition cost. A few of those activities are specification of the most cost-effective material or item of equipment, use of the appropriate specification, standardization, good sourcing and pricing practices, and professional contract and supplier relationship management.

**Processing Cost**   The cost of developing sourcing and pricing requirements and then ensuring that they arrive on time in the quality specified can be reduced significantly by applying efficient supply management processes and techniques.

**Quality Cost**   Costs are incurred in ensuring that the buying firm receives the optimal level of quality. These costs may be reduced by applying progressive quality techniques such as the design of prototypes and statistical process control. Selecting suppliers capable of producing the desired level of quality and then certifying their design and manufacturing systems can improve incoming quality while reducing administrative quality costs.

**Downtime Cost**   Downtime frequently is the largest component of the total cost of ownership for many items of production and operating equipment. One minute of downtime in a production line may cost $26,000.[5] At that rate, an hour of downtime can cost $1,560,000. Thus, when purchasing equipment, the sourcing team must place as much—or more—emphasis on reliability[6] and maintainability[7] as on purchase price.

**Risk Cost**   Many firms spend millions of dollars to minimize the risk of supply disruptions. These firms maintain needlessly large inventories and/or dual or even triple sources of supply to ensure continuity of supply. Carefully developed and managed relationships with appropriate suppliers can eliminate the need for most inventory and/or dual sources.

**Cycle Time Cost**   While this is difficult to quantify, the shorter the cycle time for virtually all activities, the lower the cost. The shorter the cycle time to bring new products to market, develop a statement of work, or select a new source, the lower the total cost.

**Conversion Cost**   Machine time, manpower, process yield loss, scrap, and rework are examples of conversion costs. These costs are every bit as real as the purchase price of an item entering the production process. A pound of brass may cost twice as much as a pound of steel, but the higher acquisition price for the brass may be more than offset by savings in machine and manpower costs during conversion of the brass to a component or end product because the brass may require less work to make it a usable product.

**Non-Value-Added Costs**   A careful analysis of all the costs involved in bringing an item or service to market frequently reveals that 40–60 percent of the costs confer no added value to the finished good! Robert Handfield indicates that estimates of the amount of time spent on non-value activities can be as high as 80 to 90 percent of the total time required to complete a cycle.[8] James P. Womack and Daniel T. Jones, in their book *Lean Thinking,* indicate that "it takes an average of 11 months for the can of cola in a domestic refrigerator to actually get there. . . . During that 11 months, the time that the material actually being converted as opposed to simply waiting is a mere three hours!"[9] All members of the supply management system (e.g., design, manufacturing and quality engineering, manufacturing, and procurement) must be on the lookout for non-value-added activities at any and all stages of the system.

**Supply Chain Cost**   The development and management of supply chains and supply networks require a significant investment, primarily in the form of human resources. The proper selection, training, and educating of the individuals involved in these activities, together with the application of software systems, can reduce the necessary investments.[10]

**Post-Ownership Cost**   These costs frequently are overlooked but must be considered in addressing the total cost of ownership. They include the disposal of scrap and other waste, customer service, warranty costs, and the cost of lost sales resulting from customer dissatisfaction with a product.

---

[5]Dave R. Nelson, Patricia E. Moody, and Jonathan Stegner, *The Purchasing Machine* (New York: Free Press, 2001), p. 27.

[6]Reliability is the degree of confidence or probability that an item will perform a specified number of times under prescribed conditions. See David N. Burt, *Proactive Procurement* (Englewood Cliffs, NJ: Prentice-Hall, 1984), p. 24.

[7]Maintainability addresses how easily an item can be repaired or restored to operational status.

[8]Robert B. Handfield and Ernest L. Nichols, Jr. *Introduction to Supply Chain Management* (Upper Saddle River, NJ, Prentice-Hall, 1999), p. 54.

[9]From a book review by David Jessop, *European Journal of Purchasing and Supply Management,* December 1997, p. 241.

[10]For an excellent collection of articles on cost reduction, see *Articles for C.P.M Exam Preparation* (Tempe, AZ: National Association of Purchasing Management, 2000), pp. 225–49.

## Supply Management and Return on Investment

Investors frequently evaluate top management's performance by calculating the return on the total capital invested in a business. Inventory, equipment, and other purchased materials constitute corporate assets attained through the investment of capital. The fact that supply management frequently is responsible for spending over half of most companies' total dollars highlights the profit-making possibilities of the purchasing and supply function. Every dollar saved in purchasing is equivalent to a new dollar of profit. Figure 1.3 illustrates this point by showing the relationships of basic elements that influence the return on investment (ROI). The figures in parentheses reflect a 5 percent reduction in the cost of materials for a manufacturing firm. Notice how, in this example, a 5 percent reduction in material cost increases ROI from 10 to 13 percent, a 30 percent increase!

As we have observed, supply management can have a significant impact on a firm's sales volume. The underlined numbers indicate the impact of a 5 percent increase in sales, holding all other variable ratios (including original material costs) constant. We see that ROI increases from 10 percent to 11.42 percent from increasing sales alone.

Now let's look at the combined impact of a 5 percent increase in sales and a 5 percent reduction in the cost of all materials purchased for this volume of activity. The figures in parentheses and underlined in Figure 1.3 show the combined impact of these two forces. We can see that the combined impact of these two realistically obtainable achievements is to increase ROI to 14.52 percent. This is nearly a 50 percent increase in the firm's return on its investment, something most CEOs would die for!

## The Progression to Strategic Supply Chain Management

### Supply Chains

Purchasing is the foundation of supply management, which in turn is the foundation of supply chain management. Through the process of acquiring goods, services, and equipment from other organizations, a chain of upstream suppliers is formed—**a supply chain** (see Figure 1.4).[11]

The firm's supply system includes all internal functions (such as operations, engineering, production control and scheduling, inventory management, demand forecasting, and marketing) plus external suppliers involved in meeting the organization's needs for materials, equipment, and services. This supply system and the firm's supply chains play a key role in helping the firm fulfill its role in its value chains and networks (see Chapter 22).

The **value chain** is a series of organizations which add value to goods and services flowing from Mother Earth to the end customer (see Figure 1.5). The value chain should be viewed as a whole, a single entity, rather than as fragmented groups each performing its own function. Money enters the value chain only when the ultimate customer buys a product or service. Transactions within the value chain simply allocate the ultimate customer's money among the members of the chain.

The supply chain is *the upstream portion* of the organization's value chain and is responsible for feeding the production or conversion process. Marketing and Distribution are the principal components of *the downstream portion* of the value chain. Marketing takes appropriate action to identify customers' wants

---

[11]For a unique and interesting article addressing this topic, see Richard L. Pinkerton, "The Evolution of Purchasing to Supply Chain Management," in John A. Woods and the National Association of Purchasing Management, eds., *The Purchasing and Supply Yearbook* (New York: McGraw-Hill, 2000), pp. 3–16.

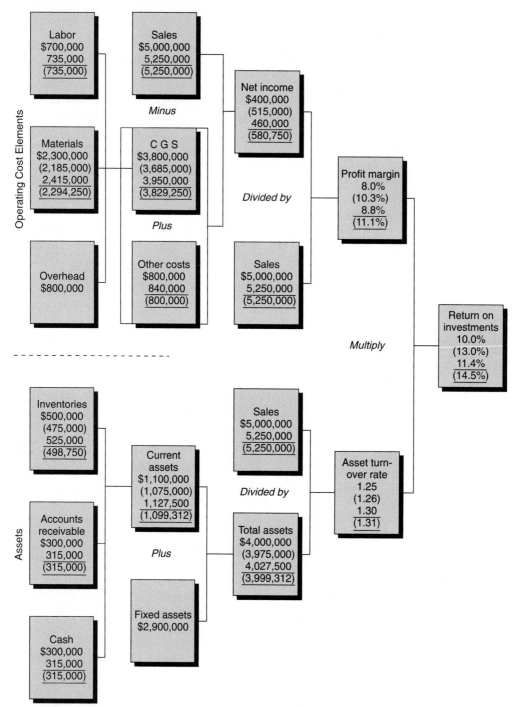

**Figure 1.3** I A Graphic View of the Relationships of Basic Elements Which Influence Return on Investment
The figures in parentheses reflect a 5 percent change in the number indicated. Changes in parentheses reflect a
5 percent decrease in material costs. Underlined figures show a 5 percent increase in sales. Numbers that are
in parentheses and underlined reflect a 5 percent decrease in material costs *and* a 5 percent increase in sales.
Note a nearly 50 percent increase in ROI resulting from these combined changes.

The Supply Chain

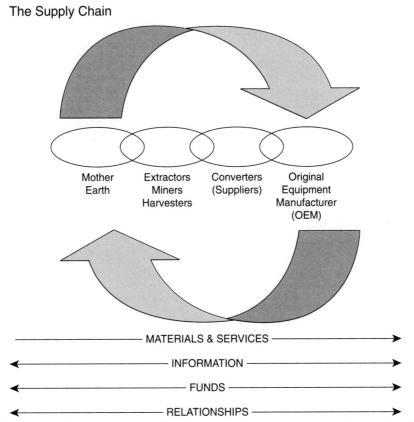

**Figure 1.4** I A firm's supply chain includes all internal functions plus external suppliers involved in the fulfillment of needs for materials, equipment, and services in an optimized fashion. The supply management system plays a key role in helping the firm fulfill its role in its supply chain.

and needs and facilitate sales to the end customer. Distribution manages the movement of finished goods from the original equipment manufacturers (OEMs) through the distribution channel to the end customer. Successful firms such as Toyota, Dell, Wal-Mart, and Procter & Gamble are aware that competition takes place between value chains. This awareness and the resulting strategic and tactical activities result in leadership in their industries.

## The Supply and Value Networks: The Next Phase of Supply Chain Management

Networks are flexible virtual systems that are linked by communication systems and alliances. Within a network, many things happen simultaneously. Final consumers also provide inputs about wants and needs which are communicated throughout the network system. These systems optimize the flow of materials and services, information, and money. Supply and value networks focus on the ultimate customer. They are designed and managed so that one member does not benefit at the expense of another. World-class value networks are highly adaptive, focus on speed, are innovative, and are tightly integrated. Value network management will be addressed in Chapter 22.

## The Value Chain

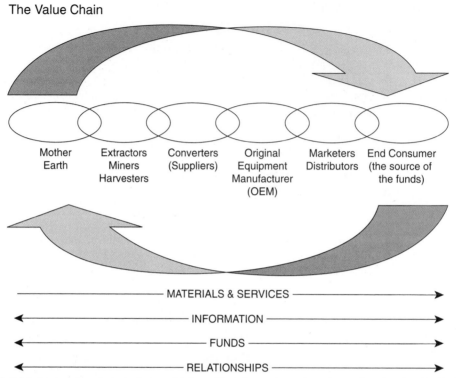

**Figure 1.5 |** A firm's value chain includes all internal functions plus external suppliers involved in the identification and fulfillment of needs for materials, equipment, and services in an optimized fashion. Also included in the value chain are the firm's distribution channel and end consumers.

In comparison to integrated supply and value networks, the traditional approach to supply chain management is more linear in concept. This approach features independent decision making as a result of gaps between the entities that constitute the supply chain. Those gaps are caused by lack of communication and information sharing and can result in excess inventories, inflated lead times, and increased costs throughout the value chain. Michigan State University (MSU) has long been regarded as one of the leaders in purchasing, supply management, and logistics research and education. Nick Little of MSU observed that the individual players in the chain are all seeking to deliver value for the end consumer. However, there are a number of elements in that value:

- *Value Creation*—through the innovation, development and launch of new products and services.
- *Value Delivery*—through the order fulfillment process.
- *Value Maintenance*—through processes to provide after sales service, support maintenance and so forth.

"These three value processes need to span your company, your suppliers and your customers in order to successfully meet the needs of end consumers."[12] It is in seeking this value that simple linear supply chains evolve into more tightly knit supply and value networks.

---

[12]"Supply Chains and Supply Networks: How Do I Win?" This research was reported by Nick Little, MCIPS, Assistant Director, Executive Development Programs, Eli Broad Graduate School of Management MSU, at the 90th Annual International Supply Management Conference, Minneapolis, MN, May 2005, pp. 3, 4.

## The Extended Enterprise

Jeffrey Dyer carries the concept of supply networks one step further. Based on eight years of study of the automotive industry, Dyer observes that when a group or network of firms collaborates in partnership (alliance) fashion, this is sometimes referred to as a *strategic network*, *virtual corporation*, or *extended enterprise*.[13] "When the group of firms views each other as partners (members of a supply alliance) and collaborates effectively for the good of the larger group, then they leave established an extended enterprise characterized by virtual integration."[14]

# Implementing Strategic Supply Chain Management

To gain the benefits of its supply chains, senior management must recognize the importance of supply chain management and support the required transformation to strategic status. One of the most visible ways of demonstrating its support of this transformation is to appoint a Chief Supply Officer at an organizational level that is equal to that of marketing, engineering, and operations. Then senior management should realign the firm's internal resources with the objective of enabling the success of the firm's supply chains. The transformation must be planned and executed carefully. Getting top management's commitment and obtaining everyone's involvement are the keys to success. The process of implementing world-class value network management will be addressed in Chapter 22.

Successful firms must know where they are in relation to where they want to be. Benchmarking best-in-class practices and developing metrics or measurements enable firms to establish a baseline of where they are, develop an appropriate action plan, and then track their progress toward Strategic Supply Management. Appropriate action plans and metrics allow the firm to focus on its vision and continuously improve the bottom line. Figure 1.6 provides a diagnostic which allows a firm to evaluate where it is on the progression to Strategic Supply Chain Management and also can serve as a road map to guide the implementation of Strategic Supply Chain Management. The left column in the figure identifies ten variables which are, or should be, of interest to management. The four columns to the right show the progression from a reactive clerical focus to a strategic focus. In each of these four stages, we see the focus of the supply management function for each of the ten variables.

# The Roles of a Supply Management Professional

Dr. Joseph Cavinato of the Institute of Supply Management provides the following thoughts on the roles of today's supply management professionals: "A supply management professional has four key roles: One is a leadership role in seeking new opportunities in the (supply) marketplace and driving them for follow-through in the organization." A second role is "being an identifier of outsource opportunities, finding the right outsource, and leading the charge to an efficient and effective relationship and oversight system for the organization."

Dr. Cavinato's third "management role is also required on a higher level than before. This is the management of systems and relationships. Having the proper eyes, ears, and antennas in place with the proper interpretive mechanisms is an essential value-added need for the organization. It is an assertive contributing role with both outsiders and insiders."

---

[13]Jeffrey H. Dyer, *Collaborative Advantage: Winning through Extended Enterprise Supplier Networks* (Oxford: Oxford University Press, 2000), p. 27.

[14]Ibid., p. 32.

## Burt-Lynch Supply Chain Evolution Model

### Building to World Class

| VARIABLE | 1. Reactive Clerical | 2. Transactional Mechanical | 3. Proactive Supply Management | 4. Strategic Supply Chain Management |
|---|---|---|---|---|
| | | | ✿ Quality, ✿ Just In Time, ✿ Total Cost of Ownership | ✿ Innovation ✿ Top and Bottom Line ✿ Internal Integration |
| Value Driver | ✿ Timely Availability, Convenience | ✿ Purchase Price | ✿ Improve Bottom Line ✿ Some Consideration of Revenue Impacts | ✿ Revenue and Bottom Line Impacts ✿ Increase Share Holder Value ✿ Transform Innovation into Value |
| Financial Impact | ✿ Overhead Cost Center | ✿ Improve Bottom Line No Consideration of Revenue Impacts | ✿ Partial Internal Integration Procurement, Logistics, Operations, Engineering | ✿ Moderate Integration Internal and External Integration: Supply, R&D, Logistics, Operations, Engineering, Marketing, Customer Service |
| Integration Level and Functional Elements | ✿ No Internal Integration Purchasing | ✿ Low Internal Integration Procurement and Logistics | | |
| Basis of Competitive Advantage | ✿ Do the Job | ✿ Leverage Size of Buyer ✿ Power Dynamics between Buyer and Seller | ✿ Through put ✿ Global Impact | ✿ Coordination and Synchronicity ✿ Interconnectedness ✿ Relationships and Trust |
| Performance Metrics | ✿ Timeliness and Efficiency | ✿ Low Component/Unit Cost, ✿ On-Time Delivery | ✿ Coordination and Cost, Develop Suppliers | ✿ Speed, Effectiveness, Monitor Supply Environment |
| Innovation Metrics | ✿ Nothing | ✿ Squeeze the Vendor ✿ Internet Auctions | ✿ Process Innovation, ✿ Develop Requirements, ✿ Near Defect-Free Supply | ✿ Speed and Integration, ✿ Design Supply Base ✿ Integrated Supply Strategy |
| Knowledge | ✿ Thomas Directory, ✿ Phone Book ✿ Rolodex | ✿ e-Commerce ✿ "Should Cost" Analysis | ✿ Understand Suppliers | ✿ Understand Industries, Supply Base |
| Supplier Relationships | ✿ Personal | ✿ Adversarial and Transactional | ✿ Transactional and Collaborative | ✿ Transactional, Collaborative, and Alliance |
| Time Focus | ✿ Isolated from Customer | ✿ Reactive to Customer | ✿ Responsive to Customer | ✿ Proactive to Customer |
| Environmental | ✿ Not Considered | ✿ Added Cost Factor | ✿ Considered As Part of TCO | ✿ Proactive as Market Differentiator for Customer |

Note: Some elements of an earlier stage are carried as a foundation into the next stage, while other elements may be discarded.

| Rating | 1.0   1.5 | 2.0   2.5 | 3.0   3.5 | 4.0   4.5 | 5.0  World Class |
|---|---|---|---|---|---|

**Figure 1.6 |** The Burt-Lynch Supply Chain Evolution Model. Evolved from *The American Keiretsu*, by David Burt and Michael F. Doyle, Business-One-Irwin, 1993, p. 21.

The fourth is "a creator role is called for in the form of identifying new opportunities and making them available to the organization. This means creating strategies, systems, and supply options of entire 'packages' of value attributes that span many departments and groups. This also includes seeking and implementing top line revenue opportunities for the organization."[15]

---

[15]Joseph L. Cavinato, "An Analysis of the Expansion of the Purchasing Field into New Value-Added Roles in Organizations," Institute for Supply Management, August 15, 2001, p. 4.

## Concluding Remarks

The field of supply management provides remarkable opportunities for fulfilling employment. Both financial and psychic rewards are readily available.

Purchasing, one of the basic activities common to all organizations, is the process of acquiring goods, services, and equipment from another organization. Purchasing is the foundation of Supply Management, a process which has an overwhelming impact on a firm's bottom line. Supply Management directly affects the two factors which control a firm's bottom line: sales and costs.

Supply chain management is the process of managing the flow of raw materials from Mother Earth to the original equipment manufacturer (OEM). It is the upstream portion of the value chain. It is our observation that supply management is the foundation of supply chain management. Marketing and distribution—the downstream side of the value chain—influence demand and sales and manage the movement of finished goods from the OEM through the distribution channel to the end customer. The value chain is a sequence of integrated activities that must be performed by various organizations to move goods from the sources of raw materials to the ultimate consumers.

An organization's success is driven by its ability to compete effectively as a member of its supply and value chain communities, not as an isolated enterprise. The ability to interact quickly with customers, suppliers, and other partners is critical to the survival and success of the firm and its chains.

Chapter 2 addresses the relationship between the organizational status of the supply management function and its ability to have an impact on a firm's success. Insight into this relationship is very useful to a job seeker who desires to join an organization in which his or her efforts will have a significant impact on the organization's success.

## Discussion Questions

1. What are three major attractions of careers in supply management?
2. Describe the five rights of purchasing.
3. What does the term "total cost of ownership" mean to you? Give an example from your personal life.
4. What role do the five M's play in the emergence of supply management as a valued business function?
5. Describe the five phases of supply management.
6. Strategic sourcing represents increasing responsibility for supply management. Describe three responsibilities.
7. Describe seven ways in which supply management has an impact on a firm's sales.
8. Describe 12 ways in which supply management has an impact on a firm's costs.
9. Explain how a 5 percent reduction in the cost of materials at a manufacturing firm can result in a 30 percent increase in the firm's ROI.
10. How does supply management's impact on sales affect a firm's ROI?
11. Strategic Supply Chain Management will increase sales while reducing the unit cost of purchased materials, services, and equipment. What is the realistic impact of these changes on a firm's ROI?
12. What are some of the advantages of a tightly integrated supply chain?
13. Why does support for strategic supply chain management have to come from the top management of an organization?
14. What are the prerequisites to bringing a firm's supply management function to "strategic" status?

# Internet Exercise

## Honda in America

Visit the "Honda in America" website below. Read how Honda values its suppliers.
(http://corporate.honda.com/america/diversity.aspx?id=diversity_supplier)

1.   How might this reflect on how Honda values its internal supply management group?
2.   What does Honda do to demonstrate to suppliers the important role they play in the company's success?

# Suggested Reading

Andraski, Joseph C. "Out of the Silos," *Supply Chain Management Review* 11, no. 3, April 2007, pp. 24–25.

Barnes, Dan. "Supply Chain Gains," *Banker* 157, no. 973, 2007, pp. 44–45.

Boyer, Kenneth, Markham Frohlich, and Thomas Hukt. *Extending the Supply Chain* (New York: AMACOM, 2005).

Budzki, Robert A., Douglas A. Smock, Michael Katzorke, and Shelley Stewart, Jr. "Supply Management: How Are You Really Doing?" *Supply Chain Management Review* 9, no. 9, December 2005, pp. 10–15.

Budzki, Robert A., Douglas A. Smock, Michael Katzorke, and Shelley Stewart, Jr. *Straight to the Bottom Line: An Executive's Roadmap to World Class Supply Management*, Copublished by *Purchasing* magazine and *Supply Chain Management Review* (Fort Lauderdale, FL: J. Ross Publishing, 2005).

Cavinato, Joseph L., Anna E. Flynn, and Ralph C. Kauffman. *The Supply Management Handbook*, 7th ed. (New York: McGraw-Hill, 2006).

Giannakis, Mihalis, and Simon R. Croomm. "Toward the Development of a Supply Chain Management Paradigm: A Conceptual Framework," *Journal of Supply Chain Management,* Spring 2004, p. 27. Giannakis and Croom describe an interesting supply chain problem domain called the 3s model. This model describes (1) the synthesis of the business and resources network, (2) the characteristics of synergy between the different actors in the network, and (3) the synchronization of all operational decisions involved in the production of goods and services.

Hammer, Michael. *The Agenda: What Every Business Must Do to Dominate the Decade* (New York: Crown Business, 2001).

Hanfield, Robert, and Ernest Nichols. *Supply Chain Redesign: Transforming Supply Chains into Integrated Value Systems* (Upper Saddle River, NJ: Financial Times/Prentice Hall, 2002).

Hugos, Michael. *Essentials of Supply Chain Management,* 2nd ed. (Hoboken, NJ: John Wiley & Sons, 2006).

*ISM Glossary of Key Supply Management Terms,* 4th ed. (Tempe, AZ: ISM, 2006). (http://www.ism.ws/glossary/index.cfm?)

Killen, Kenneth H. and John W. Kamauff. *Managing Purchasing: Making the Supply Team Work.* McGraw-Hill/Irwin, Burr Ridge, IL. 1995.

Killen, Kenneth H. and Robert L. Janson. *Purchasing Managers' Guide to Model Letters, Memos and Forms.* Prentice Hall, Englewood Cliffs, N.J. 1991. Although most of these forms are now computerized, the information is still pertinent.

Lambert, Douglas M. "The Eight Essential Supply Chain Management Processes," *Supply Chain Management Review,* Spring 2004, pp. 18–26.

Little, Nick. "Supply Chains and Supply Networks: How Do I Win?" *Proceedings of the 90th Annual International Supply Management Conference,* Minneapolis, MN, May 2005.

Monczka, Robert M, and James P. Morgan. "Quantum Leap," *Purchasing,* 131, no. 10, June 6, 2002.

Nelson, Dave, Patricia Moody, and Jonathan R. Stegner. *The Incredible Payback: Innovative Sourcing Solutions That Deliver Extraordinary Results* (New York: AMACOM, 2005).

Nelson, Dave, Patricia E. Moody, and Jonathan Stegner. *The Purchasing Machine* (New York: Simon & Schuster, 2001).

Pinkerton, Richard L. "The Evolution of Purchasing to Supply Chain Management." *Foreword to World Class Supply Management* [SM]: *The Key to Supply Chain Management*, 7ed, David N. Burt, Donald W. Dobler, and Stephen L. Starling (Burr Ridge, IL: McGraw-Hill Irwin, 2003).

Sollish, Fred, and John Semanik. *The Procurement and Supply Manager's Desk Reference* (NYC: John Wiley & Sons, 2007).

Trent, Robert J. *Strategic Supply Management: Creating the Next Source of Competitive Advantage* (Fort Lauderdale, FL: J. Ross Publishing, 2007).

# Appendix: An Overview of the Mechanics of Supply Management

## The Typical Purchasing Cycle: Materials

A supply management department buys many different types of materials and services. The procedures used in completing a total transaction normally vary with the different types of purchases. However, the general cycle of activities in purchasing most operating materials, supplies, and services is fairly standardized. The following steps constitute the typical purchasing cycle:

- Recognize, define, and describe the need.
- Transmit the need.
- Investigate and select the supplier.
- Prepare and issue the purchase order, contract, or agreement.
- Follow up the order (including expediting and de-expediting).
- Receive and inspect the material.
- Audit the invoice.
- Close the order.

Figure 1.7 outlines these steps in operational form for a requirement for materials. (Chapters 8 and 9 address the processes for the purchase of equipment and services.) More important, Figure 1.7 details the minimum flow of communications required for a system to function smoothly and efficiently. These communications may be electronic messages or paper documents, depending on the type of system used. The precise form the electronic message or the documents take varies widely from one company to another. The important point here is that a properly controlled purchase requires extensive communication with numerous work groups. Procurement procedures constitute the framework within which this task is accomplished.

## Recognition, Definition, Description, and Transmission of the Need

The need for a purchase typically originates in one of a firm's operating departments or its inventory control section. The supply management department is notified of the requirement by one of two methods: a purchase requisition or a material requirements planning (MRP) schedule. The purchase description which is transmitted to the supplier forms the heart of the procurement and is detailed on the requisition form.

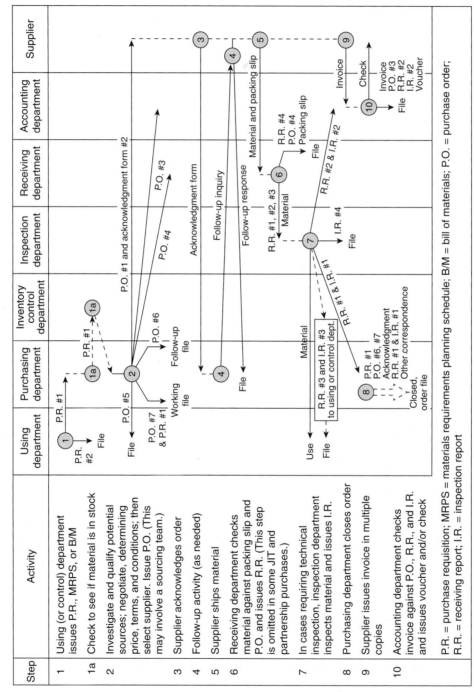

**Figure 1.7** I General Procedure and Document Flow Chart for a Typical Purchasing Cycle

### Standard Purchase Requisition

The purchase requisition is an internal document, in contrast to the purchase order, which is basically an external document. Most companies use a standard, serially numbered purchase requisition form for requests that originate in the operating departments. The requisition communicates the user's needs. The essential information communicated includes a description of the service, material, quantity, and date required. Requisitions often are transmitted electronically through the approval system to the appropriate buyer. Firms that maintain their inventory records on a computer utilize a programmed inventory monitoring system that identifies the item whose inventory level has reached the reorder point. When the computer detects this condition, it automatically prints an inventory replenishment requisition that goes to purchasing for action, and the purchasing cycle is under way.

### Material Requirements Planning Schedule

When a design engineer completes the design of a part or an assembly, he or she makes a list of all the materials (and the quantity of each) required to manufacture the item. This list is called an *engineering bill of materials.* In firms that use computerized production and inventory planning systems such as an MRP system, the engineering bill of materials first is reconfigured into a *structured multilevel* bill of materials. This structured bill of materials for each item being manufactured can be used in determining specific material requirements for a given production schedule during a specific time period. The computer program utilizes the reconfigured "bills" along with the production schedules for all items as input and calculates as output the precise time-phased requirements for each material that will be used in the manufacturing process. This schedule then is sent to purchasing for direct use in obtaining the required materials. This obviously eliminates the necessity of preparing numerous purchase requisitions and is ideally suited for use in a multi-product intermittent manufacturing operation.

## Supplier Selection and Preparation of the Purchase Order

As soon as a need has been established and described precisely, the procurement professional begins an investigation of the market to identify potential sources of supply. In the case of routine items for which supplier relationships already have been developed, little additional investigation may be required to select a good source.[16] The purchase of a new or high-value item, in contrast, may require a lengthy investigation of potential suppliers.

After qualifying a preliminary group of potential sources, the procurement professional may employ the technique of competitive bidding or negotiation or both. When competitive bidding is used, the procurement professional initiates the procedure by requesting quotations from a reasonable number of firms with which the buying group is willing to do business. Although "request for quotation" forms vary widely among firms, typically they contain the same basic information that will be included on the purchase order. These requests may be sent electronically. Chapter 11 describes this process in greater detail.

Once a supplier has been selected, the supply management department issues a serially numbered purchase order. In most cases the purchase order becomes a legal contract. For this reason, the procurement professional should take great care in preparing and wording the order. Quality specifications must be described precisely. If engineering drawings, statements of work, or other related documents are to

---

[16]In practical purchasing terminology, these types of purchases are called "rebuys" or "modified rebuys."

be considered an integral part of the order, they should be incorporated clearly by reference. Quantity requirements, price, and delivery and shipping requirements must be specified accurately. The order should include all the data required to ensure a satisfactory contract and should be worded in a manner which leaves little room for misinterpretation by either party.

In addition to the provisions that are unique to each contract, most firms include as part of every contract a series of terms and conditions that are standard for all orders (typically called "boilerplate"). These terms and conditions are designed to give legal protection to the buyer on matters such as contract acceptance, delivery performance and contract termination, shipment rejections, assignment and subcontracting of the order, patent rights and infringements, warranties, compliance with legal regulations, and invoicing and payment procedures. Each company develops its terms and conditions of purchase in accordance with its own unique needs. Consequently, there is much variation among firms. Chapter 17 describes some of the legal considerations which should be addressed in creating a contract.

After an order has been issued, changes in company requirements frequently require a change in the contract. In such cases, the supply professional issues a *change order,* following the same procedures that were used for the original order. When accepted by the supplier, the change order either supplements or replaces the original order.

## Acknowledgment and Follow-Up of the Order

In most cases, the original copy of the purchase order which is sent to the supplier constitutes a legal "offer" to buy. No purchase "contract" exists, however, until the seller "accepts" the buyer's offer. The seller's acceptance can take one of two forms: (1) performance of the contract or (2) formal notification that the offer has been accepted.

The purpose of sending the supplier an acknowledgment form along with the purchase order is twofold. First, it is a form that can be completed conveniently and returned to the purchasing firm to acknowledge acceptance of the order. Second, the supplier can indicate whether it is able to meet the desired delivery date. If a supplier ships the ordered item immediately from stock, it frequently disregards the acknowledgment form.

If shipment is not made immediately, an acceptance should be sent to the supply management department. Although the acknowledgment form usually serves this purpose, some sellers prefer to use their own forms, which state their terms and conditions of sale. In either event, the procurement professional should check the acceptance closely to see that the supplier has not taken exception to any provisions of the order. If the seller's acceptance terms are different from those on the buyer's order, the law holds that they will be incorporated automatically in the contract unless they materially alter the intent of the offer or unless the buyer files a written objection to their inclusion. In cases in which the seller's and the buyer's terms are in direct conflict, the law omits such terms from the contract, leaving settlement of the differences to private negotiation or legal adjudication. In view of the posture of the courts on this matter, it is clear that a buyer must review suppliers' order acceptances with great care.

The supply management department's responsibility for an order does not end with the making of a satisfactory contract. Supply management bears full responsibility for an order until the material is received and accepted.

Even though a supplier intends to meet a required delivery date, many problems can prevent it from doing so. When there is a reasonable chance that the supplier will not stay on schedule, important orders with critical delivery dates should receive active follow-up attention. When such orders are placed, the procurement professional should determine specific dates on which follow-up checks are to be made.

## Receipt and Inspection

The next step in the traditional purchasing cycle is receipt and inspection of the order. When a supplier ships material, it includes in the shipping container a packing slip which itemizes and describes the contents of the shipment. The receiving clerk uses this slip in conjunction with his or her copy of the purchase order to verify that the correct material has been received. The received materials often are entered electronically into the buyer's system by keyboard or the scanning of a bar code.

## Services

The procurement of services involves many of the same processes. Instead of a specification developed or adopted by engineering serving as the heart of the purchase order or contract, a statement of work serves that purpose. The statement of work is developed by a team that includes the user of the services and a procurement professional. Frequently, one or more qualified potential suppliers are involved in this effort. Receipt of services may require a technical inspection to verify that the services have been received in accordance with the contract. These inspections may be required at various points throughout the completion of the order or contract. Procurement of services can present challenges not experienced in materials buying. Chapter 9 addresses this challenging process.

## The Invoice Audit and Completion of the Order

Occasionally, a supplier's billing department makes an error in preparing an invoice or its shipping department makes an incorrect or incomplete shipment. To ensure that the purchaser makes proper payment for the materials actually received, sound accounting practice dictates that some type of review procedure precede payment to the supplier.

A typical procedure involves a simultaneous review of the purchase order, the receiving report, and the invoice. By checking the receiving report against the purchase order, the purchaser determines whether the quantity and type of material ordered were in fact received. Then, by comparing the invoice with the purchase order and the receiving report, the firm verifies that the supplier's bill is priced correctly and covers the proper quantity of acceptable material. Finally, when the arithmetic accuracy of the invoice is verified, the correctness of the total invoice figure is determined.

Auditing invoices is a repetitive, time-consuming task that should be handled as efficiently as possible. It should be conducted soon after receipt of the invoice to permit the accounting department to make prompt payment and obtain any applicable cash discounts. Prompt payment also supports the firm's efforts to establish and maintain good supplier relations. Because of the labor cost involved in auditing invoices, many companies do not verify the accuracy of low-dollar-value invoices. Invoice auditing is technically an accounting function. When possible, it is prudent to separate the responsibility for authorizing payment for an order from the responsibility for placing that order. Theoretically, the purchasing department's job is completed when the material covered by a purchase order has been received in the plant and is ready for use. In practice, however, some firms assign the responsibility for invoice auditing to accounting and others assign it to purchasing.

In the purchase of complex or technical materials or services, operationally it makes sense to assign the auditing task to the professional who handled the order. This individual is familiar with the materials or services and their technical nomenclature, prices and contract provisions, and all ensuing negotiations. Invoices for such orders often are difficult to interpret and evaluate without a detailed knowledge of these things. Auditing invoices for the purchase of most standard materials, in contrast, is a routine task that should be assigned to appropriate accounting personnel. A majority of most firms' orders fall into this category.

Figure 1.7 indicates that the supply management department closes its purchase order file before the invoice is audited. This is usually the case if accounting audits the invoice. When supply management audits the invoice, its records are closed after the audit. Closing the order simply entails consolidating all documents and correspondence relevant to the order; the completed order then is filed in the closed-order file. In most firms, a completed order consists of the purchase requisition, the open-order file copy of the purchase order, the acknowledgment, the receiving report, the inspection report, and any notes or correspondence pertaining to the order. The completed order file thus constitutes a historical record of all the activities encompassing the total purchasing cycle.

## The Small-Order Problem

Small orders are a perennial problem in every organization and a serious problem in some. An examination of a typical company's purchase order files reveals that a sizable percentage (sometimes up to 80 percent) of its purchases involve an expenditure of less than $250. In total, however, these purchases constitute a small percentage (seldom more than 10 percent) of the firm's annual dollar expenditures. For example, 75 percent of Conoco's purchase orders are for expenditures of less than $500 and 50 percent are for less than $100.[17] The Intel Corporation found that its purchasing department spent 66 percent of its time managing 1.7 percent of the firm's expenditures.[18] Kaiser Aluminum Chemical devised a system by which blank checks were sent along with their orders. This allowed the supplier to fill the order and fill out the check for payment. This system reduced the number of invoices handled and the amount of time and human capital required to process payments.[19]

Clearly, no manager wants to devote more buying and clerical effort to the expenditure of less than 10 percent of his or her funds than to the expenditure of the other 90 percent, yet this frequently is what happens. The nature of business requires the purchase of many low-value items. Nevertheless, small orders are costly to buyer and seller alike. It costs a seller only a few cents more to process a $1,000 order than it does to process a $10 order. The following sections discuss various methods a purchasing manager can use to minimize the small-order problem.

### Centralized Stores System

A stores system is the first approach typically used to reduce the volume of small-order purchasing activity. When experience shows that the same supply items are ordered in small quantities time after time, the logical solution is to order those items in larger quantities and place them in a centralized inventory for withdrawal as needed. An analysis of repetitively used production materials leads to the same action for the multitude of low-value items. If usage of an item is reasonably stable, an optimum order quantity can be computed by using a basic economic order quantity approach. This will be discussed in detail in Chapter 20. There is, of course, a limit to the number of items and the financial investment a firm can place in inventory.

---

[17]Gordon Regan, "Conoco Procurement Card Program," Presentation to the Executive Purchasing Roundtable, Phoenix, AZ, February 28, 1994.

[18]Roger A. Whittier, "How Intel's Purchasing Now Uses Plastic to Generate Cost Savings," *Supplier Selection and Management Report,* May 1994, p. 13.

[19]Anna E. Flynn, "Evolution of a Profession and a Program," *Inside Supply Management,* 14, no. 1 (January 2003), p. 29.

### Blanket Order System

A stores system solves the small-order problem only for items that are used repetitively. A *blanket order* system helps solve the problem for the thousands of items a firm cannot carry in inventory as well as some that it does carry.

Briefly, the general procedure used for this type of purchase is as follows. On the basis of an analysis of past purchases, the buyer determines which materials should be handled in this manner. After bidding or negotiating, the buyer selects a supplier for each item or family of items and issues a blanket order to each supplier. This order includes a description of each item, a unit price for each item when possible, and the other customary contract provisions. However, no specific order quantities are noted. The blanket order typically indicates only the estimated usage during the period of coverage (usually one to three years). It also states that requirements are to be delivered upon receipt of a release from the procurement professional or an other authorized person. On receiving a requisition for one of the materials, the procurement professional sends a brief release form to the supplier. On the release form are noted the blanket order number, the item number, and the quantity to be delivered. Receiving reports are filed with the original order and at the end of the month are checked against the supplier's monthly invoice. At the end of the period, the order may be renewed or placed with another firm, depending on the supplier's performance record.

Many companies develop their own unique modifications of the basic procedure. For example, instead of advising suppliers of order releases by means of a written form, some companies issue releases to local suppliers by telephone, by fax, or electronically. By noting such releases on the order, the procurement professional retains adequate control.

If material is needed immediately and the supplier is nearby, some firms allow the using department to pick up the material without notifying the supply management department. The employee obtaining the material endorses and enters the proper accounting charge on the sales receipt, a copy of which is sent to the supply management department. In many firms today, user administration of the blanket order is commonplace as it frees up time to work on more important tasks.

The blanket order system offers seven important benefits:

1. It requires many fewer purchase orders and reduces clerical work in purchasing, accounting, and receiving.
2. It releases procurement professionals from routine work, giving them more time to concentrate on value-added activities.
3. It permits volume pricing by consolidating and grouping requirements.
4. It can improve the flow of feedback information because of the grouping of materials and suppliers.
5. Because some supplier stock materials for prompt delivery, this system may reduce the buyer's lead times and inventory levels.
6. It allows the supplier to plan and buy more effectively, reducing the buyer's price.
7. It develops longer-term and improved buyer-supplier relationships.

To function effectively in the long run, however, any blanket order system must provide adequate internal control. Absence of the control element encourages petty fraud and poor supplier performance. The elements essential to effective control are

1. A numbered purchase order, including proper internal accounting charge notations
2. A record of authorized delivery releases
3. Bona fide evidence of receipt of the material

Despite the fact that blanket order systems offer both the buying and the supplying organizations a number of important benefits, organizations often fail to utilize this tool fully in dealing with small orders.

### Systems Contracting

Frequently used as a basic purchasing strategy as well as an approach for minimizing the small-order problem, systems contracting is an extension and a more sophisticated version of the concept of blanket order purchasing. Some firms call it "stockless" purchasing.

As its name implies, systems contracting involves the development of a corporatewide agreement, often a one- to five-year requirements contract, with a supplier to purchase a large group or "family" of related materials. The items to be purchased usually are described in detail in a "catalog" that becomes part of the contract. Estimated usage usually is included, along with a fixed price for each item and an agreement by the supplier to carry a stock of each item that is adequate to meet the buyer's needs. Various types of supplies and commonly used operating items, typically purchased from distributors, are the materials most often covered by these types of agreements.[20]

In addition to the benefits of blanket order purchasing, a major objective of systems contracting is to minimize both the buyer's and the supplier's administrative costs associated with the purchases. The operating procedures of the two firms are integrated to the extent practical. For example, users in the buyer's various operating locations usually send their purchase requisitions directly to the supplier that has the contract for the item. The requisition thus serves as the purchase order. The supplier maintains a list of such shipments on a "tally sheet," identifying each one by the requisition number (or a supplier-assigned number), and periodically (monthly or semimonthly) submits the tally sheet to the buyer for payment in lieu of an invoice.

These types of integrated procedures and shortcuts typically develop a closer relationship between the two firms and reduce paperwork and associated costs markedly. The buyer's inventories and carrying costs decline as well.

### Electronic Ordering Systems

The evolution of the Internet has created opportunities to purchase products and services more efficiently. Computers talking to computers replenish inventories of repetitively used items, expediting the purchasing process, reducing paperwork, and simplifying internal accounting and control.

A platform developed to facilitate electronic buying, the Trading Process Network (TPN) developed by General Electric can help buyers collaborate with suppliers by e-mail, post information to suppliers via the TPN office website, and share engineering information and other information securely. GE states that its TPN Business Services are capable of interfacing with all aspects of the supply chain and link the enterprise with the trading community by providing an electronic channel for distributing information around the world.[21]

---

[20]For a good discussion of systems contracting in MRO buying, see J. A. Lorincz, "Systems Contracts Put Control in MRO Buying," *Purchasing World,* May 1986, pp. 51–54, and Mary Lu Harding, "Designing Auto-Resupply Systems," presented at the 82nd Annual International Conference Proceedings, 1997 (available on the ISM website at www.ism.ws).

[21]George L. Harris, "Revolutionary Ways to Transfer Purchasing Responsibilities to Users and External Organizations," presented at the ISM's 82nd Annual International Conference Proceedings, 1997.

### Purchase Debit and Credit Cards

The use of corporate debit and credit cards by employees for MRO purchases and small-order buys has become commonplace. In addition to eliminating the need for most purchase orders, this technique reduces the purchasing cycle time, improves purchasing relations with operating departments, provides much faster payment to suppliers, and significantly reduces the workload in the accounts payable department.

Debit cards often offer the same protection to the buying firm without the interest that would be charged on credit transactions. Banks advertise the business debit card as being safer than cash, faster than writing a check, and easier to track. Also, it can be used to pay recurring payments such as Internet service and insurance premiums. Both debit and credit cards offer detailed records of use that allow for control and protection against unauthorized use.

Internally, cards are issued to operating department personnel with preset spending limits, variable daily limits on purchases, or tools to protect the account from fraud. Each card carries the appropriate departmental accounting charge number. The organization then receives a detailed monthly bank statement with the purchase and account number so that the account can be reconciled against expenses reported by the various users.

Many financial institutions today make it very inviting for companies to use debit and credit cards by offering perks such as purchase assurance and extended warranties, roadside assistance, travel services and assistance, and in some cases insurance coverage.

### Supplier Stores/Consignment System

If a purchaser buys a large enough volume of certain materials from a single supplier, the supplier sometimes can afford to staff a small "store" at the purchaser's plant and operate it on a consignment basis. Some suppliers find that annual purchases of approximately $100,000 justify this type a branch operation. Users then simply go to the store and sign for their purchases. At the end of the month the company is billed for its purchases. This system clearly is not a short-term arrangement. The purchaser therefore must take great care in selecting the supplier and negotiating the terms of the agreement.

### Supplier Delivery System

The supplier delivery system is somewhat similar to a supplier stores system, but it is more feasible for firms with a smaller volume of purchases. Many suppliers who are not willing to set up a store at the buyer's plant are willing to stock numerous miscellaneous materials and make daily or semiweekly deliveries. Purchase requisitions for such materials are accumulated. The supplier's delivery person then picks them up on the specified day and at the same time delivers the material ordered in the preceding batch of requisitions. This continuous shuttle service provides reasonably fast delivery and also reduces the purchaser's paperwork and inventory problems. When properly designed, the system can provide for adequate accounting control.

## Concluding Remarks

The basic steps in the purchasing cycle are the same for any buy. The time and effort put into completing each step vary with the importance of the need. With today's technology, many of these steps can be automated. The end result of this process may vary, depending on the skill of the procurement professional or the sophistication of the organization's buying process.

# 2 CHAPTER

# Organizational Issues

*After reading this chapter, you should be able to:*

1. Understand and define the terms presented in this chapter.

2. Understand where supply management fits into an organization.

3. Explain why the location of supply management within the organizational hierarchy is important.

4. Identify the four factors that influence the importance of supply management in a firm.

5. Identify the five classifications of work in a supply management operation.

6. Recognize the difference between operational activities and strategic activities.

7. Explain the advantages of centralized and decentralized supply management decision making.

8. Describe the evolution of purchasing and supply management organizational structure from materials management to supply management and supply chain management.

## VIGNETTE: A STRATEGIC SHIFT FOR XENIA

In 1998, Xenia was the leading producer of transducers worldwide. The company took pride in its marketing, product innovation, and assembly excellence. By 2002, Xenia's Asian competitor was selling its transducers for what it cost Xenia to produce comparable units. At that time, Xenia engineers designed virtually all of Xenia's components, which then were purchased from one or more of the firm's 4,000 suppliers. Widespread competition was used to obtain the best price. The selected supplier built to Xenia drawings and specifications.

Management at Xenia responded to the competitive threat. The corporation's strategy shifted to a new set of core competencies: marketing, product innovation, assembly, and supply management. The progression to supply management was enhanced by the establishment of an executive position: the Chief Procurement Officer. The CPO's organization was retitled "Supply Management." The CPO became a member of the executive committee, allowing for greater input in developing corporate strategy. Equally important, supply management was able to ensure that its strategies were aligned with those of the corporation. Over a period of three years, Xenia reduced its supply base from 4,000 to 400 suppliers. Xenia worked with those suppliers to bring them to world-class status with long-term contracts. The suppliers became involved in the development of Xenia's new transducers.

The results? Cost of goods sold was reduced 50 percent. Incoming quality problems virtually disappeared. The time required to move a new product from concept to customer was reduced 45 percent. Production lead times were reduced 65 percent. All those results were achieved in only three years! ■

## CRITICAL THINKING QUESTIONS

1. What was the most important shift in Xenia's set of core competencies?
2. What impact did the appointment of a CPO at the executive level have on the supply management function?
3. What is the impact of reducing the supply base? How is this achieved?
4. What might be some benefits of getting suppliers involved in the development of Xenia's new transducers?
5. What is the benefit of reducing cost of goods sold, time to market, production lead times, and quality problems?

In any group activity, three principal factors largely determine the level of performance attained by the group as a whole:

■ The capabilities of the individuals
■ The motivation of the individuals
■ The organizational structure within which the individuals function

This chapter focuses on the last factor. The first two factors are obvious to most businesspeople, but to many people the impact of the third is less clear. In the case of supply management, the function's location in the management hierarchy of a firm is important, for this decision either facilitates or limits the influence supply management policies and actions can have on the firm's total performance. Within the department itself, the form of organization selected influences the types and levels of expertise developed and also, to a great extent, the effectiveness with which the talents of individuals are utilized.

A firm's organizational structure reflects management's basic attitudes toward the major activities involved in its operation. Where should the supply management function fit in a firm's organizational structure?

# Placement of Supply Management Within the Organization

The location of the supply management department within an entity's organizational structure greatly influences that department's ability to function optimally and influence the decision-making process involved in effective procurement. The lower supply management is on the organizational chart, the less likely it is that it can influence corporate strategy significantly. In practice, the center for advanced purchasing studies, caps, in a study conducted in 2000 found "The supply organizational structure was forced to be congruent with the overall corporate structure," as opposed to selecting the most appropriate structure for large firms.[1]

The importance of supply management in any firm is determined largely by four factors:

**1.** *Availability of materials and services.* Are the major materials and services used by the firm readily available in a competitive market, or are some key materials and services bought in volatile markets that are subject to periodic shortages and price instability? If the latter condition prevails, creative performance by analytical supply management professionals is required; this typically is a top-level group.

**2.** *Absolute dollar volume of purchases.* If a company spends a large amount of money for materials and services, the magnitude of the expenditure means that effective supply management usually can produce significant profit. Small unit savings add up quickly when thousands of units are purchased. On the service side, a contract for IT (information technology) services can run into millions of dollars. Thus, a 10 percent saving contributes significantly to the bottom line.

**3.** *Percent of product cost represented by materials and services.* When a firm's materials and outsourced services costs account for 40 percent or more of its total operating budget, small reductions in material and service costs increase profit significantly. Well-executed supply management usually pays handsome dividends in such companies.

**4.** *Types of materials and services purchased.* Perhaps even more important than the preceding considerations is the amount of control purchasing and supply personnel have over the availability, quality, and costs of purchased materials and services. Most large companies use a wide range of materials and services, many of whose price and service arrangements definitely can be influenced by creative purchasing performance. Some firms, in contrast, use a fairly small number of standard production and supply materials or services from which even a top-flight purchasing and supply department can produce little profit through the use of creative management, pricing, and supplier selection activities.

In her article "I'm Convinced: You've Got Value!" Mary Siegfried Dozbaba emphasizes the need for purchasing and supply management departments to demonstrate to the top executive their value and commitment to improving profitability. To attain commitment and respect from the top, purchasing and supply management must shift its focus from internal processes to big-picture issues such as determining and defining the requirements, contract negotiation, supplier relations, and strategic long-term goals of the organization. "You need to be willing to let responsibility flow out of the unit. Purchasing and supply does not need to approve every requisition . . . stop being the price police," she says. "You want to . . . be called in to negotiate the multimillion dollar contracts, not just to buy pens."[2] Such activities will ensure that a purchasing and supply department is favorably positioned to support organizational needs in today's highly competitive marketplace.

---

[1]Michiel R. Leenders, P. Fraser Johnson, Anna E. Flynn and Harold E. Fearon, *"Purchasing and Supply Management: With 50 Supply Chain Cases,* 13th ed. Burr Ridge, IL: McGraw-Hill Irwin, 2006, p. 39.

[2]Mary Siegfried Dozbaba, "I'm Convinced: You've Got Value," *Purchasing Today* 10, no. 5 (May 1999), p. 44.

# Other Factors That Affect Organizational Structure

## Classification of Responsibilities and Activities

The starting point in thinking about potential organization structures is a delineation and an analysis of the work to be done by the unit: the responsibilities and activities. The six classifications of work in a purchasing operation are as follows:

**1.** *Management.* Management of the purchasing and supply function involves all the tasks associated with the management process, with an emphasis on the development of policies, procedures, controls, and the mechanics for coordinating purchasing operations with those of other departments. On an exception basis, it also involves the management of unique supplier and commodity problems.

**2.** *Buying/supply management.* This includes a wide variety of activities, such as working with users to help develop requirements and specifications, reviewing requisitions, analyzing bids, negotiating, and selecting suppliers. Additional responsibilities involve continuing work with a supplier to improve the supplier's capability and performance in the areas of cost, quality, and service.

**3.** *Contract and relationship management.* This responsibility ranges from monitoring purchase orders and working with accounts payable, to the application of project management skills, to a key procurement such as a construction project. Relationship management is appropriate for many major procurements in which the supplier's motivation, cooperation, and collaboration are essential factors in a successful relationship and a successful procurement.

**4.** *Strategic planning and research work.* A well-developed purchasing and supply management operation has a large number of research projects and systems studies that require specialized knowledge and analytical ability. The more an organization has progressed toward a supply management focus, the more emphasis it places on these strategic activities. The core activities in this area include economic, industry, and supply market studies; the development of buying strategies for material or services buying; the development and implementation of supply base and partnering plans; product research and value analysis work; and operating and information systems analysis.

**5.** *Follow-up and expediting.* Order follow-up activity involves various types of supplier liaison work, such as reviewing the status of orders and occasionally visiting suppliers.

**6.** *Clerical activities.* Every department must enter orders and maintain working files, catalogs and library material, and records for commodities, suppliers, prices, and so on.

The precise manner in which purchasing work is subdivided and grouped depends on the size of the department, which depends on the size of the company.

## Operational versus Strategic Responsibilities

In small firms, responsibilities may be handled by a purchasing or supply manager and one or two assistants; everyone wears several hats. In large organizations, the department may consist of 100 to 300 purchasing and supply professionals.[3] In 1998, R. David Nelson, Vice-President of Worldwide Supply Management at Deere & Co., hired 94 supplier development *engineers* to accomplish supplier activities, resulting in $22 million in cost savings! A major activity or responsibility for any purchasing and supply

---

[3]Large multiplant firms may employ 1,000 or more buyers and/or engineers.

| Operational Responsibilities | Strategic Responsibilities |
|---|---|
| Placement of Purchase Orders | Supplier Development Responsibilities |
| Managing Contract and Blanket Order Releases | Coordinating the Procurement Systems |
| Expediting Inbound Orders | Developing Long-Term Contracts |
| Maintaining Continuity of Supply to Production Lines | Developing and Integrating Supply Strategy |
| Managing Supplier Relationships | Managing Risks in Supply Chain |
| Transactionally Focused Activities | Strategically Focused Activities |

**Figure 2.1** | Operational and Strategic Characteristics and Activities

management department is to provide an uninterrupted flow of materials and services. The tasks required to accomplish this goal often are referred to as tactical or **operational activities.** These activities are not a great source of cost savings yet are critical in avoiding tremendous losses resulting from potential disruptions in operations. Operational activities offer minimal value-added benefits yet are often pressing and time-consuming. The focus on such tactical activities results in less time being allocated to profit-generating **strategic activities**. Figure 2.1 demonstrates various operational and strategic characteristics and activities.

Supply managers have begun to see the need for two types of resources in their organizations: (1) a team of people who manage the operational and tactical activities of purchasing and materials management and (2) supply managers who are involved in the development of broader strategic aspects of the function. Those organizations are in a position to separate operational and strategic responsibilities formally in their organizational structures. This ability to focus on the strategic sourcing process promises long-term increased profitable sales and cost savings, improving profitability, and competitive advantage.

## Organizational Authority

The placement of supply management decision-making authority affects the structure of the supply organization. **Centralized authority** exists when the decision-making process is the responsibility of a single person. This person is held accountable by top management for the proper performance of purchasing activities. **Decentralization of purchasing authority** occurs when personnel from other functional areas—production, engineering, operations, marketing, finance, and so on—make unilateral decisions on sources of supply or negotiate with suppliers directly for major purchases. As discussed in this book, this concept is concerned solely with the placement of purchasing *authority*. It has nothing to do with the location of buying personnel.

Generally, in a single-site operation, to decentralize the purchasing function needlessly is to deny a firm some of its potential profit. Centralization of the purchasing function is essential for the attainment of both optimum operating efficiency and maximum profit. Most companies today view the centralization of purchasing as a logical and desirable evolution of Frederick Taylor's basic concept of the specialization of labor. The extent to which the efficiencies of functional specialization are realized when a firm creates a supply management department, however, depends largely on the authority delegated to that department. When functioning properly, centralized purchasing produces the following benefits:

1. **Reduction of potential duplication of effort.**

2. **Leveraging of volume purchases:**  Volume discounts are possible when all company orders for the same and similar materials are consolidated. In addition, a firm is able to project a unified policy to its suppliers, gaining maximum competitive advantage from its total economic power.

3. **Consolidation:** Consolidation provides an opportunity to standardize and simplify parts. Additional benefits can be gained from value analysis and value engineering coordinated through a centralized function.

4. **Transportation savings:** Transportation savings can be realized through the consolidation of orders and delivery schedules.

5. **Allowance of specialization:** Centralization develops purchasing specialists whose primary concern is purchasing. With training, purchasing specialists inevitably buy more efficiently than less-skilled individuals can.

6. **Reduction of suppliers' costs:** Suppliers are able to offer better prices and better service because their expenses are reduced. Their sales personnel make fewer calls, prepare fewer orders, make fewer shipments, prepare fewer invoices, and do less recordkeeping.

7. **Improved inventory control:** More effective inventory control is possible because of company-wide knowledge of stock levels, material usage, lead times, and prices.

8. **Lower administrative costs:** Fewer orders are processed for the same quantity of goods purchased, reducing purchasing, receiving, inspection, accounts payable, and recordkeeping expenses.

9. **Centralized control:** Responsibility for the performance of the purchasing function is placed with a single department head, facilitating management control.

10. **Reduction in the costs of services:** Warren Norquist, while Vice President of Materials Management at Polaroid, centralized the purchase of marketing services such as advertising. As a direct result of centralization, Polaroid had savings in excess of 25 percent.

Despite the general advantages of centralization, *complete* centralized purchasing is neither always possible nor always desirable. Four types of situations justify some decentralization. The first is found in companies that process *single natural raw materials.* Many of those firms separate the purchase of key raw materials from the purchase of other materials. Firms in the textile, leather, food, beverage, and tobacco industries are good examples. In these industries, the raw materials are products of nature that are purchased in unstable markets in which prices fluctuate widely. Buying typically takes place at auctions or through commodity exchanges conducted in small local warehouses. In such markets, a practical knowledge of grades is as important as knowledge of prices. Buyers of these commodities usually guard their specialized know-how with secrecy, frequently handing it down from one generation to the next.

A second situation justifying some decentralization of purchasing authority exists in *technically oriented firms that are heavily involved in research.* In those firms some exceptions to complete centralization are always desirable. Many one-time purchases in the research, design engineering, and related departments can be handled more effectively by professional personnel in those departments. Moreover, the dollar volume of such purchases is usually relatively small.

The third situation justifying a different type of decentralization is found in the *operation of multisite institutional and manufacturing organizations.* Decentralization in this circumstance can allow for a faster response time for the requisitioner, a better understanding of the requirements unique to that plant, quicker support in product development projects, and ownership of the process and products.[4]

---

[4]Robert Monczka, Robert Trent, and Robert Handfield. *Purchasing and Supply Chain Management,* 3rd ed. (Mason, OH: South-Western, 2005), pp. 148–49.

Fifth, the *purchase of nontechnical odds and ends* often calls for a partial decentralization of purchasing. Credit card and petty cash fund purchases of less than several hundred dollars are a good example. Decentralizing through the use of these approaches can be a money saver.

The danger of losing purchasing control does not stem from partial decentralization of the purchasing function per se. Some decentralization is necessary as a matter of common sense. The use of cross-functional teams in the decision-making process is increasing. Organizations are changing to compete in the global market. Companies are seeking to take advantage of both structures by forming a **hybrid structure** that includes both centralized and decentralized decision making. This results in the best of both structures, maintaining necessary control while meeting the unique needs of the other functions or divisions.

### e-Commerce

Technology has provided a solution to the debate about centralized versus decentralized organizational structures. As computers began to appear on desktops in the late 1980s, purchasing departments were able to reduce administrative time and costs by placing purchase orders electronically. Electronic data interchange (EDI) was the early stage of e-commerce. Electronic catalogs of approved supplies or services could be created through a centralized supply management department and disseminated to decentralized locations for purchase. Electronic billing and remittance of invoices improved cash flow while reducing the cost of doing business. e-commerce allowed corporate policy and procedure to be distributed and monitored effectively while giving divisional supply management departments the authority to make purchases to meet their local requirements. e-commerce has been a catalyst, enabling organizations to benefit from the hybrid supply management structure.

## Organizational Structures

As was stated above, the position of the supply management department on a firm's organizational chart can vary. However, as materials gained in importance, becoming a larger proportion of the cost of goods sold, issues such as inflated inventories, poor quality, material stockouts, long lead times, and miscommunications provided the impetus for a movement to capture control of materials under one individual. This gave rise to the materials management approach to structuring the material portion of an organization.

### The Materials Management Organization

The concept of organizing the functions that affect the acquisition, movement, and storage of materials under one manager evolved in the early 1960s. The term **materials management** was introduced to describe an integrated systems approach to the coordination of materials activities and the control of total material costs.[5] The purchasing, planning and scheduling, transportation, and warehousing functions were organized under the control and responsibility of one individual: the materials manager. The objective was to optimize the performance of the materials system, as opposed to suboptimizing the performance of the individual functions that are parts of the materials system. The results were "great improvements in inventory levels, customer service, and communications, ultimately improving the bottom line."[6]

---

[5]For the classic reference, see Dean S. Ammer, *Materials Management and Purchasing,* 4th ed. (Homewood, IL: Richard D. Irwin, 1980).

[6]Marilyn Gettinger, "Strategic Thinking: Movin' on Up from Supply Management to the Supply Chain," 91st Annual International Supply Management Conference, ISM, Tempe AZ, May 2006, p. 2.

The materials management organization was popular during the 1960s and 1970s. This concept of integrating the functions involved in the management of materials paved the way for the more sophisticated concept of supply and supply chain management.

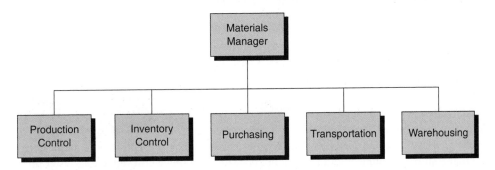

## The Supply Chain Management Structure

In the late 1980s Japan invaded the U.S. automobile market with cars assembled in Japan. This marked the beginning of globalization as we know it today. The early 1990s saw the appearance of personal computers on the desktops of organizations, putting data and information at the fingertips of managers. With the introduction of the Internet and the World Wide Web, the information age began. Through these developments, the concept of managing materials for competitive advantage flourished. The materials management structure evolved beyond the idea of managing a corporation's inventory and the functions responsible for supply. The broader concept of **supply chain management** grew to encompass the planning and management of all activities involved in forecasting, sourcing, and procurement and all incoming logistics management activities. It broke down the functional silos, creating integrated processes throughout the organization.[7] In describing the breadth of supply chain management, Marilyn Gettinger, C.P.M., president of New Directions Consulting Group, writes:

> Importantly, it also includes coordination and collaboration with channel partners such as suppliers, intermediaries, third-party service providers, and customers. In essence, supply chain management integrates supply and demand management within and across companies. It is a total system approach to facilitate coordination internally and with supply chain partners, often using enhanced communication and information technologies.[8]

## Organizing with Cross-Functional Teams

Cross-functional teams have become a common approach to addressing many supply-management-related activities, including new product development,[9] value analysis and value engineering, standardization and simplification, engineering change management, the development of statements of work describing services requirements, commodity teams, the acquisition of capital and operating equipment, make/buy and

---

[7]Ibid.

[8]Ibid.

[9]Laura M. Birou, Stanley E. Fawcett, and Gregory M. Magnam in "The Product Life Cycle: A Tool for Functional Strategic Alignment," found that "companies are striving to break down functional barriers that inhibit effective product and process design." *International Journal of Purchasing and Materials Management,* Spring 1998, p. 37.

outsourcing analysis, source selection, potential supplier field reviews, negotiation, post-award management and problem solving, supplier development, and the development of strategic alliances.[10] Since cross-functional teams require a significant investment in human resources, their use commonly is limited to time-critical and high-monetary-value activities. The appendix to this chapter addresses cross-functional teams in greater detail.

## Concluding Remarks

Foremost in developing an organizational structure is finding a structure that will allow the organization's supply chain to function effectively and efficiently. ISM Professor of Supply Chain Management Robert M. Monczka tells us in "Finding a Structure That Works," "Establishing appropriate organizational structure and governance processes for the supply management function is critical to effective supply chain management. Competitive and customer pressures, globalization, outsourcing and the need for innovation from external sources, combined with unrelenting pressure to achieve cost reduction, faster time to market and improved customer responsiveness, all increase the importance of this decision."[11]

## Discussion Questions

1.  Why is supply management's position in the corporation's organizational structure important?
2.  How do the four factors identified by the authors affect the significance of supply management in a firm? For example, is supply management more or less significant when one is buying products from a volatile market?
3.  Review the tasks identified under each of the five classifications of work in a supply management operation. Which tasks under each classification might be considered operational and which might be considered more strategic?
4.  Why are many organizations using a hybrid approach to decision-making authority in their supply management?
5.  How has the advent of the World Wide Web influenced the growth of supply chain management?
6.  Why is the organizational structure an important issue in managing the purchasing and supply function?
7.  Identify some ways in which cross-functional teams could be useful in developing new products or completing value analysis functions.

## Internet Exercise

(http://www.utc.com/press/highlights/2006-09-08_purchasing.htm)

### United Technologies: Company Highlights
### "Supply Management wins *Purchasing* medal of excellence."

1.  Why was United Technologies chosen for this honor?
2.  Would you identify UTC's approach to supply management as centralized, decentralized, or hybrid? Explain.

---

[10]"Chrysler used a team approach and chose suppliers before the parts were even designed, which meant virtually eliminating traditional supplier bidding." James Bennet, "Detroit Struggles to Learn Another Lesson From Japan," *New York Times*, June 19, 1994, p. F5.

[11]Robert M. Monczka, "Finding a Structure That Works," *Inside Supply Management* 17, no. 12 (December 2006), pp. 10–11.

3. Discuss some of the company's accomplishments that led to its receipt of the award.
4. How does UTC's corporate culture support the achievements of the supply management team?

## Suggested Reading

Dischinger, John, David J. Closs, Eileen Mcculloch, Cheri Speier, William Grenoble, and Donna Marchall. "The Emerging Supply Chain Management Profession," *Supply Chain Management Review,* January/February 2006, pp. 62–68.

Ellram, Lisa. "Supply Chain Management: The Industrial Organization Perspective," *International Journal of Physical Distribution & Logistics Management* 21, no. 1 (1991), pp. 13–22.

Gattorna, John. *Living Supply Chains: How to Mobilize the Enterprise around Delivering What Your Customers Want* (Harlow, U.K.: Pearson Education, 2006).

Giannakis, Mihilas, and Simon R. Croom. "Toward the Development of a Supply Chain Management Paradigm: A Conceptual Framework," *Journal of Supply Chain Management,* Spring 2004, pp. 27–37.

Handfield, Robert B., and E. L. Nichols. *Introduction to Supply Chain Management* (Upper Saddle River, NJ: Prentice-Hall, 1999).

Harris, George L. "Missing Links in Strategic Sourcing," *Inside Supply Management,* August 2005, pp. 27–31.

Lambert, D. M., and M. Cooper. "Issues in Supply Chain Management," *Industrial Marketing Management* 29 (2000), pp. 65–83.

Larsson, P. D., and A. Holldorsson. "What Is SCM? And, Where Is It?" *Journal of Supply Chain Management* 38, no. 4 (2002), pp. 36–44.

Lummus, R. R., and R. J. Vokurka. "Defining Supply Chain Management: A Historical Perspective and Practical Guidelines," *Industrial Management & Data Systems* 99, no. 1 (1999), pp. 11–17.

Trent, Robert J., and Robert M. Monczka. "Purchasing and Supply Management: Trends and Changes throughout the 1990's," *Journal of Supply Chain Management* 34, no. 4 (1998), pp. 2–11.

# Appendix: Benefits Resulting from Cross-Functional Teams[12]

## Synergy

The many activities identified in this chapter have one thing in common: They all benefit from a variety of functional inputs. For example, during the new product development process, marketing has information on customers' wants and needs, their willingness to purchase at different prices, and present and potential competition. Design engineering has knowledge about current and future design processes and constraints. Manufacturing engineering has information on the firm's and its suppliers' manufacturing processes and their limitations. Supply management provides a window to the supply world and its capabilities and limitations and the likely cost and availability of various materials and services under consideration. Customer service, quality, finance, information technology, and carefully selected suppliers all have many additional contributions to make during the new product development process. When these professionals come together under a capable team leader, the result is normally a synergy that results in a far more profitable new product far more quickly than would have occurred with the traditional sequential approach to new product development.

[12]Many of the ideas in this appendix were introduced by one of the authors' mentors, Professor Norman Maier of the University of Michigan, during the mid-1960s.

## Input from All Affected Functions

The cross-functional approach greatly increases the likelihood that all issues that should be considered will be addressed. For example, customer support and service frequently were overlooked in the traditional sequential approach to new product development. Standardization efforts, which are conducted or controlled by a single functional area such as manufacturing engineering, frequently overlook the procurement, manufacturing, and marketing implications of implementing new standards. The result is surplus purchased materials, manufacturing bottlenecks, or products that do not compete in the marketplace.

## Time Compression

A hypothetical example may help in understanding the traditional sequential or functional approach to many of the activities discussed above. Marketing at Alpha Corporation has identified a need for a new complex transducer. Marketing describes this need to design engineering, which designs the transducer. On completion of the design, the specifications and drawings are forwarded to manufacturing engineering, the function responsible for translating design engineering's specifications into production plans.

Manufacturing engineering determines that certain tolerances cannot be met by the firm's production equipment. Design engineering is asked to revise the specifications. Design engineering contacts marketing to determine what impact the revised tolerances (ones which the firm's equipment can meet) will have on sales. If the impact is significant, manufacturing and possibly plant engineering may become involved. They may decide that new equipment is required. This process continues on through the quality assurance function. Quality assurance reviews the specifications and production plans to ensure that the required level of quality will be obtainable. The customer service function then reviews the specifications and manufacturing plans so that it can develop plans to support the transducers in the field. Obviously, each function along the sequential path leading to production of the desired transducer may question or even challenge the design specifications and manufacturing plans. This back-and-forth process ultimately leads to a product that is late to market and overpriced.

## Overcoming Organizational Resistance

With the cross-functional approach, all functional areas are involved up front, and this helps reduce organizational resistance to decisions that will affect specific functional areas. In contrast, decisions that affect multiple functional areas, that are made without the involvement of those areas are likely to meet resistance. The representatives of each of the functional areas involved on the team constructively provide their input and are involved in the resulting agreement. In turn, each representative is responsible for ensuring acceptance by his or her functional area of the team's decisions. Experience indicates that once a team makes a decision, implementation of the resulting plan is much easier and faster than is the case with the sequential approach.

## Enhanced Problem Resolution

The cross-functional team approach is far more efficient and effective at solving problems than the traditional functional one is. For example, if a supplier, in spite of its best efforts, is unable to meet the contract schedule or quality requirements, a cross-functional team representing supply management, manufacturing engineering, and quality may be formed to work with the supplier to resolve the problem. (The solution to a surprising number of such problems is within the customer firm's control, not the supplier's!)

## Negotiations

Negotiations for critical or large-monetary-value materials, services, supplies, or items of equipment are conducted much more effectively by a well-prepared and well-coordinated cross-functional team than by the finest supply professionals alone.

## Improved Communication and Cooperation

The traditional functional approach to the activities listed in the opening paragraph of this appendix normally results in efficiency within each department. However, this approach inhibits communication and cooperation among the departments involved in the activities.

Some 40 years ago, one of the authors was the chief procurement officer (CPO) of a relatively small business unit. The organization's plant engineering department designed specifications for construction projects. Those specifications served as the basis of invitations for bids (IFBs) and the resulting contracts. Numerous questions and problems were encountered with potential suppliers during the bidding process and then with the successful bidder. The specifications were ambiguous and in several cases contained inconsistencies.

The CPO met with the plant engineer and offered to become involved in the development and review of the specifications. The plant engineer rejected the offer, stating: "Development of specifications is my responsibility. Butt out!" Interestingly, the plant engineer subsequently expressed his desire to become involved in the sourcing process. Guess what happened?

## Challenges and Problems with the Cross-Functional Approach

There are several challenges and inherent problems with a cross-functional approach.

### Additional Investment in Scarce Resources

A single professional normally requires far fewer labor hours to accomplish a task than does a team. For example, a single supply management professional can accomplish the many actions involved in selecting a critical supplier in considerably fewer labor hours than can a cross-functional sourcing team. However, a team consisting of a design engineer, a manufacturing engineer, and a quality engineer together with a supply professional will do a far more thorough job of selecting the right source.

### Role Conflict

Normally, cross-functional team assignments impose additional duties on many or all of the individuals involved. In many cases, a team member's functional manager expects that individual to perform his or her normal functional responsibilities. Such responsibilities require about 40 hours per week, and the individual also is expected to satisfy his or her team responsibilities. A number of years ago, one of the authors directed thesis research at the Graduate Logistics Division of the Air Force Institute of Technology. The research focused on minimizing role conflict between functional and team assignments. The subjects were assigned to cross-functional teams developing the B-1 bomber. The researchers focused on a multi-matrix approach to project management as a means of avoiding or minimizing the inherent role conflict. While promising, the research results were inconclusive. Some 25 years later, management is still attempting to cope with the issue of role conflict resulting from part-time assignment of individuals to cross-functional teams. Despite these issues, the benefits of teams usually outweigh the resulting problems.

### Overload for Key Team Members

Overload is an obvious result of the role conflict inherent in the additional duties assigned to key team members. Paradoxically, the most attractive team members are those individuals who are key contributors to their functional organizations. Management must be sensitive to the danger of such an overload to avoid burnout and the possible loss of such individuals.

### Continuity

Obviously, once team members have been trained and developed and have learned to work together in a synergistic manner, continuity of membership becomes critical. Retirement, departure to another firm, promotions, and layoffs can have a negative impact on the team's operation. Careful selection and assignment of team members can reduce but not eliminate such problems.

### Rewards

By now, it should be apparent that individuals who are assigned to cross-functional teams as an additional duty should be rewarded appropriately. The greatest reward is the satisfaction associated with "making a difference" in the team's success. Senior professional managers ensure that functional managers (the chief procurement officer, the director of R&D, the director of manufacturing, etc.) recognize all individuals' contributions to both their functional organizations and the cross-functional team.

A few enlightened organizations have had success with team incentives. These incentives range from team dinners, to a team vacation in Hawaii, to the award of stock options. In some cases, the team receives a bundle of rewards (such as 1,000 stock options). The team members then allocate the options according to a consensus of the members on the relative contribution of each member. More information on this subject may be found in *Rewarding Teams: Lessons from the Trenches.*[13]

## Prerequisites to Successful Cross-Functional Teams

Although there are many prerequisites, we will focus on three especially critical ones.

### Executive Sponsorship

An absolute prerequisite for successful cross-functional teams is the support of an executive sponsor. "Top management team support and political factors may be even more critical to the success of cross-functional teams than the internal team processes."[14] The individual sponsor should have all the functional areas involved reporting to him or her or have the informal ability to secure the cooperation and support of colleagues in obtaining the assignment of the appropriate human resources to the project. Additionally, the executive sponsor must track the cross-functional team's progress, run interference, and obtain additional resources as appropriate.[15]

---

[13]Glen Parket, Jerry McAdams, and David Zielinski, *Rewarding Teams: Lessons from the Trenches* (New York: Jossey-Bass, 2000).

[14]Michael A. Hitt, "Corporate Entrepreneurship and Cross-Functional Fertilization: Activation, Process and Disintegration of a New Product Design Team," *Entrepreneurship: Theory and Practice,* Spring 1999, p. 145.

[15]For additional insight, see David N. Burt and Richard L. Pinkerton, *Strategic Proactive Procurement* (New York: AMACOM, 1996), p. 33, and James W. Dean, Jr., and Gerald I. Susman, "Organizing for Manufacturing Design," *Harvard Business Review,* January–February 1989, pp. 28–36.

## Effective Team Leaders

Without skilled leadership, teams frequently become lost, flounder, get off course, lose sight of their goal, lose confidence, become mired in interpersonal conflicts, stop short of their goal, and never contribute their full potential. Surveys of highly effective teams have shown that their members rated their leaders as highly skilled. Lower-performing teams rated their leaders as being much less effective.

Ideally, a team leader has people skills, communication skills, technical knowledge, experience working with the people who will be on the team, and enthusiasm. The new role of the team leader is to build a team with vision, authority, accountability, information, skills, and a commitment to assuming more and better operational control of the team's work. The new leader expands the capabilities of the team members and the team itself. As a result, the team can perform some of the leader's traditional work roles, such as budgeting, scheduling, setting performance goals, and providing training. The team gradually assumes the day-to-day operations, allowing the leader to manage resources, ideas, technologies, and the work processes. The most challenging aspect of this new role is that the leader must give up part of his or her former, more authoritarian role. Such a shift of roles gives the leader more time to take on strategic roles. The result of the shift is that the team is able to contribute more and with greater speed.

Team leaders must assume a number of roles. They must understand people so that they can influence them. They should encourage and maintain open communication and help the team develop and follow team norms. The team leader needs to step back from his or her management role of directing employees and assume a more collaborative role as a facilitator. The leader should help guide the team and allow the team to identify problems, develop solutions, and then implement those solutions. The team members must be free to express themselves as long as that expression is not destructive in nature. The team leader should support the expression of conflicting points of view. "Team synergy begs for a conflict of ideas. Conflict can bring into being the creative tension where paradigm-shifting ideas are born."[16] While the team leader may need to retain some of the final decision making in the early stages, it should be the leader's goal to develop the team so that it can assume responsibility for the decision making entirely.

The team leader helps the team focus on the task and removes obstacles that stand in the way of the team's performance. Helping the team focus will ensure that the team progresses through productive stages of team development and will reduce the tendency for it to revert to one of the less productive stages. Effective team leaders help minimize turf issues and keep the team focused on the good of the organization. Additionally, the leader needs to make sure that the team members have all the resources they need so that they don't become distracted. The team leader also should remove any obstacles to the team's success.

Additionally, team leaders help establish a vision, create change, and unleash talent. The leader helps the team establish a mission statement and define its goals. Leaders create change within both the organization and the team. They force people to think outside the box and help develop creative solutions to problems. Leaders need to have good people skills to identify and draw out the hidden talents of the team members.

Former American League relief pitcher David Baldwin, writing in the *Harvard Business Review,* addresses the issue of "blame." He focuses on how managers in Major League Baseball employ blame.

---

[16]Tom Schulte, quoted in "Conflict Resolution, A Required Skill for Engineering Team Managers," IOMA's Report on Managing Design Engineering, January 2000, p. 2.

Baldwin contends that blame plays an important role in shaping an organization's culture. He proposes five important rules of blame, which we believe apply to most or all team leaders:

1.  Know when to blame—and when not to.
2.  Blame in private and praise in public.
3.  Realize that the absence of blame can be far worse than its presence.
4.  Manage misguided blame.
5.  Be aware that confidence is the first casualty of blame.[17]

*Meetings: Do's, Don'ts, and Donuts* (Lighthouse Point Press, 1994) offers the following suggestions to team leaders:

■  Decide whether a meeting is the best way to accomplish this. Consider circulating routine information via e-mail. If a meeting is required, distribute an agenda at least two days in advance.

■  State in one or two sentences what you would like your meeting to accomplish.

■  Set ground rules to maintain focus, respect, and order during the meeting.

■  Take responsibility for the outcome of the meeting. For example, help keep the meeting on track and help resolve conflicts.

■  If your meeting isn't working, try other tools, such as brainstorming techniques or computer software that help you create the agenda.[18]

### Qualified Team Members

Experience indicates that the most critical variable in one's ability to be a "high" contributor is willingness and desire to contribute. Baxter Health Care of Paramatta, New South Wales, Australia, ensures that team members are "willing" participants by announcing forthcoming team projects to all employees. Individuals are encouraged to volunteer for the additional assignments as team members representing their functional areas. In many cases, competition for a team position is intense. Thus, the team leader is in the enviable position of being able to select members from a pool of volunteers. Obviously, team membership has the potential for satisfaction and intrinsic and tangible rewards at Baxter.

The Wisconsin Department of Revenue has identified the following communication skills as being significant to employee success. (If an individual is deficient in one or more areas, he or she can attend training offered by the department, attend management development programs, pursue self-study, or obtain a mentor.)

*Listening* (the ability to understand, organize, and analyze what we hear)

■  Actively attend to and convey understanding of the comments and questions of others.

■  Identify and test the inferences and assumptions we make.

■  Overcome barriers to effective listening (semantic, psychological, physical).

■  Summarize and reorganize a message for recall.

■  Keep the speaker's intent, content, and process separate.

■  Withhold judgment that can bias responses to the message.

---

[17]David G. Baldwin, "How to Win the Blame Game," *Harvard Business Review,* July–August 2001, p. 57.

[18]Cited in David J. O'Shea, "Relationship-Building Skills," *NAPM InfoEdge,* September 1998, p. 9. Used with permission of the National Association of Purchasing Management.

### Giving Clear Information

■ Assess a situation, determine objectives, and give information that will best meet the objective.
■ Construct and deliver clear, concise, complete, well-organized, and convincing messages.
■ Keep on target—avoid digressions and irrelevancies and meet the aim of the communication.
■ Determine how to use persuasion effectively.
■ Maintain a climate of mutual benefit, trust, rapport, and a win-win outcome.

### Getting Unbiased Information (minimize the filtering and editing that take place when information is transmitted from person to person)

■ Use direct, nondirect, and reflective questions.
■ Identify forces that may bias the information.
■ Confirm understanding and obtain agreement and closure.

### Fostering Open Communication

■ Create an atmosphere in which timely, high-quality information flows smoothly between self and others.
■ Encourage open expression of ideas and opinions.[19]

### Team Development and Training

Each team will develop its own personality, but the key objective of all teams must be willingness to subordinate personal and functional interests to the team's goals. Having a competent leader and having well-qualified team members are two critical first steps. The third step is team development and training. This calls for investments that should pay a high return. For example, Southern California Edison (SCE) has used team development and training to create one of the best supply management systems in the utility industry. Under the leadership of Emiko Banfield, 24 cross-functional supply management teams have been established to manage supply issues. Each SCE team receives three days of team development and training as a foundation for its activities. As a result, SCE has taken over $250 million out of a spend of approximately $1 billion. Working through cross-functional teams, Banfield discovered that internal barriers could be reduced, setting the stage for successful collaboration if teams were trained properly.[20]

The Supply Chain Management Institute at the University of San Diego is pioneering an alternative approach to team development. Four-person cross-functional teams from client firms undergo interactive training on selected supply management topics. A one-hour workshop is conducted after each one-hour training module. During the workshop, each team conducts a gap analysis, comparing one of its processes with the world-class processes presented in the previous training module. The team then develops a preliminary action plan to close the gap. The plan identifies key actions, a time line, and an estimate of the bottom-line impact of the team's proposed plan. Preliminary findings indicate that cohesive teams evolve with this approach to training and organizational transformation. Although the findings are preliminary, this approach to team development appears to be very cost effective.

---

[19]O'Shea, "Relationship-Building Skills," p. 7.
[20]Emiko Banfield, *Harnessing Value in the Supply Chain* (New York: John Wiley & Sons, 1999), pp. 29–30.

### Adequate Time

Unrealistic deadlines are major problems that block the success of many cross-functional teams. As Burt and Pinkerton wrote, "Too much pressure for results too soon will almost always force a team to premature and less effective decisions."[21] The tendency for management to act now rather than allowing time for good analysis is an old habit in the United States. Many of America's global competitors have the patience to take time to nurture participative management. The results of nurturing participative management are well known. Just ask American automotive manufacturers about the cost of quick reactions without fostering participation.[22]

### Interfirm Teams

When buying and supplying organizations recognize the interdependence and the benefits to both parties of a collaborative or alliance relationship, the development of an interfirm team should be considered. In effect, a superordinate cross-functional team will result. Dan Mohr, Director of Supplier Relations for GTE, observes: "Relationship teams are the building blocks upon which the relationship prospers. Team meetings provide a forum to jointly discuss new ways to reduce process costs, improve service to our customers, and enhance time to market, which ultimately expands market share for both organizations."[23] As with cross-functional teams within each firm, the assignment of the "right" individuals and team training are essential for success. One significant difference is that two executive sponsors will be required, one at each firm. The interfirm team's first task, after receiving appropriate training, is the development of a customized effective and efficient communication system.

As we will see in the chapter on relationships, many progressive organizations are working with selected collaborative suppliers to develop and manage supply alliances. One of the keys to success with such efforts is the development and use of interfirm teams. Experience indicates that the basis of such interfirm teams must be the existence of cross-functional teams at both the buying and the supplying organizations. The development and use of interfirm teams is more challenging than are in-house cross-functional teams, but the benefits are even greater!

### Supply Management's Roles on Cross-Functional Teams

Timothy M. Laseter, vice president, Booz-Allen & Hamilton Inc. in New York, identifies four principal roles for supply management professionals who are members of cross-functional teams:

- Provide the process expertise of supply management in areas such as supply base research, supplier cost modeling, or (more typically) negotiation.
- Provide content knowledge of a specific supply market or commodity area that the supply management individual directs.
- Serve as the liaison with the supply management organization to ensure that project needs obtain priorities among other staff in the corporate organization.
- Represent the supply management point of view in considering trade-offs, setting priorities, and making decisions affecting policy.[24]

---

[21]Burt and Pinkerton, *Strategic Proactive Procurement,* p. 195.

[22]Diane Brown, "Supplier Management Teams," *NAPM Insights,* August 1994, p. 33.

[23]Mary Crews, "Relationship Management Yields Results," *Purchasing Today,* June 2000, pp. 8–9.

[24]Timothy M. Laseter, "Overcoming Conflicting Priorities," *Purchasing Today* 9, no. 1 (December 1998), p. 37.

In 210 B.C., Arbiter Petronius of the Greek Navy wrote, "We trained hard . . . but it seemed that every time we were beginning to form up into teams we would be reorganized, and I was to learn later in life that we tend to meet any new situation by reorganizing."[25] Fortunately, great progress has been made in the design and use of teams, especially in the areas of new product development, project management, source selection, and negotiation.

## End Notes

Although many variables have an impact on the success or failure of a cross-functional team, none is more critical than the team leader. Professor Robert Trent of Lehigh University has conducted extensive research on the role of cross-functional teams in purchasing and supply management. Trent defines an effective team leader as "one who is capable of satisfying a set of essential operating responsibilities and requirements while still promoting the creativity, leadership ability, and innovativeness of individual team members."

Trent identifies 10 requirements for effective team leadership:

- Work with the team to establish and make a commitment to performance goals.
- Secure individual member involvement and commitment.
- Manage internal team conflict.
- Help maintain team focus and direction.
- Secure required organizational resources.
- Prevent team domination by a member or faction.
- Deal with internal and external obstacles confronting the team.
- Coordinate multiple tasks and manage the status of team assignments.
- Clarify and help define each member's role.
- Provide performance feedback to members.[26]

The interested reader is encouraged to read Professor Trent's full article and the 1994 book *Leading Teams: Mastering the New Role.*[27]

In the spring of 1999, Michael A. Hitt reported on a longitudinal case study of a cross-functional new product development team that became dysfunctional and obtained suboptimal results. Hitt's research supports the following important conclusions:

- Top management support of the cross-functional team is essential to the success of critical projects.
- Management leadership of the cross-functional team is critical.
- Functional activities, suppliers, and key customers who have significant input should be involved throughout the project's life.
- Geographically dispersed teams are difficult to manage.[28]

---

[25]Cited in David M. Moore and Peter B. Antill, "Integrated Project Teams: The Way Forward for UK Defence Procurement," *European Journal of Purchasing & Supply Management,* September 2001, p. 57.

[26]Robert J. Trent, "Understanding and Evaluating Cross-Functional Sourcing Team Leadership," *International Journal of Purchasing and Materials Management,* Fall 1996, p. 29.

[27]John H. Zenger, Ed. Musselwhite, Kathleen Hurson and Craig Perrin, *Leading Teams: Mastering the New Role,* Homewood IL: Irwin, 1994.

[28]Michael A. Hitt, "Corporate Entrepreneurship and Cross-Functional Fertilization: Activation, Process, and Disintegration of a New Product Design Team," *Entrepreneurship: Theory and Practice* 23, no. 3 (Spring 1999), pp. 145–68.

## Concluding Remarks

Much of the success in transforming purchasing into supply chain management and then to value network management is based on embracing the power of cross-functional teams. These teams include supply management professionals, design and production engineers, and quality managers and frequently their counterparts from supply chain partners. Such teams play an essential role in the required transformations.

## Suggested Reading

Guertin, Ron, and Vince Scacchitti. "Managing Difficult Teams," presented at the 90th Annual International Supply Management Conference, May 2005.

Katzenbach, Jon R., and Douglas K. Smith. *The Wisdom of Teams—Creating the High-Performance Organization* (New York: McKinsey & Company, 1993).

Killen, Kenneth H., and John W. Kamauff. *Managing Purchasing; Making the Supply Team Work* (Tempe, AZ: Irwin Professional Publishing, 1995).

Larson, Carl E. and Frank M. J. LaFasto. *TeamWork—What Must Go Right/What Can Go Wrong* (Newbury Park, CA: Sage Publications, 1989).

Monczka, Robert M., and Robert J. Trent. "Cross-Functional Teams Reduce New Product Development," *NAPM Insights*® 5, no. 2 (February 1994), p. 64.

Monczka, Robert M., and Robert J. Trent. "Effective Cross-Functional Sourcing Teams: Critical Success Factors," *International Journal of Purchasing and Materials Management* 30, no. 4 (Fall 1994), p. 3.

Parker, Glenn M. "Success Strategies for Cross-Functional Teams: Management's Role," presented at the 80th Annual International Conference Proceedings, Anaheim, CA, 1994.

Trent, Robert J. "Individual and Collective Team Effort: A Vital Part of Sourcing Team Success," *International Journal of Purchasing and Materials Management* 34, no. 4 (Fall 1998), p. 46. Copyright © November 1998 by the Institute of Supply Management, Inc.

# Supply Management: An Organization-Spanning Activity

CHAPTER OBJECTIVES

*After reading this chapter, you should be able to:*

1. Understand the importance of integrating supply management with internal and external stakeholders.

2. Understand the role supply management plays in the supply chain.

3. Understand the importance of connecting suppliers with the ultimate customers.

## VIGNETTE: TROUBLES AT EAGLE MANUFACTURING COMPANY

It is Saturday afternoon, September 6. Ted Jones, supply manager for the Eagle Manufacturing Company, is in his office, reviewing his life at Eagle. Since becoming the head of supply management, Ted has been struggling with one crisis after another while trying to placate operations, plant maintenance, and seemingly half the management team (and their assistants). Although only age 35, Ted feels like he's 60. Eagle is expecting a large return on the salary it is paying him.

In the two years since taking over the department, Ted has put together a great team of buyers, expediters, and support staff. Their work is tops; they are all professionals. But morale has started to be a problem. On Friday, Bill Wilson, Ted's senior buyer, submitted his resignation. Bill decided to take a job with a handsome salary increase at Cable Manufacturers of America. He said, "If I'm going to get ulcers, I might as well be paid for them!"

Ted looks at the August performance data for the office: 743 transactions, 98 percent with delivery on or before the specified dates, 87 percent of supplies and material purchases at or within 5 percent of target price, 9 percent late deliveries, and a 5 percent rejection rate of materials and supplies received. Compared with the months previous to August, the trends look good, but there is still room for improvement. Ted feels that his department can have a much greater impact on the firm's profitability if he can generate more cooperation with the other departments. He also realizes that a better training program will bring along some of his own people a bit faster.

Ted thinks about some of the "big ones" that happened in August. The maintenance department submitted a purchase request for a new robot on August 29. The machine, according to the estimates supplied, would cost $5.5 million. It was to be delivered and operational in seven months. Only one source of supply was able to meet the delivery date. Ted wonders how much extra money the lack of lead time cost on that one.

Tim Raines, vice president of operations, held Ted's feet to the coals in the weekly staff meeting on August 7. Operations had run out of parts that week. The vice president of marketing, Ron Hankins, had helped to apply the coals on that one. In retrospect, Ted is puzzled about the hopscotch communication patterns among operations, material control, marketing, and his own office.

Tim confronted Ted on August 14, again during the staff meeting, saying that quality on the incoming parts was causing major production problems. Ted tried to explain the greater attrition rate inherent in new production processes, but Tim was not convinced.

In fairness, not all his problems were with operations, Ted is thinking during his Saturday afternoon reverie. The president's secretary called twice to say that the janitorial services contractor had not washed the windows properly. Ted mentioned that poorly described, unenforceable specifications were part of the problem. But the secretary was just trying to do her job in seeing that somebody else's job was done right. She didn't know about the "contractual provisions."

Mary Jacobs, head of administration, had complained to Ted on a daily basis about the new brand of reproduction paper. Mary believed that the quality of reproduction was down and that the paper was constantly jamming the machine. Machine downtime was reducing productivity and increasing frustration with her people. Ted pointed out that finance had reduced the funds available for supplies by 20 percent and that the reduction consequently forced some sacrifice in quality.

Yesterday, John McCauly, an experienced buyer who normally is as cool as a cucumber, exploded when Ted asked how everything was going. John replied, "Those blankety-blank estimators. This morning, I was negotiating with Fenwick Electronics for that robot. The maintenance department's estimate was $5.5 million. Fenwick proposed $7.2 million. You know that because of time, they were already in a 'sole-source' position. Imagine my reaction when I learned that our $5.5 million 'estimate' was not an estimate at all but merely the amount budgeted for that machine last year! I had no basis for developing a realistic negotiating objective. I literally had to throw myself on the mercy of Fenwick's marketing manager." Bringing his thoughts back to the present, Ted decides that there has to be a better way. ■

## CRITICAL THINKING QUESTIONS

1.  What might be some of the reasons other departments are not cooperating with Ted Jones's group?
2.  How will Ted's people benefit from training? How will training improve their relationships with other departments?
3.  Would a Supply Chain Management approach improve this situation?

"Purchasing is changing like it never has before in its history, [and] so are all of the other areas of the organization."[1] As businesses cope to compete in the ever-changing landscape of a global market, internal business relationships are becoming critical.

# Supply Management's Relations with Other Departments

A supply management department is the hub of a large part of a company's business activity. By its nature, supply management has continuing relationships with all the other departments in the firm as well as with the firm's suppliers. Supply management operations cut across all departmental lines. Figure 3.1 provides a graphic illustration of supply management's many interfaces within the organization.

## Supply Management and Engineering

Design engineers traditionally have played key roles throughout the supply chain management process, ranging from new product development team leaders to members of off-spec (incoming materials which deviate from the relevant specifications) review teams. However, with the advent of outsourcing of engineering tasks and projects, engineers are actively seeking ways to demonstrate value added to the organization.[2]

Supply management, engineering, and operations have many problems in common. Design engineering greatly influences the amount of time supply management has to handle a procurement assignment. Engineering has the initial responsibility for preparing the technical specifications for a company's products and services and the materials that go into them. To exercise this responsibility effectively, engineering should have the assistance of supply management and operations. A number of firms have initiated early supply management and early supplier involvement programs to ensure that supply management and suppliers contribute to the development of new products and services as they work together with the engineers in the development of a product. (Since early supply involvement and early supplier involvement have identical acronyms, we have coined the acronym ESI[2] to refer to the two terms simultaneously.) Some firms refer to this process as concurrent engineering versus sequential design work, where engineers design a product and then look to supply management and outside suppliers for input. This approach can cause incompatible designs to be sent to manufacturing and suppliers.

The product costs associated with quality, materials, fabrication, and production are inextricably linked to the design specifications. Similarly, specifications can be written in a manner that reduces or enlarges the number of firms willing to supply specific items. If costs are to be controlled and profit maximized, the materials specified by engineering must be economical both to purchase and for fabrication. Ideally, materials should be available from more than one efficient, low-cost producer. Obviously, the quality of the materials must satisfy operations and the ultimate customer.

Supply management and engineering occasionally differ in their concepts of materials problems. Their differing views are understandable. Engineers naturally tend to design conservatively; hence, their specifications may provide amply for quality, safety, and performance. By training, an engineer may be inclined to seek the "ideal" design, material, or equipment without complete regard for cost, availability, or functional need. A supply professional is more concerned with commercial issues such as cost and

---

[1]Joseph L. Cavinato, "Business Change: It Isn't Just in Purchasing and Supply," *Purchasing Today*[R] 12, no. 12 (December 2001), p. 38.
[2]Cavinato, "Business Change," p. 38.

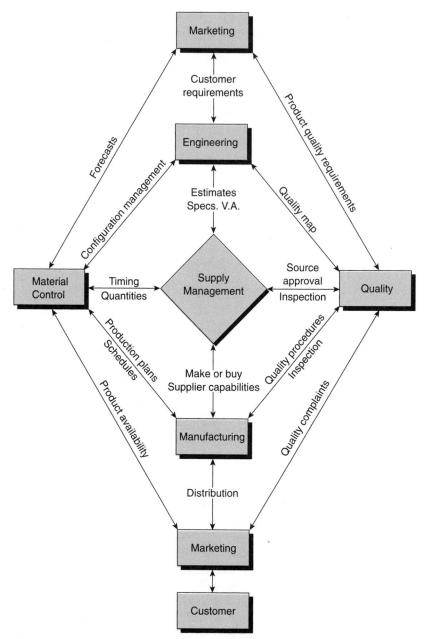

**Figure 3.1** I The Many Internal Interfaces of the Supply Management Function.[3]

---

[3]David N. Burt and Richard L. Pinkerton, *A Purchasing Manager's Guide to Strategic Proactive Procurement* (New York: American Management Association, 1996), p. 5.

availability while meeting the functional need of the customer. Several situation-specific questions asked by supply management to engineering usually can help integrate cost and availability considerations into the design process. For example, supply management may ask, "Is it possible to reduce the designer's performance goals and safety margins and to work closer to actual performance requirements? Is an expensive design with a high safety factor necessary if a less costly design with a lower but acceptable safety factor will do the job? Why use costly chrome plate if brushed aluminum is adequate?" Clearly, conflicting functional interests cannot always be resolved easily. The answers to such problems are seldom clear-cut. Mutual understanding and a willingness to give and take are required from both sides if mutually satisfactory solutions are to be reached. The key consideration *must* be the best interests of the firm, not any single functional area!

## Supply Management and Manufacturing and Operations

The supply management–manufacturing relationship begins during new product development and intensifies when manufacturing transmits its manufacturing schedule or materials requisitions to materials control, which translates those documents into a procurement schedule. Purchase timing is often a cardinal difficulty in making that translation. When the user does not give supply management sufficient time to purchase wisely, many needless expenses inevitably creep into the final costs of a company's products. When supply management has inadequate time to qualify suppliers properly, develop competition, or negotiate properly, premium prices are likely to be paid for materials. Costly special production runs, premium transportation costs, and quality problems are three common results of inadequate purchasing lead time.[4]

A production shutdown is the most serious problem stemming from insufficient procurement lead time. In most process types of operations (chemicals, cement, paint, flour, etc.), either equipment runs at nearly full capacity or it does not run at all. Consequently, material shortages in these industries can be catastrophic, resulting in a complete production stoppage. Losses resulting from material shortages in nonprocess industries are not always so disastrous or apparent. A production shutdown in a metal fabricating shop, for example, can be piecemeal. The indirect costs of such shortages, consequently, often are hidden in production costs. One or two machines from a large battery of 50 can be shut down as a routine occurrence. Conventional accounting records fail to reveal the financial impact of this kind of slow profit-draining inefficiency. Late delivery of equipment, services, or supplies also can affect the efficiency of a service organization. Imagine a dentist without the appropriate drill bit or an information technology (IT) supplier whose time to market is affected by late delivery of necessary software.

Coordination between supply management and manufacturing pays off in many ways. For example, a more expensive alternative material that will save the company money can be selected on occasion. This may sound like a paradox. "Pay more and save more"—how can this happen? Savings in manufacturing and assembling costs often can exceed the increased purchase costs. In the normal manufacturing operations of casting, forging, machining, grinding, stamping, and so on, some materials are much more economical to work with than others are. For example, government suppliers have saved thousands of dollars by using bronze instead of steel extrusions in aircraft elevator and rudder counterweights. Bronze costs more than steel, but savings in machining time more than offset the increase in material cost. In this case,

---

[4]Supply management has the responsibility to keep users informed about supply lead times for all categories of production materials.

**Table 3.1 |** Effect of Different Materials on Productivity and Cost

|  | | Costs Totals (steel) | | Costs Totals (bronze) |
|---|---|---|---|---|
| Sales | | $100 | | $100 |
| Costs of goods sold | *Man-Hours* | *Costs* | *Man-Hours* | *Costs* |
|   Raw material cost | | 5 | | 10 |
|   Direct labor (machining) | 2 | 30 | 1 | 15 |
|   Variable overhead | | 6 | | 3 |
|   Fixed overhead | | 50 | | 50 |
| Total cost | | $91 | | $78 |
| Operating income | | $9 | | $22 |

*Note 1:* Productivity Improvement: $|(.5 - 1.0)/.5| = 100\%$ improvement
*Note 2:* Profit Improvement: $|(9 - 22)/9| = 144\%$ improvement

not only is the direct cost reduced, as an added benefit skilled machinists and expensive machine tools are freed to do other high-priority work. See Table 3.1 for a comparison of these costs.[5]

Going beyond these day-to-day operational interfaces, supply management and manufacturing must coordinate effectively to achieve some of a firm's key strategic goals. For example, manufacturing management strives to achieve faster "time to market" performance and reduce the time required for product changeovers and tool and line setup work. Supply management must be able to assist in these efforts by obtaining faster responses from suppliers, working with suppliers to improve their capabilities, and so on. In these types of activities, it is imperative that manufacturing and supply management work together closely.

Information technology is simplifying the relationship between supply management and manufacturing. Computers and sophisticated software allow a firm's MRP (materials resource planning) system to communicate seamlessly with the counterpart systems at the firm's suppliers, and ERPs (enterprise resource programs) add to the necessity for data accuracy and interconnectivity. With this approach, supply management is not involved in the day-to-day tactical activity of placing orders.

As pressure continues to build for reductions in manufacturing costs, more and more products and processes will be outsourced and the supply management–manufacturing relationship will take on greater importance. Organizations will try to control the quality and quantity of outsourced materials without investing capital in equipment or having responsibility for labor. According to Joseph Cavinato, "All of this plays well into supply managers' roles, because higher and higher level relationships and arrangements are needed for these all to work efficiently and effectively. Instead of buying raw materials, they are now arranging for complete products to be produced and in many cases distributed."[6]

## Supply Management and Quality

Quality professionals should be involved in supply management from the development of new products, to involvement in sourcing, and on through supplier development with the objective of minimizing quality problems throughout the supply chain. Quality's role and responsibilities change significantly when the manufacturing function is outsourced. Quality is involved in qualifying the potential supplier. Then it

---

[5]Burt and Pinkerton, *A Purchasing Manager's Guide to Strategic Proactive Procurement,* p. 9.
[6]Cavinato, "Business Change," p. 38.

becomes responsible for monitoring the supplier's quality system and providing technical assistance if quality problems occur.

## Supply Management and Marketing

Supply management *should* be marketing's best friend! As was described in Chapter 1, supply management has a major impact on the firm's sales. The quality of the firm's products is often dependent on the quality of its suppliers. Marketing's success in generating sales is in part attributable to the firm's ability to introduce new products in a timely manner, new products that are based on technology obtained from the firm's supply base, and pricing flexibility resulting from reductions in the cost of goods sold. Many companies recognize the direct relationship between marketing excellence and profitability. In their enthusiasm to increase sales, however, companies may overlook the leaks in profit that can occur when the sales activity does not mesh properly with the supply and production activities. The sales/supply/production cycle has its genesis in a sales forecast. The forecast is the basis for the production schedule, which in turn is the basis for the materials schedule. The sales forecast also influences a firm's capital equipment budget as well as its advertising campaigns and other sales activities.

Prompt communication to manufacturing and supply management of changes in the sales forecast permits these departments to modify their schedules as painlessly and economically as possible. Likewise, changes in production schedules should be communicated immediately to sales representatives. This permits marketing to alter its distribution schedule in a manner that will not alienate customers. Supply management must immediately transmit to marketing, as well as to other management groups, information about increases in material prices. That information permits marketing to evaluate the effect of rises in price estimates given for future sales quotations on current selling prices and on plans for future product lines.

Supply management and marketing must wisely blend their interests in the delicate area of reciprocity (buying from customers). If satisfactory legal reciprocal transactions are to be developed, they must be pursued with an understanding of the true costs of reciprocity. Buying from friends can be good business, but not when it is done at the expense of product quality or higher prices for purchased materials or services. In its desire for increased sales, a company can lose sight of the fact that increased sales do not always result in increased profit. Increased sales may result in decreased profit if they simultaneously require an increase in purchase prices.

A supply management department can be of major help to the marketing or sales department by serving as its practical sales laboratory. A firm's supply management department is the target for many manufacturers' sales operations. Supply management's files are replete with the sales literature, policies, and promotional approaches of a broad range of manufacturers and distributors. Supply management professionals are aware of the personal selling methods sales representatives have used most effectively on them. They are equally aware of sales practices that fail or irritate them. Therefore, a company's supply professionals can be an excellent source of information for developing and refining the company's sales policies and procedures.

Many marketing departments spend considerable amounts of money on advertising and promotion. In many cases, the focus of those expenditures is the impact of advertising, not its cost. Several years ago Warren Norquist, former Vice President of World Wide Purchasing and Materials Management at Polaroid, demonstrated that the application of sound supply management practices to the purchase of advertising resulted in an average savings of 24 percent.[7]

---

[7] Personal discussions with Mr. Norquist, 1989.

## Supply Management and Finance

The finance department is charged with two principal responsibilities: obtaining funds and overseeing their use. Poor financial planning and execution is *the* major cause of business failure. Supply chain management is responsible for as much as 80 percent of many firms' financial resources. Thus, the CFO (Chief Financial Officer) and his or her key subordinates have a vested interest in a cost-efficient Supply Chain Management system. Though supply managers often view finance as a department with a "low-price mentality," finance has the means of identifying costs to help purchasing gain a better understanding of the total cost of ownership. Marilyn Gettinger, president of New Directions Consulting, tells us that supply should collaborate with finance because "each has the same focus: investing resources wisely with the greatest return on investment."[8]

Regardless of the price advantage available, the right time to buy from the standpoint of business conditions is not always the right time to buy from the standpoint of the company's treasury. If the supply management department makes commitments to take advantage of unusually low prices without consulting the finance department, the company can find itself paying for those purchases with funds needed for other purposes. However, if the finance department does not strive diligently to make funds available for such favorable buying opportunities, the company may have to pay higher prices later for the same material.

Finance's willingness to reimburse suppliers in a timely manner affects supply management's ability to obtain low prices and forge and maintain collaborative relationships. During the 1970s, for example, Timex had a policy of paying its suppliers the day a supplier's invoice and the receiving report arrived in the accounts payable office. As a result, Timex became a preferred customer of many of its suppliers. During two periods of material shortage in the 1970s, Timex's preferred customer status allowed it to avoid the shortage problems experienced by most firms. As a result of enlightened supply management practices, Timex never missed a beat! We see that a cooperative relationship between purchasing and finance can have an impact on the development of good supplier relations.

As discussed in Chapter 1, supply management has a major impact on 10 major components of a firm's costs. An efficient and effective supply management function significantly reduces the funds required to operate the firm. The timing of purchasing expenditures can be of significant importance to a finance department that is working diligently to protect the firm's financial ratios and solvency. Supply management and finance should coordinate on expenditures that may have a significant impact on the firm's cash position. Finance should be represented on cross-functional teams that are purchasing major equipment or construction services because of the magnitude of the expenditures involved.

Investors properly are concerned with the firm's return on investment (ROI). As shown in Figure 3.2, supply management has a major impact on this key indicator. Notice how a 5 percent reduction in a hypothetical firm's expenditures increases its ROI by 30 percent!

## Supply Management and Information Technology

Supply management and IT have an increasing number of interdependencies. In some cases, IT is outsourced. The director of IT and a supply management professional must work together closely to develop the appropriate statement of work and the sourcing and pricing processes and to manage the resulting contract and relationship.

---

[8]Marilyn Gettinger, "Supply Management and Finance—Building Bridges," *Inside Supply Management* 17, no. 1 (January, 2006), p. 6.

**Figure 3.2 |** The Relationships of Basic Elements Which Influence Return on Investment
The figures in parentheses reflect a 5 percent reduction in the cost of materials.

Many firms are purchasing B2B e-commerce buy-side software systems from firms such as Ariba and Oracle. Such software systems have a major impact on a firm's procurement processes. End users are being empowered to purchase directly from the firm's and its approved supplier's electronic catalogs. The transition from a paper-based system of requisitions, manual approval, manual citation of budgetary authorization, requests for proposals, purchase orders, receiving reports, and payment checks to electronic purchasing must be planned and implemented carefully.

Electronic communication for production materials—whether over the Internet or through electronic data interchange (EDI)—requires coordination and cooperation between supply management, IT, and manufacturing or material control.

Another example of the interdependency between purchasing and IT is the development of a database which provides timely and accurate input to supply management for strategic planning and tactical activities. Relatively few firms have developed such information systems.

Obviously, another interface exists between supply management and IT: the procurement of software, software services, and equipment. It is our observation that when the two departments operate collaboratively, a synergy results. In contrast, when IT operates in a Lone Ranger mode and does its own procurement, much waste frequently results.

## Supply Management and Logistics

When one of the authors was enrolled in the Ph.D. program at Stanford, purchasing was a component of the logistics program. At that time, both logistics and purchasing were relatively tactical. During the subsequent years, both have progressed to recognition as critical functions. Today, logistics spends approximately 10 percent of a manufacturer's income. Purchasing (supply management) spends some 60 percent.

Logistics is concerned with the movement of goods. In many cases, logistics is responsible for both incoming goods and the distribution of goods to the next member of the supply chain and frequently to the end customer itself. In virtually all cases, logistics professionals design and manage the firm's distribution system, which consists of warehouses, distribution points, and freight carriers.

The relationship between supply management and logistics tends to vary from firm to firm. In some cases, supply management plays a dominant role in sourcing and pricing logistics services. In other cases, the logistics department performs those services with little or no supply management involvement. The critical issue should not be one of jurisdiction; it should be one of professionalism and excellence. It should not matter whether supply management or logistics plays the key (or dominant) role. What does matter is that professional supply management practices are employed. Today, professional practices include hiring third-party firms to store, handle, and transport assets. "This option allows what would be fixed system costs to be incurred and paid for by the client organization on a per unit basis."[9]

Many organizations are getting tremendous results from collaboratively managing the logistics portion of their supply chains. In the service industry in particular, strategies are being utilized to improve the process of getting information and products through the supply chain. "Deerfield, Illinois-based Baxter Healthcare is in the process of leveraging its global logistics costs."[10] Their collaborative approach to logistics is working to improve forecasting and is taking a collaborative approach to the demand planning processes.

## Supply Management and Accounts Payable

The proliferation of corporate purchasing cards has had a major impact on both supply management and accounts payable. The use of those purchasing cards has had several beneficial effects: (1) It empowers end users of standard and low-value requirements to purchase directly from distributors, (2) it reduces tactical, non-value-adding purchases by the supply management department, and (3) it significantly reduces accounts payable activities.

Supply management and accounts payable frequently have conflicting interests and drivers in the area of timely payment to suppliers. Accounts payable commonly reports to the Chief Financial Officer. Finance is responsible for obtaining funds and their productive use. Finance professionals frequently take pride in seeing their "idle" funds invested at returns of 6–12 percent. This superficially "logical" thinking causes many finance professionals to keep the money entrusted to their safekeeping as long as possible.

---

[9]Personal discussions with Mr. Norquist, 1989.

[10]John Yuva, "Collaborative Logistics: Building a United Network," *Inside Supply Management* 13, no. 5 (May 2002), p. 42.

One means of achieving this apparently laudable objective is to delay paying suppliers as long as possible. For example, many suppliers to hospitals must wait six months to be reimbursed for materials, equipment, and services provided. (We assume that the accounts payable/finance people must feel good that they have earned investment income on the backs of helpless suppliers!)

Ignoring the ethical implications of that unilateral action for the moment, such action is in conflict with supply management objectives and possible breach of contract. The sophisticated supplier who has experienced delays in payment simply increases its selling price to its customers. Nobody wins. Of greater importance, nonresponsive payment often conflicts with supply management's efforts to become a preferred customer or to develop collaborative and even alliance relationships. Obviously, those conflicts can and must be overcome through open discussions between supply management and finance professionals.

## Supply Management and Lawyers

Legal professionals frequently are actively involved in contract negotiations and contract formation. In other cases, their role is one of review and approval of contracts developed by supply management professionals. Value-adding attorneys who are involved in supply management issues normally must embrace a collaborative approach to dealing with the firm's suppliers. It is the senior author's observation that a legal education is *not* a good background for the members of most negotiating teams. This is equally true of the contract formation process. Unfortunately, most attorneys are trained to look for risk and worst-case scenarios. Collaborative, pie-enhancing negotiations frequently are disrupted by attorneys who are obsessed with risk avoidance!

This is not to say that lawyers cannot add value: They most certainly can! However, care must be exercised in inviting the involvement only of lawyers who are concerned with the best interests of both parties and with enabling pie-enhancing negotiations.

# Supply Management in Nonmanufacturing Organizations

Supply management has as much—and sometimes more—impact on the success of nonmanufacturing organizations as it does on that of manufacturing firms. The timely availability of reliable equipment, supplies, and services at the right total cost of ownership affects the ability of such organizations to provide timely quality services at a profit.

In a manufacturing setting, design and manufacturing engineering professionals normally lead the new product development effort and the development of the appropriate specifications describing what is to be purchased. In a nonmanufacturing setting, supply management often must lead or facilitate the requirements process because of the absence of engineering or other qualified requirements professionals. Thus, a supply professional may need to assume the responsibility for leading a cross-functional team that is identifying or describing a nonmanufacturing need that will be satisfied through a procurement.

While the total costs of purchases compared with net income or budget authorizations may be proportionately less at a nonmanufacturing firm than at a manufacturer, such expenditures still are very significant. Supply management's impact on sales can be every bit as significant as it is in manufacturing firms. Quality implications, time to market, pricing elasticity (based on reductions in the cost of goods sold), technology inflow, and continuity of supply combine to have a major impact on a nonmanufacturing firm's sales. Thus, we see that supply management also has a major impact on a nonmanufacturing firm's bottom line!

# Supply Management in Government

Supply management (frequently called "procurement" in government circles) has a major impact on the efficient and effective use of tax dollars at all levels of government. Virtually all the problems present in manufacturing organizations are present in government procurement. Not surprisingly, many advances in the art and science of supply management originated in the federal government.

# Supply Management and the External Environment

## Business Relationships

All phases of supply management involve relations with external suppliers: early supplier involvement in the development of requirements, strategic sourcing, pricing (including cost analysis and negotiations), and post-award activities. These interfaces are explained in detail throughout the book.

## Monitoring the Supply Environment

Supply managers are responsible for protecting their firms from unexpected threats or shocks from their supply world in the form of price increases and supply disruptions. These threats include material and labor shortages which affect one or more industries that supply the firm. Shortages will affect both the price and the availability of purchased materials, supplies, and services. The firm should take actions that minimize the impact of shortages by monitoring changes in the supply environment such as the following:

- Changes in legislation that may affect the workplace. Such changes can have an impact on both price and availability. An example is a new Environmental Protection Agency regulation on toxic wastes that affects one or more suppliers.
- Wars and other conflicts that may disrupt the availability of materials and services a firm or its suppliers require. Firms that proactively monitor the environment take defensive action in anticipation of the resulting material and labor shortages and price increases.
- A consolidation among suppliers. The extreme case is consolidation to the point of monopoly. Such changes may require a change in a firm's supply strategy.
- Wages, projected wages, and possible labor relations issues.

Supply managers should have early information that will allow them to take advantage of favorable market conditions. Opportunities result both from additional capacity coming on-line and from reductions in demand for required materials, equipment, and services.[11]

The responsibility for protecting their firms from unexpected threats or shocks motivates supply professionals to develop supply monitoring systems. One of the challenges confronting today's supply professionals in monitoring is the abundance of data. "Today purchasers are literally inundated with bits of data concerning their suppliers, the markets in which those suppliers participate, and the functioning of the economy as a whole. Turning such data into meaningful, useful information—supply market knowledge—is one part of the supply professional's tasks, but so is leveraging supply information into

---

[11]The Institute for Supply Management (formerly the National Association of Purchasing Management) publishes a comprehensive report on business in *Inside Supply Management* each month. The report shows macro trends in both manufacturing and nonmanufacturing sectors and featured reports on select industries.

knowledge that increases the competitive advantage of the firm. Before attempting to understand the supply market, supply professionals must first possess a clear understanding of what is meaningful to their own organizations."[12]

Monitoring supply markets is a fascinating and challenging activity. In the late 1980s, Warren Norquist, former Vice President of World Wide Purchasing at Polaroid, assigned three researchers the responsibility of monitoring Polaroid's supply environment and then advising Polaroid buyers of potential threats and opportunities in their supply world. Frank Haluch, writing in the August 2000 issue of *Purchasing Today,* outlined a six-step environment monitoring strategy:

- Determine the cost, supply, and technology drivers of the materials and services that a supply manager is watching.
- Identify the major suppliers and customers of the materials and services.
- Determine the sources of information for those drivers.
- Build a model that predicts the material (or service) behavior.
- Monitor the model to determine its accuracy.
- Continuously make improvements as new relationships are understood and additional data becomes available.[13]

Supply environment monitoring, coupled with timely reaction to the threats and opportunities that are identified, is a key strategic activity which has a significant impact on a firm's success and survival.

## Completing the Supply Chain Linkage: Supplier Integration with the Customer

As the authors have stressed in previous chapters, supply management has a great impact on sales as well as costs. Suppliers should be major sources of innovation which results in profitable new products or services. Early supplier involvement can reduce the time required to bring a new product to market, resulting in greater market share. Supplier quality affects the quality of the firm's products, its image in the marketplace, and its sales volumes. Suppliers can help "lower costs, improve delivery, lower inventory, and problem-solve capabilities during the [customer order] fulfillment stage of production."[14] Suppliers and end user connections emerge to meet a wide variety of needs.

## Concluding Remarks

The purchasing process spans both internal and external organizational boundaries. As the process evolves to supply management, both the complexity and the strategic importance of the process increase dramatically. And as the panorama of the global business environment continues to unfold, the relationships supply managers have both inside and outside the organization will continue to evolve.

---

[12]Richard R. Young, ed., "Knowledge of Supply Markets," Chapter 5 of *The Purchasing Handbook,* 6th ed., Joseph L. Cavinato and Ralph G. Kauffman, editors in chief (New York: McGraw-Hill, 2000). For more on this report, see Ralph G. Kauffman, "Indicator Qualities of the NAPM Report on Business," *Journal of Supply Chain Management,* Spring 1999, p. 29.

[13]Frank Haluch, "Taking the Market's Pulse," *Purchasing Today,* August 2000, p. 6.

[14]Robert Monczka, Robert Trent, and Robert Hanfield, *Purchasing and Supply Chain Management,* 3rd ed. (Mason, OH: South-Western, 2005), pp. 124–25.

# Discussion Questions

1. Explain the importance of supply management relationships with other internal departments.
2. What is meant by concurrent engineering?
3. How can engineering product specifications affect the price of the product?
4. How can a product that costs more save the company money overall?
5. What impact can a company's quality department have on an outsourced part?
6. Why should supply management and marketing be best friends?
7. In what ways can finance help the supply management group purchase products and services at a lower cost?
8. In nonmanufacturing industries, who leads the requirements development process? Why?
9. How can changes in the environment affect the products you buy?
10. Identify some changes in the environment which the authors feel can have an impact on the task of procuring materials and services?

# Internet Exercise

## Reverse Auction Sites

Visit the "Reverse Auction Sites" website below. Read about one use of IT in the supply management function.

(http://www.brajeshwar.com/finance/auctions/reverse_auction_sites.html)

1. Why are these auctions referred to as "reverse"?
2. Give a brief description of how these auctions work.
3. What does the site caution sellers to guard against?

# Suggested Reading

Ayers, James B. *Handbook of Supply Chain Management,* 2nd ed. (Boca Raton, FL: Auerbach Publications, 2006).

Humphreys, P. "An Inter-Organizational Information System for Supply Chain Management," *International Journal of Production Economics* 70, no. 3 (2001), pp. 245–55.

Killen, Kenneth H. and John W. Kamauff. *Managing Purchasing: Making the Supply Team Work.* Burr Ridge, IL. Irwin Professional Books, 1995.

Lambert, Douglas M. *Supply Chain Management: Processes, Partnerships, Performance,* 2d ed. (Sarasota, FL: Supply Chain Management Institute, 2006).

Moore, Kevin R. "Trust and Relationship Commitment in Logistics Alliances: A Buyer Perspective," *International Journal of Purchasing & Materials Management* 34, no. 1 (1998), pp. 24–37.

Mentzer, John T., Matthew B. Myers, and Theodore P. Stank. *Handbook of Global Supply Chain Management* (Thousand Oaks, CA: Sage Publications, 2007).

Mentzer, John T. *Supply Chain Management* (Thousand Oaks, CA: Sage Publications, 2000).

Mentzer, John T., William DeWitt, James S. Keebler, Min Soonhoong, Nancy W. Nix, Carlo D. Smith, and Zach G. Zacharia. "Defining Supply Chain Management," *Journal of Business Logistics* 22, no. 2 (2001), pp. 1–25.

Stank, Theodore P., Scott B. Keller, and Patricia J. Daugherty. "Supply Chain Collaboration and Logistical Service Performance," *Journal of Business Logistics* 22, no. 1 (2001), pp. 29–48.

# A Portfolio of Relationships

## CHAPTER OBJECTIVES

*After reading this chapter, you should be able to:*

1. Describe the continuum of buyer-seller relationships.

2. Identify several characteristics of a transactional relationship.

3. Understand the value of developing collaborative relationships.

4. Explain why supply alliances create a win-win situation for both buyer and supplier.

5. Determine whether a relationship should be transactional, collaborative, or a strategic alliance.

6. Explain why a supplier may not see the value in a close relationship with a buyer.

7. Identify situations in which alliances are not appropriate.

8. Explain the role of power in the buyer-seller relationship.

## VIGNETTE: A SUPPLIER ALLIANCE AT QUAKER OATS

By 1998, the Quaker Oats Company of Chicago, Illinois, had captured over 82 percent of the global market in the sports beverage industry with its Gatorade brand. In an effort to increase Gatorade's market share, Quaker Oats searched for ways to bring a lower-priced product to the market. With the bottle being the biggest expense in producing Gatorade, the purchasing department established a goal of lowering the bottling cost $10 million to $15 million per year. One goal specifically was to be competitive with Coke and Pepsi in the cost of bottling.

Recognizing that good potential suppliers were the key to achieving that goal, Quaker Oats developed a strategy of seeking supplier relationships that would help it do that. In 1997 Quaker Oats was single-sourced; dual sourcing became the strategy it pursued. Quaker needed to create a competitive environment in which it would reap the benefits of the competitive bottling market. Not only could competition improve service, quality, and cost, it would drive continuous improvement in those areas.

Quaker worked to build trust and create a relationship with a second source that would result in mutual benefits. As you can imagine, the original supplier was resistant to Quaker's attempts to improve its position with the supplier. At one point it asked Quaker Oats what price it would take not to pursue a dual-source strategy. Although the existing contract contained clauses that created difficulties, Quaker Oats had learned from its mistakes in that contract and did pursue an alliance with a second source. The trust-building process Quaker Oats had employed in searching for a second source resulted in the alliance between the Quaker Oats Company and Graham Packaging of York, Pennsylvania, discussed in Appendix B in this chapter. As a result of that alliance, an in-plant bottling facility was constructed at the Gatorade plant in Atlanta, Georgia. Quaker supplied capital for the plant expansion, and Graham covered the cost of equipment in the facility. Graham agreed to operate the plant and accept responsibility for meeting quality and efficiency standards. It also agreed to be responsible for selling unused capacity in the off-season. The alliance produced savings of $20 million per year by reducing costs at the Georgia plant and helping Quaker leverage its relationship with its original single-source supplier.

The Quaker negotiation team spent a year putting the alliance in place. In addition to visiting bottling companies, plastic molding organizations, and resin suppliers, the team spent many hours holding trust-building sessions with potential suppliers. The most difficult groups to convince were the internal executive management team and the board members. The proposal for Graham to operate on-site at Quaker Oats required a cultural adjustment according to Mr. Richard Reider, currently Director of QTG Package Purchasing for Pepsico (Reider was director for Quaker Oats Purchasing at the time of those negotiations).

Quaker had been in a business relationship with the current supplier for 12 years. Because Gatorade represented 40 percent of this supplier's business, Quaker management believed it had enough leverage to obtain the most competitive price. Management's trust in the existing single-source supplier's ability to produce the least costly product available led it to question another supplier's ability to beat the current price. Senior management at Quaker Oats was uncomfortable with the level of commitment required by both parties to make Reider's onclause-site proposal work. Once Graham agreed to management's insistence on a "meet competition" and an "escape" clause in the contract and because of Reider's substantial projected savings and ability to confirm Graham's technical competence, the alliance between Quaker Oats and Graham Packaging was able to go forth. The alliance resulted in significant savings from the current supplier as well.

Quaker Oats was not the only benefactor from the alliance. Graham Packaging was able to draw on its new alliance to grow. In 2001, Graham's purchase of Owen's Illinois bottling division made Graham Packaging a giant in the bottling industry. Also in 2001, Gatorade's success was the spark that ignited much of Pepsi's interest in acquiring Quaker Oats. Quaker Oats and the Gatorade product are now part of the Pepsico family.[1] ■

## CRITICAL THINKING QUESTIONS

1.  Give an example of competition driving improvements in service, quality, and cost.

2.  Why was Quaker Oats intent on building trust in these relationships?

[1]Richard G. Reider, personal interview, June 2007.

3. With the help of your instructor, discuss the importance of Graham taking responsibility for unused capacity in the off-season.

4. Why do you think upper management would have to be convinced to accept a change that would benefit the organization?

## A Transformation in Relationships

As supply management progresses from reactive and mechanical purchasing to proactive procurement and on to Strategic Supply Chain Management, a similar transformation is evolving in relationships between buyers and suppliers. During the dark days of reactive purchasing, relations between salespersons representing suppliers and their counterparts in purchasing were reasonably cordial but frequently adversarial. A gain for one resulted in a loss for the other; that often is called a win-lose outcome. The interaction between supplier and purchaser often was characterized by highly manipulative tactics by both parties designed to maneuver the other side into a position where one's gain would be the other's loss. As purchasing became more professional, buyers and suppliers began to see benefits of more collaborative relationships in which the outcome can be a win-win relationship for both parties.

During the late 1980s and early 1990s, suppliers saw many advantages in developing "partnerships" with customer firms. Sales managers charged their salespeople with becoming partners with their key customers. However, because of a lack of clarity from management, many salespeople did not understand the implications of the term "partner." Additionally, the legal implications of that term raised further implications and concerns. For example, is a buyer partner free to solicit prices from competing suppliers? Is a supplier partner required to give all of its partners the same price and services?

While the term "partnership" is still relatively common, we avoid its use, preferring the terms "collaborative relationship" and "strategic alliance." With this new perspective, purchasing's role has changed "from a provider of the right components at the right time and lowest costs, to a manager of the supply base responsible for the generation of competitive advantages for the company."[2] Scholars such as J. Dyer and H. Singh believe that a firm's potential competitive advantage is more than its assets, technology, and resources. The emerging relational view recognizes that a firm's competitive advantage can evolve from the relationships between buyers and suppliers.[3]

## Three Types of Buyer-Supplier Relationships

Figure 4.1 portrays the three levels of relationships between buyers and sellers as they develop from a transactional arm's-length relationship to the close working relationship of an alliance. Note the shift in attitude to activity/attributes as the barriers are reduced.

---

[2]Christopher Jahns, Roger Moser, Evi Hartmann, and Martin Lockstrom, "Rent-Based Supplier Management Behavior," Eighteenth Annual North American Research and Teaching Symposium on Purchasing and Supply Chain Management, Educational Resources Committee of ISM, CAPS Research, Institute for Supply Management, and the Purchasing Management Association of Canada, Tempe, AZ, March 29–31, 2007, p. 1.

[3]Jahns et al., "Rent-Based Supplier Management," p. 5.

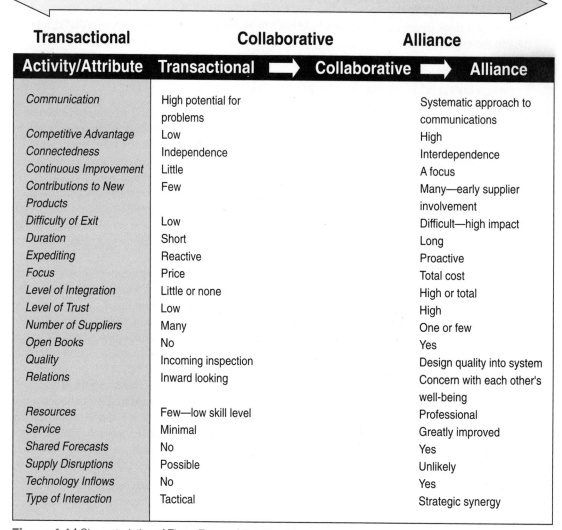

**Figure 4.1 |** Characteristics of Three Types of Relationships

| Activity/Attribute | Transactional ➡ | Collaborative ➡ | Alliance |
|---|---|---|---|
| Communication | High potential for problems | | Systematic approach to communications |
| Competitive Advantage | Low | | High |
| Connectedness | Independence | | Interdependence |
| Continuous Improvement | Little | | A focus |
| Contributions to New Products | Few | | Many—early supplier involvement |
| Difficulty of Exit | Low | | Difficult—high impact |
| Duration | Short | | Long |
| Expediting | Reactive | | Proactive |
| Focus | Price | | Total cost |
| Level of Integration | Little or none | | High or total |
| Level of Trust | Low | | High |
| Number of Suppliers | Many | | One or few |
| Open Books | No | | Yes |
| Quality | Incoming inspection | | Design quality into system |
| Relations | Inward looking | | Concern with each other's well-being |
| Resources | Few—low skill level | | Professional |
| Service | Minimal | | Greatly improved |
| Shared Forecasts | No | | Yes |
| Supply Disruptions | Possible | | Unlikely |
| Technology Inflows | No | | Yes |
| Type of Interaction | Tactical | | Strategic synergy |

## Transactional Relationships

We call the most common and most basic type of relationship "transactional." Such a relationship is neither good nor bad. It is simply an arm's-length relationship in which neither party is especially concerned with the well-being of the other and moves from one contract to another rather than developing a real long-term relationship. Virtually all buying firms have transactional relationships. Most also have collaborative ones, and some have strategic alliances.

### Transactional Relationships Have Several Characteristics:

■   An absence of concern by both parties about the other party's well-being. With transactional relationships, there is little or no concern about the other party's well-being. What one party wins, the other loses.

■   One of a series of independent deals. Each transaction is entered into on its own merits. There is little or no basis for collaboration and learning.

■   Costs, data, and forecasts are not shared. Arm's-length transactions, not openness, are characteristics of transactional relationships.

■   Price is the major focus of the relationship. Getting the best price is the focus of the transaction. Ideally, total cost analysis, as described later in this book, precedes any procurement transaction.

■   Quality of the relationship. Since there is little or no concern for the other's well-being, neither buyer nor supplier will rush to the other's assistance in bad times or when problems arise.

■   A minimum of purchasing time and energy is required to establish prices. Market forces normally establish prices in transactional relationships. Thus, little purchasing time and energy are required to establish prices.

■   Transactional purchases lend themselves to e-procurement and in some cases reverse auctions.

### The Advantages of Transactional Relationships Include:

■   Relatively less purchasing time and effort are required to establish price. As we have noted, the market forces of supply and demand establish the price with transactional procurements. Therefore, little purchasing time and effort are required to establish price.

■   Lower skill levels are required in procurement personnel. Much less judgment and less managerial expertise are required with the vast majority of transactional procurements.

### The Disadvantages of Transactional Relationships Include:

■   The potential for communication difficulties is much greater with transactional relationships than with collaborative or alliance ones.

■   A considerable investment in expediting and monitoring incoming quality is required to ensure timely delivery of the right quality.

■   Transactional relationships are inflexible when flexibility may be required. Changing technology and changing market conditions can require flexibility in buyer-supplier relationships.

■   Transactional procurements tend to result in more delivery problems than do collaborative and strategic alliance ones. Friends look out for friends, not opportunistic buyers or suppliers.

■   Quality in transactional relations will be only as good as required. Far more incentive and opportunity exist to improve quality in a collaborative or alliance relationship.

■   Transactional suppliers tend to provide the minimum service required.

■   Buyers tend to experience less effective performance from their transactional suppliers compared with those employing collaborative or strategic relationships. Transactional suppliers have much less to lose from a customer who is dissatisfied than do collaborative and strategic relationship suppliers.

■   Transactional customers are subject to more supply disruptions than are collaborative and alliance ones. Buyers who maintain continuing collaborative relations with their suppliers are much less subject to supply shortages than are opportunistic ones.

- Since the supplier recognizes the transactional and price nature of the relationship, it is not motivated to invest time and energy in the development of the potential buyer's products.
- Buyers seldom know the total cost of ownership of the items and services they are purchasing through transactional relationships.
- Frequent changes in suppliers result in hidden switching costs.[4]

## Collaborative and Alliance Relationships

Ginni Rometty, a senior vice president with IBM Global Business Services, reported the results of a global CEO study on innovation conducted by IBM. One key finding was that "76 percent of CEO's think external collaboration with business partners and customers is key to innovation."[5] For the procurement of noncommodity[6] items and services, innovative, collaborative, and alliance relationships tend to result in lower total costs than do transactional relationships. Such items may require process improvements and the adoption of technical innovations. This is difficult to achieve in transactional relationships. The risks and uncertainties present with transactional relationships reduce the likelihood of investments in research and development (R&D) and training as well as the procurement of new, more efficient equipment focused on the customer firm's needs. Thus, major opportunities for cost reduction within supplying organizations may be lost with transactional relationships.

Cost reductions resulting from value engineering and value analysis (VE/VA) are much more likely with collaborative and alliance relationships.[7] Suppliers are more likely to take the initiative to reduce costs through VE/VA when they are involved in long-term relationships than they are with short-term transactional ones.

Longer-term performance agreements give suppliers an opportunity to reduce their costs. The extended learning curve effect[8] with both production and services allows collaborative and alliance suppliers to reduce their costs and share the savings with customers.

Collaborative and alliance relations replace the market forces employed in transactional procurement with controlled competition, benchmarking, and advanced supply management pricing practices. The results are lower total costs, higher quality, reduced time to market, and reduced risk of supply disruptions.

Researchers Stanley and Pearson found that the three most important factors in a successful buyer-supplier relationship are (1) two-way communication, (2) the supplier's responsiveness to supply management's needs, and (3) clear product specifications.[9] Other research has shown that better communication and shared information regarding products purchased and new products in development stages result in better quality, faster response times, improved cost savings, and greater efficiencies.[10] Over the last 5 to

---

[4]The cost of "switching" to a new supplier. These costs may include higher initial costs since the present supplier has enjoyed the benefits of learning, the costs of working with the new supplier's production and quality people, and costs within the buying firm, including receiving and accounts payable.

[5]Ginni Rometty, "Collaboration Key to Innovation," *Leadership Excellence* 24, no. 2 (February 2007), pp. 3–4.

[6]Commodity items/services are those which are highly interchangeable with another supplier's offering. School writing tablets and noncritical fasteners (nuts, bolts, rivets, etc.) are examples of commodities.

[7]Value engineering and value analysis are addressed in Chapter 5.

[8]For more on the effects of the learning curve, see Chapter 14.

[9]Linda L. Stanley and John N. Pearson, "Buyer-Supplier Strategies and Their Impact on Purchasing Performance: A Study of the Electronics Industry," Conference 2000, Richard Ivey School of Business, University of Western Ontario, London, May 24–27, 2000.

[10]Antony Paulraj and Injazz J. Chen, "Strategic Buyer-Supplier Relationships, Information Technology and External Logistics Integration," *Journal of Supply Chain Management* 43, no. 2 (Spring 2007), pp. 2–14.

10 years, we have seen a move to improve communication, increase information sharing, and reduce the barriers that marred relationships in the past.[11]

## Collaborative Relationships

The key difference between collaborative relationships and transactional ones is an awareness of the interdependence and necessity of cooperation. "The focus on relationship management will require that all elements of relationship management, including trust building, communications, joint efforts, and planning and fostering interdependency, will be increasingly studied and managed to achieve competitive advantage."[12] Recognition of interdependency and the need for cooperation provides many benefits. Both parties are aware that money enters their supply chain (or supply network) only if the chain's end products are cost competitive. Recognizing the need for interdependence and cooperation, the customer's firm enjoys the benefits of early supplier involvement (ESI). Improvements in cost, quality, and time to market and the leveraging of supplier technology result.

Continuous improvement is far easier to implement and manage when both sides recognize their interdependence and cooperate. The end objective with continuous improvement is a reduction in total costs as the two sides strive to achieve greater value together than either could create individually.

The likelihood of disruptions in supply is reduced greatly. Collaborative suppliers look out for their friends, not for their opportunistic customers. Collaborative relationships provide a cushion in bad times. Both customers and suppliers who value each other on the basis of long-term relations and respect are more likely to come to each other's aid during times of adversity. Blockbuster, the video rental company, has become a leader in the market by forming collaborative relationships with its suppliers. In the 1990s Blockbuster revolutionized the way distributor/retailers purchased and managed the revenue of movie sales and rentals. Traditionally, a high price was paid to the supplier, with sales for the video store being generated by rentals. The cost to purchase the new tapes was so high that few tapes were purchased, and video stores were often out of stock on some of the latest releases. Blockbuster decided to collaborate with its suppliers by agreeing to share the sales revenues from rentals equally with them. The suppliers responded with a small fixed price for new videos. The availability of new releases increased dramatically, as did revenues for Blockbuster and its suppliers. Within less than a decade the entire industry was operating in this collaborative mode. It is estimated that the video rental industry's total profits increased by 7 percent. Other industries have followed Blockbuster's lead.[13]

Lower total costs are the common result of collaborative and alliance relationships. The level of certainty and the continuity of demand in collaborative and alliance relationships increase the likelihood of investments in R&D, and training and the procurement of new, more efficient equipment focused on the customer firm's needs. Cost reductions resulting from value engineering and value analysis are enhanced,

---

[11]Gregory M. Magnan and Stanley E. Fawcett, "Supply Chain Collaboration: Analyzing of Five Years of Change," Eighteenth Annual North American Research and Teaching Symposium on Purchasing and Supply Chain Management, Educational Resources Committee of ISM, CAPS Research, Institute for Supply Management, and the Purchasing Management Association of Canada, Tempe, AZ, March 29–31, 2007, p. 2.

[12]P. L. Carter, J. R. Carter, R. M. Monczka, T. H. Slaight, and A. J. Swan, "The Future of Purchasing and Supply: A Ten-Year Forecast," *Journal of Supply Chain Management*, Winter 2000, pp. 14–26.

[13]Stephan M. Wagner and Exkhard Lindemann, "Pie Sharing in Buyer-Supplier Relationships: What Determines Each Party's Share?" Eighteenth Annual North American Research and Teaching Symposium on Purchasing and Supply Chain Management, Educational Resources Committee of ISM, CAPS Research, Institute for Supply Management, and the Purchasing Management Association of Canada, Tempe, AZ, March 29–31, 2007, p. 3.

and the extended learning curve effect with both production and service activities allows collaborative and alliance suppliers to reduce their costs and share those savings with their customers.[14]

The major disadvantage of collaborative and alliance relationships is the amount of human skill, time, and energy required to develop and manage the relationships. However, firms such as Honda and Deere & Co. have demonstrated that the required investments provide very attractive returns.

## Supply Alliances

The fundamental difference between collaborative relationships and supply alliances is the presence of institutional trust[15] in alliances. The failure to develop and *manage* institutional trust is the principal reason so many supply alliances fail.

Supply alliances reap incredible benefits as a result of physical asset specialization and human specialization. Dyer defines *physical asset specialization* as "relationship-specific capital investments (e.g., in customized machinery, tools, information systems, delivery processes, and so forth) that allow for faster throughput and greater product customization. Physical asset specialization allows for product differentiation and may improve overall quality by increasing product integrity. *Human specialization* refers to relationship-specific know-how accumulated by individuals through long-standing relationships. In other words, individuals across companies have substantial experience working together and have accumulated specialized information and language that allows them to communicate and coordinate effectively with each other. They are less likely to have communication breakdowns that result in errors; this, in turn, results in higher quality, faster development times, and lower costs."[16]

### *The Primary Benefits of Supply Alliances Include:*

- *Lower total costs*    Synergies can be created in alliances that cannot happen in transactional or even collaborative relationships. The synergies result in reductions of direct and indirect costs associated with labor, machinery, materials, and overhead.

- *Reduced time to market*    Reducing the time to design, develop, and distribute products and services is a key driver that leads to improved market share and better profit margins.

- *Improved quality*    The use of both the design of experiments[17] and supplier certification[18] is the norm with supply alliances. These two activities design and manufacture quality in rather than inspecting for errors. The result is improved quality at a lower total cost.

---

[14]See Chapter 12 for insights into the learning curve.

[15]Institutional trust: The term "trust" has such a wide variety of meanings and interpretations that we have chosen to coin the term "institutional trust." Institutional trust is the key element that differentiates supply alliances from collaborative relationships. With institutional trust, the parties have access to each other's strategic plans in the area(s) of the interface. Relevant cost information and forecasts are shared. Risks and rewards are addressed openly. Informal agreements are as good as written ones. Institutional trust is measured and managed. The issue of institutional trust is addressed in grater detail in Appendix A in this chapter.

[16]Jeffrey H. Dyer, *Collaborative Advantage* (New York: Oxford University Press, 2000), pp. 42–43.

[17]The design of experiments is a quantitative approach that involves analyzing deviations from desired outcomes during the design process. Identifying deviations during this stage—before progressing to production—has a powerful positive effect on an item's quality. See Keki R Bhote, *World Class Quality,* American Management Association, New York, N.Y., AMACOM, 1991, for an excellent description of design of experiments (DOE).

[18]Supplier certification requires the customer to review a supplier's manufacturing operation carefully to ensure that it has the necessary processes in place to meet the customer's quality requirements. Items produced by a supplier whose system has been certified for the specific item can flow directly into the customer's production without being inspected.

■ *Improved technology flow from suppliers*   Openness and institutional trust enhance an inflow of technology from alliance partners that leads to many successful new products. In 1999, Dell and IBM formed an alliance worth some $16 billion over seven years. In effect, Dell was harnessing IBM's vast research, development, and production abilities. Dell was purchasing storage devices, custom logic chips, static random-access memory, and other components. The two companies were cross-licensing patents; that is, they were sharing relevant technologies.[19]

■ *Improved continuity of supply*   Alliance customers are the group least likely to experience supply disruptions.

### Alliances Share Several Attributes:

■ The focus of most supplier alliances is on achieving continuous improvements while squeezing cost out. Most alliances put major emphasis on the inflow of innovation from the supplier partner. Many have implemented programs of cocreation.

■ A high level of recognized interdependence and commitment is present.

■ An atmosphere of cooperation exists. Potential conflicts are addressed and resolved openly. When problems occur, the focus is on a search for the root cause, not the assignment of blame.

■ The alliance is controlled through a complex web of formal and informal interpersonal connections, information systems, and internal infrastructures that enhance learning.

■ There is openness in all areas of the relationship, including, cost, long-term objectives, technology, and the supply chain itself.

■ The alliance is a living system that progressively evolves with the objective of creating new benefits for both parties.

■ The alliance partners share a vision of the future in terms of how they will work together.

■ Ethics are more important than expediency.

■ The relationship is adaptable in the face of changing economics, competition, technology, and environmental issues.

■ The design of experiments and supplier certification are the norm with supply alliances. These two activities design and manufacture quality in. The result is improved quality at a lower total cost.

■ Negotiations and renegotiations occur in a cocreative manner in which the parties focus on enlarging the pie and then dividing it.

■ Executive-level commitment and alliance champions protect and nourish the alliance.

■ Suppliers and buyers agree to meet the current competition in terms of cost and technology developments and avoid conditions in long-term contracts that could prove economically destructive.

If supply alliances are so attractive, why aren't they the way to conduct all business? Alliances are a very resource-intense approach to supply management and tend to be reserved for the most critical relationships, such as the Quaker Oats–Graham alliance described in the opening vignette and in Appendix B in this chapter.

During the 1990s, Chrysler became a fascinating example of the power of alliance relationships. In 1989, Chrysler had some 2,500 suppliers in its production supply base. Chrysler was rated as the least

---

[19]"Dell to Buy $16 Billion in IBM Parts," *Los Angeles Times,* March 5, 1999, p. C-1.

desirable customer among the Big Three U.S. auto assemblers. With a surprising amount of assistance from Honda of America Manufacturing, Chrysler transitioned itself from a transaction-based buyer to a collaborative one. Results? Time to market was reduced 30 percent. Profit margins per vehicle increased an average of 750 percent.

Chrysler employed many of the principles discussed in this text: cross-functional teams, early supplier involvement, target costing, value analysis (with incentives in the form of additional profits or additional sales volume for suppliers), improved communications through techniques such as colocation of supplier engineers at Chrysler design centers, and a supplier advisory board.[20]

Unfortunately, when Daimler acquired Chrysler in the late 1990s, that level of cooperation and coordination was not in its playbook. Chrysler's approach to supply management was so far ahead of that of Daimler's Mercedes Benz (M-B) division that some people thought that M-B would have the Chrysler procurement operation become responsible for all of the new corporation's procurement! With hindsight on this disastrous acquisition we now wonder how profitable Daimler-Chrysler would have been if the firm had embraced Chrysler's visionary approach to supplier relations!

## Which Relationship Is Appropriate?

How does a supply management executive determine whether a relationship should be transactional, collaborative, or a strategic alliance? Several key questions should be asked to determine the "strategic" elements of a relationship:

**1.** Are there many relatively undifferentiated suppliers providing what amounts to interchangeable commodities? If so, a collaborative alliance or relationship would not be appropriate: Try a transactional relationship instead.

**2.** Does the potential supplier have economic power which it is willing to employ over its customers? A transactional or very carefully developed and managed collaborative relationship is usually appropriate and may be the only method the supplier will accept.

**3.** If there is recognition by both parties of the potential benefits of an alliance but adequate qualified human resources are not available at one firm or both, a collaborative relationship is usually more appropriate.

**4.** A collaborative relationship frequently is an appropriate first step on the road to a strategic alliance.

**5.** Is one supplier head and shoulders above the rest in terms of the value it provides, including price, innovation, ability to adapt to changing situations, capacity to work with your team, and task joint risks? If so, an alliance may be in order, assuming that the supplier is willing to enter into an interdependent, trusting relationship.

**6.** Are some suppliers "strategic" to your business? In other words, do they have a major impact on your competitive advantage in the marketplace? Are you highly reliant on them to provide a unique product, technology, or service? If so, an alliance may be vital.

**7.** Would your company benefit greatly if the supplier were more "integrally connected" with your company, perhaps with their engineers working side by side with yours or colocating their manufacturing facilities adjacent to or within yours? If yes, consider an alliance. (Appendix B in this chapter describes a classic example of this.)

---

[20]For more detailed insights into Chrysler's transition, see Jeffrey H. Dyer, "How Chrysler Created an American Keiretsu," *Harvard Business Review,* July/August 1996, pp. 42–53.

**8.** Do your customers require high degrees of flexibility and speed of responsiveness, causing you to demand the same performance from your suppliers? This is a classic alliance driver.

Trust is another key factor differentiating the three classes of relationships. The simplest definition of trust is "being confident that the other party will do what it says it will do." Some level of trust must be present in all three types of relationships, but the level of trust increases with collaborative relationships and becomes an essential characteristic with strategic alliances.

Few of these relationships are pure: A transactional relationship may have one or more collaborative characteristics, and a collaborative relationship may have one or more transactional as well as some alliance characteristics.

# The Supplier's Perspective

The competition for world-class suppliers is well under way. As a result, the most attractive supplier may decide that a collaborative or alliance relationship with the potential customer firm is not in its best interest. In effect, the supplier may have economic power which it desires to exercise in an effort to maximize its net income; the classic case is the monopolist. Or the preferred supplier may be unavailable since the buying firm's key competitor may have established an exclusive relationship already. World-class suppliers are careful in their selection of customer firms. The supplier will be very concerned with the potential customer firm's finances, especially as they affect its ability to pay. The customer firm's finances also provide insight into the prospects for a long-term relationship and continuing demand for the supplier's product(s) or service(s). Quality suppliers want customers who have good growth prospects.

The potential customer's demand pattern for the supplier's product is of great interest, especially in the areas of stability and fit. World-class suppliers want to ensure that potential customers' quality requirements are within their capabilities. The supplying firm is also very concerned with the buying firm's approach to problems. Does it discipline suppliers who encounter problems, or does it help solve problems together in a mutually beneficial way, deriving critical learning along the way and thus making the problem a "learning foundation" from which to improve? Suppliers are attracted to customers who have a reputation for working collaboratively with suppliers who experience a problem to identify and correct the root cause of the problem.

Suppliers want "good" customers. Several issues affect a customer firm's rating as a good customer, including the following:

- Does the customer have a reputation for timely payment? Cash flow is a major concern of all suppliers.
- Is the customer secretive? Suppliers prefer customers who are open and approachable.
- Are the buyers honest? Are they ethical, truthful, and reliable?
- Are the customer's procurement personnel responsive? Suppliers prefer customers that are available, not one whose supplier hours are 11:30–1:00, Monday–Friday.
- Are the customers known as professionals? World-class suppliers conduct themselves professionally and expect to be treated professionally.

For suppliers and buyers who comprehend the value of shifting from tactical, transactional-based relationships to strategic value-based alliance relationships, it will be essential to engage the multidimensional assessment of the elements of Total Cost of Ownership (see Chapter 13) to determine exactly where cost can be reduced, value enhanced, and substantial competitive advantage created.

## Questions to Be Addressed before Proceeding

Although strategic supplier alliances receive a great deal of media coverage and discussion in the supply management community, are they for everyone? Will the benefits of an alliance outweigh the effort, risk, and resources required? For supply management professionals and organizations that are investigating the possibility of strategic supplier alliances, it can be helpful to ask the following questions:

- Is there a danger that the supplier will act in an opportunistic manner over time?
- Do electronic systems at the purchasing and supplier organizations allow for optimum communication and sharing of information?
- Is the potential strategic alliance supplier well equipped in terms of knowledge, expertise, and resources to stay current in the industry?
- Are both the purchasing and supplier organizations willing to keep attention focused on the joint customer to establish supply chain objectives and goals?
- Are there other suppliers in the marketplace who are more accessible through e-procurement and are worth investigating before the company makes commitment to a strategic alliance?
- Has the supply manager been trained thoroughly in managing an alliance relationship?
- Is the purchasing organization proud to be aligned and associated with the supplier organization as they present a joint marketing front for the links farther downstream in the supply chain?
- Is the purchasing organization comfortable with the level of risk associated with reducing the supply base?[21]
- Are both supplier and buyer aligned in what their ultimate customer considers valuable?
- If there is substantial risk for the supplier in developing new technologies, subsystems, products, processes, or service support, is the buying firm willing to share or reduce the risks or pay for them? Are there "meet competition" provisions?
- Are both supplier and buyer aligned in their respective visions and thus able to make long-term commitments to each other?
- If an alliance is in order, are there sufficient operational points of interaction where the supplier can engage with the buying firm, such as joint development programs, just-in-time inventory, electronic communication, and colocation of service personnel?

## Developing and Managing Collaborative and Alliance Relationships

### Situations in Which Alliances May Not Be Appropriate

Obviously, alliances are not always appropriate. Professor Ralph Kauffman has identified 14 of those situations and organized them in 5 major categories[22]:

1. **Stability** of the prices, market, and buyer's demand.
   - **Price Volatility:** Commodities traded on open markets that have significant price volatility. The problem for a partnership/alliance is how to share risks and benefits that may result from

---

[21]Roberta J. Duffy with input from Dr. Joseph L. Cavinato, "Align to Be Strategic, " *Purchasing Today,* September 2000, p. 40.

[22]Ralph Kauffman, "Supplier Partnerships and Alliances, Is That All There Is? When to Consider Other Relationship Strategies," *difOrientering* 38, no. 5 (May 2001), published by the Danish Purchasing and Logistics Forum, Copenhagen.

price volatility. Some arrangements can be made to mitigate this problem, including price adjustment mechanisms based on costs or indexes and, for some commodities, hedging in futures markets.

- **Demand Volatility:** Materials or services that have significant volatility in individual buyer demand. If the buying firm's needs are not predictable, the supplier must deal with the likelihood of overstock or stockout or erratic production schedules. Doing this may generate additional costs for the supplier that must be built into the price the buyer pays.
- **High Switching Likelihood with High Switching Costs:** Situations with high switching costs that also have a high likelihood of switching being desirable. Purchases that involve changing technology or critical quality or other characteristics in which there are no strong suppliers may indicate a high likelihood of needing to switch in spite of high switching costs. In such cases, maximum flexibility is desirable.

2. **Capability** of potential suppliers.
   - **No Partnership/Alliance–Capable Supplier for the Item:** Items for which there is no full-service, world-class supplier capable of a partnership/alliance relationship. The lack of a capable supplier would dictate some other form of supply relationship. No partnership or alliance would be preferable to one with an inept supplier.
   - **No Partnership/Alliance–Capable Supplier in the Geographic Area:** Areas of the world where there is no full-service, world-class supplier capable of a partnership/alliance relationship. Depending on the material or service required, there may be regions where a partnership or alliance is not possible because of the lack of a competent supplier in the region.
   - **Rapid Technological Change:** Situations of rapid industrywide technological change in which the buyer would be disadvantaged if locked into one supplier. The buyer must have assurance that technology (that which is being purchased, that which the supplier uses in its production, or both) is maintained at the state of the art required by the buyer's industry. Not all suppliers have the ability to remain technologically competitive.
   - **Mismatch of Rates of Technological Change:** If the buying firm's industry is changing and developing more rapidly than the supplier's industry, it may be difficult to arrive at a partnership or alliance that is fully beneficial to one party or both.

3. **Competition** in the supply market.
   - **Noncompetitive Market:** Noncompetitive markets where the supplier partner may be in a position to take advantage of the buying firm. Generally, a partnership or strategic alliance will reinforce the supplier's power relative to the buying firm.
   - **Supplier Dependency Creation:** Situations in which extreme dependency on a particular supplier would be created by a partnership or strategic alliance. If the buying company is relatively small compared with the selling company and the buyer's business is not vital to the seller, the buyer may be at risk in terms of future supply. For example, a buyer becomes totally dependent on a seller through a partnership or alliance for a material vital to the supplier and for which there are few, if any, alternative suppliers. If the supplier determines at a future time that the business is not compatible with its business objectives, it may terminate the agreement and cause supply difficulties for the buyer.
   - **Neglected Areas:** Situations in which purchases have been mismanaged or not managed for years, for example, many types of indirect purchases. For these types of purchases, to obtain the lowest total cost, a relationship that leverages the free market should be used. Partnerships for such situations should be used only if there are few supply alternatives available and/or there are high supplier switching costs.

- **Suppliers Seeking to Reduce Competition:** Situations in which suppliers appear to be using partnerships/alliances as a marketing ploy to eliminate competition and reduce industry capacity. These situations may save costs in the short run, but if the supplier's strategy truly is to reduce capacity and competition, costs may increase in the long run. Being locked into such a supplier would not be desirable.

4. **Benefits** to the buying firm from the relationship.
    - **No Leverage from Partnership:** Situations in which there is nothing to leverage with a partnership/alliance. Typically, a partnership or alliance will leverage some aspect of the exchange involved. Leveraged items include volume, total cost, process or procedural cost, inventory, and innovation. If there are no leverage possibilities, there may not be a justification for the work involved in establishing and maintaining a partnership or alliance.
    - **No Hard Savings from Partnership:** Situations in which hard savings are not present as a result of a partnership/alliance. Soft savings such as nonquantifiable quality improvements and partial-person staff reductions are nice, but unless they result in other cost avoidance, they never show up on the bottom line. To justify the work involved in establishing and maintaining partnerships and alliances, there must be some hard savings.

5. **Internal buy-in** to partnership.
    - **No Internal Customer Buy-In:** Situations in which the internal customers of the buying organization do not have joint ownership with supply management of the partnership/alliance arrangement. Most purchasing organizations use a cross-functional team approach to develop, implement, and maintain partnership and alliance agreements. If that is not done or if the internal customer members of the team do not agree with all the terms of the agreement, the partnership or alliance probably will fail.

# The Role of Power

Recent books and articles on supply management largely have ignored the impact and role of power. Thus, unfortunately, relatively little is known about the role of power in collaborative or alliance relationships. At the Third Annual North American Research Symposium on Purchasing and Supply Chain Management hosted by the Richard Ivey School of Business, University of Western Ontario, in May 2000, two professors from the Netherlands observed, "Power has an ideological tinge and produces negative associations." Pfeffer (1981) recognized that power is a topic that makes people uncomfortable. Andrew Cox argues, "Power is at the heart of all business to business relationships."[23] Using power is often seen as unethical. However, power, influence, and dependence do exist. Ignoring them will not make them less important for understanding buyer-seller relationships. Power obviously is not always used, although it still can influence decisions and strategies simply because it is recognized by both trading partners. There is always a threat of (mis)use of power to which parties respond in advance. Studying networks, Thorelli (1986:38) argued that power is the central concept in networks analysis because its mere existence can condition others.[24] Thus, it is highly likely that the use and role of power in supply chain management will be the subject of research in the coming years.

---

[23] Andrew Cox, "Understanding Buyer and Supplier Power: A Framework for Procurement and Supply Competence," *Journal of Supply Chain Management,* Spring, 2001, p. 8.

[24] J. Pfeffer, *Power in Organizations* (Marstons Mills, MA: Pitman Publishing), and H. B. Thorelli, "Networks: between Markets and Hierarchies," *Strategic Management Journal,* 7 (1986), pp. 37–51.

Power plays a key role in two important subclasses of buyer-supplier relationships: the captive buyer and the captive supplier. In a captive buyer relationship, "the buyer is held hostage by a supplier free to switch to another customer."[25] The captive supplier makes investments to secure a portion of the buyer's business, with no assurance of sufficient business to recoup the investment. Cooperation and some level of recognized interdependence suggest that these two classes of relationships are subsets of the broad heading of collaborative relationships.[26]

## A Portfolio Approach

No single approach to relationship management is inherently superior. "Successful supply chain management requires the effective and efficient management of a portfolio of relationships."[27] The portfolio approach has its roots in 1950s financial investment theory.[28] One of the most useful approaches to selection of the appropriate relationships is advanced by Bensaou, who proposes three environmental factors to consider: (1) the product exchanged and its technology, (2) the competitive conditions in the upstream market, and (3) the capabilities of the suppliers available.[29] One of the most interesting phenomena of modern business is that of multidivisional firms which simultaneously buy some items and sell others to each other. Even more interesting is the fact that an array of buyer-supplier relationships may be present and appropriate.

## New Skills and Attitudes Required

Developing and managing collaborative and alliance relationships requires skilled professionals who recognize the benefits of collaboration. These individuals must be able to identify and obtain necessary data and use the data to exploit and enhance relationships. As Smith and Tracey point out, these professionals must "learn to work in and adjacent to chaos, unpredictability, and uncertainty. They must be agile, flexible, and highly adaptive."[30]

Smith and Tracey support the use of role playing, sensitivity training, diversity training, and live cases to develop the professionals who work in this area. These researchers go beyond individual development to advocate the creation of a learning organization, as discussed by Peter Senge. A learning organization is one "where people continually expand their capacity to create results they truly desire, where new and expansive patterns of thinking are nurtured, where collective aspiration is set free, and where people are continually learning how to learn together. A learning organization excels at advanced, systematic, and intentional collective learning and is effective, productive, adaptive, and very good at setting and achieving goals."[31]

---

[25]M. Bensaou, "Portfolios of Buyer-Supplier Relationships," *Sloan Management Review* 40, no. 4 (Summer 1999), pp. 35–44.

[26]The Spring 2001 issue of *The Journal of Supply Chain Management* addresses power in buyer-supplier relationships. The devoted student of supply management is encouraged to read the thought-provoking articles by Andrew Cox, Joe Sanderson, Chris Lousdale, and Glyn Watson.

[27]Bensaou, "Portfolios," p. 37.

[28]For more on portfolio theory as applied to supply management, see Appendix B.

[29]Bensaou, "Portfolios," p. 42.

[30]Kimberly A. Smith-Doerflein and Michael Tracey, "Training as a Component of Supply Chain Management," Third Annual North American Research Symposium on Purchasing and Supply Chain Management, Richard Ivey School of Business, University of Western Ontario, May 24–27, 2000.

[31]Calvert, G. Mobley and S. L. Marshall, "Grasping the Learning Organization," *Training and Development* 48, no. 5, 1994, pp. 38–43.

# e-Commerce and the "Right" Type of Relationship

We frequently are asked: "How does B2B e-commerce affect your selection of the 'right' type of relationship?" Selection of the right type of relationship and the right supplier must be a function of the requirement, not of the Internet! B2B e-commerce is an enabler, a tool that is most effective when adopted by firms that embrace strategic supply chain management. It is unfortunate that some software sales personnel and some members of customer firms mistakenly assume that B2B e-commerce will eliminate the need for professional supply management. B2B e-commerce must be seen for what it is: a powerful enabler! In the last few years, there has been an evolution from paper-driven transactions to electronic transactions as part of the transition to integrated supply management processes. Now Internet offerings will prompt even more transaction reduction initiatives and a greater transformation from paper to electronic tools. Reverse auctions are one such tool.[32] Held online, reverse auctions are a popular way to enhance competition. Companies use these auctions to encourage suppliers globally to bid on orders in the hope of reducing the price and cycle times for processing orders.[33] However, reverse auctions are not effective for all products, and the question arises of how to apply this tool without damaging supplier relationships. Also, tools are not strategies. The supply professional of the future will be first and foremost a strategic thinker and a creator of competitive advantage.

Unfolding before us is a massive array of new opportunities that will redefine the role of supply in the corporation, facilitated by a new set of tools from the worlds of computer software, electronic commerce, and the Internet. However, these tools are simultaneously alluring and deceiving.

The allure comes from the multitude of new possibilities created by e-commerce and all of its siblings, including e-procurement, e-bidding, reverse auctions, e-payment, and e-business. However, these tools can be deceptively attractive to the uncritical eye and used inappropriately with little thought given to the solution and the net effect. Therefore, three traps must be steadfastly avoided.

First, we must avoid the trap of "gilding the pig," by which we take an archaic, cumbersome procurement process and "webbize" it. The process remains ugly and inefficient despite its newfound digital disguise.

Second is the temptation to seek the holy grail of the "magic pill," the one solution that can be used to solve every procurement situation, thus circumventing the design of a more thoughtful strategy and solution tailored to fit specific goals and needs.

Third is the trap of "supplier equality." Equality may be the law in civil rights, but it makes for poor procurement. Some suppliers are simply commodity vendors and should be treated in a tactical and transactional manner, pushed on price, and managed through e-bidding auctions. Other suppliers are far more strategic to a corporation's business and should be treated as close alliance partners, integrated into a company's business processes, and challenged to create powerful value streams, such as product and process innovations and fast time to market. Alliance partners are a company's assets in creating competitive advantage for the ultimate customer. The world of procurement is splitting rapidly into supplier-based and alliance-based relationships, and procurement professionals must know how to differentiate the two.

---

[32]Reverse auctions are contrary to traditional auctions in that the seller is competing for the business and the end result is to drive the price down rather than up. This tool is used mostly in industrial B2B transactions. See S. Petcavage, "Reverse Auctions—Should You Be a Player?" *ISM Materials Management News* 3, no. 1 (February 2007), p. 9.

[33]Srinivas Talluri and Gary L. Ragatz, "Multi-Attribute Reverse Auctions in B2B Exchanges: A Framework for Design and Implementation," *Journal of Supply Chain Management,* 40, no. 1 (Winter 2004), p. 52.

While B2B e-commerce may eliminate the day-to-day sourcing and pricing aspects of procurement when a transactional relationship is appropriate, cross-functional development and sourcing teams still have many vital responsibilities with such procurements.

The Internet greatly facilitates communication and, when properly employed, enhances the development and maintenance of collaborative and alliance relationships. However, the Internet does not terminate the need for personal relationships based on face-to-face contact. Michael Dell states, "The real potential lies in its [the Internet's] ability to transform relationships within the traditional supplier-vendor-customer chain and to create value that can be shared across organizational boundaries. The companies that position themselves to build 'information partnerships' with suppliers and customers and make the Internet an integral part of their strategy—not just an add-on—have the potential to fundamentally change the face of global competition."[34]

The new world of electronic commerce holds the promise of a bold, new, and enticing future by focusing on speed, connectivity, and innovation. But we must understand and differentiate our supply base to understand what suppliers bring to the corporate table. The evolutionary integration of electronic commerce requires a new set of strategies and tools that will help make supply professionals treasured assets in the corporation. That evolution will continue to require a new type of thinking, a new set of rewards and measures, and a new set of skills. Let us not forget that it will be a challenging time, designed for those who are willing to learn, adapt, change, and take a leadership role. We must seize the Internet opportunities being offered and take risks in the electronic commerce arenas. It is acceptable to make a mistake; it is often from trial and error that we learn. As leaders, we must continue to challenge the "it won't work here" and "this too shall pass" attitudes that prevailed in the past.

Continuous learning and capability building will be the norm, not the exception. These two activities will need to be more cross-functionally oriented and work together more to select and implement the optimum buying process tools. Supply management thinking, now more than ever, needs to encompass the whole supply process, the end-to-end "need it, design it, buy it, receive it, transform it, deliver it, service it" process.

Greater focus is needed to have supply professionals become change leaders and problem resolvers rather than followers and problem identifiers. Supply personnel who over the years have been tagged as non-value-added paper pushers who have a "green eyeshade" mentality will need to overcome this stigma and change their focus to become value-added creators and analysts to support the supply strategy.

What's more, supply professionals will need to shift to a new level of understanding: They have a strategic role in the corporation. They each must keep a business focus in the forefront, understanding that long-term competitive advantage, speed to market, supplier management for cash conservation, and profit maximization are far more critical to long-term success than is their historical role of squeezing suppliers for lower prices and other concessions.

## Relationships of the Future

The terms used today—supply chain, tiers, and channels—all imply a static, rigid set of links that do not change position relative to one another. In these models, information, materials, and money flow sequentially, one link at a time, and only between adjacent links. This environment creates friction, inertia, and inflexibility. Every exchange increases the risk of error and multiplies cycle times. Incompatibility within and between supply chain member IT applications prevents fluid information flow. Compounding these

---

[34]"Michael Dell's Magic," *Industry Week,* November 16, 1998, p. 36.

problems is the fact that most companies are part of multiple supply chains. The resulting uncertainty creates mistrust among partners and leads to the withholding of critical information. High inventories, uncoordinated schedules, and dissatisfied customers are the result.

As the corporate world develops more Internet competence, there may be an uncomfortable convergence of professionals from supply management, accounts payable, information systems, and e-commerce. For the uninitiated, these professionals will interact with a set of traditions often filled with conflicting points of view. In the future, professionals from each functional area will need to reinvent the way they traditionally interacted. Supply management will need to enter the information age in a powerful, proactive, and innovative manner. Accounts payable will need to design and link its paying processes to the buying processes in a creative way. Information systems will need to be more functionally adept and user friendly. Tools such as ERP (enterprise resource planning) systems and e-commerce will need to intensify the focus on totally integrated supply process solutions instead of promoting the latest electronic solution searching for a problem or a need.

If the 1990s reengineered the internal business processes of corporations, this and the next decade will be the era of reengineering entire value chains and value networks—from the initiation of the purchase request through design, manufacturing, logistics, and service to the final customer. The winners in the future marketplace will be those networked companies which can combine their internal advantages into a powerful value network that is faster, more efficient, more agile and innovative, and ultimately more profitable than competing supply networks. The wise supply executive will recognize this shift early, knowing that supply chain/network reengineering may determine the fate of the corporation.

## Concluding Remarks

The modern supply professional is blessed with an array of relationships from which to choose. Selection of the appropriate type of relationship for a specific purchase is a matter of sound business judgment. The type of relationship selected will affect total cost, quality, timeliness, the level of cooperation, the inflow of innovation, and other variables of concern to the purchasing firm.

The next section of the book addresses the requirements process, the most critical phase of procurement. This is the phase during which 70 to 80 percent of a product's or service's cost is built in. Chapter 5 describes the process of developing a new product and describes the role supply managers must play.

## Discussion Questions

1. Why are transactional relationships often referred to as "arm's-length" relationships?
2. What is the major focus of transactional purchases? What kinds of products would you buy in using the transactional strategy?
3. What role does supply and demand play in transactional buys?
4. List five reasons a buyer might choose a more collaborative approach to the supplier relationship?
5. What are switching costs?
6. What is the key difference between collaborative relationships and transactional relationships?
7. Identify some benefits of collaborative relationships.
8. How do alliances differ from collaborative relationships?
9. Why is executive-level commitment in both companies required to make an alliance work?
10. Name three reasons a buyer might choose a more collaborative relationship with a supplier.
11. What do the authors mean when they write, "Suppliers want 'good' customers"?

**12.** Alliances are not always appropriate. Explain the five major reasons for a buyer not to pursue an alliance with a supplier.

**13.** How does Michael Dell advocate use of the Internet in managing a company's buys?

# Internet Exercise

## TradeAccess, Inc.

Visit the "TradeAccess, Inc., website. See the software being developed to allow businesses to exploit the power of the Internet in buying and selling products.

(http://www.eyedeas.net/clients/ozro/news/precommbldr.cfm)

**1.** How do you think this electronic tool could help the buyer?

**2.** Is the process described on this website the same as the reverse auction process described in this chapter? How does it differ?

**3.** Could this platform be used in transactional and more collaborative relationships as well?

# Suggested Reading

Carr, Amelia S., and John N. Pearson. "Strategically Managed Buyer-Supplier Relationships and Performance Outcomes," *Journal of Operations Management* 17 (1999), pp. 497–519.

Dyer, J., and H. Singh. "The Relational View: Cooperative Strategy and Sources of Interorganizational Competitive Advantage," *Academy of Management Review* 23, no. 4 (1998), pp. 660–79.

Ellram, Lisa M. "The Supplier Alliance Continuum," *Purchasing Today* 11, no. 2 (February 2000), pp. 8–10.

Emmett, Stuart, and Barry Crocker. *The Relationship-Driven Supply Chain: Creating a Culture of Collaboration throughout the Chain* (Hampshire, UK: Gower Publishing, 2006).

Kwon, Ik-Whan G., and Taewon Suh. "Factors Affecting the Level of Trust and Commitment in Supply Chain Relationships," *Journal of Supply Chain Management* 40, no. 2 (Spring 2004), pp. 4–13.

McHugh, Marie, Paul Humphreys, and Ronan McIvor. "Buyer-Supplier Relationships and Organizational Health," *Journal of Supply Chain Management* 39, no. 2 (Spring 2003), pp. 15–25.

Pinkerton, Richard L. "Business-to-Business Procurement—The Current Revolution within Supply Chain Management," *World Markets Series Business Briefing: European Purchasing & Supply Chain Strategies,* World Markets Research Centre, May 2001, London, UK. (www.wmrc.com)

# Appendix A: Institutional Trust

Research, including personnel interviews, and much of the current literature demonstrate the importance of trust between alliance partners.[35] Dyer points out that trust "is critical for partner success because without it suppliers and customers will spend considerable resources negotiating, monitoring, and enforcing inflexible contracts."[36] As previously noted, when institutional trust (see Figure 4.2) is present, the parties

---

[35]Nirmalya Kumar, "The Power of Trust in Manufacturing–Retailers Relationships," *Harvard Business Review,* November–December 1996, pp. 92–106, and R. M. Monczka, K. J. Peterson, R. B. Hanfield, and Gary L. Ragatz, "Success Factors in Strategic Supplier Alliances: The Buying Company Perspective," *Decision Science* 29, no. 3 (Summer 1998), pp. 553–75.

[36]Jeffrey H. Dyer, *Collaborative Advantage* (New York: Oxford University Press, 2000), p. 38.

**Figure 4.2** | Spectrum of Supply Relationships and Institutional Trust

*Note:* Institutional trust: The term "trust" has such a wide variety of meanings and interpretations that we have chosen to coin the term "institutional trust." Institutional trust is the key element that differentiates supply alliances from collaborative relationships. With institutional trust, the parties have access to each other's strategic plans in the area(s) of the interface. Relevant cost information and forecasts are shared. Risks and rewards are addressed openly. Informal agreements are as good as written ones. Institutional trust is measured and managed.

have access to each other's strategic plans in the areas of interface between the companies and their respective cross-functional teams. Relevant cost information and forecasts are shared. Risks and rewards are addressed openly. Informal agreements are as good as written ones. Institutional trust is measured and managed.

Traditional organizations that memorialize their supply agreements with detailed legal contracts often overlook the value of trust. In an ever-changing world that is moving faster and faster, trust creates a major competitive advantage in that fast decision making can be done only in an environment of trust. Further, in an ever-changing, highly uncertain business world, trust based on integrity, commitment, and common values is the only thing that remains stable while everything else—strategy, technology, people—moves. An ever-changing world requires frequent renegotiations between alliance partners. If there is no trust, the renegotiations are likely to be degenerative and antagonistic and are likely to result in a win-lose relationship, at which point the alliance dies.

In addition, innovation between buyer and supplier is typically a major strategic driver and one of the most powerful elements of competitiveness. Cocreated innovation is stymied when distrust is rampant. People communicate better in a trusting environment, and cross-functional coordination is easier. What's more, distrust causes companies to engage in additional non-value-added work, such as time wasted in legal contracts, burdensome paperwork, and redundancy. Thus, trust translates directly to more profit.

Trust in alliances is not "blind trust" but "prudent trust" that is carefully designed and planned and mutually agreed on. Initially, as alliances are formed, this trust typically is established interpersonally, usually between the alliance champions and senior executives who create the alliance entity.

This interpersonal trust, based on the vision and values of the founders, is critical at the inception of the alliance. When problems occur (and inevitably they will), trust will be the foundation for problem resolution. Similarly, as strategic or technological conditions change, as occurs in fast-moving environments, trust will be a critical ingredient in renegotiating and strategically repositioning the alliance.

However, for the alliance to survive in the long term and for supplier networks to evolve, interpersonal trust is not enough; institutional trust, a higher order of trust, must prevail. The following list is the result of six years of research on the issue of institutional trust by faculty and students at the University of San Diego.

### Attributes of Institutional Trust Include:

- Institutional trust is developed over time—part of a process.
- Internal trust is developed before external trust.
- Institutional trust is based on individual and institutional integrity.
- Institutional trust is greater than individual trust.

- Trust and the relationship are viewed as worthwhile investments.
- The partners have access to each other's strategic plans in the area(s) of the interface.
- Relevant cost information and forecasts are shared.
- When key individuals leave, fingerprints are left behind that hold the relationships together.
- Trust is visible—something for others to see, feel, and emulate.
- Informal agreements are as good as written contracts.
- Both parties are sensitive to changes which might affect the cultural bridge between the two firms.
- The relationship is adaptable in the face of changing needs of either party.
- Personnel at both firms recognize the interdependent nature of the relationship.
- Personnel at both firms consider the sharing of information to be a means of developing trust in the relationship.
- Conflict in the relationship is addressed openly and resolved.
- Both parties consider the rights, desires, and opinions of their partners during internal discussions.
- The firms have mutual goals in the area of the interface.
- Firms build a bank account of trust based on many deposits.
- Trust has different meanings in different cultures.

## Antecedents of Trust

In 2001 Fawcett and Magnan reported on a comprehensive study addressing Supply Chain Management. The study was based on both a literature review and 52 in-depth interviews with representatives of leading companies at each stage of the supply chain.

The authors observed that "trust has numerous antecedents including open and honest information sharing, commitment, clear expectations, and follow through. The passage of time, high levels of actual performance, and the fulfillment of promises also precede trust. Finally, real trust exists only when both sides agree that it does. Relationships that one party describes as trust-based are often viewed as less friendly and less mutually advantageous by the other side."[37]

### *Actions Which Are Taken to Develop and Manage Trust Include:*

- Both CEOs make a personal investment.
- Appropriate senior managers from both firms commit to nurturing the relationship.
- Either party may bring up ethical issues without fear of retribution.
- An ombudsman is assigned at both firms.
- An interfirm team consisting of representatives of relevant functional areas is appointed to develop and manage the relationship.
- Discussions between the two firms' personnel are conducted in an atmosphere of respect.
- The interfirm team receives guidance and training in the implementation of practices which facilitate the development of strategic alliances before addressing specific project details.
- Listening, understanding, time, and energy are invested to develop and maintain trust.
- Senior leaders at both firms act as a champion to the teams.
- Members of the interfirm team share in the development of the communication system between the firms.

---

[37]Stanley E. Fawcett and Gregory M. Magnan, "Achieving World-Class Supply Chain Alignment: Barriers, Bridges, and Benefits," Center for Advanced Purchasing Studies (CAPS) Focus Study, Tempe, AZ, 2001.

- Members of the interfirm team take specific actions to develop and measure trust in the relationship.
- Risks and rewards are addressed openly.
- Negotiation is used as a trust-building opportunity.
- Within the parameters of the relationship, appropriate members of both firms work together on technology plans for the future.
- Technical personnel from both firms visit their partners to learn and observe how the others' products are developed, manufactured, and utilized.
- Contractual relations are designed to enhance trust (and lawyers who engage in the contractual negotiations must be acutely tuned to the necessity of building trust into their legal interactions).
- Contractual relations focus on continuous improvement.
- Team and relationship skills are developed early.
- Both company leaders create a formal relationship agreement—an agreement that memorializes a commitment to work well together.
- A contracting philosophy and a legal infrastructure are designed to enhance buyer-supplier relationships rather than the legal mechanism (t's and c's) to protect each firm.
- Institutional trust is measured and managed.

Supply management is one of the keys to Toyota's incredible success. Toyota has perfected the art and the science of supplier relationships, with trust playing a key role. Jeffrey Dyer points out that "Toyota's ability to develop trust with suppliers is not based primarily on personal relationships between Toyota and its suppliers. Nor is it based primarily on the stock ownership it holds in its keiretsu suppliers. Rather, this trust is linked to the perceived fairness and predictability of Toyota's routines for managing external relationships."[38]

# Appendix B: Supply Management in Action

## A Supplier Alliance at Quaker Oats[39]

This appendix describes how the Quaker Oats Company of Chicago, Illinois, formed an alliance with Graham Packaging of York, Pennsylvania. Graham is a leading global manufacturer of custom blow-molded plastic containers. Plastic bottles are the largest single quantity and cost item purchased by Quaker Oats. Topics include how to select an alliance partner, how to negotiate a massive joint building construction and equipment project, and what kind of contract facilitates a win-win relationship based on trust and the sharing of cost information. This alliance actually became a joint venture with Quaker building an addition for the plastic bottle plant and Graham investing in the equipment and people required to operate the plant at the Quaker Gatorade facilities in Atlanta, Georgia.

---

[38]Dyer, *Collaborative Advantage,* pp. 15–16.

[39]Richard L. Pinkerton, Ph.D., C.P.M., Chair and Professor Emeritus of Marketing and Logistics, the Sid Craig School of Business, California State University, Fresno, and Richard G. Reider, Director, Packaging Purchasing, Quaker Oats Company. Published in the Proceedings of the 85th Annual International Purchasing Conference, April 30–May 3, 2000, ISM, Tempe AZ. This case study has been updated based on information gathered by Richard L. Pinkerton in a March 2007 interview with Mr. Richard Reider, Director, Packaging Purchasing, PEPSICO.

## Introduction

Founded in 1901, Quaker Oats had sales of $4.6 billion in 1998, produced by 11,860 employees. One of Quaker's successful brands, Gatorade, had $1.7 billion in worldwide sales and is far and away the number one brand in the sports beverage category with 82 percent share of market in the U.S. Other well-known brands include Cap'n Crunch cereal, Life cereal, Chewy Granola Bars, Quaker Fruit and Oatmeal breakfast bars, Rice-A-Roni, Near East, and Aunt Jemima syrups and pancake mixes.

## Plastic Bottles

Plastic bottles are big business at Quaker Oats. Quaker is one of the world's largest purchasers of plastic bottles for sports drinks, with Gatorade as one of the great global brands. Total U.S. case volume is roughly 100,000,000 cases purchased mostly from April through September. The incumbent bottle supplier had been supplying Quaker since 1986. Demand had grown from 100 million to over 1,400 million bottles by 1998. Because the initial emphasis had been on bottle supply and performance, the supplier had negotiated a price based on new investment and defined quantities. Over the 12-year period new negotiations had taken place, but the supplier had managed to increase/retain its high start-up margins. The incumbent supplier did offer various means of cost reduction. These were deemed not to be sufficient.

## Quaker after Snapple and Supply Chain Management

By 1997, new purchasing management was engaged to find supply chain cost efficiencies. The bottle was a logical first place to look (i.e., the low hanging fruit). A quick analysis indicated that the material cost was less than 40 percent of the bottle price to Quaker, a ratio that indicated there was tremendous opportunity for price reductions. After paying what the company thought was a reasonable price for many years, it was now immediately apparent to Quaker that the bottle price was too high.

A cross-functional team from accounting, engineering, technical, and the purchasing staff was formed to model the bottle's manufacturing cost. After numerous trips to plants and discussions with consultants, an independent cost model confirmed Quaker's initial belief that bottle prices could be reduced substantially. The current supplier was not willing to reduce the price even though Quaker demonstrated that profit was excessive. Competition for Quaker's business would be the strategy.

## The Alliance Options

Several options were examined with the objectives of reducing cost and improving quality and service:

1. Merchant supplies the total product.
2. Self-manufacture with inputs from key raw material suppliers.
3. In-house plant operated by a supplier. This option would require an alliance due to: long-term commitment needed, ongoing cost containment, and contractual issues regarding having another company operate on Quaker's premises.

Merchant supply was rejected due to:

1. Absence of lower cost alternative merchant supply (freight cost hurdle).
2. No known way to gain effective cost understanding/cultural improvement with arm's length relationship (lack of both parties' commitment).

Self-manufacture was rejected due to:

1. Not a core competency.
2. Supplier's cost of capital was generally lower than Quaker's: best to use a supplier's money.

In-house plant was chosen because:

1. Best cost–no freight, direct feeding of filling line eliminated palletizing and fresher materials.
2. Best opportunity to institutionalize continuous improvement. Alliance relationship comes from the open book need to drive improvement. Quaker and Graham (the selected supplier) agreed to act as one company on each other's behalf.

### Negotiating an Alliance

The Quaker Negotiation Team included:

- The Director of Packaging Purchasing
- Senior Manager of Purchasing
- Supervisor of Finance
- Industrial Engineer
- Manager, Supply Chain Planning

The Graham Packaging Company team included:

- Senior Vice-President and General Manager, Food & Beverage Business Unit
- Director of Sales, Beverage and Business Unit
- Director of Finance, Beverage Business Unit

Quaker visited eight bottle companies, two consulting companies, one practitioner of in-plant molding, two machinery suppliers, and two resin manufacturers. This effort took approximately one year and involved many, many sessions. In addition, Quaker refined the performance "should cost model" with the cross-functional team. Finally, trust-building sessions were held with two potential suppliers (the finalists). These sessions included senior management dinners, use of an outside consultant as a facilitator on partnering, and frequent visits to each other.

In the survey to understand the market, it was determined that Graham Packaging of York, Pennsylvania, had the capability to meet Quaker's needs because of its focus on Quaker's type of bottle and its proven record with customers. A key to begin developing an alliance was to build trust by disclosing bottle costs.

Graham and Quaker held a series of meetings to define what each company wanted from a potential business relationship. It was determined that both were aligned on views of how to jointly create value. Quaker discussed Graham's target ROI needs, and Graham acknowledged and understood Quaker's needs for low-cost bottles. A key Quaker issue was how to find a supplier who would manage the risk of unused bottle-making capacity after the substantial Gatorade seasonal peak and do it to the benefit of both parties. Graham agreed early in the discussions to price the bottle on a highly utilized machine basis in spite of Quaker's inability to commit to fill the equipment 100 percent of the year. If needed, Graham would find other customers to keep the plant running and to maintain the full economic benefit for both companies.

Although the basis for the agreement ended up to be partnering, it did not begin that way. As both parties discussed how to work to manage cost and find efficiencies, the only apparent way was to create an open-book accounting relationship based on trust.

At the core of supply chain management, the reason why trust fails to develop between buyer and supplier, and why maximum value in the relationship is not created, is because parties hide information from each other. The largest source of hidden information is cost. Opening the books is the best way to eliminate distrust and truly find a better relationship that would warrant any company's investment in developing a relationship.

## The Contract

Without divulging confidential information, the arrangement is not long term if Graham does not perform adequately. The incentive for the relationship to be constantly renewed has been built in through periodic "rewarding" of the business based on performance. While those close to the relationship know this is not needed, the board of directors at Quaker Oats needed these safeguards.

Construction on the in-plant facility at the Gatorade plant in Atlanta, Georgia, has been completed. Quaker spent $10 million in plant expansion; Graham spent $28 million on equipment and will own and operate the plant and be responsible to meet certain quality and efficiency standards. If Graham fails to meet these standards, it will bear the cost of nonperformance. Type of contract:

1. Evergreen from one fixed period to another.
2. Completely open book—Quaker pays all expenses and a fixed return on invested capital (which was mutually costed).
3. Cancelable for failure to perform.
4. Volume sensitive: Quaker will compensate for volume shortfalls. However, Gatorade has not failed to grow at least 9 percent per year over the last 18 years. Never bet against your own business.

## How Is the Alliance Working? What about Future Alliances?

The bottles produced in the in-house plant are the lowest-cost bottles in the Quaker system. The alliance has produced much better (more accurate) forecasting that helps lower costs by schedule stabilization. While this is not the only cost reduction benefit in the endeavor, it demonstrates the need to capture and analyze total cost of ownership. The few start-up quality issues were resolved very quickly, and as one would expect, the delivery and other service aspects are "perfect." Joint quality improvement initiatives enabled by the alliance are generating impressive results on the Quaker Oats filling lines as improved quality translated to increased productivity, reduced scrap, and lower costs. Joint cost savings initiatives and the "open book" approach are also already delivering bottle cost savings to Quaker that exceed project objectives by over $1 million annually.

As to other alliance possibilities, Quaker would like more in other packaging materials. Unfortunately, the packaging industry is very "old school" and adversarial. Consolidations result in frequent management changes which negate building long-term relationships. In the field of packaging, costs are driven by machinery utilization, so huge volumes are required for economies of scale. This is especially true for flexible film and folding cartons. Perhaps Quaker can partner with other noncompetitors to consolidate and achieve the volume . . . but that's another story.

## Epilogue

In a follow-up conversation between Dr. Pinkerton and Mr. Reider in March 2007, it was learned that this supplier alliance contract has been extended and the concept has been applied to other sites at various bottling plants. Mr. Reider states that one of the key aspects of the contract was the "meet competition clause." This assures that if Quaker Oats can buy bottles cheaper, Graham or any current supplier will have to meet the price or risk the execution of a cancellation provision.

# PART 2

# The Requirements Process

The ultimate cost of any product-service is largely determined at the design stage. The determination of requirements builds in much of the later costs in the production of products and the delivery of services.

The generation of requirements is the most crucial phase of the procurement process. Some 80 percent of the cost of an item or service is "built in" at this stage of the procurement. Although supply management does not have primary responsibility for this phase, it should play a major contributing role in the process. This part will look at the development of requirements for material, capital equipment, and services.

The design and development of new products is one of a manufacturing firm's most crucial activities. Profitability and even survival are affected. Supply management and the firm's suppliers have major contributions to make during this process. An increasing number of successful firms involve supply management and suppliers up front because of the contributions they can make in the areas of quality, cost, and time to market.

Both specifications and standardization play important roles in the search for the right quality and the right value. They also assist in resolving design conflicts among engineering, manufacturing, marketing, and supply management. As presented in this part of the book, specifications are the heart of the resulting procurement. The strategic dimension of specification development cannot be ignored in today's globally competitive environment. Long-term planning through organizational change and philosophical transformation must occur in most companies so that balanced specifications contribute to the viability of a firm's supply chain.

Many firms still do not fully appreciate the concepts embraced in standardization and its corollary, simplification. Nevertheless, the philosophies underlying these concepts play an important role in creating competitive advantage. It seems highly probable that these philosophies will continue to be important in the future. Aided by improved information technology and increased automation coupled with computer-aided design and computer-aided manufacturing systems, standardization is part of the way to meeting this decade's desire for customized products and services at a low cost. By further standardizing component parts, processes, and operations, companies can refine and streamline their systems. That refinement should permit the production of low-cost, high-quality differentiated products that will be competitive in the global marketplace.

It is our belief that no other functional area or system has a greater impact on the quality of an organization's products and services than supply management. Inversely, well-managed quality is a cornerstone of a competitive supply chain. Experience indicates that some 75 percent of field failures can be traced back to defects in purchased materials. Chapter 7, "Managing for Quality," demonstrates that there are many approaches to proactively mitigating quality problems. That chapter describes several philosophies, approaches, tools, and methodologies that supply management may employ to eliminate or minimize defects throughout the supply chain. The focus of Chapter 7 is on developing quality design and prevention systems rather than reactive detection systems.

In most firms, equipment is not purchased frequently. Those purchases may represent important management decisions. Equipment purchases can be major investments that lead to the manufacture of more competitive products or the delivery of more competitive services, both of which increase sales in the marketplace and/or lead to improved productivity.

The role of supply management is distinctly different in this type of buying activity than it is in production buying. In the procurement of equipment, supply management personnel function in a creative capacity as facilitators, coordinators, contract administrators, and consultants to management. Specifications must be precise and complete yet must be written as functionally as possible. Economic analyses should utilize appropriate techniques, must be thorough, and must be based on data that are as accurate as possible. In many cases, supply management becomes the champion of total cost of ownership analysis. Supply management should be actively involved and optimally guide the team through the sourcing and negotiation activities. The contract must be precise and complete. There should be no doubt about installation and start-up responsibilities, performance requirements, test and inspection methods, related post-sale responsibilities, spare part support, and warranties.

The procurement of services is one of supply management's most interesting and challenging assignments. Large sums of money are involved. Of equal or greater importance, successful operation of the organization is affected by the effectiveness with which key services are purchased. Supply Management frequently must assume a far more active role in all phases of services procurement than it does when a company purchases materials. ■

# New Product Development

*After reading this chapter, you should be able to:*

1. Understand the benefits of involving buyers and suppliers in the product development stage.

2. Recognize the steps in designing and developing new products.

3. Appreciate supply management's role in the new product development process.

4. Identify ways in which supply management can increase its role in the product development process.

## VIGNETTE: AN OPPORTUNITY AT ELITE ELECTRONICS?

Management at Elite Electronics is faced with a golden opportunity—or is it only fool's gold? Six months ago, marketing research indicated a potential market of 10,000 oscilloscopes per year if Elite's selling price could be brought down to $1,000 per unit. (Elite's lowest-priced model, the EE201, currently sells for $1,485.)

Engineering had been working day and night to develop a new model whose variable production cost would be no more than $700. Supply Management had been working with present and potential suppliers to lower the total cost of purchased material. Recently, supply management learned of the possibility of a breakthrough on material costs for the new oscilloscope. Gamma Conglomerates, while working on the development of an analog-to-digital (ADC) module for three years, developed a revolutionary new process that allowed it to produce 1,000 modules a month. To guarantee the amortization of its research and development and setup costs, Gamma offered a price of $90 per unit F.O.B. if Elite would agree to purchase all of its ADCs for the new oscilloscope from Gamma for a period of five years. Full-scale production could begin in three months.

Incorporation of the new ADC would allow the elimination of four modules required in the current model EE201 oscilloscope with only a slight loss of resolution. This would result in a system whose variable production cost would be between $650 and $700, including $200 for assembly and testing. Allocations for fixed general, administrative, and marketing expenses would add approximately $200 per unit.

Five prototype oscilloscopes that incorporated the new ADC were built and tested. The new system was an engineering success!

Both engineering and marketing were very enthusiastic about the new system. Supply management, manufacturing, and quality control shared their enthusiasm, but with some reservations. Supply management was concerned that Gamma Conglomerates would be the sole source of supply for the ADC. Quality control, production, and supply management shared another concern: the quality of incoming materials. The firm already had experienced unpleasant situations with new "state-of-the-art" materials. Many electronics items and the systems that incorporate them are extremely complex and interdependent. It is not always possible to detect defective items until they are incorporated into larger modules or even a complete system. This is an inherent aspect of the sophisticated state-of-the-art processes used to produce modern electronics components. Things go along fine for a while, and then for no apparent reason defects get completely out of control. It often takes 10 to 14 months to stabilize new production processes and eliminate the problems.

Great amounts of test and rework time may be required of Elite's production department to locate and correct this type of problem. For example, Elite currently is experiencing just this kind of situation on a new premium-quality oscilloscope. Test, rework, and assembly time is running at 400 percent of the work hours budgeted for the new oscilloscope. On the basis of his experience with state-of-the-art materials, Elite's production manager estimates that there are two chances in five of such a situation occurring with the new low-cost model if it incorporates Gamma's new ADC.

The high cost of test and rework time can have disastrous implications for a firm such as Elite. Items projected to make a profit contribution can wind up causing losses. In some ways even more damaging to such a firm, promised delivery dates may not be met. As a result, current sales, customer goodwill, and future business all can suffer.

In many industries, the first firm to market a new product successfully is able to build and maintain a much stronger market position than can firms that enter the market later. Elite believes that its likely market would be 10,000 units of the new low-priced oscilloscope for the first year of production and 6,000 per year for the next four years if it is the first firm to market such a low-priced oscilloscope. However, if the introduction is not successful for quality or manufacturing reasons, the negative impact would reduce likely sales to 4,000 units for each of the five years. Production estimates that it would take approximately one year to clear up the problem. Accordingly, it appears realistic to assume that some 4,000 units would require excessive test, rework, and assembly time. The unit variable cost of the 4,000 units would be an estimated $1,275. Marketing believes that likely sales would be 6,000 units per year for four years if Elite waited for the ADC production process to stabilize or if a less risky approach became available in approximately 10 to 14 months.

Supply management is confident that alternatives to the ADC will be available at that time. Those alternatives will use proven technology and cost approximately $45, lowering variable production costs to about $630 per unit. Management at Elite truly is in a predicament. Should it grab the new ADC and run for the pot of gold, or should it play it safe and wait for more proven technology and competitive sources? ■

## CRITICAL THINKING QUESTION

1.  Discuss whether Elite should grab the new ADC and run for the pot of gold or play it safe and wait for more proven technology and competitive sources. Consider the advantages of being first to market compared with waiting for someone else to sustain the costs of working out the issues. (Hint: Develop an expected value analysis of the two alternatives.)

T his chapter addresses four key issues: (1) early supply management and supplier involvement, (2) the process of designing and developing new products, with an emphasis on supply management's role in the process, (3) several approaches to increasing supply management's role in the new product development process, and (4) a description of supply management professionals who interface successfully with engineers during the new product development process.

World-class firms excel at a crucial triad of activities: new product development, the design of the required production process, and the development of the optimal supply chain. This chapter addresses the first member of this triad.

"Rapid changes in technology, the emergence of global industrial and consumer markets, increasing market fragmentation and product differentiation, and the increasing options for developing and producing products have increased the pressure on all firms to more effectively and efficiently develop new products."[1] In many progressive firms, the design of new products is conducted by a team representing a number of functional areas. Marketing, product planning, design engineering, reliability engineering, supply management, manufacturing engineering, quality, finance, field support, and, frequently, carefully selected suppliers and customers are involved, as appropriate. If effectively done, new product development (NDP) can be a source of competitive advantage for a firm and a competitive strategy for the internal and external partnerships in the supply chain.[2]

Anecdotal evidence indicates that the development of new products by such cross-functional teams and the use of concurrent engineering[3] have the potential of significantly improving three key objectives: time to market, improved quality, and reduced total cost.[4] The turnaround of many troubled manufacturers during recent decades was the result of replacing departmental walls with teamwork among those who should be part of the design process. Supply management professionals and carefully selected suppliers are moving to earlier involvement in the new product development process because of the important contributions they can make in the areas of quality, cost, and timely market availability. This early involvement commonly is referred to as *early supply management involvement* and *early supplier involvement* (ESI). German authorities Arnold and Essig conclude that "by involving supply management and suppliers in the simultaneous engineering process (as members of cross functional teams) at an early stage, R&D gets the chance to increase efficiency. . . . In fact, early supply management involvement helps to shorten engineering time and increase engineering quality."[5]

The lack of effective, cooperative teamwork among the functions noted above frequently has been accompanied by quality problems, cost overruns, forgone all-in-cost savings,[6] major scheduling problems,

---

[1]Michael McGinnis and R. Vallopra, "Purchasing and Supplier Involvement: Issues and Insights Regarding New Product Success," *Journal of Supply Chain Management,* Summer 1999, pp. 4–15.

[2]John E. Ettlie and Paul A. Pavlou, "Technology-Based New Product Development Partnerships," *Decision Sciences* 37, no. 2 (May 2006), pp. 117–47.

[3]Concurrent engineering is a process in which functional specialists execute their parts of the design as a team concurrently instead of in separate departments serially.

[4]Charles O'Neal, "Concurrent Engineering with Early Supplier Involvement: A Cross-Functional Challenge," *International Journal of Purchasing and Materials Management,* Spring 1993, pp. 3–9.

[5]Personal interview with Dr. Uli Arnold and Dr. Michael Essig, Stuttgart, Germany, July 1999.

[6]All-in-cost is a summation of purchase price, incoming transportation, inspection and testing, storage, production, lost productivity, rework, process yield loss, scrap, warranty, service and field failure, and customer returns and lost sales associated with the purchased item. The term "all-in-cost" is similar to "total cost of ownership" and simply "cost." All those terms recognize that the purchase price of an item is merely one component of the total cost of buying, owning, and using a purchased item.

and new products which are late to enter the marketplace. Further, early recognition of problems is difficult or impossible in the absence of cooperative teamwork. Extensive redesign, rework, and retrofit operations are common when a company is operating in the traditional functional mode. Ultimately, the absence of teamwork results in products which are a continuing burden to the firm's long-term competitiveness.

Cost overruns and forgone cost savings frequently result when the designers (or the design team) fail to consider the supply base's design, manufacturing, quality, and cost capabilities. For example, during the early 1980s, design engineers at General Electric's Jet Engine Division frequently designed materials to be purchased from outside suppliers under the mistaken belief that the outside suppliers had the same manufacturing and process capabilities as GE. In fact, that was not the case; the outside suppliers frequently did not have the same equipment, processes, and quality capabilities. The results were cost growth and schedule slippages as the suppliers, using a trial-and-error process, attempted to meet GE's specifications. Frequently, it became apparent that those specifications could not be met and that a costly and time-consuming process of reengineering would be required.[7]

A similar example of costs resulting from failure to consider supply implications during design involves IBM. In 1993, sales of IBM's PC units were just over $8 billion, with earnings of about $200 million (2.5 percent). By contrast, Compaq's profits were $462 million on sales of $7.2 billion (6.4 percent). According to *BusinessWeek,* "At least one reason . . . seems clear, IBM still does not use common parts across its product families." Another contributor to lower profits was IBM's failure to shift away from pricey Japanese components as the value of the yen rose.[8] It was noted that IBM recognized that its supply management system had been a source of significant cost overruns and forgone dollar savings. In 1994 that recognition resulted in the appointment of a new Chief Procurement Officer, Mr. Gene Richter. Under Richter, three-time Purchasing Man of the Year, IBM Procurement has undergone an incredible transformation and is now approaching "World Class" status.

Scheduling problems frequently result from the late delivery of required parts. For example, earnings at Apple Computer fell nearly 30 percent in the third quarter of 1999, largely as a result of supply shortages. Apple received only 45 percent of the G4 chips its suppliers originally had promised. This in turn led to significant reductions in the sales of Apple's Power Mac G4 computers.[9] When supply considerations are not addressed during new product development, unique nonstandard components may be specified. Those components frequently require longer lead times than do standard items. The use of nonstandard items often leads to the inability of the manufacturer to react quickly to changes in market demand, frequently resulting in lost sales. To reduce reaction time to changes in demand, firms are replacing unique components with standard "commodity" ones. In addition to being more readily available, commodity components tend to be far less expensive than the unique items they replace.

The global marketplace and global competition, coupled with advanced communication systems, computers, and sophisticated software, have generated an environment where "time to market" and first to market have significant competitive advantages. Clearly, the need to reduce development time has forced companies to look for new methods to compete. The use of supply professionals and suppliers

---

[7]Personal interview with Gene Walz, Materials Manager, General Electric, Jet Engine Division, June 1983.

[8]Ira Sager, "IBM: There's Many a Slip . . . ," *BusinessWeek,* June 27, 1994, pp. 26–27.

[9]"Apple Net May Fall Up to 30% in Quarter," *Wall Street Journal,* September 21, 2000.

earlier in the product development cycle is a key way to reduce time to market. The advantages of an integrated approach to new product development no longer can be ignored.[10]

In the early 1990s, the Chrysler Viper went from concept to production in 36 months, in contrast to an industry norm of 60 months. Chrysler did not achieve that goal by itself; it got a lot of support from its suppliers. "They were as much a part of the Viper team as anyone . . . suppliers are an integral part of the team," said Dave Swietlik, the man in charge of procurement for the Viper program. "Their processes drive design."[11] (Unfortunately, Chrysler appears to have retreated to a more adversarial approach since its takeover by Dailmer-Benz.)[12]

When a cross-functional team has the responsibility for the development of new products, a concurrent approach to the myriad of tasks involved is taken. This avoids the traditional (and time-consuming) passage of a project from concept development, to design, to manufacturing engineering, to supply management, to manufacturing, to marketing, to field support. That sequential approach requires even more time and personnel resources when changes have to be made in the product's design. The cross-functional team uses a concurrent approach in which the team members work together and collaborate throughout the process.

# The Design Process[13]

Design is the progression of an abstract notion or idea to something that has a function and a fixed form. The desired levels of quality and reliability must be "engineered in" during the design phase of the new product. "Suppliers must have access to product design as early as humanly possible in the design process to assure optimal use of any special skills or processes they can contribute."[14] The design stage is also the optimum point at which the vast majority of the cost of making an item can be reduced or controlled. If costs are not minimized during the design stage, excessive cost may be built in permanently, resulting in expensive, possibly noncompetitive products that fail to realize their profit potential.

The new product development process is a series of interdependent and frequently overlapping activities which transform an idea into a prototype and on to a marketable product. The process is much more fluid and flexible than is portrayed in the flow diagrams in this chapter. As the original idea progresses through the development process, it is refined and constantly evaluated for technical and commercial feasibility. Trade-offs between the various objectives (price, cost, performance, market availability, quality, and reliability) are made throughout the process. These days, one hears a great deal about designing for manufacturability; however, invariably, the focus is on the firm's internal manufacturing process. However, when those responsible for design ignore the manufacturing process and technological capabilities of outside suppliers, problems with quality, time to market, configuration, control, and cost are

---

[10]Chong Leng Tan and Michael Tracey, "Collaborative New Product Development Environments: Implications for Supply Chain Management," *Journal of Supply Chain Management* 43, no. 3 (Summer 2007), pp. 2–15.

[11]Ernest Raia, "The Chrysler Viper: A Crash Course in Design," *Purchasing*, February 20, 1992, p. 48.

[12]"The Tight Squeeze at Chrysler," *BusinessWeek,* October 9, 2000, p. 54.

[13]Portions of this section are based on David N. Burt, *Proactive Procurement: The Key to Increased Profits, Productivity, and Quality* (Englewood Cliffs, NJ: Prentice Hall, 1984) and David N. Burt and Richard L. Pinkerton, *Proactive Procurement* (New York: AMACOM, 1996).

[14]John A. Carlisle and Robert C. Parker, *Beyond Negotiation: Redeeming Customer-Supplier Relationships* (Chichester, U.K.: John Wiley & Sons, 1989), p. 127.

inevitable. If optimal design performance is to be achieved, suppliers must be active from the beginning, when they can have a major impact on performance, time, cost, and quality. Selected suppliers should participate in feasibility studies, value engineering, and prototype, failure, and stress analysis, among other product development tasks.

There is a growing trend among manufacturers toward developing an "envelope" of performance specifications for suppliers. For example, instead of determining the materials, manufacturing processes, and engineering drawings for a seat for one of its motorcycles, in the 1980s Kawasaki began specifying the environmental conditions and the maximum weight the seat had to withstand together with a drawing showing how the seat was to attach to the motorcycle frame. The suppliers' engineering and CAD/CAM[15] tools, not the buying firm's, were dedicated to designing selected components. This approach allows engineers at the buying firm to focus on the development of more sophisticated core technologies and proprietary systems. The customer firm's engineers do not prepare engineering drawings for nonstrategic components. However, they review and approve the supplier's designs. That not only redirects critical engineering resources to higher-value activities but places responsibility for manufacturability and quality with the supplier.

To involve suppliers effectively and early, manufacturing companies invite carefully selected suppliers' engineers into their own engineering departments. In a 1995 *Harvard Business Review* article, management guru Peter Drucker described William Durant as the inventor of the keiretsu. Durant designed and built General Motors during the early 1900s. "Durant deliberately brought the parts and accessories makers into the design process of a new automobile model right from the start. Doing so allowed him to manage the total cost of the finished car as one cost stream."[16] Manufacturers should allow key suppliers to review the design of the entire subassembly before committing to it. Not only does this tease out new ideas, it also helps the supply partner understand the customer's real needs—and likely future needs.

Involving suppliers in the new product development process is more challenging than one might imagine. Handfield and Ragatz observe, "Successful supplier integration initiatives result in a major change to the new product development process. Further, the new process must be formally adapted by multiple functions within the organization to be successful. One of the most important activities in the new development process is understanding the focal supplier's capabilities and design expertise, conducting a technology risk assessment, weighing the risks against the probability of success."[17]

The changing competitive environment requires that much more planning, coordination, and review take place during the design and development process than previously was the case. Complexity of product lines must be addressed. Lower levels of complexity result in higher schedule stability, a prerequisite to just-in-time manufacturing. Feasibility studies, computer simulations, prototype analysis, failure analyses, stress analyses, and value engineering all must be conducted in an effort to develop producible, defect-free products quickly at the lowest possible total cost.

The new product development process has undergone a tremendous change during the last several years. The process is described in Figures 5.1, 5.2, and 5.3 and discussed below.[18]

---

[15]Computer-assisted design/computer-assisted manufacturing.

[16]Peter F. Drucker, "The Information Executives Truly Need," *Harvard Business Review,* January–February 1995, p. 56.

[17]Robert B. Hanfield and Gary L. Ragatz, "Involving Suppliers in New Product Development," *California Management Review,* Fall 1999, p. 60.

[18]Some world-class firms prepare a report at the end of a new product development project to document the major lessons learned—ones which can be applied to future projects.

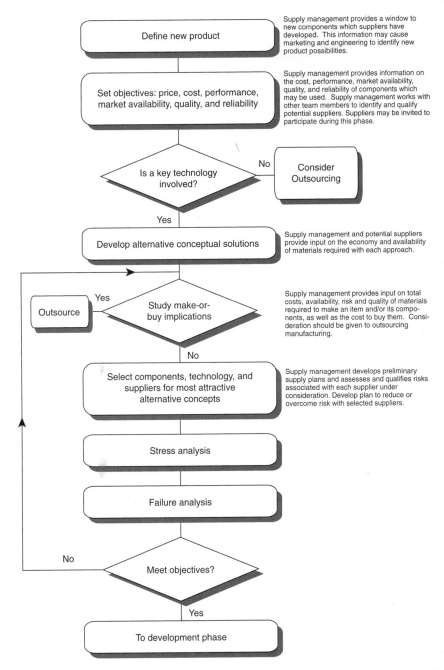

**Figure 5.1** | Team and Supply Management Activities during New Product Development *(NPD) Investigation Phase*
Source: Adapted from David N. Burt and Richard L. Pinkerton, *A Purchasing Manager's Guide to Strategic Proactive Procurement* (New York: AMACOM, 1996), p. 27.

## The Investigation or Concept Formation Phase

There are several types of new product design. The first is the one used for a totally new product. This is the least common approach since completely new products are the exception. Most new product design is actually an adaptation or an expanded feature set for a previous design. Advancing technology, process improvements, and market expansion drive the majority of new product design activity. The process described is equally applicable to a totally new product or a "new improved one."

**Defining the New Product**    The design and development process begins with the investigation phase. First, the product is defined. This function normally is performed with considerable marketing involvement. Intel carries marketing to its logical extreme: It emphasizes design ethnography, which focuses on understanding the customer and the culture in which a product is to be used.[19] The design and development process has been formally titled "customer-focused product and process development" at some firms, and "quality function deployment" at others.[20] Marketing authority Regis McKenna has been quoted as saying:

> Companies need to incorporate the customer into product design. That means getting more and more members of an organization in contact with the customer—manufacturing and design people, as well as sales and marketing staff. You can, for example, have customers sitting in on your internal committee meetings.[21]

Designers can make up for some of the shortcomings of consumer input, since they usually understand more about future technological possibilities and look at a longer time line. They are also in a better position to know what competitors may offer. For example, consumers may desire a "user-friendly" personal computer that is easy to get started with, but the designer realizes that the computer also should meet longer-term needs. Therefore, designers should have the freedom to create innovative product designs that not only meet current user requirements but are also up to the demands of future consumer expectations. This give-and-take requires a delicate balance between designers and consumers since research has shown a high correlation between inadequate feedback from users and the failure of new products that contain technical innovations.[22]

One of a supply management professional's key responsibilities is to acquire, assimilate, digest, and share information about new or forthcoming developments in the supply markets for which he or she is responsible. Interviews with present and potential suppliers, visits to suppliers (with emphasis on their research and development and production activities), attendance at trade shows, weekly reviews of relevant literature, and discussions with colleagues at local supply chain management organizations and American Production and Inventory Control Society meetings help a professional remain current. Through such activities, a supply management professional will become aware of new products and new technologies which may be of interest. This information may help product managers in marketing and senior design personnel responsible for identifying and developing new products. While being careful to screen out inappropriate information, the buyer should share potentially attractive information with marketing and engineering.

---

[19]Peter Tarasewich and Saresli Nair, "Designing for Quality," *Industrial Management,* July–August 1999, p. 18.

[20]The interested reader is referred to John R. Hauser and Don Clausing, "The House of Quality," *Harvard Business Review,* May–June 1988, pp. 63–67.

[21]Interview with Regis McKenna by Anne R. Field, "First Strike," *Success,* October 1989, p. 48.

[22]Tarasewich and Nair, "Designing for Quality," p. 18.

**Statement of Objectives**   Next, a statement of needs, desires, and objectives is developed. Needs are based on marketing's perception or knowledge of what customers want (or the customer's direct input if the customer is a member of the design team), balanced against the company's objectives and resources. Needs that are potentially compatible with the firm's objectives (profit potential, sales volume, etc.) and resources (personnel, machines, and management) are considered for development. Product objectives, including performance, price, quality, and market availability, are established and become the criteria that guide subsequent design, planning, and decision making. A well-informed procurement professional is the key source of information on the cost, performance, market availability, quality, and reliability of supplier-furnished components which may be used in the new product.

Establishing a realistic target cost at this stage of the new product development process is mandatory at world-class firms. (Target cost = Targeted market selling price − Targeted profit.)

Purchasing authority Lisa Ellram writes, "By establishing the target cost up front, purchasing, the supply base, designers, and marketing can all work toward a common goal in the value engineering, design for purchasing, and early supplier involvement processes."[23] The planned product life cycle typically includes not only the original product but several future products that will incorporate improvements in design, function, features, and so on. These new products are driven by advances in technology, design, and/or materials; competitive offerings; and customer expectations. These desired advances frequently are known at the time of the original product design, but they are not included in the design because the technology does not exist or requires additional development to be production-ready. This product feature design "wish list" is very important to the design engineer since he or she best understands the design trade-offs and compromises that were included in the original design. This wish list of technology requirements is extremely important. Unfortunately, most firms do not document the technical interests that eventually drive a subsequent iteration through their product development process. Not only should these data be documented, they must become an important focus for a supply partner's R&D efforts. Quick development will drive new product offerings that add additional sales volume, frequently at premium prices, for both the manufacturer and the supplier.

**Key Technology**   The development team should determine whether a key technology is involved. If it is not, the team may decide to have an outside supplier develop both the technology and the product.

**Development of Alternatives**   Alternative ways to satisfy these needs, desires, and objectives should be developed and then evaluated against the criteria established in the preceding step.

There is an unfortunate tendency to proceed with the first approach that appears to meet a need even though less obvious alternatives may yield more profitable solutions. Alternative approaches should be evaluated on the basis of suitability, producability, component availability, economy, and customer acceptability.

■ *Suitability* refers to technical considerations such as strength, size, power consumption, capability, maintainability, and adaptability. Engineering has primary responsibility for these issues.

■ *Producability* is the ease with which a firm can manufacture an item. In the past, designs needed to be changed to accommodate the firm's or its suppliers' ability to produce the item economically. Problems arose when the needed changes were implemented. Early manufacturing engineering involvement in the design is needed to ensure the producability of items made internally, and early supplier involvement helps ensure the producability of items furnished by suppliers.

---

[23]Lisa Ellram, "Cost Reduction: Match the Tool to the Purchase," *Purchasing Today,* October 1998, p. 34. For more insight into this process, see Lisa M. Ellram, "Purchasing and Supply Management's Participation in the Target Cost Process," *Journal of Supply Chain Management,* Spring 2000, pp. 39–51.

■ *Component availability* is the time at which components are available, while component economy describes the cost of an item or service. Component availability and economy are the responsibility of purchasing.

■ *Customer acceptability* is defined as the marketability of an item to potential customers.

The selection of components, technologies, and suppliers for the most attractive conceptual solutions is a complex process. At progressive firms such as GE, Hewlett-Packard, and Deere & Co., this selection process is a team effort, with design engineering providing the majority of the staffing and the team leadership.

Often, an engineer has a need that must be filled: a power transmission gear ratio, a structural component, a capacitance, a memory requirement. This need usually can be met in more than one way, yet the engineer may not be aware of the options available. In such a case, a supply management professional may be able to offer suggestions. A gear, for example, might be machined from bronze or steel, die cast in aluminum or zinc, molded from plastic, or formed by powder metallurgy. All these options may meet engineering's constraints while offering a wide range of cost, availability, and reliability choices. Supply management and potential suppliers can provide information on the economy and availability of the materials and subassemblies to be purchased under each approach.

The Internet is playing an increasingly critical role in compressing development time. In 2000, Spin City began providing its customers a service which allowed customers to search electronically for current data sheets, free symbols, pricing, and availability for more than 1 million components. Electronics parts suppliers were able to communicate product and service information directly to an engineer's desktop in real time, reducing costs and development time.[24] Practiced by leading firms today, early supplier involvement (ESI) is a key contributor to the product development process.

With ESI, suppliers are carefully prequalified to ensure that they have both the desired technology and the right management and manufacturing capability. Before inviting an outside supplier to participate in the development of a new product, the cross-functional development team will ask the following and related questions:

■ Will the supplier be able to meet our cost, quality, and product performance requirements?

■ Does the supplier have the required engineering capability?

■ Will the supplier be able to meet our development and production needs?

■ Does the supplier have the necessary physical process and quality capabilities?

■ Does the supplier have both the resources and the reputation of being able to overcome problems and obstacles as they arise?

■ Is the supplier financially viable?

■ Are the supplier's short- and long-term business objectives compatible with ours?

■ If a long-term relationship appears desirable, are the technology plans of the two firms compatible?

■ If a long-term relationship appears desirable, is it likely that we can build a trusting relationship?

When a component or subsystem is to be developed by an outside supplier under an ESI program, normally two or three potential suppliers will be requested to design and develop the required item.

---

[24]Personal interview with Pat Guerra, CEO, Spin City, October 10, 2000.

Potential suppliers are given performance, cost, weight, and reliability objectives and information on how and where the item will fit (interface) in the larger system. These potential suppliers must develop quality plans during the design of the item to ensure that the item can be produced in the quality specified. Selection of the "winning" supplier is a team effort, with supply management, design engineering, reliability engineering, product planning, quality, manufacturing, finance, and field support participating. Performance, quality, reliability, and cost are all considered during the selection process. When a carefully crafted strategic alliance for the item or the commodity class (e.g., fasteners, resistors, safety glass) exists, the alliance supplier alone will be invited to design and develop the required item.

Early supply management and supplier involvement can reduce the well-known start-up problems that occur when the design and the supplier's process capability are poorly matched. Ideally, supplier suggestions will be solicited and the matching of design and manufacturing process will take place during the investigative phase of the design process. The support that suppliers provide in the early stages of design is a critical factor in squeezing the material costs out of a product, improving quality, and preventing costly delays.

**Make-or-Buy and Outsourcing Analysis**    The make-or-buy and outsourcing issues should be addressed for all new items which can be either purchased or produced in-house. Every job release and every purchase request implies a decision to make or to buy. Supply management plays a key role in the make-or-buy process by providing information on the cost, quality, and availability of items. For more on this critical issue, see Chapter 10.

**Select Components, Technologies, and Supplies**    Several options may meet engineering's constraints while offering a wide range of cost, availability, and reliability choices. Supply management professionals and selected suppliers provide information on the availability of the materials and subassemblies to be purchased under each approach. The Internet allows engineers to check for component capability and product attributes in real time. The early involvement of quality engineers allows advanced quality planning to commence in a timely manner. Quality standards are developed to ensure that the components and products that are being designed can be produced at the quality specified.

The selection of required standard components is facilitated by the availability of a current internal catalog of standard items and sources which have been prequalified.[25] The use of such a catalog simplifies the design engineers' job while supporting the efforts of standardization engineering or materials management to standardize the items used. The use of standard materials, production processes, and methods shortens the design time and lowers the cost of designing and producing an item. In addition, standardization reduces quality problems with incoming materials, inventories, administrative expenses, inspection, and handling expenses while achieving lower unit costs.

The selection of technologies is a complex issue because of inherent cost/benefit trade-offs and functional orientations. Engineers are eager to incorporate the latest technology. The marketplace often richly rewards those who are first to market with innovative products; therefore, there is a strong case for incorporating new technology or processes before they are perfected. But as was seen at Elite Electronics, the

---

[25]This catalog is developed and maintained through the joint efforts of design engineering, reliability engineering, supply management, and manufacturing engineering. It reflects the technical and commercial implications of the items included. The catalog typically classifies components as low, medium, or high risk in an effort to dissuade design engineers from using high-risk components in new products. The internal catalog is in contrast to a supplier's catalog, which, while simplifying the engineer's efforts to describe an item, places the firm in an unintentional sole-source posture catalog which, while simplifying the engineer's efforts to describe an item, places the firm in an unintentional sole-source posture.

cost of such a decision can be high. Not only does that approach result in a proliferation of components to be purchased and stocked, it frequently results in the use of items whose production processes have not yet been stabilized; quality problems, production disruptions, and delays frequently result, increasing project risk. Engineering, quality, supply management, and manufacturing personnel must ensure that both the costs and the benefits of advanced developments are considered properly. The design team should design new products to the requirements of the customer, not necessarily to the state of the art.

**Stress Testing and Failure Analysis**   Once candidate component and subsystem items have been identified, they are subjected to stress testing and failure analysis. Failures are caused by failure mechanisms which are built into the item and then activated by stresses. Studying the basic stresses and the failure mechanisms they activate is fundamental to the design of effective reliability tests. The correct design approach is to find and eliminate the fundamental causes of failure. This means that the most successful stress tests are the ones that result in failures. Successful tests also are tailored to look for particular failure mechanisms efficiently by selectively accelerating the tests.

Every failure has a cause and is a symptom of a failure mechanism waiting to be discovered. The tools of failure analysis are both statistical and physical; used together, they are a potent means for detecting the often unique fingerprint of the underlying source of the failure.

## The Development Phase

Rapid advances in computer technology and software have made large-scale, complex computer simulations possible. Manufacturers typically conduct extensive computer simulations to identify interferences, fit issues, functionality, algorithmic logic accuracy, and so forth, before the development of prototypes. As the technology continues to advance, computer modeling and simulation may replace prototype development.

Despite these technical advances, breadboard and/or hardware prototypes commonly are developed so that the design team may conduct tests on the integrated system to eliminate performance and quality problems. The selected approach is reviewed in detail for feasibility and likely risk. Efforts are made to reduce risk to acceptable levels by developing and testing prototypes.

**Prototypes**   As shown in Figure 5.2, the first complete prototypes of the new product are designed, built, and tested. Documentation such as materials lists, drawings, and test procedures is created. It is not unusual to repeat this phase more than once, perhaps building the first prototype in the laboratory to test the design and building the second prototype in manufacturing as a test of the documentation. The design should not exit this phase until a prototype has met all the design goals set for it, although it may not be possible to demonstrate the reliability goal because of the small number of prototypes available for testing.

**Design Reviews**   The design review is the point at which the new design can be measured, compared with previously established objectives, and improved. Supply management participates in design reviews and provides information on the effect of specifications and the availability of items that are standard production for or are inventoried by suppliers. The supply professional must ensure that the specification or other purchase description is complete, is unambiguous, and provides necessary information on how items furnished under it are to be checked or tested. He or she should be satisfied that the purchase description is written in terms that are relevant to and understandable by potential suppliers.

Boeing provides an example of how computers have an impact on new product development. It can design a commercial aircraft entirely by computer. It solves nearly all of its design issues through computer

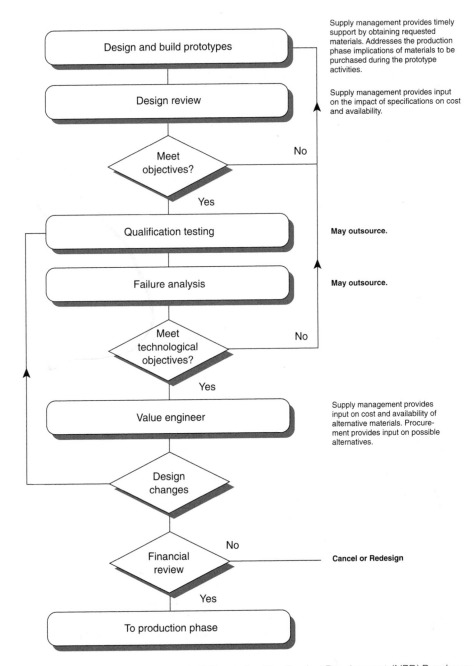

**Figure 5.2 |** Team and Supply Management Activities during New Product Development *(NPD) Development Phase*
Source: Adapted from David N. Burt and Richard L. Pinkerton, *A Purchasing Manager's Guide to Strategic Proactive Procurement* (New York: AMACON, 1996), p. 28.

animation, avoiding the need to build physical prototypes. This approach reduces the cost of making design changes during production. This practice cut the time required to design the 777 by 50 percent.[26]

**Qualification Testing**   Qualification tests are conducted on the prototype equipment. There are two different types: (1) margin tests and (2) life tests. *Margin tests* are concerned with assuring that the threshold of failure—the combination of conditions at which the product just begins to malfunction—is outside the range of specified conditions for the product's use.

*Life tests* are intended to find patterns of failure which occur too infrequently to be detected by engineering tests on one or two prototypes. These tests differ from margin tests primarily in the number of units tested and the duration of the test.

**Failure Analysis**   The stress testing and failure analysis techniques described in the investigation phase are applied to the prototype.

**Meet Objectives?**   The design team determines whether the prototype meets the objectives established in the investigation phase. If the prototype fails this analysis, the project reenters the design process and a new or upgraded prototype is developed.

**Value Engineering**   During World War II many critical materials and components were difficult to obtain, and most manufacturers were required to incorporate numerous substitutions in their design and production activities. Harry Erlicher, then vice president of purchasing for the General Electric Company, observed that many of the substitutions required during that period resulted not only in reduced costs but also in product improvements. Consequently, Erlicher assigned to L. D. Miles the task of developing a systematic approach to the investigation of the function/cost aspect of existing material specifications. Larry Miles not only met the challenge successfully but subsequently pioneered the scientific procurement concept General Electric called "value analysis."[27]

In 1954 the U.S. Navy's Bureau of Ships adopted a modified version of General Electric's value analysis concept in an attempt to reduce the cost of ships and related equipment. In applying the concept, the Navy directed its efforts primarily at cost avoidance during the initial engineering design stage and called the program "value engineering" (VE) even though it embodied the same concepts and techniques as GE's value analysis (VA) program. In an operational sense, however, the two terms typically are used synonymously in industry today; only the timing differs. Hence, throughout this book when the term "value analysis" is used, it has the same conceptual meaning as the term "value engineering" except for the practical matter of timing.

## Value Engineering vis-à-vis Value Analysis

As practiced in U.S. firms for many years, value analysis techniques were used most widely in programs designed to engineer unnecessary costs out of existing products. Finally, more progressive firms began to follow the Navy's lead by establishing what they too called value engineering programs: programs that applied the value analysis concept during the early stages of the new product design process. Clearly, this is the first point at which it should be applied. This is where the greatest benefits are produced for both the firm and its customers.

---

[26]"The Economy," *Fortune*, October 2, 2000.

[27]The classic book on value engineering and analysis is Lawrence D. Miles, *Techniques of Value Analysis and Value Engineering*, 2nd ed. (Mc-Graw-Hill, 1972). This book is still the best on the subject.

What is the mix of value analysis and value engineering applications in American industry today? No one really knows. However, the numbers of both programs have grown markedly in the last decade, with value engineering programs setting the pace.

The VE concept finds its most unique use in two kinds of companies: those which produce a limited number of units of a very expensive product and those which mass-produce products that require expensive tooling. In these types of companies, value analysis of an item already in production is often impractical because it is too late to incorporate changes in the product economically. In manufacturing certain electronic instruments used in defense systems, for example, the production run is often so short that it precludes the effective use of value analysis after production has been initiated. In fact, the Federal Acquisition Regulations now stipulate that most major defense procurement contracts be subjected to value engineering studies before initial production.[28]

A somewhat different situation that produces similar operating results is used in firms that mass-produce automobiles. For example, in manufacturing the body panel for a car, once the design is fixed and the dies are purchased, it is normally too costly to change them even though value analysis studies subsequently may disclose design inefficiencies.

Value engineering utilizes all the techniques of value analysis. In practice, it involves very close liaison work among the supply, production, and design engineering departments. This liaison is most frequently accomplished through the use of product design teams or supply and production coordinators who spend considerable time in the engineering department studying and analyzing engineering drawings as they are produced. Once coordinators locate problem areas, value analysis techniques are employed to alleviate them.[29]

Value engineering (VE) is a systematic study of every element of cost in a material, item of equipment, service, or construction project to ensure that the element fulfills a necessary function at the lowest possible total cost. Ideally, the value engineering thought process is instilled in all members of the new product design team through appropriate training. (World-class firms provide 40 to 50 hours of VE training per year to those who can benefit from it!) The team members (including selected suppliers) apply VE as the product development project evolves. In some instances, value engineers are assigned to the development teams to ensure that these powerful tools are applied.

The inclusion of the value engineering step in Figure 5.2 is a safeguard: If VE thinking has been incorporated throughout the development process, a separate VE review may not be necessary. However, experience indicates that a VE review at the indicated point will result in significant savings and improved quality and/or performance. Two tools aid those involved in the VE process:

■ Design analysis
■ The VE checklist

**Design Analysis**   Design analysis entails a methodical step-by-step study of all phases of the design of a particular item in relation to the function it performs. The philosophy underlying this approach is not

---

[28]For an interesting discussion of how the Department of Defense utilizes value engineering, see "DOD Honors ASD Value Engineering Program," *Skywriter,* August 1991, p. 7.

[29]For a complete discussion of this topic see D. W. Dobler, "How to Get Engineers and P.A.'s Together," *Purchasing World,* November 1980, pp. 48–51, D. N. Burt, *Proactive Procurement* (Englewood Cliffs, NJ: Prentice-Hall, 1984), chapter 2, and David N. Burt and Richard L. Pinkerton, *A Purchasing Manager's Guide to Proactive Procurement* (New York: AMACOM, 1996), chapter 11.

concerned with the appraisal of any specific part per se. Rather, the appraisal focuses on the function which the part or the larger assembly containing the part performs. This approach is designed to lead the analyst away from a traditional perspective which views a part as having certain accepted characteristics and configurations. Instead, it encourages the analyst to adopt a broader point of view and consider whether the part performs the required function both as effectively and as efficiently as possible. Both quality and cost are objects of the analysis.

A technique that many firms use in analyzing component parts of a subassembly is to dismantle, or "explode," the unit and then mount each part adjacent to its mating part on a pegboard or a table. The idea is to demonstrate visually the functional relationships of the various parts. Each component thus can be studied as it relates to the performance of the complete unit rather than as an isolated element. Analysis of each component in this fashion is done to answer four specific questions:

1. Can any part be *eliminated* without impairing the operation of the complete unit?
2. Can the design of the part be *simplified* to reduce its basic cost?
3. Can the design of the part be changed to permit the use of simplified or less costly *production methods?*
4. Can less expensive but equally satisfactory *materials* be used in the part?

Design simplifications frequently are more apparent than is possible under the original design conditions when viewed from the standpoint of the composite operation. (This in no way reflects unfavorably on the work done initially by the design engineer.) The discovery of such potential improvements is simply the product of an analysis with a substantially broader orientation than that of the original designer. An organized VE study usually utilizes a number of individuals with different types of backgrounds, experience, and skills impossible to combine in the person of a single designer. The resulting design changes often permit the substitution of standardized production operations for more expensive operations that require special setup work. In some cases, considering the volume of parts to be produced, an entirely different material or production process turns out to be more efficient than the one originally specified. Figure 5.3 shows the logic underlying a VE study.

**The Value Engineering Checklist**   Most companies develop some type of checklist to systematize the value engineering process. Literally hundreds of questions and key ideas appear on those lists. Some of the checklists are highly specialized for particular types of products. Illustrative of the more general questions is the following checklist:

Determine the function of the item and then determine the following:

1. Can the item be eliminated?
2. If the item is not standard, can a standard item be used?
3. If it is a standard item, does it completely fit the application, or is it a misfit?
4. Does the item have greater capacity than is required?
5. Can the weight be reduced?
6. Is there a similar item in inventory that could be substituted?
7. Are closer tolerances specified than are necessary?
8. Is unnecessary machining performed on the item?
9. Are unnecessarily fine finishes specified?

Figure 5.3 | A Generalized Procedural Model of the Value Engineering Process[30,31]

**10.** Is "commercial quality" specified? (Commercial quality is usually more economical.)

**11.** Can you make the item less expensively in your plant? If you are making it now, can you buy it for less?

**12.** Is the item properly classified for shipping purposes to obtain the lowest transportation rates?

**13.** Can the cost of packaging be reduced?

**14.** Are suppliers contributing suggestions to reduce cost?[32]

---

[30]Most items perform more than one function—usually a basic function plus several supporting functions. Experience has shown that often the basic function constitutes 20 to 25 percent of the cost of the item and supporting functions account for the rest of the cost. Consequently, it is important to identify clearly these two types of functions. Use of the FAST (function analysis system technique) diagram approach provides an easy way to organize functions and subfunctions in their logical relationships. Details are available in Carlos Fallon, *Value Analysis* (New York, N.Y.: Wiley Inter-Science Publishers, 1991), and Gary Long, *VA/VE Workshop Workbook* (Society of American Value Engineers, Dayton OH, September 24, 1993), Phase One and Phase Two.

[31]The development of alternative materials and processes is the most challenging but perhaps the most stimulating phase of value engineering. Creativity and brainstorming should be encouraged and supported. Professor Alvin Williams and his colleagues suggest a number of other techniques that readers may find helpful. For details see Alvin J. Williams, Steve Lacey, and William C. Smith, "Purchasing's Role in Value Analysis: Lessons from Creative Problem Solving," *International Journal of Purchasing and Materials Management,* Spring 1992, pp. 37–41.

[32]*Basic Steps in Value Analysis,* a pamphlet prepared under the chairmanship of Martin S. Erb by the Value-Analysis-Standardization Committee, Reading Association, NAPM, Tempe, AZ, pp. 4–18.

In using this or similar checklists, those involved evaluate the component under investigation with respect to each item on the checklist. When a question is found to which the answer is not entirely satisfactory, this becomes a starting point for more detailed investigation. The checklist focuses the analyst's attention on those factors which past experience has proved to be potentially fruitful cost reduction areas.[33]

**Viability**   Before proceeding to production, a careful business analysis must be completed. In effect, the development team asks: "Will the product provide our firm's required return on its investment?"

## The Production Phase

**Manufacturing and Production Plans**   In the production phase, as shown in Figure 5.4, the manufacturing plan and the procurement plan (frequently in the form of a bill of materials) are finalized.

As a result of its early involvement in the design and specification development process, supply management also should have been able to develop contingency plans that will satisfy the firm's needs if the first source doesn't work out. The appropriate plans are now formalized and implemented.

**Knowledge Transfer**   Manufacturing engineering applies experience from similar projects and new developments from other manufacturers to the firm's production process. Manufacturing engineers also work with suppliers to share new and improved production techniques.

**Process Control**   Contrary to popular opinion, the design is not finished when the transfer from development to production takes place—quite the contrary. Unfortunately, changes at this stage of product development are very costly and tend not to be evaluated with the same thoroughness as the original alternatives. Finding a quick fix typically is the order of the day, preferably a fix that does not require extensive retooling or scrap. Still, there are legitimate reasons why changes in the design occur after release to production. For example, there may be phenomena that occur so infrequently that they are not discovered until a large number of products are manufactured. Another reason for changes at this point is the pressure to develop new products in a shorter time. This time compression frequently results in concurrent engineering. This means that a new manufacturing process is developed simultaneously with a new product that uses that process, as opposed to the more traditional sequential approach. This is a risky approach but one that is gaining popularity because it saves time and results in earlier new product release.

When manufacturing problems arise, whether in the buying firm or in the supplier's manufacturing operations, there is a tendency to look for a quick fix. One type of solution is to adjust the manufacturing process to minimize the problems rather than change the design. Perhaps this approach is taken because the process documentation is internal and not shipped to the customer along with the product. More likely, such changes in manufacturing processes are made because the process is under the jurisdiction of production and consequently the change does not require design engineering's approval.

This approach can create problems. The situation can deteriorate to the point where there is a customized process for each product—nothing is standard, and the process is out of control most of the time. When design rules and process parameters are being varied at the same time, the situation quickly becomes too complex to understand or control, and quality suffers.

---

[33]For an interesting list of suggestions, see Dave A. Lugo, "Boost Your Creativity with Divergent Thinking and Checklists," *NAPM Insights,* May 1994, p. 12.

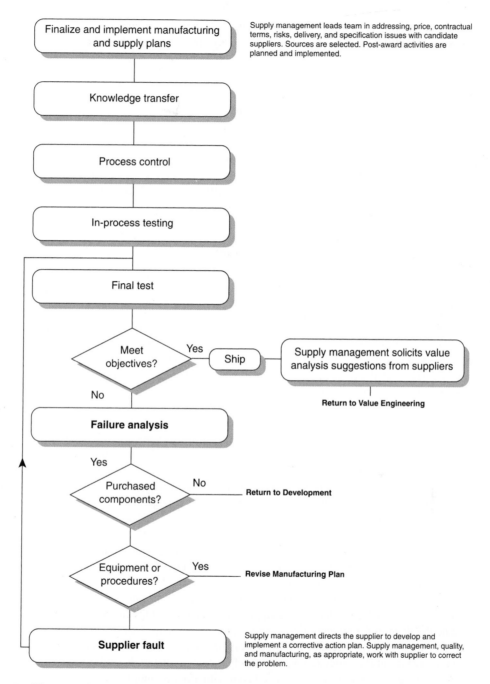

**Figure 5.4 |** Team and Supply Management Activities during New Product Development *(NPD) Production Phase*
Source: Adapted from David N. Burt and Richard L. Pinkerton, *A Purchasing Manager's Guide to Strategic Proactive Procurement* (New York: AMACOM, 1996), p. 30.

The correct solution is to optimize the process, get it under control, and keep it that way. Then the designs can be modified so that they fit the standard process, producing stable and predictable yields day after day.

**In-Process and Final Testing**    There are two objectives for in-process testing: (1) adjust or calibrate the performance in some way and (2) eliminate defects before much value is added to the product. Final product testing ensures that the item meets its performance objectives.

Every failure has a cause and is a symptom of a failure mechanism waiting to be discovered. For example, if failure analysis identifies a purchased component as the source of the failure, further analysis is required to determine whether (1) faulty equipment or procedures are to blame or (2) the problem resides with the supplier. Failure analysis also may identify a latent defect in the product's design that requires redesign.

## Engineering Change Management

Any changes in components or in the product itself may have profound effects on its cost, performance, appearance, and acceptability in the marketplace. Changes, especially at the component or subassembly level, can have a major impact on manufacturing. Unless changes in the configuration of an item or its components are controlled, manufacturers may find themselves in trouble. They may possess inventories of unusable raw materials or subassemblies. They may possess materials that require needlessly expensive rework to be adapted to a new configuration. They may produce an end item that will not meet the customer's needs. Uncontrolled changes generally mean that quality and reliability requirements have been compromised without appropriate retesting.

*Engineering change management,* a discipline which controls engineering changes, has been developed to avoid such problems.[34] How often engineering change management is required is a matter of managerial judgment, but for most modern technical items, engineering change management is a necessity. In some cases, it will be imposed on the manufacturer by its customer. When engineering change management is used, changes are controlled and recorded. Marketing and all activities involved in the purchase, control, and use of purchased materials are told about any proposed changes to the item's characteristics. These organizations then comment on the effect of the proposed change. Such control and coordination is especially important when production scheduling and the release of purchase orders are controlled by a material requirements planning system.

There are many ways to organize an engineering change management group. Ideally, an engineering change management board is established with engineering, manufacturing, marketing, production planning, inventory management, and supply management represented. When there is a materials management organization in the firm, a senior representative of production planning and inventory control is a logical candidate to chair this board. It is crucial that supply management and the function responsible for materials control be involved in the review of proposed engineering changes for three reasons: (1) to provide input on the purchased materials implications of a proposed change, (2) to discuss the timing of proposed changes to minimize the costs associated with unusable incoming materials, and (3) to be aware of forthcoming changes so that appropriate action can be taken with affected suppliers.

---

[34]Engineering change management controls the changes to a product's design—specifically, its form, fit, and function.

Adherence to this or a similar design process is key to the firm's success in the development of new products. Product quality, cost, and availability all must receive proper attention. Engineering, manufacturing, marketing, quality assurance, and supply management all have vital roles to play in the design process.

## How to Expand Supply Management's Contributions

This chapter has described the design and development process. In too many firms, the design engineer attempts to address not only the technical and functional issues of design and development but also manufacturing considerations, marketing implications, and the commercial considerations of economy and availability. Many of these individuals enjoy interacting with suppliers on both technical and commercial issues, and most believe they are serving their employer's best interests even when making sourcing and specifications decisions that turn out to be suboptimal in the long run.

It is important to note that the effectiveness of early supplier involvement appears to be a function of the industry involved. Researchers McGinnis and Vallopra found that "supplier involvement is not a panacea for every new product development effort." They also found that the potential for supply management's "contribution to new product development is substantial. These potentials can be realized if the supply management staff has the abilities to successfully participate in (and lead) multi-functional teams; has the skills needed to identify, screen, and select suppliers to include in new product development; and the competence to manage, control, and coordinate supplier involvement in a multi-functional team environment."[35] Supply management professionals have their work cut out for them. They must develop and maintain cooperative relations with engineering that protect the profitability of the firm. Early involvement of supply management is an essential ingredient of the program to maximize a firm's profitability.

Supply management professionals must understand the orientation and dedication of the typical design engineer. Obviously, an ability to speak the engineer's language (i.e., *engineeringese*) is very helpful. In a study conducted by one of the authors, it was found that supply management personnel who think in the same manner as engineers have a much higher success rate in dealing with engineers than do other individuals. Such thought processes can be identified through established testing procedures.

Whenever feasible, supply professionals should provide advice on the commercial implications of the designs under consideration in a positive and constructive manner. They must learn to co-opt their engineering counterparts by providing value and service. Supply management then is seen as a partner that takes care of business problems, allowing engineers to concentrate on technical issues. Several successful approaches to obtaining the desired level of supply management input during the design process are described below.

### Design or Project Teams

When the importance of a project or program warrants, a dedicated project team is the ideal means of ensuring early supply management involvement. These teams often are referred to as cross-functional design teams.

---

[35]Michael A. McGinnis, "New Product Development with and without Supplier Involvement: Factors Affecting Success in Manufacturing and Nonmanufacturing Organizations," *Purchasing 2000 Conference* (London, Ontario, May 24–27), Richard Ivey School of Business, University of Western Ontario, pp. 455–61.

## Materials Engineers

Individuals with an engineering background are good candidates for supply management positions whose responsibilities include involvement with design engineering. Some supply management organizations divide buying responsibilities into two specialties: (1) materials engineering and (2) the supply management activities of sourcing, pricing, and negotiating. The materials engineer is responsible for coordinating with design engineering, prequalifying potential sources (usually with the assistance of quality assurance), and participating in value management.

## Colocation

This approach calls for the placement of members of the supply management staff in locations where design engineering and development work are done. These individuals are available to collaborate with design engineers and others by obtaining required information from prospective suppliers and advising designers on the procurement implications of the different materials and suppliers under consideration. When Harley-Davidson opened its product design center in 1997, it colocated design engineering, supply management, manufacturing, marketing, and key supplier personnel. Cross-functional teams are the order of the day. The result? Faster time to market, reduced total cost, and improved quality.[36]

# Supply Management Professionals Who Interface Successfully with Engineers

The supply professional is the key to successful early supply management involvement in the new product development process. Management directives, policies, and procedures supporting early supply management involvement all help. But it is only when design engineers realize that the early involvement of a supply professional is a productive asset, not a nuisance or an infringement on their territory, that early supply management involvement makes its full contribution.

A supply management professional who recognizes the importance of being involved early in the process must acquire the necessary skills and knowledge to be seen and accepted as a contributor. Courses in the development and interpretation of engineering drawings, as well as in a wide variety of technologies, can be taken via correspondence, at night school, or in a few degree-granting programs.[37] Sales personnel love to talk and are glad to help a willing listener gain technical insight into their products. Visits to suppliers' operations provide further insight and understanding.

# Concluding Remarks

The design and development of new products is one of a manufacturing firm's most crucial activities. Profitability and even survival are affected. Supply management and the firm's suppliers have major contributions to make during this process. An increasing number of successful firms involve supply management and suppliers up front because of the contributions they can make in the areas of quality, cost, and time to market.

---

[36]Personal interviews with Leroy Zimdars, former Director of Product Purchasing, Harley-Davidson, 1997 and 1998.

[37]A small but growing number of universities now offer integrated procurement and engineering management programs.

# End Notes

Simon Croom of the Warwick Business School, Coventry, U.K., and the University of San Diego establishes the need for two types of competencies during product development: operational and relational. He defines operational competencies as those related to the design, manufacture, and delivery of a product. Relational competencies are involved in communication, interaction, problem resolution, and relationship development. Croom demonstrates the importance of relational competencies in achieving successful collaborative product development.[38]

European researchers Finn Wynstra, Bjorn Axelsson, and Arjan van Weele argue that authors in the fields of purchasing, procurement, and supply management have failed to identify many of supply management's activities in product development. These highly respected researchers identify 21 supply management activities related to product development. The interested reader is encouraged to review their provocative articles in the Summer 1999 and Autumn 2000 issues of the *European Journal of Purchasing and Supply Management*.

Handfield, Ragatz, Petersen, and Monczka address the complex issue of evaluating the capabilities of suppliers that are being considered for early involvement in new product development. The interested reader is encouraged to review this insightful article.[39]

Charles Fine, the author of *Clockspeed,* advocates that firms design their supply chains strategically and concurrently with their products and production processes. "When firms do not explicitly acknowledge and manage supply chain design and engineering as a concurrent activity to product and process design and engineering, they often encounter problems late in product development, or with manufacturing launch, logistical support, quality control, and production costs. In addition, they run the risk of losing control of their business *destiny*."[40] We agree with Dr. Fine.

# Discussion Questions

1. What is meant by the term "concurrent engineering"?
2. What are the three likely benefits of early supplier and early supply management involvement in new product development?
3. What were the results of the failure of GE's Jet Engine Division to consider its supply bases' design, manufacturing, quality, and cost capabilities?
4. What supply consideration was *not* addressed by Apple?
5. What was the impact of the early involvement of Chrysler suppliers in the early 1990s?
6. What is the optimum point at which the vast majority of the cost of making an item can be reduced or controlled?
7. What products are included under the heading "new product development"?
8. How do supply professionals gain insight into and information about forthcoming supplier developments and new technologies?

---

[38]Simon R. Croom, "The Dyadic Capabilities Concept: Examining the Process of Key Supplier Involvement in Collaborative Product Development," *European Journal of Purchasing and Management* 7 (2001), pp. 29–37.

[39]Robert B. Handfield, Gary L. Ragatz, Kenneth J. Petersen, and Robert M. Monczka, "Involving Suppliers in New Product Development," *California Management Review* 42, no. 1 (Fall 1999), pp. 59–82.

[40]Charles H. Fine, *Clockspeed* (Cambridge MA: Da Capo Press, 1998), p. 133.

9. Why should target costs be established in the development process? Describe the process of developing target costs.
10. What is the danger of adopting the first apparently viable method for meeting established needs, desires, or objectives?
11. On what basis should alternatives be evaluated?
12. Describe the process of prequalifying suppliers.
13. Describe stress testing and failure analysis.
14. What is the relationship between computer modeling, simulation, and prototype development?
15. Describe value engineering.
16. At what point do firms receive the greatest return on their investment in value engineering?
17. When problems arise during the production phase, it is very tempting to implement a quick fix. Why is this a bad practice?
18. What is the single most powerful way for supply managers to co-opt their engineering counterparts?
19. Under what conditions can supply management make its full contribution during new product development?
20. How can supply personnel acquire the necessary skills and knowledge to be seen as contributors during new product development?

## Internet Exercise

### New Product Development: WIKIPEDIA

Visit the website below and see how Wikipedia defines "NPD." If you have taken a marketing course, you can see that this definition is from the marketing/sales perspective.
(http://en.wikipedia.org/wiki/New_product_development)

List five things not listed on this site that the supply manager would need to consider.

## Suggested Reading

Crawford, Merle, and Anthony Di Benedetto. *New Products Management,* 7th ed. (New York: McGraw-Hill, 2003).

Ettlie, John E., and Paul A. Pavlou. "Technology-Based New Product Development Partnerships," *Decision Sciences* 37, no. 2 (May 2006), pp. 117–47.

Kahn, Kenneth B. *PDMA Handbook of New Product Development,* 2d ed. (Hoboken, NJ: John Wiley, 2005).

Karol, Robin, and Beebe Nelson. *New Product Development for Dummies* (Hoboken, NJ: Wiley, 2007).

Kono, Toyohiro, and Leonard Lynn. *Strategic New Product Development for the Global Economy* (Basingstoke, U.K., and New York: Palgrave Macmillan, 2007).

Lakemond, Nicolette, Christian Berggren, and Arjan vanWeele. "Coordinating Supplier Involvement in Product Development Projects: A Differentiated Coordination Typology," *R & D Management* 36, no. 1 (January 2006), pp. 55–66.

McGinnis, M. A., and R. M. Vallopra. "Purchasing and Supplier Involvement in Process Improvement: A Source of Competitive Advantage," *Journal of Supply Chain Management* 35, no. 3 (1999), pp. 42–50.

Nellore, Rajesh. "The Impact of Supplier Visions on Product Development," *Journal of Supply Chain Management,* 37, no. 1 (Winter 2001), pp. 27–36.

Petersen, K. J., R. B. Handfield, and G. L. Ragatz. "Supplier Integration into New Product Development: Coordinating Product, Process and Supply Chain Design," *Journal of Operations Management* 23, no. 3–4, (2005), pp. 371–88.

Rainey, David L. *Product Innovation: Leading Change through Integrated Product Development* (Cambridge, UK, and New York: Cambridge University Press, 2005).

Rogers, D. S., D. M. Lambert, and A. M. Knemeyer. "The Product Development and Commercialization Process," *International Journal of Logistics Management* 15, no. 1 (2004), pp. 43–56.

Schilling, M. A., and C. W. Hill. "Managing the New Product Development Process: Strategic Imperatives," *Academy of Management Executive* 12, no. 3 (1998), pp. 67–81.

Tan, Chong Leng, and Michael Tracey. "Collaborative New Product Development Environments: Implications for Supply Chain Management," *Journal of Supply Chain Management* 43, no. 3 (Summer 2007), pp. 2–15.

# 6 CHAPTER

# Purchasing Descriptions and Specifications

## CHAPTER OBJECTIVES

*After reading this chapter, you should be able to:*

1. Understand the purpose of and the need for developing clear descriptions and specifications.

2. Identify a balanced specification.

3. Define the categories of specifications.

4. Give examples demonstrating when the various categories would be used in describing a need.

5. Identify approaches to avoiding conflicts in specification development.

6. Explain the term "standardization" in relation to the product specification process.

7. Explain how standardization differs from simplification.

## VIGNETTE: THE SIMPLE SANDWICH

In a recent training session for Chili's restaurant chain, prospective employees were asked to write a description for making a peanut butter and jelly sandwich. One of the trainees then was summoned and asked to select a description randomly. The instructor asked the trainee to follow the description to make a sandwich, using the vast resources in the restaurant's kitchen.

What was the result? Complete chaos! The trainee could not even start because the materials specified did not state whether the bread was wheat, white, rye, Texas, toast, or a hamburger bun. The author of the specifications assumed that everyone knew that a peanut butter and jelly sandwich was made with white bread, creamy peanut butter, and grape jelly.

After the assumption was made to use Rainbow brand white bread, Skippy crunchy peanut butter, and Welch's grape jelly, the specifications still failed to state how the materials were to be assembled and with what tools. Does the peanut butter go on the edge of the bread? Should a spoon be used for spreading the jelly? Should one, two, or three pieces of bread be used? The manager at Chili's had made her point: Don't assume that the specifications given by a customer to you or by you to the kitchen are readily understood. In an analogous way, don't assume that you, as a supply manager, understand all the specifications given to you by an internal customer. In addition, do not assume that suppliers will understand your descriptions in a purchase order or contract. ■

## CRITICAL THINKING QUESTIONS

1. In the Chili's example, what is the analogy for supply managers?
2. How might an employee of Chili's prevent the "simple sandwich" problem on the job?
3. Try this exercise outside of class. Get a few friends together and write a description for making a peanut butter and jelly sandwich. Document the results. Where did you have problems?

# Specifications and Standardization

Participation by both critical suppliers and supply management in the development of clear specifications and comprehensive standardization is required for an organization to evolve to Strategic Supply Chain Management. Proactive development of specifications and standardization can help an organization reduce the total costs of a product or service developed either in-house or externally. The importance of including supply management in the design process was discussed in Chapter 5.

In a manufacturing firm, when specifications for a tangible product are fixed, the final design of the product is also fixed. The final design of the product often dictates fixing other costs, such as packaging and required service for the product. Therefore, when the final design is fixed, the product's competitive position and profit potential are also fixed. As was stated in Chapter 5, it is estimated that 75 to 85 percent of avoidable total costs are controllable at the design stage. Consequently, early involvement of supplier professionals is essential in a firm's effort to reduce total cost.[1]

Specifications and standardization are two related topics in the field of supply management. Specifications form what is called the purchase description. Standardized parts, components, and services may be included in the purchase description, but standardization goes beyond mere inclusion in that description. Standardization is treated in many companies and supply chains as a philosophy for creating competitive advantage. As will be discussed in this chapter, the development of specifications and standardization requires strategic action as well as tactical vigilance. This chapter discusses first specifications and then standardization.

---

[1]David N. Burt and Michael F. Doyle, *The American Keiretsu* (Homewood, IL: BusinessOne-Irwin, 1993), p. 158.

# Purposes of Specifications

The purchase specification forms the heart of a procurement. Whether a purchase order or contract will be performed to the satisfaction of the buying organization frequently is determined at the time the specification is selected or written. Purchase specifications serve a number of purposes, including the following:

- Communicate to professionals in the supply management department what to buy.
- Communicate to prospective suppliers what is required.
- Establish the tangible goods to be provided.
- Establish the intangible services to be provided, such as warranty, maintenance, and support.
- Establish the standards against which inspections, tests, and quality checks are made.
- Balance the specification goals of individual departments, relevant suppliers, desired product or service performance, and cost.

Recognition that procurements should be made with an understanding of the total cost of ownership (as discussed further in Chapter 13) requires supply managers to consider specifications that go beyond the tangible good or primary service needed. For example, laptop specifications should include the desired warranty and support levels.

## Collaborative Development

The development of specifications should be done with cross-functional teams whenever it is economically justified. Through collaborative interactions of various departmental representatives and relevant suppliers, the specifications output can balance goals that often conflict with one another. Performance goals such as quality and delivery should be balanced against cost. Individual department goals should be balanced. Supplier goals should be considered. The balancing concept is illustrated in Figure 6.1. The

**Figure 6.1 |** Considerations in Developing Balanced Specifications

balancing process is best done in an atmosphere of collaboration and mutual desire to develop specifications outcomes in which "win-win" opportunities are maximized.

As suggested by Figure 6.1, multiple goals are balanced simultaneously. For example, in the design of a DVD player, high quality and timely delivery goals may conflict with cost containment goals. The objective in collaboratively developing the specifications would be to achieve the quality, delivery, and cost goals simultaneously. Perhaps a supplier suggests that a standard part that the buying firm was unaware of could be used where the original specification used a nonstandard part. The standard part would decrease production time, improve quality, and cost less than the nonstandard part. Unfortunately, many companies do not pursue balanced specifications through collaborative efforts.

## Categories of Specifications

Purchase specifications can be classified into two broad categories of simple and complex, also referred to as low detail and high detail. The classification as simple or complex reflects the specification development itself, not the complexity of the product or service or the fulfillment of the specification. Both simple and complex specifications require a balancing of departmental differences, along with quality, delivery, and cost. However, in most cases, simple specifications require less balancing than do complex specifications.

In contrast to simple specifications, complex or detailed specifications are used when a simple specification is not possible or preferable. A complex specification requires more resources and more time to develop. Complex specifications are discussed after simple specifications in this chapter. All categories of specifications are presented in Figure 6.2, since combinations of the categories of specifications are possible.

**Figure 6.2** | Categories of Specifications

## Simple Specifications

Simple specifications require fewer resources and less time to develop than do complex specifications. In many cases, simple specifications are completed in one sentence and do not require collaboration between functional areas or supply chain members. For example, the specification of an accounting department for supply management to purchase "12 Dell Latitude D 630 laptops with their Intel Core 2 duo processor and warranty" is a complete yet simple specification. Nothing other than the brand name, model and package type, and warranty is needed. The astute reader will recognize that supply management could contribute to the specification by working with accounting to meet its needs with a lower-cost manufacturer or a prequalified supplier. The six categories of simple specifications are desired performance, function and fit, brand or trade names, samples, market grades, and qualified products.

**Performance Specifications**    A performance specification in theory is the perfect method for describing a requirement. Instead of describing an item in terms of its design characteristics, performance specifications describe in words—and quantitatively where possible—what the item is required to do. This type of description is used extensively in buying highly technical military and space products. For example, the product wanted could be a missile capable of being launched from a submarine with a designated speed, range, and accuracy. Potential suppliers are told only the performance that is required. Though performance is specified in precise detail, suppliers are not told how the product should be manufactured or what material should be used in its manufacture.

Performance specifications are not limited to complex items such as spacecraft. Electronics, aircraft, and automobile companies, for example, frequently use this method to buy common materials such as electrical wire, batteries, and radios. A performance specification for wire may require it to withstand a given temperature, have a designated resistance to abrasion, and have a particular conductivity capability. No mention is made in the specifications of what materials are to be used or how the wire is to be manufactured or insulated to give it the required characteristics. Manufacturers are free to make those choices as they see fit.

Industry uses performance specifications extensively in buying expensive, complicated machines and machine tools. Today, more production machines are replaced because of technological obsolescence than because of wear. Therefore, in buying such a machine, a firm should make every effort to obtain the ultimate in technological advancement. Often this can be done best by using performance specifications. To reduce and control the expense associated with this approach to describing requirements, descriptions should be written as explicitly as possible. Also, the product being purchased should be sectionalized into the greatest practical number of distinct components, with potential sellers required to provide a quote for each component. This practice helps solve the difficult problem of comparing sellers' prices by allowing a comparison of the prices of individual components.

There are two primary advantages to describing quality by performance specifications: (1) ease of preparing the specifications and (2) assurance of obtaining the precise performance desired. For complex products, it is by far the easiest type of specification to write. It assures performance, and if the supplier is competent, it assures the inclusion of all applicable new developments. The clarity of a performance specification also brings clarity into any legal or liability issue that may ensue if the supplier does not meet the specification as agreed. A potential disadvantage occurs when the performance specification is out of date in light of current technology. For example, a late-model computer hard drive often costs more than a current technology hard drive that stores more and has faster access rates and a lower price.

Proper supplier selection is essential when performance specifications are used. In fact, the ability to select capable and honest suppliers is a prerequisite to the proper use of performance specifications.

Because the supplier assumes the entire responsibility for designing and making the product, quality is entirely in its hands. If the supplier is not capable, it cannot apply the most advanced technical and manufacturing knowledge. If it is not honest, materials and workmanship may be inferior. When using performance specifications, supply managers must solicit competition among two or more capable sellers. Capable suppliers ensure quality; competition ensures reasonable prices.

**Function and Fit Specifications**     These purchase descriptions are a variation of performance specifications and are used in *early supplier involvement (ESI)* programs. With this approach, the design team describes the function(s) to be performed and the way the item is to fit into the larger system (e.g., automobile, computer), together with several design objectives (cost, weight, and reliability).

Robert May supports the argument that ESI best meets the needs of companies by giving suppliers performance specifications. According to May, "The optimal use of suppliers' special skills and processes is experienced when suppliers are provided with a set of performance specifications."[2]

As ESI becomes more common, this approach to describing requirements undoubtedly will increase in popularity. With careful prequalification of suppliers, there are no significant disadvantages with this approach.

**Brand or Trade Names**     When manufacturers develop and market a new product, they must decide whether to brand it. Branding or differentiating a product generally is done to develop a recognized reputation and thus gain repeat sales, protect the product against substitutes, maintain price stability, and simplify sales promotion.[3] The primary reason most manufacturers brand their products is to obtain repeat sales. Consumers develop a preference for brands. Therefore, branded products generally can be sold at prices higher than those of unbranded products of similar quality. A brand represents the manufacturer's pledge that the quality of the product will be consistent from one purchase to the next. A supply manager can be certain that a reputable manufacturer will strive to keep that pledge.

Brand name products are among the simplest to describe on a purchase order. Thus, they save time and reduce supply management expense. Inspection expense is also low for branded products. The only inspection required is sight verification of the brand labels. The brand is the quality ordered. The higher prices usually paid for name brands thus are offset to some extent by reduced description preparation and inspection costs.

A supplier's success in maintaining a consistent quality level is greatest in situations in which production and quality control are under its own supervision. If a supplier buys an item from several manufacturers, the quality variation in all probability will be larger than would be the case if the supplier made the item or bought it from a single source. For this reason, it is important for supply managers to know who is responsible for the production and quality control of all branded products that the company buys. In situations in which tight quality control is essential, multiple sources of production should be avoided if possible.

It often is said that when a supply manager purchases by brand name, he or she eliminates competition by limiting the purchase to a single source of supply. If a supply manager had to limit purchases to a single brand from a single source, that would represent a major disadvantage of purchasing by brand name. In fact, however, there are very few situations in which only one brand is acceptable for a particular purpose.

---

[2]Robert E. May, C.P.M., Senior. Consultant, Harris Consulting, Inc., "Top Ten Approaches to Cost Reduction," presentation at the 1998 NAPM International Purchasing Conference, May 1998. See www.ism.ws for a full transcript of the proceedings paper.

[3]Manufacturers also produce merchandise for wholesalers and retailers who market it under their own private brand labels. In such arrangements, the manufacturer is relieved of marketing and promotional responsibilities.

A profitable market for any item in a competitive enterprise economy attracts other manufacturers to make that item. Competition therefore is available by brands just as it is by other types of quality descriptions. In addition, the same branded product may be available from different wholesalers or jobbers who are willing to compete on price and service to get a buying company's order.

Making a specification of "brand A or equal" on the bid forms usually ensures competition among brands. What does "or equal" mean? This question has generated many arguments. Realistically, it means materials that are of equal quality and are capable of performing the function intended. Equal quality means similar quality of materials and similar quality of workmanship. Comparing the quality of materials is relatively easy, but comparing the quality of workmanship is particularly difficult. Here nebulous considerations such as precision of production, fit with and matching of adjacent parts, types of finish, and shades of color must be resolved. The key to the "or equal" consideration is, "Can the 'equal' perform the function for which the specified brand is desired?" If it cannot, it certainly is not equal; if it can, it is equal.

One practical way to resolve the "or equal" problem is to let the using department decide which products are equal before prices are solicited. Only companies whose products are accepted by using departments as equal are requested to submit prices. This technique helps avoid wounded feelings among potential suppliers. It also allows requisitioning departments to make more objective decisions.

In some situations, purchasing by brand name can be done more effectively by including additional references or limitations in the purchasing description. For example, if the supply manager suspects that other materials can perform the desired function, reference in the description should give prospective suppliers an opportunity to offer those other materials for consideration. When limitations concerning physical, functional, and other characteristics of the materials to be purchased are essential to the buying company's needs, they should be set forth clearly in the brand name description. For example, in many purchases of equipment, interchangeability of repair parts is essential. When this is the case, the limitation described above should be spelled out in the brand name description. The invitation for bids or requests for proposals should include the right to examine and test the proffered item if an "or equal" product is offered.

For small quantities, brand buying is excellent.[4] The primary disadvantage of purchasing by brands frequently is higher price. Many categories of branded items sell at notoriously high prices. Antiseptics and cleaning compounds are common examples of such items. For these products, another type of purchase description is preferable. When they are purchased with detailed or performance specifications, savings often exceed 50 percent. In recent years, buying drugs by generic name rather than by brand has resulted in spectacular savings for many hospitals; savings up to 70 percent are not uncommon.

**Samples**   Samples have been called the lazy person's method of describing requirements. When samples are used, the supply manager does not have to look for an equal brand, pick a standard specification, or describe the performance wanted. Samples are neither the cheapest nor the most satisfactory method of purchase. Usually the money spent on inspection costs substantially exceeds the money saved in description costs. It usually is difficult to determine by inspection that the product delivered is in fact the same as the sample. Quality of materials and quality of workmanship are generally exceedingly difficult to determine from routine inspection. Therefore, in many cases, acceptance or rejection becomes a matter of subjective judgment.

---

[4]Brand buying is mandatory in some situations. Common examples are when a supplier's production process is secret, when its workmanship exceeds that of all competitors, and when testing competitive items is too costly.

Samples generally should be used only if other methods of description are not feasible. Color and texture, printing, and grading are three broad areas in which other methods of description are not feasible. A precise shade of green, for example, is difficult to describe without a sample. Proposed lithographic work is best judged by the supplier's proofs. Establishing grades for commodities such as wheat, corn, and cotton through the use of samples has proved to be the best method of describing those products.

**Market Grades**    Grading is a method of determining the quality of commodities. A grade is determined by comparing a specific commodity with previously agreed on standards. Grading generally is limited to natural products such as lumber, wheat, hides, cotton, tobacco, and food products. The value of grades as a description of quality depends on the accuracy with which the grades can be established and the ease with which they can be recognized during inspection. There are, for example, 13 grades of cotton, each of which must be determined from an examination of individual samples. Trade associations, commodity exchanges, and government agencies all expend great effort in establishing and policing usable grades.

In buying graded commodities, industrial supply managers often use personal inspection as part of their buying technique. Just as individuals select by inspecting the shoes, dresses, and shirts they buy, industrial supply managers select by inspecting some of the commodities they buy in primary markets. There can be a significant difference between the upper and lower grade limits of many commodities. The difference is so great in some cases that materials near the lower limit of the grade may be unacceptable. Hence, inspection is critically important in buying many materials by market grade. Brewers and millers, for example, usually inspect all the grains they buy. Inspection is necessary if they are to obtain raw materials of the quality needed to produce a finished product with consistent quality.

Beef is an excellent illustration of the wide quality spread that can exist within a grade. Normally, 700-pound steers dressed and graded as "U.S. Prime" have a spread of roughly 40 pounds in fat content between the beef at the top of the grade and the beef at the bottom of the grade. Such a wide spread may be a minor consideration to the purchaser of a 1-pound steak. However, to an industrial food service manager buying millions of pounds of beef, the difference can be thousands or hundreds of thousands of dollars.

**Qualified Products**    In some situations, it is necessary to determine in advance of a purchase whether a product can meet specifications. These situations normally arise when (1) it takes too long[5] to conduct the normal post-purchase inspections and tests that are required to ensure quality compliance, (2) inspection to ensure compliance with the quality aspects of the specifications requires special testing equipment that is not commonly or immediately available, and (3) the purchase involves materials concerned with safety equipment, life survival equipment, or research equipment or materials described in performance specifications.

When advance qualification is indicated, suppliers are prequalified by a thorough review and test of the entire process by which they ensure compliance with their specifications. After qualification, the products of the approved suppliers are placed on what is called a *qualified products list (QPL)*. Trade name, model number, part number, place of manufacture, and similar identifying data describe approved products on the QPL.

## Complex Specifications

Complex or detailed specifications are descriptions that tell the seller exactly what the buyer wants to purchase. A simple specification for buying ketchup might be "12-ounce plastic bottle of Heinz tomato

---

[5]The federal government and some large industrial firms have defined "too long" as a period exceeding 30 days.

ketchup." In contrast, ketchup specifications become complex if the actual recipe is given with ingredients and production procedures. A complex specification often goes beyond the design of a product to include specifications regarding methodology, packaging, transport, delivery schedules, warranty, and service.

There are four principal types of complex specifications: commercial standards, design specifications (generally accompanied by engineering drawings), engineering drawings, and material and method-of-manufacture specifications.

**Commercial Standards**  Recurring needs for the same materials have led industry and government to develop commercial standards for those materials. A commercial standard is nothing more than a complete description of the item that has been standardized. The description includes the quality of materials and workmanship that should be used in manufacturing the item, along with dimensions, chemical composition, and so on. It also includes a method for testing both materials and workmanship. Commercial standards are a cornerstone of the mass production system; therefore, they are important to efficient supply management and to the standard of living in the United States.

All nuts, bolts, pipes, and electrical items that are made to standard specifications can be expected to fit all standard applications regardless of who manufactured them. Materials ordered by standardized specifications leave no doubt on the part of either the buyer or the seller about what is required. Standard specifications have been prepared for many goods in commercial trade. National trade associations, standards associations, national engineering societies, the federal government, and national testing societies all contribute to the development of standard specifications and standard methods of testing. Commercial standards are applicable to raw materials, fabricated materials, individual parts and components, and subassemblies.

Purchasing by commercial standards is somewhat similar to purchasing by brand name. In both methods, the description of what is wanted can be set forth accurately and easily. Commercial standards are more complex because they require greater detail in the description. With the exception of proprietary products, most widely used items are standard in nature; hence, they are highly competitive and readily available at reasonable prices. There are many users of standard products; therefore, manufacturers that make them can safely schedule long, low-cost production runs for inventory. They do not need specific sales commitments before production. They know that materials will be ordered under these standard specifications when they are needed.

Inspection is only moderately expensive for materials purchased by commercial standards. Commercial standard products require periodic checking in addition to sight identification to assure firms that they are getting the quality specified.

Commercial standard items should be used whenever possible. They contribute greatly to the simplification of design, supply management procedures, and inventory management, as well as to cost reduction. Copies of standard specifications can be obtained from a number of government, trade association, and testing association sources. In fact, the easiest way to get a particular specification is to ask a manufacturer to provide a copy of the standard specification for the material or product that it recommends for the supply manager's intended need.

**Design Specifications**  Not all items and materials used in industry are covered by standard specifications or brands. For many items, therefore, a large number of buying firms prepare their own specifications. By doing this, those firms broaden their field of competition. All manufacturers capable of making the item described in the firm's specifications are potential suppliers.

By preparing its own specifications, a company often can avoid the premium prices of brand name items and the sole-source problems of patented, copyrighted, and proprietary products. When preparing its own specifications, a company should attempt to make them as close as possible to industry standards. If any special dimensions, tolerances, or features are required, every effort should be made to attain those "specials" by designing them as additions or alterations to standard parts; this will save time and money.

Describing requirements with chemical or electronic specifications or with physical specifications and accompanying engineering drawings entails some risk. For example, if a buying company provides the exact chemical specifications of the paint it wants, it assumes complete responsibility for the paint's performance. If the paint fades in the first month, it is the buyer's responsibility. If a buying company specifies for a metal fabricator the exact dimensions wanted in a part, the buyer assumes all responsibility for that part's fitting and functioning. If it happens that to fit and function properly, a part must be 26.045 inches long rather than 26.015 inches as specified in the purchase order, the responsibility for failure rests solely with the buying firm.

The very nature of the materials purchased under this method of description tends to require special inspection. The cost of inspection to assure compliance with company-prepared specifications can be high.

**Engineering Drawings**   Engineering drawings and prints occasionally are used alone but more typically are used in conjunction with other physical purchase descriptions. Engineering drawings may be part of the design specifications described above. Where precise shapes, dimensions, and spatial relationships are required, drawings are the most accurate method of describing what is wanted. Despite their potential for accuracy, exceptional care must be exercised in using them. Ambiguity, which sometimes is present in this method of description, can produce costly repercussions. All dimensions, therefore, must be completely covered, and the descriptive instruction should be explicit.

Engineering drawings are used extensively in describing quality for construction projects, foundry and machine shop work, and a myriad of special mechanical parts and components. There are four principal advantages to using drawings for description: (1) They are accurate and precise, (2) they are the most practical way of describing mechanical items that require extremely close tolerances, (3) they permit wide competition (what is wanted can be communicated easily to a wide range of potential suppliers), and (4) they clearly establish the standards for inspection.

**Material and Method-of-Manufacture**   When this method is used, prospective suppliers are instructed precisely about the specific materials to be used and how they are to be processed. The buying firm assumes full responsibility for product performance. Further, the buying firm assumes that its own organization has the latest knowledge about materials, techniques, and manufacturing methods for the item being purchased. In this case, purchasers see no reason to pay another company for that knowledge.

Material and method-of-manufacture specifications are used extensively by the armed services and the Department of Energy. A modified version of those specifications is used by industry. Large purchasers of paint, for example, frequently ask the manufacturers of a standard paint to add or delete certain chemicals when producing paint for them. Purchasers of large quantities of steel make the same type of request when purchasing special steels. Chemical and drug buyers, for reasons of health and safety, sometimes approach full use of the material and method-of-manufacture technique in describing quality. Also, these specifications are used most appropriately in situations in which technically sophisticated large companies deal with small suppliers that have limited research and development staffs. Normally, however, this technique is used infrequently in industry because it puts such great responsibility on the buying firm. It can deny a company the latest advancements in both technical development and manufacturing processes. Specifications of this type are expensive to prepare; inspection generally is very expensive.

There are two important features of this method of description. First, the widest competition is possible, and thus good pricing is assured. Second, since the product is nonstandard, the provisions against discrimination in the Robinson-Patman Act pose no barrier to obtaining outstanding pricing and service.

## Combination of Methods

Many products cannot be described adequately with the use of a single method. In such cases, a combination of two or more methods should be used. For example, in describing the quality desired for a space vehicle, performance specifications could be used to describe numerous overall characteristics of the vehicle, such as its ability to withstand certain temperatures, perform certain predetermined maneuvers in space in precise time sequences, and stay in space for a specific period. Physical specifications could be used to describe the vehicle's configuration as well as the television cameras and other instruments it will carry. Commercial standards or brand names might be used to describe selected pieces of electrical or mechanical hardware used in the vehicle's support systems. A chemical specification could be used to describe the vehicle's paint. Finally, a sample could be used to show the color of that paint.

Few products are as complex as space vehicles; nevertheless, an increasing number of industrial products require two or more methods of quality descriptions. For instance, something as commonplace as office drapes could require chemical specifications to describe the cloth and fireproofing desired, physical specifications to describe the dimensions desired, and samples to describe the colors and texture desired.

# Development of Specifications

Developing specifications can be a difficult task because it involves many variables, including the problem of conflicting human sensitivities and orientations. Many departments are capable of contributing to specifications development; however, they frequently are thwarted from fully doing so because of conflicting views. Before the optimum in design can be achieved, these major conflicting views must be reconciled.

## Organizational Approaches

Several approaches to developing balanced specifications are used individually or jointly by most companies. The approaches, in order of collaborative orientation from lowest to highest, include the informal approach, the supply management coordinator approach, early supply management involvement (formerly EPI), early supplier involvement (ESI), consensus development, and the Cross-Functional team approach.

**Informal Approach** The informal approach emphasizes the concept of a supply manager's responsibility to "challenge" materials requests. At the same time, top management urges designers to request advice from supply managers and work with them on all items that may involve commercial considerations. The emphasis at all times is on person-to-person communication and cooperation between individual supply managers and designers. When this approach is used, a company-oriented, cost-conscious attitude is developed at the grassroots level throughout the organization.

There are two potential problems with the informal approach. The first and most obvious is that the lack of formalization through corporate policy or organizational structure may render the supply manager powerless and make the approach completely ineffective. The second problem is that the supply manager may create animosity when it is appropriate to challenge a specification.

**Supply Management Coordinator Approach**    One or more positions are created in the supply department for individuals, frequently called *materials engineers,*[6] to serve in a liaison capacity with the design department. Typically, the materials engineer spends most of his or her time in the engineering department reviewing design work as it comes off the drawing boards. The materials engineer searches for potential supply management problems in an attempt to mitigate them before the specifications have been completed.

The supply management coordinator approach is highly structured as well as expensive. It also is very effective. Therefore, it should be used whenever coordination problems stemming from the technical nature of a firm's product or the magnitude of its cost justifies the investment.

**Early Supply Management Involvement**    As we discussed in Chapter 5, progressive firms increasingly are creating design policies to involve supply management in the early stages of new product development. Early supply management involvement was popularized in industry through the now-dated term EPI,[7] which stands for early purchasing involvement.

Too often design engineers and production engineers resolve between themselves all four of the major departmental considerations of specifications preparation without consulting supply management. This is regrettable because professional engineers seldom have the commercial experience and market information required to resolve the supply management considerations of specifications. In their attempts to do so, they frequently develop stringent specifications that do not provide sufficient latitude to allow effective competition.

**Early Supplier Involvement**    Early supply involvement (ESI) is used widely in industry. To implement ESI properly, a buying company should start by establishing the policy of involving supply management in the design process. After that policy is enacted, ESI can be actively engaged. ESI coupled with early supply management involvement can improve product quality and reliability while compressing development time and reducing total material cost.[8]

**Consensus Development Approach**    Consensus development calls for specifications to be agreed on by the department managers. This collaborative approach falls short of the development of a formal team. Although department managers disagree occasionally, compromise and consensus usually can be worked out when the various aspects of the problem are understood and the organizational mechanism for reaching consensus has been established. When specifications conflicts arise and a consensus cannot be reached, final authority for the decision should rest with the department that has responsibility for the product's performance.

**Cross-Functional Team Approach**    The cross-functional team (CFT) approach recognizes that a good specification is a compromise of basic objectives. A specifications CFT is established, with representatives (as appropriate) from design engineering, production engineering, supply management, marketing, operations (including production control), quality, and standards. As described in Chapter 5, members of the

---

[6]The reader should not infer from this discussion any intent to denigrate the work of design engineers; none is intended. Often, for reasons of policy, tradition, or expediency, the design engineer is required to make decisions alone that could be made more effectively in collaboration with others. Billions of dollars are lost annually through the adoption of unnecessarily stringent specifications at the design stage.

[7]While we expect the acronym EPI to continue to be used over the next several years, we believe the term "purchasing" has become associated primarily with tactical activities. The involvement of supply management in the design process is clearly a strategic activity, thus requiring the shift in terminology.

[8]Burt and Doyle, *op. cit,* p. 116.

design team are involved as appropriate throughout the development of the product and its specifications. A common variation to this approach is for the development of the specification to be delegated to an appropriate technical expert, with the resulting specification being reviewed and approved by the CFT.

## Supply Management Research

Once a need has been identified and functionally described and when the size of the contemplated purchase warrants, supply management research and analysis should be conducted to investigate the availability of commercial products that can meet the need. This research and analysis also should provide information to aid in selecting a strategy appropriate to the situation. Supply management research and analysis involves obtaining the following information, as appropriate:

- The availability of standard products suitable to meet the need (with or without modification).
- The terms, conditions, and prices under which such products are sold.
- Any applicable trade provisions or restrictions or controlling laws.
- The performance characteristics and quality of available products, including quality control and test procedures followed by the manufacturers.
- Information on the satisfaction of other users with similar needs.
- Any costs or problems associated with integration of the item with those currently used.
- Industry production practices such as continuous, periodic, or batch production.
- The distribution and support capabilities of potential suppliers.

## Writing Specifications

After the design of a product has been determined, the next step is to translate the individual part and materials specifications into written form. Optimal performance in all departments is contingent on good specifications. To meet the needs of all departments, a specification must satisfy many requirements:

- Design and marketing requirements for functional characteristics, chemical properties, dimensions, appearance, and other features.
- Manufacturing requirements for workability of materials and manufacturability.
- Inspection's requirements to test materials for compliance with the specifications.
- Stores' requirement to receive, store, and issue the material economically.
- Supply management's requirement to procure material without difficulty and with adequate competition from reliable sources of supply.
- Production control's and supply management's requirement to substitute materials when such action becomes necessary.
- The total firm's requirements for suitable quality at the lowest overall cost.
- The total firm's requirement to use commercial and industrial standard material whenever possible and to establish company standards in all cases in which nonstandard material is used repetitively.

## Common Specifications Problems

Several common problems frequently arise in companies after specifications have been developed. Three of these problems are discussed below. If present, they should be addressed in the specifications development process, before the specifications have been completed.

**Lack of Clarity**    Specifications should be written in clear and unambiguous terms. Clarity in written expression is not always easy to achieve. One company lost $65,000 on a closed-circuit television installation because its written specifications misled the supplier into believing that a more expensive installation than the buyer really wanted had been specified.

**Limiting Competition**    In addition to achieving clarity, care must be exercised to ensure that specifications are not written around a specific product in a way that limits competition. Several years ago, a fire chief wrote into the specifications for a new fire truck the requirement that the supplier of the truck manufacture the truck's 12-cylinder engine. This completely restricted competition, since only one supplier of fire engines manufactured 12-cylinder engines in its own plant. If the fire chief had specified what was wanted in terms of performance characteristics, such as speed and acceleration, competition would have been plentiful. This example typifies one of industry's most common forms of specifications abuse: slanting specifications to one supplier's product, thus reducing or precluding competition. In this case, fortunately, the situation had a happy ending: The supply management department challenged the specifications, and the fire chief agreed to rewrite them in a form that permitted maximum competition. Significant savings resulted from that change.

**Unreasonable Tolerances**    Specifying an unreasonable tolerance is another common specification difficulty. Unnecessary precision pyramids costs! It costs more to make materials to close tolerances, it costs more to inspect them, and more rejects typically result. The best method of avoiding such unnecessary costs is to adhere to the most economical method of manufacture while using standard specifications wherever possible. For example, in procuring 1,000 drive pulleys for use in vacuum motors, the first decision would be to determine whether a casting process could be used to manufacture the pulleys satisfactorily. Although this method dictates the use of looser tolerances, in large volumes its unit cost is considerably lower than that of a second alternative: machining the pulley from bar stock. The second decision would be to select an industrial standard for the part regardless of the method of manufacture used. This decision leads directly to a consideration of standardization.

**Unreasonable Tolerances Example**    Ben Rogers, a Ph.D. student in production operations management, was excited to start gathering research data at a manufacturer of heavy construction equipment in Illinois. The goal of the research was to develop a model to forecast product costs on the basis of specifications given in designs. Yesterday, he had met the managers in operations, design, and quality to decide what data to accumulate. Today he hoped to start the data accumulation process with a senior design engineer, Keith Sampson.

As Ben walked up to the engineering department, he heard a loud and angry argument between Keith and Gary Hamm, a production manager. In an agitated tone Gary said, "Keith, we are on the floor reworking another nonstandard bore from our supplier that once again did not meet the tolerances your group specified. For four years these tolerances have given us headaches. The tighter tolerances on the bores sure haven't reduced the complaints from customers about the road grader. Heck, there weren't any complaints that I can recall that were ever related to the old tolerances for this part anyway. I still don't understand why you never consulted our department on the change to begin with. One thing is for sure: The tighter tolerance has increased frustration on the factory floor; angered our supplier, who we keep charging for the reworks; and screwed up my schedule so I continuously miss due dates. I am fed up. It's time you changed this tolerance back to the old standard!"

Keith replied in a terse voice, "Gary, you know that to compete we needed to continuously improve quality, and that means tightening tolerances. There is no way I am going to change the design again! If your supplier is incapable of producing to our specifications, then dump the supplier. You are the operations manager, so start managing your operations and deal with it!"

Gary bumped Ben as he stormed out of Keith's office. Ben quietly walked on by, deciding that this was not the time to ask Keith for data. As Ben walked away, he wondered if he had just had a foretaste of the problems he would discover in the next six months.

This true story[9] illustrates what can happen when internal functions do not work together to develop specifications. The overspecification problem is a common one that has been discussed for the last 30 years but still exists in most companies. Regardless of the method(s) used to describe specifications, only the minimum quality needed for the product to perform the function intended should be specified. Overspecifying and including restrictive features in purchase descriptions cause delays and increase costs.

The importance of developing balanced specifications and standards through interfunctional and relevant chain member participation is paramount for companies that need to improve their competitive position. The balancing act is accomplished by meeting the needs of the functional areas while balancing performance measures such as quality and delivery against cost.

# Standardization

A uniform identification that is agreed on is called a *standard*. In business practice, the concept of standardization is applied in either industrial or managerial standardization. *Industrial standardization* can be defined as "the process of establishing agreement on uniform identifications for definite characteristics of quality, design, performance, quantity, service, and so on." *Managerial standardization* deals with things such as operating practices, procedures, and systems.

## History of Standardization

Eli Whitney contributed to the development of standardization in 1801, when he accepted a contract to furnish 10,000 muskets to the U.S. government. When it appeared that Whitney had fallen behind on his contract, he was summoned to Washington by Thomas Jefferson to explain the delay. Whitney took with him a box containing the parts from 10 muskets. On a table before his congressional interrogators, he separated the parts into piles of stocks, barrels, triggers, firing hammers, and so on. He asked a representative to pick a part from each pile. Whitney then assembled the parts into a finished musket, repeating the process until all 10 muskets had been assembled. After his demonstration, it was easy for Whitney to explain the apparent delay. Rather than furnishing a proportional number of guns each month, as an artisan gunsmith would have done after individually making the parts for each gun and then assembling each gun in turn, Whitney had been working to design machine tools and dies with which he could mass-produce parts which were interchangeable. He had standardized the parts. When his machine tools were completed, he was able to produce the muskets in a period during which an artisan gunsmith could have produced only a few muskets.

Whitney discovered that when parts were standardized, the skills of artisans could be transferred to machines that could be operated with less skilled labor. This in turn reduced the need for highly skilled labor, which at that time was in extremely short supply. His discovery revolutionized technology and led to the development of industrial standards.[10] Even more important, this practice led to mass production and sizable industrial growth to the United States.

---

[9]The actual names of the individuals and company involved in the story are not given in the case. The story is true with respect to the events that occurred.

[10]Robert Schwarzwalder, "Searching the Industrial Standards," *Database Magazine* 20, no. 2 (April/May 1997), p. 69.

The burning to the ground of Baltimore's business district in 1904 clearly illustrates the need for standards in urban living. Like the battle that was lost for the lack of a horseshoe nail, Baltimore was lost for the lack of standard fire hose couplings. Washington, New York, and Philadelphia all responded to Baltimore's cry for help. When their pumping equipment arrived in Baltimore, however, the rescuers stood by helplessly because there was no way to connect the different size hose couplings to Baltimore's fire hydrants.

Eli Whitney introduced mass production in the United States; Henry Ford made it universal. Ford, however, misinterpreted one important relationship of standardization to mass production: He visualized mass production to mean a standard product produced on an assembly line. Ford thought he was speaking correctly when he said, "The customer can have any color car he wants as long as it is black." Actually, he missed the full implication of mass production. Mass production is the production of many diverse products assembled from standardized parts that have been mass-produced.

Standardization has become a way to create competitive advantage through mass customization. Perhaps no company exemplifies this more than Dell, the largest assembler and seller of personal computers in the world. Dell works with many suppliers to design and produce parts, components, and modules that can be used in multiple models. For example, several laptop models use the same DVD player module. A supply chain standard design was developed to allow interchangeability of several suppliers' modules and ease of installation and support.

## Types and Sources of Standards

In industry, there are three basic types of materials standards: (1) international standards, (2) industry or national standards, and (3) company standards. If a designer or user cannot adapt a national or international standard for his or her purpose, the second choice is to use a company standard. If the required part is truly a nonrepetitive "special," use of a standard is impossible.

Where can one get standard specifications? Specifications for items that have been standardized can be obtained from the organizations that have developed them, such as those listed below:

- International Organization for Standardization
- National Bureau of Standards
- American National Standards Institute
- American Society for Testing and Materials
- American Society for Quality
- Society of Automotive Engineers
- Society of Mechanical Engineers
- American Institute of Electrical Engineers
- Federal Bureau of Specifications
- National Lumber Manufacturers' Association

The European-based International Organization for Standardization (ISO) has several hundred specialized committees that develop a wide variety of standards that are promulgated by ISO and usually are accepted worldwide. Many of these standards are adaptations of standards from the American National Standards Institute (ANSI), the German Institute for Standards, the British Standards Institute, and other national standards organizations around the world.

A catalog of U.S. standards, international recommendations, and other related information is published annually and distributed without charge by the American National Standards Institute.[11] The institute is a federation of more than 100 nationally recognized organizations, trade associations, and technical societies or groups of such organizations. Its members can gain ANSI assistance in developing any standard desired. Recommendations for establishing a standard can be made at any time. If, after appropriate research and debate, ANSI approves a recommended standard, it will be adopted as a U.S. standard.

Both the civilian and the military departments of the U.S. government participate in standardization work that greatly assists industry. For example, the National Bureau of Standards (NBS), among other things, was established to serve "any firm, corporation, or individual in the United States engaged in manufacturing or other pursuits regarding the use of standards."

The need for international standards is fundamental; by eliminating technical trade barriers, international standards facilitate increased international trade and prosperity. The ISO 9000 series of quality standards, now used voluntarily worldwide, is a good illustration. The economic stakes associated with the development of international standards are so high in terms of increased international trade and prosperity that progress, albeit slow, is inevitable. Because private organizations, national and regional governments, and other international organizations are all involved in the adoption process, political infighting is inescapable.

Metric system measurements are among the important international standards. In December 1975, Congress passed the Metric Conversion Act, which provided for only voluntary action. The voluntary conversion appears to be working, but at a very slow pace. In many industries, the United States already has gone metric. The shutters of thousands of 8-, 16-, and 35-millimeter cameras daily click across the nation. Work is done daily in hundreds of repair shops on thousands of foreign automobiles manufactured to metric standards in foreign countries. U.S. pharmaceutical companies went metric over 20 years ago, and the electronics industry has used the metric system since 1954.

More recently, in 1996, the International Organization for Standardization adopted ISO 14000 to establish environmental performance standards. Conflicting environmental regulations across national borders have long been a problem for international supply management. Like the ISO 9000 series, ISO 14000 series focus on processes, not outcomes, and both involve audit by a third party.[12]

## Benefits of Standardization

Standardization benefits an organization in a variety of ways: It enables mass production, enables customization, improves supplier coordination, improves quality, enables simplification, enables delayed differentiation, and, as a result of many of the other benefits, lowers inventories.

- ■ *Enables mass production.*   As the example of Eli Whitney showed, mass production becomes possible through the creation of interchangeable parts. Standardized parts and components enable management to stabilize production processes and focus on continuous improvement, thus reducing costs.

- ■ *Enables customization.*   Standardized parts and modules enable manufacturers to make a wide variety of finished products from a relatively small number of parts. With standardization, the wide variety of finished products may be assembled when ordered, reducing inventory carrying costs and increasing

---

[11]ANSI, 1430 Broadway, New York, NY 10018.

[12]Frank Montabon, Steven A. Meinyk, Robert Sroufe, and Roger J. Calantone, "ISO 14000: Assessing its Perceived Impact on Corporate Performance," *Journal of Supply Chain Management,* National Association of Purchasing Management, Spring 2001.

flexibility to meet specific consumer demands. Dell exemplifies this capability in its ability to customize computers for customers on the same day an order is placed. Dell accomplishes customization largely by using standard components and modules.

- *Improves supplier coordination.* Standardized parts and components provide a very clear specification for the supplier. The dimensions, characteristics, and performance of a standard part or component improve the ability to communicate between the buying and selling companies.

- *Improves quality.* Standard parts and components are manufactured repetitively to the same design, enabling investment by the producing company in better machinery, training, and materials. The result is a significantly lower defect rate.

- *Enables simplification.* Once standard parts have been identified, simplification can be used to identify redundant standard parts that can be eliminated. Simplification is discussed in the next section.

- *Enables delayed differentiation.* When customization of a product is accomplished as close to customer demand as possible, the differentiation of the product or service is delayed. For example, suppose a customer purchases a computer online with a customized configuration of standard parts and modules. The manufacturer has two choices to meet the demand. The manufacturer can pre-assemble hundreds or even thousands of computer configurations that customers may want so that they are ready to ship when the demand occurs. The second choice is delayed differentiation, in which the manufacturer stocks standard components and modules that can be assembled quickly into customized configurations. Delayed differentiation results in much lower inventory levels.

- *Lowers inventories.* The lowering of inventories is primarily a result of carrying fewer parts because the number of distinct parts being carried has been reduced. Several other reasons for lower inventories from standardization exist. Better quality resulting from greater use of standard parts and components reduces safety stock. Delayed differentiation reduces the need to carry as many finished goods in stock, reducing overall inventory levels. Standard parts and modules usually have more certain and shorter supplier order lead times. Reduced uncertainty in production lead time reduces the need for additional inventories required for unreliable lead times. Shorter lead times directly translate into smaller order quantities.

The use of standards permits a firm to purchase fewer items, in larger quantities, and at lower prices. Thus, fewer items are processed and stocked. This reduces supply management, receiving, inspection, and payment costs. Stocking fewer items makes controlling inventories easier and less costly. The use of standardized approved items drastically reduces the number of defects in incoming materials. Consequently, the purchase of standardized materials reduces total costs in four ways: lower prices, lower processing costs, lower inventory carrying costs, and fewer quality problems. The benefits of standardization are presented in Figure 6.3.

## Simplification

Simplification, a corollary of standardization, is another term for which recognized authorities have varying definitions. Most frequently, simplification means reducing the number of standard items a firm uses in its product design and carries in its inventory. For example, a company used 27 different kinds of standard lubricating greases in the maintenance of its machinery. Analysis showed that in some cases the same grease could be used for several different applications and that only six kinds of grease were needed. Hence, through simplification the number of standard greases used was reduced from 27 to 6. Similar analysis showed that the number of standard bearings and fasteners used in production could be reduced by about 50 percent. Reductions of this scope are commonplace.

**Figure 6.3 I** Benefits of Standardization

Simplification savings result primarily from reduced inventory investment, more competitive prices, greater quantity discounts (because of larger-volume purchases and the use of blanket orders), and reduced clerical and handling costs (because fewer different items have to be handled and controlled).

Some authorities consider simplification an integral part of standardization rather than a corollary of it. They visualize the simplification process as taking place primarily at the design level rather than at the stocking level. They think in terms of simplifying (or reducing) the number of related items that are approved as standards in the first place.

## Developing a Standardization Program

The benefits of standardization cannot be fully realized when they are developed internally only by design engineers. The next level up is to involve cross-functional team with internal members from supply management, marketing, quality, and other relevant functional areas. However, to gain all the benefits of standardization discussed earlier, standardization should be addressed across the supply chain through cross-functional teams containing chain members.[13] A standardization program can be approached in various ways, but because so many departments and suppliers are affected by decisions about standards, a team effort is the most appropriate approach.

---

[13]An assumption is made that standards exist at the industry, national, or international level that a supply chain team can use in its standardization decisions. If no such standards exist, the supply chain members should consider addressing the industry's reasons for not having industry standards and lead the development of such standards in conjunction with developing standards within their own supply chain.

## Standards Team

A standards team normally consists of representatives from engineering, supply, operations, marketing, and transportation. Relevant suppliers also should be included on the team under the guidance of supply management. The standards team typically is charged with the responsibility of obtaining input from all user departments and relevant suppliers, reconciling differences between them, and making the final standards decisions.

Theoretically, a member of any department could serve as head of the team. Supply management is particularly well qualified to head the team in companies in which materials that comply with national standards or maintenance, repair, and operating (MRO) items form a large portion of the company's total purchases. In companies that manufacture highly differentiated technical products assembled from parts made to company standards, engineering is well qualified to head the team.

## Importance of Supply Management

Regardless of the organization employed, the supply management department occupies a focal point in the process. Only in supply management are duplicate requests for identical or nearly identical materials, overlapping requests, and "special buy" requests from all departments visible. Hence, no program for standardization can be optimally successful unless supply management is assigned a major role in the program.

## Materials Catalog

Once the decision to implement a standardization program has been made, the most common approach is to work toward developing a comprehensive materials catalog. A current, easily accessible materials catalog or database of approved standard items is the logical output of a standardization program. The catalog greatly aids the firm's design efforts. There are many benefits of developing a materials catalog; the most obvious are the following:

- *Improved quality.* The documentation of materials is the first step toward accumulating data to determine which materials have quality problems. The availability of such a catalog virtually eliminates the possibility that designers will incorporate materials that previously caused problems.
- *Reduction in design time.* Access to a materials catalog provides designers with a resource that will shorten the materials selection process in the design stage, reducing total design time.
- *Reduction of nonstandard parts.* The exercise of developing a materials catalog facilitates the use of standard parts.
- *Reduction of standard parts.* Simplification is easier since the standard parts documentation is centrally maintained. See the discussion on simplification earlier in this chapter.
- *Reduction of inventory.* Through standardization and simplification, two activities enabled by the development of a materials catalog, inventories are reduced. The reduction is due primarily to the decrease in the variety of parts carried and the improved quality.
- *Benefits of centralization.* Development of a materials catalog for a company with several physically separated facilities provides an opportunity to take advantage of centralization benefits, including pricing leverage.

## Electronic Materials Catalogs

An emerging trend in companies is to move the materials catalog from a hardcopy form to an electronic file. A simple electronic materials database can be created in virtually any software package capable of organizing and maintaining data. The complexity of the software is directly related to the complexity of the data. Included in the term "data" are graphical images such as photos, drawings, and designs. The designs may be quite complex. For example, the rail industry (railroads) chose to include vector drawings in its electronic catalogs. Vector drawings are created by using a computer-aided design software package in which arcs and lines are generated from mathematical formulas. The rail industry decided that converting an image from a vector drawing to an image resulted in a loss of underlying intelligence.[14]

A simple database software package such as Microsoft Access is sufficient and allows for relatively sophisticated data maintenance, centralization, queries, and graphics. On the more complex end of the materials database continuum are enterprise resource planning (ERP) systems, which can centrally locate materials catalog information for access, updating, and utilization by all departments. Most ERP systems already have converted to Web-based interfaces, allowing maximum access to centralized materials information in even the most remote regions of the world.

**Benefits of Electronic Catalogs**   Materials catalogs that are electronically maintained are superior to hardcopy versions since they can be centralized in one location, updated easily, electronically disseminated, queried using search techniques, and used to provide links to activate ordering and obtain additional information. The increasing dissemination of information using technologies such as secured intranets and extranets, data warehouses, and database-driven websites enables greater growth of electronic materials catalogs. As companies move much of their intellectual property to cyberspace, the use of electronic materials catalogs is on the rise.

## Concluding Remarks

Both specifications and standardization play important roles in the search for the right quality and the right value. They also assist in resolving design conflicts between engineering, manufacturing, marketing, and supply management. As presented in this chapter, specifications are the heart of the resulting procurement. The strategic dimension of specification development cannot be ignored in today's globally competitive environment. Long-term planning through organizational change and philosophical transformation must occur in most companies so that balanced specifications contribute to the viability of the firm's supply chain.

Many firms still do not fully appreciate the concepts embraced in standardization and its corollary, simplification. Nevertheless, the philosophies underlying these concepts play an important role in creating competitive advantage. It seems highly probable that these philosophies will continue to be important in the future. Aided by improved information technology and increased automation coupled with computer-aided design and computer-aided manufacturing systems, standardization is part of the answer to this decade's desire for customized products and services at a low cost.[15] By further standardizing

---

[14]Dennis Smid and Jo-Anne Kane, "Another Link in the Chain—Electronics Parts Catalogs," *NAPM 81st Annual International Conference Proceedings,* 1996. For proceedings papers, see www.ism.ws.

[15]Recall the discussion in Chapter 1 describing the direct relationship between reductions in material costs and increases in profit margins and return on investment.

component parts, processes, and operations, companies can refine and streamline their systems. That refinement should permit the production of low-cost, high-quality differentiated products that will be competitive in the global marketplace.

## Discussion Questions

1. Explain the authors' statement, "When specifications for the tangible product are fixed, the final design of the product is also fixed."
2. Why is standardization treated as a philosophy rather than a procedure in some companies and supply chains?
3. What are the purposes of specifications?
4. What does the term "balanced" imply in balanced specifications?
5. How can a collaborative approach to developing specifications result in a better description of the need?
6. List and define the categories of specifications.
7. A specification for the purchase of a Toyota that can go from zero to 60 miles per hour in 7 seconds is what type of simple specification?
8. What type of specification is it when the specification describes the function to be performed and the way the item is to fit into the larger system, together with several design objectives?
9. In what way does specification by brand name potentially eliminate competition?
10. Why have samples been called the lazy person's method of describing requirements?
11. What are the situations that require the development of qualified products?
12. Which of the following is usually a more complex specification: brand name, sample, commercial standard, or engineering drawings?
13. What are the potential problems of the informal approach to the development of specifications?
14. What should a company do before implementing ESI?
15. What are the common problems in developing specifications?
16. How can specifications limit competition?
17. In the unreasonable tolerances example in this chapter, what was the source of the problem between the two managers?
18. In the unreasonable tolerances example, do you agree with the senior design engineer's definition of quality?
19. Discuss the impact of Eli Whitney's use of standardized parts in making products.
20. How is standardization applied in business today?
21. Define how simplification differs from standardization. What additional benefits does simplification contribute to supply management?
22. Describe how standardization and simplification can benefit the entire supply chain.
23. When should samples be used as specifications?
24. In buying market graded commodities, why is inspection important?

## Internet Exercise

### About ANSI
Access the website below and discover the voice of U.S. standards.
(http://www.ansi.org/about_ansi/overview/overview.aspx?menuid=1)

1. Identify what ANSI is and what it does.
2. Explore the website and describe how ANSI can strengthen the U.S. position in the global economy.

## Suggested Reading

Brunsson, Nils, Benqt Jacobsson, and Associates. *A World of Standards* (New York: Oxford University Press, 2000).

Hoyle, David. *ISO 9000 Quality Systems Handbook* (Burlington, MA: Elsevier Butterworth-Heinenmann, 2006).

Kerzner, Harold. *Project Management Best Practices: Achieving Global Excellence* Hoboken, NJ: John Wiley & Sons, 2006).

Pacelli, Lonnie. *The Project Management Advisor: 18 Major Project Screw-Ups and How to Cut them Off at the Pass* (Upper Saddle River, NJ: Prentice Hall/Pearson, 2004).

Schwarzwalder, Robert. "Searching the Industrial Standards," *Database Magazine* 20, no. 2 (April/May 1997).

Spivak, Steven M., and F. Cecil Brenner. *Standardization Essentials: Principles and Practice* (New York: Marcel Dekker, 2001).

Publications from the Society of American Value Engineering, SAVE, SAVE International, 136 South Keowee St., Dayton, OH 45402 USA, Phone: 937-224-7283, Fax: 937-222-5794, E-mail: CAO@value-eng.org.

# Managing for Quality

## CHAPTER OBJECTIVES

*After reading this chapter, you should be able to:*

1. Understand quality as it relates to industrial and commercial value.

2. Recognize the contributions of the quality gurus.

3. Understand how TQM links quality, productivity, and profits.

4. Explain the concept of Six Sigma.

5. Explain the concept behind the International Organization for Standardization.

## VIGNETTE: THE QUALITY WALK

Beth Stuart noticed that employees were disappearing into their offices and down connecting aisles as she walked through the supplier's facility with her escort, Michael Spade. Spade, the youngest vice president of manufacturing in the supplier's history, had agreed to meet with Beth to show her the facility in North Carolina where the parts would be produced.

Beth had set up the meeting to evaluate the supplier's facility personally before her company, Epic Communications, entered into a long-term contract for a rough demand of 1,200,000 high-speed communications printed circuit boards in 2009. Follow-on contracts would be negotiated each year thereafter if the relationship benefited both parties. On paper, the potential supplier, PushTel Technology, appeared to be a viable supplier. PushTel's marketing department had provided Beth and Epic with information about its pending ISO 9001 registration, high quality standards, activity based costing system, and satisfied customers. Further, PushTel appeared to be a company on the rise, based on its financial reports.

Reflecting on the way Michael's employees were avoiding him, Beth recalled the last supplier facility she had visited, where, as she walked through the plant, the quality manager who gave her the tour greeted workers by name. The workers there went out of their way to say hello. Employees did the complete opposite with Michael.

Moving from the office area into the production facility, Beth could not help noticing area rugs and posters on the walls that had slogans encouraging workers to produce high-quality products. The rug at the entrance stated "Zero Defects" with a smiling cartoon character holding a wrench. Two posters near the entrance stated, "Think" and "Quality Is Job One." Beth asked, "Michael, did you or some of your upper managers go through Crosby philosophy training?" Michael replied, "We sure did, about eight years ago. Why do you ask, Beth?" "Whenever I see rugs and posters with exhortations and goals, it is an indication to me that Crosby's teachings influenced the organization. Deming was adamantly against that practice, so you tend not to see that practice in Deming-influenced facilities."

Suddenly, a loud spraying noise could be heard about 20 feet away. A high-pressure hose had come off a machine, and fluid was pouring out onto the factory floor. Beth watched in amazement as the operator of the machine quickly reattached the hose and proceeded to clean the floor—as if the breakdown was business as usual. Embarrassed and angry, Michael went straight over to the operator and criticized him for his ineptness.

As he walked back over to Beth, he quickly changed his composure to make it seem as if nothing of significance had happened. "Beth, breakdowns like that rarely happen here. We are ISO 9001 registered, after all," Michael said in defense of his plant. Beth replied, "Yes, I know that sometimes we can't control everything, but could I see documentation on the maintenance of your production line?" A little shocked, Michael said, "Sure. Let's go over to the supervisor's desk for the information." Sure enough, Michael was able to retrieve the maintenance schedule and records; however, the records for preventive maintenance were mixed in with the records for repairs. Beth asked, "Michael, how are you able to discriminate between preventive maintenance and repairs?" Michael replied, "I am sure the supervisors know how to tell the difference." Beth then observed, "Also, just glancing over the report, I notice that about six weeks of data are missing." Looking at the supervisor's desk, she noticed similar-looking data sheets placed under one leg of the desk to balance the desk. "Is that the data?" she asked. Overhearing the conversation, the supervisor quickly grabbed the papers from under the leg and handed them to Beth. "Sorry," he said. "The desk was a bit wobbly, and I forgot about the data being there." Visibly angry with the supervisor, Michael said to Beth, "Let's continue with the tour."

Walking through the facility, Beth noticed as many employees conducting what appeared to be testing and inspection as were actually producing the products. In addition, she noticed parts that had been pulled from the line to be reworked or scrapped sitting to the sides of the production lines. She thought to herself, "Lots of inspection, rework, scrap, and work-in-progress—all indications of processes that are either incapable or out of control." Pointing to a rack of printed circuit boards, she asked, "Michael, can I see the scrap records for these parts?" "I don't think all the parts are scrap; some may be reworks," Michael replied. He continued, "Let's go to the QC [quality control] department and have those records pulled for you."

As they walked to the QC department, Beth saw out of the corner of her eye an employee drop a printed circuit board, instinctively catch it by crushing it with his elbow against a conveyor belt casing, and then place the board back on the production line as if nothing had happened. She decided to not bring the event to Michael's attention after his reaction to the machine breakdown earlier.

After asking several QC employees who was responsible for the scrap records, Michael traced the records to Martha Ryder, a QC employee who worked in a cramped little room about 40 yards away from the QC offices. Martha managed the quality records in a small, enclosed area of the factory with no windows. Tagged parts were strewn throughout the room. Martha was able to retrieve the scrap records for the process in question very quickly. She handed the manila folder for the last month to Beth.

Looking through the records, Beth noticed that on average, the scrap forms were dated about three weeks after a part was pulled from the production line. Scanning down the forms, she expected to find bogus causes for the scrap listed. Sure enough, the causes were written in the shortest form possible, with "operator error" listed most of the time. Beth knew that there was no way the company could possibly trace the causes and improve the processes with the data sheets. She thanked Martha for her time. Michael and Beth then left and resumed the tour.

Curious, she asked Michael, "Can I see descriptions of the processes for how you handle scrap?" Michael replied, "Sure. I can give you that information, but it will take me a couple of days to get it together. I'll e-mail it to you." She recalled a visit to a supplier in San Jose who had been able to pull up specific process information in an instant with an online ISO 9001 documentation system.

Finally, they reached the end of the production and assembly lines, where quality control conducted the final inspection. Michael stated with a hint of pride, "We maintain high inspection levels, usually 100 percent, to assure that you as the customer get the highest quality possible."

Beth left the facility thankful that she had taken the time to visit. "The irony," she thought, "is that the new manager has plans to reduce the number of facility visits because according to him, 'The cost of visiting suppliers is really eating into my budget!'"[1] ▮

## CRITICAL THINKING QUESTIONS

1. What did Beth learn from her "quality walk"?
2. Why might upper management be reluctant to invest in visits to suppliers? How can that reluctance be overcome?

# Evolution of Quality Management

Firms have taken many different pathways to world-class quality management, but the end destination has been very much the same. A frequently overheard phrase is "same wine, different bottles." The wine in this case is quality, and the different bottles are the different approaches and pathways. The fact that new bottles continue to sell is proof that quality still is and always will be critically important.

In historically understanding the evolution of the quality management movement over the last 50 years, it is useful to reflect on the multiple pathways that companies have taken to achieve competitive capability on a quality basis. The beginning of almost all pathways can be traced to a relatively small number of individuals who essentially "preached" about quality when very few companies recognized quality as a source of competitive advantage. Instead, many companies, such as General Motors, did not heed the call of the preachers and waited until quality was required for survival. Some companies, such as American Motors Company, never heeded the call and went out of business. In companies that decided to survive, the chief executive officer administered one or more management approaches that adhered to the philosophical

---

[1]The case is based on a combination of real events observed independently at two supplier facilities by one of the authors while conducting research. Unfortunately, the telecommunications company (the buying firm) did not visit the supplier's plant, but it did enter into a "partnership" with the supplier. The result? Catastrophic costs caused by poor quality and missed deadlines. The results of the contract were observed at the telecommunications company two years after research at the supplier's facility. The dates, company names, and individuals presented in the case are fictional. It is doubtful that all the events in the case would have been discovered in one visit, but one thing is for sure: The telecommunications company would have been far better off if it had invested the time and money to do "the quality walk."

understanding of the "religion" he or she had accepted. The management approach then determined which methodologies and tools the companies used to implement, improve, and maintain quality. The remainder of this chapter follows the pattern of influence by presenting philosophers, approaches, methodologies, and tools.

# Philosophies of the Gurus

Quality management has been blessed with many visionaries who have helped develop the field to its current importance within companies. These visionaries often are referred to as gurus or preachers. The reason for this reverence is rooted in the fact that quality management investment in the past often was decided on within companies on the basis of belief or "gut feelings," not hard costs. (The issue of the costs of quality is addressed later in the chapter.)

The influences of gurus such as Deming, Crosby, Juran, Taguchi, and Imai are still evident in corporate cultures. As was noted in "the quality walk" in the opening vignette, a supply manager can identify which guru influenced any specific company the most simply by listening to managers and observing their processes. From a supply management perspective, understanding the influence of one or more gurus on a supplier aids in evaluating, selecting, understanding, and helping that supplier. Although their teachings were directed at managers who were trying to improve their own internal quality, most of the concepts are general enough to apply across supply chains.

## W. Edwards Deming

W. Edwards Deming was perhaps the most influential quality guru of the last century. Ironically, his message was ignored by Western countries until the 1980s. Before that time he spent most of his career in Japan as a consultant, helping the Japanese rebuild their industries after World War II. Deming is best known for the 14 points summarizing the philosophy of quality management that he developed over time in Japan.[2] The 14 points are general enough that they are still applicable, and many of the concepts are directly transferable to modern supply management.

**Statistical Methods**   In his seminars on the 14 points, Deming always stressed the use of statistical methods to identify when a process is becoming unstable or unpredictable so that the problem can be identified and the process can be prevented from producing defects. This important topic is discussed later in this chapter in the section on statistical process control (SPC). Showing that he was far ahead of his time in supply management (it was called purchasing back then), he advocated the use of SPC at the supplier's facilities as well as at the buying firm's facilities.

**Causes of Defects**   Deming contended that the vast majority of defective or poor products produced in processes are directly traceable to poor-quality input materials, parts, and components. These, according to Deming, are often the result of poorly coordinated design specifications and poorly managed processes after the design is in production. From a supply management perspective, this means that better coordination with suppliers in specifications development and usage will improve quality and decrease costs. In addition, developing suppliers to use statistical techniques such as SPC can help reduce costs and maintain high quality after the design stage. Deming also felt that buying materials primarily based on price contributed to the selection of suppliers with quality problems.[3]

---

[2] N. Logothetis, *Managing for Total Quality: From Deming to Taguchi to SPC*, Manufacturing Practitioner Series (United Kingdom: Prentice-Hall International, 1992). The authors highly recommend this book for its conciseness, straightforward clarity, and global view.

[3] David N. Burt and Richard L. Pinkerton, *Strategic Proactive Procurement*, AMACOM, New York, 1996. p. 185, A letter from Deming to Pinkerton, Oct. 14, 1982.

## Philip Crosby

Philip Crosby is another American quality guru who rose to international fame as a management consultant. Before he became a consultant, he had worked his way up from line inspector to corporate vice president and quality director of ITT. Crosby authored several seminal books; among the best known are *Quality Is Free* and *Quality without Tears.*[4]

**Zero Defects**  Crosby is best known, and misunderstood, for championing the zero defects standard and popularizing many slogans, such as "Do it right the first time." The focus of the zero defects standard is on defining quality from the customer's perspective as conformance to requirements and then improving processes through prevention activities to meet the requirements. Crosby pushed the idea of measuring the costs of quality to support efforts toward zero defects, which culminated in his zero defects management approach (presented later in this chapter).

Crosby intended the zero defects approach to be a management performance standard, not a motivational program. Despite his intentions, it was treated as a motivational program in many companies; those companies eventually gave up on the program because they could never reach perfection. Deming believed the zero defects standard created anxiety, fear, frustration, and mistrust of management when it was not accompanied by the means to achieve the standard.

## Masaaki Imai

Like Deming and Crosby, Masaaki Imai became one of the world's leading management consultants. Imai introduced the world to continuous improvement through his book *Kaizen: The Key to Japan's Competitive Success.*[5] In a working environment, kaizen means continuous process improvement that involves everybody.

**Kaizen and Supply Management**  Kaizen calls for everyone in an organization to work for constant and gradual improvement in every process. Since processes span supply chains, we believe that kaizen should be extended to calling for everyone in the chain to work for constant and gradual improvement in every process. When a new standard is achieved, management should make certain it is maintained and that conditions are present that ensure the attainment of even higher standards. Kaizen improvement is, by Imai's definition, a long-term and long-lasting improvement resulting from team efforts focused on processes. Since it draws from existing employees, it usually requires less investment than do other management approaches but great internal effort to maintain.[6]

## Genechi Taguchi

Genechi Taguchi served as the director of the Japanese Academy of Quality and is a four-time recipient of the Deming Prize. Taguchi notes that as the level of conformance moves out toward the upper and lower limits, there is a quadratic increase in costs. Taguchi referred to this as the "quadratic loss function."

Taguchi advocates identifying target values for design parameters and producing robust designs by using statistical experimentation. The approach focuses on consistency in hitting the target values rather

---

[4]Ibid.

[5]M. Imai, *Kaizen: The Key to Japan's Competitive Success* (New York: Random House, 1986).

[6]Logothetis, *Managing for Total Quality*, p. 90.

than being within a band of tolerance. Taguchi's "loss to society" model is presented in greater detail in the tools and methods section of this chapter.

### Joseph Juran

Joseph Juran is perhaps best known for his *Quality Control Handbook*. First published in 1951, the book is revised periodically to remain relevant. Like Deming and Crosby, Juran is an American consultant with international fame. Also, like Deming, Juran worked in post–World War II Japan, conducting seminars for top-level and middle-level executives.

The main principles of Juran's message are to focus on planning, organizational issues, creating beneficial change (breakthrough), preventing averse change (control), and management's responsibility.[7] He recommends a formula for results which has four important stages, as follows:

1. **Establish specific goals to be reached**—identify what needs to be done, the specific projects that need to be tackled.
2. **Establish plans for reaching goals**—provide a structured process.
3. **Assign clear responsibility**—make clear who is responsible for meeting the goals.
4. **Base the rewards on results achieved**—feed results information back and utilize the lessons learned and the experience gained.

Planning for quality is seen by Juran as an indispensable part of what he calls the quality trilogy: quality planning, quality control, and quality improvement. He believes that objectives should be set yearly for increased performance and decreased costs. To develop the habit of always striving for those yearly goals, a company needs quality planning and a quality structure. Juran believes that the development of the goals, plans, and structure is the responsibility of top management.

Juran countered Crosby's approach by stating that simplistic slogans and exhortations do not constitute a structure. According to Juran, "There are no shortcuts to quality." The emphasis should be on the results and the experience gained from those results, not on the quality campaign itself. Juran insists that "the recipe for action should consist of 90 percent substance and 10 percent exhortation, not the reverse!"[8]

Juran's approach to quality received widespread acceptance because of the clear setting of responsibility and the detailed focus on planning. Juran's approach is especially popular with managers who feel that the teachings of Deming and Crosby are vague and difficult to evaluate.

## Management Approaches

Six Sigma, Total Quality Management (TQM), continuous improvement, zero defects, the Quality Management System (QMS), and just-in-time (JIT) are management systems that continue to make large contributions to the improvement and maintenance of quality internally in companies and across supply chains. As was pointed out earlier, the system a company or chain chooses is greatly dependent on the philosophical views of upper management as influenced either directly or indirectly by the gurus. It should be noted that the type of production or service a company provides also influences which system is chosen. In addition, companies may implement several approaches sequentially or simultaneously. In the automobile industry, for example, continuous improvement in a just-in-time framework coupled with

---

[7]Ibid., p. 62.

[8]Ibid., p. 64.

Total Quality Management is fairly common. Among companies that bought into the zero defects movement, many now use the similar "set an ambitious goal" approach of Six Sigma. All the systems may be used in manufacturing or service environments, but service operations are less likely to have a comprehensive quality management system because of the lack of physical outputs.

Management usually believes it needs a new approach to "rally the troops" much in the same way that psychologists discovered that painting the walls of a factory temporarily increases productivity. New quality management systems will always appear in corporations. In most cases, the latest approach will incorporate lessons learned from past systems, and so new initiatives should not be ignored. For example, Six Sigma incorporates the best tools and methodologies of the other approaches, such as cause-and-effect analysis and statistical process control, while advancing several newer tools and methodologies, such as balanced scorecards and project charters. The most recent incarnation of a quality system is the Quality Management System as defined by the International Organization for Standardization.

**Role of Supply Management**   So how does a supply professional fit into a comprehensive system such as TQM or Six Sigma? In most cases, supply managers play a critical role in making the entire program work effectively. Most quality experts agree that poor quality of incoming materials causes approximately 75 percent of the problems and related costs associated with final product quality.[9] It is clear that the quality consultant Joseph Juran is correct when he writes: "The assurance (for good quality) must come from placing the responsibility on the supplier to make the product right and supply proof that it is right."[10] Consequently, supply management becomes the "point" player or the "playmaker" in a firm's quality program.

## Total Quality Management

Total Quality Management received recognition and adaptation in the 1980s because of the increasing need for firms to compete on the basis of quality. By the late 1980s and early 1990s publications were writing about the reasons why TQM had succeeded or failed in many organizations. The reviews were mixed but generally were in favor of a comprehensive quality management system. Most quality experts agree that the reasons for failure of TQM are usually poor management execution of the system.

By the late 1990s, TQM essentially had matured and management needed new "bottles for its wine." Six Sigma appears to be the latest new bottle, or management system. Although Motorola initiated Six Sigma in the 1980s, the management approach did not gain widespread recognition until the late 1990s. Six Sigma is discussed later in this section of the chapter. Although the terminology of TQM eventually will pass, the management approach will never die since quality management in everything a company does is a requirement for competing today and in the future. In fact, this entire chapter is essentially about TQM if one goes by the vague definitions that once were in vogue. For example, the International Organization for Standardization offered the following definition of TQM:[11] *A management approach to an organization centered on quality, based on the participation of all its members and aiming*

---

[9]While a majority of a firm's quality problems commonly can be attributed to purchased materials and subassemblies, the root cause of most of these problems is in the design and resulting specifications of the items and their production processes. Supply management professionals have two areas of responsibility in the design/quality issue: They and invited suppliers must work cooperatively with the firm's design engineers to design appropriate quality characteristics into the materials to be purchased, and (2) this group must ensure that suppliers design variability out of their production processes to the extent that is practical.

[10]As quoted by Paul Moffat in "Quality Assurance," in *The Purchasing Handbook* (New York: McGraw-Hill, 1992), p. 421.

[11]As quoted by Greg Hutchins, *ISO 9000* (Essex Junction, VT: Oliver Wight-Publications, 1993), p. 4.

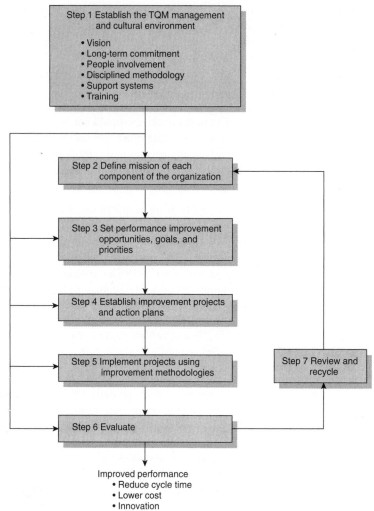

**Figure 7.1 |** A Generalized Total Quality Management Model

*at long-term success through customer satisfaction, and benefits to the members of the organization and to society.* A generalized TQM model is presented in Figure 7.1.[12]

## Continuous Improvement

The concept of continuous improvement was introduced in the section on Imai, the champion of kaizen. Kaizen is synonymous with continuous improvement. Although Imai brought continuous improvement to the world through his books, Taiichi Ohno, the pioneer of the kanban system at Toyota, developed continuous improvement into a viable, tangible management approach. In this section, continuous improvement

---

[12]James F. Cali, *TQM for Purchasing Management* (New York: McGraw-Hill, 1993), p. 36.

is presented within the just-in-time (JIT) framework. Continuous improvement is a concept that is independent from JIT. It can be implemented without JIT, but it has received its most publicized adopters in companies that run JIT systems.

**Just-in-Time**   Two major tenets form the basis for just-in-time as practiced at Toyota: respect for people and elimination of waste. Ohno is credited with identifying categories of waste which are avoidable: waste of overproduction, waste of unneeded motion and transportation, waste in needless processing and machine time, waste in holding excessive inventory, and waste resulting from defects.[13] In taking the quality walk described in the opening vignettes in this chapter, a supply manager with a solid grasp of these wastes can see them quickly on the factory floor of a supplier. Often managers working within the supplier's facilities have become so complacent about their systems and their inherent wastes that they no longer see them. A knowledgeable supply manager needs to be able to see what the managers of the facilities cannot.

Ohno demonstrated that most wastes can be eliminated if a kanban system is coupled with continuous improvement. A kanban system also can be called a "pull" system. In a pull system, units needed by an upstream stage of production are transported to that stage only when needed and in the exact amount needed. This is in contrast to traditional "push" production systems, in which units are transported to the next stage as soon as they have completed the previous stage. Using the kanban system, the operator of each stage is responsible for the collection of the units from the previous stage; hence, the operator "pulls" the material through the system. A kanban (signpost) is attached to the box of parts as they go to the assembly line, and the same kanban is returned when the parts are all used to serve as an order for more and as a record of work done.

Supply managers must understand that JIT can be extended to subcontractors and external suppliers. Extending JIT across a supply chain requires supply professionals and suppliers to work collaboratively so that only enough units to meet demand (that is, small lots) are produced and moved from one stage to another. The supply chain members should work together to assure that the need for speculative, just-in-case production is eliminated.

**Elimination of Waste**   In eliminating waste with a continuous improvement methodology, a company may choose to use the following steps: First, form a small team that will go through kaizen training using the tools and methods discussed later in this chapter. The people in the group are usually factory floor workers, hence the tenet of respect for people. Second, the team will gather data on existing systems to discover where waste is and what the wasteful activity is costing the company. Many managers do not believe in assigning a cost to waste because they believe it does not matter—waste is waste no matter how small or large, and it should be eliminated. Juran and Crosby would argue that we need to know the cost of the waste to prioritize projects to eliminate it. Third, once a project for eliminating a waste is identified, the P-D-C-A (Plan, Do, Check, Act) cycle often is used. After the P-D-C-A substeps are completed, the group returns to step two again and selects a new project.

## Six Sigma

In the book *The Six Sigma Way,* Six Sigma is defined as a broad and comprehensive system for building and sustaining business performance, success, and leadership.[14] The key focus of Six Sigma is on processes, but with measurement of both processes and products. With Six Sigma, companies strive to

---

[13]Logothetis, *Managing for Total Quality.*

[14]Peter S. Pande, Robert P. Neuman, and Roland R. Cavanagh, *The Six Sigma Way* (New York: McGraw-Hill, 2000), p. 77.

| Sigma | Corresponding Yield | DPMO |
|-------|---------------------|---------|
| 1 | 30.9% | 690,000 |
| 2 | 69.2% | 308,000 |
| 3 | 93.3% | 66,800 |
| 4 | 99.4% | 6,210 |
| 5 | 99.98% | 320 |
| 6 | 99.9997% | 3.4 |

**Figure 7.2 |** Sigma Quality Levels and Corresponding Yields

achieve the statistical six sigma goal of near perfection as measured by 3.4 defects per million opportunities (DPMO). The corresponding yield from the six sigma process is 99.9997 percent, as shown in Figure 7.2. This lofty goal, very reminiscent of the zero defects management philosophy, is used by Six Sigma advocates as a driver of organizational change.

Six Sigma was developed at Motorola in the late 1980s as a way to accelerate the company's rate of improvement, provide a clear and objective goal for improvement, and create a stronger focus on the customer. The success of the six sigma measure as a mantra for change led Motorola to institutionalize the goal into a comprehensive management system. While the objective of statistical "six sigma" is the overarching goal, Six Sigma as a management system shifts the attention to the rate of improvement in processes and products. According to supporters of the Six Sigma management approach, there are some clear measurement benefits.

1. *Six Sigma starts with the customer.*   Measures demand a clear definition of customers' requirements.
2. *Six Sigma provides a consistent metric.*   Once you've defined the requirement clearly, you can define a "defect" and measure almost any type of business activity or process. For example, some measures from a supply management perspective could be late deliveries, incomplete shipments, and parts shortages.
3. *Six Sigma links the effort to an ambitious goal.*   Having an entire organization focused on a performance objective of 3.4 defects per million opportunities can create significant momentum for improvement.[15]

## DMAIC Cycle

Similar to the P-D-C-A cycle discussed in the previous section, Six Sigma offers a cyclical improvement model called DMAIC that focuses on improving processes. DMAIC stands for Define, Measure, Analyze, Improve, and Control.[16] In contrast to P-D-C-A for continuous improvement, the Six Sigma model has elements of both continuous and discontinuous (reengineering) improvement. Six Sigma's focus on processes is evident from the combination of process improvement and design (including redesign), "incorporating them as essential, complementary strategies for sustained success." The process design approach is reminiscent of reengineering, in which the objective in Six Sigma is not to fix but to replace a process (or a piece of a process) with a new one. Six Sigma also calls for addressing product and service design through what the approach calls "Six Sigma Design." Six Sigma Design principles are intended to link the creation of new goods and services to customer needs and validate the linkage by means of data and testing.[17]

---

[15]Ibid., p. 29.

[16]Ibid., p. 37.

[17]Ibid., p. 33.

**Six Sigma Blackbelts**   A differentiator of the Six Sigma management system from other quality management approaches is the designation of levels of understanding of Six Sigma into belts: green, black, and master. The excitement that the belts cause is very real and, to put it bluntly, is shrewd marketing. Taking the term from the martial arts, a color of belt is a level attained through intensive training and experience. Although no solid definition of the levels exists, a master blackbelt is essentially an individual who has attained the highest level of understanding of Six Sigma and is capable of training others and working as an internal consultant in a corporation. Regular blackbelts become the primary drivers of Six Sigma improvements within companies by essentially managing specific projects. A greenbelt is a training level that is encouraged by Six Sigma advocates for all workers.

At GE, blackbelts receive three weeks of training, with follow-up exams and continued learning through conferences and other forums. A greenbelt at GE is the lowest commitment, which involves training for a minimum of two weeks in Six Sigma. At GE, every management employee is required to at least become a greenbelt in Six Sigma.[18]

**Six Sigma Themes**   In the book *The Six Sigma Way,* the authors present six themes or principles of Six Sigma that can be summarized as follows:

■ *Theme One: Genuine Focus on the Customer.*   In Six Sigma, customer focus becomes the top priority. For example, the measures of Six Sigma performance begin with the customer. Six Sigma improvements are defined by their impact on customer satisfaction and value.

■ *Theme Two: Data- and Fact-Driven Management.*   Six Sigma discipline begins by clarifying *what* measures are key to gauging business performance; then it applies data and analysis to build an understanding of key variables and optimize results. Six Sigma helps managers answer two essential questions to support fact-driven decisions and solutions: What data/information do I really need? How do we use those data or information to maximum benefit?

■ *Theme Three: Process Focus, Management, and Improvement.*   Whether designing products and services, measuring performance, improving efficiency and customer satisfaction, or even running the business, Six Sigma positions the process as the key vehicle for success.

■ *Theme Four: Proactive Management.*   Proactive management means making habits out of what are too often neglected business practices: defining ambitious goals and reviewing them frequently, setting clear priorities, focusing on problem prevention versus firefighting, and questioning why we do things instead of blindly defending them as "how we do things here."

■ *Theme Five: Boundaryless Collaboration.*   The opportunities available through improved collaboration within companies and with suppliers and customers are huge. Billions of dollars are left on the table (or on the floor) every day because of disconnects and outright competition between groups that should be working for a common cause: providing value to customers.

■ *Theme Six: Drive for Perfection; Tolerance for Failure.*   No company will get anywhere close to Six Sigma without launching new ideas and approaches—which always involve some risk. If people who see a possible path to better service, lower costs, new capabilities, and so on (i.e., ways to be closer to perfect), are too afraid of the consequences of mistakes, they'll never try.

Successes with Six Sigma are being published in a variety of industries. One of the most outspoken advocates of Six Sigma is former General Electric chairman John F. Welch. According to Welch, "Six

---

[18]Ibid. and see John F. "Jack" Welch Jr, with John A. Byrne, *Straight from the Gut* (New York: Warner Business Books, 2001).

Sigma has forever changed GE. Everyone—from the Six Sigma zealots emerging from their Black Belt tours, to the engineers, the auditors, and the scientists, to the senior leadership that will take this company into the new millennium—is a true believer in Six Sigma, the way this company now works."[19] At GE, the best Six Sigma projects begin "not inside the business but outside it, focused on answering the question—how can we make the customer more competitive? What is critical to the customer's success? . . . One thing we have discovered with certainty is that anything we do that makes the customer more successful inevitably results in a financial return for us."[20]

## Quality Management System

The International Organization for Standardization (ISO) released its ISO 9000:2000 standards with radical revisions that justify the inclusion in this section of what ISO calls a Quality Management System (QMS). The principles are intended for use as a framework to guide organizations toward improved performance. According to ISO, the principles are derived from the collective experience and knowledge of international experts. They form the foundation of a QMS approach to managing quality. The principles are as follows:[21]

- *Principle 1. Customer Focus:* Organizations depend on their customers and therefore should understand current and future customer needs, meet customer requirements, and strive to exceed customer expectations.
- *Principle 2. Leadership:* Leaders establish unity of purpose and the direction of the organization. They should create and maintain an internal environment in which people can become fully involved in achieving the organization's objectives.
- *Principle 3. Involvement of People:* People at all levels are the essence of an organization, and their full involvement allows their abilities to be used for the organization's benefit.
- *Principle 4. Process Approach:* A desired result is achieved more efficiently when activities and related resources are managed as a process.
- *Principle 5. System Approach to Management:* Identifying, understanding, and managing interrelated processes as a system contributes to the organization's effectiveness and efficiency in achieving its objectives.
- *Principle 6. Continual Improvement:* Continual improvement of the organization's overall performance should be a permanent objective of the organization.
- *Principle 7. Factual Approach to Decision Making:* Effective decisions are based on the analysis of data and information. Applying the principle of factual approach to decision making typically leads to assurance that data and information are sufficiently accurate, reliable, and accessible.
- *Principle 8. Mutually Beneficial Supplier Relationships:* An organization and its suppliers are interdependent, and a mutually beneficial relationship enhances the ability of both to create value.

---

[19] Address to General Electric Company Annual Meeting, Cleveland, OH, April 21, 1999.

[20] General Electric Company Annual Meeting, Charlotte, NC, April 23, 1997.

[21] www.iso.org, the website for the International Organization for Standardization, February 2008.

# Tools and Methodologies

The quality movement, whether embraced through TQM, continuous improvement, Six Sigma, or another management approach, is accomplished in the "trenches" on the floors of factories, warehouses, offices, and any other places where business is accomplished. To accomplish quality, a plethora of tools and methodologies have been developed that are used whenever needed by middle management and the general workforce. Improvement-focused tools and methodologies all have contributed to and continue to contribute to quality improvement.

**Terminology and Usage**    The term "tool" emerged from the use of the methodologies in small group improvement efforts, such as quality circles, in which the group would focus on solving a problem by using a mix of the methodologies. Some of the methodologies would be used in the same problem-solving session, like a screwdriver being used for many phases of a construction project. Some of the tools are better used to discover where the focus should be. For example, a cost of quality analysis helps clarify what areas of investment may require attention. If there is downtime as a result of breakdowns, perhaps increasing investment in maintenance or training is warranted. We can view these "tools" as available in our "quality toolbox" for use when appropriate to help us achieve quality. Not all tools will be used on every project. Some may never be used.

**Implications for Supply Management**    Why should a supply professional need to be aware of the tools and methodologies of quality management? Some companies talk a great deal about quality at the upper-management level, but real improvements in quality occur in the trenches where the tools and methodologies are used. Physically seeing that these activities are occurring provides reassurance that the company is investing in its quality system and the people running the system. When a supply manager does the quality walk through a supplier's facility, he or she often will discover meeting rooms or factory walls pasted with diagrams, charts, and lists that are outputs of using these tools and methodologies.

## Common Tools

The most commonly used tools of quality are Pareto charts, cause-and-effect diagrams, process flow charts, run plots, frequency histograms, correlations plots, and control charts. These are often called the "seven tools of quality."

1.  *Pareto Charts* are used to distinguish between critical and trivial problems. For example, a company could use Pareto charts with checklists to identify the number of occurrences or quality costs for each variable that causes their products to be scrapped. The variables themselves could be identified by using cause-and-effect diagrams.

2.  *Cause-and-Effect Diagrams* show the possible causes of a problem. Also called a fishbone diagram, a cause-and-effect diagram is an aid to brainstorming and hypothesis generation. For example, the causes of defects that cause product to be scrapped could be identified by using this method. Always try to find the underlying causes of causes. Ask, "Why is this a cause?" several times until the true underlying cause is discovered.

3.  *Process Flow Charts* are useful for showing linkages among the parts of a process. This is a good tool for identifying bottlenecks and non-value-added activities in processes. Simulation is a natural extension of flow and run charting to increase knowledge about the flows of a process.

4. *Run Plots* graph samples over time of a variable that is thought to be important. A run plot can be examined to see whether the process is subject to change or behaves consistently over time. Noting when changes occur may suggest hypotheses about their cause.

5. *Frequency Histograms* show the distribution of a variable that is thought to be important. Frequency histograms are useful for hypothesis testing. For example, how do the distributions of process times for manufacturing processes compare with the ones you would expect?

6. *Scatter Diagrams* show correlations between two variables, typically a problem and a potential cause. To examine interactions between more than two variables, multiple regression should be used. For example, a negative correlation between increased quality and increased total costs could be investigated by using a simple scatter diagram.

7. *Control Charts* are similar to run plots but are used for operational control. Control charts show the upper and lower allowable limits for a process variable. When the process exceeds those limits or shows a recognizable pattern, action should be taken to adjust that process. Once set up, control charts are effective tools for day-to-day monitoring and management of a process. They are discussed in greater detail later in this chapter.

**Example Using the Tools**　Consider a supplier who recently installed a new production process and assigned several operators to a team to manage improvement projects. The team decides to map the process stages by using a flow chart to identify where data should be gathered. The decision is made to gather data at each of the inspection points. After data are gathered on where failures are occurring and the costs of the failures (costs of quality) are estimated, a Pareto chart may be used to identify which problem is generating the greatest failure costs. A cause-and-effect diagram then could be used to help identify the root causes of the highest-cost failure. Through cause-and-effect analysis and brainstorming, the team determines that higher levels of maintenance of the tools used in the production process are needed. To prevent the problem from occurring in the future, the team decides to implement statistical process control to measure the process outputs and identify when the process is in need of additional maintenance before new defects are produced. Data are accumulated on the new solution, and a decision is made at a later date about whether the project has been a success. If it has been a success, the team moves on to the project with the next highest priority. If the project has not been a success, the team restarts the improvement process. Regardless of the success or failure of the project, the team maintains detailed documentation of the effort so that the gains can be maintained, lessons can be learned, and the information can be disseminated to other production processes within the company.

The successful use of the seven tools has partly been the result of the simplicity and ease of use they facilitate while revealing much about a process. They are designed so that little training is required. Still, they do require commitment on the part of management to provide time and resources for small-group members to utilize them properly.

**Design of Experiments (DOE)**　A brilliant quality control engineer at Motorola, Keke Bhote, used the DOE techniques developed by Dohan Shainin, another brilliant quality control engineer who worked for United Aircraft (now United Technologies). DOE tools discover key variables in process-product design and then find solutions to reduce the variations they cause substantially or totally while reducing tolerances on the lesser variables to reduce costs.[22]

---

[22]Keki R. Bhote, *World Class Quality* (New York: AMACOM, 1991). Also see the book review by Richard L. Pinkerton published in the *International Journal of Purchasing Materials Management,* Summer 1993, pp. 51–52.

## Costs of Quality

Since the introduction of the traditional quality cost model in the 1950s, managers have been urged to base quality-related decisions on the hypothesized trade-off between the costs of prevention and appraisal and the costs of internal and external failure.[23,24] From a supply management standpoint, understanding the costs associated with quality decision making enables a better understanding of both the total cost of ownership and how suppliers make decisions in their production facilities. (See Chapter 13 on the total cost of ownership.)

According to the traditional costs of quality (COQ) model, a company that is producing poor-quality products can reduce nonconformance or failure costs by investing in prevention and appraisal activities. The model resolves a hypothesized trade-off by specifying a nonzero optimal level of defects at the point where the marginal cost of increased prevention and appraisal activities equals the marginal benefit from reductions in failure costs. An important note here is needed with respect to the optimum point. In many progressive quality systems, the optimal levels of defects are very close to zero.[25] A six sigma process, for example, should have 3.4 defects per million opportunities. The cost categories in the COQ model are as follows:[26]

- *Prevention costs* are the costs of all activities specifically designed to prevent poor quality in products or services. Examples are the costs of maintaining equipment and supplies, new product reviews, quality planning, supplier capacity surveys, process capability evaluations, quality improvement team meetings, quality improvement projects, quality education, and training.

- *Appraisal costs* are the costs associated with measuring, evaluating, and auditing products or services to assure conformance to quality standards and performance requirements. These costs include the costs of incoming and source inspections; tests of purchased material; in-process and final inspection; product, process, and service audits; calibration of measuring and test equipment; and the cost of associated materials and supplies.

- *Failure costs* are the costs resulting from products or services that do not conform to requirements or customer or user needs. Two categories of failure costs exist: internal and external. Internal failure costs are costs that occur before the delivery or shipment of the product or the furnishing of a service to the customer. Examples are the costs of scrap, disposing of scrap, rework, redoing inspection, redoing testing, material review, and downgrading. External failure costs are costs that occur after delivery or shipment of the product or during or after furnishing a service to the customer. Examples are the costs of processing customer complaints, customer returns, warranty claims, and product recalls. Opportunity costs of lost customers as a result of poor quality sometimes are included as an external failure cost but are extremely difficult to estimate.

## Loss to Society

In continuing the COQ discussion, Taguchi taught that a traditional "conformance to specifications" definition of costs underestimates failure costs. The conventional conformance to specification definition assumes that no loss occurs as long as output lies within upper and lower specification limits. This view also has been referred to as the "goalpost philosophy."

[23]A. V. Feigenbaum, "The Challenge of Total Quality Control," *Industrial Quality Control*, May 1957, pp. 17–23.

[24]J. M. Juran, *Quality Control Handbook,* 1st ed. (New York: McGraw-Hill, 1951).

[25]Many textbooks present figures for the COQ showing a plot where the optimum point as plotted somewhere midway between 0 percent and 100 percent good; this has led many students over the years to believe that the optimal point is somewhere around 50 percent good.

[26]Jack Campanella, ed., *Principles of Quality Costs*, 2nd ed. (Milwaukee, WI: ASQC Quality Press, 1990).

**Tolerance Stacking**   One problem with the goalpost philosophy is tolerance stacking. Tolerance stacking occurs when two or more parts are to be fit together; the size of their tolerances often determines how well they will match. If one part falls at a lower limit of its specification and a matching part falls at its upper limit, a good fit is unlikely.

Taguchi developed a way to confront the stacked tolerances conformance problem. Taguchi begins with the idea of "the loss function," a measure of losses from the time a product is shipped. The theoretical notion is that "losses to society" occur whenever output deviates from its target value.[27] In more tangible terms, these losses include warranty costs, nonrepeating customers, and other problems resulting from performance failure. Taguchi then compares such losses to two alternative approaches to quality. The first approach is simple conformance to specifications. The second approach is a measure of the degree to which parts or products diverge from the ideal target or center. Taguchi demonstrates that tolerance stacking is worse when the dimensions of parts are more distant from the ideal target of a specification than when they cluster around it, even if some parts fall outside the tolerance band entirely. Knowing that the problem of stacked variances exists and understanding Taguchi's loss function causes managers to focus on reducing the variances of parts and processes.

## Process Capability Analysis

No operations activity can produce identical results time after time. This is true even for machine-based production processes. Every process has some natural variability as a result of things such as machine part clearances, bearing wear, and lubrication, and variations in operator technique. In the language of statisticians, these are "chance" or "common" causes that produce *random variations* in the output. Over time, this natural variability in the output of a process will produce a distribution of outputs around the mean quality level. In many cases this distribution approximates the normal bell-shaped curve. The difference between the two extremes of the curve, the high and low values, is defined as the *natural tolerance range* of the process. As long as the process is properly adjusted and is not affected by outside nonrandom forces—as long as the process is "in control"—the distribution it produces is predictable, as shown in Figure 7.3.

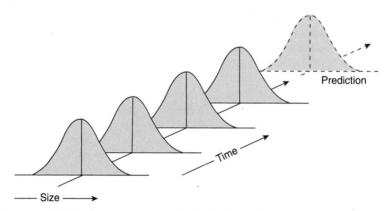

Prediction

Time

—— Size ——➤

**Figure 7.3 |** The Output Distribution of a Process That Is "in Control"

---

[27]G. Taguchi, and D. Clausing, "Robust Quality," *Harvard Business Review*, January–February 1990, pp. 65–75.

If a buying firm's desired range of quality for a particular purchased part is compatible with the natural tolerance range of a potential supplier's production process, the supplier should have little difficulty providing the buying firm with parts that meet specifications. In contrast, when the buying firm's required quality range is narrower than the natural capability range of the process, the supplier is bound to produce some unacceptable parts.

**Implications for Supply Management**    Alert supply managers recognize the direct economic relationship between their specified quality requirements and the producer's ability to perform consistently at the specified level. In the case of a nonstandard item, before selecting a supplier, a supply manager must determine (1) whether the potential supplier in fact knows what the natural capability range for its production process is, (2) if so, whether the buying firm's *desired* range of quality is compatible with the supplier's natural capability range, and (3) if so, how the supplier plans to monitor the process to ensure that it stays in control so that it will produce satisfactory output consistently. The following examples should clarify this concept.

In Figure 7.4a, assume that a supply manager wants to purchase 100,000 metal shafts that are 1 inch in diameter with a tolerance of $\pm 0.005$ inch. Assume further that the supplier has studied its process, has stabilized it, and knows that its natural capability for this type of job is 1 inch $\pm 0.004$ inch. In Figure 7.4a, the supply manager sees that as long as the supplier's process operates normally and remains centered on 1.0 inch, every piece produced will fall within his or her acceptable range of quality. In this example, then, if the supplier is able to keep the process in control, this situation appears to represent a sound purchase for the buying firm from a quality point of view. In this case, the supplier's process is said to be "capable."

Assume now that the supply manager wants to purchase 100,000 shafts that are 1 inch in diameter with a tolerance of $\pm 0.003$ inch. Examination of Figure 7.4b reveals that by dealing with the same supplier under normal operating conditions, the production process cannot entirely satisfy the buying firm's requirement. Some shafts will be produced with diameters less than 0.997 inch, and some with diameters larger than 1.003 inches. It is important for the supply manager to understand this type of situation. Unusable shafts, whether reworked or scrapped, create cost that eventually must be recovered by the supplier.

(a)                    (b)

**Figure 7.4 |** An Illustrative Comparison of Quality Requirements with Process Capability (Process Frequency Distribution Curves for Shafts Are Shown)

In the long run, it will be the buying firm that pays. Assuming that the buying firm's requirements cannot be compromised, the supply manager is faced with two alternatives:

1. Negotiate with the supplier to determine whether the natural range of process capability can be narrowed economically to a point closer to the buying firm's requirements.
2. Seek another supplier whose process can meet the requirements more economically.

**Process Capability Index** Another way to express a process's capability relative to a buying firm's specific design requirement is to use a *process capability index (Cp)*. This index is defined as

$$Cp = \frac{\text{Buying firm's absolute design tolerance}}{\text{Natural capability range of the process}^{28}}$$

A *Cp* value of 1 indicates that the capability range of the process matches *exactly* the quality range required by the buying firm. From a practical point of view, this is a very marginal fit for the buying firm. A value of more than 1 reveals excess process quality capability, while a value of less than 1 indicates insufficient process capability. Consider the examples in Figure 7.4:

$$Cp(\text{a}) = \frac{1.005 - 0.995}{1.004 - 0.996} = \frac{0.01}{0.008} = 1.25$$

$$Cp(\text{b}) = \frac{1.003 - 0.997}{1.004 - 0.996} = \frac{0.006}{0.008} = 0.75$$

In case (a), the *Cp* = 1.25, indicating that the quality capability of the process, if it stays centered and stable, exceeds the buying firm's requirement. In case (b), the *Cp* = 0.75, showing clearly that the process is not capable of satisfying the buying firm's quality requirement. In case (a), the process is "capable," whereas in case (b), the process is "incapable."

The preceding discussion makes the important assumptions that the manufacturer's process is stable and that the average can be adjusted to line up with the center point (the target value) of the buying firm's specification (as is the case in Figure 7.4). In some operating situations this is not possible. Suppose, in the situation discussed in Figure 7.4*a*, that after a great deal of experimentation, the best process average the supplier was able to achieve was 0.999 inch. This condition is depicted in Figure 7.5. One can see by inspecting the sketch that there is adequate excess quality capability at the upper end of the scale (1.005 − 1.003) but that at the lower end there is no excess (0.995 − 0.995). Any movement of the process distribution to the left will produce out-of-specification shafts.

Thus, we see that one additional factor is important in making a process capability analysis: the location of the process average relative to the buying firm's target specification value. That means that the previously calculated capability index (*Cp*) must be adjusted for the off-center location of the process average.

---

[28]In practice, the natural capability range of the process frequently is *estimated* by taking the mean output quality value ±3 standard deviations of the output values. In the case of normally distributed output values, this means that the process capability range includes 99.7 percent of the expected population values. In other words, there are 3 chances in 1,000 that the process output will fall outside the estimated process capability range. Some firms with high precision requirements estimate the natural capability range of a process by using the mean output value ±4, ±5, or ±6 standard deviations.

**Figure 7.5** | An Illustrative Comparison of Quality Requirements with Process Capability When the Process Mean Is Not Centered

The adjusted $Cp$ is called the *process capability/location index (Cpk)*. It can be calculated as follows:

$$Cpk = Cp(1 - k)$$

$$\text{where } k = \frac{\text{Buying firm's target value } - \text{ process mean}}{\text{Buying firm's absolute design tolerance divided by 2}}$$

For the situation in Figure 7.5, the location index is

$$k = \frac{1.000 - 0.999}{(1.005 - 0.995)/2} = \frac{0.001}{0.005} = 0.2$$

$$Cpk = 1.25(1 - 0.2) = 1.25 \times 0.8 = 1.0$$

The *Cpk* value is interpreted just like the *Cp* value: A value less than 1 indicates an incapable process, and a value greater than 1 indicates a capable process. In this case the fit is marginal because of the absence of any leeway on the lower end of the distribution.

## Statistical Process Control

The preceding discussion about the natural process capability range was based on the premise that the supplier could keep the process operating in a stable manner, that is, "in control."

At this point in the discussion, it is necessary to point out that in addition to the random variations that occur naturally in any process, during the course of operation some *nonrandom* variations caused by external factors also occur. At times a machine goes out of adjustment, cutting tools become dull, the hardness or workability of the material varies, human errors become excessive, and so on. When these things happen, they usually take the process out of control. What really happens is that *the quality capability of the process changes because of these unplanned events*. The process output distribution changes. It may spread out, increasing the range; it may shift up or down, altering the mean and the extreme values; or a combination of these things may occur. The end result is that the characteristics of the distribution no longer can be predicted; statistically, *the process is out of control*.

The statistical process control technique has the ability to detect these process shifts caused by outside forces, or assignable causes, as they occur. When the changes are detected, the process is stopped and an investigation is initiated to find the cause of the problem. An operator who is familiar with the process and the equipment typically can locate the problem fairly quickly. This technique thus enables the operator to detect the problem, make the necessary corrections, and continue operation, with the production of few, if any, defective products.

After a supply manager locates a potential supplier whose process capability matches his or her needs, as discussed in the previous section, the final step for a supply manager is to persuade the supplier to use an SPC system that will keep the process in control and ensure the consistency of the process's output quality.

The following paragraphs discuss the basics of SPC theory and application.

**Control Charts**   Several different types of control charts are used for different kinds of applications. The most common, however, are the $\bar{X}$ and $R$ control charts for variables. These typically are applied in situations in which the quality variable to be controlled is a dimension, a weight, or another measurable characteristic. Operationally, the two charts are used together. The $\bar{X}$ chart monitors the absolute value, or the location, of the process average, and the $R$ chart monitors the spread (range) of the output distribution, that is, the piece-to-piece variability.

Figure 7.6 illustrates an $\bar{X}$ chart and an $R$ chart in simplified form. Before the charts are constructed for operating use, *the process must be studied carefully to determine that it is in fact stable*—that it is in statistical control. This usually is done by quality assurance and maintenance specialists and often is a time-consuming experimental task. Once the process has been stabilized—that is, its operation is influenced only by natural, random variations—its natural capability range can be determined and process control limits can be calculated.

*At this point, the operating procedures are established.* Usually the operator will inspect a small sample of output units every 15 minutes or so. Sample size typically runs between 3 and 5 units. The idea is to sample sequentially produced units in a manner that tends to minimize the quality variation within a specific sample subgroup and maximize variation between the periodic sample subgroups.

*The measurements are recorded as they are taken* in the upper portion of the table shown below the $R$ chart. (For illustrative purposes, hypothetical shaft dimension data from the example in Figure 7.6 are included in the first three subgroup columns.) The measurements for the *subgroup sample* are then summed and the average, $\bar{X}$, is computed. The range for the subgroup also is determined and entered in the table. After 20 to 25 subgroups have been inspected, enough data are available to provide good estimates of the process average and spread. At this point, an average of the subgroup $\bar{X}$ values is computed as $\bar{\bar{X}}$ (the average of the averages), and an average of the subgroup $R$ values is computed *as $\bar{R}$*. The $\bar{\bar{X}}$ value represents the mean value of the average shaft diameter sizes determined in each subgroup; *this is the value used as the process average on the $\bar{X}$ chart.* The $\bar{R}$ value represents the mean value of the range of the shaft diameter sizes found in each subgroup; *this is the value used as the average range on the R chart.*

In most applications, $\bar{X}$ *control chart limits are set at* $\bar{\bar{X}} \pm 3$ standard deviations of the $\bar{X}$ values (3 sigma limits). The reader should note that the frequency distributions used in constructing control charts are distributions of averages, not distributions of the individually measured values produced by the process. This fact ensures the existence of a normal distribution of control chart values when the process is in control.[29] Thus, the 6 sigma range of the chart encompasses 99.7 percent of the $\bar{X}$ values that will result from the process operation as long as only natural random process variations are occurring.

---

[29]The central limit theorem states that the *means of small samples* tend to be normally distributed regardless of the type of distribution from which the individual sample values are taken.

**Figure 7.6** I An Illustration of $\bar{X}$ and $R$ Charts in Simplified Form

The 3 sigma control chart limits can be determined by calculating the standard deviation of the $\bar{X}$ values, multiplying by 3, and subtracting and adding to $\bar{\bar{X}}$. In practice, however, this calculation has been simplified by the construction of a table of constant factors (for various sample sizes) that can be applied to $\bar{R}$ (and $\bar{\bar{X}}$) to obtain the control limit values directly. This can be done quickly and easily.

The same rationale and procedure apply to the construction of $R$ chart control limits. In this case, however, it should be noted that only the upper control limit is of practical significance in operation.

After the control charts are constructed, *as the operation continues, data are plotted and the charts are interpreted.* As shown in Figure 7.6, the operator plots both the $\bar{X}$ value and the $R$ value on their respective charts after his or her inspection and computations for each subgroup sample.

In the majority of cases, interpretation of the charts is a relatively simple matter. Any points falling outside the control limits usually indicate the existence of nonrandom variation. (If the process were actually in control, this would happen only 3 times in every 1,000 subgroup inspections.) The appearance of other nonrandom patterns also may be observed. For example, an unusually large number of points in sequence on the same side of the average line may indicate a shift in the process average or an expansion of the spread. As a rule of thumb, a run of seven points usually indicates an out-of-control situation. Clear-cut trends of points in one direction may indicate a tool wear or adjustment problem. As was noted previously, when the operator suspects an out-of-control situation, he or she stops the process and investigates the potential problem.

# Quality Movement Support

Support for the quality movement over the last several decades has come from three sources: organizations, standards, and awards. Organizations such as the American Society for Quality (ASQ) have helped support the quality management movement through seminars, local meetings, conferences, certifications, and research. Standards institutions such as the International Organization for Standardization, the American National Standards Institute (ANSI), and the British Standards Institute (BSI) have helped support the quality management movement through the development of common standards and registration bodies for certifying the quality of company systems. Awards such as the Deming Prize, the Malcolm Baldrige National Quality Awards, and the European Quality Awards all support the quality management movement through documentation and recognition of companies that achieve world-class status. These awards serve to motivate others and disseminate the best practices of companies to society.

## Organizations

Worldwide, there are many organizations that support quality initiatives and education. In Europe, the European Organization for Quality and the European Foundation for Quality Management (EFQM) are two excellent sources. The main quality-focused organization in the United States is the American Society of Quality (ASQ), formerly called ASQC, the American Society for Quality Control.

Most supply professionals receive quality training, education, and networking through a variety of sources. In the United States, most supply management professionals who receive quality training or education do so through the Institute for Supply Management[30] which integrates almost everything discussed in this chapter into its teachings. The Educational Society for Resource Management, more commonly referred to as APICS,[31] is another source.

## Standards

The standards in quality management referred to in this section are process-based standards or norms that do not deal with the technical specifications of products and materials but with how they are made. Globally, there are quite a few standards-developing institutes and organizations. The International Organization for Standardization's ISO 9000 system is currently the most dominant standards system for quality control.[32]

---

[30]Formerly the National Association of Purchasing Management. www.ism.ws, February 2008.

[31]APICS stood for the American Production and Inventory Control Society. After the society changed its name, it decided to continue using its well-known acronym APICS.

[32]Steven Casper and Bob Hancke, *Global Quality Norms within National Production Regimes: ISO 9000 Standards in French and German Car Industries, Organization Studies* (Berlin: Walter De Gruyter and Company, 1999).

**International Organization for Standardization**    The International Organization for Standardization (ISO), headquartered in Geneva, Switzerland, is an international body composed of members who represent standards organizations.[33] The objective of the ISO is to promote the development of standards, testing, and certification to encourage the international trade of goods and services.[34] The global emphasis on economic competitiveness, the unification of the European market, and a broad array of different quality standards among countries led to concentrated ISO work in the quality area over the last 20 years. The main product of this work was the issuance of the ISO 9000 series of *quality system* standards in 1987, which are revised periodically to maintain their relevancy. The ISO 14000 series addresses aspects of environmental management. The intent is to provide a framework for a holistic strategic approach to an organization's environmental policy, plans, and actions.[35]

A firm that adopts one or more of the standards is required to document what its quality management procedures are for each element in the standards. The firm then must be able to prove to an ISO auditor that the procedures are followed in practice. Recall the underlying eight principles of the ISO 9000:2000s series presented earlier in this chapter in the section on the Quality Management System. ISO 9001:2000 requires that you plan and manage the processes necessary for the continual improvement of your quality management system. Continual improvement is defined by the International Organization for Standardization as "a process of increasing the effectiveness of your organization to fulfill your quality policy and your quality objectives." ISO 9004:2000 goes beyond ISO 9001:2000 to deal with improving the efficiency of your operation. ISO 9001:2000's focus on continual improvement of the quality management system is a major departure from the past reputation of the ISO 9000 series, about which a commonly heard joke was "As long as you document it and make it as your documentation says you make it, you can make cement life preservers and still get ISO 9000 certified!" The new standards do not allow companies to pass registration without showing tangible efforts to improve products. As with the ISO 9000 certifications, there is a series of ISO 14000 standards aimed at managing the business environment.

**Additional ISO Standards**    The International Organization for Standardization has created thousands of standards during its existence. Among some of the topic-specific standards that may be applicable to supply management are ISO 10006 for project management, ISO 10007 for configuration management, ISO 10012 for measurement systems, ISO 10013 for quality documentation, ISO/TR 10014 for managing the economics of quality, ISO 10015 for training, ISO/TS 16949 for automotive suppliers, and ISO 19011 for auditing. A large number of sources are available to learn more about the ISO's many standards. Probably the best starting point is the ISO website at www.iso.org.

**Impact on Supply Managers**    Since their inception in 1987, the ISO 9000 standards have had implications for supply professionals, but the revisions to ISO 9000:2000 have an even greater focus on supply management.

■    The new standards promote the adoption of a process approach as opposed to the procedural approach described in the 1994 versions. This is important to supply management since processes are what span supply chain boundaries and are as a result a responsibility of supply professionals.

■    Changes also have occurred in terminology. The most important changes concern the use of the term "organization" instead of "supplier" and the use of the term "supplier" instead of "subcontractor."

[33]The American National Standards Institute (ANSI) is the U.S. member of the International Organization for Standardization.

[34]Greg Hutchins, *ISO 9000* (ESSEX Junction, VT: Oliver Wicht Publications, 1993), p. 3.

[35]www.iso.org, website for the ISO, February 2008.

According to ISO, these changes were made in response to the need to be more consistent and friendly with the normal use and meaning of the words.

■  The number of requirements for documented procedures has been reduced in ISO 9001:2000, and the emphasis is on the organization demonstrating effective operation. This reduces the barriers to suppliers in achieving ISO 9000 registration and brings greater relevancy to the outcomes.

■  The standards have become a competitive weapon in global business. Consequently, if a firm wants to do business in the global marketplace, the chances are good that it will have to be ISO 9000:2000 registered.

■  While the standards do not require that a registered firm's suppliers also be registered, the revisions make it clear that registration of supply chain members is preferable.

■  The implications of the "continual improvement" emphasis in the standards includes suppliers, and this places greater importance on supply management's role in meeting the ISO 9000:2000 series challenge whether suppliers are registered or not.

## Awards

**Malcolm Baldrige Award**   In 1987, President Ronald Reagan signed into law the Malcolm Baldrige National Quality Act. The act called for the establishment of a national quality award that would provide a comprehensive framework of guidelines that an organization could use to evaluate its quality program and quality improvement efforts. Additionally, the award was designed to provide recognition for U.S. organizations that had demonstrated excellence in the attainment and management of quality. Each year firms compete for this recognition in three categories in each of which up to two firms per year can be recognized:

1.  Large manufacturing companies or subsidiaries
2.  Large service companies
3.  Small manufacturing or service companies

On balance, the program has been extremely popular and certainly has elevated the awareness and interest of American businesspeople in the importance of quality. Most managers recognize that quality improvement is a developmental process that takes time and that there are seldom any quick fixes. But clearly, the Baldrige Award format provides a helpful road map. Part of the significance of the award has been in the way companies have used it to audit themselves to see where they stand and target the weak areas uncovered.[36] Additionally, previous award winners are required to share their success stories with other interested firms.

**European Quality Award**   Following the trend of establishing geopolitically driven awards, the European Foundation for Quality Management (EFQM) in partnership with the European Commission and the European Organization for Quality announced the creation of the European Quality Award in 1991.[37] The award consists of two parts: the European Quality Prize and the European Quality Award. The prize is given to companies that demonstrate excellence in quality management practice by meeting the award criteria. The award goes to the most successful applicant. The award is very similar to the Malcolm Baldrige Award, with the exception of results criteria that address people satisfaction and impact on society.

---

[36]Robert E. Cole, "Learning from the Quality Movement," Harvard Business Publishing, Boston MA, 1998, p. 67.

[37]James R. Evans and William M. Lindsay, *The Management and Control of Quality* (Southwestern College Publishing, 1999), pp. 143–44.

**Deming Prize** In appreciation for Dr. W. Edwards Deming's contributions to Japanese industry, in 1951 the Japanese technical community established this prestigious award that bears Deming's name. The Deming Prize is designed to recognize both individual and organizational achievements in the field of quality, with a unique emphasis on the use of statistical techniques. Any firm that meets the requirements is eligible to receive the award, including individuals and firms outside Japan. Past recipient companies include Nissan, Toyota, Hitachi, Nippon Steel, and Florida Power and Light.[38]

# Supply Management Issues

Supply managers who were trying to make their efforts more proactive came to realize in the late 1990s that working with suppliers to improve their quality management systems yielded greater benefits than did trying to control an existing system fraught with waste. Collaborative quality management enables supply chains to gain competitive advantage over other chains. Supply management is central to that collaboration.

Generally speaking, four factors determine the long-run quality level of a firm's purchased materials:

1. Creation of complete and appropriate specifications for quality requirements.
2. Selection of suppliers that have the technical and production capabilities to do the desired quality/cost job.
3. Development of a realistic understanding with suppliers of quality requirements and creation of the motivation to perform accordingly.
4. Monitoring of suppliers' quality/cost performance and the exercise of appropriate control.

Supply management is directly responsible for factors 2 and 3, and it should play a strong cooperative role in factors 1 and 4.

## Requirements Development

Quality often is perceived in as many ways as there are people pondering its meaning. Quality can be defined in three primary ways:

1. In absolute terms
2. Relative to a perceived need
3. As conformance with stated requirements

In *absolute terms,* quality is a function of excellence, intrinsic value, or grade, as determined over time by society generally or by designated bodies in specialized fields. Hence, most people consider gold a high-quality precious metal. In a more utilitarian sense, "prime" beef generally is considered to be among the highest-quality meats in the meat market. While few absolutes endure the test of the ages, for a particular period in a specific culture, most people hold absolute views about the quality of many things.

In business and industrial activities, generally quality is defined first in terms of its *relationship to a need* or a function. In these cases the important thing is not the absolute quality of an item but the suitability of that item in satisfying the particular need at hand. Thus, design engineers, users, and supply managers attempt to develop a material specification in which the quality characteristics of the specified material match closely the quality characteristics needed to fulfill the functional requirements of the job satisfactorily. Consequently, in the *development* of product or material specifications, quality is defined relative to the need.

---

[38]Logothetis, *Managing for Total Quality,* p. 28.

Once the specifications have been finalized, the specific requirements have been set for those who subsequently work with the specifications. For these people, especially supply management personnel and suppliers, quality is defined very simply as *conformance with the stated requirements.* A supply manager's responsibility and a supplier's job is to deliver material whose quality conforms satisfactorily to specification requirements.

The last two definitions are the ones with which supply managers regularly contend. As supply management works with users and suppliers in the development of material specifications, it is concerned with quality relative to a functional need. In dealing with suppliers' output quality levels, supply management is concerned with quality in the sense of its conformance to requirements.

A sound material specification represents a blend of four different considerations: (1) design requirements, (2) production factors, (3) commercial supply management considerations, and frequently, (4) marketing factors. When dealing with the commercial considerations, supply management personnel should make the following investigations with respect to quality:

- Study the quality requirements.
- Ensure that quality requirements are stated completely and unambiguously in the specifications.
- Investigate their reasonableness relative to cost.
- Ensure that specifications are written in a manner that permits competition among potential suppliers.
- Determine whether existing suppliers can build the desired quality into the material.
- Ensure the feasibility of the inspections and tests required to assure quality.

For some materials and components, such investigations are relatively simple. For others, they are extremely complex, involving highly technical considerations. Some firms, for example, include "reliability or quality engineers" on the supply management staff to assist with analysis of the more complex problems. When technical quality problems arise, a reliability engineer and a supply manager jointly review the specifications to determine the appropriateness of the quality requirements. Working in a coordinating capacity, they make their recommendations to the design engineer, directing to his or her attention the potential quality problems arising from commercial considerations.

As was discussed earlier, many firms utilize a cross-functional product development team in the overall design process. This approach is ideal for integrating the views of supply management, as well as those of the other appropriate functions, in the process of specifications development. In some cases it is desirable to involve appropriate designers or application engineers from the supplier's organization in the specifications development process before the specs are finalized. Early cooperative involvement of these individuals frequently provides technical and manufacturing input from the supplier's perspective that is useful in reducing costs or avoiding subsequent processing and quality problems in the supplier's operation. This type of cooperative activity is becoming more common in progressive buying organizations. Clearly, supply management is responsible for planning and coordinating this type of supplier involvement.

## Supplier Quality Analysis

Most firms can minimize their material quality problems by selecting competent and cooperative suppliers in the first place. The following paragraphs discuss briefly some of the methods used to achieve this objective.

**Product Testing**   A practical approach used in determining potential suppliers' quality capabilities is to test their products before purchasing them. The quality of most purchased materials can be determined with *engineering tests* or *use tests.* Usually those tests can be conducted by the buying firm; when this is not practical, commercial testing agencies can be used.

The object of product testing is twofold: (1) to determine that a potential supplier's quality level is commensurate with the buying firm's quality needs and (2) where feasible, to compare the quality levels of several different suppliers. This permits the development of a list of qualified suppliers that the supply manager can compare on the basis of the quality/cost relationship.

Supply managers frequently utilize their own operating departments for the performance of use tests. It is not uncommon, for example, for a manager to test several brands of tires on his or her firm's vehicles during the course of regular operations. Although feasible, use testing of most *production* parts and components is more difficult because tests often cannot be conducted until the buying firm's finished product has been placed in service. In many cases, though, the buying firm's sales force is able to obtain feedback data on operating performance from customers. In those cases, various kinds of use tests can be conducted to compare the performance of different suppliers' components. Regardless of the method used, supply management usually needs the cooperation of other departments in setting up and conducting the tests. Consequently, the supply manager typically functions as an organizer and an administrator in coordinating the efforts of others.

A word of caution is appropriate, however, for practitioners who are not skilled in experimental testing. Test results for the products being compared must be obtained through well-designed experiments that permit *valid* comparisons. For example, mileage data on two sets of tires, each taken from a different truck, are not comparable if the two trucks were operated under significantly different conditions. The variables in the testing situation must be controlled to an extent where the results are truly comparable. A "comparison of apples with oranges" is of little value in the decision-making process.

Unfortunately, in conducting use tests without the benefit of controlled laboratory conditions, it may be difficult to generate truly comparable test data. Consequently, experience and judgment play an important role in determining the extent to which test results are comparable and hence useful. At times, interpretation of test data also may require a basic knowledge of statistical inference. While many supply managers have this background, it is essential to recognize when the help of an experienced statistician is required.

In firms that have testing laboratories for their engineering and research work, the supply management department has an additional resource to support its quality management activity. Such laboratories can take much of the experimental and interpretive burden off supply management's shoulders. In addition, they usually are equipped to conduct more precise and sophisticated tests with greater speed and ease than use testing allows. An example will illustrate the point. One of IBM's computer-manufacturing plants has an electronic testing laboratory that is used primarily for research and development work. The laboratory, however, also serves the supply management department. Before new electronic components are purchased for assembly into IBM products, a sample of each new component is subjected to rigorous tests in that laboratory to determine whether its performance characteristics meet the company's quality specifications. Firms without testing laboratories frequently use one of the many commercial testing laboratories throughout the country. A directory of those laboratories, indicating their locations and types of services, is published annually by the U.S. Department of Commerce.

First article inspection involves requiring the first part to be shipped and inspected by the buying plant. If the part passes, full production is authorized. The problem lies in determining whether the trial part is made by the same methods and procedures as the actual production run. The question becomes whether the trial part is "handmade" by special craftsmen and not made on production machines by ordinary workers. If this is the case, the production parts that follow may not meet the expectations of the buying firm.

**Proposal Analysis** A second point at which supply management can assess a potential supplier's quality capabilities is in the proposal analysis. Firms indicate in their proposals, either directly or indirectly, how they intend to comply with the quality requirements of the purchase. A supply manager must be especially alert in detecting areas of misinterpretation or areas of possible overemphasis by the prospective supplier that could result in excessive costs. In purchases in which quality requirements are critical, the trend today is to *require* potential suppliers to state *explicitly* how they plan to achieve the specified quality level with consistency.

For potential suppliers whose written proposals survive the supply manager's analysis, the next step in evaluating quality capabilities is an on-site capability survey. Because of the time and expense involved, most companies conduct this survey only for their more important purchases and for government contracts that require it. In inspecting a prospective supplier's facilities and records and in talking with management and operating personnel, the buying firm's investigating team attempts to answer questions such as these:

- What is the firm's basic policy with respect to product quality and quality control?
- What is the general attitude of operators and supervisors toward quality? Does the firm use a specific quality program that focuses attention on the attitudes and responsibilities assumed by each individual for high-quality work?[39]
- Does the prospective supplier use statistical methods to reduce process variation?
- What is the prospective supplier's engineering/production experience and ability with respect to this specific type of work?
- Is the production equipment capable of consistently producing the quality of work required?
- Exactly how is the firm organized to control quality, and to what extent does quality receive management support?
- What specific quality measurement techniques and test equipment does the prospective supplier employ? Is statistical process control utilized effectively?
- Is quality training continuous? Is the quality environment a way of life?

These questions make it clear that a supply manager alone usually cannot conduct an effective survey; the endeavor must be a *team effort.* Specialists from design and process engineering, quality assurance, and sometimes maintenance are needed to provide a professional interpretation of the facts the survey uncovers. The supply manager's major responsibility in this endeavor is to organize and coordinate the efforts of those specialists and make a composite evaluation of the potential supplier, considering the findings of all team members.

## Inspection Dependence

Even with the continuing improvement of quality systems to prevent defects, most firms maintain a traditional inspection department. In addition, some selected operations in both the buying firm's and the supplying firm's plants still may require either 100 percent or sampling inspection. This is particularly true after certain types of assembly or final assembly operations. In any case, to some extent inspection

---

[39]For two classic discussions about the individual's responsibility for quality, see William Ouchi, "The Q-C Circle," in *Theory Z.* (Reading, MA: Addison-Wesley, 1981), pp. 261–68, and Robert M. Smith, "Zero-Defects and You," *Management Services,* January–February 1966, pp. 35–38.

activities are still part of a supply manager's world, and for this reason, the topic is discussed briefly in the next few paragraphs.

**Receiving and Inspection Procedure**    If a shipment is coming from a certified or a JIT supplier, it may go directly to the point of use, bypassing the traditional receiving and inspection operations. In a majority of cases, however, when a purchase order is issued, the receiving and inspection departments both receive electronic or paper copies of the order that specify the inspection the material is to receive. When a shipment arrives, receiving personnel check the material against the supplier's packing slip and against the purchase order to ensure that the firm has received the material ordered. This is the basis for subsequent invoice/payment approvals. The receiving clerk then visually inspects the material (looking for shipping damage and so on) to determine its general condition. Finally, a receiving report is prepared on which the results of the investigation are noted. In some cases, no further inspection is required. In the case of more complex materials, a copy of the receiving report is forwarded to the inspection department, advising it that the material on a particular order has been placed in the "pending inspection" area and is ready for technical inspection.

The inspection department performs the specified technical inspection on a sample or on the entire lot as appropriate and prepares an inspection report that indicates the results of the inspection. If the material fails to meet specifications, a more detailed report usually is completed that describes the reasons for rejection. In some cases, rejected material is clearly useless to the buying firm, and the supply management department immediately arranges with the supplier for its disposition. In other situations, the most desirable course of action is less clear-cut. The buying firm often has three alternative courses of action:

1. Return the material to the supplier.
2. Keep some of the more acceptable material and return the rest.
3. Keep all the material and rework it to the point where it is acceptable. (From a strategic point of view, this is not a good alternative. It says to the supplier that it is permissible to ship off-spec material and can be interpreted as an invitation to do that again.)

Cases involving rework may be sent to a materials review board for study and decision. A typical board is composed primarily of personnel from production, production control, quality, and supply management. After the board reaches its decision, the appropriate papers are sent to the supply manager, who concludes final cost negotiations with the supplier. Rework costs should be charged back to the supplier.

**Technical Inspection**    Before a contract or a purchase order is issued, quality control personnel, in conjunction with engineering and supply management, should decide what type of inspection the incoming material requires to ensure that it meets specification requirements. If the supplier is certified, perhaps no inspection will be required. If the supplier is using statistical process control in the item's production, it may be sufficient simply to review the supplier's control charts for selected processing operations to determine whether further inspection is required. In other cases sampling inspection may be desirable,[40] and

---

[40]Industry uses a wide variety of statistical sampling plans. Two of the more commonly used sources are Harold F. Dodge and Harry G. Romig, *Sampling Inspection Tables-Single and Double Sampling* (New York: John Wiley & Sons), 1959 and H. A. Freeman, Milton Friedman, and Frederick Mosteller, and Wallis, *Sampling Inspection* (New York: McGraw-Hill), 1948. The Dodge and Romig tables are designed specifically to minimize total sampling. *Sampling Inspection* contains plans which are particularly useful in inspecting material coming from statistically controlled production processes. These plans tend to minimize the "consumer's risk" of accepting off-spec material.

in still other situations 100 percent inspection may be required.[41] The most common sampling methods are single, double, and sequential. In all cases, quality personnel should prepare a technical inspection plan. Key information from the plan should then be communicated to the supplier in the purchase order or a related contractual document. In this way, the appropriate people in both organizations are fully aware of the procedures to be followed and can work together toward that end.

**Defect Detection System**    To control the quality of production materials entering a manufacturing or assembly operation, companies historically have utilized defect detection systems that employ inspection. That is, after a batch of items has been produced at one step in the process, the items are inspected to identify the ones that do not meet the design specification. Those which do not are reworked or scrapped, and the good items pass on to the next processing operation. Frequently, though not always, a similar inspection is conducted after this operation, and so on through the entire manufacturing process until a finished product is produced.

Three basic problems are inherent in the defect detection type of operation. First, there tends to be some duplication of inspection activity both within the supplier's manufacturing operation and between the buying firm's and the supplier's operations. Second, a very large number of items are inspected. Third *and most important,* defective items are found only after they are finished (or semifinished)—after the mistakes have been made and after substantial processing costs have been incurred.

Defect detection systems are inefficient and expensive. Because they require time and resources to execute, there is a tendency to cut back on inspection and reduce the standards, resulting in the acceptance of some off-spec items. Cutbacks usually occur in the interest of cost control and maintenance of production schedules. The bottom line is that in many firms that use this system, quality levels tend to be inconsistent and perhaps lower than originally planned.

In Deming's 14 points discussed earlier in this chapter, one of the points is to stop dependending on inspection. To alleviate the problems inherent in most defect detection systems, Deming proposed the use of a *defect prevention system.* The idea here is to identify operating (process) problems that may produce defective items, preferably before any defective products are produced. This approach monitors the output of a process as it occurs and identifies unacceptable process changes soon after they occur. When an unsatisfactory situation is identified, the process is stopped and the operating cause (tool wear, machine adjustment, operator error, etc.) is determined. Appropriate corrective action on the operating system is taken to prevent the production of more defectives. The specific technique Deming suggested to use to detect such process changes was *SPC.* A defect prevention system utilizing SPC is shown in simplified graphic form in Figure 7.7.[42]

Another approach to preventing defects and reducing the need for inspection in a repetitive manufacturing environment is to implement jidohka, which was championed by Ohno while he was with Toyota. Jidohka uses an automatic mechanism to stop the entire production system whenever a defective part is found along the process line. Appropriate adjustments then take place so that major problems are prevented from arising in the future. This concept, apart from adhering to the principle of prevention rather than cure, can save substantially on work allocation times, since the worker needs to attend to the machine only when it stops because of a problem. Jidohka forces resolution of the cause of a problem at the source when it

---

[41]In many types of inspection activities involving human operation or judgment, experience indicates that 100 percent inspection may detect only 80 to 95 percent of the defects present. Consequently, when quality is extremely critical, a second inspection operation may be required.

[42]Figure 7.7 was developed from material in Gordon K. Constable, "Statistical Process Control and Purchasing," *Freedom of Choice*, National Association of Purchasing Management, Tempe, AZ, 1987, p. 15.

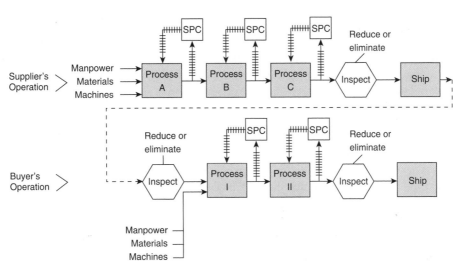

**Figure 7.7 |** Defect Prevention Concept

happens and is still traceable. The fact that jidohka can shut down a production line highlights the importance of resolving the cause of the discrepancy, whereas defects discovered through traditional inspection frequently are not traced to the source. As a result, traditional inspection procedures rarely reduce the need for the same inspection in the future.

Jidohka usually is coupled with the use of poka-yoke, which could be called another form of inspection; however, most poka-yoke methods do not delay the product flow in the way that traditional inspection does since poka-yoke builds the inspection into the process. In the early 1960s Shingo developed the concept of poka-yoke (or defect = 0), meaning mistake-proofing: Source inspection is employed actively to identify process errors before they become defects; when an identification takes place, the process is stopped until the cause is determined and eliminated. Monitoring potential error sources takes place at every stage of the process so that errors that lead to defects are detected as soon as possible and corrected at the source rather than at a later stage.

Needless to say, Ohno's and Shingo's techniques can be effective only if a certain (high) level of quality already has been built into the process as early as possible. This can be achieved through the use of appropriate statistical tools by the workers, who should be allowed to take the initiative to eliminate bottlenecks and interruptions, and also through cooperation with the suppliers of the process components. Otherwise, jidohka or poka-yoke will cause a prohibitively large number of stoppages, and cost-efficient production will never materialize.[43]

**Critique** In summary, it is important that a buying organization develop some type of system that monitors a supplier's quality performance. Historically, defect detection systems have been used widely, but they are expensive and the results frequently are not as effective as desired. In his classic book *Quality Is Free*, Philip Crosby summarizes the attitudes in American industry in the following statement:

> A prudent company makes certain that its products and services are delivered to the customer by a management system that does not condone rework, repair, waste, or nonconformance of any sort. These are expensive

[43]Logothetis, *Managing for Total Quality,* pp. 97–98. A new technology to automatically adjust machines, i.e., self-correcting developing errors is ADRC or Active Disturbance-Rejection Control currently being developed by engineering Prof. Zhiqiang Gao at Cleveland State University, Cleveland, OH. *The Plain Dealer*, Sept. 2, 2008. pp. c1, c3 fbentayou@plaind.com.

problems. They must not only be detected and resolved at the earliest moment, they must be prevented from occurring at all.[44]

Once a defect prevention system is in place, the benefits of improved quality control capability and reduced costs of quality flow to both the buying firm and the supplying firm. Properly implemented, it should be a win-win situation that tends to improve cooperation and set the stage for a continuing relationship that is mutually beneficial.

## Supplier Development

A *cooperatively* developed defect prevention system, including appropriate training of suppliers' personnel by the buying firm, creates a situation that should enhance a supplier's motivation to perform satisfactorily for the buying firm. The anticipated prospect of follow-on business in a longer-term continuing collaborative relationship normally provides a significant incentive for the supplier to perform well in the quality area. We mention supplier development here to stress its importance and refer the reader to Chapter 11 for further discussion of supplier development.

## Certification

The concept of supplier certification has been used by a number of progressive firms for years. However, the increased emphasis on quality in the last two decades has sharpened the focus on the real values of a certification program. The certification concept recognizes the fact that a supplying firm's and a buying firm's quality systems are two parts of a larger quality system and that through integration of the two the total costs associated with quality can be reduced.

Certification agreements take many forms, ranging from a simple supplier's guarantee of quality to a formally negotiated document that specifies the responsibilities of both parties for specifications, process design inspection procedures, SPC applications and training, reporting and correction procedures, and so forth. Although certification programs vary widely from firm to firm, the general approach to supplier certification involves three steps:

1. Qualification
2. Education
3. The certification performance process

**Qualification**   Because of the mutual trust and dependence in a certification relationship, a supplier is not considered for certification until the buying organization has had a fairly lengthy positive experience with that firm. In addition to quality and reliability performance, the supply manager again verifies the broader supplier characteristics that are important to the relationship: management philosophy, financial stability, R&D capability, shop organization and management, manufacturing support capabilities, including supply management, and so on.

The technical qualification requirements for certification typically are rigorous. They start with product and process design, tightened process capability studies, and a stringent quality capability survey to ensure mutual agreement on the quality system the supplier will employ. Applications for the potential

---

[44]Philip B. Crosby, *Quality Is Free* (New York: Mentor New American Library, 1979), p. 106.

design of experiments and statistical process control are identified, and the procedures are detailed. At this point in the process, the supply manager's quality personnel work with their counterparts in the supplier's organization to fine-tune the system and develop the procedures that will be used in the final inspection.

**Education**   Two types of supplier education typically are required. The first deals with the buying organization's structure, people, and mode of operation and the resulting expectations for a certified supplier's performance. The second focuses on specific quality concepts and techniques that may be new to the supplier but that are needed for successful operation, such as various applications of SPC, unique inspection measurement techniques, and the philosophy of Six Sigma or TQM.

The extent to which education is required obviously varies from supplier to supplier. The important point is that the buying firm must assume responsibility for ensuring that the education function is accomplished. In some cases, this education must continue up the supply chain to the supplier's suppliers.

**The Certification Performance Process**   To use an old operations expression, this is where "the rubber meets the road." The supplier must demonstrate that it can meet the buying firm's requirements for certification.

After the manufacturing and assembly processes are stabilized and the quality assurance system is in place, the supplier's test period begins. Initially, both parties subject the supplier's output to 100 percent inspection. This facilitates the identification and correction of unanticipated problems. When the predetermined quality level has been maintained for a specified period, full inspection is replaced by sampling inspection of declining severity as quality levels are maintained. At some point in the process, the supplier provides key evidence of implementing proactive quality management methods, such as SPC control charts, to the buying firm for continued analysis. Periodically, the buying firm's quality expert visits the supplier's plant to ensure that control tests are being conducted appropriately. This process is continued for a period of perhaps six months to several years, depending on the specifics of the operation, until the predetermined quality performance requirements have been fulfilled.

Once a supplier has gained certification, the buying firm's goal is to do very little, if any, inspection of incoming materials. When possible, material is delivered directly to the point of use after the required receiving activities. Periodically, however, the buying organization checks supplier performance in one of several ways: (1) by reviewing the supplier's critical manufacturing operations through control charts and other statistical outputs, (2) by using a minimal sampling inspection program, (3) by reviewing test reports from the buying firm's laboratories, and (4) by making periodic visits to the supplier's plant.

The concept of supplier certification fits logically with supplier quality and collaborative arrangements, but there are potential problems:[45]

- Once a process has been "certified," it tends to be perceived as "unchangeable."
- The process of documentation and then certification can be long and resource-consuming so that once documentation does exist, companies don't want to commit the additional resources to improve it.
- Quite a few organizations have a team of full-time staff dedicated to maintaining certification documents and conducting internal compliance audits but have fewer or no people who focus on actually improving the processes.
- Some companies use their certification efforts to improve their processes, but this is relatively rare.

---

[45]Pande et. al., *The Six Sigma Way,* p. 63.

Despite these potential problems, firms that have used certification programs generally have experienced favorable results. Inspection costs typically are reduced, and quality levels usually remain high. Most suppliers take pride in being included on a customer's certification list. They are also aware that good performance places them in a favored position to receive additional business.

## Concluding Remarks

Quality management is a major component of supply management's supplier performance management responsibility. Quality failures lead directly to costly difficulties that reduce productivity, profit, and often market share. To preclude such losses, supply management should participate creatively in the corporate quality management program and in the firm's critical supplier quality efforts.

It is important to remember that quality assurance programs and procedures are the same whether a company is outsourcing overseas or using domestic suppliers. If your supplier is in China, it is critical to establish who monitors the quality programs and how it is verified that they are being followed.

To contribute most effectively to the organizational effort, supply management's role in the program should include (1) participation in the development of specifications, (2) participation in the selection of appropriate quality control, inspection, and test requirements, (3) active involvement in analysis and development of proactive prevention measures at the supplier's facility, (4) the selection and motivation of qualified suppliers, and (5) the subsequent monitoring and nurturing of the ongoing relationships between the buying and supplying firms.

Beth's experience in her quality walk at the beginning of this chapter stressed the importance of assessing quality management before entering into long-term contracts with suppliers. All supply managers should have at least a rudimentary understanding of quality systems, tools of quality, process capability analysis, and statistical process control (SPC) concepts. A world-class supply management firm views its quality system and the supplier's quality system as two parts of a single integrated system. The supply manager responsible for developing the relationship between the buying and selling firms is the middle person in this integrated system. He or she first must be able to cooperate with in-house quality people in designing and making operating decisions about the firm's quality system. Finally, because the supply manager is the key communication link with suppliers, he or she must be able to deal with them effectively on a wide variety of quality issues.

## Discussion Questions

1. Define quality.
2. How did the gurus of quality affect the management of supplier quality? Explain for each guru.
3. What does "elimination of waste" mean? Give a tangible example using a process that you are familiar with, such as the production process of a hamburger at the local fast-food restaurant.
4. Define the concept of total quality management.
5. What are the key elements of a TQM operation? Are the elements still relevant today?
6. Why has Six Sigma become one of the most popular approaches to the management of quality in the last decade?
7. Describe what it takes to be a "Six Sigma blackbelt" at General Electric.
8. What is the Quality Management System? How does it differ from the other quality management approaches?
9. Which quality management approach do you belief best fits the needs of today's businesses? Why?

10. Describe how the costs of quality model could be used to create support for quality initiatives and investment in a firm.
11. Discuss the role the supply management department should play in a firm's overall quality program.
12. What is the supply management department's interest in its firm's material specifications as far as quality is concerned?
13. What is a quality capability?
14. Supply managers frequently visit suppliers at their plants. Is there any reason why a supply professional might want to ask a supplier's representative to visit him or her at the supply manager's plant? Explain.
15. What is a defect detection system? Discuss.
16. What is a defect prevention system? Discuss.
17. What is statistical process control?
18. What are the ISO standards with respect to quality management?
19. What are the implications of ISO standards for supply managers?
20. Briefly discuss the concept of supplier certification. What possible dangers do you see in the use of this concept by a supply management department?
21. Outline the basic elements of a supplier certification program.
22. Discuss the Baldrige Award.
23. Discuss the Deming Prize.
24. Why should a firm try to reduce and maybe eliminate its dependence on inspection? Why is this especially critical for suppliers?
25. What do you think went wrong in the importing of toys, toothpaste, and some food items from China in 2007? What actions could have prevented those disasters?

## Internet Exercise

### ISO: Latest News

It's been around since 1987, and the ISO is still going strong. Visit the website below and read about its latest activities.
(http://www.iso.org/iso/pressrelease.htm)

1. Select an article from the list and submit a paragraph summarizing what you've learned. Be prepared to share it with your classmates.

## Suggested Reading

The American Society for Quality (ASQ) Milwaukee, WI, www.asq.org, Excellent books and Publications.

Adams, Cary W., Praveen Gupta, and Charles E. Wilson. *Six Sigma Deployment* (Woburn, MA: Butterworth-Heinemann, 2003).

Akao, Yoji. *Quality Function Deployment: Integrating Customer Requirements into Product Designs* (Florence, KY: Productivity Press, 2004).

Basu, Ron, and J. Nevan Wright. *Quality beyond Six Sigma* (Woburn, MA: Butterworth-Heinemann, 2003).

Brue, Greg. *Six Sigma for Managers* (New York: McGraw-Hill, 2002).

Cali, James F. *TQM for Purchasing Management* (New York: McGraw-Hill, 1993).

Crosby, Philip B. *Quality Is Free: The Art of Making Quality Certain* (New York: McGraw-Hill, 1979).

Deming, W. E. *Out of the Crisis* (Cambridge, MA: MIT Center for Advance Engineering Study, 1986).

Fernandez, Richard R. *Total Quality in Purchasing and Supplier Management* (Boca Raton FL: St. Lucie Press, 1995).

Garvin, David A. *Managing Quality: The Strategic and Competitive Edge* (New York, Free Press, 1988).

Greico, Peter, Jr., Michael W. Gozzo, and Jerry W. Claunch. *Supplier Certification II: A Handbook for Achieving Excellence through Continuous Improvement,* 3d ed. (Plantsville, CT: PT Publications, 1992).

Harry, Mikel, and Richard Schroeder. *Six Sigma: The Breakthrough Management Strategy: Revolutionizing the World's Top Corporations* (New York: Doubleday, 2000).

Juran, I. M. *Juran on Planning for Quality* (New York: Free Press, 1988).

Keller, Paul A. *Six Sigma Demystified* (New York: McGraw Hill, 2005).

Martin, James W. *Lean Six Sigma for Supply Chain Management: The 10-Step Solution Process* (New York: McGraw Hill, 2007).

Ruamsook, Kusumal, Dawn Russell, and Evelyn Thomchick. "U.S. Sourcing from Low-Cost Countries: A Comparative Analysis of Supplier Performance," *Journal of Supply Chain Management* 43, no. 4 (Fall 2007), pp. 16–29.

# The Procurement of Equipment

## CHAPTER OBJECTIVES

*After reading this chapter, you should be able to:*

1. Understand the differences between production buys and capital equipment buys.

2. Explain what drives the need for expenditures on capital equipment.

3. Identify various costs and factors to consider in managing an equipment buy.

4. Develop basic specifications for an equipment buy.

5. Understand the benefits of leasing versus buying equipment.

## VIGNETTE: THE IMPACT OF EQUIPMENT ACQUISITION

Keith Erickson, supply manager for Bath Straits Petroleum Company, sat in his office in Melbourne. Keith was studying a purchase requisition that his equipment buyer, Mandalay Curry, had just brought him. The requisition merely stated "buy one Tow Lift High Rise fork lift truck as per the attached specifications to be delivered by July 10, 2010." Erickson called Curry into his office and asked "is this equipment in the capital budget, what other brands are available and what payoff period is anticipated?" Erickson reminded Curry "The acquisition of equipment has an impact far beyond the dollars involved." ■

## CRITICAL THINKING QUESTIONS

1. What are some of the factors that contribute to the total cost of capital equipment?

2. Will a team buy be better than just one buyer analysis and who should be on this team?

3. Why is financial analysis so important in equipment procurement?

# The Nuances of Capital Equipment Procurement

## Nonrecurring Purchases

The purchase of a particular piece of capital equipment typically occurs no more than once every three to five years or so. For example, a supply manager recently purchased a unique high-temperature electric furnace for use in her company's research and development laboratory. Since the furnace is used only periodically for experimental work, it is very unlikely that another purchase of this kind of equipment will be made in the foreseeable future.

In contrast, a few industrial operations require the use of many identical machines in their production processes. For example, in petroleum and chemical processing plants, the product is transported by pipeline throughout most of the production operation. This requires dozens, at times hundreds, of similar pumps which vary only in size and details of construction. To keep capital expenditures at a fairly uniform level from year to year and minimize maintenance costs, pumps often are replaced on a continuing basis rather than all at once. Although relatively uncommon, this type of operating equipment purchase has some of the characteristics of conventional production purchasing.

The lead-time requirement is a unique feature of most equipment purchases. While some types of equipment are standard off-the-shelf products, many are not. Much production machinery and prime moving equipment is built, at least in part, to operate under specific conditions that are peculiar to each purchaser's operation. Consequently, manufacturing lead time for potential suppliers is usually a matter of months or perhaps years. The production of a large steam turbine generating unit, for example, may require negotiating and expediting work substantially different from that normally required in production procurement.

## Nature and Size of Expenditure

An expenditure of company funds for capital equipment is an investment. If purchased wisely and operated efficiently, equipment generates profits for its owner. Because it affects the costs of production, the selection of major capital equipment should be a matter of significant concern to top management.

The purchase of most major equipment involves the expenditure of a substantial sum of money. The purchase price for a piece of equipment, however, frequently is overshadowed by other elements of cost. Since a machine often is used for many years, the cost of operation and maintenance during its lifetime may far exceed its initial cost. For example, downtime costs easily may exceed the equipment's purchase price. An auto assembler estimates its downtime cost as $26,000 *per minute*. Hence, the *total life cost* of a machine relative to its productivity frequently is the cost factor of primary importance.[1] Although estimating the operating and maintenance costs which will be incurred in future years is not easy, such costs will be incurred and must be addressed when one is comparing the total cost of ownership of two or more items of equipment which will satisfy the firm's needs. Thus, post sale technical and the availability and cost of replacement parts may be critical supplier selection criteria.

---

[1] This type of analysis is also called life cycle costing. The term and the concept originally were developed and refined in military procurement. Subsequently, industry adopted the concept, and now it is used widely in most industries. This topic is discussed in more detail shortly. The terms "total life cost" and "life cycle cost" are virtually identical to the total cost of ownership described in Chapter 13.

The timing of many equipment purchases often presents a paradoxical situation. Typically, the general supply capabilities of equipment producers cannot be adjusted quickly to changes in demand. Thus, because most firms' equipment purchases are made infrequently and often can be postponed, producers of industrial capital goods frequently find themselves in a "feast or famine" type of business. When a potential purchaser's business is good, it needs additional production equipment as quickly as possible to satisfy customers' burgeoning demands. But because other purchasers are in the same situation, the buyer may find that equipment prices are rising in a market with short supply. Conversely, when a buyer's business is down and additional production equipment is not needed, equipment is in plentiful supply, often at reduced prices.

Finally, the installation cost may be as much as 30–50% of the total cost and involve multiple contractors for site preparation. The contract must cover all such details.

## Building the Foundation

### Identify the Need for a Procurement

At least five functional areas may identify a need for the acquisition of equipment: the using department, marketing, process engineering, supply management, and plant engineering (see Figure 8.1). The using department may desire equipment which is more productive, that is, requires less equipment or operator time (or both) per unit of throughput. Marketing may identify new products whose production processes require new equipment. Process engineering (or operations) is concerned with the equipment's ability to meet new and changing requirements. Supply management is responsible for monitoring threats and opportunities in the supply world. In the process, supply management may identify relevant new technology and new equipment. Additionally, supply management should be potential suppliers' primary point of contact. Supply management should be both a filter and a conduit for suppliers whose products may be of interest to other functions within the firm. Plant engineering may stimulate equipment procurement by identifying the potential risks of downtime if an item of equipment is not replaced.

### Project Management

If the equipment is critical on the basis of either cost or schedule, a project manager should be selected to drive the process. Ideally, that individual will champion and oversee the project to success. Good people, communication, leadership, and project management skills should be a requirement for the person who will fill this position.

### Selection of an Equipment Sourcing Team

Depending on the criticality of the procurement, the following functional areas may be represented on the team responsible for obtaining the equipment: operations, process engineering, finance, supply management, and plant engineering.

Operations is responsible for identifying the required and desired operating characteristics of the equipment. (These characteristics are described in greater detail in the next section.) Process engineering, which also is known as manufacturing engineering, is concerned with the equipment's ability to meet current and likely future needs. The process engineer must balance two frequently conflicting forces: A very specialized piece of equipment may be the most productive one but may be incapable of being adapted to possible future production needs.

**Figure 8.1 |** Capital Equipment Procurement Phase 1: Build the Foundation

Finance's involvement is based on four primary interests in equipment purchases and leases. First, this department usually administers the firm's capital budget; it therefore is concerned with the allocation of funds for the proposed purchase. If the budget contains a provision for such equipment, all is well; if it does not, the team will have to secure a budget authorization. Second, the finance department has the responsibility for deciding how to finance such purchases. Is enough cash available internally? Can a long-term loan be arranged? Will it be necessary to raise the money through a bond issue? For large purchases, the answers to these questions bear heavily on the final equipment selection decision. Third, the finance department should be involved in the economic analysis of alternative machines. Fourth, finance normally chairs the lease versus buy analysis. In some firms, the finance department conducts the original analyses; in others, the analyses are done by engineering or supply management. In any case, the finance department normally is involved in these activities in connection with its capital budgeting responsibility.

Supply management plays many roles: It is the primary point of contact with potential suppliers and a conduit for the flow of information. Supply management ensures that the statement of work or specification that is developed to describe the firm's needs is sufficiently specific to protect the firm's interests and broad enough to ensure competition, assuming that competition is appropriate. Supply management normally guides the sourcing process and leads the negotiating team, and it also is responsible for the post-award activities.

Plant engineering is concerned with both current and future issues. Immediate considerations include physical issues such as size, foundation, and power requirements. Future concerns include reliability, maintainability, service support, and the availability of replacement and spare parts.

## Build and Train the Team

The careful selection of the "right" representatives from the appropriate functional areas is an essential task. Unless the representatives have recent successful experience working as a team, an internal or external trainer should be called on to build and train the team.

# Identify Objectives and Estimate Costs

## Identifying Objectives

As is true with production requirements, some 80 percent of the costs associated with the procurement of equipment are built in during the requirements development stage! See Figure 8.2 for further explanation. Estimating the acquisition cost (purchase price, installation, spares, and training costs) and the total cost of ownership is always difficult. It is especially challenging at this early stage. However, it is strongly recommended that the team agree on both a target acquisition cost and a target total cost of ownership. Normally, the total cost of ownership is based on the present value (P.V.) of the anticipated stream of expenditures and downtime minus the P.V. of the item's estimated salvage value.

The desired operating and engineering characteristics are by far the most influential factors in selecting the supplier for a particular item of equipment. The user and appropriate engineering personnel must clearly establish the function the equipment is to perform and its design and operating capabilities. Operating characteristics include the equipment's capacity, setup and run times, product yields, operator ease of use, and adaptability to meet unforeseen requirements.

Closely related to the equipment's operating characteristics are its engineering features. *Ideally, these features will be compatible with the buying firm's existing equipment, process, and plant layout.* They also must comply with standards established by state and federal regulatory agencies such as the Occupational Safety and Health Administration (OSHA) and the Environmental Protection Agency (EPA). Some major engineering considerations are reliability (how long will it operate before requiring maintenance or replacement?), size and mounting dimensions, interface with other equipment, power and maintenance requirements, safety and OSHA requirements, and pollution and EPA requirements.

## Used Equipment

A buying firm is by no means restricted to the purchase of new capital equipment. Purchases of used machinery constitute an important percentage of total machinery sales.

**Reasons for Purchasing Used Equipment**   The firm may consider buying or leasing used equipment for several reasons. First, the cost of used machinery is substantially less than that of new equipment. Analy-

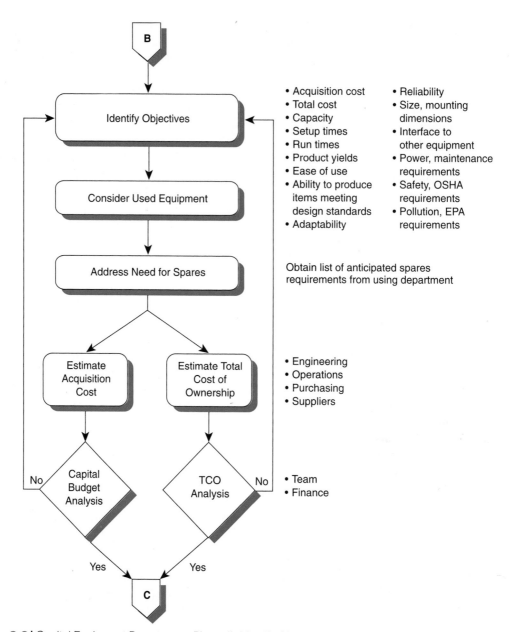

**Figure 8.2 |** Capital Equipment Procurement Phase II: Identify Objectives and Estimate Costs

sis of payback or return on investment may well reveal that a piece of used equipment is a better buy than a new machine. Even if this is not the case, a firm's financial position may dictate the purchase or lease of a lower-priced used machine. Second, used equipment frequently is more readily available than new equipment. In some situations, availability may override all other considerations.

A third and very common reason for the purchase or lease of used equipment is that used equipment may satisfy the purchasing firm's need, in which case there is no point in acquiring new equipment. In cases in which operating requirements are not severe, a used machine in sound condition frequently provides economical service for many years. If equipment is needed for standby or peak-capacity operation or for use on a short-lived project, more often than not used equipment can satisfy the need very well. The used equipment must not affect the manufacturing process negatively (i.e., the equipment is not a critical "technology"-dependent item).

**The Used Equipment Market**    Used equipment becomes available for purchase for a number of legitimate reasons. When a firm buys a new machine, it frequently disposes of the old one. Although the old machine may be obsolete relative to the original owner's needs, it is often completely adequate for the needs of many potential buyers. If significant changes are made in the previous owner's product design or production process, it may be advantageous to the original owner to purchase or lease more specialized production equipment. Finally, some used equipment becomes available because the owner lost a contract or has discontinued operations altogether.

Whatever the reason, a great deal of used equipment is available and commonly is purchased from one of four sources: (1) used equipment dealers, (2) the owner, (3) brokers, and (4) auctions. In recent years, the majority of these purchases have been made from used equipment dealers who specialize in buying, overhauling, and marketing certain types of equipment. Dealers usually are located in large industrial areas, and as a rule, they periodically advertise the major equipment available.

*Used Equipment Dealers*    These dealers typically specialize in certain kinds of equipment and sell two types of machines: "reconditioned" machines and "rebuilt" machines. Generally, a reconditioned machine carries a minimal dealer warranty and sells for approximately 40 to 50 percent of the price of a similar new machine. The machine usually has been cleaned and painted, broken and severely worn parts have been replaced, and the machine has been tested under power. A rebuilt machine typically carries a more inclusive dealer warranty and sells for perhaps 50 to 70 percent of a new machine's price. A rebuilt machine usually has been completely dismantled and built up from the base. All worn and broken parts have been replaced, wearing surfaces have been reground and realigned, the machine has been reassembled to hold original tolerances, and it has been tested under power.

*Sale by Owner*    Some owners prefer to sell their used equipment directly to the next user because they think they can realize a higher price than they would get by selling to a dealer. Some buying firms also prefer this arrangement because it permits them to see the machine in operation and learn something about its usage history before making the purchasing decision.

*Brokers*    A broker is an intermediary who brings buyers and sellers together but generally does not take title to the equipment. Brokers sometimes liquidate large segments of the equipment of a complete plant. Occasionally, an industrial supply house or a manufacturer's agent will act as a broker for a good customer by helping the firm dispose of an odd piece of equipment which has a limited sales market.

*Auctions*    Auction sales represent still another source of used equipment. Several types of auction firms are in operation. Some actually function as traders, buying equipment and selling from their own inventory. More common, however, are firms which simply provide the auction sale service. Their commission is usually somewhat less than a broker's commission. Generally, buying at auction is somewhat more risky than is using the other supply sources because auctioned machines usually carry no warranty and it rarely is possible to have a machine demonstrated. In some cases, however, machines can be purchased at auction via videotape or closed-circuit TV; this permits the buyer to see the machine operating in a distant plant.

**Cautions in Purchasing Used Equipment**    The age-old adage of caveat emptor—let the buyer beware—is particularly applicable when one is purchasing used equipment. It may be difficult to determine the true condition of a used machine and estimate the type and length of service it will provide. For this reason, it is wise to have one supply professional specialize in used equipment. Moreover, it is virtually essential to enlist the cooperation of an experienced production or maintenance specialist in appraising used equipment. It is always sound practice to check the reputation of a used equipment supplier and to shop around, inspecting several machines before making a purchase. Whenever possible, a machine should be observed under power through a complete operating cycle. Finally, a prospective buyer should determine the age of a machine. If it is not available in the seller's records, the age of a machine can be traced through the manufacturer by means of serial number identification. The combined knowledge of age and usage history is a key guide to the future performance of a used machine.

In preparing a purchase order or contract for used capital equipment, one must take care to include all essential data. In addition to an adequate description of the machine, an order should specify the accessories included, warranty provisions (if any), services to be performed before shipment, and financing as well as shipping arrangements. Generally, sellers do not provide service for used equipment after the purchase. All transportation, handling, installation, and start-up costs, as well as risk, usually are borne by the purchaser.

## Spares

When is the optimal time to obtain prices on spares and service agreements? Obviously, when competition is present! Wise supply professionals obtain a list of anticipated spare parts and service requirements from the prospective user of the equipment so that they can solicit prices for those items when soliciting the price of the equipment itself. Otherwise, excessive prices frequently become the norm when the need for the spare part or service arises.

## Estimating Acquisition Costs and the Total Cost of Ownership

After the desired operating and engineering objectives have been identified, the team should develop both acquisition cost and total cost of ownership (TCO) estimates as explained in Chapter 13. If the item to be purchased is a standard one, supply management will obtain estimates of the purchase price from its files or from potential suppliers. If customized or nonstandard equipment is to be purchased, it is desirable for supply management to obtain informal estimates from potential suppliers. These estimates are compared with the budget authorization and are input into the total cost of ownership analysis. If these analyses indicate that either cost is likely to be excessive, the team must reexamine the list of desired objectives and make appropriate adjustments. Ideally, those analyses and adjustments are made before the development of the appropriate specifications.

# Develop Specifications and Initiate Sourcing, Pricing, and TCO Analysis

## Develop Specifications

Normally, a performance specification is developed by the team. As was seen in Chapter 6, a performance specification describes the desired performance (160 units per minute, setup time of 5 minutes, specific tolerances, etc.) together with the required engineering features. *If* another type of specification is

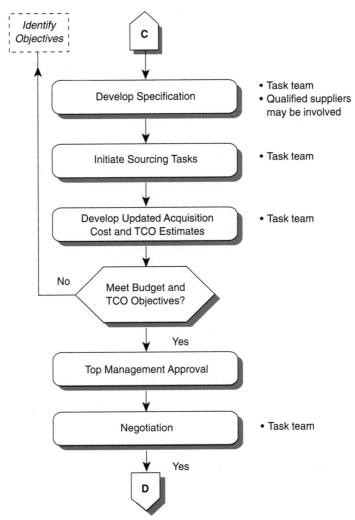

**Figure 8.3** | Capital Equipment Procurement Phase III: Specifications, Sourcing, Pricing, and TCO Analysis

determined to be appropriate, one or more qualified potential suppliers may become involved in the process of developing the specification (see Figure 8.3).

One of the advantages of formally establishing a sourcing team is the fact that more *cooperative* action usually is generated in attacking the procurement. This can be extremely useful in the development of the equipment specifications. Quality/cost trade-offs are best addressed by a team. When specifications are nearing completion and requests for proposals are to be issued, a good supply management professional should function in the role of an informal auditor. Although technical requirements predominate, the supply management professional should make every effort to see that specifications are written as functionally as possible. Most equipment users are biased toward or against specific types of equipment. Every effort should be made to exclude personal biases from the specifications. The nature of many equipment requirements limits the number of possible suppliers. This number should not be reduced further by arbitrarily excluding certain potential suppliers on the grounds of personal prejudice. After development of the appropriate specification, sourcing, pricing, and negotiations are accomplished.

## Sourcing

The sourcing of equipment suppliers involves the quantitative and qualitative analyses described in detail in Chapter 11. Briefly, the first step in equipment sourcing is the development of a request for proposal. Once proposals are received, they are evaluated for responsiveness. The supplier or suppliers that appear to be most attractive are identified. Some suppliers are more qualified in the "soft," or qualitative, area than are others. The degree of qualification should be considered carefully by the team in deciding which machine to buy. The team must determine the level of a supplier's *technical, production,* and *commercial* capabilities. The team also must assess the supplier's capability and willingness to provide any engineering service required during the installation and start-up of the new equipment. This is an extremely important financial consideration when complex expensive equipment such as steam turbines and numerically controlled machine tools is involved. Closely related to this factor is the necessity of training operators. What service is the supplier willing to provide in this area? The reliability of a supplier in standing behind its guarantees is another important consideration. A combination of the supplier's history of satisfactory performance and financial viability must be addressed. Once the equipment is installed, unexpected problems beyond the purchasing firm's control sometimes add significantly to the total cost of a machine. Finally, what is the supplier's policy on providing spares and replacement parts? When the purchased machine is superseded by a new model, what will be the availability of obsolete parts? The policy of one pump manufacturer, for example, is to produce a small stock of replacement parts for obsolete equipment once every six months. The semiannual production policy of this manufacturer, combined with its low inventory levels, forces some customers to carry unreasonably large stocks of major replacement parts. The other costly alternative for the customer is to risk occasional breakdowns, which may leave a machine out of service as long as three or four months, waiting for the next run of parts. In practice, unfortunately, such considerations frequently play a minor role in the initial selection of equipment suppliers, only to assume major proportions at a later date. It is the responsibility of the supply management department to evaluate potential suppliers in light of these qualitative factors and to bring significant considerations before the evaluating group.

## Develop Updated Acquisition Cost and TCO Estimates

When proposals are received, a supply management professional tabulates them and makes the necessary calculations so that they can be interpreted on a comparative basis by the team responsible for the final recommendation. Because administration and control of such activities are clearly related to the capital budgeting function, the finance department frequently assumes responsibility for conducting a total profitability study. The authors' view, however, is that once management has selected the types of analyses to be used, the supply management department can perform the analyses more easily and effectively. Those analyses are a logical extension of the supply management department's proposal analysis activities. Clearly, the supply management professional is familiar with any proposal complications. Through his or her involvement in the preceding technical discussions, that professional also should understand any technical problems involved in developing estimates for maintenance and operating costs. Consequently, an individual with a good understanding of the total cost situation may effectively prepare, interpret, and present the complete package of price, cost, and profitability data for the group's consideration.

**Table 8.1** | Total Cost of Ownership for Items X and Y

|  | X | Y |
|---|---|---|
| Acquisition cost | $1,000,000 | $1,200,000 |
| Present value of future costs for spares, maintenance, operator labor, downtime, etc. | $2,000,000 | $1,300,000 |
| Total | $3,000,000 | $2,500,000 |

The team now has considerable information to update its TCO estimate, including all likely acquisition costs and data on actual operating characteristics. As a result, a reasonably accurate TCO estimate can be developed. One of the most challenging issues confronting the team responsible for the selection of an expensive item of equipment is the possible conflict between the budget authorization and the total cost of ownership. The budget focuses on "now" costs (purchase price, transportation, installation, training, and initial spares); the total cost of ownership addresses both now and likely future costs. Compare the total cost of ownership for items X and Y in Table 8.1. If the budget authorizes the expenditure of $1,000,000, the sourcing team will tend to acquire X, incurring a likely $500,000 excess cost, based on the total cost of ownership for the two alternatives.

## Meet Budget and TCO Objectives?

The team now ensures that the updated acquisition and TCO estimates are at or below its objectives. If they exceed either objective, the project is returned to the objectives phase for revision (see again Figure 8.2).

## Top Management Approval

If significant funds are involved, once the project satisfies budgetary and total cost considerations, it should be forwarded for top management's review and approval.

## Negotiation

Once appropriate approvals have been received, the team proceeds to negotiate all the terms and conditions of a contract with the most attractive potential supplier, as discussed in Chapter 16. During negotiations, the negotiating team may explore the advantages of leasing.

# Leased Equipment

In addition to the possibility of purchasing new or used equipment to satisfy a firm's requirements, an equipment customer has a third alternative: *leasing* the equipment (see Figure 8.4). In recent years, leasing has become a big business. It is now a $190 billion industry whose volume of business has doubled in the last five years. Approximately 20 percent of the new office and industrial equipment used in American business today is leased. Generally accepted reasons underlying this trend appear to be the heavy demand for capital in most firms, the cost of capital, and the increased flexibility that can be negotiated in the contract.

## Types of Leases

If one looks at leases in terms of the basic purposes for which they are used, most fall into one of two categories: operating leases and financial leases.

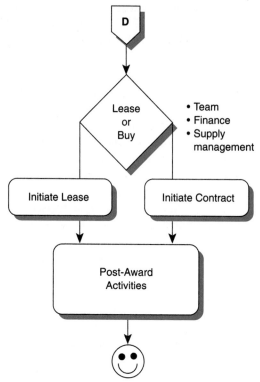

**Figure 8.4 |** Capital Equipment Procurement Phase IV: Sourcing, Lease/Buy Analysis, and Post-Award Activities

As the name implies, an *operating lease* is used by most firms as a vehicle to facilitate business operations. The focus typically is on operating convenience and flexibility. Frequently, a firm has a temporary need for equipment that will be used in the office or on a special production or maintenance job. The firm requires the use of the asset but is not interested in owning it. In some cases, the need stretches beyond the temporary period but the firm still is not interested in ownership and the risks and responsibilities that accompany it. Equipment obtained by means of an operating lease may fit the firm's needs well. Most operating leases are *short term,* for a fixed period of time that's considerably less than the life of the equipment being leased. In many instances, an operating lease is used when the customer firm wants the freedom of being able to avail itself of new and unexpected technology.

A *financial lease* in most cases is used for a very different purpose. When operating equipment is obtained by means of a financial lease, the primary motivation is to obtain financial leverage and related longer-term financial benefits.[2] Relatively speaking, a financial lease is a *long-term* lease that usually covers a period just a bit shorter than the approximate life of the equipment being leased. Many financial leases

---

[2]For the financial analysis of leases, see R. A. Brealey and S. C. Myers, *Principles of Corporate Finance,* 6th ed. (Burr Ridge, IL: Irwin/McGraw-Hill, 2000), Chapter 25. Note, there is a 2009 edition of this text.

are noncancelable. Several purists argue that such leases distort the firm's financial reports by reducing debt, which might otherwise be required to finance major purchases. Additionally, assets will be understated, resulting in a lower asset base in calculating the firm's return on assets.

## Factors Favoring Leasing

**Operating and Managerial Convenience**   While there are different types of leasing organizations, most industrial leasing firms are called *full-service* lessors. This means that the leasing organization owns the equipment, has its own continuing source of financing, and is prepared to assume all the responsibilities of ownership for the lessee. Hence, the lessee has full use of the equipment and can concentrate on its regular business operations without having to worry about maintenance, special service, and other administrative tasks associated with equipment ownership. This can be a major benefit in the case of complex equipment that requires highly specialized technical support.

**Operating Flexibility**   With relatively short-term leases for selected pieces of operating equipment, a lessee is not locked into long-term commitments resulting from large capital investments. The lessee can maintain maximum flexibility in its operations to respond to changing business conditions and the subsequent production requirements. It can use a leasing arrangement to meet temporary operating needs with relative ease, and in the same manner it can test new equipment before making a longer-term purchasing decision.

**Obsolescence Protection**   Leasing substantially reduces the risk of equipment obsolescence. In many businesses, particularly those which use high-tech equipment, some machines become technologically obsolete in a very short period. In leasing things such as data processing equipment, for example, an arrangement usually can be made with the lessor to replace or upgrade the old equipment. This can be an extremely important consideration in a highly competitive industry.

**Financial Leverage**   A major advantage of leasing expensive equipment stems from the fact that a leasing decision typically replaces a large capital outlay with much smaller regularly timed payments. This frees working capital for use in meeting expanded operating costs or investment in other segments of the business operation. Leasing equipment reduces the up-front start-up cost for new businesses.

Viewing the lease strictly as a financing mechanism provides a cash flow advantage over a conventional bank loan financing arrangement. Most equipment leases can be stretched over a longer payment period, reducing the relative size of the monthly payments.

In the United States, the Financial Accounting Standards Board (FASB) requires that all financial leases be capitalized. This means that the present value of all the lease payments must be shown as part of the firm's debt.

**Income Tax Considerations**   If a lease fulfills the Internal Revenue Service's requirements for a "true lease" from an accounting point of view, lease payments are recorded as operating expenses. As long as lease payments exceed the value of allowable depreciation (if the asset were owned), an additional tax shield is provided for the lessee. Comparatively speaking, the amount of taxable income is reduced by the difference between the lease expense payments and allowable depreciation expenses. Therefore, if a lessee plans to obtain this tax benefit, it is important to compare the proposed lease payments with the corresponding allowable depreciation figures (if the asset were owned) over the life of the lease to ensure that the anticipated positive relationship actually exists.

It is important to bear in mind that the IRS has established rather stringent guidelines to distinguish between a true lease and a lease which is intended to be a disguised conditional sales contract. Whenever it appears that the actual intent of the parties is simply to use the lease as a financing arrangement for a subsequent purchase of the equipment, no incremental tax benefit is allowed.

The Tax Reform Act of 1986 has had a significant influence on the lease/buy decision for some firms. The 1986 tax law eliminated the investment tax credit and modified the allowable depreciation preferences, forcing many firms into an alternative minimum tax position. The combined effect of these two provisions has made it more costly, from a tax perspective, for some capital-intensive firms to buy capital equipment. Although the situation is different for each firm, experience to date indicates that the 1986 law has made leasing a more attractive alternative for many firms.

## Factors Weighing against Leasing

Cost    As a general rule, the primary disadvantage of leasing is its cost. "Margins" are typically higher on leases than interest rates are on direct loans. This is understandable, because in addition to covering financing charges, the lessor must bear all the risks associated with ownership (including obsolescence and inflation risks). The typical financial lease runs for approximately three-quarters of the equipment's estimated useful life, and monthly fees total approximately 120 to 135 percent of the purchase price over the life of the lease contract.

Control    A second disadvantage arises from the fact that the lessor retains control of the equipment. This loss of control often places restrictions on the manner in which the equipment is operated; it also requires that the lessee give the lessor access to the equipment for inspection and maintenance. There are usually times when such control by the lessor creates inconveniences for the lessee. Closely related to this fact is the possibility that the lessee may have its purchasing prerogatives constrained with respect to the purchase of operating supplies for the leased equipment. A lessor normally wants to have the equipment operated with its own supplies. If use of other manufacturers' supplies could conceivably impair the machine's performance, the lessee usually agrees to such an arrangement. Frequently, higher prices are paid for such supplies than would be paid if they were purchased on the open market.

## To Lease or to Buy?

Cost Comparison    It is imperative for the supply and/or finance professional to make a comparative analysis of the cost to lease and the cost to own. A discounted cash flow analysis of the two alternatives over the life of the lease is the most accurate and straightforward approach to use.

Procedurally, the same approach is used in this analysis that is used in making a life cycle cost analysis. Basically, all cost and savings factors for the lease alternative are identified and quantified and then are projected to appropriate future dates when they actually will be incurred. This produces a cost matrix over the life of the lease. All future costs are discounted to their present values and subsequently summed to express the total cost in present value terms.[3] The same procedure is followed for the "buy" alternative. Total present value costs then can be compared directly to determine the additional true cost (or saving) associated with the leasing alternative.

The Decision    The lease-or-buy decision should be made just as any other sound purchasing decision is. First, the merits of the alternative items of equipment must be assessed relative to the buying firm's functional needs. The total cost of each then is considered in light of the preceding functional analysis. To these factors are added the relevant qualitative considerations that may vary among suppliers, markets, economic

---

[3]The cost of capital for evaluating lease cash flows is the firm's after-tax cost of debt. See Brealey and Myers, *Principles of Corporate Finance,* Chapter 25.

conditions, and so on. A decision then is made on the basis of the relative cost/benefit assessments. In the case of a lease-or-buy decision, this process can be summarized in the following four steps:

1. Determine the *operating* (including financing considerations) advantages and disadvantages of leasing and owning. Input from operations, finance, and supply management is required.
2. Compare the two alternatives and answer the question: From an operating point of view, is leasing the preferred alternative?
3. If leasing is preferable, calculate and compare the *present value costs* of the two alternatives.
4. Make the decision: Are the operating benefits of leasing worth the additional cost?

More often than not, the final decision will center on a determination of whether the extra cost entailed in leasing is justified by the avoidance of the major risks and responsibilities associated with ownership.

## Initiate Lease or Contract

The purchase order, contract, or lease agreement should be written with care, specifying the responsibility of both the buying firm and the supplying firm for equipment performance and post-sale activities. Acceptance testing and inspection methods, acceptance timing, machine specifications and performance standards, and guarantee conditions should be addressed during negotiations and in the resulting contract. In the aviation industry, it is common for penalties to be paid by the supplier if performance standards are not met. For example, International Aero Engines, when selling its new engine (V2500), agreed that if the fuel consumption was above specifications, it would pay a penalty to the engine user. Similarly, supplier responsibility for post-sale services pertaining to installation, start-up, operator training, maintenance checks, and replacement parts should be spelled out clearly so that there is no question about what is to be furnished and at what price.

If the purchase or lease involves a lengthy manufacturing period, a special follow-up and expediting program should be developed. This may call for periodic plant visits and in-process inspection of the work. Responsibility for monitoring this activity normally rests with supply management.

## Post-Award Activities

We strongly recommend that the key individuals from the buying and supplying firms who are concerned with timely delivery, installation, training, and delivery of spares meet to ensure total understanding of each firm's and each function's responsibilities. Normally, supply management will assume responsibility for the day-to-day management of the contract and the relationship.

After a machine is purchased, a wise supply professional works closely with plant engineering in keeping and interpreting historical records (part by part) of machine performance. Data of this kind are valuable in making similar future analyses. (That information may indicate that reimbursement under the warranty is appropriate.)

## Concluding Remarks

In most firms, equipment is not purchased frequently. Such purchases may represent important management decisions. Equipment purchases can be major investments that lead to the manufacture of more competitive products or the delivery of more competitive services, both of which increase sales in the marketplace and/or lead to improved productivity.

The role of supply management is distinctly different in this type of buying activity from what it is in production buying. In the procurement of equipment, supply management personnel function in a creative capacity as facilitators, coordinators, contract administrators, and consultants to management. Specifications must be precise and complete yet must be written as functionally as possible. Economic analyses should utilize appropriate techniques, must be thorough, and must be based on data that are as accurate as possible. In many cases, supply management becomes the champion of total cost of ownership analysis. Supply management should be actively involved and, optimally, guide the team through the sourcing and negotiation activities. The contract must be precise and complete. There should be no doubt about installation and start-up responsibilities, performance requirements, test and inspection methods, related post-sale responsibilities, spare part support, and warranties.

## End Notes

For a comprehensive analysis of the lease/buy question, see William L. Ferrara, James B. Thies, and N. W. Dirsmith, *The Lease-Purchase Decision* (New York: National Association of Accountants, 1979).

## Discussion Questions

1. List several factors unique to most equipment purchases.
2. Identify five areas that may initiate the need for acquiring capital equipment.
3. What functional areas should be represented on the team responsible for obtaining a $10 million item of equipment for a firm's production line?
4. What four interests does finance address during the acquisition of capital equipment?
5. What five responsibilities does supply management have during the acquisition of equipment?
6. Describe and discuss five operating characteristics which frequently should be addressed when a company is acquiring an item of capital equipment.
7. What are three important reasons for purchasing or leasing used equipment?
8. When is the optimal time to obtain prices on spares and service agreements? Why?
9. Describe a performance specification. Why is this normally the preferred basis of equipment procurement?
10. Describe the sourcing process as it applies to equipment procurement.
11. Describe the possible conflict between a budget authorization and the total cost of ownership.
12. Discuss the characteristics of operating leases and financial leases.
13. Identify and discuss five factors which favor leasing.
14. What is the primary disadvantage of leasing?
15. What is a second disadvantage of leasing?
16. Describe post-award activities as they apply to the procurement of equipment.

## Internet Exercise

### Overview: Buying and Accounting for Capital Equipment

Access the website below and read an overview of how Stanford University manages the process of procuring capital equipment.

(http://financialgateway.stanford.edu/staff/capitalequip/buy_cap_equipment.html)

1. How do they categorize their capital equipment buys?
2. List the various areas involved in these buys and describe the roles they play in the process.
3. Why would Stanford have such an elaborate process for the accountability of capital equipment?

## Suggested Reading

Auguston Field, Karen. "Calculating ROI: Hope for Best, Plan for Worst: By Examining a Proposed Investment's Financial Performance over a Range of Conditions, You'll Know How Wrong You Can Be and Still Be Right." *Supply Chain Management Review* 6, no. 2 (March–April 2002), p. S54.

Contino, Richard. *The Complete Equipment-Leasing Handbook* (New York, AMACOM, 2002).

Harding, Mary Lu. "Applying TCO to Capital Equipment," *NAPM InfoEdge* 5, no. 3 (May 2000).

Menezes, Sanjit. "Calculating the Total Cost of Ownership," *Purchasing Today*® 12, no. 5 (May 2001), p. 16.

Newman, Richard G., and Robert J. Simkins. *Capital Equipment Buying Handbook* (New York: AMACOM, 1998).

Woodside, Arch G., Timo Liukko, and Risto Vuori. "Organizational Buying of Capital Equipment Involving Persons across Several Authority Levels," *Journal of Business & Industrial Marketing* 14, no. 1 (Winter 1999), p. 30.

**CHAPTER**

# Purchasing Services

## CHAPTER OBJECTIVES

*After reading this chapter, you should be able to:*

1. Explain the purpose of a Statement of Work (S.O.W.).

2. Prepare a simple S.O.W.

3. Identify issues to consider in selecting a service contractor.

## VIGNETTE: LESSONS LEARNED

Al Carpenter, Materials manager at Captiva Conglomerate, has called a meeting with his Inventory and Spares manager, Sam Sliderule, and his Supply manager, Aaron Blumencranz. Jason Patel, vice president of Operations, Monica Stein, vice president of finance, and Jana Perry, director of Information Technology, are also in attendance. The topic: the contract with S.O. Software (SOS), the developer/supplier of a custom inventory management and spare parts management system.

Al begins: "Here's our agenda: I. Status of the SOS contract; II. Development of a corrective action plan; III. Lessons learned. Any questions?"

"How did we get in such a mess?" Monica asks.

Al interrupts: "Let's save this for agenda item III. Let's start with a status report. Sam, you're the user. Begin."

Sam answers, "We just completed a test of the spares management module. It's a disaster! It might be an Okay system, but it's four months behind schedule, and my people can't use it."

"Well, I certainly can use it. I think it's great!" Jim comments.

"Yes, but you have an M.S. in Information Technology. My guys want to access the relevant data without all the hassle the system requires," Sam continues.

"How about the regional and centralized inventory management system?" asks Al.

"It's 10 months late," Sam says.

"Aaron, sounds like we should sue them," Al adds angrily.

Aaron replies, "Under the contract Gerry [Captiva's president] signed, we don't have a leg to stand on. The contract calls for 'best efforts,' 'whenever possible,' etc. Oh, and one additional small item: The project manager at SOS says they've used up the $1 million called for in the contract. In fairness to the supplier, there have been 17 unpriced change orders."

Jason Patel (VP Operations) joins the discussion: "This system was supposed to provide me with better support. 'More uptime' were your words, Jana. And you said, 'We should be able to cut our inventory while providing the improved support.' Who wrote the specs for the software?"

"When we received the contract from Gerry, the specs looked like they were drafted by SOS. But Jana [IT manager] had initialed each page," Aaron answers. ■

## CRITICAL THINKING QUESTION

1. What do you think is *the main cause* of Captiva's problem?

The procurement of services is an activity of increasing importance. Expenditures on services by commercial firms, not-for-profit organizations, and government increase each year. In some cases, services procurements represent more than 25 percent of an organization's expenditures. Purchased services play key roles in the successful operation of those organizations. In many instances, the impact of the services on the success of the organization's operation is far greater than the impact of the dollars spent. Services ranging from architectural engineering, promotion and advertising, and the development of software to the maintenance and repair of production equipment are of critical importance to the operation of the organization. More mundane purchases such as cafeteria and janitorial operations affect the morale of all employees.

A tidal wave of "outsourcing" of services is taking place in the United States and abroad. At one level, services which are not at the core of the organization's competencies, such as management information systems, payroll, travel services, delivery services, and even the procurement of MRO supplies and services, are being outsourced to service providers. Those suppliers have expertise and economies of scale that allow them to provide the services at the same or a higher quality level than the purchasing firm and at a lower total cost. At another level, in economies that traditionally have been characterized by a high level of government participation in service delivery in the provision of health, transport, utilities, and municipal services, there has been large-scale outsourcing to private sector providers. This move to outsourcing adds a new dimension to procurement. Expenditures on such third-party service provision can reach 60 to 70 percent of total organizational expenditure and require higher-level supply management skills than has been imagined.

Obtaining services is one of supply management's most challenging responsibilities. In no other area is there a more complex interdependency between the purchase description (statement of work), method of compensation, source selection, contract administration, and a satisfied customer.[1] The purchasing of services frequently leads to relationships with suppliers that focus on trust rather than the transaction and can "stretch" supply professionals beyond their traditional zones of comfort and competence.

---

[1]This material is based in part on David N. Burt, Warren E. Norquist, and J. Anklesaria, *Zero Base Pricing™: Achieving World Class Competitiveness through Reduced All-in-Cost* (Chicago: Probus Publishing, 1990).

# Hidden Opportunities

Warren Norquist, former vice president of International Materials Management at Polaroid, involved his staff in many of the following nontraditional procurements:

- Print ad production
- General consultants
- Computer consultants
- Computer network management
- Design of exterior of products
- Television ad production
- Outplacement agencies
- Training consultants
- Network TV time
- Market research
- Financial auditors
- Training courses
- Per diem help
- Placement agencies
- Technical consultants
- Spot TV and radio time
- Telephone customer service
- Annual reports
- Logistics and inventory control

Mr. Norquist's experience was that when qualified procurement personnel were involved in the planning and procurement of such services, savings of approximately 25 percent were achieved with equal or improved quality and service.[2] In addition, an increasing number of proactive supply management operations now purchase services such as utilities, disposal services, and insurance.

Stephen Sutton, Supply manager for Ok Tedi Mining Limited (OTML) in Papua New Guinea, talks of the increasing significance of services procurement in world-class organizations. OTML's spend on services now exceeds 50 percent of total expenditures. Sutton cites examples of outsourcing major areas of core on-site activity at OTML such as blasting (where a contractor now delivers a total drilling, charging, and explosives detonation service) and major equipment maintenance, for which a contractor has total responsibility on site for activities that include buying and holding inventory and the provision of the associated maintenance labor requirements. Such examples clearly indicate the shift in the manner in which leading-edge organizations operate in their supply markets today.[3]

# The Statement of Work

As is true in the purchase of production requirements and capital equipment, the most critical prerequisite to a successful procurement of services is the development and documentation of the requirement—the statement of work (S.O.W.). And as is true with production requirements and capital equipment, one of the keys to success is the involvement of qualified supply management personnel at this point in the procurement process. In fact, supply professionals know that many of their service customers lack training and experience in the development of service requirements or specifications. Accordingly, a supply professional can provide invaluable assistance during this phase of the procurement. In many instances, supply professionals invite two or three carefully prequalified potential contractors to aid in the development of the statement of work. Their early involvement helps the internal customer fully understand the organization's

---

[2]Ibid., p. 177.

[3]Personal interview with Laurie LeFevre, October 14, 2000.

true needs. At the same time, the potential contractor gains insight into the nature and level of the effort required.

The statement of work identifies what the contractor (supplier) is to accomplish. The clarity, accuracy, and completeness of the S.O.W. and the way the effectiveness of delivery will be measured determine to a large degree whether the objectives of the contract will be achieved. The S.O.W. clearly identifies first the primary objective and then the subordinate objectives so that both the buyer and the seller know where and how to place their emphasis. Those responsible for developing the S.O.W. must ask themselves questions such as the following: Is timeliness, creativity, or artistic excellence the primary objective? How will customer satisfaction be measured?

One of the objectives of writing a statement of work is to gain understanding and an agreement with a contractor concerning the specific nature of the technical effort to be performed. Satisfactory performance under the contract is a direct function of the quality, clarity, and completeness of its statement of work and of the contractor's understanding of the outcome required.

The S.O.W. also affects the administration of the contract. It defines the scope of the effort, that is, what the contractor is to do and what the buyer is to receive and how satisfaction is to be measured. The manner in which the scope of work is defined governs the amount of direction that the supply professional can give during the contract's life.

A well-written statement of work enhances the contractor's performance in pursuit of S.O.W. objectives. Before writing it, those responsible must develop a thorough understanding of all the factors that will bear on the project and are reflected in the S.O.W.

## Four Formats for Statements of Work

The majority of formats fall into four basic types of statements of work, plus a combination of those four types called a "hybrid" S.O.W. The four S.O.W.s are as follows:

- **Performance S.O.W.** details everything wanted by the buyer. This statement of work is broken down into tasks describing the required outcome performance of the task(s).

- **Functional S.O.W.** defines what the buyer is "trying to do," leaving the seller free to come up with the most efficient means to do it.

- **Design S.O.W.** is the most detailed type of statement of work; it is used mainly in the construction and manufacture of goods or equipment projects. Statements of work of this type require the inclusion of plans, blueprints, CAD designs, or specifications.

- **Level-of-Effort S.O.W.** is a specialized version of the performance statement of work, generally used in research and development or studies contracts.[4]

## Planning the Statement of Work

A statement of work frequently is described as a document that details a strategy for contractor and buyer accomplishment of the objectives of a project. However, before any strategy can be developed, certain basic questions must be answered and understood:

- What are the objectives of the project?

- Where did the objectives come from, who originated them, and why were they originated?

---

[4]Janet Sickinger, "Writing a Complete and Effective Statement of Work," *InfoEdge*, November 1997, p. 3.

- What is the current status of the effort?

- Based on current status, what risks are associated with the achievement of the project objectives?

The planning phase of S.O.W. preparation is aimed at a thorough investigation of the why and what of the project. The following checklist will assist the program manager and the buyer in this determination:

- Identify the resource, schedule, and compensation constraints for the project.

- Identify all customer and contractor participation needed for the project and define the extent and nature of their responsibilities. All customer support, such as customer-furnished equipment, materials, facilities, and approvals should be stated specifically.

- Challenge the tasks identified, including the sequencing and interrelationships of all required tasks. For example, on a janitorial services contract, should the contractor be required to wash (versus completely erase) blackboards every evening or only once a week? On a landscape maintenance contract, should the contractor be required to furnish expendables such as fertilizer?

- Identify contractor delivery requirements at specified points in time; include details about the type and quantity of any deliverables.

- Identify specific technical data requirements such as plans, specifications, and reports.

- Identify realistic desired or required service levels.[5]

O'Reilly, Garrison, and Khalil provide the following list of typical elements that may be in a statement of work:

- Description of the work

- Schedule

- Specifications and requirements

- Quality requirements

- Performance measurements

- Deliverables

- Delivery and performance schedule

- Service levels

- Changes and modifications

- Bonds

- Charges and costs

- Project management

- Reporting requirements

- Safety

- Supplier responsibilities

---

[5]A desired service level might call for response within three hours 97 percent of the time.

- Buyer responsibilities
- Work approvals
- Use of subcontractors
- Authorized personnel
- Exhibits, schedules, and attachments[6]

## Writing the Statement of Work

As a result of a thorough planning effort, the individuals writing the S.O.W. should have determined the tasks and details that have to be included. These items must now be documented. This is even more important as the Uniform Commercial Code (UCC) does not apply to services; there is more on this distinction in Chapter 17.

Writing a quality statement of work is not an easy task. The S.O.W. must maintain a delicate balance between protecting the customer's interests and encouraging the supplier's (contractor's) creativity during both proposal preparation and contract performance. For example, when purchasing janitorial services, some well-intended firms specify the number of personnel the contractor must supply in the questionable belief that this provision will guarantee satisfactory performance. But that action blocks the supplier's creativity and generally results in needlessly high prices. The use of a carefully developed S.O.W. which specifies the required performance and procedures for monitoring (inspecting) the contractor's performance allows the contractor to apply its experience and creativity—usually resulting in significant savings. To complicate the task, those developing the S.O.W. must remember that it will be read and interpreted by customer and contractor personnel with widely varying experience and expertise.

The following issues merit special attention on a case-by-case basis. Required provisions may be in either the S.O.W. or the special terms and conditions included in the request for proposal and the resulting contract.

- *A performance plan.* The contractor is required to develop a nonsubjective, quantifiable blueprint for providing the services. Staffing, equipment, and supplies should all be identified. After developing the blueprint, the contractor must identify all required processes.

- *Quality monitoring system.* The contractor will be required to specify and implement fail-safe measures to minimize quality problems.

- *Personnel plan.* The contractor is required to develop and maintain recruiting and training programs that are acceptable to the customer.

- *Performance and payment bonds.* The contractor must provide performance and payment bonds equal to a specified percentage of the value of the contract amount.

- *Metrics.* When possible, performance objectives should be quantified.

- *Progress reviews.* If progress reviews appear to be appropriate, how, when, where, and by whom should be specified.[7]

---

[6]Peter O'Reilly, David H. Garrison, and Frediric Khalil, "Purchasing Professional Services," *InfoEdge,* May 2001, p. 8.

[7]Sickinger, "Writing a Complete and Effective Statement of Work, " p. 2.

## Artificial Intelligence

While executive director of Purchasing at Pacific Bell, colleague Joe Yacura began the development of artificial intelligence applications used to develop specifications for statements of work for both services and products. He carried this effort forward while SVP of Purchasing at American Express. His efforts have progressed to the point where an individual requiring a service to be purchased from an outside provider can go to a website which answers a number of detailed questions. The system algorithm and business rules then generate a statement of work together with a set of performance metrics and a total life cycle cost model.[8]

## Tips on Writing an Effective S.O.W.

Experience indicates that a clause such as the following should be added to the bidder's instructions section of the request for proposal (RFP) to ensure that the bidder's proposal will be responsive to the mandatory requirements:

> This RFP describes the minimum content and general format for responding to our RFP. Your reply shall be submitted on the forms and in the formats requested (or equivalent) with all questions answered in detail. Elaborate format and binders are neither necessary nor desired. Legibility, clarity, and coherence are more important. Your proposal should present information in the order requested in the RFP. It is mandatory that the Bidder use the same numbering format as used in this RFP so that responses correlate to the same paragraph in the RFP requirement. This will make your proposal more "evaluator friendly" to the evaluation team conducting the evaluation of the proposals.

Whenever a question is asked in the RFP subparagraphs or a requirement is stated by the use of the phrase "The Bidder Shall," the Bidder is expected to answer these as fully and completely as possible. Failure to do so may deem your proposal as "nonresponsive" to that requirement.

Responsiveness will be measured by the Bidder's response to the requirements in each paragraph of the RFP. Merely "parroting" back the RFP requirements statement in the Bidder's proposal may deem the response as nonresponsive. The Bidder's response must demonstrate an understanding of the requirements. This might be done by providing what was asked for or citing how the Bidder has achieved the requirements in its normal business practices (such as submitting samples of procedures or award letters).[9]

To make sure the S.O.W. accurately reflects what the contracting parties have agreed to, follow these suggestions:

- Be clear—use simple, direct language. Avoid ambiguity.

- Use active, not passive, voice. (The seller "shall conduct a test," as opposed to "a test should be conducted by the seller.") Active verbs assign responsibility more clearly than passive verbs do.

- Be precise, especially about task descriptions. The clarity of the S.O.W. affects the administration of the contract since it defines the scope of work to be performed. Work outside this scope will involve new procurement, probably with increased costs.

- Spell out the buyer's obligations carefully. Don't infer or "back into" a work requirement.

- Limit abbreviations to those in common use and spell them out at the first usage with the abbreviation in parenthesis. Provide a list of abbreviations and acronyms to be used at the beginning of the S.O.W.

---

[8]Mr. Yacura currently is CEO of Ridgewood Development Corporation.

[9]Sickinger, "Writing a Complete and Effective Statement," p. 9.

■ Include procedures. When immediate decisions cannot be made, it may be possible to include a procedure for making them (for example, "as approved by the purchaser" or "the seller shall submit a report each time a category B failure occurs").

■ Do not overspecify or overstate. Depending on the nature of the work and the type of contract, the ideal situation may be to specify results required or end times to be delivered and let the contractor propose the best method.

■ Eliminate extraneous statements. If a statement has no practical value, it shouldn't be in the S.O.W.

■ Include all relevant reference documents.

■ Don't mix general/background information, guidance, and specific direction/requirements.

■ Don't sole-source the work statement unless competition isn't desired.

■ Describe requirements in sufficient detail to assure clarity not only for legal reasons but for practical application, such as in closing loopholes.

■ Be aware that contingent actions may have an impact on price as well as schedule.

■ Provide a ceiling on the extent of services or work out a procedure that will ensure adequate control where appropriate (for example, a level of effort, pool of labor hours).

■ Avoid incorporating extraneous material and requirements which may add unnecessary cost. (Data requirements are common examples of problems in this area.)

■ Don't repeat detailed requirements or specifications which already are spelled out in applicable documents. Instead, incorporate them by reference.

■ Explain the interrelationship between tasks and indicate how tasks are related to required results and deliverables.

■ Identify all constraints and limitations.

■ Include standards that will make performance measurement possible and meaningful.

■ Be clear about phase requirements, if applicable, and the timing used to gauge work phases.

■ Proofread for errors and omissions, as well as for format and information consistency.[10]

## Selecting Service Contractors

Selecting the "right" source is much more of an art in purchasing services than in purchasing materials. Because of the complexity of many service procurements and the unexpected problems that tend to arise, it usually is prudent to select only established, reputable firms. Exceptions may be made occasionally in cases involving promising new suppliers who have not established a reputation yet. Unless the potential supplier has a truly unique skill or reputation, competition typically is employed. In some service markets, however, experienced supply managers find that the competitive process is not completely effective because of the structure of the market. This issue is discussed later in the chapter.

When a large number of potential contractors are available and the dollars involved warrant the effort, the customer firm's sourcing team normally reduces the list to three to five firms. Ideally, a weighted scorecard will be

---

[10]Ibid., p. 11.

**Table 9.1 |** Total Costs for the Construction Project

|  | Firm X | Firm Y |
|---|---|---|
| Construction cost | $10,000,000 | $11,000,000 |
| Design fee | 739,200 | 660,000 |
| Total cost | $10,739,200 | $11,660,000 |

developed to facilitate the process. The team interviews prospective contractors' management, talks with previous customers, and checks out employees through random interviews. The supply manager then invites proposals only from the potential suppliers with which the buying firm would be comfortable doing business.

During the evaluation process, emphasis should be placed on the total cost and total benefits to the purchasing organization. Assume, for example, that two architect-engineering (A-E) firms are under consideration for the development of plans and specifications for a new building estimated to cost approximately $10 million. Firm X has a reputation for designing functional buildings whose costs are relatively low. Firm Y, in contrast, has a reputation for designing more elaborate and aesthetically attractive buildings whose costs tend to run about 10 percent more than X's. For the sake of illustration, however, assume that firm X's professional fees tend to run about 12 percent more than Y's. Table 9.1 illustrates these cost differentials and shows the overriding influence of construction costs in the complete analysis. Hence, in this case, the contractor's design fee is a relatively minor item in the total cost package.

In addition to the traditional concerns about a prospective contractor's financial strength, management capability, experience, and reputation, the area of technical capabilities requires special analysis. An article in *Purchasing World* identifies the following issues that should be addressed in selecting a contractor for computer maintenance. This list of issues is introduced simply as an example of the depth of analysis required in selecting a contractor for this specialized service.

- Will the contractor maintain all the equipment in your computer installation?

- Can the contractor correct the problem quickly?

- How close to your facilities is the contractor's field engineering office? Does the contractor specialize in your type of equipment?

- Does the contractor have a prescribed schedule of service calls?

- Does the contractor have troubleshooting escalation procedures, skilled field engineers, and ready availability of spare parts?

- If there is any possibility of having to move the computer equipment, does the contractor have proven successful experience moving computers?

- Does the contractor offer equipment brokerage?

- Does the contractor have the technical ability to make low-cost modifications to your equipment? If so, can the firm support the resulting system?

- Will the contractor service refurbished equipment?

- Does the contractor have high hiring standards, require appropriate training, and equip field service personnel with appropriate tools and equipment?

- Does the contractor supply maintenance documentation?

■ Will the contractor develop custom products for your special needs?

■ Is the contractor flexible in meeting your specific requirements?[11]

The selection of suppliers for repair services depends on the situation. The best way to cope with emergency services is to anticipate them. Vehicles, office machines, and plant equipment do break down; sewer lines do get clogged. In many cases, it is possible, and certainly desirable, to establish the source and the price or dollar rates for such services before an emergency occurs. In purchasing transportation services, consistent on-time pickup and delivery, equipment availability, and service to particular locations typically are more important than price.[12]

Competitive prices should be solicited every two or three years for recurring services. This tends to prevent complacency and helps maintain realistic pricing. More frequent changes in contractors often cause service disruptions.

## Tips from a Professional

Barbara Stone-Newton, Purchasing manager for the State of North Carolina, provides the following tips:

■ *Partner with users.* Be sure you understand their needs, goals, and constraints. You will be the bridge between them and potential service providers. If users are not already familiar with your organization's procurement procedures (and possible options), use this time to go over them.

■ *Learn from the past.* For ongoing services, review the prior specifications and any comments in the contract administration file. If there were questions during the previous procurement, try to incorporate the answers into your new request for proposal (RFP) or invitation for bid (IFB).

■ *Update specifications.* Service standards and environment often evolve over the contract term. Generic specs may leave out important features that users have come to expect and thus create problems. For example, the current contractor may price for today's level of service (assuming rightly or wrongly that you want that to continue) while others submit costs for exactly what's in the specs. Be equally cautious about overspecifying, since that can increase costs or limit competition.

■ *Minimize assumptions.* Be specific about deliverables, schedule, performance measures, and similar expectations. The "fudge factor" is a particular concern in service procurements.

■ *Encourage questions.* Provide some mechanism for questions: a deadline for written inquiries, a site visit, or a preproposal conference. Issue a summary addendum formalizing substantive questions and answers so that all potential suppliers have the same information.

■ *Facilitate comparison.* Make it easy for prospective suppliers to provide everything you need to evaluate their responses. Include a checklist, outline, or similar section detailing what information is to be included in the responses. A "fill-in-the-blanks" format is great for simple procurements.

■ *Plan evaluation.* Outline the evaluation process and any weighting or scoring method to be used.

■ *Reduce surprises.* Include contractual terms and conditions in the solicitation document. This counters the mind-set of "we'll fix it with the contract" and streamlines the award process.

---

[11]"How to Choose a Computer Maintenance Service," *Purchasing World,* August 1987, p. 73.

[12]James R. Stock and Paul H. Finszer, "The Industrial Purchase Division for Professional Services," *Journal of Business Research,* February 1987, p. 3.

■ *Check yourself.*   When you think the RFP or IFB is ready to go, put it aside (at least for a few hours) and then take a fresh look. Read it from the suppliers' viewpoint. Does it contain everything they'll need to offer a competitive response? Finally, look forward to contract administration. Are the deliverables, standards, and so on, defined clearly so that both parties can measure performance? If the answers are positive, you probably have a good solicitation document.[13]

## The Ideal Services Supplier

The ideal services supplier listens to what users complain about most and then designs service products that supply the market's missing ingredients. Satisfaction is built into service products rather than added as an afterthought. Employees of ideal services providers are given every conceivable form of automation to help them deliver a consistently satisfactory service product. The ideal services supplier invests to increase both employee productivity and customer satisfaction.

If an ideal services supplier or contractor is not available, the purchasing firm should consider the development of a long-term relationship with a supplier that is willing and able to grow into an ideal provider.

# Pricing Service Contracts

Procurement authority Louis J. DeRose writes that "the competitive process is not truly efficient in services markets. It is constrained by three forces and factors of supply."

■ "One of the strongest factors influencing competition and prices—a continuing or cumulative supply—is absent."

■ "Interchangeable services generally are not available due to the personal effort and involvement of the supplier."

■ "The supply of services is more easily restricted or restrained than is the supply of commodities or products."

It is for these reasons, DeRose writes, "that buyers must negotiate service agreements."[14] Yet there are some situations in which competitive bidding is an effective method of determining both source and price. A janitorial services contract for which competition is intense is an example. Again, the supply professional's judgment plays a key role: Are all the conditions required for the use of competitive bidding (as discussed in Chapter 11) satisfied? Are time and qualified resources available to prepare for and conduct negotiations? Are supply management's internal customers prepared to play a constructive role in professional negotiations? In most instances, negotiation results in better pricing and the supply of a more satisfactory service.

Too frequently, the pricing of service contracts is not tailored to motivate the supplier to satisfy the organization's principal objective. Once the primary requirement (artistic excellence, timeliness, low cost, and so on) is identified, the supply professional must ensure that the resulting contract motivates the supplier to meet that need. When conditions require, the contract should reward good service and penalize poor service.

---

[13]Barbara Stone-Newton, quoted in Julie Roberts, "Services Purchases in the Public Sector," *Purchasing Today,* February 2001, p. 57.

[14]Louis J. DeRose, "Not by Bids Alone," *Purchasing World,* November 1985, p. 46.

## Professional Services

Architect-engineering firms, lawyers, consultants, and educational specialists are representative of the individuals and firms that provide professional services. Supply professionals pay particular attention to the relationship between the price mechanism (firm fixed price, cost plus incentive fee, fixed price with award fee, and so on) and the contractor's motivation on critical professional services contracts. For example, fixed price contracts reward suppliers for their cost control. Every dollar that the supplier's costs are reduced results in a dollar of additional profit for the supplier.

Assume that you are selecting an individual or a firm to prepare a fairly complex personal income tax return for a gross income of $125,000. Firm C advertises that it will prepare any tax return, regardless of its difficulty, for a guaranteed maximum of $200. Firm D offers a rate of $75 per hour. Discussion with a representative of firm D indicates that approximately five hours will be required to prepare your return. If forgone tax savings are considered a cost, which firm is more likely to provide the service at the lowest total cost? The use of firm D will cost an estimated $375 ($75 × 5 hours), or $175 more than firm C. Assuming that firms C and D have similar hourly costs, it is likely that D will spend about two hours more preparing the tax return. Most individuals with a $125,000 income would pay the extra $175 in the hope of offsetting the outlay with a larger tax saving.

Cost-type contracts should be considered when there is significant uncertainty about the amount of effort that will be required or insufficient time to develop a realistic S.O.W. Obviously, the dollar amount involved must warrant the administrative cost and effort involved. For smaller dollar amounts, a time and materials or labor-hour contract should be considered to avoid contingency pricing. Such contracts require close monitoring to ensure that the specified labor skill is furnished and that the hours being billed are in fact required.

Administratively, it may be impractical to use anything except a fixed price contract or an hourly rate price for relatively small professional services contracts. Even on larger dollar amounts, the supplier's reputation may allow the use of a fixed price contract. However, supply managers should be aware of the potential effect of the pricing mechanism on the contractor's performance.

## Technical Services

Technical services include things such as the following:

- Research and development
- Software development
- Machine repairs
- Printing services
- Payroll services
- Mailroom services maintenance
- Elevator maintenance services

- Pest control
- Energy management
- Accounting and bookkeeping services
- Advertising and promotion
- Heating and air-conditioning
- Copyroom and message

R&D services normally are purchased through one of two methods of compensation: a fixed price for a level of effort (e.g., fifty days) or a cost plus fixed or award fee. Software development lends itself to cost plus award fee contracts. This approach rewards excellent performance and punishes poor performance while ensuring the contractor that its costs will be reimbursed and at least a minimum fee will be received.

In a competitive market, once a good S.O.W. is available for services such as printing, promotional services, and the development of technical manuals, competition should be employed to select the source and determine the price, using a fixed price contract.

## Operating Services

Janitorial, security, landscaping, and cafeteria operations are typical operating services. Experience has shown that obtaining effective performance of such services can be very challenging for contract administrators. Accordingly, the compensation scheme should reward the supplier for good service and penalize it for poor service. (The use of a fixed price award fee scheme, as described in Chapter 15, may be appropriate.) That approach to pricing greatly aids in the administration of the contract and frequently results in a far higher level of customer satisfaction.

Insurance, plant and equipment maintenance, and anticipated emergency services should be sourced and priced through the use of competition among carefully prequalified suppliers. Unanticipated emergency repairs normally are purchased on a "not-to-exceed" time and materials basis, as described further in Chapter 15.

## Third-Party Contracts

Contracts for the provision of a service to a third party may result in a nonlinear supply chain and create ambiguities in contract relationships, for example, between the supplier and the end user. While a contract may exist between an organization and its customer and between an organization and its supplier, it does not necessarily follow that a contract will exist between the supplier and the customer unless that is provided for explicitly in the contract.

An example is a nationwide automobile insurer that puts in place across all regions of the country arrangements with suppliers for the provision of windshields for its customers. The question of whether a contract exists between the windshield supplier and the customer of the insurance company probably will be incidental if the relationship between the insurance company and its supplier is well managed. But if that is not the case, the relationship between the insurer and the customer may be at risk.

## So Your Services Contract Is about to Expire

The requirement for many services continues beyond the duration of the service contract. If a collaborative, mutually beneficial relationship has been established, many members of the purchasing firm may want to extend the contract. Additional pressure to extend the contract results from switching costs. We estimate that it may cost as much as 5 percent of the face value of some services contracts to switch to a new supplier.

But what should the price be for such an extension? If we have an open book relationship, we could study the present supplier's costs and use this information as the basis of a contract extension. A more objective and more scientific basis for determining the price of a contract extension is to apply the "experience" or "learning curve," as discussed in Chapter 14. The supplier, its site management, and its direct labor should learn how to do things more efficiently the more times they do a task or activity. Supply management should work with the supplier to develop a realistic estimate of what performance "should cost," based on past and future learning. While the mechanics of such approach are beyond this chapter, we emphasize that our readers should be sensitive to some of the subtleties of extending service contracts.

# Contract Administration

The four keys to successful service contract administration are (1) a sound S.O.W., (2) selection of the "right" source, (3) a fair and reasonable price, and (4) aggressive management of the contract. The administration of many service contracts can be a very challenging responsibility. The supply professional needs to monitor and have a realistic degree of control over the supplier's performance. Crucial to success in this area is the timely availability of accurate data, including the contractor's plan for performance and the contractor's actual progress. The supply professional must manage the relationship proactively to ensure success.

# Services Purchases and the Internet

Clearly, the Internet is becoming increasingly important in the purchase of services. Firms are employing electronic requests for proposals and receiving proposals electronically. Electronic collaboration both within a firm and with potential suppliers is becoming increasingly common. The Internet allows purchasing firms to obtain increased competition and thus lower prices for some services. When used properly, the Internet has the potential of reducing total cost of ownership, reducing order processing costs, compressing the sourcing cycle time, and improving the flow of information required to manage the resulting contract. Electronic marketplaces can provide a directory of services suppliers and frequently can play the role of matchmaker.

Leading firms use the prospect of incorporating the Internet as a stimulus to optimize their services supply chains. Reengineering is frequently appropriate. One Fortune 500 company reengineered its temporary labor service process before going digital. The documented savings was in the millions of dollars. This and a host of similar experiences cause us to encourage firms to reengineer to optimize the process before developing (or acquiring) the enabling e-solution.

There are some services that lend themselves to reverse or "E-auctions". The critical aspect of this sourcing technique is the complete S.O.W. to ensure comparing apples to apples.*

# Construction Services

The purchase of new facilities is a commitment for the future. Quality, productivity of the new plant or office, the time required to affect the purchase, and cost all must be considered. Aesthetic requirements, time requirements, and the availability of highly qualified designers and builders all tend to influence the selection of a purchase method.

There are five common methods of purchasing construction; however, it is unlikely that any one of those methods consistently will be the proper choice for all building requirements. Figure 9.1 provides a graphic presentation of the various steps involved in each method from start to completion of a construction project.

## Conventional Method

This is the most frequently employed approach to buying building construction in the United States. With this approach, design of the required facility is done by architects and engineers without the involvement of a builder. The design of the facility is completed before potential suppliers are requested to submit bids. Two separate organizations are responsible: one for the design work and one for the construction phase of the project.

Many architects are not noted for being cost-conscious. Nevertheless, the cost factor can be controlled in several ways. A common approach involves employment, on a consulting basis, of a "cost-control architect" who is concerned solely with cost reduction. Naturally, the general architect typically does not

---

*Bryan Robinson, "How to E-Auction the Intangible" *Inside Supply Management* July, 2005, pp. 10–11.

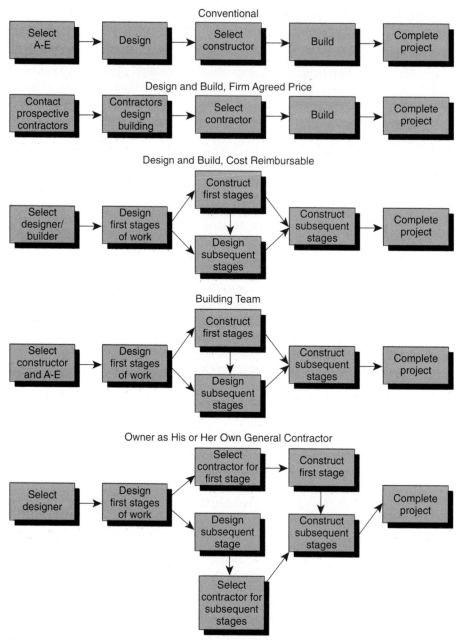

**Figure 9.1** | Sequence of Steps Involved with Alternative Methods of Purchasing Construction

appreciate having his or her work reviewed or "second-guessed." However, use of a consulting architect undeniably tends to make the primary architect more cost-conscious.

If a consulting architect is not used because of the general architect's sensitivity, alternative methods of cost control are available to a supply professional. For example, for major interior furnishings, the architect or interior decorator can be required to specify three manufacturers' products that can be purchased through competitive bids (with any one of the specified products being satisfactory). The actual purchasing can be done by the customer's organization, the architect, or the interior decorator. The three-bid requirement ensures competitive pricing. As an added bonus, this practice helps eliminate conflicts of interest, unreasonable personal bias, and the specifying of low-volume proprietary items.

## Design and Build, Firm Agreed Price Method

This approach could be described as construction with gratuitous design. The owner determines the basic facility requirements, such as size, temperature, electrical, and mechanical. Those requirements become the basis of a performance specification. That specification is furnished to carefully prequalified builders who, with their prospective subcontractors, prepare a bid package consisting of a design and price proposal. The purchasing firm awards a fixed price contract for construction to the builder whose bid is most attractive.

## Design and Build, Cost-Reimbursable Method

With this method, only one contract is awarded for both design and construction. Design is accomplished by architects and engineers employed by the general contractor. Thus, the builder has ample opportunity to influence the design of the required facility. With this approach, construction of a work element (excavation, structural work, and so on) proceeds when the design of that element has been completed. It is not necessary to wait for design of the total project since one firm is responsible for both the design and construction phases. This approach is particularly useful when a structure is required within a very short time and the design and build, firm agreed price method is not applicable.

## Building Team

With this approach, the owner retains both a designer and a builder concurrently. In contrast to the conventional method, the builder is retained during the design phase and is expected to contribute information on costs, procedures, and time requirements to the designer. As the A-E firm completes the plans and specifications for a work element, the builder either accomplishes the work with its own crews or obtains prices from several specialists and awards the work to the qualified subcontractor that makes the best offer (price, time, and quality considered). As with the other methods, the general contractor oversees and integrates the efforts of the subcontractors.

## The Owner as a Contractor

With this method, the owner contracts directly for the various work elements (including design) and performs the functions of integrating and controlling that otherwise would be accomplished by a general contractor. Since purchase orders and contracts are awarded on a work element basis, it is possible for construction to proceed before completion of the total design phase.

*Findings:* Research conducted by one of the authors on these five methods shows that the conventional method is by far the most costly approach to purchasing construction. Savings of approximately 25 percent were found to result when the design and build, firm agreed price method was used rather than the conventional method. Savings of 9 percent resulted when either the design and build, cost-reimbursable or

**Table 9.2 |** Purchase Price of a Hypothetical Building under Five Compensation Methods

| Method | A&E Fee | Construction Contract(s) | Total | Time (months) |
|---|---|---|---|---|
| Conventional | $740,000 | $12,300,000 | $13,040,000 | 16 |
| D&B (firm agreed price) | — | 9,750,000 | 9,750,000 | 11.5 |
| D&B (cost reimbursable) | — | 11,830,000 | 11,830,000 | 12 |
| Building team | 670,000 | 11,160,000 | 11,830,000 | 12 |
| Owner as his or her own general contractor | 600,000 | 11,800,000 | 12,400,000 | 15.5 |

the building team method was used in lieu of the conventional method. Savings of about 5 percent resulted when the owner acted as his or her own general contractor (see Table 9.2).

The amount of time from first contacting the designer or builder until completion of the facility frequently is as important as or more important than the price paid. Availability of the required facilities varies significantly with the methods used. On a typical 130,000-square-foot manufacturing plant, 16 months was required with the conventional method; 11.5 months with the design and build, firm agreed price method; 12 months with both the design and build, cost-reimbursable method and the building team method; and 15.5 months when the owner acted as the general contractor.

Supply professionals know that selection of the most appropriate method of purchasing plant facilities can reduce the cost and time required to purchase new facilities significantly. Their early involvement in such projects is a key to saving both time and money.

## Construction Purchasing Entails Unique Problems

Construction purchasing is a highly specialized field. Of particular importance is the fact that proper financial, legal, and planning actions must be undertaken to prevent possible losses. For example, a purchasing organization sometimes discovers that after completion of a new building a mechanic's lien is filed against the firm. In such cases, the organization typically has paid the general contractor but the general contractor has not paid its subcontractors. Under the law, if a "general" does not pay its "subs," the owner of the building is financially responsible.

The proper financial and legal steps that must be taken differ among states and municipalities; hence, the specific steps must be determined individually in each case. In general, though, the first step that must be taken in selecting the supplier is to analyze carefully the financial status of all prospective contractors. Next, the supply professional should consider the desirability of utilizing protective devices such as bid, performance, and payment bonds,[15] liquidated damages contract clauses, and the development of construction cost estimates by the organization's own engineering personnel (perhaps with the assistance of a specialized consultant). Finally, legal protection is achieved when the organization properly files all required completion and related reports, at the appropriate times, at the appropriate courthouses.

**Construction Insurance**    Because construction is a high-risk business, the insurance a purchasing organization requires the contractor to carry is very important. All construction contracts should stipulate specific insurance responsibilities. For example, a contract clause may require the contractor, at its expense, to maintain in effect during performance of the work certain types and minimum amounts of insurance coverage with insurers that are satisfactory to the customer.

---

[15]Some organizations require performance bonds on all construction contracts, mistakenly believing that performance bonds per se assure quality performance.

In addition, the contract should specify that before the performance of any work, the contractor must provide certificates of insurance as evidence that the required insurance is actually in force and that it cannot be canceled without 10 days' written notice to the customer organization. Failure to require any of these insurance provisions could be very costly. Other unique legal nuances in construction include the concept of Promissory Estoppel. A good example of this legal principle is a sub contractor cannot "at will" revoke a quote offer, which is part of a prime contractor's proposal, prior to a reasonable time period. For example, a plumbing company offers to do the plumbing for a general contractor and it knows the general contractor has used this offer as part of the general contract proposal. The plumbing company must allow a reasonable time to lapse to allow the general contractor's proposal to be accepted or rejected, i.e. the offer from the plumber is "irrevocable" until notified by the general contractor.*

## Performance Contracting

There are many opportunities to correlate the design and construction fees to the "performance" of the resulting facility. Throughput and productivity are obvious examples. Energy conservation is an especially "hot" example today, although it has been around since the 1970s. An article in *Facilities Design and Management* cites an example of how performance contracting saves the facility owner money while reducing energy demands. When the owner of one of the largest high-rise office/retail complexes in the United State—comprising two 51-story buildings and an underground retail center for a total of 1.56 million square feet—undertook a major facilities upgrade to reduce operating costs and retain Class A tenants, it used a performance contract to execute the project. Not only did the performance contract provide turnkey delivery for design, construction, and maintenance, it also allowed the owner to finance the project off its balance sheet, secured against operations costs and installed equipment value; that would have been difficult to arrange under a traditional design/construction contract.

The project included the design and installation of a direct digital-controlled energy management control system, variable frequency drives, variable air volume terminal units, fire-and life-safety control upgrades, utility control and monitoring systems, a fiber-optic Ethernet network with multiple workstations, and the development of custom software drivers to third-party terminal unit controllers. After completion of the project, operating savings were 10 percent overall, more than double the owner's target.[16]

# Concluding Remarks

The procurement of services is one of supply management's most interesting and challenging assignments. Large sums of money are involved. Of equal or greater importance, successful operation of the organization is affected by the effectiveness with which key services are purchased. Supply management frequently must assume a far more active role in all phases of a services procurement than in purchasing materials.

---

[16]Trevor Foster, "Performance Contracting Can Yield Significant Returns," *Facilities Design and Management*, January 2000, p. 34.

*Richard A. Mann and Barry S. Roberts, *Smith & Roberson's Business Law 13th Ed.*, Mason, OH. West, Thomson/South-Western, 2006, pp. 176, 214, 259–260.

# Discussion Questions

1. Give two examples of the statement "the impact of the services themselves on the success of the organization's operation is far greater than the impact of the dollars spent."
2. Several years ago, Polaroid demonstrated a 25 percent reduction in cost when qualified procurement personnel were involved in the planning and procurement of nontraditional services. Identify three contributions you believe supply professionals can make which would lead to such savings.
3. What is the primary objective of the statement of work?
4. Why is it essential to differentiate between the primary objective and subordinate objectives while developing the statement of work (S.O.W.)?
5. How does the S.O.W. affect administration of the contract?
6. Describe the balancing act which must be performed in developing the S.O.W. Give two examples.
7. Describe the sourcing process when competition is appropriate and a large number of potential contractors are available and a significant amount of money is involved.
8. Describe the use of a total cost of ownership approach during the sourcing process for services.
9. What is the "best" way to cope with emergency services?
10. Why should competitive prices on recurring services be solicited every two or three years?
11. Describe the ideal services supplier.
12. Describe the ideal state in an organization preparing for negotiations with a prospective services provider.
13. Describer the relationship between a contract's price mechanism and the contractor's motivation.
14. Describe the ideal compensation scheme in purchasing operating services.
15. What is meant by the term "switching costs"?
16. Describe how you would approach negotiating a two-year extension to a two-year contract for landscaping services which is due to expire in three months.
17. What data must the contract administrator possess to administer a services contract proactively?
18. Identify six ways in which the Internet can aid in the procurement of services.
19. What issues must be considered in purchasing construction services?
20. Describe the conventional method of buying construction.
21. What disadvantages do you see with the conventional method?
22. What advantages do you see with the design and build, firm agreed price method?
23. Describe how a supply manager can help reduce or eliminate many of the unique problems involved in purchasing construction services.

# Internet Exercise

## Procuring Services and Outsourcing Agreements

Visit the following website:
(http://www.bakerdonelson.com/Content.aspx?NodeID=200&PublicationID=129)

1. Identify the disconnect Kelly Frey believes exists between the buyer and the supplier of a service. Click on "read more . . . " (which should take you to the address below):
   (http://www.bakerdonelson.com/Documents/Procuring%20Services%20and%20Outsourcing%20Agreements.pdf)

2. List and define the elements in service agreements.

## Suggested Reading

Axelsson, Bjorn, and Finn Wynstra. *Buying Business Services* (West Sussex, U.K.: John Wiley & Sons, 2002).

Duffy, Roberta J., and Anna E. Flynn. "Services Purchases: Not Your Typical Grind," *Inside Supply Management*® 14, no. 9 (September 2003), p. 28.

Hatfield, Jo Ellen. "Purchasing Services on the Internet: Is There a Fit?" *Inside Supply Management*® 13, no. 5 (May 2002), p. 20.

O'Reilly, Peter, David H. Garrison, and Frederic Khalil. "Introduction to Purchasing Services," *NAPM InfoEdge* 6, no. 3 (May 2001).

Roberts, Julie S. "Service Purchases in the Public Sector," *Purchasing Today*® 12, no. 2 (February 2001), p. 53.

Smeltzer, Larry A., and Jeffrey A. Ogden. "Purchasing Professionals' Perceived Differences between Purchasing Materials and Purchasing Services," *Journal of Supply Chain Management* 38, no. 1 (Winter 2002), p. 54.

# Sourcing:
# Sourcing Perception and
# Corporate Outsourcing

It is often said that *sourcing* is the most important purchasing activity. If the wrong supplier has been selected, one who either has poor quality, late delivery, weak service or worse, all three problems, no contract can overcome these basic flaws.

In recent years, sourcing has become much more proactive than it once was. Today professional supply managers work with an organization's internal customers and engineers to ensure that the firm's supply base will support the firm's technology requirements now and in an uncertain future. The organization's information system allows supply managers to study the aggregation of its supply requirements. Professional supply managers then determine the most appropriate type of buyer-supplier relationship for each relevant commodity class, study the existing supplier base, and plan action to ensure that the base will meet the organization's needs efficiently and effectively. Those activities, which frequently are called "strategic sourcing," are key components of effective supply management.

Chapter 10 addresses the incredibly complex issue of outsourcing. Its predecessor, the make-or-buy analysis, pales by comparison in both complexity and strategic implications. The make-or-buy issue is largely tactical, but the outsourcing of manufacturing product design and services has strategic long-term implications which all too frequently are ignored.

Sourcing, as discussed in Chapter 11, appears to be far less challenging. By and large, there is agreement on world-class sourcing practices. The most impactful aspect of sourcing is that it prequalifies suppliers who become involved in the new product development process and the development of statements of work for service requirements. Extreme caution must be exercised.

The growth of the Internet and electronic commerce has changed global supply management forever. Today, there is virtually no way to avoid going global somewhere in a firm's supply chain. Chapter 12 addresses several benefits of global sourcing, the use of intermediaries, the problems and dangers which may be involved, and the world-class processes required. Even though we have dedicated a chapter to the topic, global supply management is addressed throughout the book. Regardless of whether a firm's products and services are sold globally, world-class supply managers pursue global supplier relationships. As with all supplier relationships, those relationships must be based on fairness, honesty, and trust. ■

# Outsourcing

## CHAPTER OBJECTIVES

*After reading this chapter, you should be able to:*

1. Understand what outsourcing entails and why companies outsource.

2. Identify and define strategic issues to consider in deciding to outsource manufacturing.

3. Explain why a company may favor making a product in-house.

4. Explain why a company would favor buying a service or product from the outside.

5. Explain what is meant by what the authors call the "volatile nature of the make-or-buy decision."

## VIGNETTE: MAKING OR OUTSOURCING PUMP HOUSINGS

When a firm considers which components, subsystems, or services it should make and which it should buy, it should analyze the issue at two levels: strategic and operational or tactical. The strategic level obviously is the more important of the two as far as the future of the firm is concerned. This initial analysis thus has a forward-looking, future-oriented aura about it. This chapter focuses initially on the strategic analysis and later on the tactical analysis. But first, let's look at a typical make-or-buy scenario.

The Muenster Pump Company has manufactured high-quality agricultural pumps for over 40 years. The firm's only plant is in the small midwestern city of Muenster. The company is Muenster's largest employer. Bob Dorf, president of the firm, is the grandson of Emil Dorf, the founder. Bob and his family, along with all key personnel, live in or near Muenster. Cordial relations exist between the firm and the city officials.

Since its founding, the firm has always been as self-sufficient as possible. Shortly after setting up the business, Emil Dorf established a foundry to cast pump housings and related items. Today, the foundry provides virtually all the required pump housings.

Bob's cousin, Terri, is the purchasing manager for Muenster Pump. After graduating from State University, Terri worked as a buyer at a large appliance manufacturer in the southwestern corner of the state, but after two years of life in the big city, Terri returned to Muenster. Bob was delighted to have Terri back in town. He established the position of purchasing manager by consolidating the buying functions previously performed by himself and other members of the firm. Terri is an aggressive and conscientious buyer. Materials costs have come down from 60 percent of the cost of sales to 50 percent in the two years since she assumed responsibility for purchasing.

Recently a representative of Union Foundry, a firm in the southeastern part of the state, contacted Terri. The rep was aware that Muenster Pump made its own cast pump housings, but he claimed that new developments in casing pouring allowed his firm to offer extremely attractive prices.

Terri requested a price on the L-1012 case housing, Muenster's most popular size. The L-1012 represents 60 percent of Muenster's demand for casting housings. The pump that incorporated the L-1012 is sold to distributors for $500. Within a week of the meeting, a letter arrived from Union Foundry, quoting a price of $90 F.O.B. Muenster. Delivery was promised in 120 days after receipt of the first order. Thereafter, delivery would be made in 60 days after receipt of an order. Minimum orders were established as 100 units. Terri contacted two other foundries and obtained quotations for the L-1012 housing. The prices were $94 and $98 F.O.B. Muenster.

Terri met her uncle Ned, discussed her findings with him, and asked how much it cost Muenster to produce the casting housings internally in its own foundry.

Ned Dorf was not at all enthusiastic about Terri's efforts in this area of the business. He said, "Terri, I appreciate your interest and efforts at reducing cost, but a lot more is involved here than meets the eye. We produce a quality housing that is not equaled in the industry. It's one of the primary keys to our success! Furthermore, we can respond to requirements much quicker than those city boys."

Terri responded, "Ned, let's assume that all your doubts could be overcome. How much does it cost us to make the housings?" Ned replied, "Terri, there is something else involved. We have 16 men working in that foundry. If we stop making our own housings, we'll have to close down the foundry, and there's no other place in the firm where these men could work."

At that point, Terri thought that discretion would be the better part of valor. She thanked her uncle Ned for the information and returned to her office.

Later that day, her cousin Bob stopped by. In the ensuing conversation, she learned that the L-1012 housing cost Muenster about $180. Total overhead at Muenster was calculated to be approximately 200 percent; hence, direct costs for material and labor for the housings would be about $60. Approximately 70 percent of the overhead is for fixed costs such as depreciation, taxes, and executive salaries. Terri sat in her office debating with herself the political, human, and cost implications of making or outsourcing the casting housing. ■

## CRITICAL THINKING QUESTIONS

1. Should Muenster consider the political and human costs? Why or why not?
2. Should Muenster make or outsource the case housing? Why? (Conduct an in-depth analysis using the available data.)

# Outsourcing: A Growth Industry

The use of outsourcing by both manufacturing and service industries is increasing rapidly. An increasing number of business functions are being outsourced. To meet competitive challenges, corporations are outsourcing to highly specialized firms that can use their expertise to increase the efficiency of an outsourced function. The increase in outsourcing has resulted in lower staffing levels, reduced costs, and more flexibility. Outsourcing is more than a means of cutting costs; it provides an opportunity to achieve innovation. Managers are transforming from their traditional roles into brokers or facilitators of outsourced activities. The 'make/buy' decision continues to be one of the key strategic issues and options confronting the purchasing function.[1]

# Strategic Issues

The starting point most firms use in conducting a strategic outsourcing analysis is to identify the major strengths of the firm and then build on them. Senior management needs to ask, "What is it we really do better than most firms?"

A firm's competitive advantage is often defined as cost leverage, product differentiation, or focus. It is important to perform a competitive analysis before initiating the outsourcing analysis. A competitive analysis will provide a report of the firm's strategic position relative to the market, the industry, and its competitors.

## Core Competencies

Do our strengths lie in certain design skills, unique production skills and equipment, or different types of people skills? A thorough investigation of these types of questions is what many people today call identifying a firm's existing core competencies. The next step in the process is to look at the current and expected future environment in which the firm operates, including the competition, the governmental regulatory climate, and the changing characteristics of sales and supply markets. Subsequently, the bottom-line question management must answer is, "Precisely what business do we really want to be in to maximize the use of our core competencies as we proceed into the future?"

Once a clear answer to this question has been formulated, the supply manager must identify expected competency requirements necessary for future operations. Competency requirements then are compared with existing core competencies to determine which ones need to be refined and which ones need to be supplemented with related competencies that must be developed to create a competitive advantage. Two researchers place these ideas in sharp focus when they say, "Senior managers must conceive of their companies as a portfolio of core competencies rather than just as a portfolio of businesses and products."[2] The products and the nature of the business flow from the core competencies.

In considering what to make and what to buy, the decisions should nurture and exploit the firm's core competencies. The items or services that should be made or done in-house are those which require capabilities that are closely linked with the core competencies and are mutually reinforcing, as opposed to those which can be separated. This is the fundamental strategic consideration that guides the original make-or-buy decisions that ultimately shape the character of the firm.[3]

---

[1]Lisa Ellram, Ph.D., and Arnold Maltz, Ph.D., "Outsourcing Supply Management," *Journal of Supply Chain Management,* vol 35, # 2, Spring 1999, pp. 4–17.

[2]C. K. Prahalad, "Core Competence Revisited," *Enterprise,* October 1993, p. 20.

[3]Robert B. Hays and Gary Pisano, "Beyond World Class: The New Manufacturing Strategy," *Harvard Business Review* 72, no. 1 (January–February 1994), pp. 77–87.

## Supplier Dominance

Chris Lonsdale at the Centre for Business Strategy and Procurement at the University of Birmingham in the United Kingdom observes that a majority of the problems outsourcing firms have experienced can be traced to suppliers who exploit the leverage they gain through the relationship. Lonsdale writes, "The significance of asset specificity for outsourcing is that if activities that require 'transaction-specific investments' are outsourced, the firm will find itself locked into its supplier, as it will not want to write off those investments by revisiting the market. This lock-in can then be exploited by the supplier, by renegotiating the terms of the contract or insisting on different terms next time around. This post-contractual lock-in (dependency) will cause the power relation between the two parties to change—the situation can become one of supplier dominance."[4] We share Lonsdale and his colleague Andrew Cox's concerns about the potential for suppliers to exercise the power they gain through such relationships. However, we believe that a carefully crafted and managed alliance will prevent such problems.

## The Creation of Strategic Vulnerabilities

Michael E. Porter, author of the landmark book *Competitive Strategy,* inserts a timely cautionary note by observing that "when you outsource something, you tend to make it more generic. You tend to lose control over it. You tend to pass a lot of the technology, particularly on the manufacturing or service delivery side, to your suppliers. That creates strategic vulnerabilities and also tends to commoditize your product. You're sourcing from people who also supply your competitors."[5]

## The Dangers of Vertical Integration

If a decision to "make" or "insource" results in vertical integration, the critical connection between output and rewards is broken. Cost and responsiveness both suffer. Vertical integration frequently results in a loss of flexibility and responsiveness.

# Horizontal Integration

A general trend in competitive strategy is emerging in which all noncritical activities are outsourced to achieve significant cost advantages. Known as critical dependencies, these activities are the same in other businesses and are not a unique part of a firm's product. For this approach to be successful, the minimum resources and value-added activities that are key to supporting the firm's core competencies must be identified and defined. All other activities (noncore activities) are potential candidates for outsourcing.

Companies are outsourcing a large range of services, including customer service, warehousing, training, and travel. Horizontal integration, which often is referred to as a "virtual corporation," involves outsourcing nearly everything except a few core activities. Companies that separate intellectual activities from the resulting processes and then outsource those processes create virtual corporations. Cisco Systems is an ideal example of this type of organization. The company outsources most of its manufacturing, order fulfillment, and distribution. New product development is outsourced to small companies that frequently are acquired by Cisco Systems. This company has developed a competitive advantage over competitors and

---

[4]Chris Lonsdale, "Locked in to Supplier Dominance: On the Dangers of Asset Specificity for the Outsourcing Decision," *Journal of Supply Chain Management,* May 2001.

[5]Michael E. Porter, quoted in John A. Byrne, "Caught in the Net," *BusinessWeek,* August 27, 2001, p. 35.

established a standard for the virtual corporation. The company is able to provide its products faster and at a lower cost than its competitors because of its flexibility.

## New Product Development and Outsourcing

The option to make or buy is first presented at the beginning of a product's life cycle, during new product development. The process of designing a new or modified product often is accompanied by new technologies, minimal information, and a high level of uncertainty. It is important that supply managers conduct an analysis that is based on the availability of resources in terms of timeliness and optimal cost. Extensive supplier market research should be conducted on new technologies and innovations. The firm's technological core competencies must be identified and defined. Often suppliers will develop technology and new innovations that are beyond the reach of the firm's core competencies. To take advantage of new technology, many manufacturers outsource development to suppliers. By utilizing suppliers during the development of new and modified products, manufacturers are gaining a competitive advantage and developing dependencies. To maintain a technological competitive advantage, manufacturers need suppliers to continue developing innovative designs.

A great deal of project planning is involved in the make-or-buy decision for new product development. Although outsourcing is considered a long-term activity, it can be considered in the context of finite projects. A project's strict deadlines may force a firm to make the decision to outsource. Coordination of the development activities of selected suppliers may be necessary, depending on the number of suppliers involved and the type of development required. The supply manager will need to coordinate horizontal suppliers that are producing parts that will affect the product as a whole. Vertical coordination is necessary for suppliers that are interacting on different tiers when technological collaboration is required.[6]

## Lean Manufacturing

If one steps back to assess the current situation in American industry, it is clear that the concept of "lean manufacturing" is widely embraced for competitive purposes. This means that lean firms increasingly buy more and make less. A rule of thumb used by some firms is to outsource subsystems and components unless they fall into one of the following three categories:

1. An item that is critical to the success of the product, including customer perceptions of important product attributes.
2. An item that requires specialized design and manufacturing skills or equipment and for which the number of capable and reliable suppliers is extremely limited.
3. An item that fits well within the firm's core competencies or within those the firm must develop to fulfill its plans for the future.

Components or subsystems that fit into one of these categories are considered strategic and are produced in-house if possible. The analytical procedure used in making these decisions is straightforward and is shown in Figure 10.1.

If the analysis to this point indicates that a make decision is desirable from a strategic point of view, before that decision is made, several additional factors must be analyzed. These practical considerations

---

[6]Bjorn Axelsson, Ph.D., Finn Wynstra, Ph.D., and Arjan van Weele, Ph.D., "Purchasing Involvement in Product Development: A Framework," *European Journal of Purchasing and Supply Management* 5, nos. 3/4 (September/December 1999), pp. 129–41.

**Deal first with subsystems of the product:**

**Figure 10.1 |** Analyzing Strategic Outsource Decisions

*In some cases, in the short run it is not possible to make such an item in-house. This may be due to budget constraints, capability problems, capacity limitations in-house technical skills, equipment needs and so on. In these cases, until the problem is resolved, the item must be outsourced under a carefully crafted and managed contract.

focus on a comparison of the firm's current situation with that of potential suppliers with respect to the matters of design, manufacturing, and quality capabilities. Similarly, relative costs and volume requirements also need to be compared and evaluated as supplementary information to be used in conjunction with the strategic analysis in reaching a final decision.

This, then, is the approach used at the strategic level of analysis to determine whether a firm should make an item or outsource it. These are the crucial decisions that to a great extent shape the destiny of the firm.

Let us turn now to make-or-buy decisions that are made at the operating level.

# Tactical Decisions

After the strategic make and outsourcing decisions are finalized and as operations progress, a number of situations inevitably arise that require additional make-or-buy analyses at something less than a strategic level. Unsatisfactory supplier performance in the case of some outsourced items, cost considerations, changing sales demands, restricted manufacturing capacity, and the modification of an existing product are just a few of the operating factors that generate these needs. As a general rule, from a make perspective, these tactical make-or-buy situations involve items for which the firm already has most of the necessary production resources. Small investments in tooling, minor equipment, or a few additional personnel usually are all that would be needed to do the job in-house. Consequently, these investigations tend to be driven by operating considerations of efficiency, control of quality and reliability, cost, capacity utilization, and so on.

In any case, the make-or-buy possibility requiring only a small expenditure of funds in the event of a make decision is the type most commonly encountered by supply managers. A decision of this type usually does affect a firm's resource allocation plans; however, its effect on the firm's future is minimal compared with a decision requiring a major capital investment. Although the decision requiring a nominal expenditure of funds does not require direct top-management participation, it does require coordinated study by several operating departments, perhaps using a team approach. Top management's responsibility is to develop an operating procedure which provides for the pooling and analysis of information from all departments affected by the decision. In other words, management should ensure that the decision is made only after all relevant inputs have been evaluated.

# Factors Influencing Make-or-Buy Decisions

Two factors stand out above all others in considering the make-or-buy question at the tactical level: total cost of ownership and availability of production capacity. A good make-or-buy decision nevertheless requires the evaluation of many less tangible factors in addition to these two basic factors. The following considerations influence firms to make or to buy the items used in their finished products or operations.

### Considerations Which Favor Making

1. Cost considerations (less expensive to make the part).
2. Desire to integrate plant operations.
3. Productive use of excess plant capacity to help absorb fixed overhead.
4. Need to exert direct control over production and/or quality.
5. Design secrecy required.
6. Unreliable suppliers.
7. Desire to maintain a stable workforce (in periods of declining sales).

### Considerations Which Favor Buying

1. Limited production facilities.
2. Cost considerations (less expensive to buy the part).
3. Small-volume requirements.
4. Suppliers' research and specialized know-how.
5. Desire to maintain a stable workforce (in periods of rising sales).
6. Desire to maintain a multiple-source policy.
7. Indirect managerial control considerations.
8. Procurement and inventory considerations.

## Cost Considerations

In some cases, cost considerations indicate that a part should be made in-house; in others, they dictate that it should be purchased externally. Cost is obviously important, yet no other factor is subject to more varied interpretation and greater misunderstanding. A make-or-buy cost analysis involves a determination of the cost to make an item and a comparison of that cost with the cost to buy the item. The following checklist provides a summary of the major elements which should be included in a make-or-buy cost estimate.

### To Make

1. Delivered purchased material costs.
2. Direct labor costs.[7]
3. Any follow-on costs stemming from quality and related problems.

---

[7]It is assumed that all inspection costs associated with the make operation are included in the direct labor costs.

4. Incremental inventory carrying costs.
5. Incremental factory overhead costs.
6. Incremental managerial costs.
7. Incremental purchasing costs.
8. Incremental costs of capital.

*To Buy*

1. Purchase price of the part.
2. Transportation costs.
3. Receiving and inspection costs.
4. Incremental purchasing costs.
5. Any follow-on costs related to quality or service.

To see the comparative cost picture clearly, the analyst must evaluate these costs carefully, considering the effects of time and capacity utilization in the user's plant.

**The Time Factor**   Costs can be figured on either a short-term or a long-term basis. Short-term calculations tend to focus on direct measurable costs. Therefore, they frequently understate tooling costs and overlook indirect materials costs such as those incurred in storage, purchasing, inspection, and similar activities. Also, a short-term cost analysis fails to consider the likely future changes in the relative costs of labor, materials, transportation, and so on. Consequently, in comparing the costs to make and to buy, the long-term view is the correct one. Cost figures must include all relevant costs, direct and indirect, and reflect the effect of anticipated cost changes.

Since it is difficult to predict future cost levels, estimated average cost figures for the total period in question generally are used. Even though an estimate of future costs cannot be completely accurate, the following example illustrates its value.

Suppose the user of a stamped part develops permanent excess capacity in its general-purpose press department. The firm subsequently decides to make the stamped part that previously was purchased from a specialized metalworking firm. Because this enables the firm to reactivate several unused presses, the additional cost to make the item is less than the cost to buy it. However, the user finds that the labor segment of its total cost is much higher than the labor segment of the automated supplier's cost. If labor costs continue to rise more rapidly than the other costs of production, the user's cost advantage in making the part may soon disappear. Therefore, an estimate of future cost behavior can prevent a make decision that may prove unprofitable in the future.

Another factor that should be considered is the need for time-based competition. Many companies, especially high-tech firms, compete by reducing the amount of time necessary to produce or complete activities. The ability to reduce cycle time is a key strategy for gaining competitive advantage. Time is a critical issue in developing new products and bringing them to market. Making the decision to outsource research and development or the manufacturing or distribution of a product will affect the time required to bring new technology to market. Make-or-buy decisions have a strong impact on reducing cycle time in all aspects of a business.

**The Capacity Factor**   When the cost to make a part is calculated, determining the relevant overhead costs poses a difficult problem. The root of the problem lies in the user's capacity utilization factor. As in most managerial cost analyses, the costs relevant to a make-or-buy decision are the incremental costs. In this case, incremental costs are those costs which would not be incurred if the part were purchased outside. The overhead problem centers on the fact that the incremental overhead costs vary from time to time, depending on the extent to which production facilities are utilized for existing products.

For example, assume that an automobile engine manufacturer currently buys its piston pins from a distant machine shop. For various reasons, the engine producer decides that it wants to make the piston pins in its own shop. Investigation reveals that the machine shop is loaded to capacity with existing work and will remain in that condition in the foreseeable future. If the firm decides to make its own piston pins, it will have to purchase additional machining equipment or free existing equipment by subcontracting to an outside supplier a part currently made in-house. In this situation, the incremental factory overhead cost figure should include the variable overhead caused by the production of piston pins, plus the full portion of fixed overhead allocable to the piston pin operation.[8]

Now assume that the engine manufacturer wants to make its own piston pins and has enough excess capacity to make the pins in its machine shop with existing equipment. Investigation shows that the excess capacity will exist for at least the next two or three years. What are its incremental overhead costs to make the pins in this situation? Only the variable overhead caused by production of the piston pins! In this case, fixed overhead represents sunk costs which continue to accumulate whether piston pins are produced or not. The total machine shop building continues to generate depreciation charges. Heat, light, and janitorial services are still furnished to the total machine shop area. Also, property taxes for the machine shop remain the same regardless of the number of machines productively employed. The firm incurs these fixed costs regardless of the make-or-buy action on which it decides. Such costs, under conditions of idle capacity, are not incremental costs and, for purposes of the make-or-buy decision, must be omitted from computation of the cost to make a new part.

The concept can be observed from a slightly different point of view in the graphic representation in Figure 10.2. Note that a 12½ percent increase in production volume (an increase from 80 to 90 percent of capacity) can be achieved with a total cost increase of only 10 percent. This favorable situation results simply because the 12½ percent increase in production is accomplished by activating unused capacity. Fixed overhead costs are incurred regardless of the decision to make piston pins by utilizing unused capacity.

Finally, consider a third common situation in which the engine manufacturer wants to make its own piston pins. Investigation in this case reveals that there currently is enough excess capacity in the machine shop to permit production of the piston pins. However, management expects a gradual increase in business during the next several years, which will eliminate all excess capacity by the end of the second year. How should the make-or-buy decision be approached in this case?

As always, the starting point of the analysis is an estimate of the costs to make versus the costs to buy. For the first one to two years, the cost to make piston pins will not include fixed overhead because excess capacity exists. Beyond two years, however, the cost to make must include fixed overhead; if piston pins are not made, increased production of some other part will, in the normal course of business, carry its full share of fixed overhead. One alternative is to consider the make-or-buy decision separately for each of the two time periods. While the analysis may indicate that it is profitable to make the pins in both cases, it probably will reveal that it is profitable to make the pins only for the first two years and buy them beyond that date. In this case, several qualitative factors must be investigated to determine the practical feasibility of a split course of action. If that course of action does not appear feasible, a second alternative is to

---

[8]If piston pin production replaces the production of another part, the piston pin operation should carry the same absolute amount of fixed overhead that was carried by the part that was replaced. If new equipment is purchased to produce piston pins, the piston pin operation should be charged with the additional fixed overhead arising from acquisition of the new equipment.

**Figure 10.2 |** A Representative Case Illustrating the Incremental Costs Resulting from a Make Decision When Operating at 80 Percent of Production Capacity

compute a weighted average cost to make the pins during both periods. The cost data can then be used in considering the total make-or-buy question.

In practice, an infinite number of situations exist between the two extremes of excess capacity and full capacity. There is no simple, absolutely accurate solution to any of these problems. Each situation must be analyzed in its own dynamic context.

In summary, an analyst should be guided by several basic ideas. First, incremental costs are virtually always the costs relevant to the managerial decision-making process. Second, the determination of a realistic cost to make an item requires a realistic estimate of the future conditions of capacity. When capacity can be utilized by existing business or by alternative new projects, incremental overhead costs to make a new item must reflect total overhead costs. During any period when this condition does not exist, the incremental overhead to make consists only of variable overhead. When conditions of capacity normally fluctuate frequently between partial load and full load, it is likely that the make-or-buy decision for a new project of substantial duration will turn largely on considerations other than comparative cost.

**Precautions in Developing Costs**    If a firm decides to buy a part that it has made in the past, it must exercise particular care in interpreting the quotations it receives from potential suppliers. Some suppliers may prepare the quotation carelessly, with the mistaken idea that the user does not really intend to buy the part. Other suppliers may bid unrealistically low in an attempt to induce the user to discontinue making the part in favor of buying it. Once the user has discontinued its make operation, resumption of the operation in the future may be costly. Thus, the user may be at the mercy of the supplier if the supplier later chooses to increase the price.[9] It is essential that the supply management professional carefully evaluate the reliability of all quotations in his or her attempt to determine a realistic estimate of the total cost to buy the part.

In estimating the cost to make a part, an analyst must be sure that the firm has adequate equipment and technical know-how to do the job. Moreover, in an industry in which technological change occurs rapidly, a firm can find its equipment and know-how competitively outmoded in a few short years. Thus, the

---

[9]A partnering arrangement or a long-term requirements contract may be used to control such price increases.

factor of obsolescence should be given adequate consideration in determining the ultimate costs of equipment and personnel training.

The proper equipment to make an item sometimes may be easier to acquire than the properly skilled manpower. Large-volume requirements, complex skill requirements, and unique geographic locations can precipitate shortages of adequately skilled manpower. In preparing cost-to-make estimates, the local manpower situation must be evaluated. If it is necessary to import adequately skilled personnel, total labor costs can exceed initial estimates substantially.

In the case of a make decision, it is equally important to investigate the availability and price stability of required raw materials. Large users of particular materials generally find the availability and price structure of those materials much more favorable than do small unspecialized users. Wise analysts ensure that their estimates for raw material are realistic.

Finally, in estimating the cost to make a part for the first time, the analyst must investigate several practical production matters. The first deals with a partnering arrangement or a long-term requirements contract that may be used to help control price increases such as the cost of unacceptable production work. What is the expected rate of rejected and spoiled parts? Equally important, what learning curve can the production department reasonably expect to apply? Answers to these questions may vary substantially, depending on the complexity of the job and the types of workers and equipment available. The resulting influence on the make-buy cost comparison can be considerable, however, and realistic answers should be sought.

## Control of Production and Quality

Consider now some of the factors other than costs that influence make-or-buy decisions. Two conditions weigh heavily in some firms' decisions to make a particular part: control of production and control of quality.

**Production Requirements**   The need for close control of production operations is particularly acute in some firms. A company whose sales demand is subject to extreme short-run fluctuations finds that its production department must operate on unusually tight time schedules. This kind of company often produces a small inventory of parts used in several different products. However, it produces to individual customer order the parts unique to a particular product or customer specification. Sales fluctuations for products that use unique parts therefore influence the planning and scheduling of numerous assembly and subassembly operations as well as single-part production operations. Efficient conduct of assembly operations depends on the firm's ability to obtain the unique unstocked parts on short notice.

Most suppliers that serve a number of customers normally cannot tool up and fit an order for a unique part into existing schedules on a moment's notice unless they are operating under some type of JIT or partnering arrangement. If a user cannot tolerate suppliers' lead-time requirements, its only major alternative is to control the part production operations itself. Thus, by making the item, the user acquires the needed control. It then is possible to revise job priorities quickly, reassign operators and machines to specific jobs, and require overtime work as conditions demand.

Some firms also choose to make certain critical parts to assure continuity of supply of those parts to succeeding production operations. This type of integration guards against production shutdowns caused by supplier labor problems, local transportation strikes, and miscellaneous supplier service problems. These are particularly important considerations in dealing with parts that feed an automated production operation whose downtime is tremendously expensive. If such an action reduces the risk of a production stoppage, it may justify the incurrence of extra materials costs.

**Quality Requirements** Unique quality requirements often represent a second condition requiring control of part production operations. Certain parts in technical products are occasionally quite difficult to manufacture. Compounding this difficulty at times is an unusually exacting quality specification the part must meet. In certain technological fields or in particular geographic areas, a user may find that the uniqueness of the task results in unsatisfactory performance by an outside supplier. Some companies find that their own firm is in a better position to do an acceptable production job than are external suppliers.

A user normally understands more completely than an outside supplier the operational intricacies connected with use of the part. Therefore, if the using firm makes the part itself, there can be greater coordination between the assembly operation and the part production operation. Conducting both operations under one roof likewise eliminates many communications problems which can arise between a supply management professional and a supplier whose operations are geographically separated. Finally, large users often have technological resources superior to those of smaller suppliers. Those resources may be needed in solving new technical problems in production.

For example, one producer of hydraulic systems makes a practice of subcontracting production of some of the valves used in its systems. The production of one particular subcontracted valve involved difficult interior machining operations as well as tight quality requirements. In the supplier's first four shipments, the systems manufacturer rejected 80 percent of the valves for failure to meet quality specifications. During the ensuing months, the systems manufacturer worked closely with the subcontractor to solve the quality problem. With the passage of time, however, it became clear that the systems manufacturer was contributing considerably more to the solution of the problem than was the supplier. Eventually, the systems firm decided to make the valve. Although production of the valve remained a difficult task, the systems manufacturer was able to develop the techniques necessary to produce a valve of acceptable quality, with a greatly reduced reject percentage.

The American Airline Industry has learned that outsourcing of critical operations such as aircraft maintenance can be very dangerous causing major investigations by the Federal Aviation Administration (FAA). Outsourcing may require more quality control supervision than internal operations.

## Business Process Outsourcing

As outsourcing has gained in popularity, the opportunity to outsource business processes has increased greatly. Lisa Ellram and Arnold Maltz have described business process outsourcing as the transfer of responsibility to a third-party of activities which used to be performed internally.[10] Many consulting firms are competing to be external providers of these services because of the "commoditization"of generic services. Companies that formerly outsourced only information technology (IT) now outsource many business processes that are not core competencies. Advertising, accounting, maintenance, auditing, travel, and human resources are functional services that commonly are outsourced. In addition, companies are beginning to outsource major business systems, including logistics, real estate, and software systems development. Companies are realizing more than cost reduction by outsourcing these activities; they are able to take advantage of innovative, specialized suppliers. James Brian Quinn has stated, "Proper outsourcing of entire business processes can speed and amplify major innovative changes."[11]

The success that has resulted from outsourcing business processes has encouraged many firms to outsource entire operational functions. Firms have been outsourcing supply management without receiving

---

[10]Ellram and Maltz, "Outsourcing Supply Management," *op cit.*

[11]James Brian Quinn, Ph.D., "Outsourcing Innovation: The New Engine of Growth," *Sloan Management Review,* July 1, 2000, pp. 13–28.

much improvement in cost reduction or innovation. Often internal purchasing has proved to be more effective than using a third-party supplier for supply management. Firms that use programs such as JIT and VMI (vendor-managed inventory) have the most success outsourcing the activities associated with those programs. MRO purchasing is another activity that often is outsourced successfully.

The high-tech industry may benefit the most by outsourcing supply chain management activities. The need for faster cycle times and flexibility was the reason for Toshiba's decision to combine operations with a supply management provider. Toshiba outsourced responsibility for supplier management, logistics, manufacturing, testing, and order processing. Yasuo Morimoto, president and CEO of Toshiba Semiconductor Co., explained, "To be successful in this extremely competitive environment, it is absolutely essential to have the most efficient and flexible method to service the customer, wherever the customer need arises."[12] The business model Cisco Systems established relies on the outsourcing of many supply management activities to strategic partners.

While the outsourcing of some supply activities is beneficial, the need to perform critical sourcing activities internally has become apparent. Loss of control over performance or cost is important to consider when a company is deciding whether to outsource supply management activities. A third party may not be aggressive in seeking improvements. Supply management skills are strategic, hard to duplicate, lead to success in multiple business units, and can lead to dominance over competitors.[13]

**Design Secrecy Required**   Although their number is small, a few firms make particular parts primarily because they want to keep secret certain aspects of a part's design or manufacture. The secrecy justification for making an item can be found in highly competitive industries in which style and cost play unusually important roles. Also, a firm is more likely to make a key part for which patents do not provide effective protection against commercial copying.

If design secrecy is really important, however, a firm may have nearly as much difficulty maintaining secrecy when it makes a part as it does when a supplier makes it. In either case, a large number of individuals must be taken into the firm's confidence, and once information leaks to a competitor, very little can be done about it. Nevertheless, a firm usually can control security measures more easily and directly in its own plant. In either case, however, the element of trust is extremely important. World-class firms work hard to create an atmosphere of trust for both internal and external activities.

## Technology Risk and Maturity

Technology life cycles are an important factor in the make-or-buy decision. Technology that is changing continually is not mature and has short life cycles. It may be too risky to make parts that use this type of technology internally. The investment in capital equipment would not be reasonable. Outsourcing technology that is changing rapidly places the risk on the supplier. Such suppliers are less likely to invest in the production of a part that uses mature technology. The life cycle of mature technology is reasonably stable and long term. Supply management professionals closely survey expected changes in technology. It is important to obtain insight into technology life cycles of potential materials and processes on a continuous basis.

Outsourcing is not a viable option for products with specifications that fluctuate as a result of continually developing technology or technology that is truly new. For example, Cisco Systems has decided to make many of the products in the demanding industry of optical networks. Cisco Systems is forced to integrate and perform product development internally to be competitive in this industry. Fiber optic technology is still

---

[12]"Toshiba and Kingston Establish New Supply Chain Management Model," *Business Wire,* February 29, 2000.

[13]Ellram and Maltz, "Outsourcing Supply Management." *op cit.*

in a fluctuating stage, which makes it difficult to define the specifications required to outsource development and manufacturing successfully.[14] Technology life cycles are a function of customer demand and technological advances.

## Unreliable Suppliers

Some firms decide to make specific parts because their experience has shown that the reliability record of available suppliers falls below the required level. The likelihood of encountering that situation 30 years ago was infinitely greater than it is now. Today, competition in most industries is so keen that grossly unreliable performers do not survive the competitive struggle. With one major exception, unreliable delivery or unpredictable service is confined largely to isolated cases in new, highly specialized lines of business in which competition has not become established. Those businesses usually are characterized by low sales volumes, the requirement for highly specialized production equipment, or the unique possession of new technological capabilities.

The one major exception mentioned above is the case of a firm that purchases only an insignificant fraction of a specific supplier's total volume of business. Even the most reputable suppliers are forced at times to shortchange very small accounts to give significant attention to their major accounts. Regardless of the reasonableness of the cause, however, consistently unreliable performance by a supplier is sufficient grounds for switching suppliers or possibly reconsidering the original make-buy decision.

## Suppliers' Specialized Knowledge and Research

A primary reason underlying most decisions to buy a part rather than make it is the user's desire to take advantage of the specialized abilities and/or research efforts of various suppliers.

Lest the preceding discussion of make decisions distort the total procurement picture, bear in mind that the typical American manufacturing firm spends more than 50 percent of its sales dollar for purchases from external suppliers. Modern industry is highly specialized. No ordinary firm, regardless of size, can hope to possess adequate facilities and technical know-how to make a majority of its production part requirements efficiently. Large corporations spend millions of dollars on product and process research each year. The fruits of this research and the ensuing technical know-how are available to customers in the form of highly developed and refined parts and component products. A firm that considers forgoing these benefits in favor of making an item should, before making its final decision, carefully assess the long-range values that accrue from industrial specialization.

## Small-Volume Requirements

When a firm uses only a small quantity of a particular item, it usually decides to buy that item. The typical firm strives to concentrate its production efforts in areas where it is most efficient and areas it finds most profitable. The work of designing, tooling, planning, and setting up for the production of a new part is time-consuming and costly. These fixed costs are recovered more easily from long production runs than from short ones. Consequently, more often than not, a small-volume user searches for a potential supplier that specializes in the production of the part and can produce it in large quantities economically. Such specialty suppliers can sell to a large number of users in almost any desired quantity at relatively low prices.

---

[14]Clayton M. Christensen, Ph.D., "Limits of the New Corporation," *BusinessWeek*, August 28, 2000, pp. 180–81.

Small-volume production of unique, nonstandard parts also may be unattractive to external suppliers. Every supplier is obligated to concentrate first on its high-volume, high-profit accounts. Thus, cases may develop in which a user is virtually forced to make a highly nonstandard part it uses in small quantities. Generally, however, as a part tends toward a more common and finally a standard configuration, the tendency to buy increases proportionally.

## Limited Facilities

Another reason for buying rather than making certain parts is the physical limitation imposed by the user's production facilities. A firm with limited facilities typically attempts to utilize them as fully as possible on its most profitable production work. It then depends on external suppliers for the balance of its requirements. Thus, during peak periods a firm may purchase a substantial portion of its total requirements because of loaded production facilities, and during slack periods, as internal production capacity opens up, its purchases may decrease markedly.

## Workforce Stability

Closely related to the matter of facilities is the factor of workforce stability. A fluctuating production level forces a firm to face the continual problem of contracting and expanding its workforce to stay in step with production demands. Significant continuing fluctuation, moreover, negatively affects the quality of the workers the firm is able to employ. The less stable an operation is, the more difficult it becomes to retain a competent workforce.

At the time when a firm sizes the various parts of its production operation, many make-buy decisions are made. One factor which often bears heavily on the decision is the firm's desire to develop an interested, responsible group of workers with a high degree of company loyalty. Awareness that stable employment helps attain this objective sometimes prompts a firm to undersize its production facility by a slight margin. Its plan is to maintain as stable an internal production operation as possible and to buy requirements in excess of its capacity from external suppliers. This policy is most effective in firms whose products require a considerable amount of general-purpose equipment in the manufacturing operation. Equipment, as well as personnel, that can perform a variety of different jobs provides the internal flexibility required to consolidate or split work among various production areas as business fluctuates. This capability is necessary for the successful implementation of such a policy. As business increases, it is not feasible to place small orders for a large number of different parts with outside suppliers. It is much more profitable to farm out large orders for a small number of parts.

Firms that solve their workforce problems in this way frequently create problems in the purchasing area. External suppliers, in effect, are used as buffers to absorb the shocks of production fluctuations. This action transfers many of the problems associated with production fluctuations from the user to the supplier. The supplier's ability to absorb these production shocks is therefore an important consideration. In some instances, it may be able to absorb them reasonably well; in others, it may not.[15] In all cases, however, the supplier prefers, as does the user, to maintain a stable production operation. Consequently, many suppliers

---

[15]Two factors largely determine a supplier's ability to absorb fluctuating order requirements from a user:

1. The similarity of the work involved in producing a particular user's requirement and in producing other customers' orders. The more similar the requirements are, the lower is the expense of planning setup work for a particular user.

2. The extent to which other customers' orders offset the peaks and valleys in the supplier's production operation. The more stable the supplier's total production operation is, the less disturbing is the effect of an occasional fluctuating account.

are not interested in a customer that buys only its peak requirements. The question naturally arises, "Will a supplier ever be motivated to perform well for a purchaser who uses the supplier only for surplus work?" This question should be considered carefully before a buy decision of this type is made.

A third choice is available for maintaining a stable workforce. A company may choose leased labor to alleviate the need to maintain a steady number of employees during fluctuations in production. External temporary manpower support is utilized instead of permanent employees or complete outsourcing of the task or function. Leased labor can run the gauntlet from clerical help to highly skilled professionals. Quality is maintained by selecting leased employees who are competent in the areas required. A supply management professional must be aware of all aspects of the leased-labor business. Agencies providing leased labor should be analyzed and selected with great care. Payment terms, temporary to permanent employment options, and functional variations should be determined before the implementation of a plan to use leased labor.

## Multiple-Source Policy

Some firms occasionally make and buy the same nonstandard part. This policy is followed for the explicit purpose of having available a reliable and experienced second source of supply. Firms that adopt a make-and-buy policy recognize that they may not always be able to meet their internal production schedules for certain parts. In an emergency, an experienced outside source usually is willing to increase its delivery of the part in question on a temporary basis until the situation is under control.

## Managerial Control Considerations

Companies occasionally buy and make the same part for the purpose of developing managerial control data. Some firms use outside suppliers' cost and quality performance as a check on their own internal production efficiency. If internal costs for a particular part rise above a supplier's cost, the user knows that somewhere in its own production system some element of cost is probably out of line. An investigation frequently uncovers one or more problems, some of which may extend to other production areas. These consequent improvements may have a compounding effect as they reach into other operations where inefficiencies might have gone undetected.

## Procurement and Inventory Considerations

A buy decision produces several significant benefits in the management of supply and inventory activities. For supply management, a buy decision typically means that it has fewer items to buy and fewer suppliers to deal with. Usually, though not always, when a component is made in-house, a number of different materials or parts must be purchased outside to support the make operation. A corresponding buy decision usually involves only one or two suppliers and a relative reduction in the associated buying, paperwork, and follow-up activities. The same relative reduction in workload occurs in receiving, inspection, stores, and inventory management groups. Typically, inventory investment also is reduced.

# Netsourcing

The Internet has enabled companies to manage supply more efficiently and effectively. A supply management professional now can locate and research new suppliers by accessing information on the Internet. The Internet has become an open market for electronic business transactions. Many tactical supply management activities can be replaced by the use of electronic forms and direct connections with suppliers. Intranets have become a way to provide services to personnel by connecting employees directly with preferred providers. The Web offers an aggregation of common business tools that allow more efficient management of many business processes. The Internet can replace many different services and functions, including human resources, accounts payable and receivable, and document storage systems. The online business revolution requires companies to develop infrastructures and websites quickly.

# The Volatile Nature of the Make-or-Buy Decision

Although make-or-buy investigations normally begin with a cost analysis, various qualitative factors frequently foretell more far-reaching consequences than does the cost analysis. Therefore, a correctly approached make-or-buy decision considers the probable *composite effect* of all factors on the firm's total operation.

A thorough investigation is complicated considerably by the dynamics and uncertainties of business activity. Certain factors can have very different implications for a make-or-buy decision at different points in time and under different operating conditions. As has been pointed out, changing costs can turn a good decision into a bad one in a very short period. In addition, future costs, complicated by numerous demand and capacity interrelationships, are influenced substantially by variable factors such as technological innovation and customer demand. The availability of expansion capital also influences make-or-buy decisions. An "easy money" policy, a liberal depreciation policy, and liberal government taxing policies tend to encourage make decisions. The opposite policies promote buy decisions. These federal policies fluctuate with economic and political conditions.

The tendency toward favoring make decisions to stabilize production and workforce fluctuation is usually greater in small firms than in large ones. In some small shops, the loss of just a few orders results in the temporary layoff of a sizable percentage of the workforce until additional orders can be obtained. Generally, larger organizations do not have such severe problems because their fluctuations in production volume relative to total capacity are smaller. As large firms adopt compensation plans that move toward a guaranteed wage structure, however, they too feel a similar pressure to favor make decisions.

Finally, the labor-relations climate within a firm can influence its make-or-buy decisions. A hostile union may seize the opportunity to irritate management as a result of the decision to buy an item that previously was made in-house. An amicable labor-management climate may generate a very different reaction.

To summarize, beware of rigid formulas and rules of thumb that claim to produce easy make-or-buy decisions. The make-or-buy question is influenced by a multitude of diverse factors that are in a constant state of change. Under such conditions, few easy decisions turn out well in both the short run and the long run. Moreover, the relevant factors vary immensely from one firm to another. For these reasons, every company should evaluate the effectiveness of its past decisions periodically to generate information helpful in guiding future courses of make-buy action. Some make/buy experts feel the "make" decision is usually weaker, more risky than the "buy" decision because make costs are usually estimates and could be much higher than expected.

## Insourcing

Core competencies change. Thus, periodic reevaluation of outsourcing decisions is a strategic necessity. Although it is often expensive and difficult to bring an activity back in-house, changes in core activities, technology, or strategy may require a company to reverse a make-or-buy decision. Continued involvement is always necessary when a buy decision has been implemented. Managing the supplier relationship for an outsourced activity will allow a company to make adjustments when problems arise. Change management has been recognized as a needed skill for handling the transition of such activities. Implementing the decision to outsource or bring an activity back in-house involves a formal transition process that affects the organizations of both the firm and the supplier.

## Dangers of Outsourcing

**Loss of Control**   Entrusting an entire process to an external provider may cause loss of control and skills, resulting in overdependency. A firm may lose key information resources if it does not engage in continuous and active management of the outsourcing contract. Information that is required to manage the business and future growth effectively will not be communicated. Inadequate involvement is often the cause of this problem. Supply professionals must be good at supplier management for an outsourcing program to work. The airline industry has outsourced significant percentages of aircraft maintenance causing great concern to the FAA over major maintenance problems.

**Loss of Client Focus**   The goals and objectives of the selected external provider may differ from the firm's goals. Eventually the provider will lose touch with the firm's business plan and strategy. The provider may cause a conflict of interest if similar outsourced functions are performed for other organizations. Key resources from one firm may be used to support other clients. These activities affect the timely and successful performance of the outsourced function.

**Lack of Clarity**   Failure to articulate clearly the responsibilities of the selected external provider is a major concern. A formal service level agreement (SLA) contract must be developed before services are outsourced. Without a clear and agreed on contract, the outsource provider can cause costly and disruptive disputes with claims of "out of scope" work. A formal agreement avoids the extra charges for every change or request that such providers can assess. The agreement should specify how changes and requests will be processed and include a mechanism or formula for pricing such changes.

**Lack of Cost Control**   Many outsourcing decisions are made in an effort to lower overall costs. Changes in company objectives and rising prices can take costs beyond the estimates made for the initial analysis. If the outsourcing contract does not include long-term pricing with appropriate incentives, the outsource provider will not be motivated to control costs or maintain quality. This problem is affected by an inflexible contract. The buying company should specify in the outsourcing contract the degree to which it desires to manage costs and the appropriate mechanics. It can be very difficult to disengage from a poorly structured outsourcing contract. Inflexible conditions limit the ability to support changing business strategies and objectives. If a company is unable to manage an outsourcing contract appropriately, it may need to insource to regain control of those activities. Bringing a function or service back in-house is expensive, and the organization usually lacks employees with the required skill sets.

**Ineffective Management**   The selected external provider may not perform the outsourced function better than the client organization can. Many companies have outsourced a function without carefully prequalifying the provider on the basis of efficiency, effectiveness, and total capabilities. Careless outsourcing ultimately costs more than keeping a function in-house. Without proper analysis and consideration, a function may be outsourced for the wrong reasons. Managers may decide to outsource because of a problem they are experiencing with a function in-house only to find that the selected provider cannot solve the problem. For example, management may believe that the internal IT department is not sensitive to the needs of the users. An external provider is not necessarily going to be more sensitive to those needs. This type of problem can be avoided by developing a precise statement of work, carefully researching and prequalifying providers, and utilizing a clear service level agreement.

**Loss of Confidentiality**  Outsourcing often means off-loading sensitive functions involving proprietary corporate data. Concerns about loss of control of these functions and the protection of the underlying information are valid, particularly in an environment where hacking is a blood sport. This raises several issues:

- Is the outsourcing service provider's system secure against external and internal threats?
- What kind of security monitoring is in place?
- How will the service provider prevent intentional and unintentional disclosure of private data?
- What may the service provider do with data it has received from your company?
- How will your company know if sensitive data have leaked from the service provider's system?

Service providers must answer all these questions satisfactorily, and executives charged with outsourcing IT functions should validate all claims before retaining any service provider.[16]

**Double Outsourcing**  The practice of double outsourcing essentially involves the subcontracting of an outsourcing contract. This type of arrangement can backfire if the client does not manage the agreements with both companies. Double outsourcing is common with functions that are outsourced frequently, such as IT. The external provider may not have the necessary technical skills to perform all the outsourced work and will subcontract to fulfill the contract requirements. If the selected external provider is considering the use of a third party, the supply manager should select and manage the subcontractor. Problems occur when the provider utilizes a subcontractor without involving the client. This leaves the client firm with little control over problems caused by the outsource provider's subcontractor.[17]

# Administration of Make-or-Buy Activities

It is not difficult to find otherwise well-managed firms in which many tactical make-or-buy decisions are delegated inadvertently to an operating person in inventory control or production control. It should be apparent that this is a poor practice. In the first place, such a person normally does not have adequate information with which to make an intelligent decision from a companywide point of view. Second, even if adequate information is available, this type of person typically lacks the breadth of experience to evaluate fully the significance of the information and the resultant decision.

## Chief Resource Officer

Strategic outsourcing is an emerging trend in the business world. A new management role is being developed as a result of this trend: the Chief Resource Officer.[18] The CRO manages and initiates outsourcing for direct support to the company's bottom line. Outsourcing deals are accounting for an increasingly large amount of corporate expenditures. Both the overall risks and the rewards are becoming greater with increased outsourcing activity. The need for active management and skilled leadership is increasing. The CRO, essentially the director of external resources, is responsible for all outsourcing relationships and for ensuring that they live up to expectations. Companies that are embracing strategic outsourcing are beginning to realize the need for a dedicated team of individuals to oversee outsourcing activities. John Chiazza,

---

[16]Scott J. Nathan, "Reducing the Risk of Outsourcing," *Supply Strategy,* May/June, 2001, p. 20.

[17]"Getting into Outsourcing," *NAPM InfoEdge,* January 1998, pp. 1–16.

[18]Frank Casale, "The Rise of the Chief Resource Officer," *Business Briefing: European Purchasing and Logistics Strategies,* July 1999, pp. 81–82.

Chief Information Officer at Kodak, advocates establishing relationship management groups to "research potential outsourcers, negotiate terms, and address other matters of policy . . . individual relationship managers interact with the outsourcing providers on a day-to-day basis."[19] These outsourcing professionals have three essential skills: negotiation, communication, and project management skills.

## Framework for Outsourcing

Many frameworks have been developed for successful outsourcing. All of them involve information gathering, developing a strategic road map, and a decision flow chart.[20] Developing a "transition back" plan is an important step that often is ignored. It is less costly to have a plan in place in the event that the outsourced function needs to be brought back in-house. It will be easier to transfer the function back in-house or to another provider if such a contingency was planned for initially. In addition to providing an operational framework within which make-or-buy alternatives are investigated, a review system is necessary. The system should provide procedures for three important additional activities: (1) the entry of projects into the study system, (2) the maintenance of essential records, and (3) a periodic audit of important decisions.

Procedures should be established as part of a firm's product development program, compelling high-value and strategically oriented parts in new products to enter the make-or-buy analysis process. In some cases, this analysis can be integrated effectively with preproduction value engineering investigations. Similarly, existing production parts should be subjected to a systematic review which searches for borderline make-or-buy items that warrant careful study.

Regardless of the source of entry, all make-or-buy investigations should be classified as "major" or "minor" on the basis of the value and strategic nature of the part. In one firm, all items involving expenditures under $25,000 are classed as minor. Subsequent studies of minor items involve personnel from production, supply management, quality control, and occasionally design engineering. Major items entail expenditures over $25,000 and additionally involve personnel from finance, marketing, and other production areas.

Summary records are essential to full utilization of the data developed in make-or-buy investigations. The record should be designed to serve as a useful future reference. A brief discussion of all the factors pertinent to the decision that was made should be included, as well as the primary reasons for the decision. Assumptions about future conditions should be stated. An accurate summary of cost data always should be included. Records of this type provide the information required when a firm is forced to make quick decisions about subcontracting work under peak operating conditions or about bringing work back into the shop when business slumps. Accurate records can make the difference between a profitable decision based on facts and a hopeful decision based on intuition and hunches. Finally, investigation records provide the basic data for post-decision audits.

## Executive-Level Involvement

In most cases, make-or-buy decisions should be made or at least reviewed at the executive level. The decision maker must be able to view such decisions with a broad companywide perspective. Many progressive firms use a team or committee approach to analyze make-or-buy alternatives. The important point to keep in mind is that all departments that can contribute to the decision or that are affected by it should have a voice in making it. A team or committee accomplishes this directly. In other cases, a formal mechanism must be established which facilitates and perhaps requires all interested departments to submit relevant data and suggestions

---

[19]Scott Leibs, "Special Report on Outsourcing: How You Slice It," *CFO Magazine*, February 2001, pp. 81–86.

[20]For more information see Eric Sislian and Ahmet, Satir, "Strategic Sourcing: A Framework and a Case Study," *Journal of Supply Chain Management*, Summer 2000.

to the decision maker. Moreover, to ensure thoroughness and consistency, the system must detail the cost computation procedures to be used and assign cost investigations to specific operating groups.

## The Special Disadvantages of Outsourcing Business Processes

While many of the negatives involved in make-or-buy decisions have been discussed in this chapter, there are special risks involved in business process outsourcing (BPO), the moving of "back office" functions such as accounting to third-party providers. "Many companies overweight the cost factor in their original analysis and underweight (or ignore) the other relevant variables."[21] The other variables include the quality of delivered services, risk to branding, loss of in-house knowledge and skills necessary to evaluate the service effort, connections to the other business functions, and documentation of the process for the handoff to the supplier. Several firms have had to bring back telephone service centers at the insistence of their customers. In all buy and outsourcing decisions, there is some, and at times serious, loss of control.

## Concluding Remarks

If one takes a broad view of the American industrial scene over the last several decades, three characteristics stand out clearly: (1) Firms are becoming more aware of the strategic dimension of the make-or-buy decision; management is more proactive in identifying and exploiting the firm's core competencies as organizations adopt lean manufacturing strategies; (2) most manufacturing firms have become much more specialized as technology has advanced—in the words of researchers Peters and Waterman, they "stick to their knitting";[22] and (3) the cost of materials, expressed as a percentage of total product cost, has continued to increase in many industries. These three factors lead to the inevitable conclusion that in the aggregate, American firms are buying more and making less. Planned or unplanned, the trend continues to develop.

Yet at the managerial level, many successful firms have not handled the recurring make-or-buy issue in a well-organized, systematic manner. Instead, many have elected to deal with specific cases on an ad hoc basis as they arise.

This situation is understandable yet ironic. In earlier years when the cost-price squeeze was less severe for many firms, poor decisions in this area did not affect earnings dramatically. Yet in the aggregate, make-or-buy decisions significantly affect a firm's ability to utilize its resources in an optimal manner. Past practices are changing. Three forces will continue to stimulate this change:

- *Pressures on profit margins* are severe and will continue to increase. Resources must be utilized more effectively.

- *Firms continue to become more highly specialized* in products and production technology, producing greater cost differentials between making and buying for many users.

- Computer modeling capability is becoming commonplace; make-or-buy evaluation and control systems can be developed and handled quasi-automatically with this capability.

Just as materials management organizations, MRP systems, and JIT systems have developed over the last several decades, implementation systems for recurring make-or-buy analysis are being developed.[23]

---

[21]Steve Matthesen, "It's Not Just about Cost," *Inside Supply Management,* March 2006, pp. 12–14. Matthesen is Vice President and Global Leader for Supply Chain, Boston Consulting Group (BCG), in Los Angeles.

[22]T. J. Peters and R. H. Waterman, *In Search of Excellence* (New York: Harper & Row, 1982), pp. 292–305.

[23]Readers interested in a detailed examination of the make-or-buy issue should review the classical study conducted some years ago by J. W. Culliton, *Make or Buy?* Research Study 27, Graduate School of Business Administration, Harvard University, Boston, 1942 (4th reprint, 1956).

## Discussion Questions

1. Why is outsourcing becoming increasingly common?
2. What is meant by the term "core competencies"?
3. Why is it a mistake to view a firm as a portfolio of businesses and products?
4. What strategic danger resulting from outsourcing does Chris Lonsdale identify?
5. What three dangers does Michael Porter identify?
6. What three dangers does vertical integration introduce?
7. What is meant by the term "virtual corporation"?
8. When is the make-or-buy issue first encountered?
9. What frequently is the impact of strict deadlines during new product development?
10. An increasing number of firms outsource subsystems and components unless they fall into one or more of certain categories. Describe those categories.
11. What two issues are critical in conducting a make-or-buy cost analysis at the tactical level?
12. What is the relationship between make-or-buy decisions and cycle time reduction?
13. What should be the basis of operational make-or-buy cost analyses?
14. What is meant by the term "business process outsourcing"?
15. What is the inherent danger in attempting to maintain a stable workforce by outsourcing peaks in demand?
16. What are the likely staffing implications of an increase in outsourcing at a firm?
17. What are the implications of the online business revolution?
18. What is the likely impact of "easy money" on the make-or-buy decision? Why?
19. What is the likely impact of a "guaranteed annual wage" on the make-or-buy decision? Why?
20. Describe the "insourcing" process. How is it best conducted?
21. Describe the following dangers of outsourcing:
    a. loss of control
    b. loss of client focus
    c. lack of clarity
    d. lack of cost control
    e. ineffective management
    f. loss of confidentiality
22. Describe "double outsourcing."
23. Describe the ideal amount of executive level involvement in the make-or-buy process.

## Internet Exercise

### Business Process Outsourcing

#### Procter & Gamble: Case Study

Visit the following website outlining Procter & Gamble's outsourcing of the accounts payable function. Read the article and answer the following questions.
(http://h20219.www2.hp.com/services/cache/83969-0-0-225-121.html)

1. Why is Procter & Gamble concerned about HP's culture and values?
2. What would you identify P&G's core competencies to be? What does P&G see as HP's core competencies?
3. Who do you think will benefit from this relationship?

# Suggested Reading

Berry, John. *Offshoring Opportunities: Strategies and Tactics for Global Competitiveness* (Hoboken, NJ: John Wiley & Sons, 2006).

Carter, Joseph R., William J. Markham, and Robert M. Monczka. "Procurement Outsourcing: Right for You?" *Supply Chain Management Review* 11, no. 4 (May–June 2007), p. 26.

Cohen, Linda, and Allie Young. *Multisourcing: Moving beyond Outsourcing to Achieve Growth and Agility* (Boston: Harvard Business School Press, 2006), http://www.HBSPress.org.

Corbet, Michael F. *The Outsourcing Revolution: Why It Makes Sense and How to Do It Right* (Chicago: Dearborn Trade Publishing, 2004).

Duening, Thomas N., and Rick L. Click. *Essentials of Business Process Outsourcing* (Hoboken, NJ: John Wiley & Sons, 2005).

Engardio, Pete, Michael Amdt, and Dean Foust. "The Future of Outsourcing," *BusinessWeek*, "Special Report: Outsourcing," January 30, 2006.

Fine, C. H., and D. E. Whitney. "Is the Make-Buy Decision Process a Core Competence?" MIT Center for Technology, Policy, and Industrial Development, Cambridge, MA, 1996.

Gietzmann, M. B. "Make or Buy Revisited: Some Lessons from Japan," *Management Accounting* 73, no. 1 (1995), pp. 24–25.

Greaver, Maurice F. *Strategic Outsourcing: A Structured Approach to Outsourcing Decisions and Initiatives* (New York: AMACOM, 1999).

Halvey, John K., and Barbara Murphy Melby. *Business Process Outsourcing: Process, Strategies, and Contracts,* 2nd ed. (Hoboken, NJ: John Wiley & Sons, 2007).

McIvor, R. T., and P. K. Humphreys. "A Case-Based Reasoning Approach to the Make or Buy Decision," *Integrated Manufacturing Systems* 11, no. 5 (2000), pp. 265–310.

Parker, David W., and Katie A. Russell. "Outsourcing and Inter/Intra Supply Chain Dynamics: Strategic Management Issues," *Journal of Supply Chain Management* 40, no. 4 (Fall 2004), p. 56.

Perrons, R. K. "The Long-Term Irrelevance of Trust in Outsourcing Decisions for New Technologies: Insights from an Agent-Based Model," *Supply Chain Forum: An International Journal* 6, no. 2 (2003), pp. 30–37.

Perrons, R. K., and K. Platts. "Make-Buy Decisions in the Face of Technological Change: Does Industry Clockspeed Matter?" *International Journal of Management and Enterprise Development* 2, no. 1 (2005), pp. 1–11.

Perrons, R. K., M. G. Richards, and K. Platts. "What the Hare Can Teach the Tortoise about Make-Buy Strategies for Radical Innovations," *Management Decision* 43, no. 5 (2005), pp. 670–90.

Quinn, J. B. "Outsourcing Innovation: The New Engine of Growth," *Sloan Management Review* 41 (Summer 2000), pp. 13–28.

Tompkins, James A., Steven W. Simonson, Bruce W. Tompkins, and Brian E. Upchurch. "Creating an Outsourcing Relationship: Successful Outsourcing Depends as Much on the Kind of Relationship Developed as It Does on the Details of the Operational Execution," *Supply Chain Management Review* 10, no. 2 (March 2006), p. 52.

# 11 CHAPTER

# Sourcing

*After reading this chapter, you should be able to:*

1. Understand the importance of the supplier selection process.

2. Know where to find potential suppliers when developing a supply base.

3. Evaluate potential suppliers to determine their strengths and capabilities.

4. Know when to bid competitively versus negotiate with suppliers.

5. Recognize strategic issues encountered in developing a strategic sourcing plan.

## Supply Management and Strategy

In a Certificate in Purchasing Management (CPM) seminar attended by 29 supply managers from Silicon Valley area firms, the instructor asked several strategic supply management questions. The first was on the topic of the seminar: "How many of you are involved in developing the materials budget?" Having recently graduated with a Ph.D. and having little real-world experience, the instructor expected about half the hands to rise, but only two did. Surprised, he then asked, "How many of you are involved in the design process for your products and services?" The same two hands went up. Clearly rattled by the low number of responses, he asked, "How many of you are involved in any strategic activities?" This time half the hands went up, but that was still not as many as he expected in light of the general nature of the question. No wonder the economic downturn of 2001 resulted in so many high-tech corporations having problems with bloated inventories, unreliable "hard-times" suppliers, and massive layoffs.

Unfortunately, strategic planning in the area of supply management has not been a high priority for upper management, and it is upper management that must provide support to pursue strategic activities. Regardless of the reasons, almost all supply managers will tell you that they firmly believe in strategic planning. Among the most critical of those plans is the strategic sourcing plan.

**Strategic Sourcing Plan Stages**

**Figure 11.1** | Strategic Sourcing Plan Stages

# The Strategic Sourcing Plan

Development of a strategic sourcing plan is driven by the recognition that tactical sourcing will not succeed in developing a supply base that will yield the benefits[1] of collaborative relationships and alliances. Development of collaborative relationships and eventually world-class supply management requires concerted strategic planning. This chapter presents a generic road map that details how supply management can develop a strategic sourcing plan that will enable it to discover, evaluate, select, develop, and manage a viable supplier base. The road map is presented in Figure 11.1.

Before pursuing the development of a supplier base for any material or service, the buying firm must determine whether the material or service should be outsourced at all. Chapter 10 addressed this issue in detail. World-class firms conduct a strategic analysis of what their core competencies are. They analyze the skills and processes which form the basis of their success and competitive advantage. As Prahalad and Hamel say, "Core competencies are the wellspring of new business development."[2] If an item or service represents a core competency or supports or interfaces with such a competency, the source of supply should be the firm itself.

Also before a strategic sourcing plan is developed, companywide support and financial backing must be provided by the chief executive officer. The strategic sourcing plan is doomed to fail without companywide support from the various departments and financial backing that will allow supply management time to be spent on essential planning activities.

# Discovering Potential Suppliers

Before the information age and the globalization of markets, the discovery process for potential suppliers was limited. Today, suppliers throughout the world can be found simply by typing several key words into a World Wide Web search engine or letting suppliers find your company through a variety of posting methods.

---

[1]The benefits of collaborative relationships and alliances were presented in Chapter 4.

[2]For more insight into this important strategic issue, see C. K. Prahalad and Gary Hamel, "The Core Competence of the Corporation," *Harvard Business Review,* May–June 1990, pp. 79–91.

While the opportunities to source via the Web are amazing, supply managers should not ignore other sources of information. Many leading supply management organizations maintain existing information about present and potential suppliers in soft and hardcopy media. The following information sources should prove helpful to a supply manager in establishing a robust list of potential suppliers.

■ *Supplier Websites*   Today, most suppliers have websites that provide detailed information about their products and services. The sites usually are registered with search engine providers such as Lycos and Yahoo! Search engines enable supply managers to type in key words such as "third-party logistics" and receive a "hit list" of sites that contain the key words. The World Wide Web has become one of the primary ways to discover new sources of supply.

■ *Supplier Information Files*   Supply management departments should keep supplier information files on past and present suppliers which include the name of each supplier, a list of materials available from the supplier, the supplier's delivery history, the supplier's quality record, the supplier's overall desirability, and general information about the supplier's plant and management. In addition to a departmental file, supply managers usually maintain a personal supplier file for their own use. Supplier information files are important because many supply management operations are repetitive; hence, it would be poor management indeed if supply managers spent time repeatedly recapturing information which was once available to them but had gotten needlessly lost. Web-enabled centralized databases make the maintenance and dissemination of supplier information files a relatively easy task compared with the hardcopy alternative.

■ *Supplier Catalogs*   Because catalogs are a commonly used source of supplier information, many supply management departments maintain a hardcopy catalog library. An alternative that is gaining in popularity is the use of electronic catalogs. Regardless of the storage medium, users may examine the catalogs to locate the materials they need. The firm's supply managers also use catalogs to determine potential sources of supply and, on occasion, to estimate prices and total cost of ownership.

■ *Trade Registers and Directories*   *Thomas' Register of American Manufacturers* is typical of several widely known trade registers and directories. These registers are available in book and searchable compact disk and website formats. They contain information on the addresses, number of branches, and affiliations of all leading manufacturers. Financial standings of firms are frequently given. The registers are indexed by commodity, manufacturer, and trade name or trademark description of the item. Kompass Publications in Europe provides similar information for European firms.[3]

■ *Trade Journals*   Trade journals are another excellent source for information about possible suppliers. Advertisements in trade journals are often a supply manager's first contact with potential suppliers and their products. For example, a supply manager in the aircraft industry would read *Aviation Week*. Many journals have moved or are moving to the World Wide Web and compact disks, where archived editions are easily searched for specific sourcing needs.

■ *Phone Directories*   Before the 1990s this source of information was of limited value to industrial supply managers because local telephone books list only local companies and searching through volumes of telephone books was a cumbersome activity. Today, phone directories are available online and on searchable compact disks that are available for purchase in computer retail stores. Phone directories can serve as a useful starting point if other sources have proved fruitless or if local sources are desired.

---

[3]Kompass Publications, Ltd., Windson Court, East Grimstead House, East Grimstead, Sussex, RH19-IXD, United Kingdom.

■ *Filing of Mailing Pieces* Many mail advertisements are worth saving. These ads should be given a file number, dated, and indexed by the name and number of each publication. When supply managers seek a new source, they can refer to the index and review the appropriate brochures and booklets. Some supply management departments ask prospective suppliers to complete a simple form that gives basic information about themselves and their products. This information, which includes company name, address, officers, local representatives, and principal products, is kept in a set of loose-leaf notebooks or preferably in a searchable database or spreadsheet. By referring to these standardized data, a supply manager can obtain immediate current information about potential new sources.

■ *Sales Personnel* Sales personnel are excellent sources for information about suppliers and materials. Not only are they usually well informed about the capabilities and features of their own products, they also are familiar with similar and competitive products. Because of their specialized knowledge, salespeople often can suggest new applications for their products which will eliminate the need to search for new suppliers. From their contacts with many companies, salespeople learn much about many products and services, and all that information is available to an alert, receptive supply manager. This is a key reason why sales personnel should be treated courteously and given ample time to make their sales presentations. To deny them this opportunity is to risk the loss of valuable information, including information about new and reliable sources of supply.

■ *Trade Shows* Regional and national trade shows are another way for supply managers to learn about possible sources of supply. Trade shows provide an excellent opportunity for supply managers to see various new products and modifications of old products. They also offer supply managers an opportunity to compare concurrently similar products of different manufacturers. Regional trade shows are sponsored periodically by many manufacturers, distributors, and trade organizations. Information about trade shows usually is sent to all interested supply management and technical personnel in the area. If it is not, a quick search of the World Wide Web usually will yield information about upcoming shows.

■ *Company Personnel* Personnel from other departments in a supply manager's firm often can provide supply management with helpful information about prospective suppliers. Through their associations in professional organizations, civic associations, and social groups, these employees often learn about outstanding suppliers. Scientific, technical, and research personnel who use sophisticated materials or services can make many valuable suggestions regarding possible sources of supply. From their attendance at conventions and trade exhibits and from their discussions with associates, these personnel are particularly well informed about new products, methods, and manufacturers.

■ *Other Supply Management Departments* Supply management departments in other firms can be helpful sources of information about suppliers. Information exchanged among individuals from these departments can be mutually beneficial for all the participating companies; therefore, this source of information should be developed actively.

■ *Professional Organizations* Local supply management associations such as the local affiliates of the Institute for Supply Management (formerly NAPM), the Purchasing Management Association of Canada, the National Institute of Governmental Purchasing, and the National Association of Educational Buyers publish lists of their members. One of the basic objectives of a supply management association is that its members help one another in every possible way. Accordingly, members usually will do everything possible to help fellow members locate and evaluate new sources of supply.

This list of sources for suppliers left out the possibility that an existing supplier could be developed as a new supplier. Jim Wehrman, assistant vice president of purchasing at Honda America Manufacturing, points out that "a top-level supply chain management effort must focus heavily on the development of current suppliers, and must devote significant resources to strengthening current suppliers and improving their capabilities."[4] An existing supplier may have the ability to fulfill new sourcing needs, and if this supplier is selected, it will strengthen the existing relationship.

# Evaluating Potential Suppliers

After developing a comprehensive list of potential suppliers, the supply manager's next step is to evaluate each prospective supplier individually. The type of evaluation required to determine supplier capability varies with the nature, criticality, complexity, and dollar value of the purchase to be made. The evaluation also varies with the supply manager's or sourcing team's knowledge of the firms being considered.

In some cases, an evaluation is uneccessary. For many uncomplicated, low-dollar-value purchases, an examination of basic information that is readily available, such as a mailing or website, is sufficient. For complex, high-dollar-value, and perhaps critical purchases, additional evaluation steps are necessary. Marc Ensign, Director of Strategic Sourcing for Honeywell IAC, provides the following guidelines for determining whether an assessment is necessary.

- Is the supplier strategically important? If the supplier provides a product or access to a future product that is critical to the buying firm's success, take the time.

- Is the product or service being procured considered strategic? If yes, take the time to perform the evaluation.

- Are there other short-term alternatives available? If supply management can modify the request (with the concurrence of the internal customer) to allow another product, service or supplier to be substituted quickly, they can reduce the thoroughness of the evaluation.[5]

Steps for complex, high-dollar-value, and other critical purchases can include surveys, financial condition analysis, third-party evaluators, evaluation conferences, plant visits, and selected capability analyses. Usually surveys and an analysis of the financial condition come first. Companies that have positive survey results and good financial standing still may require facility visits. As necessary, visits are followed by even more detailed analyses of the most promising suppliers' management, quality, capacity, service, just-in-time, and information technology capabilities. The approaches and analyses given here are by no means an exhaustive list, but they provide a starting point for supply managers in evaluating potential suppliers. The approaches and analyses are discussed in greater detail below.

- *Supplier Surveys* A survey should provide sufficient knowledge about the supplier to make a decision to include or exclude the firm from further consideration. A survey is based on a series of questions which often cover the following areas: principal officers and titles, bank references, credit references, annual history of sales and profit for the last five years, a referral list of customers, number of employees, space currently occupied, expansion plans (including sources of funds), an indication of the use of Design of Experiments (DOE), current production defect rate for similar products, number of inspectors used, quality methods adopted, and a list of all equipment and tools which would be used to manufacture, test, and inspect the purchase in question. Appendix A at the end of this chapter provides a sample supplier survey that can be used to develop other surveys.

---

[4]Roberta J. Duffy, "The Future of Purchasing and Supply: Supply Chain Partner Selection and Contribution," *Purchasing Today,* November 1999.

[5]Marc Ensign, "Breaking Down Financial Barriers," *Purchasing Today,* July 2000, vol 11, #7, p. 10.

■ *Financial Condition Analysis*    Preliminary investigation of a potential supplier's financial condition often can prevent the expense of further study. A qualified supply manager or professional from the finance department conducts these investigations. A review of financial statements and credit ratings can reveal whether a supplier is clearly *incapable* of performing satisfactorily. Financial stability is essential for suppliers to assure continuity of supply and reliability of product quality. Imagine the difficulty of getting (1) a financially weak supplier to maintain quality, (2) a supplier who does not have sufficient working capital to settle an expensive claim, or (3) a financially unsound supplier incapable of working overtime to meet a promised delivery date. For additional information on financial ratio calculations, refer to Appendix B at the end of this chapter.

■ *Third-Party Evaluators*    Independent third-party firms can be hired to conduct many of the analyses listed in this section. For example, a Dun & Bradstreet Information Services supplier evaluation typically contains sections describing the company's address, size, organizational structure, officers, financial condition, bankruptcies, suits, liens, newsworthy events, performance versus industry competitors, operations, facilities, subsidiaries, corporate relations, minority ownership, payments, and other information in the public record. As the databases, accumulation procedures, and query procedures of third-party evaluators improve over time, the use of this source of information for evaluating suppliers will continue to grow.

■ *Evaluation Conference*    For an extremely critical purchase, a supplier evaluation conference frequently is held at the supply manager's plant to discuss the purchase. From such a discussion, it is usually easy to differentiate among suppliers who understand the complexities of the purchase and those who do not. When those who do not are eliminated, the search for the right supplier is narrowed further.

■ *Facility Visits*    By visiting a supplier's facility, the sourcing team can obtain firsthand information about the adequacy of the firm's technological capabilities, its manufacturing or distribution capabilities, and its management's technical know-how and orientation. Depending on the importance of the visit, the company may send representatives from only supply management and engineering, or it also may include some combination of representation from those functions and finance, operations, quality assurance, marketing, and industrial relations. For example, engineering's task may be to review and assess the technological capability of the potential supplier. Occasionally, top management may participate in the visit and the evaluation. When the concurrent approach to the design of new products is utilized, appropriate members of the cross-functional team conduct the visit and evaluation. See Appendix C.

■ *Quality Capability Analysis*    The potential supplier's quality capability is a critical factor to examine. If the prospective supplier's process capability is less than the buying firm's incoming quality requirements, the supplier typically does not merit further investigation. An obvious exception occurs when no supplier possesses the required process capability. In this case, the two firms will have to work together to improve the supplier's process capability. An analysis of the quality capability also should include an investigation of upper management's philosophy towards quality, the quality department (if one exists), and the firm's abilities with quality assurance techniques and DOE (Design of Experiments). These critical issues were discussed in detail in Chapter 7. According to Forker, Ruch, and Hershauer, "Managers in customer firms should not underestimate the importance of a supplier's top management and its quality department in shaping and implementing quality improvement efforts. Top management support has been shown repeatedly to be paramount to the success of a quality improvement program."[6]

---

[6]L. Forker, W. Ruch, and J. Hershauer, "Examining Supplier Improvement Efforts from Both Sides," *Journal of Supply Chain Management,* Summer 1999, pp. 40–50.

■ *Capacity Capability Analysis*   Ensuring continuity of supply is one of the most fundamental objectives of supply management. A supply manager rarely is noticed if materials arrive on time, but if materials are late so that expensive operations grind to a halt, the supply manager can become infamous and perhaps unemployed. Unscrupulous suppliers often promise that they can meet future demands when in fact they do not have the capacity. Some suppliers' salespeople do not have a solid understanding of their firms' manufacturing capacity and the demands on that finite capacity. In 2000, one large telecommunications company did not investigate its second largest supplier's capacity before entering into a "partnership length and quantity" contract for the critical components in DSL kits. The supplier did not have the capacity to meet the buying firm's demands. The buying firm's parts and components from other suppliers arrived, but those parts could not be kitted since some of the parts were not available.

■ *Management Capability Analysis*   Evaluating an organization's management style and compatibility usually requires several visits to the potential supplier's facilities. A quick way to draw conclusions that often hold true is to evaluate the management capability of the firm by evaluating the sales representative, the facility grounds, and even the parking lot.[7] A properly trained sales representative knows his or her product thoroughly, understands the buying firm's requirements, gives useful suggestions to the supply manager and appropriate members of the buying team, commits the company to specific delivery promises, and follows through on all orders. The presence of this type of sales representative indicates that the supplier's firm is directed and managed by responsible and enterprising executives. Even a parking lot analysis can yield information about a potential supplier's management. Few cars, poorly maintained landscaping, poor quality of structures, and irregular condition of pavement can be indicators of problems. A well-maintained and well-managed firm seldom experiences the instability that results from continual labor problems and always strives to reduce its costs. This type of company can be a good supplier. In addition, the supplier's purchasing expertise is a major factor in cost control.

■ *Service Capability Analysis*   "Service" is a term that varies in meaning, depending on the nature of the product being purchased. Specifically, good service means delivering on time, treating special orders specially, filling back orders promptly, settling disputes quickly and fairly, and informing supply managers in advance of impending price changes or developing shortages. In some situations, it means exceptional post-sale service. Service also can include actions such as stocking spare parts for immediate delivery, extending suitable credit arrangements, and warranting the purchased item's quality and performance to a degree beyond what normally is required. In the aggregate, good service means that a supplier will take every reasonable action to ensure the smooth flow of purchased materials between the supplying and buying firms.

■ *Flexibility Capability Analysis*   One issue that emerged from the stock market turmoil of 2001 was the importance of supplier flexibility to adjust production volumes with short notice and remove inventory from the chain. Flexibility is achieved through methods encapsulated in the just-in-time philosophy, also known as lean strategy. According to a 10-year forecast for the 2000s, "Lean supply chains will be a competitive strategy."[8] When properly implemented, a just-in-time (JIT) system results in the following *supply chain* benefits: reduced inventory, increased quality, reduced lead time, reduced scrap and rework, and reduced equipment downtime.[9] JIT requires a high degree of integration of the customer's and supplier's

---

[7]M. Ensign, "Breaking Down Financial Barriers."

[8]P. L. Carter, J. R. Carter, R. M. Monczka, T. H. Slaight, and A. J. Swan, "The Future of Purchasing and Supply: A Ten-Year Forecast," *Journal of Supply Chain Management,* Winter 2000, pp. 14–26.

[9]Caron H. St. John and Kirk C. Heriot, "Small Suppliers and JIT Purchasing," *International Journal of Purchasing and Materials Management,* Winter 1993, p. 12.

operations. The inevitable changes in a customer's production plans and schedules affect the supplier's schedules. Experience has demonstrated that dependable single-source collaborative relationships are virtually essential for the required level of integration to result. A firm that is considering the adoption of JIT manufacturing must focus on its suppliers' abilities and willingness to meet the stringent quality and schedule demands imposed by the system. The sourcing team must carefully investigate a potential supplier's capability as a JIT manufacturer.[10]

■ *Information Technology Capability Analysis*   Information sharing is a key enabler of effective supply chain management. Information sharing does not require technology, but technology increasingly is being employed as the "vehicle of use." As reported in the *European Journal of Purchasing and Supply Management,* "Without a doubt, competitive advantage accrues to those who effectively adapt information technology to better disseminate information within the supply chains. In a number of industries, the ability to link electronically has become a right of entry and a prerequisite just to be considered as a potential supply chain partner."[11] The type of analysis that is required depends greatly on the buying firm's technology capability.

The analyses above should not necessarily be limited to potential first-tier suppliers. Today's supply chains have multiple tiers which may be critical to the success of the procurement. In a 10-year forecast of the future of supply management, several noted academicians stated, "Determination of first-, second-, and possibly third-tier suppliers will become more critical to supply chain dominant companies in the future."[12]

A common approach to summarizing the analyses above or to conducting them on an individual basis is a weighted-factor analysis, as discussed below

# Selecting Suppliers

After one or more potential suppliers have passed the evaluation process, the selection process must begin. The supply manager or the sourcing team will invite potential suppliers to submit bids or proposals. A decision must be made whether to use competitive bidding or negotiation (or a combination of the two) as the basis for source selection.

## Bidding versus Negotiation

When competitive bidding is used by private industry, requests for bids traditionally are sent to three to eight potential suppliers, depending on the dollar size and complexity of the purchase. Requests for bids ask suppliers to quote the price at which they will perform in accordance with the terms and conditions of the resulting contract if they become the successful bidder. The traditional bidding process is usually one pass. Government supply managers generally are not able to restrict the number of bidders to only eight.

---

[10]A follow-up study to the 10-year forecast warns that companies need to consider factors beyond operational excellence. The authors predict companies will turn to "value-based" sourcing to leverage a supplier's full capabilities for competitive advantage. See P. L. Carter, J. R. Carter, and R. M. Monczka, "Key Supply Strategies for Tomorrow," ATKearney, Chicago, 2007.

[11]R. E. Spekman, J. Kamauff, and J. Spear, "Towards More Effective Sourcing and Supplier Management," *European Journal of Purchasing and Supply Management* 5 (1999), p. 105.

[12]Carter et al., "The Future of Purchasing and Supply: A Ten-Year Forecast. "

Rather, all suppliers that wish to bid are permitted to do so (for large purchases of standard commodities, the numbers are literally in the hundreds). Under competitive bidding, industrial supply managers generally, *but not always,* award the order to the lowest bidder. By law, government supply managers routinely are required to award the order to the lowest bidder provided that the lowest bidder is deemed qualified to perform the contract.

**Prerequisites to Bidding**   The proper use of competitive bidding is dictated by five criteria. When all five criteria prevail, competitive bidding is an efficient method for source selection and pricing. The criteria are as follows:

1. The dollar value of the specific purchase must be large enough to justify the expense, to both buying and selling firms, that accompanies this method of source selection and pricing.

2. The specifications of the item or service to be purchased must be explicitly clear to both the buying and selling firms. In addition, the seller must know from actual previous experience, or be able to estimate accurately from similar past experience, the cost of producing the item or rendering the service.

3. The market must consist of an adequate number of sellers.

4. The sellers that make up the market must be technically qualified and *actively want* the contract—and therefore be willing to price competitively to get it.

5. The time available must be sufficient for using this method of pricing: Suppliers competing for large contracts must be given time to obtain and evaluate bids from their subcontractors before they can calculate their best price. Thirty days is not an uncommon amount of time; however, the increasing use of online bidding using the World Wide Web is forcing compression of bid preparation time.

**Conditions Demanding Negotiation**   In addition to satisfying the preceding five prerequisites, four other conditions should *not* be present in employing competitive bidding as the means of source selection:

1. Situations in which it is impossible to estimate costs with a high degree of certainty. Such situations frequently are present with high-technology requirements, with items that require a long time to develop and produce, and under conditions of economic uncertainty.

2. Situations in which price is not the only important variable. For example, quality, schedule, and service may well be negotiable variables of significant importance.

3. Situations in which the buying firm anticipates a need to make changes in the specification or some other aspect of the purchase contract.

4. Situations in which special tooling and setup costs are major factors. The allocation of such costs and title to the special tooling are issues best resolved through negotiation.

If these nine conditions are satisfied, competitive bidding usually will result in the lowest price and is the most efficient method of source selection. To ensure that the lowest prices are obtained, the competing firms must be assured that the firm submitting the low bid will receive the award. If the buying firm gains a reputation for negotiating with the lowest bidders *after* bids are opened, future bidders will tend *not* to offer their best prices initially, believing that they may do better in subsequent negotiations. They will adopt a strategy of submitting a bid low enough to allow them to be included in any negotiations, but the initial bid will not be as low as it will be when they are confident that the award will be made to the low bidder without further negotiation.[13] When any of the prerequisites to the use of competitive bidding are not satisfied, the *negotiation process* should be employed to select sources and arrive at a price.

In his now famous lectures in Japan, W. E. Deming recommended that organizations "end the practice of awarding business on the basis of price tag alone."[14] Several progressive supply management professionals offer two additional arguments that favor the use of negotiation over competitive bidding for critical procurements:

1. The negotiation process is far more likely to lead to a complete understanding of all the issues of the procurement. This improved understanding greatly reduces subsequent quality and schedule problems.

2. Competitive bidding tends to put great pressure on suppliers to reduce their costs so that they can bid a low price. This cost pressure may result in sacrifices in product quality, development efforts, and other vital services.

Normally the competitive bidding system itself, when all the prerequisite criteria prevail, evaluates the many pricing factors that bear on the purchase being made quite accurately. These factors include determinants such as supplier production efficiency, willingness of the seller to price this particular contract at a low profit level, the financial effect on the seller of shortages of capital or excesses of inventories, errors in the seller's sales forecast, and competitive conditions in general.

## Reverse Auctions

In contrast to standard competitive bidding, reverse auctions use the Internet for online "real-time" interaction in which the number of bids submitted is limited primarily by the time provided by the buyer for the process. In addition, the number of bidders in reverse auctions can be very large. Reverse auctions often are used to help drive prices down on products and services that are believed to be above the true market value. The results are reported to be an average of 15 percent savings.[15] However, as with competitive bidding, reverse auctions are not appropriate for all situations. Managers in industry urge caution in opening the bidding process to unqualified suppliers.[16] Suppliers must be prequalified for reliable completion of the contract. The reverse bid process can have adverse effects on long-term supplier relationships. Amid the frenzy of the bid process, suppliers can inadvertently bid below their costs. While this may be appealing for the short term, economics dictate that it cannot be sustained in the long run. Reverse auctions, as well as some bidding situations, also assume all the participating suppliers and their products-services are identical and equal, very risky assumptions.

## Two-Step Bidding/Negotiation

On occasion, large, technically oriented firms and the federal government use a modified type of competitive bidding called "two-step bidding." This method of source selection and pricing is used in situations in which *inadequate specifications* preclude the initial use of traditional competitive bidding. In the first

---

[13]On occasion, a supply manager may intend to use the initial proposal solicitation process to identify firms with which he or she plans to conduct follow-on negotiations. In this case, professional ethics and good business judgment dictate that the initial solicitation state clearly that follow-on negotiations will be conducted.

[14]Larry Weinstein, "Single-Source Successes and Snafus," *Purchasing Today*, April 2000, p. 68.

[15]Srinivas Talluri, and Gary L. Ragatz, "Multi-Attribute Reverse Auctions in B2B Exchanges: A Framework for Design and Implementation," *Journal of Supply Chain Management,* 40, no. 1 (Winter 2004), p. 52.

[16]Chain Management Forum: Focus on Supply Management, University of San Diego, 2001.

step, bids are requested only for technical proposals, without any prices. Bidders are requested to set forth in their proposals the technical details describing how they would produce the required materials, products, or services. After these technical bids are evaluated and it is determined which proposals are technically satisfactory, the second step follows.

In the second step, requests for bids are sent only to sellers who submitted acceptable technical proposals in the first step. Those sellers now compete for the business on a price basis, as they would in any routine competitive-bidding situation. The price is determined in one of two ways: (1) Award may be based solely on the lowest price received from those competing, or (2) the price proposals for the accepted technical approaches may be used as the beginning point for *negotiations*. It is important that the supply manager specify *at the outset* which of the two procedures will be used.

## The Solicitation

Once it has been decided whether to use competitive bidding or negotiation as the means of selecting the source, an *invitation for bids (IFB)* or a *request for proposal (RFP)* is prepared. The IFB or RFP normally consists of a purchase description of the item or service required, information on quantities, required delivery schedules, special terms and conditions, and standard terms and conditions. The legal implications of these documents and processes are discussed in Chapter 17.

When an RFP is used in anticipation of cost negotiations with one or more suppliers, the supply manager should request appropriate cost data in support of the price proposal. The supply manager also must obtain the right of access to the supplier's cost records that are required to support the reasonableness of the proposal. The cost data and the right of access must be established during the RFP phase of the procurement, at a time when potential suppliers believe that there is active competition for the job.

## Weighted-Factor Analysis

In many instances, one prospective supplier is obviously superior to its competition, and selection is a very simple matter. Unfortunately, though, the choice is not always so clear. In these cases, a numerical weighted-factor rating system can facilitate the decision process greatly.

A weighted-factor system calls for four activities: (1) the development of the factors that serve as the selection criteria and the weight those factors carry in the decision-making process, (2) the development of subfactors or performance factors within the broader selection criteria and the weighting of those factors, (3) the development of a scoring factor to evaluate potential suppliers, and (4) the scoring or evaluating of the supplier.

The first activity—identification of the key factors to be considered in the selection decision, along with their respective weights— and the second activity—the development of subfactors and weights—typically are accomplished by a committee of individuals involved in the purchase. Factors to consider are specific to the particular buy and could include technical, financial, managerial, quality, and capability factors. Weights are assigned according to the importance of each factor. If technology outweighs cost in a particular buy, technical factors will be given more weight.

The subfactors indicate activities under each main factor or category. As shown in Table 11.1, subfactors of the technical factor would include understanding the problem, the technical approach to the product, the level of technology in the production facilitites, the operator's technical capabilities, and the maintenance requirements. Weights for these subfactors would result from assigning a portion of the total weight for the overall factor or category.

**Table 11.1** | An Illustration of the Weighted-Factor Rating Approach

| Factors | Weights and Subweights | Score* 0–10 (A) | Weighted Score (Supplier A) | Score 0–10 (B) | Weighted Score (Supplier B) |
|---|---|---|---|---|---|
| Technical | 40 | | | | |
| Knowledge of problem | 10 | 9 | 9 | 7 | 7 |
| Approach | 20 | 9 | 18 | 8 | 16 |
| Production facilities | 5 | 8 | 4 | 6 | 3 |
| Operators | 3 | 6 | 1.8 | 6 | 1.8 |
| Maintenance | 2 | 10 | 2 | 10 | 2 |
| | | | Total 34.8 | | Total 29.8 |
| Delivery | 20 | | | | |
| Requested date | 10 | 10 | 10 | 8 | 8 |
| Lead time | 10 | 10 | 10 | 8 | 8 |
| | | | Total 20 | | Total 16 |
| Price | 20 | | | | |
| Cost structure available | 10 | 8 | 8 | 10 | 10 |
| Value analysis efforts | 10 | 8 | 8 | 10 | 10 |
| | | | Total 16 | | Total 20 |
| Managerial capability | 10 | | | | |
| Labor relations | 5 | 10 | 5 | 8 | 4 |
| Financial strength | 5 | 9 | 4.5 | 8 | 4 |
| | | | Total 9.5 | | Total 8 |
| Quality | 10 | | | | |
| Quality control processes | 5 | 9 | 4.5 | 8 | 4 |
| Acceptable defect rate | 5 | 9 | 4.5 | 8 | 4 |
| | | | Total 9 | | Total 8 |
| RATING TOTALS | | | 89.3 | | 81.8 |

*Scoring: A score of 9/10 possible is 90 percent of available points. Ninety percent of 10 available points of the subweight for "Knowledge of problem" earns Supplier A 9 points. Supplier B received a score of 7/10, or 70 percent of the 10 available points in the subfactor "Knowledge of problem." Supplier B earns 7 points.

Step 3 requires the developing of a numerical rating system with which to evaluate each supplier on each factor and subfactor. Generally, a scale to assess these issues would be a 5- or 10-point scale, clearly defined to reduce subjectivity in the process. Clearly defined would include a defined rating of 0 to 5 where 0 is "not able to conform" and 5 is "supplier meets all needs of customer." The better defined the factors and rating system, the more optimal the decision outcome.

The last step requires the assignment of numerical ratings for each of the competing firms. These assessments are based on the collective judgments of the evaluators after they have studied all the data and information provided by the potential suppliers, as well as the information obtained in field investigations.

In effect, a weighted-factor rating system breaks a complex problem down into its key components and permits analysis of each component individually. The approach is used widely in practice and generally leads to a fair and reasonably objective result.

## Responsibility for Source Selection

While supply management normally has the ultimate responsibility for selecting the "right" source, the process is handled in many ways. Procedurally, the simplest approach is to have a single *supply manager* conduct the analysis and make the selection. A second common approach calls for the use of a *cross-functional team* consisting of representatives of supply management, design engineering, operations, quality, and finance. The third common approach is the use of a commodity team. Commodity teams are created to source and manage a group of similar components. Commodity teams frequently consist of supply managers, materials engineers, and production planners. Larger commodity teams include a commodity manager (normally from supply management) and representatives of materials, design and manufacturing engineering, quality, and finance. Commodity teams are essentially a type of cross-functional team. The principal difference is that commodity teams tend to be fairly permanent, whereas cross-functional teams tend to be one-time assignments.

# Developing Suppliers

Most suppliers have come to realize that their ability to be competitive on cost, quality, timeliness, and service is dependent on their suppliers' ability to be contributing members of their supply chains. Not all suppliers need development assistance, but to reach the optimum collaborative relationship, development assistance frequently is required. Even suppliers recognized as the "best of the best" require investment on the part of the buying firm to realize the full benefit of the collaborative relationship. In major corporations such as General Electric, John Deere, Chrysler, and Honda of America, supply managers help their suppliers "improve quality, enhance delivery performance, and reduce costs."[17]

At Silicon Valley's Sun Microsystems, management treats the development of suppliers as a two-way effort. In the late 1990s, Sun started having suppliers measure their performance by using scorecards modified from the ones Sun used to evaluate its suppliers. The benefits to Sun were numerous. Suppliers felt that Sun finally had started to listen to their ideas instead of trying to push the Sun way of doing business on them. Suppliers now could contribute to developing Sun and improving the collaborative relationship to find "win-win" opportunities. The proactive efforts of Sun bring up the issue that the term "development" is actually a misnomer that implies a one-way interaction in which the buying firm "develops" the supplying firm. The process of development also should include the development of the buyer in collaborative relationships.

In many instances, the buying firm may be unable to identify a world-class supplier that is willing (or able) to meet its needs. If the requirement is sufficiently important, the buying firm will select the most attractive suppliers and then develop them into suppliers capable of meeting its present and future needs. Training in project management, teamwork, quality, production processes, and supply management may prove to be a worthy investment. That kind of training has been provided by several leading customer firms for well over a decade.

# Managing Suppliers

The challenging issue of managing suppliers is dealt with in several chapters in this book. At this point, however, it is essential to recognize that a supply manager has many responsibilities associated with the management of his or her suppliers. Satisfying these responsibilities should ensure that suppliers perform

---

[17]Janet Hartley and Gwen Jones, "Process Oriented Supplier Development: Building the Capability for Change," *International Journal of Purchasing and Materials Management* 33, no. 3 (Summer 1997), p. 24.

as required or that appropriate corrective action is taken to upgrade them or eliminate them from the firm's supplier base.

In addition, on a periodic basis, supply management must analyze its suppliers' abilities to meet the firm's long-term needs. Areas that deserve particular attention include the supplier's general growth plans, its future design capability in relevant areas, the role of supply management in the supplier's strategic planning, the potential for future production capacity, and its financial ability to support such growth.

If present suppliers appear to be unlikely to meet future requirements, the firm has three options: (1) It may assist the appropriate supplier(s) with financing and technological assistance, (2) it may develop new sources that have the desired growth potential, or (3) it may develop the required capability internally.

# Additional Strategic Issues

The buying firm must consider many factors in selecting sources of supply. This section presents several areas of concern. All the issues described here have impacts beyond the supply management department. Accordingly, other departments must be involved in the decision making, and approval of the strategic outcomes should be sought from management above the functional areas that are affected.

## Early Supplier Involvement

As presented in the Chapters on new product development and specifications and standardization, early supplier involvement (ESI) is an approach in supply management to bringing the expertise and collaborative synergy of suppliers into the design process. Early involvement of the supplier is used to find "win-win" opportunities in developing alternatives and improvements to materials, services, technology, specifications and tolerances, standards, order quantities and lead time, processes, packaging, transportation, redesigns, assembly changes, design cycle time, and inventory reductions. Today, early supplier involvement is an accepted way of life at many proactive firms and a requirement for "Proactive Supply Management" status. ESI helps in developing trust and communication between suppliers and the buying firm. ESI normally, but not always, results in the selection of a single source of supply. At most progressive companies, this selection process is the result of intensive competition between two or three carefully prequalified potential suppliers. The company selected becomes the single or primary source of supply for the life of the item that uses its material. The results of ESI translate into tangible cost savings. According to Dave Nelson, former senior vice president of purchasing and corporate affairs for Honda of America, suppliers helped design the 1998 Accord and, as a result, lowered the cost of producing the car by over 20 percent.[18]

## Supply Base Reduction

One of the interesting transitions taking place in supply management is the shift from enlarging a firm's supply base to downsizing that base. Reduction of the supply base usually is achieved through both reducing the variety of items procured and consolidating items previously procured from different suppliers into one supplier.

Supply base reduction success stories are abundant. For example, Xerox reduced its supply base by 92 percent in the early 1980s—from 5,000 to 400 suppliers. Chrysler winnowed its supplier base from a mass of 2,500 in the late 1980s to a lean, long-term nucleus of 300. During the 1990s, before its ill-fated

---

[18]Spekman, Kamauff, and Spear, "Towards More Effective Sourcing and Supplier Management."

acquisition by Daimler, suppliers loved working for Chrysler, and for obvious reasons: The company's production volume was growing rapidly. Chrysler included suppliers in development activities from day one and listened eagerly to their suggestions for design improvements and cost reductions. Chrysler had replaced its adversarial bidding system with one in which the company designated suppliers for a component and then used target pricing to determine with suppliers the component prices and ways to achieve them. Most parts were sourced from one supplier for the life of the product.[19]

Applied Materials reduced its supply base from 1,200 suppliers in the early 1990s to 400 by 2001. Applied Materials stated that the reduction resulted in significant cost reductions in manufacturing and supply chain operations. Applied Materials develops and works with preferred suppliers that pass a series of qualification criteria. The reduced risk that comes with being a preferred supplier empowers the company to invest in long-term strategies such as early supplier involvement in design, materials research, process value analysis, and workforce education.

Similar supply base reductions have occurred at other major corporations. IBM uses 50 suppliers for 85 percent of its production requirements, and Sun Microsystems uses 40 suppliers for 90 percent of its production material needs.[20] Such accomplishments generally require significant research and development expenditures and/or capital investment.

Two benefits of supply base reduction cited by John Deere are increased leverage with suppliers and better focus and supplier integration in product development. According to Deere, the increased leverage results primarily from the increased volume of business with the supplier.[21] However, as observers of Deere over the last several years, the authors of this book can safely state that the increased leverage also is due to the increased involvement with the suppliers, which builds goodwill and trust.

## Single versus Multiple Sourcing

Few strategic sourcing issues ignite more debate in corporate boardrooms around the world than the issue of single versus multiple sources. Such decisions are larger than the supply management department, the commodity team, or the cross-functional team responsible for source selection. These decisions may affect the success or even the survival of the firm.

The major argument for placing all of a firm's business with *one supplier* is that in times of shortage, that supplier will give priority to the needs of a special customer. Additionally, single sources may be justified when:

- Lower total cost results from a much higher volume (economies of scale).
- Quality considerations dictate.[22]
- The buying firm obtains more influence—clout—with the supplier.
- Lower costs are incurred to source, process, expedite, and inspect.
- The quality, control, and coordination required with just-in-time manufacturing require a single source.
- Significantly lower freight costs may result.

---

[19]James P. Womack and Daniel T. Jones, "From Lean Production to the Lean Enterprise," *Harvard Business Review,* March–April 1994, p. 97.

[20]James Carbone, "Evaluation Programs Determine Top Suppliers," *Purchasing*, November 18, 1999.

[21]Bill Butter Field, "Supplier Development at John Deere," Presentation at the 16th Annual Supply Chain Forum, San Diego, CA. November, 2001.

[22]James Dairs, manager of Transportation Programs at G.E.'s Plastics Group, Pittsfield, MA, quoted in Somerby Dowst, "The Winning Edge," *Purchasing*, March 12, 1987, p. 57.

- Special tooling is required, and the use of more than one supplier is impractical or excessively costly.
- Total system inventory will be reduced.
- An improved commitment on the supplier's part results.
- Improved interdependency and risk sharing result.
- More reliable, shorter lead times are required.[23]
- Time to market is critical.[24]

A common approach to multiple sourcing that can yield many of the benefits of single sourcing is the "70-30" approach. Through the award of 70 percent of the volume to one supplier and 30 percent to a second supplier, economies of scale are obtained from the "big supplier" while the "little supplier" provides competition. In the 70-30 strategy, when the 70 percent supplier "misbehaves," its volume is reduced and the smaller supplier is awarded an increase. (An interesting approach to discipline!)

Although the 70-30 strategy is reported to have started in Japan in the 1970s with just-in-time firms, it is firmly established in many world-class companies. For example, visits in 2001 by one of the authors of this book verified that Solectron, Applied Materials, and Cisco Systems all cognitively use the 70-30 approach in sourcing selected materials. Dual or multiple sourcing may be appropriate:

- To protect the buying firm during times of shortages, strikes, and other emergencies.
- To maintain competition and provide a backup source.
- To meet local content requirements for international manufacturing locations.
- To meet customer's volume requirements.
- To avoid lethargy or complacency on the part of a single-source supplier.
- When the customer is a small player in the market for a specific item.
- When the technology path is uncertain.
- In areas where suppliers tend to leapfrog each other technologically.[25]

Note that the term "collaborative relationship" implies neither the presence nor the absence of a single-source relationship. That is, the buying firm may have one, two, or three "partners" for the same item, although the trend is toward single sourcing.

## Share of Supplier's Capacity

Many highly regarded firms try to not exceed more than 15 to 25 percent of any one supplier's capacity. That percentage refers to the company's entire capacity, not to one individual product or service. For example, Palm may contract for 15 percent of Flextronics' production capacity but purchase 100 percent of a specific product from Flextronics. Palm might reason that if its purchases represent too large a share

---

[23]Larry Weinstein, "Single-Source Successes and Snafus," interview with Ron Reese of Haliburton Energy Services, *Purchasing Today*, April 2000, p. 68.

[24]Bob Bretz, former director of Corporate Purchasing for Pitney Bowes and 1994 Shipman Medalist, indicates that "'single sourcing' is much simpler. There's less effort on the part of the seller and it's easier to resolve issues." Patrick Robert Bretz, quoted in Patrick Flanagen, "The Rules of Purchasing Are Changing," *Management Review*, March 1994, p. 30.

[25]Several large corporations use a dual or multiple approach to sourcing items with dynamic technology. See "Buyers Beef Up Supplier Management Skills," *Purchasing*, October 21, 1993, p. 28.

of the supplier's business and the supplier discontinues a product or purchases an item from another supplier, it could put Flextronics in a very difficult financial situation.

This issue became all too relevant in the early 2000s with the economic downturn. Many companies canceled orders that had long supplier lead times, which resulted in suppliers being caught with, in some cases, hundreds of millions of dollars of work-in-process. Cisco Systems, for example, had outstanding orders that totaled nearly $2 billion! Unlike many companies during the early 2000s, Cisco paid for almost all of its orders and maintained its reputation as a good business partner. If Cisco had not paid its suppliers, the financial ruin that would have spread would have been even more staggering. Still, Cisco's suppliers had to contend with few, if any, follow-on orders since demand for Cisco's products had diminished greatly.

## Local, National, and International Sourcing

Before the discovery process for building a supply base, the company must consider the issue of local versus national versus international sourcing. Local sourcing implies that the firm's headquarters and all facilities are located in the city or region (such as northern California) where the materials or services will be used. Local sources are usually relatively small in contrast to national and international sources. National sourcing implies that the source is headquartered within the country and has facilities in multiple regions throughout the country. National sources are also larger companies as defined by the buying firm. For example, a national firm may be defined by a company as having a presence in at least two regions other than the region of the buying firm, have at least 2,000 employees, and have annual revenues in excess of 100 million U.S. dollars. The delineation between a national source and an international source also should be defined by the buying firm. The common definition is that an international source is headquartered outside the buying firm's country, but this does not define where the company has its operations. For example, Flextronics is headquartered in Singapore but has virtually no manufacturing in Singapore.[26] The lines between local, national, and international sourcing have become blurred in the last 30 years.

**Buying Locally**    Most supply managers prefer to patronize local sources whenever that action is prudent. In a Stanford University research study, approximately three-fourths of the 152 supply managers surveyed indicated a preference to buy from local sources whenever possible. Many of them were willing to pay slightly higher prices to gain the advantage of better service and immediate availability of materials offered by some local suppliers, thus lowering their total cost.

Just-in-time manufacturing requires dependable sources of defect-free materials which arrive within a very tight time frame. Suppliers to JIT customers meet their requirements in three ways: (1) They are locating close to their customers;[27] (2) suppliers are implementing responsive manufacturing systems; and (3) they are taking aggressive action to control the transportation of their materials to their customers. In summary, local buying has the following advantages:

1. Closer cooperation between buying and selling firms is possible because of close geographic proximity. JIT deliveries thus are facilitated.

2. Delivery dates are more certain since transportation is only a minor factor in delivery.

3. Lower total costs can result from consolidated transportation and insurance charges. A local supplier in effect brings in many local buying firms' orders in the same shipment.

---

[26]The tax benefits of headquartering in Singapore make Singapore a popular location choice.

[27]For example, during the 1980s Chrysler built additional buildings on-site and leased them to its suppliers. Robert M. Faltra, "How Chrysler Buyers Make Quality a Standard Feature," *Electronics Purchasing,* 101 (July 10, 1986), p. 62A15.

4. Shorter lead times frequently can permit reductions in or the elimination of inventory. In effect, the seller produces just in time.

5. Rush orders are likely to be filled faster.

6. Disputes usually are resolved more easily.

7. Implied social responsibilities to the community are fulfilled.

**Buying Nationally**    National buying has the following advantages:

1. National sources, as a result of economies of scale, in some situations can be more efficient than local suppliers and offer higher quality or better service at a lower price.

2. National companies often can provide superior technical assistance.

3. Large national companies have greater production capacity and therefore greater production flexibility to handle fluctuating demands.

4. Shortages are less likely with national companies because of their broader markets.

**Buying Internationally**    This important sourcing consideration is discussed in detail in Chapter 12. It is mentioned here only to note that it is an important factor in supplier selection.

## Manufacturer or Distributor?

In deciding whether to buy from a manufacturer or a distributor, a supply manager should focus largely on the distributor's capabilities and services, not on its location. In the steel industry, for example, distributors pay the same prices for steel that other buying firms pay. Distributors, however, buy in carload lots and sell in smaller quantities to users whose operations do not justify purchasing carload lots. The distributors realize a profit because large lots sell at lower unit prices than small lots. If a buying firm wishes to purchase steel directly from the mill and bypass the distributor, it is free to do so; however, when it does, it usually forgoes certain special services that a competent distributor is equipped to offer. Distributors, for example, have cutting and shaping tools and skilled personnel to operate them. They maintain large, diverse inventories. They also are able to perform numerous customer services.

When the materials ordered from a distributor are shipped directly to the user by the manufacturer (a *drop shipment*), an additional buying decision becomes necessary. In this situation, the distributor does not handle the materials physically; it acts only as a broker.[28] In such circumstances, a supply manager is strongly motivated to buy directly from the manufacturer—if the manufacturer will sell to his or her firm.

Supply managers should be aware that distributors stock many manufacturers' products. Hence, ordering from a distributor can significantly reduce the total number of orders a supply manager must place to fill some of his or her materials requirements. If there were no distributors, orders for production as well as maintenance, repair, and operating (MRO) requirements would all have to be placed directly with many different manufacturers. This obviously would increase direct supply management costs. Furthermore, for every additional purchase order placed, an additional receiving, inspection, and accounts payable operation is created.

In the final analysis, the manufacturer–distributor decision centers on one critical fact: The functions of distribution cannot be eliminated. The supply manager needs most of these functions; therefore, the

---

[28]Manufacturers' representatives, who usually deal only in technical items, also effect deliveries by drop shipments, and they act as brokers. Manufacturers' reps also aid a supply manager by being able to furnish numerous product lines from a single source.

supply manager should pay for them once—but should not pay for them twice. Either the distributor or the manufacturer must perform the essential distribution functions of carrying the inventory, giving technical advice, rendering service, extending credit, and so on. The supply manager must decide for each individual buying situation how best to purchase the functions needed. The supply manager must answer the question: Is it my company, the distributor, or the manufacturer that can perform the required distribution services satisfactorily at the lowest cost?

## "Green" Supply Management

Environmentally sensitive supply management can make good business sense. Many of us have heard of the story of the young Henry Ford. It seems that Ford was very explicit about the dimensions and quality of the lumber used to construct the packing crates his suppliers used to ship parts to Ford. One day, one of the suppliers asked a Ford employee why a throwaway packing crate had to be made to such explicit specifications. The answer was, "Because we use the wood to build the floorboards of our Model T." Was Mr. Ford an environmentalist or a good businessman? Quite obviously, he was both!

Environmentally sensitive supply management has two components: (1) the purchase of materials and items which are recyclable and (2) the environmental and liability issues associated with the use and discharge of hazardous materials anywhere in the supply chain.

**Environmental and Liability Issues**   Supply management, the firm's environmental engineer (or environmental consultant), and the firm's attorney should study the firm's value chain to identify the possible uses of and disposal methods for environmentally hazardous substances and materials. It is entirely possible, for example, that a supplier who disposes of hazardous waste in an environmentally unsafe manner while producing a product for the buying firm may subject the buying firm to financial liability if the supplier has limited financial resources. Current statutes cover present and previous operators and owners.

Additionally, supply management has a responsibility to ensure that a supplier's salvage and disposal contractors meet OSHA standards both before award and during performance under the contracts. One way of dealing with this challenging issue is to require the supplier to post adequate performance and liability bonds.

## Minority- and Women-Owned Business Enterprises

Many forces motivate a buying firm to develop and implement programs designed to ensure that minority- and/or women-owned businesses receive a share of the firm's business. These motivators include federal and state legislation, set-aside quotas in government appropriations, the actions of regulatory bodies such as the state public utilities commission, chambers of commerce, civil rights activists, and a firm's "corporate social consciousness." Perhaps one of the most significant motivators is the recognition by a firm's management that *its customer base* includes minority- and women-owned business enterprises and their employees. Companies that can demonstrate minority supplier content in their products are more likely to receive business from minority customers.[29] In addition to a sense of social responsibility, MWBE should be focused on bottom-line profitability and good business sense.[30]

---

[29]Ginger Conrad, John F. Robinson, and Forrest Walker, Jr., " Conquering the M/WBE Challenge," *Purchasing Today*, April 2000, p. 6.

[30]Debbie Newman, Patricia Richards, and Linda Butler, "Shared Commitment to MWBE Development," *NAPM Conference Proceedings*, Tempe, AZ, 1994, p. 300.

## Ethical Considerations

Supply managers must be aware of potential conflicts of interest when selecting suppliers. A conflict of interest exists when supply managers must divide their loyalty between the firm which employs them and another firm. In supply management, this situation can occur when a supply manager is a substantial stockholder in a supplier's firm or when he or she makes purchases from close friends and relatives. The subject is introduced here solely to remind the reader that such conflicts always should be avoided in all source selection decisions.

Supply managers should keep themselves as free as possible from unethical influences in their choice of suppliers. It is very difficult to maintain complete objectivity in this matter, for it is only human to want to favor one's friends. On occasion, friends make unusually good suppliers. They will respond to emergency needs more readily than will suppliers without a strong tie of personal friendship. However, supply managers tend not to discipline friends who perform poorly to the same degree as they discipline other suppliers. A detailed discussion of ethical issues and social responsibilities is contained in Chapter 19.

## Reciprocity

When supply managers give preference to suppliers that are also customers, they are engaging in a practice known as *reciprocity*.[31] The practice can be illegal, and the line between legal and illegal reciprocal practices frequently is very thin. It is entirely legal to buy from one's customers at fair market prices, without economic threat, and without the intent of restricting competition. A key criterion used by the courts in determining illegality is the degree to which reciprocal activity tends to restrict competition and trade. Hence, those who engage in reciprocal practices must do so with care and legal consultation.

Most supply managers disapprove of the practice of reciprocity, even when it is legal, because it restricts their ability to achieve competition among potential suppliers. However, proponents of reciprocity contend that it is simply good business. They believe that if a supply manager buys from a friend, both the supply manager and the friend will profit in the long run. They maintain that service is better from suppliers who are also customers. They argue that reciprocity is a legitimate way to expand a company's markets. Consequently, some U.S. firms proclaim a reciprocity policy similar to this one: "When important factors such as quality, service, and price are equal, we prefer to buy from our customers."[32]

In the final analysis, reciprocity is neither a marketing problem nor a supply management problem; it is a management problem. If management believes that it can expand its markets permanently and add to the firm's profit *legally* by means of reciprocity, this is the decision management should make. Conversely, if management believes that buying without the constraints of reciprocity will increase profit, that is the policy management should adopt. Although reciprocity can benefit a firm, no economist would argue that it benefits a nation's total economy.

## Consortium Purchasing and Group Buying

Historically, group or cooperative buying as it was commonly called, was largely restricted to collective contracting or pooled requirements of non profit entities such as schools, hospitals and local government units. This procurement method was based on the obvious principle of leveraged volume discounts of standard

---

[31]Reciprocity becomes more insidious when it involves more than one tier of suppliers. For example, A is asked to buy from B not because B is A's customer but because B is C's customer, and C is A's customer, and B wants to sell to A. Obviously, it is possible for reciprocal relationships to extend to four or more tiers.

[32]Some firms use vague phrases such as "Buy from customers when doing so will contribute to the greatest economic good of the firm."

"shelf items" and generic commodities. For example, all of the secondary schools in a local district could combine their requirements for desks, lockers, janitorial supplies and computers, etc. and have a team negotiate a master contract with a supplier to achieve the lowest price for the combined quantity of items and materials. The groups were very careful to obtain exemptions from Federal and State Anti Trust law, which forbids conspiracy to restrict competition, set prices and other such restraints of trade as explained in Chapter 17 of this text. In recent years, many procurement personnel call group buying the collaborative model. The E-Commerce boom of the 1990's triggered profit organizations such as manufacturers to form collective buying organizations for vertical buying within one industry. Often called exchanges or consortiums, they primarily used reverse auctions to drive the price to the lowest point for any particular "event" as they called their auction rounds. There were consortiums for utilities, aircraft parts and many other industries.

The most dramatic example was COVISINT, the rather strange name for the joint effort by Ford, GM and Chrysler to standardize selected automotive parts and supplies for all three and then hold reverse auctions and negotiate to achieve the lowest possible price. This enormous effort started with a rather large staff in Southfield, MI around 2002 and failed in late 2004. The major reasons for this failure and other similar vertical consortiums appear to be:

1. The difficulty of forcing long time competitors to agree on the same specifications.
2. Reluctance and even refusal of many major suppliers to participate in a scheme to drive the price down in a return to adversarial purchasing.
3. The lack of enthusiasm and support by plant level supply—purchasing managers.
4. The added "middleman" expense of the consortium buying group.
5. The lingering (and very legitimate) fear of Federal and State Anti Trust action. Many corporate attorneys were horrified at the thought of such obvious "conspiracy among competitors to fix prices".

Several purchasing executives have told the authors of this text that many of the vertical industry consortiums have either ceased operation or have evolved into data collection services tracking prices and sources for materials.[33]

However, the third party horizontal group buying ventures, those that combine volume requirements of indirect material from firms in several different industries appear to be successful. It is interesting to note these ventures do *not* use the term *consortium*. One of the best examples is Corporate United, Inc. in Cleveland, Ohio. Since 1997, Corporate United has managed indirect purchases for its member companies such as (MRO) Maintenance Repair and Operating supplies and services such as human resources, marketing and communication, IT and telecom, engineering and laboratory and even consulting. Using several sourcing methods including personal negotiation, bidding and when appropriate, reverse auctions, Corporate United provides member companies with pre-negotiated master agreements and then manages these contracts throughout the contract life cycle.[34]

---

[33]Richard L. Pinkerton, "Creating Value with Consortia and Reverse Auctions: Fact or Fiction?" A presentation given at the Technology Procurement Conference, July 21–23, 2004, New York, New York. Sponsored by ICN, Winter Park, FL. Also *see E-Commerce Exchanges: Making Informed Decisions, Applying Best Practices*, Caps and McKinsey & Co., Tempe, AZ. May, 2002, and James M. Johnstone "The Consortium: Basic Anti Trust Issues," *Purchasing Today*, May, 1996, pp 18–19 and Bob Wooten "Cooperative Purchasing in the 21st Century," *Inside Supply Management*, Feb. 2003, pp 4–5.

[34]Telephone conversation between Richard L. Pinkerton and David B. Clevenger, Vice President, Corporate United, Sept 2, 2008. Also see the website www.corporateunited.com.

# Concluding Remarks

A supply manager's first responsibility in source selection is to develop and manage a viable supply base. Before development of the supply base, many strategic issues need to be addressed, such as supply base size, single versus multiple sourcing, supplier involvement in design, negotiation versus bidding, share of supplier's capacity, whether to source internationally, manufacturer versus distributor, whether to pursue "green" supply management, and policies related to diversity, ethics, and reciprocity. These issues should be addressed in the strategic sourcing plan where relevant. In the plan, details about how suppliers will be discovered, evaluated, selected, developed, and managed should be committed to paper.

Clearly, the activity of developing a strategic sourcing plan affects many functional areas as well as supply chain members. Therefore, the strategic sourcing plan should not be developed in a supply management vacuum. The plan should be developed in a collaborative environment that includes all relevant functional area representatives and supply chain members.

Selection of the right source is more important today than ever before, since more firms are entering into long-term collaborative relationships with a single source of supply. The benefits of such collaborative relationships are many, but the risks are great. Careful selection of suppliers and professional management of the relationships are essential as supplier performance has a significant impact on customer satisfaction.

Finally, all sourcing decisions must include an analysis of the industry involved in the purchase. The standard industrial classification system (S.I.C.) has been replaced by the North American Industry Classification System (NAICS) which is the basic source for industry statistics.*

# Discussion Questions

1. Identify five key means of identifying potential suppliers.
2. What issues should a supply manager consider in determining whether a comprehensive evaluation of a potential supplier is appropriate?
3. What source screening activities are available to a supply manager for critical procurements? Describe each one.
4. Why is the analysis of a potential supplier's financial condition so important?
5. What are the benefits of a properly implemented just-in-time (JIT) system?
6. What abilities must JIT suppliers demonstrate?
7. Describe the competitive bidding process.
8. Describe the five key prerequisites to competitive bidding.
9. Identify and describe four conditions which, if one or more is present, dictate that competitive bidding not be employed.
10. How can buying firms help ensure that competitive bidding is efficient and will result in the lowest price?
11. Describe "two-step" bidding. What circumstances may call for its use?
12. Describe the role of sourcing in early supplier involvement.
13. Describe supply base reduction at Chrysler during the 1990s.
14. What is the major argument favoring single sourcing?

---

*Richard L. Pinkerton, "Industry Analysis for Materials Management," *ISM Materials Management News*, vol 1, # 4, October 2005, pp. 12–16. Sheila D. Petcavage, Ed. Tempe AZ.

15. What are the advantages of a 70-30 approach to sourcing a critical item?
16. What arguments favor dual sourcing?
17. Why should a buying firm be sensitive to the percentage of a supplier's capacity that it is purchasing?
18. What issues should be addressed in deciding whether to purchase from a distributor or a manufacturer?
19. How was Henry Ford a forerunner of "green" supply management?
20. Describe reciprocity. When is it illegal? Why do supply managers tend to disapprove of its use?
21. Describe the Pros and Cons of group buying.

## Internet Exercise

### The Supplier Selection Process

This website is published by the U.K. government. Look it over thoroughly and compare the advice they give the potential supply manager with what you read in this chapter.
(http://www.businesslink.gov.uk/bdotg/action/layer?topicId=1073920782)

1. In what ways do you find it helpful to a supply manager?

## Suggested Reading

Benton, W. C. *Purchasing and Supply Management* (New York: McGraw-Hill Higher Education, 2007).
http://www.mhhe.com/benton1e

Beall, S., C. Carter, P. L. Carter, T. German, T. Hendrick, S. Jap, L. Kaufman, D. Maciejewski, R. Moncka, and K. Petersen. *The Role of Reverse Auctions in Strategic Sourcing*, CAPS Research focus study, Tempe AZ, 2003.

Choi, T. Y., and J. L. Hartley. "An Exploration of Supplier Selection Practices across the Supply Chain," *Journal of Operations Management* 14, no. 4 (1996), pp. 333–43.

De Boer, L., E. Labro, and P. Morlacchi. "A Review of Methods Supporting Supplier Selection," *European Journal of Purchasing and Materials Management* 7 (2001), pp. 75–89.

Dunn, Steven C., and Richard R. Young. "Supplier Assistance within Supplier Development Initiatives," *Journal of Supply Chain Management* 40, no. 3 (Summer 2004), p. 19.

Ellram, Lisa M. "The Supplier Selection Decision in Strategic Partnerships," *International Journal of Purchasing and Materials Management* 26, no. 4 (Fall 1990), pp. 8–14.

Hartley, Janet L., and Thomas Y. Choi. "Supplier Development: Customers as a Catalyst of Process Change," *Business Horizons* 39, no. 4 (July–August 1996), p. 37.

Heriot, Kirk C., and Subodh P., Kulkarni. "The Use of Intermediate Sourcing Strategies," *Journal of Supply Chain Management* 37, no. 1 (Winter 2001), pp. 18–26.

Kannan, Vijay R., and Keah Choon Tan. "Supplier Selection and Assessment: Their Impact on Business Performance," *Journal of Supply Chain Management* 38, no. 4 (Fall 2002), p. 11.

Kaufman, Lutz and Craig R. Carter. "Deciding on the Mode of Negotiation: To Auction or Not to Auction Electronically," *The Journal of Supply Chain Management*, Spring, 2004, pp. 15–26.

Krause, Daniel R., and Thomas V. Scannell. "Supplier Development Practices: Product- and Service-Based Industry Comparisons," *Journal of Supply Chain Management* 38, no. 2 (Spring 2002), p. 13.

Krause, D. R., T. V. Scannell, and R. J. Calantone. "A Structural Analysis of the Effectiveness of Buying Firms' Strategies to Improve Supplier Performance," *Decision Sciences* 31, no. 1 (2000), pp. 33–56.

Nelson, David, Patricia E. Moody, and Jonathan R. Stegner. *The Incredible Payback: Innovative Sourcing Solutions That Deliver Extraordinary Results* (New York: AMACOM, 2005).

Paquette, Larry. *The Sourcing Solution: A Step-by-Step Guide to Creating a Successful Purchasing Program* (New York: AMACOM, 2004).

Park, Seungwook, and Janet L. Hartley. "Exploring the Effect of Supplier Management on Performance in the Korean Automotive Supply Chain," *Journal of Supply Chain Management,* 38, no. 2 (Spring 2002), pp. 46–53.

Sarkis, Joseph, and Srinivas Talluri. "A Model for Strategic Supplier Selection," *Journal of Supply Chain Management,* 38, no. 1 (Winter 2002), p. 18.

Vonderembse, M., and M. Tracey. "The Impact of Supplier Selection Criteria and Supplier Involvement on Manufacturing Performance," *Journal of Supply Chain Management* 35, no. 3 (Summer 1999), p. 33.

# Appendix A: Illustrative Plant Survey

After preliminary surveys of potential suppliers of critical materials, equipment, or services have been conducted, it frequently is desirable to conduct a plant visit to one or two of the most attractive candidates. The purpose of such visits is to gain firsthand knowledge of the supplier's facilities, personnel, and operations. Such a visit normally is conducted by a team from the buying firm. Each member will study his or her area of expertise at the potential supplier's operation.

The plant survey shown below is used by a high-tech manufacturer. The evaluation form calls for yes or no answers to specific questions and evaluation ratings for all the other questions, asking the team member to evaluate how well the supplier is doing in a particular area. The evaluation ratings are described below.

| Rating | Description |
|--------|-------------|
| 10 | The provisions or conditions are extensive and function is excellent. |
| 9 | The provisions or conditions are moderately extensive and function is excellent. |
| 8 | The provisions or conditions are extensive and are functioning well. |
| 6/7 | The provisions or conditions are moderately extensive and are functioning well. |
| 4/5 | The provisions or conditions are limited in extent but are functioning well. |
| 2/3 | The provisions or conditions are moderately extensive but are functioning poorly. |
| 1 | The provisions or conditions are limited in extent and are functioning poorly. |
| 0 | The provisions or conditions are missing but needed. |

Assume that the buying firm's quality manager is rating a potential supplier on the sections titled quality management and quality information. When these phases of the study are complete, the quality manager is in a position to assign an average or overall rating for quality management on the first sheet of the survey.

This type of evaluation is used in at least two ways: (1) It now is possible to compare competitors' operations, with a major emphasis on quality, and (2) actual or potential problem areas for an otherwise attractive supplier may be identified. The buying firm then may require that the area of concern be corrected or upgraded before award or as a condition of award.

## Design Information

Control of design and manufacturing information is essential for the control of product. That control consists of making sure that operating personnel are furnished with complete technical instructions for the manufacture and inspection of the product. This information includes drawings, specifications, special purchase order requirements, engineering change information, inspection instructions, processing instructions, and other special information. A positive recall system usually is considered necessary to prevent the use of superseded or obsolete information.

1. ( ) How well do procedures cover the release, change, and recall of design and manufacturing information, including correlation of customer specifications, and how well are procedures followed?
2. ( ) How well do records reflect the incorporation of changes?
3. ( ) How well does quality control verify that changes are incorporated at the effective points?
4. ( ) Is the design of experiments employed to ensure robust designs before the release of designs to manufacturing and supply management?
5. ( ) How well is the control of design and manufacturing information applied to the procurement activity?
6. (Y/N) Is there a formal deviation procedure, and how well is it followed?
7. (Y/N) Does your company have a written system for incorporating customer changes into shop drawings?
8. (Y/N) Does your company have a reliability department?
9. (Y/N) Are reliability data used in developing new designs?
10. (Y/N) Is quality history fed back to engineering for improvements in current or future designs? Does quality management review new designs?
11. (Y/N) Does your company have a sample or prototype department?
12. (Y/N) Does QA review sample prototypes?
13. (Y/N) Is this information used in developing shop inspection instructions?
14. (Y/N) Are customer specifications interpreted into shop specifications?
15. (Y/N) Do drawings and specifications accompany purchase orders to suppliers?
16. (Y/N) Are they reviewed by quality management?
17. (Y/N) Are characteristics classified on the engineering documents as to importance?
18. (Y/N) Does QA review new drawings with the intent of designing gauging fixtures?

## Procurement—Control of Purchased Material

It is essential for the assurance of quality that outside suppliers meet the standards for quality imposed on the firm's own operations department. Sources should be under continuous control or surveillance. Incoming material should be inspected to the extent necessary to assure that the requirements have been met.

19. ( ) How well are potential suppliers evaluated and monitored?
20. ( ) How well are quality requirements specified?
21. ( ) How well are inspection procedures specified, and how well are they followed?
22. ( ) How adequate are inspection facilities and equipment?
23. ( ) Have you certified (approved) key suppliers' design manufacturing and quality processes so that their shipments to you do not require inspection and testing?
24. ( ) How adequate are the "certifications" which are used in lieu of inspection?
25. ( ) How well are certifications evaluated by independent checking?
26. ( ) How well are inspection results used for corrective action?
27. (Y/N) Do you have an incoming inspection department? (If yes, list personnel) Inspectors _____, Supervisors _____, Quality Engineers _____
28. (Y/N) Are purchase orders made available to incoming inspection?
29. (Y/N) Is there a system for keeping shop drawings up to date?
30. (Y/N) Are written inspection instructions available?
31. (Y/N) Is sample inspection used?
32. (Y/N) Is gauging equipment calibrated periodically?
33. (Y/N) Is gauging equipment correlated with suppliers' equipment?
34. (Y/N) Are suppliers' test records used for acceptance?
35. (Y/N) Are commercial test records used for acceptance?
36. (Y/N) Is material identified to physical and chemical test reports?
37. (Y/N) Are records kept to show acceptance and rejection of incoming material?

38. (Y/N)   Does your company have a supplier rating system?
39. (Y/N)   Is it made available to the supply management department?
40. (Y/N)   Is the supplier notified of nonconforming material?
41. (Y/N)   Does your company have an approved supplier list?
42. (Y/N)   Does your company survey supplier facilities?
43. (Y/N)   Does the incoming inspection department have adequate storage space to hold material until it is inspected?
44. (Y/N)   Is nonconforming material identified as such?
45. (Y/N)   Is nonconforming material held in a specific area until disposition can be made? Who is responsible for making disposition of nonconforming material? _____

## Material Control

Control of the identity and quality status of material in stores and in process is essential. It is not enough that the right materials be procured and verified; they must be identified and controlled in a manner that will assure that they also are used properly. The entire quality program may be compromised if adequate controls are not maintained throughout procurement, storage, manufacturing, and inspection.

46. (   )   How adequate are procedures for storage, release, and movement of material, and how well are they followed?
47. (   )   How well are incoming materials quarantined while under test?
48. (   )   How well are materials in stores identified and controlled?
49. (   )   How well are in-process materials identified and controlled?
50. (   )   How well are materials in inspection identified and controlled?
51. (   )   How adequate are storage areas and facilities?
52. (   )   How well is access to material controlled?
53. (   )   How well do procedures cover the prevention of corrosion, deterioration, or damage of material and finished goods?
54. (   )   How well are they followed?
55. (   )   How well are nonconforming items identified, isolated, and controlled?

## Manufacturing Control

In-process inspection, utilizing the techniques of quality control, is one of the most satisfactory methods yet devised for attaining quality of product during manufacture. Because many quality characteristics cannot be evaluated in the end product, it is imperative that they be achieved and verified during the production process.

56. (   )   How well are process capabilities established and maintained?
57. (   )   How well is in-process inspection specified?
58. (   )   How effectively is it performed?
59. (   )   How adequate are inspection facilities and equipment?
60. (   )   How well are the results of in-process inspection used in the promotion of effective corrective action?
61. (   )   How adequately are equipment and facilities maintained?
62. (   )   How adequate are housekeeping procedures, and how well are they followed?
63. (   )   Does your company have a process inspection function? (If yes, list on a separate sheet inspectors and supervisory and quality engineering personnel.) To whom does process inspection report? _____
64. (Y/N)   Are inspection stations located in the production area?
65. (Y/N)   Are shop drawings and specifications available to inspection?
66. (Y/N)   Is there a system for keeping the documents up to date?
67. (Y/N)   Are written inspection instructions available?

68. (Y/N)    Is there a system for reviewing and updating inspection instructions?
69. (Y/N)    Is sample inspection used?
70. (Y/N)    Do production workers inspect their own work?
71. (Y/N)    Are inspection records kept on file?
72. (Y/N)    Is inspection equipment calibrated periodically?
73. (Y/N)    Is all material identified (route tags, etc.)?
74. (Y/N)    Is defective material identified as such?
75. (Y/N)    Is defective material segregated from good material until disposition is made?
76. (Y/N)    Are first production parts inspected before a job can be run?
77. (Y/N)    Is corrective action taken to prevent the recurrence of defective material?
78. (Y/N)    Who is responsible for the disposition of nonconforming material?
79. (Y/N)    Does your company use $\overline{X}$ and $R$ charts?
80. (Y/N)    Does your company use process capability studies?
81. (Y/N)    Are standards calibrated by an outside source that certifies traceability to NBS?
82. (Y/N)    Are standards calibrated directly by NBS?
83. (Y/N)    Are packaged goods checked for proper packaging?

## Quality Management

The key to the management of quality lies in philosophy, objectives, and organization structure. The philosophy forms the primary policy and should include the broad principles common to good-quality programs. The objectives should be clearly stated in specific terms and should provide operating policies which guide the activity of the quality program. The organizational structure should clearly define lines of authority and responsibility for quality from top management down to the operating levels.

84. (  )    Does the potential supplier embrace total quality management?
85. (  )    How adequate is the quality philosophy, and how well is it explained in operating policies and procedures?
86. (  )    How adequate is the technical competence in the quality discipline of those responsible for assuring quality?
87. (  )    How well does the organizational structure define quality responsibility and authority?
88. (  )    How well does the organizational structure provide access to top management?
89. (  )    How adequate is the documentation and dissemination of quality control procedures?
90. (  )    How adequate is the training program, including employee records?

Does the quality department have:

91. (Y/N)    Written quality policy and procedures manual?
92. (Y/N)    Written inspection instructions?
93. (Y/N)    A quality engineering department?
94. (Y/N)    Person or persons who perform vendor surveys?
95. (Y/N)    Incoming inspection department?
96. (Y/N)    In-process inspection department?
97. (Y/N)    Final inspection department? To whom does the inspection department report? _____
98. (Y/N)    A quality audit function?
99. (Y/N)    A gauge control program?
100. (Y/N)    A gauge control laboratory?
101. (Y/N)    Other quality laboratories? (If yes, specify type) _____
102. (Y/N)    A quality cost program?
103. (Y/N)    A reliability department?
104. (Y/N)    Does the quality department use statistical tools (control charts, sampling plans, etc.)? Explain _____
105. (Y/N)    Is government source inspection available to your plant? Resident _____ Itinerant _____ No _____

## Quality Information

Records should be maintained of all inspections performed, and the data should be analyzed periodically and used as a basis for action. Quality data should always be used, whether it is to improve the quality control operation by increasing or decreasing the amount of inspection, to improve the quality of product by the initiation of corrective action on processes or suppliers, to document certifications of product quality furnished to customers, or to report quality results and trends to management. Unused or unusual data are evidence of poor management.

| | | |
|---|---|---|
| 106. | ( ) | How well are records of inspections maintained? |
| 107. | ( ) | How adequate is the record and sample retention program? |
| 108. | ( ) | How well are quality data used as a basis for action? |
| 109. | ( ) | How well are quality data used in supporting certification of quality furnished to customers? |
| | | How well is customer and field information used for corrective action? |
| 110. | ( ) | How well is it reported to management? |

## Calibration—Inspection and Testing

Periodic inspection and calibration of certain tools, gauges, tests, and some items of process control equipment are necessary for the control and verification of product quality. Controlled standards periodically checked or referenced against national standards will assure the compatibility of vendor and vendee measurements. Inaccurate gauges and testers can compromise the entire quality control program and may result in either rejection of good material or acceptance of defective material.

| | | |
|---|---|---|
| 111. | ( ) | How well do internal standards conform to national standards or customer standards? |
| 112. | ( ) | How well are periodic inspections and calibrations specified? |
| 113. | ( ) | How adequate are calibration facilities and equipment? |
| 114. | ( ) | If external calibration sources are utilized, how adequate is the program and how well is it executed? |
| 115. | ( ) | Does your company have a gauge control function? |
| 116. | ( ) | Does your company have written instructions for operating inspection and test instruments? |
| 117. | ( ) | Are all inspection instruments calibrated at periodic intervals? |
| 118. | ( ) | Are records of calibration kept on file? |
| 119. | ( ) | Is there a system to recall inspection instruments when they are due for calibration? |
| 120. | ( ) | Are the inspection instruments used by production calibrated? |
| 121. | ( ) | If so, are these instruments removed from use until they can be repaired or recalibrated? |
| 122. | ( ) | Are shop masters calibrated at periodic intervals to secondary standards traceable to NBS? |

## Inspection of Completed Material

| | | |
|---|---|---|
| 123. | (Y/N) | Does your company have a final inspection function? If yes, list inspection, supervisory, and quality engineers on a separate sheet. To whom does the final inspection department report? _____ |
| 124. | (Y/N) | Are shop drawings and specifications available to inspection? |
| 125. | (Y/N) | Is there a system for keeping the documents up to date? |
| 126. | (Y/N) | Are written inspection instructions available? |
| 127. | (Y/N) | Is there a system for reviewing and updating inspection instructions? |
| 128. | (Y/N) | Is sample inspection used? |
| 129. | (Y/N) | Are inspection records kept on file? |
| 130. | (Y/N) | Are records of inspection results used for corrective-action purposes? |
| 131. | (Y/N) | Is inspection equipment calibrated periodically? |

132. (Y/N)  Is all material identified (route tags, etc.)?
133. (Y/N)  Is defective material identified as such?
134. (Y/N)  Is defective material segregated from good material until disposition is made? Who is responsible for making disposition of nonconforming material? _____
135. (Y/N)  Who is responsible for making disposition of nonconforming material? _____
136. (Y/N)  Is reworked material submitted for reinspection?

## Final Acceptance

Final inspection, testing, and packing are critical operations to assure the acceptability of material. The specifications must form the basis for these activities. To the extent that certifications or in-process inspections are used in lieu of final inspection, records of those activities should be reviewed to verify conformance.

137. (  )  How well are specifications used in determining the acceptability of material?
138. (  )  How well are certifications and in-process inspection records used in the final acceptance decisions?
139. (  )  How adequate are inspection procedures? How well are they followed?
140. (  )  How adequate are inspection facilities and equipment?
141. (  )  How well are inspection results used for corrective action?
142. (  )  How adequate are packing and order-checking procedures?
143. (  )  How well are they followed?

# Appendix B: Financial Statement Analysis[35]

The following information is useful during preliminary sourcing. These ratios and measures are useful for analyzing company-specific trends and for making comparisons among competing suppliers. Comparative data for specific industries may be obtained from Dun & Bradstreet or Robert Morris Associates.

*Liquidity Measures.* Liquidity refers to a company's ability to pay its bills when they are due and provide for unanticipated cash requirements. In general, poor liquidity measures imply short-run credit problems. From a supply management perspective, short-run credit problems could signal possible decreases in quality or difficulties in meeting scheduled deliveries. Three common liquidity measures are:

1. **Working capital** = Current assets − Current liabilities
   Working capital measures the amount of current assets that would remain if all current liabilities were paid.
2. **Current ratio** = Current assets/Current liabilities
   The current ratio is a standardized measure of liquidity. In general, the higher the ratio is, the more protection a company has against liquidity problems. However, the ratio can be distorted by seasonal influences and abnormal payments on accounts payable made at the end of the period.
3. **Quick ratio** = Quick assets/Current liabilities
   The quick ratio is a standardized measure of liquidity in which only assets that can be converted to cash quickly (e.g., cash, accounts receivable, and marketable securities) are included in the calculation.

---

[35]This appendix was prepared by Donn W. Vickrey of the University of San Diego.

# Funds Management Ratios

The financial position of a company depends on how it manages key assets such as accounts receivable, inventory, and fixed assets. As a business grows, the associated expansion of these items can lead to significant cash shortages even for companies that maintain profitable operations. As was implied previously, short-term cash problems may signal future decreases in quality or delays in scheduled deliveries. Six frequently used measures of funds management are:

1. **Receivables to sales** = Accounts receivable/Sales

   In the absence of detailed credit information, the receivables-to-sales ratio can be used to analyze trends in a company's credit policy.

2. **Average collection period** = (Accounts receivable/Sales) $\times$ 365

   The average collection period is used to assess the quality of a company's receivables. The average collection period may be assessed in relation to the company's own credit terms or to the typical credit terms of firms in its industry.

3. **Average accounts payable period** = (Accounts payable/Purchases) $\times$ 365

   The average accounts payable period is used to assess how well a firm manages its payables. If the average days payable is increasing or is large in relation to the credit terms offered by the company's suppliers, it may signal that trade credit is being used as a source of funds.

4. **Inventory turnover** = Cost of goods sold/Average inventory

   The inventory-turnover ratio indicates how fast inventory items move through a business.

5. **Average days in inventory** = 365/Inventory turnover

   The average days in inventory is a simple conversion of the turnover ratio to a more intuitive measure of inventory management.

6. **Fixed asset turnover** = Sales/Average fixed assets

   The fixed asset turnover provides a crude measure of how well a firm's investment in plant and equipment is managed relative to the sales volume it supports. Unfortunately, interpreting the fixed asset turnover ratio is not always a straightforward proposition. For example, a decrease in the firm's turnover ratio could result from poor management of fixed assets *or* from an investment in new technology (e.g., computer integrated manufacturing).

## Profitability Measures

Profitability refers to the ability of a firm to earn positive cash flows and generate a satisfactory return on shareholders' investments. Profitability measures provide an indication of a firm's long-term viability. Profitability measures may be used to infer quality in the sense that to generate a satisfactory return, a firm must ensure that it provides quality products from year to year. Profitability measures also may be used, to some extent, to infer a company's pricing policies. Thus, they may be useful for negotiating contract prices and, in particular, the profit portion of such prices.

1. **Profit margin** = Net income/Sales

   The profit margin percentage measures the amount of net income earned on a dollar of sales.

2. **Gross profit margin** = Gross margin/Sales

   The gross margin percentage measures the gross profit earned on each dollar of sales. Thus, this ratio may be used to infer the typical markup percentage used by a supplier.

3. **Return on assets** = Net income/Average total assets

   Return on investment measures how efficiently assets are used to produce income.
4. **Return on equity** = Net income/Average stockholders' equity

   Return on equity measures the percentage return on the stockholders' average investment.

### Measures of Long-Term Financial Strength

The ability to deliver quality products over time is contingent on the long-term financial strength of the supplier. Difficulties meeting long-term obligations also may signal insolvency. The disruptions caused by insolvency can cause major delays in shipments, decreases in quality, or complete inability to perform.

1. **Debt to equity** = Total liabilities/Stockholders' equity

   Since debt requires periodic interest payments and eventual repayment, it is inherently more risky than equity. The debt-to-equity ratio measures the proportion of the company that is financed by creditors relative to the proportion financed by stockholders.
2. **Times interest earned** = Operating profit before interest/Interest on long-term debt

   The times-interest-earned ratio measures the extent to which a company's operating profits cover its interest payments. A low times-interest-earned ratio may signal difficulties in meeting long-term financial obligations.

# Appendix C: Planning a Facility Visit

In planning facility or plant visits, only a few outstanding potential suppliers' plants should be chosen for observation because of the time and costs involved. In addition to observing production equipment and operations, there are other compelling reasons for plant visits. It is vital, for example, to determine a supplier's managerial capabilities and motivation to meet contractual obligations. The buying firm wants suppliers whose management is committed to excellence. Making such a determination properly requires an overall appraisal.

Among the factors to be addressed are the following:

- Attitude and stability of the top- and middle-management teams.
- R&D capability.
- Appropriateness of equipment.
- Effectiveness of the production control, quality assurance, and cost control systems.
- Competence of the technical and managerial staffs.

Other important factors include:

- Morale of personnel at all levels.
- Industrial relations.
- Willingness of the potential supplier to work with the buying firm.
- Quantity of back orders.
- Effectiveness of supply management and materials management operations

And past performance:

- Past major customers.
- General reputation.
- Letters of reference.

The plant visit should be planned carefully to provide the required level of knowledge and insight into the potential supplier's operations, capacity, and orientation. The efficiency with which the plant visit is planned and conducted reflects on the buying organization. To provide the reader with a sense of the detail in which some plant visits are conducted, one firm's evaluation form is reproduced in Appendix A of this chapter. This evaluative instrument is used by a high-tech firm that has a number of single-source collaborative relationship arrangements.

Although it varies with the firm's size and organizational structure, the *initial orientation meeting* typically is attended by the sourcing team members and their management counterparts from the potential supplier's organization. In smaller firms, the president often leads the supplier group. In this session, the sourcing team provides general information and explains the interests of its company: its kind of business, a brief history, kinds of products, the importance of the item(s) to be purchased, and volume, quality, and delivery requirements.

The prospective supplier usually is requested to provide additional information on the company's history, current customers, sales volume, and financial stability. If classified or confidential data might be involved during design and production operations, the sourcing team must review the supplier's security control system.

In the quality area, the supply manager and his or her sourcing teammates should attempt to understand the *supplier's attitude* toward quality by asking questions such as: How do you feel about zero defects and total quality management? Are you ISO 9000 certified? Do you employ the design of experiments during new product development? Do you employ statistical process control? Have you adopted a total quality commitment plan? How do you measure customer satisfaction? Show us how you've implemented these concepts. Do you have a quality manual? Copies of the manual and the policy should be reviewed by the buying team's quality representative. The potential supplier also should be asked to describe *its own* supplier quality control program. The more technical aspects of supplier quality are addressed in Chapter 21.

An increasing number of firms, including Motorola and many other leading-edge manufacturers, require that potential suppliers be registered under the appropriate ISO 9000 quality standard(s). It is important that the supply manager and members of the sourcing team understand that ISO 9000 is a series of process standards and that an ISO certificate is not necessarily a guarantee of high product quality.[36]

If the sourcing team is satisfied with the results of the introductory meeting, a tour of the facilities typically is made. Before the tour, the sourcing team should get permission to talk freely with various individuals working in the operation, not just handpicked managers.

The potential supplier's management often assumes that satisfactory operating controls are in place. In reality, however, experience frequently shows that some of these controls may not have been implemented or may have been discontinued. When management describes these things, the sourcing team should respond, "That sounds excellent; we'd like to see them." The team also should check controls by asking such questions as, "How do you ensure that the most current drawing is in use?" "How do you segregate rejected materials?"[37]

As a cross-check on the specific information obtained in the initial meeting, perceptive team members often ask shop and staff personnel similar types of questions. When the potential supplier's managers are

---

[36]"Does the ISO 9000 Need Fixing?" Industry Forum Supplement to the June 1994 issue of *Management Review.*

[37]Warren E. Norquist, director of Worldwide Purchasing and Materials Management, Polaroid Corporation, personal interview, October 1987.

not present, operating personnel should be asked about *their* understanding of the firm's quality systems, schedules, cost control efforts, and related requirements. Workers also can be asked about working conditions and turnover, the firm's commitment to quality, quality tools, and training.

When observing plant equipment, the sourcing team should determine whether the equipment is modern, whether it is in good operating condition, whether tolerances can be held consistently, and what the output rates are. The sourcing team also should look for special modifications or adaptations of equipment; these things often provide clues to the ingenuity of operating management personnel.

The first impression of a supplier's operation is generally obtained by observing the housekeeping of the plant itself. Is it clean and well organized? Are the machines clean? Are the tools, equipment, and benches kept orderly and accessible? Good housekeeping tends to be an indication of efficiency. Many sourcing team members responsible for source selection believe it is reasonable to expect that a firm that displays pride in its facilities and equipment also takes pride in the workmanship that goes into its products.

During the visit, responsible sourcing team members should investigate production methods and efficiencies. Is a just-in-time system utilized to a significant extent? Is material moving freely from storage to production areas? Are there any production bottlenecks? Is the production scheduling and control function organized and functioning well? Is reserve production capacity available? Is it available on a regular or an overtime basis? Does the potential supplier have a competent maintenance crew? Finally, the sourcing team should determine whether inventory levels for both production materials and finished goods are adequate for the company's needs.

Employee attitudes are extremely important. In the long run, production results often depend more on people than on the physical plant. Do the employees seem to work harmoniously with one another and with their supervisors? Are they interested in quality and in improving the products they make? Is enthusiasm at a reasonable level? In short, do the people take pride in their jobs and in the firm, or do they view it as an eight-to-five clock-punching operation?

# Global Supply Management

## CHAPTER OBJECTIVES

*After reading this chapter, you should be able to:*

1. Explain why global sourcing is here for the long term.

2. Understand and identify how companies benefit from buying globally.

3. Recognize potential issues that can arise in buying globally.

4. Determine which products and services are best suited for buying offshore.

5. Explain how to get started in the international arena.

6. Explain how to identify possible sources of supply.

7. Understand potential issues with payment and how to avoid them.

8. Explain the concept of countertrade.

9. Identify the major economic alliances around the world and explain what drives them.

## VIGNETTE: SOPRAFFINO GOES GLOBAL

Pam grimly looked over her spreadsheet analysis for her first year's profits. Her business, Sopraffino, which means "super-fine" or "first-class" in Italian, was started in 1998 in Danville, California, with about $10,000. The original idea was to sell gallery items, beautiful gifts, and furniture. Pam hoped that the Italian name coupled with her artistic background, Italian heritage, and imported dried flowers and gifts would give Sopraffino a niche in Danville's heavily saturated retail market. But after six months of business, Pam discovered that the gallery items did not sell very well. In fact, Sopraffino had a net income of only $4,000 in the first year of business because of high costs and low sales.

Although she kept the name, the store shifted to selling mostly dried floral arrangements, along with soaps, lotions, containers, cards, and similar items. The growth for sales of dried floral arrangements appeared to have a 71 percent annual rate if extrapolated over the following year. Customers loved the dried floral arrangements that could be customized to each customer's home by using a raw material inventory of about 30 varieties of dried flowers.

As with all products sold in the store, the dried floral materials were purchased in San Francisco through wholesalers. When the store opened, Pam was unable to research more direct sources of supply, and so using wholesalers as intermediaries made economic and managerial sense. The manufacturers that supplied wholesalers were clearly labeled on the boxes of dried flowers. In every case, the suppliers were overseas, primarily in Israel and Holland. Once a week, Pam would awake at 4:00 A.M. to drive to San Francisco to purchase and transport dried flowers in her Suzuki Sidekick four-door. Sometimes, she would have to make two or more trips in a week if she could not fit all the flowers in her car or if the wholesalers were out of stock for a specific flower. After unloading the flowers at her store, she would use them throughout the week to make arrangements for custom orders and stock for the store. The traveling created a strain on her marriage and made for difficult 16-hour workdays, but the thrill of making products customers were excited about and readily bought made the sacrifices worthwhile.

Using spreadsheet data from the first year, she forecast expected profits for the next year. She discovered that sales nearly would have to double from $88,000 to $160,000 for her to start making a significant profit. The prospect of doubling sales seemed remote. She did not want to close the business. Could increasing sales be the only answer?

Then she remembered a discussion on global supply management she once had had with a professor of supply chain management at California State University, Hayward. He had said that when intermediaries such as wholesalers outlived their usefulness, she could move to direct buying. She had dismissed the comment at the time in the belief that manufacturers would not sell directly to her because wholesalers had exclusive rights to the northern California region. Surely that was the case, she thought. After all, why would the wholesalers sell her boxes with the manufacturers' names on them? Now it was time to verify that assumption.

First, she typed the names of the manufacturers into a search engine and visited their websites. Next, she contacted them and quickly discovered that not only could she buy directly from them at about 40 percent less, they would deliver the boxes to her door. The issues with global sourcing that she had worried about were virtually nonexistent. In the span of one hour, she had found the profit she needed to keep her business open without unrealistic increases in sales. In addition, she no longer would need to take early-morning trips. She wondered how many other companies use intermediaries after their usefulness no longer exists. It was time to research her other products. ■

## CRITICAL THINKING QUESTIONS

1. What issues might Pam encounter with global sourcing that she is not expecting?

2. What does Pam mean by "wholesalers outliving their usefulness"?

3. Why is Pam able to save 40 percent by buying offshore? What is different about the overseas transaction versus the local transaction?

# Global Management Perspective

The supply management profession operates in an environment characterized by at least four important driving forces: (1) an economic landscape increasingly driven by transnational issues and concerns, a truly mutually interdependent "global economy"; (2) a supplier selection and development process that seeks collaborative and collaborative-based relationships with the best suppliers worldwide; (3) the formulation and positioning of supply management strategies which reflect forward-looking, long-term global supplier relationships; and (4) an orientation toward supply chain management (SCM) which extends supplier selection and relationship management issues well beyond the traditional business perspective of buyer-seller to those characterized by multitiered, highly interdependent supplier selection and relationships which span the globe.

## Future of Global Supply Management

In an ambitious consideration of what the future holds for the supply management profession, the Center for Advanced Purchasing Studies (CAPS) concluded that

> much has happened to change the world of business and supply management in particular—with much more expected to come.[1]

The CAPS studies also stated that

> global sourcing is increasing. In 2000, firms in this study sourced between 21 percent and 30 percent of their total annual spend on a worldwide basis. In 2005, total nondomestic spend increased to between 31 percent and 40 percent. It is projected that in 2010 the total dollar amount of purchased items obtained from nondomestic sources will be between 41 percent and 50 percent.[2]

The CAPS studies support the conclusion that the main reasons for global sourcing are driven by a desire to reduce costs. "On average, respondents achieved cost reductions of 19 percent and a total cost-of-ownership reduction of 12 percent."[3] Consequently, "China, India, Eastern Europe and Brazil will continue to gain importance as sources of supply over the next five years, while sourcing from U.S., Canadian and Western European markets will decline."[4]

Supply managers face increased challenges in this new environment. Global turbulence and the risks inherent in many new supply chain practices will present increased supply chain risks. Changes in market segments will drive suppliers to be more selective about which customers they decide to service. One study predicts that supply managers "will face more aggressive and powerful suppliers in some markets."[5]

Procuring products and services of foreign origin can be extraordinarily challenging. Virtually all the practices and procedures described in this book are applicable, but many new issues must be addressed for a supply team to ensure that its organization receives the right quality, in the right quantity, on time, with the right services, at the right cost. As with other areas in purchasing and supply chain management, the process of global sourcing is experiencing massive changes.

---

[1]Philip L. Carter, Joseph R. Carter, and Robert M. Monczka, "Key Supply Strategies for Tomorrow," research study done by A. T. Kearney in conjunction with CAPS Research, Institute for Supply Management, Tempe, AZ, 2007, p. 1.

[2]Robert M. Monczka, Robert J. Trent, and Kenneth J. Petersen, "Effective Global Sourcing and Supply for Superior Results," CAPS Research, Institute for Supply Management, Tempe, AZ, 2006, p. 7.

[3]Ibid.

[4]Carter, Carter, and Monczka, "Key Supply Strategies for Tomorrow," p. 8.

[5]Ibid.

## Stages to Global Supply Management

At a number of leading firms, international sourcing is being replaced with a broader terminology called "global supply management."[6] Joseph Carter suggests three stages of worldwide sourcing, as follows:

- *Stage One*: International Purchasing—Organizations focus on leveraging volumes, minimizing prices, and managing inventory costs. These areas are characteristic of an organization first entering the global purchasing arena.

- *Stage Two*: Global Sourcing—Organizations focused on global opportunities will place more emphasis on supplier capability, supporting production strategies, and servicing customer markets. Most organizations which have sourced offshore for some time are at this stage.

- *Stage Three*: Global Supply Management—Here, organizations optimize supply networks through effective logistics and capacity management. These organizations have effectively minimized risks in offshore sourcing and have sourced worldwide for technology leadership.[7]

## Reasons for Global Sourcing

Global sourcing requires additional efforts compared with domestic sourcing, but those efforts can yield large rewards. One of the complexities of buying goods and services of foreign origin is the wide variability among the producing countries in characteristics such as quality, service, and dependability. Quality, for example, may be very high in products from one country but inconsistent or unacceptably low in products from a neighboring land. This is particularly apparent today in the quality and safety issues the domestic toy maker Mattel is experiencing with products manufactured in China.[8] With this caveat in mind, let us look at six common reasons for purchasing goods and services from global sources.

- *Superior quality.* A key reason for using global supply management is to obtain the required level of quality. Although this factor is declining in significance, supply managers in a variety of industries still look to global sources to fulfill their most critical quality requirements. Refer to Chapter 7 for more details.

- *Better timeliness.* A second major reason for global sourcing is to improve the certainty of the supplier about meeting schedule requirements. Order lead-time lengths and variability in lead-time estimations may be better than those available from domestic sources. As with quality, the timeliness capability of suppliers around the globe has improved steadily. Once the initial difficulties of the new business relationship have been overcome, many international sources have proved to be remarkably dependable in meeting schedules.

- *Lower total cost.* While lower cost is often the major reason for importing, it must be remembered that international sourcing generates expenses beyond those normally encountered in sourcing domestically. Examples include additional communications and transportation expenses, import duties, and greater costs of investigating the potential supplier's capabilities, all of which add to the buying firm's total costs. The total cost for goods to arrive at the point of use must be calculated, not just the unit price. To illustrate this point, one major computer manufacturer uses a rule of thumb

---

[6]Robert M. Monczka and Robert J. Trent, "Global Sourcing: A Development Approach," *International Journal of Purchasing and Materials Management*, Spring 1991, p. 3.

[7]Joseph R. Carter, Ph.D., "The Global Evolution," *Purchasing Today*, July 1997. p. 33.

[8]"Mattel Recalls 9 Million Toys from China," *Plain Dealer* (Cleveland), August 14, 2007.

that a foreign material's price must be at least 20 percent lower than the domestic price of that material to compensate for these additional costs. Nonetheless, after all the additional costs of "buying international" are considered, in the case of many materials it frequently is possible to reduce the firm's *total cost* of the material significantly through global sourcing.

■ *More advanced technology.* No country holds a monopoly on advanced product and process technology. Developing countries are expanding their capabilities into design, finance, and distribution.[9] Global sources in some industries are more advanced technologically than their North American counterparts. Failure to take advantage of such product or process technologies can result in a manufacturer's losing its competitive position to competitors that incorporate the more advanced technologies.

■ *Broader supply base.* Sourcing globally increases the number of possible suppliers from which the buying firm can select. Increased competition for the buying firm's business will better enable the firm to develop reliable low-cost suppliers. Broadening the supply base does not mean increasing the number of suppliers. Broadening the supply base actually increases the opportunity to find better suppliers, enabling the buying firm to decrease the number of contracted suppliers and pursue collaborative or alliance relationships when appropriate.

■ *Expanded customer base.* Sourcing globally can create opportunities to sell in countries where the buying firm's suppliers are based. In areas where trade restrictions are minimal, the interaction itself may yield some of the sales opportunities. However, in some countries, trade restrictions are in place that require nondomestic suppliers to procure materials in the buying country as part of the sales transaction. These arrangements commonly are called *barter, offsets*, or *countertrade*. The tying of *sales into a country* with *the purchase of goods from that country* makes both marketing and supply management far more challenging than is the case when pure monetary transactions are involved. For a firm to compete and make sales in many countries, increasingly it is necessary to enter into agreements to purchase items made in those countries. Countertrade is discussed in detail later in this chapter.

## Potential Problems

The following potential problems must be kept in mind:

■ *Cultural issues.* Cultural issues can be a problem in global sourcing because of the wide variety of approaches to conducting business in different regions of the world. A colleague recently stayed in a hotel in Hong Kong that did not have a fourth floor. The floor was there, but it was completely empty, with no walls! The number four has a variety of connotations, depending on whom you speak to in Asia. The explanation given by management at the hotel was that four means "death," and therefore it would be bad luck to have a fourth floor. Cultural issues are very real and should not be ignored in global sourcing; they are discussed later in this chapter.

■ *Long lead times.* Variable shipping schedules, unpredictable time requirements for customs activities, the need for greater coordination in global supply management, strikes by unions, storms at sea (which can cause both delays and damage), and increased security procedures usually result in longer lead times. Airfreight may be used to offset some of the problems of variable shipping schedules, but probably at an increase in cost.

---

[9]Carter, Carter, and Monczka, *op cit*, "Key Supply Strategies for Tomorrow".

■ *Additional inventories.*   The quantity of additional inventory required to buffer the effects of such long lead times can be difficult to determine. Quite often, however, the additional inventories are not as large as one might expect. Nevertheless, inventory-carrying costs must be added to the purchase price, the freight costs, and the administrative costs to determine the true total cost of buying from global sources. Occasionally, when a domestic industry is producing at full capacity, it is possible to get both faster delivery and lower prices from global sources. Routinely, however, additional lead times, which traditionally exceed 30 days, must be considered in planning foreign purchases when surface transportation is involved. It should be noted that some supply managers do *not* add buffer stocks, relying on airfreight in emergencies.

■ *Lower quality.*   As was mentioned previously, global suppliers frequently are utilized because many of them can provide a consistently high level of quality. But problems do exist. For example, the United States is the only major nonmetric country in a metric world. This frequently leads to manufacturing *tolerance problems* for buyers of U.S. products and U.S. buyers of products from metric countries. Additionally, nondomestic suppliers tend to be less responsive to necessary design changes than are their domestic counterparts. In many cases, there is the risk that production outside the domestic firm's control will result in "off-spec" incoming materials. Potential rework or scrap costs could add substantially to the total cost of doing business with global suppliers.

■ *Social and labor problems.*   In Europe and the United States, unions and some politicians are pushing for retaliatory measures against exporting countries where workers lack clout and labor laws are weak or are flouted routinely. Retailers such as Levi, Nordstrom, and Reebok discern a greater tendency by some customers to shun production from "sweatshops." Documentaries by the news media of working conditions in some international plants have made U.S. retailers sensitive to working conditions in those plants. It seems highly likely that manufacturers in other developed countries soon will have similar concerns about their global suppliers.

■ *Higher costs of doing business.*   The need for translators, communications problems, the distances involved in making site visits, and so on, add to the cost of doing business with global suppliers. Port-order services are more complicated because of currency fluctuations, different methods of payment, customs issues, and the use of import brokers and international carriers. Inadequate local (international) logistical support functions such as communication systems (telephones, fax machines, Internet), transportation systems, and financial institutions can complicate communications and product distribution.

■ *High opacity.*   Investors, chief financial officers, bankers, equity analysts, and supply managers involved in global activities have long been aware that the risk of conducting business in different countries varies. A risk factor called the Opacity Index has been developed to address the risk costs associated with conducting business in a specific country.[10] The Global Opacity Index addresses the following areas: (1) corruption in government bureaucracy; (2) laws governing contracts or property rights; (3) economic policies (fiscal, monetary, and tax-related); (4) accounting standards; and (5) business regulations. China, for example, has high opacity in comparison to the United States. The United States has less bureaucracy, fewer government-imposed restrictions, fewer monetary transaction constraints, and very little corruption.

---

[10]"The Opacity Index: Launching a New Measure of the Effects of Opacity on the Cost and Availability of Capital in Countries World-Wide (Executive Summary)," Price Waterhouse Coopers, London, January 2001, pp. 1–13. http://www.opacityindex.com/.

## Questions before Going Global

Several years ago, Raul Casillas of the Alps Manufacturing organization suggested that to help determine whether a part, product, or process is a candidate for global sourcing, one should ask the following questions:[11]

1. Does it qualify as high-volume in your industry?
2. Does it have a long life (two to three years)?
3. Does it lend itself to repetitive manufacturing or assembly?
4. Is demand for the product fairly stable?
5. Are specifications and drawings clear and well defined?
6. Is technology not available domestically at a competitive price and quality?

If the answer to all six questions is yes, the supply manager may want to evaluate the support network within his or her firm by asking the following questions:

- Does sufficient engineering support exist to facilitate engineering change orders (ECOs) efficiently when they occur?
- Will the buyer be able to allow sufficient time to phase out existing "in the pipeline" inventory?
- Will the supply manager's firm take the responsibility for providing the necessary education and training for those who will have to interact with and support foreign suppliers?
- Is the firm prepared to make a financial commitment for trips to the supplier?
- Is management willing to change the approach, in some cases even the policy, to the way business and related transactions are conducted?
- Is the buyer aware of the environment, including current and forecast exchange rates, the general impact of tariff schedules, available technologies, and products from other countries as well as their political climates and leading economic indicators both domestically and abroad?

If the answers to both sets of questions are positive, global sourcing may be a realistic possibility. A significant number of negative responses indicate the potential for real problems if a global sourcing arrangement is developed. Before a decision is made, however, the buyer needs to explore several issues with top management. First, do the required procedural and policy changes mesh satisfactorily with the firm's existing mode of operation? More important, is the global sourcing concept, along with its underlying rationale, compatible with the firm's long-term plans? It is important that the program contribute positively to the achievement of the firm's long-range goals and that the commitment be more than a short-term-strategy decision. In some cases, unions must be consulted.

## Supply Channels

The next step after deciding to source globally is to decide what supply channels to use. The lowest-price method for procuring goods globally usually is to procure them directly. Direct procurement requires the buying firm to deal with all the issues associated with getting the goods to its facilities. Although direct

---

[11]Raul Casillas, "Foreign Sourcing: Is It for You?" *Pacific Purchaser*, November–December 1988, p. 9. Also, for a more recent analysis, see Robi Bendorf, C.P.M., "The Global Sourcing Process—On the Road to World-Class," 86th Annual International Purchasing Conference Proceedings, May 2001, Orlando, FL.

procurement may result in a low price, the total costs may be prohibitive. In addition, limited resources in supply management may make direct procurement infeasible. The simplest way to source globally is through the use of an intermediary. The value of using intermediaries dissipates over time as learning by the buying firm increases.

## Global Trade Intermediaries

Selection of the appropriate intermediary is a function of availability and of the services required. The use of such intermediaries typically adds a significant cost to the overall cost of the transaction, but in most cases that use prevents many unforeseen problems.[12] A supply manager who is venturing into global sourcing is well advised to solicit the advice of colleagues from the local supply management association.

Some typical intermediaries are described below:[13]

■ *Import merchants* buy goods for their own accounts and sell through their own outlets. Since they assume all the risks of clearing goods through customs and performing all the intermediate activity, their customers are relieved of import problems and in effect can treat those transactions as domestic purchases.

■ *Commission houses* usually act for exporters abroad, selling in the United States and receiving a commission from the foreign exporter. Those houses generally do not have goods billed to them, although they handle many of the shipping and customs details.

■ *Agents* or *representatives* are firms or individuals that represent sellers. Since the seller pays their commission, their primary interests are those of the exporter. They generally handle all shipping and customs clearance details, although they assume no financial responsibility of the principals.

■ *Import brokers* act as "marriage brokers" between buyers and sellers from different nations. Their commissions are paid by sellers for locating buyers and by buyers for finding sources of supply, but they are *not* involved in shipment or clearance of an order through customs. They also may act as special purchasing agents for designated commodities on a commission basis. Like agents, import brokers do not assume any of the seller's fiscal responsibility.

■ *Trading companies* are large companies that generally perform all the functions performed individually by the types of agencies listed above. The worldwide operations and know-how of such firms offer significant advantages and convenience. Standard directories and trade publications list those firms, their capabilities, and their areas of service.

■ *Subsidiaries* are established by multinational corporations in countries where a physical presence is needed to improve competitive capability and/or meet host government restrictions. For example, Hitachi, a Japanese company, created a Hitachi Americas subsidiary to serve North American markets. Subsidiaries can increase sales and lower costs through employing a workforce with unique training and education and through reduced transport distances and tariffs. Subsidiaries usually start with a large percentage of expatriate managers, who are competent in the local language, which lessens over time as qualified managers from the host country are developed. Subsidiaries serve to buffer the supply manager from

---

[12]Dick Locke, "Get the Purchasing Channel You Want," *Electronics Components*, October 1993, p. U-12. Note: Dick Locke also wrote *Global Supply Management: A Guide to International Purchasing* (Chicago: Irwin Professional Publishing, 1996), which is an excellent resource on global supply management.

[13]N. A. DiOrio, "International Procurement," *Guide to Purchasing, National Association of Purchasing Management*, Tempe, AZ, 1987, p. 7.

both language and time-zone problems. They offer to set prices in the local currency and deliver material to buyers with all duties paid. Unfortunately, they are often remote from manufacturing and marketing decision makers and can block the flow of technical information. They also can add 5 to 35 percent for their services.

## International Procurement Offices

When an organization's purchases in a foreign country or region warrant, consideration should be given to establishing an international procurement office (IPO), also called an international purchasing office.[14] An IPO is an office in a foreign country that is owned and/or operated by the parent company to facilitate business interactions in the foreign country and the surrounding region.

Supply management professionals at an IPO quickly become familiar with qualified sources, expanding the buying firm's potential supplier base. IPO personnel can evaluate suppliers physically and personally, negotiate for price and other terms, and monitor quality and job progress through direct site visits. IPO personnel are in a position to develop and maintain better information on local conditions such as materials shortages, labor issues, and governmental actions than are domestically based supply managers. An IPO facilitates payments to the suppliers, provides on-site support at the supplier's site if problems arise, and provides logistical support.

Expatriates who have worked for the domestic manufacturer, usually in a technical role, normally staff IPOs; however, this is changing as the percentage of locals staffing IPOs is increasing. IPOs normally are established as cost centers, charging a percentage markup (typically 2 percent) for their services. Competition from other channels (foreign trade intermediaries and direct relations) tends to keep IPOs efficient. The one weakness of IPOs that has been observed is their tendency to represent the local supplier's interests over those of the parent company.

Deere & Co. undertook an aggressive globalization program under the direction of Dave Nelson, former Vice President of Worldwide Supply Management. Under Nelson's leadership, Deere's International Supply Management Services established IPOs around the world. A John Deere newsletter stated that the International Supply Management Services "group's mission evolved into leveraging opportunities around the world for strategic sourcing teams and for all of Deere's 75 factories."[15] Three of the group's key responsibilities were (1) "maintaining cross-cultural relationships and training sourcing team members in global supply management," (2) "serving as the main link between supply management activities and the Deere & Company functions that global trade requires: customs, law, finance, and others that deal with such murky issues as quotas and duties, world economic forecasts, business development, risk management, currency and taxes," and (3) establishing and facilitating International Purchasing Offices. According to Dave Nelson, "These offices will link local manufacturing to common enterprise processes, work to improve supplier capability by accessing and applying proven John Deere programs (such as Achieving Excellence and Supplier Development), and facilitate understanding of in-country trade and regulatory requirements, as well as cultures."[16]

---

[14]Before publishing this book, the authors debated whether to use another term for IPO, since IPO is popularly used for "initial public offering." The decision to keep the acronym IPO is based on its entrenchment in supply management literature and the lack of a better term. We considered the obvious, GPO (global procurement office), but quickly realized that GPO already means group purchasing organization.

[15]"Global Surge," *Supply Management Linkages: A Newsletter from John Deere*, Summer 2000.

[16]Ibid.

# Direct Suppliers

Dealing directly with the supplier usually results in the lowest *purchase price*, including transportation and import duties. It eliminates the markups of global trade intermediaries. However, it requires an investment in travel, communications, logistics, and interpretation of costs. Direct relations with the supplier should be undertaken only after a cost/benefit analysis has been conducted carefully. It is important to note that conditions in developing countries are often problematic. Buyers should anticipate problems. For example, China, India, South America, and Eastern Europe have relatively poor transportation infrastructure systems in comparison to North America, Western Europe, and the Pacific Rim.

## Eliminating Intermediaries

After the buying firm has gained confidence in the quality of the imported materials and volume increases, the firm typically attempts to discontinue the use of global trade intermediaries for major procurements. Its major motivation is to avoid an intermediary's markup. The supply manager should inform its supplier of this new policy and then visit each of the manufacturers, *without the intermediaries*, to negotiate new contracts. While cost and the desire for direct dealings on technical issues may motivate the buying firm to deal directly with the supplier, the final decision will be made at the supplier's headquarters. The supply manager should anticipate resistance by both the intermediaries and their manufacturers, but that resistance normally can be overcome. In some cases, new suppliers may have to be developed because of the tight ties the global trade intermediaries may have with the existing supplier. Before taking such action, the supply manager must ensure that his or her company is set up to handle items such as traffic, customs clearance, and international payments.

Direct procurement requires the involvement of the company in all aspects of the transaction; when properly conducted, it eliminates the added profit of the middleman. Outside agencies may be engaged to perform specialized services. For example, *customs brokers* can be used to handle entry requirements, *export brokers* to handle foreign clearances, and *freight forwarders* to arrange for transport. Those agents do not take title to the goods. Most direct purchasers whose scale of activities does not warrant such in-house capability use outside agencies.

Definitions of terms which the supply manager may encounter when dealing globally may be obtained by visiting the following websites:

CISG — Table of Contracting States   http://www.cisg.law.pace.edu/cisg/countries/cntries.html

Dictionary of International Trade Terms   http://www.itds.treas.gov/glossaryfrm.html

International Chamber of Commerce   http://www.iccwbo.org/

International Trade Administration of the U.S. Department of Commerce   http://trade.gov/index.asp

OANDA — The Currency Site   http://www.oanda.com/

The International Monetary Fund (IMF)   http://www.imf.org/

The U.S. Central Intelligence Agency's World Factbook
http://www.odci.gov/cia/publications/factbook/

The World Trade Organization (WTO)   http://www.wto.org/index.htm

Understanding Incoterms   http://www.iccwbo.org/incoterms/understanding.asp

## Identifying Direct Suppliers

Global trade intermediaries also are an excellent source of information. Unfortunately, these organizations have a vested interest in maintaining their position in the supply channel. The best way to prepare to bypass an intermediary is to develop direct contacts with key players at the division responsible for the design, manufacture, and marketing of the item or commodity class. The supply manager should provide performance feedback *directly* to the supplier. The supply manager should tell the intermediary that he or she wants to visit with the supplier's key personnel the next time they are in the country or the next time the key personnel are in the buyer's country. International purchasing authority Dick Locke recommends meeting the supplier's key personnel and presents other tips in his paper "Get the Purchasing Channel You Want," as summarized in the following list:

■  Use the meeting to provide performance feedback and explain your company's purchasing goals and values. Take care not to appear to be an unreasonable company to work with even if you must deliver a critical message. Work to make foreign visitors to your company feel as welcome as possible.

■  As part of the strategy, consider the timing of your request. The ideal time is when you are considering a change in suppliers or are selecting a supplier for a new project. The possibility of a major increase in business will give you more leverage.

■  If you're dealing with a new supplier, state your intention to deal directly right from the start. Once a subsidiary or representative has started to handle your business, it is difficult to dislodge. It's easier to change your mind and start dealing through reps than the other way around.

■  Once your company has established a relationship with the business and technical staff of the supplier, make the request to deal more directly. You might be requesting to deal through an IPO (referred to as GPO in this book), or you might be asking to deal directly. This request should go to the supplier's sales management, and specifically to an individual you already know.

■  Be prepared to give reasons. These might be that you need a lower cost and believe that both parties can benefit by removing intermediaries. Another reason might be that the representative or subsidiary doesn't add enough value to the transaction to justify the markups it must be charging.[17]

Potential direct global suppliers can be located through a wide variety of sources. Chapter 11 has a detailed section on discovering sources of supply and discusses the increasing use of the Internet in identifying sources. The use of the Internet is particularly advantageous in discovering global sources.

## Qualifying Direct Suppliers

Before additional energy is invested in dealing with a global supplier, two issues should be addressed: *country and regional stability* and the *potential supplier's financial condition.*

For approximately $750, Dun & Bradstreet will prepare a Country Analysis Report for its clients. The report includes some 70 pages of in-depth research, information on the current and historical economy and government, import and export practices, trading partners, and monetary policies.

Most experts recommend a survey of a region as well as the company and country because factors such as political and monetary stability, currency transfer laws, and trade and product liability policies may be crucial to doing business there. According to Heidi Jacobs and Barbara Ettorre,

> The client should also ask what is needed to engage in commerce in a particular country. Credit professionals cite such factors as: required documentation for transactions, the transportation and distribution infrastructure, religious customs, quality standards and existing regulations that may restrict sale of the client's product or service. Will there be overseas agents to facilitate a deal? How reliable and experienced are they? Many a deal has been

---

[17]Locke, "Get the Purchasing Channel You Want."

derailed by such cross-border questions as whether the desired country prohibits sales of products whose *components* originated in a certain country.[18]

The supply manager or buying team is cautioned not to judge the creditworthiness of the potential supplier by the ability of its key personnel to speak fluent English. A careful financial analysis must be conducted. Jacobs and Ettorre list the following sources of information for such analyses: Dun & Bradstreet, Owens On Line, and Justitia International Inc.[19] International credit specialists representing U.S. firms also caution their clients to familiarize themselves with the Foreign Corrupt Practices Act, which bars U.S. companies from engaging in bribery and other practices when doing business overseas.[20]

## Preparing for Direct Relations

Preparation for direct relations includes all the issues raised in Chapter 11, as well as intercultural preparation, the hiring of a competent translator, and an exhaustive technical and commercial analysis.

**Cultural Preparation**   Virtually all supply relationships with global suppliers are the result of negotiations. The success of each negotiation is influenced in part by the negotiator's ability to understand the needs and ways of thinking and acting of representatives of global firms. What is considered ethical in one culture may not be ethical in another. The intention of filling commitments, the implications of gift giving, and even the legal systems differ widely.

In addition to the conventional preparation for any negotiation, it is essential to conduct an extensive study of the culture(s); this study should focus on the culture, not the language. The ability to understand a supplier's cultural background is of great practical advantage for several reasons. Negotiators perform more effectively if they understand the cultural and business heritage of their counterparts and the effect of that heritage on their counterparts' negotiation strategies and tactics. Cultural awareness on the part of the buyer or buying team puts the supplier off his or her guard. Talk with others who have experience living or working in the culture. Learn what the holidays are, what the units of measure are, what the currency exchange is, what topics are taboo, and so on.

Another aspect of cultural preparation becomes important in cases in which there is a strong likelihood of continuing relations (i.e., one or more transactions that would require a year or more for completion). In such circumstances, the supplier's representatives (accompanied by their spouses) frequently visit the domestic firm. The buying firm's hosts should go to considerable lengths to become acquainted with their counterparts (and their spouses) on a social basis. Americans, for example, should entertain the visitors in their homes (a rarity in Europe and the Far East). This will give the Americans and their spouses an opportunity to develop good relations with their counterparts. This bank of goodwill, while not a means of co-opting the foreign supplier, projects a desire and willingness to understand, which frequently proves to be invaluable during subsequent transactions.

One other aspect of cultural preparation needs to be emphasized here: It takes much longer to negotiate with foreign suppliers than with a supplier from North America. This is especially true if the supplier has not had extensive exposure to the buying firm's business practices and specifications. The time required varies with the mode of operation. In the case of European firms, it usually takes at least twice as much time as with U.S. and Canadian firms, and up to six times as much time often is required with firms

---

[18]Heidi Jacobs and Barbara Ettorre, "Evaluating Potential Foreign Partners." Cited by permission of publisher. From *Management Review*, October 1993, p. 60. American Management Association, New York. All rights reserved.

[19]Ibid., p. 61.

[20]Ibid., p. 60.

in the Far East. As a result, U.S. negotiators must be aware of the requirement for additional time and plan accordingly.

Cultural preparation is specific to the country in which a supply professional is planning to conduct business. As a result, a detailed discussion is beyond the scope of this book. Several excellent resources are provided in the footnote below to aid the reader in his or her efforts.[21]

**Interpreters** Language frequently poses a significant barrier to successful global business relations. Bilingual business discussions usually require a third-party interpreter even when both of the principal parties are fluent in one of the two languages. Differences in culture, language, dialects, or terminology may result in miscommunication and cause problems. Both parties may think they know what the other party has said, but true agreement and understanding may be missing. Think, for instance, of the confusion the simple word "ton" can create. Is it a short ton (2,000 lb), a long ton (2,240 lb), or a metric ton (2,204.62 lb)? The use of textbook English raises innumerable interesting problems. For example, in the Far East, the word "plant" is used to mean only a living organism, not a physical facility. "Yes" means only "I understand" to many Japanese, not "I agree."

When there are language differences between cultural groups, many busy executives believe that a competent interpreter is all that is necessary to overcome those differences. While a good interpreter can speed negotiations, an ineffective interpreter or one ineptly used can convert even simple matters into interminable wrangles. Complex discussions may grind to a halt amid a haze of miscommunication. An inexperienced supply manager risks wasting inordinate amounts of time for very little gain while acquiring the necessary communication skills. According to Hal Porter, a specialist on interpreters, "One or two words with a double meaning can certainly change the entire content of a statement." Executives experienced in international trade usually have learned these lessons, if only by trial and error. The use of native-born interpreters, while allowing communication to take place, does not obviate the need for an understanding of the supplier's culture. Even when one overcomes the natural barriers of language difference, it is possible to fail to understand and be understood.[22]

**Technical and Commercial Analysis** Technical and commercial analysis is discussed in greater detail in Chapter 11. *Before* dealing with identified global candidate suppliers, the supply management team should do the following:

- Prepare and review specifications and drawings.
- Pack samples or photos of required materials if they would help in communicating requirements.
- Clearly prepare the quality requirements.
- Identify specific scheduling requirements.
- Determine (as a group) what percentage of the annual requirements for the item can be placed offshore.

---

[21]Four sound investments to help prepare for cultural issues are: Dick Locke, *Global Supply Management: A Guide to International Purchasing* (Chicago: Irwin Professional Publishing, 1996).

Fons Trompenaars and Charles Hampden-Turner, *Building Cross Cultural Competence: How to Create Wealth from Conflicting Values* (New York: McGraw-Hill, 2000).

Fons Trompenaars and Charles Hampden-Turner, *Riding the Waves of Culture: Understanding Diversity in Global Business*, 2d ed. (London: McGraw-Hill, 1998).

Edward T. Hall and Mildred Hall, *Understanding Cultural Differences* (Boston, MA: Intercultural Press, 1990).

[22]Hal Porter, "Interpreters: What They'll Do for You," *Across the Board*, October 1993, p. 14.

- ■ Determine requirements for special packaging.
- ■ Identify likely lead times.
- ■ Develop a clear idea of the price objective.
- ■ Prepare a briefing on your (the buying) firm. Frequently, much effort will be expended selling the potential suppliers on doing business with the buying firm. The briefing should include:

    Information on the relevant product line and related lines.

    Actual and forecasted sales volume.

    Customers.

    Market share.

    Unclassified corporate strategy information.

    Annual reports.

    An indication of why the buying firm is soliciting the potential global supplier's interest (quality? price?).

    Business cards in English on one side and in the relevant language on the other side.

    A North American's title on his or her card should be "adapted" to the situation. Most non–North Americans are extremely rank-conscious. Thus, a supply manager may be titled Supply Manager, Director, Vice President, and so on, for a specific situation. One supply manager has seven different business cards with seven different titles!

## The Initial Meeting

Adequate preparation as detailed in the previous section will increase the probability of a smooth, efficient, and successful initial meeting. At the initial meeting it is good practice to conduct a facility tour or visit of the potential supplier's facilities and meet with critical personnel. Be certain the plant you visit is the one that will make the parts you are buying. Plant visits are discussed in detail in Chapter 11. For large procurements with complex specifications, the buying firm's technical people clearly must be part of the visiting team. The potential supplier will be judging the buying firm just as much as the buyer will be judging the potential supplying firm. Experience has shown that the controller of the target supplier usually occupies a very influential position. To gain his or her support, the supply manager or buying firm's team should describe how and when the supplier's firm will get paid! Currency and payment issues are discussed in the next section.

# Currency and Payment Issues

From the buying firm's point of view, the preferred time of payment is after receipt and inspection of the goods. However, it is customary in many countries for advance payments to be made before the work begins. Such a provision ties up the purchaser's capital. Letters of credit also are common in global commerce. Again, the purchaser's funds may be committed for a longer period than would be the case if a domestic source were involved. Not surprisingly, a cost is incurred in obtaining the letter of credit.

## Exchange Rates

The absence of fixed exchange rates can be a problem; it creates at least two potential situations, as described below.

**Case 1** A contract calls for *payment in a foreign currency (Euros)*. The exchange rate moves against the U.S. dollar during performance of the contract. For example, assume that a contract was awarded to a supplier in Germany for 1 million euros. Assume further that the rate of exchange was U.S. $1.00 = Eur 0.689;[23] that is, one U.S. dollar purchased 0.69 Eur at the time the contract was awarded. Ignoring all other costs, the dollar cost to the U.S. buyer would be

$$\frac{\text{Eur } 1,000,000}{\text{Eur } .69/\$} = \$1,451,590$$

**Case 2** Assume that the U.S. dollar strengthens to the point that $1.00 buys Eur 1. The cost in dollars then becomes

$$\frac{\text{Eur } 1,000,000}{\text{Eur } 1.0/\$} = \$1,000,000$$

This is a decrease of $451,590, or a 30 percent decrease in the cost of the item in U.S. dollars. Note that the German supplier is no better off, since it receives only Eur 1 million, while the U.S. purchaser has benefited from the 30 percent decrease in the cost of the item in *U.S. dollars*.

The issue of currency risk is examined in greater detail in the Appendix to this chapter.

## Payments

Payments to a global supplier are simplified when a trade intermediary or an IPO is involved. When payment is to be made directly by the buying firm to the supplier, a letter of credit frequently is used.

**Letters of Credit** As part of the negotiations, many global suppliers will request that the buying firm obtain a letter of credit from its bank. A letter of credit is an instrument issued by a bank at the request of a buyer. It promises to pay a specified amount of money upon the presentation of documents stipulated in the letter. A letter of credit is not a means of payment, merely a promise to pay. Actual payment is accomplished through a draft, which is similar to a personal check. It is an order by one party to pay another party. Documents commonly stipulated in the letter of credit include the bill of lading, a consular invoice, and a description of goods. In effect, if the purchaser defaults, the bank has to foot the bill. Thus, any risk of nonpayment is transferred to the bank. Frequently, the global supplier will use the purchase order (contract) together with the letter of credit as security when obtaining a loan for working capital for the required labor and materials.

Letters of credit are classified in three ways:

- *Irrevocable versus revocable.* An irrevocable letter of credit can be neither canceled nor modified without the consent of the beneficiary.
- *Confirmed versus unconfirmed.* A bank that confirms a letter of credit assumes the risk. The best method of payment for an exporter in most cases is a confirmed, irrevocable letter of credit. Some banks may not assume the risk, preferring to take an advisory role. Such banks and their correspondents believe that they are better able to judge the credibility of the issuing bank than the exporter is.
- *Revolving versus nonrevolving.* Nonrevolving letters of credit are valid for one transaction only. When relationships are established, a revolving letter of credit may be issued.

---

[23]This reflects the exchange rate as of November 4, 2007, quoted on ADVFN Currency Converter (www.advfn.com); 1 EUR = 1.4516 USD.

Obtaining a letter of credit may take three to five business days. A detailed application must be completed. Since a letter of credit is an extension of credit from the bank, it is processed much as a loan is processed. If no line of credit has been established with the bank, the applicant must prepay the specified amount. Typical charges involved include an application fee—0.008 percent on a $125 minimum—plus a negotiation charge—0.0025 percent on a $110 minimum. In case of cancellation, a charge of $100 is common.

# Countertrade

The term "countertrade" refers to any transaction in which payment is made partially or fully with goods instead of money. Countertrade links two normally unrelated transactions: the sale of a product into a foreign country and the sale of goods out of that country. Foreign governments normally impose countertrade requirements in an effort to gain foreign exchange or foreign technology.[24] Countertrade has several distinct definitions:

- *Barter.* This form of transaction preceded the use of money. Goods are exchanged for other goods, with no money involved. This is the simplest form of countertrade. If goods are bartered to save on transportation costs, the arrangement is called a swap.

- *Offset.* With this form of transaction, some, all, or even more than 100 percent of the value of the sale is *offset* by the purchase (or the facilitation of purchases by others) of items produced in the buying country. Offsets are categorized as direct and indirect. A *direct offset* involves close technological ties between the items sold and purchased. For example, when the government of Australia purchased helicopters made by Boeing, Boeing agreed to buy ailerons for the 727 from an Australian supplier. An *indirect offset* involves the purchase or facilitation of sales of commodities unrelated to the purchasing country. When the Swiss purchased F-5 aircraft, the manufacturer (Northrop) facilitated sales of Swiss elevators and other nonaircraft products in North America.

- *Counterpurchase.* With this type of transaction, unrelated goods are exchanged. The U.S. manufacturer purchases goods in the foreign country from a supplier who is paid in local currency by the buyer of the manufacturer's goods. Counterpurchase normally involves two separate but linked contracts: one for purchase and one for counterpurchase.

- *Buy-back/compensation.* Buy-back (or compensation) is an agreement by the seller of turnkey plants, machinery, or other capital equipment to accept as partial or full payment products produced in the plants and/or on the capital equipment.

Laura Forker, in her 1991 report on countertrade, identifies the following advantages and disadvantages:

**Countertrade's Advantages** Companies involved in countertrade frequently have enjoyed a variety of marketing, financial, and manufacturing advantages that have resulted in increased sales, increased employment, and enhanced company competitiveness. By accepting goods or services as payment instead of cash, countertrade participants have been effective in (1) avoiding exchange controls, (2) selling to countries with inconvertible currencies, (3) marketing products in less-developed, cash-strapped countries

---

[24]The interested reader is encouraged to read *Creative Countertrade: A Guide to Doing Business Worldwide* by Kenton W. Elderkin and Warren E. Norquist (Cambridge, MA: Ballinger Publishing Co., 1987), and the more recent study by Laura Forker: "Countertrade: Purchasing's Perceptions and Involvement," Center for Advanced Purchasing Studies/National Association of Purchasing Management, Inc., Tempe, AZ, 1991. Single copies are available gratis by written request to the Center for Advanced Purchasing Studies, P.O. Box 22160, Tempe, AZ, 85285-2160.

(with centrally planned economies) that could not make such purchases otherwise, and (4) reducing some of the risks associated with unstable currency values. By overcoming these financial obstacles, counter-trading firms have been able to enter new or formerly closed markets, expand business contacts and sales volume, and dampen the impact of foreign protectionism on overseas business.

Countertrade also has engendered goodwill with foreign governments concerned about their trade balances and hard currency accounts. Finally, Western participants in countertrade have enjoyed fuller use of plant capacity, larger production runs, and reduced per-unit expenses because of the greater sales volume. Their expanded sales contacts abroad sometimes have led to new sources of attractive components and at other times to valuable outlets for the disposal of declining products. Countertrade has opened up many new opportunities for American firms willing to become involved in it.

**Countertrade's Disadvantages** Experienced companies have encountered a number of problems unique to or exacerbated by countertrade. Countertrade negotiations tend to be lengthier and more complex than conventional sales negotiations and must be conducted at times with powerful government supply agencies that enjoy negotiating strength. Additional expenses in the form of brokerage fees, additional transaction costs, higher supply management involvement, and transactions in goods problems reduce the profitability of countertrade deals. For example, countertrade contracts that use goods as payback often result in difficulties with the quality, availability, and disposal of the goods. Countertrade also introduces pricing problems associated with the assignment of values to products and/or commodities received in exchange. Commodity prices can vary widely over the lengthy negotiation and delivery periods, and trading partners may differ about the worth of particular products. All these drawbacks result in higher risk and greater uncertainty about the profitability of a counter-trade deal.

Offsets entail further concerns in the form of technology transfer requirements, local procurement conditions that favor local suppliers, and the rigidities that offsets introduce into the buying process. The result for Western firms is often increased competition. Offset customers can become competitors later on. And some offset requirements divert a Western firm's resources to less-than-optimal suppliers. These additional costs must be considered when a proposed deal is being evaluated.[25]

## Supply Management's Role

Historically, a firm's marketing people who are intent on making a sale have coerced reluctant supply managers to engage in a countertrade transaction. One of the authors was involved in such transactions during the 1970s. Little thought was given to the domestic seller's countertrade obligations until the purchasing government brought economic and political pressure to bear. At that point, the domestic firm's supply managers frantically began to see what could be purchased in the foreign country. As a result, a very uncomfortable relationship developed between the customer country and the seller.

Both marketing and supply managers must recognize that they need to work as a team if countertrade is to operate to the firm's benefit. When countertrade is used to facilitate sales, supply management should be involved *up front*. Supply managers should review the items their company requires. Similar requirements must be levied on the firm's suppliers so that they are in a position to assist the manufacturer in meeting its present or potential obligations.

---

[25]Forker, "Countertrade," pp. 11–12.

## Creative Countertrade

Elderkin and Norquist define traditional countertrade as focusing "on existing goods to be brought out of the host country and sold in existing world markets. Traditional countertrade must deal with the limitations of fitting what already exists into unresponsive markets."

"Creative countertrade," in contrast, with its focus on creating future goods for *new market niches*, has greater flexibility and wider possibilities. Creative countertrade is broader than traditional countertrade. It includes not only traditional countertrade but also international investment and joint venture activities. It carefully analyzes the needs of all the major parties, including the potential development of new global suppliers, and creatively applies existing business tools to meet those needs.

Traditional countertrade provides quick-fix solutions to ongoing trade problems but lacks the depth and longer time horizons of creative countertrade. It seems likely that progressive firms will embrace creative countertrade as a means of both increasing sales and developing new dependable sources of supply.[26]

# Political and Economic Alliances

Global political and economic changes are constant issues for supply managers to identify and address. Countries in various regions of the world have restructured trade laws and developed compromise-based agreements in efforts to stabilize trade, open markets, and create a body for addressing trade issues. The new laws and agreements have had and will continue to have an impact on global supply management. Among the more prominent economic alliances are the European Union (EU), the North American Free Trade Agreement (NAFTA), MERCOSUR, South American Free Trade Area (SAFTA), the Association of Southeast Asian Nations (ASEAN), and Asia Pacific Economic Cooperation (APEC).[27] Most of the discussion in this section is on the European Union since it is the largest economic alliance in the world.

## European Union[28]

The European Union is based on a treaty that calls for "common foreign, security and, eventually, defense policies, and a common central bank and single currency."[29] The inspiration for the EU is thought by many to have been the example of the United States and the need to prevent European wars. Others argue that the EU had its roots in the 1957 Treaty of Rome and first was envisioned as a "Common Market of Western Europe." Regardless of how the EU came into being, the impact of the EU has been profound on the field of supply management, creating opportunities as well as new challenges. William L. Richardson, former director of Commercial Services for British Steel, Inc., in London, made the following comments in 1993 that still hold true:

---

[26]Elderkin and Norquist, *Creative Countertrade*, pp. 122–23.

[27]Current maps of the countries included in the alliances listed above are readily available at a variety of websites, such as cnn.com as of August 2001. We have chosen not to include maps because of frequent changes in the alliance countries.

[28]The European Community, now called the European Union, consists of the following countries (as of September 2007): Austria, Belgium, Bulgaria, Cyprus, the Czech Republic, Denmark, Estonia, Finland, France, Germany, Greece, Hungary, Italy, Latvia, Lithuania, Luxembourg, Malta, the Netherlands, Poland, Portugal, Republic of Ireland, Romania, Slovakia, Slovenia, Spain, Sweden, and the United Kingdom.

[29]Sally Jacobsen, "Europe Finally to Be United, but Federation Is a Loose One," *Arizona Republic*, October 13, 1993, p. A10.

For the American purchaser, the European Single Market offers considerable opportunities and it makes purchasing easier. . . . First, it will strengthen or create new effective alternatives to existing large manufacturers, be they in the U.S.A., Japan, or elsewhere. Second, it makes purchasing easier by virtue of the creation of European standards where as many as 12 different national standards can exist. This is a huge aid to the cost of reducing and simplifying the quality and performance comparisons purchasers have to make when evaluating the advantages of different supply sources.

If the U.S.A. fears the European Single Market, it is a misplaced fear. In a sense Europe has looked at the U.S.A., seen how America has created a giant manufacturing base and said to itself, what is it that prevents us Europeans from achieving similar growth and prosperity? The European answer is, first, to tear down its own internal barriers and then to open up its market to world trade fairly conducted within international law.[30]

Richard L. Pinkerton, in the conclusion to his article on the history and evolution of the European Community (EC) and the implications for purchasing managers, writes:

Supply managers should be prepared to join their firm's EC strategy/tactics team. Each supply management professional must investigate the specific EC technical directives and the implications of the ISO 9000 standards as they apply to his or her firm. Subsequently, the development of implementation plans should be undertaken as an integral part of the firm's overall EC strategy and plan.

In many respects, the standardization directives and programs of EC 92 will facilitate trade with Europe by reducing a number of different codes into a single code. Not only does this "harmonization" reduce the need for 12 different sets of paperwork, including border documents, and for a variety of rules and regulations, it should also reduce the costs of products bought and sold. Additionally, a more efficient and uniform European transportation system is expected to develop. Although some product variation will always be present as a result of differing styles, tastes, languages, and other cultural nuances among the member nations, it is very clear that Europe is moving toward essentially the same type of free market that currently exists in the United States. Sourcing should be accomplished more quickly, with fewer suppliers, as customers in all 12 countries utilize a common set of standards and procedures, coupled with the growth of mass distribution centers.[31]

The words of Richardson and Pinkerton have not been proved wrong, but the advancement of the EU's objectives has been slow, though it is gaining momentum.

**The Euro** The European Monetary Unit (EMU) called the euro was launched on January 4, 1999, with 11 EU member countries voting to join: Austria, Belgium, Finland, France, Germany, Ireland, Italy, Luxembourg, the Netherlands, Portugal, and Spain. The United Kingdom and Sweden did not join, and the other members were not qualified. Slovenia and Greece have now joined, and the euro is used by a total of 13 of the 27 EU members as of Jan, 2007.

Initially, it was an electronic currency which could be bought and sold on markets in which consumers could establish bank accounts and credit cards. In January 2001, the euro (in cash and coin form) began circulating alongside national currencies for up to two months until national notes and coins were withdrawn.

Economically, the euro is meant to complete the European single market, bolstering cross-border mergers, improving price transparency, and eliminating exchange-rate risk. Enthusiasts also hope it will

---

[30]Quoted in Richard L. Pinkerton, "EC 92: It's Official," *NAPM Insights,* July 1993, pp. 25–27.

[31]Richard L. Pinkerton, "The European Community—'EC 92': Implications for Purchasing Managers," *International Journal of Purchasing and Materials Management*, Spring 1993, p. 25. Note: The EC was renamed the European Union in 1994.

be a rival to the hegemony of the U.S. dollar. Though its performance has been rocky, the potential for the euro to become the first international reserve currency in the near future is being debated among economists. "Former Federal Reserve Chairman Alan Greenspan gave his opinion in September 2007 by stating that the euro could indeed replace the U.S. dollar as the world's primary reserve currency. He said that it is absolutely conceivable that the euro will replace the dollar as reserve currency, or will be traded as an equally important reserve currency."[32] The euro continues to strengthen against the dollar. On November 2, 2007, the dollar was posted at $1.4489 against the euro.[33]

The euro has both a political and an economic rationale, but several key European countries do not support it. The United Kingdom has not adopted the euro as its official currency, although many stores throughout that country accept the euro.

What possible consequences could the euro and its adoption pose for supply management professionals in non-EU states? Richard L. Pinkerton studied the potential risks and advantages for U.S. supply managers.[34] The potential advantages of the euro for U.S. supply management personnel were given by Pinkerton as follows:

■ *Greatly reduced transaction costs.* The U.S. firm is now dealing with one exchange rate versus 12. This is especially significant when U.S. firms in the 12 EMU countries buy from one another on an intra- or extra-firm basis.

■ *Increased Competition.* (The level playing field concept). This should produce lower prices as firms are forced to be more productive as a result of price transparency.

■ *Reduced exchange rate risk.* U.S. firms will have to hedge against only one versus 12 countries. This also reduces transaction costs, as was noted previously.

■ *Increased trade and capital movement.* The euro will create a greatly increased capital bond and stock market and reduce the historical EU reliance on government and bank loans. Price stability and lower interest rates with controlled inflation should stimulate capital investment and, as a result, a sustainable economic growth rate in the 12 countries. However, increasing unemployment within the EU, especially France and Germany, is a major concern. *Note:* as of Jan, 2007, 13 EU countries use the euro.

In looking back over the first 50 years of this historic union of European countries, the *Economist* provided an excellent evaluation of the euro in the year 2007 in its article "Europe's Mid-Life Crisis: A Special Report." "Within the euro area a debate is in progress over whether the single currency itself encourages or discourages reforms. Most of its progenitors had hoped for the first. The euro has clearly boosted intra-EU trade by somewhere between 5 and 15% according to the Organization for Economic Cooperation and Development. It has also been a spectacular success from a technical point of view, establishing itself not just as a viable currency but as the only plausible rival to the dollar. For example,

---

[32]http://www.reuters.com/article/bondsNews/idUSL1771147920070917. Reuters: "Euro Could Replace Dollar as Top Currency—Greenspan." Retrieved on September 17, 2007.

[33]ECB: Euro foreign exchange reference rates: http://www.ecb.eu/stats/exchange/eurofxref/html/index.en.html.

[34]Richard L. Pinkerton. "Implications of the Euro for U.S. Supply Management Personnel." Presented at the NAPM Global Supply Management Conference, November 8–9, 1999, Phoenix, AZ, and published in the *World Market Series, Business Briefing: Global Purchasing and Supply Chain Management,* October 1999, pp. 46–52. World Markets Research Centre, London, U.K., www.wmrc.com. Also see Cherish Karoway White "The Euro Launched: Now What?" *Purchasing Today,* August 1999, pp. 48–51.

it now accounts for 25% of global foreign currency reserves."[35] While the European Union struggles with current issues such as agreement on a constitution, grassroots support to counter mistrust of the union, and the poor performance of its economies in recent years, supply executives must continue to study and understand this political and economic union as it represents the world's largest market and is here to stay.[36]

## North American Free Trade Agreement

In June 1990, the presidents of the United States and Mexico endorsed the idea of a comprehensive United States–Mexico Free Trade Agreement to guarantee that the positive effects of export growth and industrial competitiveness, which already had begun, would continue to expand. In 1991, Canada joined the talks, leading to the three-way negotiation known as the North American Free Trade Agreement, or NAFTA. This agreement was designed to create a Free Trade Area (FTA) comprising the United States, Canada, and Mexico. Consistent with World Trade Organizations (WTO) rules, all tariffs will be eliminated within the FTA over a transition period. NAFTA involves an ambitious effort to eliminate barriers to agricultural, manufacturing, and service trade; remove investment restrictions; and protect intellectual property rights effectively. In addition, NAFTA marks the first time in the history of U.S. trade policy that environmental concerns have been addressed directly in a comprehensive trade agreement. By accelerating the integration of the three markets, NAFTA should enable North American businesses to produce goods that are more competitive with goods produced in Asia and the European Union and will allow North American consumers to benefit from a greater selection of higher-quality, lower-priced goods.[37]

**Implications of NAFTA**   Canada and the United States have long been sources of supply to each other. Modern-day Mexico has pockets of expertise that are world-class. Many U.S. buyers already avail themselves of Mexican sources of supply.

When a global analysis of potential suppliers reveals that it makes sense to develop a world-class supplier in Mexico, a joint venture with carefully developed plans, objectives, action plans, and milestones is the appropriate way to develop the supplier. (Obviously, these principles apply to the development of suppliers in many parts of the world.) This approach brings together the social, political, and economic strengths of the supplier with the knowledge, technology, systems, and commercial expertise of the global buyer.

## Mercosur

MERCOSUR was founded in 1988 as a free trade pact between Brazil and Argentina. The modest tariff reductions in its first years led to an 80 percent increase in trade between the two partners. In 1990, Paraguay and Bolivia joined MERCOSUR, and in 2005, Uruguay was admitted. The ambitious goal is to invite other Latin American nations into the pact to form the Union of South American Nations. That union will unite two existing free-trade organizations, MERCOSUR and the Andean Community.

---

[35]"Europe's Mid-Life Crisis: A Special Report," *The Economist*, March 17–23, 2007, p. 8.

[36]Ibid, pp. 5–6.

[37]*NAFTA, the Beginning of a New Era*, Business America (partial extract), August 24, 1992, National Trade Data Bank, March 27, 1994.

## Association of Southeast Asian Nations

The Association of Southeast Asian Nations (ASEAN) was formed in 1967 by Indonesia, Malaysia, the Philippines, Singapore, and Thailand to promote political and economic cooperation and regional stability. The ASEAN Declaration, signed in 1976 by ASEAN leaders in Bali and considered ASEAN's foundation document, formalized the principles of peace and cooperation to which ASEAN is dedicated. Brunei joined in 1984, shortly after its independence from the United Kingdom. In the 1990s, Vietnam, Laos, Burma, and Cambodia became members as well.

Also in 1976, ASEAN heads of state signed the Treaty of Amity and Cooperation in Southeast Asia (TAC). The stated goal of the treaty is to foster a peaceful, cohesive region and promote regional economic cooperation. In July 1998, ASEAN Foreign Ministers signed the Second Protocol to the TAC, which permits accession by non–Southeast Asian countries. ASEAN then invited, and has since been urging, the Dialogue Partners to accede to the treaty.

ASEAN has established 10 "Dialogue Partner" relationships with other countries. The two sides meet at a Post-Ministerial Conference (PMC), which follows the annual ASEAN Ministerial Meeting (AMM). In 1994, ASEAN established the ASEAN Regional Forum, which focuses on regional security issues. This left the PMC to deal with international economic and political issues and transnational issues.

## Asia Pacific Economic Cooperation

Asia Pacific Economic Cooperation (APEC) was established in 1989 in response to the growing interdependence of Asia-Pacific economies.

Begun as an informal dialogue group, APEC has become the primary regional vehicle for promoting open trade and practical economic cooperation. Its members define the geographic littoral of the Asia-Pacific Basin. Its goal is to advance Asia-Pacific economic dynamism and sense of community. APEC's 21 member economies had a combined Gross Domestic Product of over US$18 trillion in 1999 and 43.85 percent of global trade.[38] This makes APEC the world's largest free trade area. Of the many issues before APEC's membership is a focus on streamlining intergovernmental procurement policies. "APEC members are now working individually and collectively (through the Government Procurement Experts Group, established in 1995 to manage APEC's work in this area) to fulfill these and other commitments articulated in the OAA. Indeed, this initiative, which aims to enhance the transparency of members' existing government procurement systems, is one of the agreed collective actions included in the OAA meant to serve the above objectives. Another is the development, completed in 1999, of a set of nonbinding principles (NBPs) on government procurement (comprising transparency; value for money open and effective competition; fair dealing; accountability and due process; and non- discrimination)."[39]

# Concluding Remarks

A firm's approach to global supply management normally progresses from a reactive mode to a proactive one. Under reactive global sourcing, the firm reacts to opportunities in the supply marketplace. If an internationally produced good or service is the most attractive buy, it is purchased. As the firm embraces a proactive approach to procurement, it develops supply strategies and supply plans for its requirements.

---

[38]APEC homepage. August 31, 2001.

[39]"Government Procurement in APEC," APEC website, August 31, 2001.

The development of these strategies and plans calls for the analysis of all possible sources of supply, both domestic and international.

Perhaps it is the level of difficulty and the degree to which global perspectives may conflict with one another that have warned off in-depth studies of global supply management. The shift from a tactical to a strategic business focus is no less profound than the shift in perception implicit in the terms "purchasing" and "procurement" when contrasted with "supply management." Nonetheless, it is this very complexity that requires our serious attention as we attempt to conduct global supply management strategies successfully.

Far from merely conducting an "inorganic" study of the various "tools" involved in the practice of global purchasing, we must seriously examine the professional competencies required to be effective in the global supply management environment. Supply management professionals must have the ability to (1) develop a strategic point of view with regard to global supply management; (2) deal with change and chaotic, shifting environments effectively; (3) deal with diverse cultures effectively; (4) work with and within distributed organizational structures; (5) work with others in teams and act as team leader/project manager; and (6) learn to communicate effectively with those who may have cultural beliefs and exhibit values very different from their own.

Recalling Socrates' entreaty that we are all "citizens of the world," the time has come to improve our understanding of world events as influenced by powerful political, economic, social, and cultural influences. Not only will we become better supply management professionals, we will become better human beings as well.

## Discussion Questions

1. What is the number one reason for global sourcing?
2. What other reasons do the authors offer for global sourcing?
3. Describe the biggest risk in buying foreign-made goods and services. What problems might we incur?
4. How do we get started when buying from another country?
5. List and describe five international intermediaries.
6. What are the advantages of establishing an IPO?
7. Why would a buying firm prefer to buy directly from an international supplier?
8. What two issues should be addressed in qualifying potential international suppliers? Why?
9. What three things should be done to prepare for direct relations with global sources?
10. How can the rate of currency exchange affect a contract agreement?
11. When are letters of credit typically required? How are they classified?
12. Describe countertrade. What are its major advantages to a manufacturer from a developed country with a pegged currency? What are the major disadvantages?
13. What impact has the European Union had on international sourcing? What impact will it have in the future?

## Internet Exercise

### One Red Paper Clip

In this chapter we talk about countertrading, which is a form of bartering. Visit this website to see how one individual bartered his way from one red paper clip up to a house!

(http://oneredpaperclip.blogspot.com/2005/11/one-instant-party.html)

## Suggested Reading

Assaf, Michael, Cynthia Bonincontro, and Stephen Johnsen. *Global Sourcing and Purchasing Post 9/11*, (Fort Lauderdale, FL: J. Ross Publishing, 2006.)

Ball, Donald, Michael Geringer, Paul Frantz, Wendell McCullock, and Michael Minor. *International Business: The Challenge of Global Competition* (New York: McGraw-Hill/Irwin, 2005).

Berry, John. *Offshoring Opportunities: Strategies and Tactics for Global Competitiveness* (Hoboken, NJ: John Wiley & Sons, 2006).

Cook, Thomas A. *Global Sourcing Logistics: How to Manage Risk and Gain Competitive Advantage in a Worldwide Marketplace* (New York: AMACOM, 2007).

European Union Data. The website for the New York EU office is www.europa-eu-un.org and in Washington, D.C., it is www.eurunion.org. The Washington office includes a large EU bookstore, and most of the publications are free.

Global Logistics and Supply Chain Strategies (excellent website): http://www.intracen.org/tradstat/welcome.htm. International Trade Centre—International Trade Statistics

*Global Logistics and Supply Chain Strategies* (trade magazine). Keller International Publishing.

"Global Sourcing to Grow—but Slowly," *Purchasing*, 18 (May 2001), pp. 24–32.

Hickman, Thomas K., and William M. Hickman, Jr. *Global Purchasing: How to Buy Goods and Services in Foreign Markets* (Homewood, IL: Business One Irwin, 1992).

Hinkelman, Edward G. *Dictionary of International Trade,* 7th ed., (Petaluma, CA: World Trade Press, 2006).

INCOTERMS 2000—Chart of Responsibility: http://www.i-b-t.net/incoterms.html.

Locke, Dick. *Global Supply Management: A Guide to International Purchasing* (New York, NY: McGraw-Hill, 1996).

Monczka, Robert M., Robert J. Trent, and Kenneth J. Petersen. "Effective Global Sourcing and Supply for Superior Results," CAPS Research, Institute for Supply Management, 2006.

Overholt, William H. *The Rise of China: How Economic Reform Is Creating a New Superpower* (New York: W.W. Norton & Company, 1993).

Pooler, Victor H., David J. Pooler, and Samuel D. Farney. *Global Purchasing and Supply Management: Fulfill the Vision*, 2d ed., Boston: Academic Publishers (Springer), (2004).

Ramberg, Jan. *Guide to INCOTERMS 2000 (INternational COmmercial TERMS)* (New York: International Chamber of Commerce, 1999).

Schaffer, Richard, Beverley Earle, and Filiberto Agusti. *International Business Law and Its Environment*, 6th ed. (Mason, OH: SouthWestern Publishing, 2005).

Schary, Philip B., and Tage Skjott-Larsen. *Managing the Global Supply Chain*, 2d ed. (Herndon, VA: Sopenhagen Business School Press, 2001).

Schuster, Camille, and Michael Copeland. *Global Business: Planning for Sales and Negotiations* (Orlando, FL: Harcourt Brace and Company, 1996).

Supplychainbrain.com: http://www.supplychainbrain.com/content/index.php.

Walker Danielle, and Thomas Walker Joerg Schmitz. *Doing Business Internationally: The Guide to Cross-Cultural Success*, 2d ed. (New York: McGraw-Hill, 2003).

## Appendix: Currency Risk

Locke and Anklesaria write:

> U.S. purchasing departments are at a disadvantage compared to their more sophisticated counterparts . . . in countries [which] deal in foreign currencies as a matter of course . . . U.S. buyers' unfamiliarity in dealing in foreign currencies leads to higher costs in two ways. First, they attempt to put all currency risk on the supplier,

which causes the supplier to include charges for hedging, or to add an extra margin for contingencies into the price. Second, in an attempt to avoid dealing in foreign currencies, buyers use suppliers' U.S. subsidiaries and representatives, who will accept payment in dollars, but who also charge high markups. . .

Buyers and finance staffs of firms should understand when to buy in foreign currencies and when to buy in U.S. dollars. They should know the measures to take to avoid major increases in dollar cost and to be flexible enough to get decreases when possible. They should understand methods of reducing short-term risk through hedging. They should have analytical tools available to help them choose between various hedging strategies.[40]

The biggest advantage comes from the choice of the best pricing currency (the currency in which prices are set). The payment currency (you actually may pay an equivalent amount of a different currency) does not make a big difference in prices. To choose a pricing currency, you must answer two questions.

First, what are you buying? Product prices can be divided into cost-driven and market-driven categories. Cost-driven prices are those for which the supplier can set prices on the basis of his or her costs. Market-driven prices are those for which prices are set on a world market, usually in U.S. dollars, and the supplier cannot sell at a higher price. Second, where is the product built? Some countries have currencies that are pegged to the U.S. dollar. Other currencies float freely. If a currency is truly pegged to the dollar, there should be no need for currency protection. Table 12.1 shows the possibilities.

## Floating Currency, Cost-Driven Product

These products are typically custom or semicustom products. An example would be a printed circuit assembly from Japan or South Korea. By pricing in the supplier's currency, the supplier is relieved of the currency risk. This should enable a buyer to negotiate a lower initial price than it could if the supplier took on the risk. It is better to start with the lower price, because one doesn't know if the dollar will strengthen or weaken. The buying firm can protect itself against dollar cost increases by using low cost hedging; an escape clause is needed in the purchase agreement.

**Table 12.1** | Best Buying Currency

| | Type of Currency | |
|---|---|---|
| **Pricing Driver Currency** | **Pegged Currency** | **Floating Currency** |
| Cost-based products | Dollars or supplier's currency | Supplier's product |
| Dollar market-based product | Dollars | Dollars |

## Floating Currency, Market-Driven Product

These products are typically commodities whose price is nearly the same anywhere in the world. Examples are gold, oil, and DRAMs. For this type of product, a buyer should not hedge. The buying firm is better off negotiating one worldwide price and keeping the price the same around the world. This works best if the firm has a purchasing presence in various regions, so that hedging does not work as it does with cost-driven parts. If the dollar strengthens, the price in another currency goes up.

---

[40]Richard Locke, Jr., and Jimmy Anklesaria, "Selection of Currency and Hedging Strategy in Global Supply Management," *Proceedings,* International Conference of Purchasing and Materials Management, Atlanta, GA, May 1994, pp. 294–99.

### Pegged Currency, Cost-Driven Product

Countries with pegged currencies are generally smaller ones. They include Taiwan, Thailand, Hong Kong, and Korea. There is little need to hedge these currencies, because they are unlikely to move against the dollar. In addition, the foreign exchange market is thin and not well developed. Instead of hedging, a buyer should have an escape clause in the contract, because these currencies do have occasional controlled changes in value against the dollar.

### Pegged Currency, Market-Driven Product

If the market is dollar-based, these products need not be hedged. Similar techniques to those used for market-driven products from floating currency countries are the best choice.

## Hedging

Hedging protects the dollar value of a future foreign currency cash flow. The reason to hedge is to protect against major swings in the value of a purchase. A buyer can achieve this via forward or futures contracts or via currency options. The buyer enters into contracts to sell dollars for foreign currency at the time the supplier is paid. It's easiest to think in terms of using the foreign currency that was purchased in the hedge to pay the supplier, but this is not what happens. There is a profit or loss on a hedge contract that takes place behind the scenes. This profit or loss is applied to a material price variance that results from exchange rate changes and offsets higher or lower part costs.

Forward contracts give a fixed cost for foreign currency and therefore for foreign currency purchasing. If the interest rates in the foreign country are higher than they are in the United States, the forward rate is at a discount to the spot rate, and this reduces the dollar cost still more.

Forward contracts also have the advantage of being suitable for internal transactions. If the buying company exports to the country it is buying in and wants to sell in local currency, purchasing in local currency reduces the company's currency exposure. The purchasing flow of funds offsets the sales office flow of funds. If an internal forward agreement is made between the two departments, only the difference between the two flows needs to be hedged at banks.

Options allow a buyer to take advantage of an increase in the value of the U.S. dollar but protect against a decrease. Unfortunately, they are expensive. A six-month option on a volatile currency typically costs about 5 percent, and most people choose not to buy them. An added difficulty is that option prices for the European-style options that buyers need are not well listed in financial newspapers.

### Risk of Buying in Dollars

Buying in dollars is not as safe a solution to global buying as many want to believe. A dollar buyer may start off with a higher price than necessary. If the dollar weakens, the buyer is paying even more. A more sophisticated competitor would be paying less. A supplier's competitors will soon let buyers know that they are paying too much. Other channels of distribution could also open up. Finally, supplier promises of fixed dollar pricing often are broken when the value of the dollar declines.

### Length of Hedging

Hedging for too long a period with forward contracts can lead to the same problems as buying in dollars. If the dollar increases in value, a buyer will be paying too much. Hedging for too long with options is expensive, because the option premium increases with time. Three months of orders plus three months of lead time gives six months of hedging, a typical period.

### Risks in Hedging

Hedging does involve some risks, but they are limited and can be controlled if one pays attention to the fundamentals. Risk arises from forecast inaccuracy and can lead to unexpected price variations, either up or down. If a company overforecasts purchases and hedges with forwards, there will be larger profit or loss on the hedge than the variance on part cost. With overforecasts, there will be a loss on forward contracts if the dollar strengthens and a gain if the dollar weakens. The total unexpected gain or loss will be approximately the percent overforecast times the percent that the dollar changed. For example, a 20 percent overforecast and a 15 percent currency strengthening will result in a 3 percent (15 percent of 20 percent) extra cost of the parts.

With underforecasts, some of the parts must be purchased at the spot rate without an offsetting hedge. If the dollar weakens, they will be more expensive, and if it strengthens, they will be cheaper.

### Choosing a Hedging Strategy

The biggest gains in currency management come from choosing the right currency. A good negotiator should be able to get an initial price reduction of 5 percent or more against a volatile currency such as the yen or the peso. The next most consequential decision is whether to hedge. Not hedging opens the buyer to dollar price swings that are often as much as 20 percent in six months. This uncertainty is unacceptable to most companies.

The third decision is to choose a hedging strategy![41]

Joseph Carter and his coauthors demonstrated the benefits of choosing a hedging strategy that is based on a Bayesian statistical analysis of probable outcomes. In the study, Carter showed that choosing a hedge strategy would have saved 3.6 percent compared with paying in the supplier's currency.[42]

---

[41]Locke and Anklesaria, "Selection of Currency and Hedging Strategy in Global Supply Management."

[42]Joseph R. Carter, Shawnee Vickery, and Michael P. D'Itri, "Currency Risk Management Strategies for Contracting with Japanese Suppliers," *International Journal of Purchasing and Materials Management,* Summer 1993, pp. 19–25.

# Cost Management

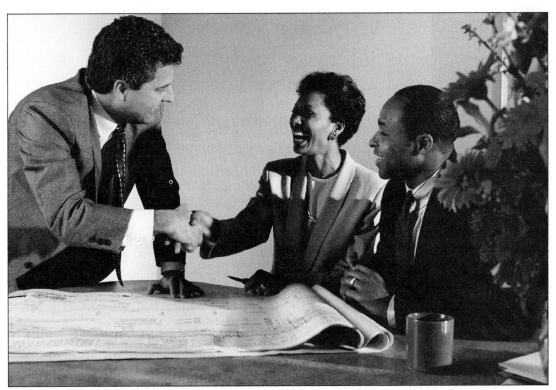

Historically, purchasing managers and buyers treated price as the only cost, ignoring the total cost of ownership (TCO). Almost all material, parts, sub assemblies and even services have significant costs beyond the initial price. Think of the simple example of the automobile life cycle costs of mileage, maintenance, insurance, etc.

To maintain global competitiveness, supply professionals must become enablers at revealing synergistic opportunities while balancing customer desires against cost. Some 40 years ago, the U.S. Air
Force introduced the concept of life cycle costing. Instead of addressing only operating characteristics and flyaway costs, we analyzed the cost of owning and operating a weapon system over its expected
life. The private sector has learned much from the Department of Defense in what has come to be known
as the Total Cost of Ownership. We believe that every supply manager, every program manager, every design engineer—in fact, every decision maker—must be familiar with and support the principles described
in Chapter 13, "Total Cost of Ownership."

Obtaining the *right* price is one of supply management's most important responsibilities. As described
in Chapter 14, a supply professional has a wonderful and evolving arsenal of tools to help satisfy this role.

As addressed in Chapter 15, the traditional tools of price and cost analysis have been augmented with
sophisticated ways of dealing with cost and technology uncertainty. Some of these compensation methods,
together with the award fee, help align buyer and supplier objectives.

Negotiation techniques, as discussed in Chapter 16, have evolved to a set of principles and practices
which help buyers and suppliers plan for and address all issues of the forthcoming relationship, ensure an
understanding of all issues, and arrive at an agreement in which both parties reap synergistic opportunities
and rewards—a truly win-win outcome. ■

# Total Cost of Ownership

## CHAPTER OBJECTIVES

*After reading this chapter, you should be able to:*

1. Recognize the critical value of determining the *total* cost of buying and/or owning a service or product.

2. Recognize and identify the major components that make up the total cost of a good or service.

3. Recognize and identify the subcomponents of total costs.

4. Explain why those cost components should be addressed when one is considering the true cost of an item or service.

## VIGNETTE: PURCHASE PRICE: JUST *ONE* COMPONENT OF COST

Ray Hummell, the supply manager of Tangential Reprographics (TR), is in the market for a new copier. The current copier, a five-year-old Xero model PDS 10/10 (known by the staff as the Pretty Darn Slow 10 copies/10 minutes) is down again. It's 8:15 A.M. and the coffee maker hasn't finished filling the first pot. The service firm can't come out until tomorrow morning, and there is a backlog of customers' orders.

Ray knows he has to take fast yet appropriate action. One choice is to get a new copier as quickly as possible. Another is to find the least expensive copier designed to handle TR's current monthly copy requirements. Perhaps the best choice is to spend some time and analyze the near-term and long-term copier requirements with regard to purchase price, ownership costs, and post-ownership costs.

Purchase price alone is not a guarantee of meeting office copier needs. In this case, ownership *costs,* both quantitative and qualitative, should play a major role in the selection. Those factors may be related to per-copy costs, reliability, copy quality, warranty, service response time, operator frustration, financing (e.g., leasing versus buying), upgradability, ease of use, and functionality. Post-ownership costs may include those related to trade-in or disposal value and environmental waste concerns. A generally accepted figure is that the purchase price makes up 30 to 50 percent of the total cost of ownership of a capital purchase.[1]

---

[1]Lisa M. Ellram, "A Structured Method for Applying Purchasing Cost Management Tools," *International Journal of Purchasing and Materials Management*, vol. 32, no. 1, Winter, 1996, p. 11.

Ideally, Ray should minimize the total cost of ownership over the life of the copier. In some cases, a low purchase price may be only the beginning of inefficiency and frustration. Durable/capital goods purchases such as copiers, cars and trucks, production machinery, computers, furniture, and fixtures will benefit from a TCO analysis. Direct and indirect materials (manufacturing) and services also will benefit from such an analysis. Actually, almost any purchase decision will benefit when one embraces the *philosophy* of TCO.[2] ■

## CRITICAL THINKING QUESTION

1.  After reading this chapter, develop a cost of ownership analysis for two new cars which catch your fancy. Be sure to select cars in the same category. Try to capture all acquisition, ownership, and post-ownership costs. The significant differences in the resale values of various cars might amaze you.

Total cost of ownership (TCO) includes all the costs related to the procurement and use of a product, including any related costs in disposing of the item after its usefulness ends. This concept can be applied to a company's costs singularly or viewed more broadly to encompass costs throughout the supply chain. This will be discussed in detail later in this chapter.

## The Three Components of Total Cost

There are three components of cost that must be captured in developing a TCO model: acquisition costs, ownership costs, and post-ownership costs.

### Acquisition Costs

Acquisition costs are the initial costs associated with the purchase of materials, products, and services. They are not long-term costs of ownership but represent an immediate cash outflow. Scrutinizing purchase price, planning costs, and quality costs to determine the lowest total cost of ownership/usage may provide significant savings.

Purchase Price    The price paid for direct and indirect materials, a product, or a service is frequently the major component in an item's total cost. Acquisition costs may include freight and delivery, site preparation (capital purchases), installation, and testing. Supply management professionals can reduce acquisition costs by negotiating effectively, obtaining quantity discounts, standardizing specifications, and completing a value analysis. In addition, strategic cost analysis offers methods to analyze and understand suppliers' costs, allowing for more fruitful negotiations and enhancement of supplier relationships. The purchase of used materials and equipment of acceptable quality is another way to lower acquisition costs.

---

[2]"A TCO analysis is generally not worthwhile with low-value or low-impact items it tends to be fairly time-consuming to complete. However, if an organization has a fully automated approach to capturing costs this technique can and should be applied to all major purchase decisions. This technique can also be a useful tool for continuous improvement when used as a strategic cost analysis technique." Ibid.

A supply management professional must not compromise long-term ownership costs by focusing on the purchase price alone.

**Planning Costs**    Costs incurred during the acquisition process include the costs of developing requirements and specifications, performing price and cost analysis, supplier selection/sourcing, contract determination, initial order processing, and monitoring. Increasing spending in these areas at times can reduce future ownership/use costs. For example, during the development phase of a new product, time spent with engineering representatives and the supplier to replace custom parts with standardized ones generally will reduce the initial purchase price as well as lower future repair, replacement, and inventory carrying costs.

Subscribing to e-procurement, B2B e-commerce, or electronic supply networks provides many businesses with a means to lower acquisition costs by reducing or eliminating overhead such as the time-consuming research and paperwork often associated with ordering the best product or service to satisfy specifications. The higher initial development and start-up costs are negated by the potential benefits of better communication, more information, reduced clerical overhead, and lower purchase costs.

**Quality Costs**    The higher initial cost of engineered-in quality during the design phase generally lowers future ownership and post-ownership costs for both the purchaser and the customer. Selecting and certifying a supplier to obtain the optimal level of quality and monitoring the results by using, for example, design of experiments and statistical process control ensure the achievement of the desired quality. In addition, the *quality* of the relationship established during this process can have long-run benefits. Long-term strategic relationships improve communications and may facilitate product innovation and cost reduction, especially in a cross-functional environment. The costs associated with quality were discussed in detail in Chapter 7.

**Taxes**    According to Richard Janis, a partner with KPMG LLP, a firm that sources internationally must address the impact of taxes, both direct (e.g., duties, processing fees) and indirect (e.g., foreign fuel taxes, tolls, facility fees), on the cost of procured materials and products. "Companies spend endless hours haggling over freight rates, the cost of warehousing services, and the purchase price of goods. But they typically pay little attention to the hidden expenses that can inflate a supply chain's costs. One of the most pervasive of these hidden expenses is taxes. Supply chain managers need to sit down with their tax colleagues to minimize the global impact of all taxes on supply chain operations."[3] Janis adds that when sourcing nationally, a firm must consider differences in state and local taxes. Experienced tax professionals must be included in the cross-functional team when taxes are a concern. Janis provides examples of ways to reduce acquisition costs by minimizing taxes:

- *Customs duties and tariffs*—focus on compliance to eliminate penalties and on planning to ensure that the proper tariff classifications with the lowest rates are applied.
- *Regional trade agreements*—source and/or produce in free trade areas that reduce or eliminate duties on all or part of a product.
- *Income-base shifting*—use transfer pricing to shift income legally from high-tax areas to lower-tax areas.

The impact of taxes can be significant. The added cost of addressing domestic and international tax issues up front may have a significant effect in reducing the purchase price.

---

[3]Richard Janis, "Taxes: The Hidden Supply Chain Cost," *Supply Chain Management Review*, Winter 2000 pp. 72–77.

**Financing Costs**   Whether purchasing inventory and materials, opening new facilities, or investing in equipment, the acquisition team should consider the quantitative and qualitative costs of financing alternatives, which are considered ongoing acquisition costs. A business can finance an acquisition by using surplus cash, debt financing (secured and unsecured term loans, mortgages, revolving lines of credit, capital leases, sale-leaseback arrangements, bonds, securitization of receivables, etc.), or equity financing (issue different classes of stock, form new partnerships and joint ventures, etc.). Each form of financing has costs and benefits. The creditworthiness of the firm (cash flow, profitability, debt load, future sales) and the expected return on the investment are key variables in making this determination. The cost of money is normally not a supply management professional's concern but must be considered by the firm.

## Ownership Costs

Ownership costs are the costs, after the initial purchase, associated with the ongoing use of a purchased product or material. Ownership costs are both quantitative and qualitative. Examples of costs that are quantifiable include energy usage, scheduled maintenance, repair, and financing (lease versus buy). Qualitative costs, although difficult to quantify, are important considerations in making purchases. Examples of qualitative costs include ease of use (is it a time-saver?), aesthetic factors (psychologically pleasing to the eye), and ergonomic factors (maximize productivity, reduce fatigue). The sum of both types of costs may exceed the initial purchase price and have a significant bearing on cash flow, profitability, and even employee morale and productivity. Understanding and minimizing these costs can have strategic significance. A supply management professional considers the following additional cost categories before making a significant purchase decision.

**Downtime Costs**   Making a purchase decision solely on the basis of the purchase price may have long-run implications, depending on the reason for the lower price. A seller may discount a premium item to move excess inventory and increase sales. It also may want to dump a troublesome product on an unsuspecting purchaser. A new entrant in the market may discount an unproven product in an effort to gain market share. Often the selling price is representative of the quality of the product; presumably, the higher the price, the higher the quality. Whatever the reason, the long-run costs associated with a purchase may include non-value-added downtime. Costs associated with downtime include, for example:

■ Reduced production volume and idle resources in a manufacturing environment. Downtime often is caused by unreliable and/or inflexible equipment or direct materials that are substandard or wrongly specified in the design stage. Downtime for an automobile production line can run $27,000 or more per minute.[4]

■ Opportunity cost of lost sales as a result of lower production volume.

■ Goodwill costs caused by undelivered or late orders, resulting in unhappy customers.

Careful scrutiny of reliability and dependability problems can reduce the cost of downtime.

**Risk Costs**   Weighing the risk of an inventory stockout in a retail or manufacturing business against the opportunity cost of maintaining excess inventory is an important issue. Keeping extra inventory *just in case* can be a stopgap decision or a needlessly costly move. In just-in-time literature, just-in-case inventory is treated as a form of waste that a company should endeavor to reduce or eliminate. Some costs of

---

[4]Personal interview with R. David Nelson, former Senior VP of Purchasing at Honda America Manufacturing, October 14, 1998.

excess inventory include those associated with financing, reduced cash flow, lost interest on cash flow, obsolescence, theft, and additional floor space.

It is important to consider risk costs when purchasing from new suppliers (issue: dependability; risk avoidance maneuver: multiple sourcing); using new materials, processes, and equipment in manufacturing (issues: reliability, flexibility, suitability; risk avoidance maneuver: parallel processing); hiring new employees (issue: adaptability; risk avoidance maneuver: additional training and backup personnel); or choosing legal representation (issue: expertise; risk avoidance maneuver: multiple representation).

Careful investigation and the development of appropriate sources of supply will reduce the inherent risk associated with the unknown, untried, and unproven. The appropriate place to begin is in the planning or acquisition stage, in which a risk assessment study should be conducted. Spending up front to reduce risk is an investment in the long-run efficiency and profitability of any firm.

**Cycle Time Costs**    Whether decreasing a new product's time to market or increasing the number of items produced in an hour (throughput), reducing cycle time can increase profitability and return on investment (ROI) through lower total costs. An organization with vision will apply the principles discussed throughout this text to shorten the time to complete all relevant purchasing and production activities. Practices that a supply management professional can employ that may have a significant impact include implementing JIT materials management, forming strategic alliances with key suppliers, and establishing cross-functional alliances within the organization. The higher initial cost of establishing and implementing these goals will provide long-run savings in the cost of direct material, direct labor, and manufacturing overhead. In addition, qualitative *savings* may accrue in the form of a smoother-running, more *user-friendly* organization.

**Conversion Costs**    Buying the wrong material, whether in quality, form, or design, can increase the cost of conversion (the application of direct labor and manufacturing overhead to direct materials to create a product or service). As was discussed earlier, material that is not optimized for the production process can increase labor and overhead use and thus, because throughput is decreased and the cost of maintaining the quality of the finished product is increased, the total cost of production is increased. In addition, machine time, labor requirements, scrap, and rework may add to the unit cost. Spending too little time and money in the acquisition of materials may result in spending more time and money during production.

Other areas that affect conversion costs include production methods (assembly lines versus cells, labor-intensive versus automated production), employee training and working environment, and methods of accounting for product costs, especially in the application of overhead costs to units of product. A well-informed and well-trained supply management professional may have the ability to influence decision making in these areas when working in a cross-functional environment.

**Non-Value-Added Costs**    Non-value-added costs flourish in most businesses. It is estimated that some 40 percent of all costs add little or no value. Examples of non-value-added activities that add costs to a product or service include the following:

- Moving and stockpiling batches of direct materials and work-in-process inventory because of a poor factory layout, poor scheduling, and a variety of wastes that increase uncertainty in the outputs of the system.
- Maintaining cumbersome operating procedures that duplicate efforts and steps for no apparent reason.
- Routing daily service appointments in a random fashion rather than designing routes that minimize travel time.

Total quality management (TQM), continuous improvement, activity based costing (ABC), and activity based management (ABM) are incremental change approaches that help identify non-value-added activities. Process reengineering is a more radical approach to change that focuses on simplification and elimination of wasted effort.

Supply management professionals with a background in management, operations, manufacturing, finance, information technology, and logistics are qualified to make suggestions to suppliers (and suppliers' suppliers) that reduce non-value-added costs. A successful strategy, when possible and cost-effective, is to visit a supplier's manufacturing site and observe how production takes place. Careful scrutiny may reveal a number of non-value-added costs that the supplier can reduce or eliminate, thus allowing for negotiations on lowering the supplier's price. Observing a service provider's processes either on-site or at its place of operation may reveal non-value-added costs that, when eliminated, will provide savings for both parties.

**Supply Chain/Supply Network Costs**   "If you process-map a supply chain and examine the material movement alone, such as the ins and outs of material flow from one organization to another, you will find many opportunities to eliminate waste."[5] Of course, waste adds unnecessary costs to purchased materials and services, as well as to logistics.

James E. Morehouse, a vice president for A. T. Kearney in Chicago, asserts that extended enterprises are beginning to develop and will hasten the development of improved efficiency and cost reductions along the supply chain. He believes that "organizations will be outsourcing transportation, purchasing operations, manufacturing, warehousing, order entry, and customer service. As a result, organizations will be more integrated with their suppliers and customers in order to manage the total supply chain from raw materials to the ultimate customer, the only source of revenue."[6] A supply management professional should consider the following interrelated areas for developing better strategies for cost reduction:

- *Forecasting*—Improving customer demand forecasting and sharing the information downstream will allow more efficient scheduling and inventory management.

- *Administration*—Implementing EDI (electronic data interchange) within an organization and between members of the supply chain will facilitate communication, reducing purchasing time, paperwork, and errors.

- *Transportation*—Streamlining material movement through the chain will reduce supply chain cycle time.

- *Inventory*—Embracing a JIT-type philosophy will help reduce unnecessary stockpiling and movement of inventory; suppliers can share inventory type and level information.

- *Manufacturing*—Improving capital budgeting procedures and designing and developing manufacturing processes that provide quality, efficiency, and reliability will lower costs and improve quality.

- *Customer service*—Listening to the customer will help identify supply chain inefficiencies and blockages.

- *Supplier selection and relationships*—Determining the appropriate source of supply and type of relationship (transactional, collaborative, or strategic alliance) with each supplier will minimize administrative overhead and help the company focus on the lowest cost at the required quality.

---

[5]Leroy Zimdars, CPM, former Director of Supply Chain Management for Harley-Davidson, quoted in John Yuva, "Reducing Costs through the Supply Chain," *Purchasing Today,* June 2000, p. 48.

[6]Ibid.

■ *Global sourcing*—Expanding sourcing internationally will provide cost savings and quality improvements by focusing on an international supplier's comparative advantage and utilizing EDI and low-cost transportation.

Well-trained supply management professionals armed with this knowledge can bring fresh insight to the table when developing TCO models and negotiating throughout the supply chain.

## Post-Ownership Costs

In the past, salvage value and disposal costs were the major inputs required in estimating the post-ownership costs of capital purchases. Those costs could be estimated as cash inflows (the sale of used plant and equipment) or outflows (such as demolition of an obsolete facility). For many purchases, there was an established market that provided data to help estimate reasonable future values, such as the Kelley Blue Book for used automobiles. An appraiser of industrial equipment could help estimate the future worth of plant and equipment. Often companies made investments with *absolute certainty* of future appreciation, although estimating actual appreciation required more information than was available (e.g., property in a major metropolitan area). Today, supply management professionals must address these issues. In addition, three other factors with potential long-term impact must be addressed in performing a TCO analysis on equipment, a plant, direct materials, a product, or a service: long-term environmental impact, unanticipated warranty and product liabilities, and the negative marketing implications of low customer satisfaction.

**Environmental Costs**   Gasoline stations in California have faced the unplanned expenditure of replacing their underground gas storage tanks with more environmentally friendly models. They also have been required to sanitize the soil near a tank if leakage has occurred. This expenditure has cost many independent operators their businesses, devalued their property (if polluted and unsafe), and increased the margin required on each gallon of gas sold to help recover such expenditures. This type of post-ownership cost is becoming more common as environmental problems persist.

**Warranty Costs**   A poorly designed and produced product may have unanticipated warranty-related costs. Tire tread difficulties that occurred between 1978 and 1980 and again in 2000 resulted in that kind of problem for Firestone. In 2000, General Electric, in cooperation with the Consumer Product Safety Commission, recalled selected dishwashers manufactured between April 1983 and January 1989 to rewire a defective slide switch (as an option, GE offered a rebate toward the purchase of a new unit). After-sale costs such as replacements, returns, and allowances can accrue to service providers (e.g., a carpet cleaning company whose poorly trained employee inadvertently uses a cleaning solution that fades the carpet fibers) and retail companies (e.g., a department store that misrepresents a product's capabilities). A well-trained supply management professional participating in a cross-functional team in product or service design may point out potential warranty/recall costs early enough that more emphasis is placed on designing and producing a defect-free and reliable product or service.

**Product Liability Costs**   Companies engaged in all types of business have faced unanticipated product liability costs resulting from poorly designed and/or produced products and services: fuel tanks that explode on impact because of poor design; tire treads that separate as a result of poor design or manufacture, inferior materials, and/or improper inflation by end users; faulty ignition switches that cause cars to stall at inopportune moments; ground beef infected with the *E. coli* bacillus because of improper processing; lawyers and accountants who have not performed their services according to professional standards;

and retail outlets that sell defective merchandise. This list is long, and the remedies usually require expenditures that often are not covered by insurance reimbursement.

**Customer Dissatisfaction Costs**   Some 75 percent of field failures in consumer goods can be attributed to defects in purchased materials. Field failures lead to customer dissatisfaction. When a customer is dissatisfied with a product, he or she frequently shares that dissatisfaction with many friends and acquaintances, some of whom may be potential customers. This flow of negative publicity frequently results in lost sales or "customer dissatisfaction" costs.

## TCO, Net Present Value Analysis, and Estimated Costs

When one is trying to consider the true TCO, one method of evaluating a potential capital investment is to combine the present values of the initial expenditure (initial cash payment), the future revenue streams (cash receipts or the reduction or elimination of expenses), and future expenditure streams (cash payments or the reduction or elimination of revenues). Analysts discount the positive and negative streams by using an interest rate that usually is referred to as the opportunity cost of holding capital: the minimum required rate of return a business expects to receive on its investment. The opportunity cast of capital is linked to the riskiness of the investment and the firm's capital structure.[7]

TCO and net present value (NPV) analysis are very similar in philosophy. Both are used in an attempt to estimate and analyze the acquisition cost, operating costs, and post-ownership costs in terms of value likely to be received by the company; in addition, NPV analysis is used to analyze revenues and other cash inflows. NPV uses the present value of a sum of future cash flows discounted by a required rate of return; the larger the positive net present value is, the more likely it is that the investment will return more than required over its life. A net present value of zero (NPV = 0) is the point of indifference. An NPV greater than zero usually suggests that the investment should be accepted. A negative NPV indicates that the overall return will be less than the minimum rate of return required by the company for the investment. An example of an NPV analysis is presented in Table 13.1.

Table 13.1 provides an example that demonstrates, based on actual and *accurately* estimated cash inflows and outflows, that this machine would be an unattractive investment—the required rate of return is 20 percent, and this investment returns 15.66 percent. Alternatively, the NPV is negative, and so the investment opportunity should be rejected. Other potential investments may be more attractive.[8] Qualitative considerations, which cannot be used in this calculation, may support or not support this purchase. Obviously, poorly constructed estimates of future cash flows and discount rates may provide meaningless information.

TCO, like NPV, requires an analysis of the holding period of the asset. TCO focuses on estimating and analyzing the ownership and post-ownership costs. The following formula represents a simplified approach to TCO analysis:

$$\text{TCO} = A + P.V. \sum_{i=1}^{n} (T_i + O_i + M_i - S_n)$$

---

[7] In financial management literature, the opportunity cost of capital is referred to as the weighted-average cost of capital, or WACC.

[8] This example does not consider the income tax on the revenue generated by the copier or the tax savings that accrue by depreciating the copier (known as the *depreciation tax shield*). Including the tax effects in this analysis will change the NPV results.

where:

TCO = Total cost of ownership

$A$ = Acquisition cost

P.V. = Present value

$T_i$ = Training costs in year $i$

$O_i$ = Operating cost in year $i$

$M_i$ = Maintenance cost in year $i$

$S_n$ = Salvage value in year $n$

Using the data presented in Table 13.1, the TCO calculation is shown in Table 13.2.

This type of analysis can be repeated for competing copiers. The copier with the lowest TCO should be the best choice, other considerations being equal.

This analysis focuses on costs or cash outflows, not cash inflows. Additionally, it considers the present value of those outflows. Incorporating NPV analysis, when applicable, into a TCO analysis will provide additional input that will allow the analyst to make a sound recommendation between alternatives.

**Table 13.1** | Net Present Value Analysis—*Copier*

| **Required Rate of Return** | **20.00%** | | | | | | | |
|---|---|---|---|---|---|---|---|---|
| **Year** | **NOW** | **1** | **2** | **3** | **4** | **5** | **6** | **Present Value** |
| Cost of machine including installation and testing (actual) | (120,000) | | | | | | | (120,000) |
| Manufacturer required overhaul (estimated) | | | | (9,000) | | | | (5,208) |
| Cash inflows generated by using machine (estimated) | | 40,000 | 40,000 | 40,000 | 40,000 | 40,000 | 40,000 | 133,020 |
| Cash outflows incurred by using machine (estimated) | | (7,000) | (7,000) | (7,000) | (7,000) | (7,000) | (7,000) | (23,279) |
| Salvage value (estimated) | | | | | | | 7,500 | 2,512 |
| Net present value of potential investment | | | | | | | | (12,955) |
| **(Alternative Method)** | | | | | | | | |
| Total of annual streams (from above) | (120,000) | 33,000 | 33,000 | 24,000 | 33,000 | 33,000 | 40,500 | |
| Required rate of return | | 20% | 20% | 20% | 20% | 20% | 20% | |
| Sum of present value of annual streams equals net present value of potential investment | (120,000) | 27,500 | 22,917 | 13,889 | 15,914 | 13,262 | 13,563 | (12,955) |
| Internal rate of return | (120,000) | 33,000 | 33,000 | 24,000 | 33,000 | 33,000 | 40,500 | 15.66% |

**Table 13.2 |** Sample TCO Calculation

| | Acquisition Cost = | $120,000 | Present Value Formulas |
|---|---|---|---|
| Present value of cash outflows for years 1–6 = | | 23,279 | $7,000[1/.20 - (1/.20(1+.20)^6)]$* |
| Present value of overhaul in year 3 = | | 5,208 | $9,000/(1 + .20)^{3\dagger}$ |
| Present value of salvage value in year 6 = | | (2,512) | $7,500/(1 + .20)^6$ |
| | TCO = | $145,975 | |

*$PV_{Annuity} = CF[1/r - 1/r(1 + r)^t]$

$CF$ = periodic cash inflow or outflow (must be the same each period)

$r$ = discount rate per period (annual rate divided by the number of periods in one year)

$t$ = total number of periods

$\dagger PV = FV/(1 + r)^t$

$FV$ = future value of single cash inflow or outflow

$r$ = discount rate per period (annual rate divided by the number of periods in one year)

$t$ = total number of periods

A note about estimated costs: Since TCO and NPV analyses require estimates of future costs of cash outflows, their reliability in providing useful information is only as good as the quality of the input data. A well-conceived analysis relies on inputs provided by cross-functional representatives with specific knowledge of and interest in the subject of the analysis. The most interested team member should provide the estimate. For example, supply management provides data on the purchase price, plant engineering provides an estimate of potential downtime costs, marketing provides an estimate of support costs, manufacturing provides an estimate of productivity or efficiency costs, and so on. A good rule of thumb is to include relevant participants who want to be part of the process.

Another method of arriving at estimates is for the leader of the cross-functional team to propose a cost figure and submit it for discussion. Frequently, one or more team members will react by saying, "No, $x$ is too much. It would be closer to $y$." Two other approaches to arriving at the estimated costs are parametric (several variables which affect costs are addressed) and Delphi (the cross-functional team members reflect on and refine an initial guesstimate). Both approaches, when applied in a strict sense, tend to be needlessly costly.

Neither of these methods can quantify many intangible variables that may affect a choice between alternatives or influence the decision whether to proceed with an investment. For example, in choosing between a sports car and a sports utility vehicle, a cost analysis is often not enough. Many people use a vehicle to make a statement about themselves, and so ego may have more substance than cost in this instance. Similarly, a company may want to project an image that only an automobile with a higher TCO can provide. This image may or may not be quantifiable in terms of increased future sales or executive image. It can be difficult at times, if not impossible, to quantify cash inflows on purchases; in these instances, a strict NPV analysis may be pointless.

## The Importance of Total Cost of Ownership in Supply Management

As Ray learns in the opening vignette, purchase price is only one component of the cost of purchasing material, a product, or a service. TCO should be a permanent concept in every supply management professional's mind in a service, retail, or manufacturing firm. Overemphasis on acquisition cost/purchase price frequently results in failure to address other significant ownership and post-ownership costs. Total cost of ownership is a philosophy for understanding all supply chain–related costs of doing business with a particular supplier for a particular good or service.[9]

Typical ownership costs include those associated with processing inventory (direct materials), repair, maintenance, warranty, training, operating, inventory carrying, contract administration, and downtime cost for operating equipment. Post-ownership costs may include those for disposal and environmental cleanup. The addition of risk and its associated costs adds yet another dimension. These costs and others must be estimated and included in a total cost analysis.

TCO is relevant not only for a firm that wants to reduce its cost of doing business but also for a firm that aims to design products or services that provide the lowest total cost of ownership to end customers. For example, some automobile manufacturers have extended the tune-up interval on many models to 100,000 miles, reducing the vehicle operating cost for car owners.

TCO analysis draws from a variety of academic disciplines, such as finance (NPV analysis), accounting (product pricing and costing), operations management (reliability and quality), marketing (understanding and meeting customer wants), information technology (systems integration and e-commerce), and economics (minimum average total unit cost of production). The best and, perhaps, only way to address all relevant costs is to employ a cross-functional team representing the key stakeholders.

Supply management personnel can facilitate the TCO analysis by combining their broad-based analytical skills with those of other team members to ensure that all relevant costs are considered. A brief examination of each type of business together with supply management's vision and role in minimizing total costs is a good place to begin.

## Service Providers

Service firms provide seemingly intangible products to satisfy human wants and needs. Service providers run the gamut from the accounting, legal, and medical professions to federal, state, and local governments to window washers, gardeners, and taxi drivers. Service providers procure capital equipment, products, and services as well as hire employees and provide employee benefits such as health and life insurance.

Like all businesses, service firms enhance profitability by increasing sales at a faster rate than costs, maintaining sales and reducing costs, or increasing sales and reducing costs while maintaining the desired quality and timeliness. Understanding what drives the cost of overhead expenditures is crucial to any service business. Service revenue must cover the direct costs, material and labor, and overhead to generate a profit. Depreciation is a key element of overhead. We define depreciation as the systematic transfer of the cost of a capital expenditure (an asset on the balance sheet) to an expense (the income statement). Another important cost element is the cost of maintaining capital and operating equipment. A TCO analysis of equipment purchases may help reduce expenditures for maintenance and parts over the lives of the investments.

Another important consideration in service businesses, as well as in retail and manufacturing businesses, is the total cost of maintaining the employee base. Paying the lowest wage does not necessarily result in the most cost-effective employees. The cost of getting a new and inexperienced employee "up to speed" can be high, and the learning curve can be long. Paying more for an experienced person with a short "ramp-up" time may be the best long-run solution for a position. A total cost/total benefit analysis of company-sponsored health insurance programs can reap rewards in terms of lower per-person total costs, greater benefits for covered employees, and improved morale.

---

[9]Lisa M. Ellram, Seminar on Strategic Cost Management for Purchasing Professionals held at The NAPM Convention, San Diego, CA, May 1999.

## Retail

The considerations that apply to service businesses also apply to retailers. Retail businesses sell a product that often must be ordered, received, inventoried, sold, and perhaps delivered to the customer. The choice of a system that facilitates the processes involved in inventory ordering and turnover will influence the total cost of inventory ownership. Many major retailers have empowered select suppliers to manage their product inventory for them,[10] thus reducing purchasing overhead and inventory carrying costs without necessarily increasing product cost. Embracing the just-in-time (JIT) philosophy is another way to improve QCT (quality, cost, and time) while reducing TCO. Lowering the cost of goods sold and the overhead costs associated with procurement, inventory carrying costs, and sales improves the bottom line. It is often easier to lower costs than to increase sales in a competitive business environment.

A retail business may own a product for a short time but may be responsible for after-sale adjustments, warranty claims, and the maintenance of general customer satisfaction for an indefinite period. If a retailer selects an item or product for sale solely on the basis of price,[11] thus ignoring reliability and product liability issues, customer satisfaction and future sales may suffer. Further, the retailer may incur an increased risk of financial and/or moral liability. Retailers must know their customer base and tailor the products they sell to satisfy that base. Retailers also must consider the long-term effects of every purchase made for resale.

## Manufacturing

Manufacturing businesses are concerned with the same TCO issues as are service and retail firms. In addition, they procure direct materials (raw materials, products, subassemblies, etc.) and incur overhead in the production of their finished goods inventory and other activities required to conduct business. Managerial accountants place emphasis on the variance between what something should cost or is expected to cost and what it actually costs. Price variance analyses are often misleading. For example, a favorable price variance (the material cost less than anticipated), compared with an unfavorable quantity variance (more material was used than anticipated), may indicate that although the material was less expensive, it was of a lower quality and therefore more was used. If you compare this with an unfavorable labor efficiency variance (more labor was used to work with the material than was anticipated), it becomes clear that a lower acquisition price may translate into higher production costs. By considering all costs simultaneously, supply management professionals and other members of the product development team can better determine the right specifications for the material and ensure that suppliers meet those guidelines.

The accurate allocation of manufacturing overhead is a major factor in calculating the true unit cost of a product. Using the wrong cost driver (process or activity that creates the need for overhead) can make a product seem more or less expensive than it actually is. Activity based costing (ABC), although initially somewhat complicated and expensive to implement, can return long-run benefits by providing more accurate unit cost information that serves as the basis for better decisions. Careful budgeting and procurement of overhead items from the purchase of capital equipment to that of lubricants used in production and the implementation of systems to ensure the timely availability of accurate information are methods used in obtaining the lowest total cost of production.

---

[10]The acronym for suppliers managing inventory at the buyer's site is VMI, which stands for vendor managed inventory.

[11]Usually, this reflects the reliability and quality of the product; that is, "you get what you pay for."

## Supply Chains/Supply Networks

A supply chain is a set of three or more entities (organizations or individuals) directly involved in the up-stream and downstream flows of products, services, finances, and/or information from a source to a customer.[12] A supply network is a less linear, more flexible virtual system that is linked by advanced communication systems and enhanced supplier relations. A supply management professional/organization can apply the philosophy and practice of TCO to the strategic optimization of costs within the chain or network. For example, an American company with the option of making a new product in Asia (potentially lower manufacturing costs) and shipping it to its customer base in the United States (higher transportation costs) or manufacturing it in the United States (potentially higher manufacturing costs) with minimal shipping (lower transportation costs) will have to determine the total cost of each alternative before making a decision. This TCO analysis should include[13] the study of the following:

- The manufacturability of the product (value engineering/value analysis).
- The manufacturing infrastructure requirements (the basic facilities, services, and installations needed for the optimal functioning of the manufacturing operation).
- Whether to outsource or self-manufacture.
- The abilities/location/responsiveness of potential tier two, three, and so on, suppliers relative to the manufacturing operation.
- The structure of foreign and domestic tariffs/duties/taxes.
- The costs of transportation and the timeliness of delivery.
- Foreign business/labor/environmental regulations.
- Foreign political/economic stability.
- Foreign exchange risk.
- Language/communication requirements.
- Volatility of end-customer demand and responsiveness of the network to changes in that demand.
- Inventory carrying costs (investment versus service levels).
- Inventory risk (relocation, damage, obsolescence, shrinkage).
- Quality costs.
- Managerial travel costs.

Although much of this analysis is ultimately quantifiable in dollars, some elements require a qualitative evaluation that offers less certainty. In this example, Asia may seem at first the logical choice, but distance from the customer base and other international issues may guide the decision toward domestic production.

## Concluding Remarks

TCO is an analytical tool and a philosophy that supports management decision making. A supply management professional can modify the TCO approach to support each major purchase decision as well as integrate it into strategic cost analysis to support make or buy (outsourcing), pricing and costing, critical direct material purchases, and other decisions that require analysis of costs over time. TCO is also a powerful

---

[12]John T. Mentzer, W. Dewitt and J. S. Keebler, *Journal of Business Logistics* 22, no. 2, 2001, p. 4.

[13]The bulleted list provides some general consideration and is by no means exhaustive.

adjunct, for example, in evaluating employee benefit programs and aiding in analyses such as the total cost of implementing an integrated activity based costing system in a manufacturing business. Estimates are the basis of most ownership and post-ownership costs. The care with which a supply management professional on a cross-functional team estimates these costs will determine the effectiveness of the resulting analysis.

As a philosophy, TCO can become an active part of everyday decision making. For example, TCO can help a family determine the total costs of maintaining a pet or choosing kitchen appliances. If the expression "There's no such thing as a free lunch" is true, everything people do has a tangible or intangible cost that can be analyzed if necessary.

## Discussion Questions

1. Define total cost of ownership.
2. What organizations benefit from a focus on total cost of ownership?
3. What is the best, and perhaps only, way to address all relevant costs?
4. What are three components of the total cost of ownership?
5. What are five components of acquisition costs?
6. Describe each of the following ownership costs:
   a. Downtime costs
   b. Cycle time costs
   c. Conversion costs
   d. Non-value-added costs
   e. Supply chain costs
7. Describe each of the following post-ownership costs:
   a. Disposition of used plant and used equipment
   b. Environmental costs
   c. Warranty costs
   d. Product liability costs
   e. Customer satisfaction costs
8. In your own words, describe a quantitative approach to a TCO analysis.
9. How should TCO affect service firms?
10. How should TCO affect retail firms?
11. How should TCO affect manufacturing firms?
12. Why is it important to consider the entire supply chain when one is considering TCO?

## Internet Exercise

### Total Operating Costs

Go to this website and have a little fun while you learn:

(http://db.theautochannel.com/db/newcarbuyersguide/total_operating_costs.php)

While exploring the ownership costs of various makes and models of cars, consider the following:

1. Why do they ask for the state in which you plan to drive the vehicle most?
2. Were you surprised by the results?
3. Are there other costs you might need to consider that are not included in the list?

# Suggested Reading

Barkman, Sandra and Bryon S. Marks. "Getting What You Pay For?—Total Cost of Ownership Model," presented at the 91st Annual International Supply Management Conference, San Antonio, TX, May 2006.

Cavinato, J. "A Total Cost/Value Model for Supply Chain Competitiveness," *Journal of Business Logistics* 13, no. 2 (1992), pp. 285–301.

Degraeve, Z., and F. Roodhooft. "Effectively Selecting Suppliers Using Total Cost of Ownership," *Journal of Supply Chain Management* 35, no. 1 (1999), pp. 5–10.

Ellram, L. M. "Activity Based Costing and Total Cost of Ownership: A Critical Linkage," *Journal of Cost Management* 9, no. 1 (1995), pp. 22–30.

Ellram, L. M. "A Taxonomy of Total Cost of Ownership Models," *Journal of Business Logistics* 15, no. 1 (1994), pp. 171–91.

Ellram, L. M. "Total Cost of Ownership: Elements and Implementation," *International Journal of Purchasing and Materials Management* 29, no. 4 (1993), pp. 3–10.

Ellram, Lisa M. "Total Cost Modeling in Purchasing," Center for Advanced Purchasing Studies, 1994 CAPS Focus Study.

Ellram, L. M., and S. P. Siferd. "Purchasing: The Cornerstone of the Total Cost of Ownership Concept," *Journal of Business Logistics* 14, no. 1 (1993), pp. 163–85.

Ellram, L. M., and S. P. Siferd. "Total Cost of Ownership: A Key Concept in Strategic Cost Management Decisions," *Journal of Business Logistics* 19, no. 1 (1998), pp. 55–76.

Ferrin, Bruce G., and Richard E. Plank. "Total Cost of Ownership Models: An Exploratory Study," *Journal of Supply Chain Management* 38, no. 3 (Summer 2002), p. 18.

Harding, Mary Lu. "Defining and Calculating TCO," *NAPM InfoEdge,* May 2000, www.ism.ws/ResourceArticles/2000/IE050001.cfm.

Harding, Mary Lu. "Total Cost of Ownership—MRO," *Purchasing Today* 12, no. 8 (August 2001), p. 15.

Harding, Mary Lu, "Understanding Total Cost of Ownership," *NAPM Info Edge* 5, no. 3 (May 2000), Tempe, AZ, National Association of Purchasing Management.

Hurkens, Krisje, Wendy Vandervalk, and Finn Wynstra. "Total Cost of Ownership in the Services Sector: A Case Study," *Journal of Supply Chain Management* 42, no. 1 (Winter 2006), pp. 27–37.

Milligan, B. "Tracking Total Cost of Ownership Proves Elusive," *Purchasing* 127, no. 3 (1999), pp. 22–23.

Roberts, Julie S. "The Supply Chain of Dollar and Cents," *Inside Supply Management,* June 2002, p. 38. www.ism.ws/ResourceArticles/2002/060238.cfm.

# Appendix: Supply Management in Action

## Implementing and Using TCO at Scott Paper: Prepared by Robert Porter Lynch[14]

Before being acquired by Kimberly Clark several years ago, Scott Paper was one of the world's largest producers of paper, with 20 plants in nearly 20 countries.

The papermaking process requires that wet pulp slurry be deposited uniformly on a continuously moving fabric belt. The fabric belt (known as "fabric" in the industry) is approximately 12 feet wide, and the

---

[14]Case study contributed by Robert Porter Lynch, President, the Warren Company (http://www.warrenco.com).

belt is about 60 feet in circumference. Fabrics are woven to enable the water in the pulp to be drawn out through the fabric so that when the pulp leaves the end of the belt, it is in a semisolid, rather gelatinous form. After leaving the fabric belt, the pulp goes onto other machines, which further dry and then press it into paper. Fabrics cost approximately $25,000 each.

For years, each plant's procurement team had negotiated with fabric suppliers. Knowing that the sales price was about $25,000 (a simple "component cost" to Scott), the procurement directors were always rewarded for driving costs down. Every buyer was trained in being a tough negotiator; they all knew that there was 5 to 10 percent that should be driven out of the sales price. Each year the procurement group aimed to push prices down, thus driving down the profit for the fabric manufacturers. At the end of the year, rewards were allocated to the buyers who got the most favorable pricing. Moreover, for years, Scott Paper's procurement department patted itself on the back for doing a wonderful job at keeping both the supplier's profits and Scott's prices low.

Scott Paper's profitability was among the lowest in the industry, making it ripe as a takeover target. Nevertheless, the purchasing managers were all confident that they were doing their part to get costs down to the lowest level possible.

In 1994, a new VP of Procurement, Ted Ramstad, arrived on the scene and began challenging the traditional thinking. In an effort to understand the real cost of the fabric, Ted conducted a reevaluation of cost. Internal data were gathered:

- While replacing fabrics, the paper machine must be shut down, at a cost of nearly $100,000/day to the paper company (because paper manufacturing requires a continuous process and the machine is considered efficient only when it runs 24 hours a day).
- It takes about eight hours to put fabric on a paper machine.
- Fabrics lasted an average of 40 days.
- Most fabrics broke on the machines.
- When a fabric broke, it normally had less than 10 percent wear.
- Seventeen companies supplied fabrics to Scott around the world. Each plant manager had a "favorite" supplier, but there was no compelling reason for using one supplier over another. Procurement assumed it could use the large number of suppliers in a competitive manner to keep the costs low.
- Cost of Goods Sold (COGS) for most suppliers was about 35 percent, and R&D was 3 to 5 percent.
- Most plants had four to six fabrics in inventory.

While most of the buyers were unconcerned about this information, Ramstad and his team, applying TCO thinking, began probing and asking more questions:

- How can we lengthen the time a fabric lasts on a machine?
- How long should a fabric last?
- Are we getting the *best* fabrics from our suppliers or just the *cheapest?*
- What suppliers are providing the research and development to give us better performance from our fabrics?
- Would fewer suppliers give us volume-purchasing power?
- Could we build win-win incentives to get more value from our suppliers and their fabrics?
- Where is there significant "non-value-added" in the system?
- What benchmarks should we be using to be "best in class"?
- If the "absolute component cost" of a fabric is $25,000, what is the "Total Cost of Ownership," and how does this compare as a "relative competitive advantage (or disadvantage)"?

Armed with a new focus and an energetic spirit, Ramstad's team began a worldwide search for answers. Fabric suppliers were interviewed, and information about competitors was gathered, indicating the following:

- The industry average fabric life span was 60 days.
- The industry benchmark fabric life span for one paper producer was 470 days.
- Only three suppliers were interested in helping Scott increase fabric longevity.
- None of the suppliers believed their fabrics were at fault for the low life span of Scott's Fabrics; all blamed either the operators or the machinery manufacturers.

## A Crucial Juncture

Now came the real test. In a "Simple Accounting, Component-Cost" world, fabrics clearly cost $25,000 apiece. However, Ramstad stuck his neck way out and maintained that this was true only in a narrow, "absolute" sense. In a broader, "relative advantage" perspective, the formulation of cost looked radically different. Here's what Ramstad's TCO calculations looked like:

- *Fabric Cost:*   If the highest standard benchmark life is 470 days and Scott's standard is only 40 days, the relative cost of the fabrics Scott has been purchasing is really 470/40, or 11.75 times that of the highest benchmarked competitor.

  Therefore, 11.75 × 25,000 unit purchase cost = $293,750.

  (To understand Relative Competitive Advantage, think of relative motion. Consider the analogy of driving down a highway at 40 miles per hour in the right-hand lane. The average competitors are in the middle lane, passing you at 60 mph. But the Best-in Class competitor flies by in the left lane at 470 mph. This is the Relative Competitive Advantage view of costing.)

- *Downtime Cost:*   Add an additional 8-hour portion of $100,000 per day to reflect the downtime for changing the fabric (8 hrs/24 hrs × $100,000 = $33,333). Relative to the best in class competitor, Scott has to make 11.75 changes of the fabric to the best-in-class competitor's one change.

  Additional relative cost to Scott is 11.75 × $33,333 = $391,663.

- *Burdened Labor Costs:*   It takes two men 8 hours to change a fabric. At a burdened labor rate of $45/hour, the labor costs are 2 × $45 × 8 = $720. Relative to the best in class competitor, Scott has to make 11.75 changes to the best-in-class competitor's one change.

  Additional relative cost to Scott is 11.75 × 720 = $8,460.

- *Incremental Cost of Purchasing the Low-Price Fabric:*   Adding these figures, the results are overwhelming. Relative to the best in class, Scott's "relative disadvantaged cost" is $693,873![15] That is very different from what was thought by procurement to be a $25,000 belt.

The procurement group had naively engaged in myopic thinking; they were playing the game "too small." Squeezing the supplier for a 5 to 10 percent discount made no sense when the issue was really how to gain an advantage of nearly $700,000. This is a "strategic systems" view of cost versus a "component cost" view.

---

[15]Fabric cost ($293,750) + downtime ($391,663) + labor ($8,460) = $693,873.

Ramstad did not stop there. He saw the relative disadvantage to be multiplied by the number of plants globally. Therefore, multiplying the "relative single plant competitive disadvantaged cost" by the 20 plants throughout the world, there was nearly $14 million of advantage to be gained on this single line item alone.

(Note: the standard accounting systems at Scott could not measure this factor, and therefore it was "invisible" to the Chief Financial Officer, who steadfastly called this accounting hocus-pocus.)

Undaunted, Ramstad pressed on. He insisted that the problem was even worse, since much of this inventory was actually scrapped because of product redesign before the inventory was utilized. What's more, he took the position that if Scott bothered to add the time value of money for financing the inventory of belts (because of frequent breakage several extra belts had to be kept on hand), it was clear that, the extra inventory was tying up capital. Eventually Ramstad was able to eliminate $20 million in inventory.

And it didn't stop there. By selecting the best-in-class suppliers, thereby reducing the number of suppliers to two globally, and negotiating long-term contracts, Ramstad was able to convince suppliers that they no longer needed to make sales calls on Scott's procurement officers. Because sales costs were 35 percent of the component price, he persuaded the remaining suppliers to lower their prices 25 percent, increase their R&D budgets to provide better products, provide technical support, and work with the machinery companies to improve sensing and tuning devices. Because of the higher volumes for the remaining two suppliers, their actual profits were substantially higher under the new model than they had been before. In addition, by not handling a continuous stream of bidding and purchasing, which previously accounted for 3 to 5 percent of the cost of ownership, Ramstad was able to reduce the procurement force as well.

CHAPTER 14

# Price and Cost Analysis

## CHAPTER OBJECTIVES

*After reading this chapter, you should be able to:*

1. Understand how economic conditions drive competitive conditions and price.

2. Explain how variable-margin pricing can result in overpriced purchases.

3. Identify and define the various categories of cost that influence price.

4. Identify and define the tools for conducting a price analysis.

5. Explain how a cost analysis can be used to obtain a fair and reasonable price.

6. Differentiate between direct costs and indirect costs.

7. Define which costs are direct and which are indirect.

8. Explain why it is important that a supplier make a reasonable profit.

## VIGNETTE: A PROBLEM OF PRICE

Sue Jones sat at her desk, reflecting on a pricing problem. Sue was a graduate of State University, where she majored in materials management. After joining the small manufacturing firm of Prestige Plastics in Des Moines, she was promoted from assistant buyer to buyer. In that position she was responsible for purchasing the chemicals used in producing the firm's plastic products.

    Sue was perplexed by a particular procurement involving the purchase of X-pane, a chemical that was formulated specifically for Prestige Plastics. Thirty-one days ago, she forwarded a request for bids to six suppliers for Prestige's estimated annual requirement of 10,000 drums of X-pane. Yesterday morning, Sue opened the five bids that had been received. The bids, F.O.B. Des Moines, were as follows:

|  | Price per Drum ($) | Total Price ($) (For Estimated Annual Requirement of 10,000 Drums) |
|---|---|---|
| Greater Sandusky Chemical | 312 | 3,120,000 |
| Chicago Chemical Co. | 297 | 2,970,000 |
| Tri-Cities Chemical | 323 | 3,230,000 |
| St. Louis Industries | 332 | 3,320,000 |
| St. Paul Plastics | 340 | 3,400,000 |

The Chicago Chemical Company was the low bidder for the fifth straight year. On the face of it, a decision to award the annual requirements contract to Chicago Chemical looked obvious. The day after the bid opening, the sales engineer from Greater Sandusky Chemical threw Sue a ringer. He said that no one would ever be able to beat Chicago Chemical's price. His firm estimated that the setup costs associated with producing X-pane would be approximately $750,000. He went on to say that because of the uncertainties of follow-on orders, his firm would have to amortize that cost over the one-year period of the contract to preclude a loss.

Sue checked with the other unsuccessful bidders. They said substantially the same thing: $700,000 to $850,000 in setup costs was included in their prices.

Next, Sue looked at the history of past purchases of X-pane. She saw that on the initial procurement five years ago, Chicago Chemical's bid was $202 per barrel, $3 lower than the second lowest price. Since that time, bid prices had increased, reflecting cost growth in the materials required to produce X-pane. Each year, Chicago Chemical's prices were $3 to $15 per drum lower than those of the unsuccessful competitors.

Knowing that the Chicago Chemical Company should have the lowest cost, Sue has decided to negotiate a more favorable price with the firm. She is puzzling over how to determine her objective target price. ■

O btaining materials at the right price can mean the difference between a firm's success and failure. Price, also referred to as acquisition cost, is frequently the largest component of total cost. Professional supply managers define the right price as a price that is fair and reasonable to both the buyer and the seller. Unfortunately, there is no magic formula for calculating precisely what constitutes a "fair and reasonable price." The right price for one supplier is not necessarily the right price for another supplier either at the same time or at different points in time. To determine the right price for a specific purchase, a number of constantly changing variables and relationships must be evaluated. This chapter discusses the most important of those variables and their relationships.

# General Economic Considerations

## Conditions of Competition

Economists of the classical school speak of a competitive scale that includes three fundamental types of competition: pure, imperfect, and monopoly. At one end of the scale is *pure* (or *perfect*) *competition*. Under conditions of pure competition, the forces of supply and demand alone, not the individual actions

**Figure 14.1** I Categories of Competition

of buyers or sellers, determine prices. In this environment, producers are price takers: They have no control over the price they receive for their products.[1]

At the other end of the competitive scale is monopoly. Under conditions of a *monopoly*, one seller controls the entire supply of a particular commodity and thus is free to maximize its profit by regulating output and forcing a supply-demand relationship that is most favorable to the seller. In this environment, producers are price makers and exert varying degrees of control over the price they receive for their products.

The competitive area between the extremes of pure competition and monopoly is called *imperfect competition*. Imperfect competition takes two forms: (1) markets characterized by few sellers and (2) those in which many sellers operate. When there are just a few sellers, an *oligopoly* is said to exist. The automobile, steel, and tobacco industries are examples of oligopolies. Generally, oligopolistic firms produce relatively few different products.

In contrast to oligopolies, the second form of imperfect competition exists when many sellers produce many products. This form of competition is referred to as *monopolistic competition*. Most of the products sold in this market are *differentiated* (distinguished by a specific difference), although some are not. Sellers, however, spend large sums on major promotional efforts to persuade buyers that their products are different. The majority of the products sold in the United States are traded in this market. These economic principles are portrayed in Figure 14.1.

In practice, the three categories of competition are not mutually exclusive; that is, they can overlap. When one considers both the buying side and the selling side of the total market, it is apparent that the number of market arrangements between individual buyers and sellers is very large.

It frequently is suggested that oligopolists conspire and act together as monopolists to thwart price competition. In fact, the U.S. Department of Justice does uncover a few conspiracies every year. The facts, however, indicate that price conspiracies among oligopolists are not the normal order of business. Any buyer who has purchased in oligopolistic markets knows that both price and service competition can be intense. Chevrolet strives intensely to outsell Ford, and vice versa. This is not to say that oligopolistic industries do not periodically exercise monopolistic tendencies to their own advantage. They do. For example, in times of recession, it requires only a basic knowledge of economics, not a conspiracy, for oligopolies to lower production rates and thus direct a balance of the forces of supply and demand in their favor. (One might reflect on how OPEC uses supply to affect oil prices.)

It should be noted that oligopolistic industries frequently hold firmly to their prices for long periods and appear to be noncompetitive. This appearance may be deceptive, however. Frequently, to gain a competitive advantage without notice, oligopolists shift their competitive efforts to other areas, such as service. Sellers may agree to perform additional services such as carrying customers' inventories, extending

---

[1]Pure competition exists only under the following circumstances: The market contains a large number of buyers and sellers of approximately equal market power. The products traded are homogeneous (a buyer would not desire one particular seller's product over any other's). The buyers and sellers always have full knowledge of the market. The buyers always act rationally, and sellers are free to enter and leave the market at will.

the payment time of their bills, and absorbing their freight charges. Those indirect price reductions often are not advertised.

Consequently, the amount of service a firm is able to obtain usually correlates directly with the perception and skills of its supply management personnel. Foreign competitors also greatly influence the freedom of U.S. oligopolies to raise their prices above fair market prices. For example, the freedom of U.S. automobile, steel, and electronic companies to raise prices is noticeably restrained because of foreign imports. For a number of items, specialty suppliers also compete effectively with oligopolies. Consequently, a competent buyer who learns to operate successfully within the practices of oligopolistic industries can influence a firm's total cost of materials.

It is important to understand that oligopoly is not characteristic of industry as a whole. Most firms and industries operate somewhere in the area of imperfect competition. Millions of people, working in thousands of factories, produce hundreds of thousands of products substantially without governmental or any other outside direction. The firms that make up this market exercise almost complete control over their prices, and price conspiracies in this market are extremely rare. In fact, aside from utilities, transportation, and some manufacturing industries, the concentration of oligopolistic power is rare.

**Most Prices Are Subject to Adjustment**   Because most firms are free, within broad limits, to adjust their prices at will, competent buyers can obtain better prices in direct proportion to their ability to analyze costs, markets, and pricing methodologies. Prices can be negotiated very little with firms operating in the markets of pure competition or monopoly. They can be negotiated a great deal with firms operating in the markets of imperfect competition. The question then is: What proportion of the nation's total market falls within the area of imperfect competition? What percentage of a buyer's total purchases is subject to price flexibility?

Studies made at the Graduate School of Business at Stanford University show that the nation's economy is approximately 70 percent free and exists in the area of imperfect competition. The results of similar studies by other authorities support this conclusion. Buyers in most purchasing situations therefore have considerable latitude for negotiating both price and service with their suppliers. However, every buyer should guard against the inducement of illegal price concessions. Buying personnel must understand the operation of federal and state restraint of trade laws.

## Variable-Margin Pricing

Most industrial firms sell a line of products rather than just a single product. Very few firms attempt to earn the same profit margin on each product in the line. Most firms price their products to generate a satisfactory return on their whole line, not on each product in the line. This variable-margin pricing policy permits maximum competition on individual products. The profits from the most efficiently produced and "successfully priced" items often are used to offset the losses or the lower profit margins of the inefficiently produced items.

Recently, during a research project at a printed circuit manufacturer, one of the authors traced overhead for 188,000 boards consisting of about 4,000 designs. The overhead generated by the production was applied by the company to the boards on an equal basis; however, about 20 percent of the boards drove 80 percent of the overhead. As expected, the 20 percent consisted of the low-volume boards produced in small lots. Since the company based its prices on the cost estimates, the high-volume boards were significantly overpriced.

An understanding of the theory of variable-margin pricing is essential if buyers are to obtain the right price. Whenever possible, sellers use average profit margins for pricing orders because that is usually advantageous to them. In some cases, this practice results in prices that sophisticated buyers realize are too high, particularly when low-cost, efficiently produced items are being purchased. Invariably when average margins are used, prices considerably above fair prices result for large, long-term purchases. When dealing with large multiproduct firms which utilize this pricing approach, a buyer also must know which of the items purchased is a high-margin item and which is a low-margin item. Such facts are learned by noting the differences in volumes, manufacturing skills, and costs of the various producers.

The following case illustrates the practical concepts of the preceding discussion. A large high-technology research firm successfully negotiated a $2.8 million annual contract for medical and scientific supplies. At the outset, the seller proposed that the contract be priced at cost plus the firm's annual gross profit margin of 19 percent. After several hours of negotiation, the contract was priced at cost plus a 6 percent profit margin. If the supply manager had not understood the concept of variable-margin pricing and not known which items the seller produced efficiently, the contract would have cost her company an additional $320,000.

In their search for optimum prices, competent buyers are aided by analyzing the pricing methods of both full-line and specialty suppliers. Regrettably, only buyers from a few progressive firms actually make such in-depth analyses of the entire product line of the industries in which they do business. Instead, most buyers focus their analyses on one product at a time (the product currently being purchased). Buyers are rewarded by directing their efforts toward the development of savings produced by recurring long-term cost reductions rather than focusing on savings from short-term cost reductions. In short, optimal pricing comes to buyers who understand the pricing processes for complete product lines, in all firms, in all industries from which they buy.

*In the long run*, a firm must recover all of its costs or go out of business. In the long run, for any particular item, the price is roughly equal to the cost of the least efficient producer that is able to remain in business. In the short run, however, prices in the free, competitive segment of the economy (roughly 70 percent of the whole) are determined primarily by competition, that is, by supply and demand, not by costs.

## Product Differentiation

There are many basic differences between the kinds of products marketed in the various segments of the economy. Some products in the competitive segment are *undifferentiated* (not distinguished by specific differences), while others are *differentiated*. In some cases, the products are intrinsically different (differentiated); in others, manufacturers are successful at making their products appear different from those of their competitors. Even in cases in which a product cannot be made different in substance, producers can get premium prices if they can persuade customers *to believe* that their products are superior. Some producers spend huge sums of money on sales personnel and advertising to accomplish that purpose. In the jargon of the economists, "they attempt to make the demand curve for the products of their firm somewhat inelastic." If their efforts are successful, they can charge higher prices for their products. However, if their efforts are defeated by the counterefforts of competitors, as is frequently the case, price competition comparable to that in pure competition can result. Grocers, for example, are well acquainted with this economic fact.

For both differentiated and undifferentiated products, producers compete on quality and service as well as price. The consumer market is more susceptible to producers' advertising claims than are buyers in the industrial market; therefore, the major portion of advertising effort is directed toward the consumer market. Nonetheless, industrial supply management professionals must be aware of advertising and sales tactics and be very careful to determine quality from an analysis of facts, not from unsupported claims.

## Six Categories of Cost

A supply professional knows that Price = Cost + Profit. He or she also must understand variable, fixed, semi-variable, total, direct, and indirect costs and how those costs influence prices.

**Variable Manufacturing Costs**   These are items of cost that *vary directly and proportionally with the production quantity* of a particular product. Variable manufacturing costs include direct labor (unless fixed by contract), direct materials (raw materials, subassemblies, etc.), and variable manufacturing overhead (e.g., plant utilities if they vary with machine use/output). For example, if a specific cutting tool costs $10 and lasts for 100 cuttings, each cut represents a variable cost of 10 cents. If three cuts were required in machining a specific item, the variable cost for cutting would be 30 cents. Variable costs may decrease as a result of economies of scale (e.g., purchase discounts on direct materials) and increase as a result of dis-economies of scale (e.g., too many workers in a confined workspace). Variable costs exist not only in the manufacturing environment but also in the selling, general, and administrative areas (nonmanufacturing costs). In summary, variable costs are fixed per unit but vary in total as the activity level changes.

**Fixed Manufacturing Costs**   Fixed costs *do not vary with volume* but change over time. Fixed costs are costs sellers must pay simply because they are in business. They are a function of time and are not influenced by the volume of production.[2] Fixed costs generally represent either money the seller already has spent for buildings and equipment (e.g., depreciation) or money the seller will have to spend for unavoidable expenses (e.g., rent and insurance) regardless of the plant's volume of production. For example, if the lathe that held the cutting tool in the preceding example depreciates at a rate of $250 a month, this is a fixed cost. The seller has this $250 expense every month whether or not any turnings are made during that period. Fixed selling, general, and administrative costs may include advertising and research and development; these are classified as nonmanufacturing costs. Fixed costs may be increased or decreased from one time period to another regardless of production volume. Fixed costs are fixed in total but vary per unit as the activity level changes (fixed costs per unit decrease as more units are produced).

**Semi-Variable or Mixed Manufacturing Costs**   Generally, it is not possible to classify all production costs as being either completely fixed or completely variable. Many others, termed semi-variable or mixed costs, fall somewhere between those extremes. Costs such as maintenance, utilities, and postage are partly variable and partly fixed. Each is like a fixed cost because its total cannot be tied directly to a particular unit of production, yet it is possible to sort out specific elements in each of these costs that are fixed as soon as the plant begins to operate. When the fixed portion is removed, the remaining elements frequently vary closely in proportion to the production volume. For example, if a plant is producing an average of 5,000 items a month, it may have an average light bill of $700 a month. If the number of units produced is increased to 8,000, the light bill may increase by $100 to $800. The $100 increase is not proportional to the production increase because a certain segment of the light bill is fixed whether any production occurs or not. Above this fixed segment, however, light costs may vary in a fairly consistent relationship with production volume. Mixed selling, general, and administrative costs may include selling salary (fixed) and commission (variable), telephone service (fixed) and metered local and long distance calls (variable), and so on.

---

[2]Fixed costs usually are "fixed" over the relevant range of production. The relevant range extends from the minimum to the maximum capacity/output of a manufacturing facility. Increasing production beyond maximum capacity requires the purchase of additional plant capacity and results in increased fixed costs.

**Total Production Costs**    The sum of variable, fixed, and semi-variable costs constitutes total costs. As the volume of production increases, total costs increase. However, the cost to produce *each unit* of product decreases. This is the case because the fixed costs do not increase; they are spread over a larger number of units of product. Suppose, for example, that a single-product firm has the following cost structure:

| | |
|---|---|
| Variable manufacturing costs, per unit | $    2.25 |
| Fixed manufacturing costs, per month | $1,200.00 |
| Mixed manufacturing costs: | |
| Variable portion, per unit | $    0.30 |
| Fixed portion, per month | $ 450.00 |
| Variable selling, general, and administrative costs, per unit | $    0.35 |
| Fixed selling, general, and administrative costs, per month | $ 700.00 |

Under these circumstances, Table 14.1 shows how unit costs change as volume changes; this example assumes a $7 per unit selling price. A contribution format income statement used by managerial and cost accountants may help illustrate these costs. Notice how manufacturing cost per unit and total cost per unit decrease as production increases to plant capacity. Also, notice how the income generated per unit increases as production increases. To understand the intricacies of the cost-volume-profit relationship fully, it is essential to understand variable, fixed, and semi-variable costs.

Since it is difficult to allocate costs specifically as fixed, variable, and semi-variable, accountants generally classify costs in two categories: direct costs and indirect costs. These costs are discussed briefly below.

**Table 14.1 I** Cost, Volume, Profit Relationships

| Number of Units Produced | *Per Unit* | 500 | 1,000 | 1,500 | 2,000 | 2,500 |
|---|---|---|---|---|---|---|
| Revenue | 7.00 | $3,500.00 | $7,000.00 | $10,500.00 | $14,000.00 | $17,500.00 |
| Variable Manufacturing Costs | 2.25 | 1,125.00 | 2,250.00 | 3,375.00 | 4,500.00 | 5,625.00 |
| Variable Portion of Mixed Mfg. Costs | 0.30 | 150.00 | 300.00 | 450.00 | 600.00 | 750.00 |
| Variable Selling, General, & Administrative Costs | 0.35 | 175.00 | 350.00 | 525.00 | 700.00 | 875.00 |
| Total Variable Cost | 2.90 | 1,450.00 | 2,900.00 | 4,350.00 | 5,800.00 | 7,250.00 |
| Contribution Margin (the remainder, after deducting variable costs from revenue, to cover fixed costs and return a profit or minimize a loss) | 4.10 | 2,050.00 | 4,100.00 | 6,150.00 | 8,200.00 | 10,250.00 |
| Fixed Manufacturing Costs | | 1,200.00 | 1,200.00 | 1,200.00 | 1,200.00 | 1,200.00 |
| Fixed Portion of Mixed Mfg. Costs | | 450.00 | 450.00 | 450.00 | 450.00 | 450.00 |
| Fixed Selling, General, & Administrative Costs | | 700.00 | 700.00 | 700.00 | 700.00 | 700.00 |
| Total Fixed Cost | | 2,350.00 | 2,350.00 | 2,350.00 | 2,350.00 | 2,350.00 |
| Operating Income | | −$300.00 | $1,750.00 | $3,800.00 | $5,850.00 | $7,900.00 |
| Total Cost Per Unit | | 7.60 | 5.25 | 4.47 | 4.08 | 3.84 |
| Manufacturing Cost Per Unit | | 5.85 | 4.20 | 3.65 | 3.38 | 3.21 |
| Income Generated Per Unit | | −0.60 | 1.75 | 2.53 | 2.93 | 3.16 |

*Assumptions:*
- *Selling price remains constant*
- *All Manufacturing and Nonmanufacturing Costs are Included*
- *Variable Costs do not change with volume*
- *Fixed Costs do not change within the relevant range of production, 0–2,500 units*
- *All units produced are sold*
- *Taxes are not considered*

**Direct Costs**    Direct costs are specifically traceable to or caused by a specific project or production operation. Two major direct costs are direct labor and direct materials. Although most direct costs are variable, conceptually, direct costs should not be confused with variable costs; the two terms are rooted in different concepts. Direct costs relate to the *traceability* of costs to specific operations, while variable costs relate to the *behavior* of costs as volume fluctuates. The salary of a production supervisor, for example, can be directly traceable to a product even though the supervisor is paid a fixed salary regardless of the volume produced. Returning to the illustration of the cutting tool, if a firm pays a worker 15 cents for making the three cuts required for each item, direct labor costs are 15 cents. If the value of the piece of metal being cut is 85 cents, direct costs for the item are $1.00.

**Indirect Costs (Overhead)**    Indirect costs are associated with or caused by two or more operating activities "jointly" but are not traced to each of them individually. The nature of an indirect cost is such that it is either not possible or not practical to measure directly how much of the cost is attributable to a single operating activity.[3] Indirect costs can be fixed or variable, depending on their behavior (property taxes are fixed, but the proportion of energy consumption that varies with the level of production is variable). Therefore, it is important that the reader not confuse indirect costs with fixed costs.

## Regulation by Competition

From a buyer's point of view, competition is the mainspring of good pricing. As was discussed previously, most producers do not have the same real costs of production. Even when their costs are the same, their competitive positions can be quite different. Hence, their prices also can be quite different. Consider the following example. Assume that a supply manager is ready to purchase 10,000 specially designed cutting tools. He sends the specifications to five companies for quotations. All five respond. For the sake of simplicity, assume that direct costs in those five companies are identical. Further, assume that each company uses the same price-estimating formula; overhead is figured as 150 percent of direct labor, and profit is calculated as 12 percent of total cost. Each company could then lay out its figures as follows:

| | | |
|---|---|---|
| Cost of materials | $12,000 | |
| Cost of direct labor | 3,000 | |
| Cost of overhead | 4,500 | (150 percent of direct labor) |
| Total cost | $19,500 | |
| Profit | 2,340 | (12 percent of total cost) |
| Price | $21,840 | |

To simplify the example, assume that all overhead is classified as fixed; that is, it remains constant over a given range of production.

Even with all the controlling figures fixed, the companies more than likely would not quote the same price, because *the cost of production and profit are only two of the factors a seller considers in determining an asking price*. In the final analysis, the factors stemming from competition ultimately determine the exact price each firm will quote. That is, when faced with the realities of competition, the price any specific firm will quote will be governed largely by *its need for business* and by *what it thinks its competitors will quote*, not by costs or profits.

---

[3] Many costs treated as indirect by organizations are traceable and could become direct costs through improvements in the measurement system. The authors contend that the reasons for not tracing costs directly have diminished with advances in information technology.

Who is responsible for the final determination of the price to be quoted? Generally, it is a marketing executive; in some cases, it is the president of the company. Pricing is one of the most important management decisions a firm must make. As an objective, a firm tends to seek the highest price that is compatible with its long-range goals. What is the possible price range for the order in the preceding example? The out-of-pocket (variable) costs for this order are $12,000 for materials and $3,000 for direct labor, for a total of $15,000. This is the lowest price any company should accept under any circumstances. The highest price is $21,840, based on the assumption that a profit in excess of 12 percent is not in the long-range interest of the firm. (Such a profit may attract additional competition to enter this market, which would erode the profitability of the market.)

What could cause one of the firms to consider a price of $17,000? Keen competition among suppliers could do that. However, keen competition among buyers could drive the price higher. This is why competition, as a leveler, is such a dominant factor in pricing. If the firm was unable to obtain a satisfactory volume of other business, it would gladly take this order for a price of $17,000. As a result of the order, the $15,000 out-of-pocket costs would be covered, the experienced workforce could be kept working, and a $2,000 contribution could be made to overhead. Remember that the fixed overhead would continue whether or not the firm received this order.

*In the long run* a firm must recover all costs or go out of business, for in the long run plant and machinery must be maintained, modernized, and replaced. *In the short run*, however, it is generally better for a firm to recover variable costs and some portion of overhead than to undergo a significant decline in business. Of course, this would not be true if the additional business would affect the pricing of other orders the firm already has filled or is going to fill.

Business in good times ordinarily is not done at out-of-pocket (or variable cost) prices. A more common situation would be for each of the five firms to bid prices above the total cost figure of $19,500. How much above this figure each would bid would depend on the specific economic circumstances and expectations applicable to each firm. Firms hungry for business would bid just slightly above the total cost figure of $19,500. Those with large backlogs and growing lists of steady customers (and therefore not in need of new business in the short run) would bid a larger profit margin (perhaps 14 percent). Sellers can be expected to evaluate competitive situations differently, depending on how much they want or need the business. Therefore, even with the simplifying assumption of identical costs, it is reasonable to expect bids in this situation to range from approximately $19,700 (1 percent profit) to $21,840 (12 percent profit). Prices close to out-of-pocket costs could be offered if the seller was attempting to obtain a desirable and prestigious account, if the supplier wanted to gain experience in a situation in which additional large orders are expected to follow, or if the supplier wanted to keep its workforce employed.

**Varying Profit Margins**   A seller must recover *all* costs from his or her total sales to make a profit. However, *each* product in the line does not have to make a profit, and not all accounts have to yield the same profit margin. Bearing these thoughts in mind, the principal cost/competition implications of pricing can be summarized as follows: *Sound pricing policy dictates that sellers, in accordance with their interpretation of the prevailing competitive forces, quote prices that are high enough to include all variable costs and make the maximum possible contribution toward fixed costs and profit.*

Similarly, sound pricing policy dictates that for any specific purchase, supply professionals should use their knowledge of products, markets, costs, and competitive conditions to estimate the price range in which sellers reasonably can be expected to do business. Finally, with this information, knowledge of the value of the buyer's ongoing business to a seller, and an appreciation of the value of this specific order, the supply professional applies all relevant purchasing principles and techniques to purchase at prices as close as possible to the bottom of the estimated price range.

# Price Analysis

Some form of price analysis is required for every purchase. The method and scope of analysis required are dictated by the dollar amount and circumstances attending each specific purchase. Price analysis is defined as the examination of a seller's price proposal (bid) by comparison with reasonable price benchmarks without an examination and evaluation of the separate elements of the cost and profit making up the price.

A supply professional has five tools which can be used to conduct a price analysis: (1) analysis of competitive price proposals; (2) comparison with regulated, catalog, or market prices; (3) use of Web-based e-procurement; (4) comparison with historical prices; and (5) use of independent cost estimates.

## Competitive Price Proposals

Chapter 11 describes the conditions that should be satisfied before competitive bidding is used as a means of selecting the source of supply. When this approach is employed and the following additional conditions are satisfied, the resulting low bid normally provides a fair and reasonable price:

- At least two qualified sources have responded to the solicitation.
- The proposals are responsive to the buying firm's requirements.
- The supplier competed independently for the award.
- The supplier submitting the lowest offer does not have an unfair advantage over its competitors.
- The lowest evaluated price is reasonable.

The buyer cannot apply this approach to pricing in a mechanical manner. He or she clearly must use common sense and ensure that the price is reasonable compared with past prices, independent estimates, or realistic rules of thumb.

## Regulated, Catalog, and Market Prices

**Prices Set by Law or Regulation**   When the price is set by law or regulation, the supplier must identify the regulating authority and specify the regulated prices. With regulated prices, a governmental body (federal, state, or local) has determined that the prices of certain goods and services should be controlled directly. Normally, approval of price changes requires a formal review, hearings, and an affirmative vote of the regulatory authority. No supplier may charge more or less than the approved price.

**Catalog Price**   An established catalog price is a price that is included in a catalog, a price list, or some other place that is regularly maintained by the supplier. The price sources must be dated and readily available for inspection by potential customers. The buyer should request a recent sales summary demonstrating that significant quantities are sold to a significant number of customers at the indicated price before accepting a catalog price. See Appendix B for the role of discounts in pricing.

**Market Price**   A market price results from the interaction of many buyers and sellers who are willing to trade at a given (market) price. The forces of supply and demand establish the price. A market price generally is used for an item or a service that is generic in nature and not particularly unique to the seller. Prices for eggs and lumber, for example, are based on the market. Normally the daily market price is published in local newspapers or trade publications that are independent of the supplier.

## Internet/e-Commerce II

Advanced communications using the Internet allows supply management personnel to view up-to-date pricing, as well as catalogs, specification sheets, video presentations, and other information the seller has on a material, product or service. Since the Internet does not have geographic constraints, the information is available worldwide. Of particular interest here are buying exchanges, reverse auctions, and the search capability of the Internet.

*Buying exchanges* (often referred to as B2B e-commerce) offer purchasing firms a list of pre-approved sellers that offer identical and/or similar products or services, usually within a specific category, from which to choose. Normally, prices or discounts from list prices are provided.

*Reverse auctions* identify materials, equipment, or services required and request carefully prequalified suppliers to submit bids. Potential suppliers are able to see the prices submitted by their competitors and revise their bids until the preestablished closing time for the auction. Caution must be used in employing reverse auctions since they ignore the relationship dimension of the transaction.

*Tailored global searches* allow expanded Internet search capabilities. Supply management professionals can investigate products or services by simultaneously scanning all *relevant* public and private websites worldwide. Obtaining the right price, quality, and delivery is becoming easier and faster as the Internet expands and more procurement-specific portals are developed.

## Historical Prices

Price analysis may be conducted by comparing a proposed price with historical quotes or prices for the same or a similar item. It is essential to determine that the base price was fair and reasonable (as determined through price analysis) and is still a valid standard against which to measure the offered price. The fact that a historical price exists does not automatically make it a valid basis for comparison. Several issues must be considered:

- How have conditions changed?[4]
- Were there one-time engineering, setup, or tooling charges in the original price?
- What should be the effect of inflation or deflation on the price?
- Will the new procurement create a situation in which the supplier should enjoy the benefits of learning? (The concept of learning curve analysis is discussed in Appendix A to this chapter.)

## Independent Cost Estimates

When other techniques of price analysis cannot be utilized, a supply manager may use an independent cost estimate as the basis for comparison. He or she must determine that the estimate is fair and reasonable.[5] If

---

[4]The Bureau of Labor Statistics in Washington, D.C., provides thousands of different price indexes every month. Available are indexes by stage of processing, industry, and individual commodity grades. A commonly used series for these purposes is the producer price index (PPI). Also, import and export price indexes broken down into the major subcategories are available. These indexes allow a price analyst to adjust historical prices by appropriate changes over time.

[5]The development and use of independent cost estimates is described in detail in Chapter 4 of D. N. Burt, W. Norquist, and J. Anklesaria, *Zero Base Pricing™: Achieving World Class Competitiveness through Reduced All-in-Cost* (Chicago: Probius, 1990).

price analysis is impractical or does not allow the buyer to conclude that the price is fair and reasonable, cost analysis should be employed.

# Cost Analysis

Cost analysis should be employed when price analysis is impractical or does not allow a supply management professional to conclude that a price is fair and reasonable. Cost analysis is generally most useful when one is purchasing nonstandard items and services. This section focuses on the application of cost analysis to the acquisition cost of materials, products, and services.

## Cost Analysis Defined

We have seen that price analysis is a process of comparisons. *Cost analysis* is a review and an evaluation of actual or anticipated costs. This analysis involves the application of experience, knowledge, and judgment to data in an attempt to project reasonable estimated contract costs. Estimated costs serve as the basis for buyer-seller negotiations to arrive at mutually agreeable contract prices.

The purpose of cost analysis is to arrive at a price that is fair and reasonable to both the buying firm and the selling firm. Estimates can be made with the help of one's engineering department or by analyzing the estimates submitted by the seller. To analyze a supplier's costs, a supply manager must understand the nature of each of the various costs a supplier incurs. The supply manager must compare the labor hours, material costs, and overhead costs of all competing suppliers as listed on their cost-breakdown sheets. Most important, he or she must determine the reasons for any differences, focusing on three principal elements of cost: direct, indirect (overhead), and profit.

A supply manager always should be conscious of the fact that costs vary widely among manufacturing firms. Some firms are high-cost producers; others are low-cost producers. Many factors affect the costs of specific firms as well as the cost of individual products within any particular firm. Some of the most important elements affecting costs are:

- Capabilities of management.
- Efficiency of labor.
- Amount and quality of subcontracting.
- Plant capacity and the continuity of output.

Each of these factors can change with respect to either product or time. For this reason, a specific firm can be a high-cost producer for one item and a low-cost producer for another item. Similarly, the firm can be a low-cost producer one year and a high-cost producer another year. These circumstances make it extremely important for a supply manager to obtain competition among potential suppliers when appropriate. Competition can be a supply manager's key to locating the desired low-cost producer.

## Capabilities of Management

The skill with which management plans, organizes, staffs, coordinates, and controls all the personnel, capital, and equipment at its disposal determines the efficiency of a firm. Managements utilize the resources available to them with substantially different degrees of efficiency. This is one basic reason why finding the correct supplier (and price) is so rewarding for astute supply management professionals.

## Efficiency of Labor

Anyone who has visited a number of different suppliers has noticed the differences in attitudes and skills between various labor forces. Some are cooperative, take great pride in their work, have high morale, and produce efficiently, while others do not fit that profile. The skill with which management exercises its responsibilities contributes greatly to these differences between efficient and inefficient labor forces. Supply managers are well rewarded for pinpointing suppliers with efficient labor forces.

## Amount and Quality of Subcontracting

When a contract has been awarded to a supplier (the *prime contractor*), the supplier frequently subcontracts some of the work required to complete the job. The supplier's subcontracting decisions are important to the buying firm because they may involve a large percentage of prime contract money. The first decision a prime contractor must make regarding subcontracts is which items should be made and which items should be bought. If the prime contractor decides to buy some of the items that could be made more efficiently, and vice versa, the buyer will suffer financially. Even if the prime contractor makes the correct "make" decision, it is responsible for selecting the subcontractors that are needed for the "buy" items.

Subcontractor prices and performance directly influence the prices the buying firm pays the prime contractor. Hence, the prime contractor's skills in both making and administering its subcontracts are of great importance to the supply manager. For this reason, supply managers must review their major suppliers periodically to ensure that they have effective supply management and subcontracting capabilities of their own.

## Plant Capacity

A plant's overhead costs are influenced directly by its size. A plant can get too large for efficient production and, as a result, lose its competitive ability. In contrast, plants with large capital investments and those manufacturing products on a mass production basis can be too small to attain the most efficient production levels. A supply professional must be alert to detect firms whose operations are affected adversely by size.

Plant output is clearly one of the controlling elements in the cost/profit picture. Table 14.2 illustrates this concept numerically. Note how volume affects profit when variable costs change because of inefficient

**Table 14.2 I** How Production Volume Affects Fixed Costs, Variable Costs, and Profit

| Production Quantity | Selling Price | Sales Revenue | Fixed Costs | Variable Costs | Total Cost | Total Profit | Profit per Unit of Added Production |
|---|---|---|---|---|---|---|---|
| 0 | $20 | $ 0 | $4,000 | $ 0 | $4.000 | −$4,000 | $15 |
| 100 | 20 | 2,000 | 4,000 | 500 | 4,500 | − 2,500 | 15 |
| 200 | 20 | 4,000 | 4,000 | 1,000 | 5,000 | − 1,000 | 15 |
| 300 | 20 | 6,000 | 4,000 | 1,500 | 5,500 | + 500 | 15 |
| 400 | 20 | 8,000 | 4,000 | 2,000 | 6,000 | + 2,000 | 15 |
| 500 | 20 | 10,000 | 4,000 | 2,500 | 6,500 | + 3,500 | 15 |
| 600 | 20 | 12,000 | 4,000 | 3,000 | 7,000 | + 5,000 | 14 |
| 700* | 20 | 14,000 | 4,000 | 3,600 | 7,600 | + 6,400 | 12 |
| 800* | 20 | 16,000 | 4,000 | 4,400 | 8,400 | + 7,600 | 10 |
| 900* | 20 | 18,000 | 4,000 | 5,400 | 9,400 | + 8,600 | |

*Plant begins to strain capacity and administrative capabilities. The result is less efficient operation; that is, overtime is required, less experienced workers are utilized, scheduling and handling of materials become less efficient, and variable costs per unit rise. Consequently, although profit continues to increase beyond a production quantitiy of 600, it increases at a decreasing rate.

use of facilities beyond optimum plant capacity. Note also that while total profit continues to increase as production output increases, beyond a certain output, profit increases at a decreasing rate. This relationship is an important one for supply professionals to keep in mind.

## Sources of Cost Data

There are three primary sources of cost data: (1) from potential suppliers as a precondition of submitting proposals and bids, (2) from suppliers with which the firm has developed preferred or strategic supplier relationships/alliances, and (3) cost models.

### Potential Suppliers

When a supply manager anticipates that a cost analysis will be required, he or she should include a request for a cost breakdown with each request for a quotation. *This is the proper time to make such a request, not after negotiations have started.* This is critical! Suppliers cannot complain that making this breakdown is an extra burden at this time, since they must perform such an analysis to prepare their bids. A simple procedure used by a number of progressive firms for obtaining cost breakdowns is to include the following statement with their request for quotations: "We will not consider any quotation not accompanied by a cost breakdown." Not all suppliers readily provide cost-of-production information; however, the number refusing to do so for non-standard items is declining. An example of a typical cost breakdown request form is shown in Figure 14.2.

### Supply Partners

As firms develop open relationships built on trust and collaboration, the purchasing firm shares information on forecasts, schedules, the way purchased items are integrated into its product or process, and so on. The supply partner shares information on its design, production, and quality processes and its *design and production costs.*

### Cost Models

On some occasions, it may not be possible to obtain cost data from a supplier. In other cases, the cost data obtained may appear unrealistic or support prices that are unacceptable. Under these conditions, it may be necessary for the purchasing firm to develop its own cost models to estimate what the supplier's costs should be. (The U.S. Navy and U.S. Air Force call such models "should-cost models." Both services have found that this approach to pricing is extraordinarily powerful.) The development of such models requires the application of both accounting and industrial engineering skills and is beyond the scope of this chapter. It is sufficient at this point simply to say that this approach, though not used extensively by small and medium-size firms, is used commonly by leading-edge firms that have the technical resources available.[6]

## Direct Costs

Except in industries with heavy fixed capital investments, direct costs normally constitute the major proportion of product or service costs and are the most easily traceable. Thus, they generally serve as the basis on which sellers allocate their overhead costs. An astute supply manager therefore must investigate a seller's

---

[6]The interest reader is referred to Chapter 8 of Burt, Norquist, and Anklesaria, *Zero Base Pricing™: Achieving World Class Competitiveness through Reduced All-in-Cost.*

| COST ANALYSIS | CHECK APPROPRIATE BOX<br>ESTIMATED COST ☐ HISTORICAL COST ☐<br>PERIOD COVERED: | | |
|---|---|---|---|
| NAME OF SUPPLIER | INQUIRY OR<br>PURCHASE REQUISITION NO. | | |
| ADDRESS (Street, City, State) | QUANTITY | AT<br>$    EACH | AMOUNT<br>$ |
| ARTICLE | | | |
| TERMS AND DISCOUNT | NET TOTAL OF QUOTATION $ | | |
| ANALYSIS OF COST AS OF _____, 20 ___ INDICATE WHETHER:<br>COST PER ITEM ☐  OR TOTAL COST ☐ | | | |

| ITEM | AMOUNT | PERCENT<br>OF COST |
|---|---|---|
| 1. DIRECT MATERIAL | | |
| 2. LESS SCRAP OR SALVAGE | | |
| 3. NET DIRECT MATERIAL | | |
| 4. PURCHASED PARTS - FROM SUBCONTRACTORS | | |
| 5. DIRECT PRODUCTIVE LABOR          HOURS AT $ | | |
| 6. DIRECT FACTORY CHARGES: | | |
| (A) TOOLS AND DIES | | |
| 1. DIRECT WAGES          HOURS AT $ | | |
| 2. TOOLING BURDEN | | |
| 3. MATERIALS | | |
| (B) SPECIAL MACHINERY | | |
| (C) MISCELLANEOUS | | |
| 7. INDIRECT FACTORY EXPENSES (Burden), ON BASIS OF          See Note[a] | | |
| 8. ENGINEERING AND DEVELOPMENT EXPENSES • DIRECT: | | |
| (a) SALARIES AND WAGES          HOURS AT $ | | |
| (b) BURDEN | | |
| (c) OTHER | | |
| TOTAL MANUFACTURING COST | | |
| 9. GENERAL AND ADMINISTRATIVE EXPENSE:<br>PERCENT OF          See Note[b] | | |
| 10. SELLING EXPENSE          See Note[c] | | |
| 11. CONTINGENCIES          See Note[d] | | |
| 12. OTHER EXPENSES          See Note[e] | | |
| 13. | | |
| 14. | | |
| 15. | | |
| 16. | | |
| 17.          TOTAL COST | | |
| 18. SELLING PRICE | | |

19. (a) Are the wage rates used in estimating the direct labor of the unit cost break-down
the same as those now prevailing?
(b) If "No", explain difference and indicate approximate amount thereof.

20. (a) What operating rate has been used in calculating the above estimate?
Hours of operation per week?
(b) At what rate is your plant now operating?
Hours of operation per week?

_____          _____
(Supplier)                                    (Signature and title)

_____
(Date)

[a] State basis of allocation.
[b] State nature of expenses included and basis of allocation.
[c] State nature of expenses included and amount of advertising, if any, separately, and basis of allocation.
[d] Explain in detail.
[e] State nature of expenses, basis of allocation, and why related to the cost of this item.

**Figure 14.2 |** A Typical Request for a Cost Breakdown

**Table 14.3** | Direct Costs and Prices

| Cost Elements | Situation 1 | Situation 2 |
|---|---|---|
| Material | $ 8.00 | $ 8.00 |
| Direct labor | 8.00 | 6.00 |
| Fixed overhead at 150 percent | | |
| of direct labor | 12.00 | 9.00 |
| Manufacturing cost | $28.00 | $23.00 |
| General and administrative overhead | | |
| at 10 percent of manufacturing cost | 2.80 | 2.30 |
| Total cost | 30.80 | 25.30 |
| Profit at 10 percent of total cost | 3.08 | 2.53 |
| Price | $33.88 | $27.83 |

direct costs carefully. *A tiny reduction here (because they are relatively large) is worth more (pricewise) to the buying firm than is a major reduction in the percentage of profit* (which is relatively small). Referring to Table 14-3, a 25 percent reduction in the $8 direct labor cost of situation 1 to the $6 direct labor cost of situation 2 results in a $6.05 ($33.88 − $27.83) reduction in price. A 25 percent reduction in profit would result in only a 77-cent reduction in price (0.25 × $3.08 = $0.77).

## Direct Labor

During the development and production phase of a new item, a supplier typically experiences a heavy design and production engineering effort. These efforts peak and then decrease. As they do, tooling and setup efforts increase, peak, and decline. Machining, assembly, and test efforts then become the predominant users of labor. A supply professional should be cognizant of these factors and should analyze a supplier's estimate to ensure that it is based on proper planning, applying reasonable expectations of efficiency in this regard. When analyzing direct manufacturing labor estimates, a supply manager should pay particular attention to the following:

■  Allowances for rework
■  Geographic variations
■  Variations in skills

**Allowances for Rework**    A supply manager should review a bidder's estimate of rework costs carefully. Modern production techniques make it possible to reduce scrap rates drastically. Effective purchasing by a supplier's organization can reduce the defect rates on incoming materials as much as 95 percent. The combined effect of reduced incoming quality problems and improved production and quality systems should reduce a supplier's requirement for rework markedly.

**Geographic Variations**    Wage rates vary significantly from one country to another as well as within a country's borders. A buyer must ensure that the wage rates proposed are in fact the wage rates applicable in the areas where the work is to be performed. The Bureau of Labor Statistics provides current wage rates in the United States for a variety of trades in different locations.

**Variations in Skills**  A supply manager, with assistance from the firm's industrial engineering or production department, should review the types of labor skills proposed to ensure that they are relevant and necessary for the accomplishment of the required tasks.

## Direct Materials

Direct materials are consumed or converted during the production process. Sheet metal, fasteners, electrical relays, and radios for automobiles are examples of direct materials. In most cases, such materials are purchased from a wide variety of suppliers. In some cases, the materials may have been produced or partially processed in other plants or divisions of the supplier's operation. The resulting costs should be scrutinized carefully for internal transfer charges and markups.

Further analysis of proposed materials costs frequently reveals a difference between the buyer's cost estimate for a bill of materials and the supplier's estimate for that bill. In such cases, the supply manager should request supporting data from the supplier. In some cases, the labor component of the proposed materials costs should reflect a learning effect as more units are produced (this topic is discussed later in this chapter). In any case, careful analysis and discussion should help identify the source of the variance.

## Tooling Costs

Most procurement authorities advocate that the buying firm pay for and take title to special tooling. That approach gives the buying firm maximum control. Analysis of production costs is easier, and the tooling can be moved if circumstances dictate.

There should be an inverse relationship between the investment in tooling and the number of hours required to produce a unit of output. The supply manager should ensure that the supplier plans to use sufficient tooling to minimize labor hours but at the same time avoids investments that are not recovered through labor savings.

## Learning Curves

In many circumstances, labor and supervision become more efficient as more units are produced. The *learning curve* (sometimes called the *improvement curve*) is defined as an empirical relationship between the number of units produced and the number of labor hours required to produce them. Production managers can use this relationship in scheduling production and in determining manpower requirements for a particular product over a specific period. Supply managers can use the relationship to analyze the effects of production and management "learning" on a supplier's unit cost of production.

Traditionally, the learning curve has been used primarily for purchases of complex equipment in the aircraft, electronics, and other highly technical industries. Recently, its use has spread to other industries. The learning curve is useful in both price analysis and cost analysis. It is probably most useful in negotiations as a starting point for pricing a new item. In addition to providing "buyer's insurance" against overcharging, the learning curve is used effectively by government and commercial supply professionals in developing (1) target costs for new products, (2) make-or-buy information, (3) delivery schedules, and (4) progress payment schedules for suppliers.

### The Cumulative Curve and the Unit Curve

In practice, two basic forms of the learning curve exist. The first curve, "the cumulative average cost curve," is used commonly in price and cost analysis. This curve plots cumulative units produced against

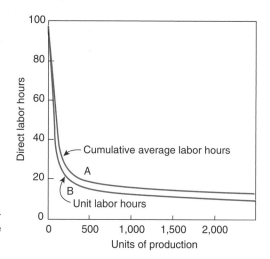

**Figure 14.3** I Comparison of a Cumulative Average Learning Curve (A) and a Unit Learning Curve (B), Plotted on an Arithmetic Grid

the average direct labor cost or *average labor hours required per unit for all units produced.* The second, "the unit or marginal cost curve," also is used in labor and cost-estimating work. The unit curve plots cumulative units produced against the *actual labor hours required to produce each unit.* Figure 14.3 illustrates and compares the two types of curves.

Selection of the learning curve technique to use tends to be based on an organization's past experience. Ideally, whether one should use a cumulative curve or a unit curve is a function of the production process. Some operations conform to a cumulative curve; others conform to a unit curve. The only way to know which to use is to record the actual production data and then determine which type of curve fits the data the best. The relationship is strictly an *empirical* one.

## Target Cost Estimation

If a new product is custom-made to unique specifications, what should be paid for the 50th item? The 500th item? Obviously, costs should decline, but by how much? Analysis of the learning curve provides an answer. Cost reductions and estimated prices can be obtained merely by reading figures on a graph.

The learning curve is a quantitative model of the commonsense observation that the unit cost of a new product decreases as more units of the product are made because of the learning process. The manufacturer, through the repetitive production process, learns how to make the product at a lower cost. For example, the more times an individual repeats a complicated operation, the more efficient he or she becomes in both speed and skill. This means progressively lower unit labor costs. Familiarity with an operation also results in fewer rejects and reworks, better scheduling, possible improvements in tooling, fewer engineering changes, and more efficient management systems.

Suppose a supply manager knows that it took a supplier 100 hours of labor to turn out the first unit of a new product, as indicated in Figures 14.4 and 14.5. The supplier reports that the second unit took 80 hours to make, and so the average labor requirement for the two items is 180 ÷ 2 = 90 hours per unit. The production report for the first four units is summarized in Table 14.4.

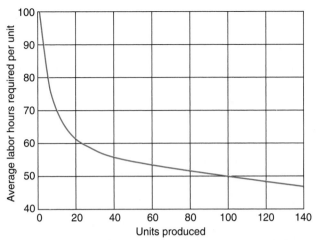

**Figure 14.4** | A 90 Percent Cumulative Average Learning Curve, Plotted on an Arithmetic Grid

**Figure 14.5** | The 90 Percent Cumulative Average Learning Curve of Figure 14.4, Plotted on a Log-Log Grid

**Table 14.4** | Ninety Percent Cumulative Learning Curve Data

| Unit Produced | Labor Hours Required | Cumulative Labor Hours Required | Average Labor Hours Required per Unit |
|---|---|---|---|
| 1st | 100 | 100 | 100.0 |
| 2d | 80 | 180 | 90.0 |
| 3d | 74 | 254 | 84.7 |
| 4th | 70 | 324 | 81.0 |

Observe that the labor requirement dropped to 74 hours for the third unit and to 70 hours for the fourth unit. Column 4 shows that the average number of labor hours required for the first four units was 81 hours per unit. Investigation of the learning rate shows the following relationships:

- As production doubled from one to two units, *the average labor hours required per unit* dropped from 100 to 90, a reduction of 10 percent.
- As production doubled from two to four units, *the average labor hours required per unit* dropped from 90 to 81, a reduction of 10 percent.

Figure 14-4 indicates that the same learning rate continues as production of the new item increases. Each time production doubles, the average labor requirement for all units declines by 10 percent. Thus, the product is said to have a 90 percent learning rate, or a 90 percent learning curve. Note that this is based on the *cumulative average* learning curve phenomenon. The basic point revealed by the learning curve is that a *specific and constant percentage reduction in the average direct labor hours required per unit results each time the number of units produced is doubled.* It is an established fact that specific learning rates occur with reasonable regularity for similar groups of products in many different industries.

Studies made in the aircraft, electronics, and small electromechanical subassembly fields indicate that learning rates of 75 to 95 percent are typical. However, learning curves can vary anywhere within the practical limits of 50 to 100 percent. As more units are produced, the effect of a constant learning rate on unit costs gradually diminishes. After several thousand units, the absolute reduction in cost from learning becomes negligible. Note in Figure 14.4 how the curve flattens out as the number of units produced increases. This is why learning curve analysis is of greatest value for new products.[7]

Most analysts prefer to plot the data for learning curves on log-log graph paper, as in Figure 14.5. The logarithmic scales on both the horizontal and vertical axes convert the curve in Figure 14.4 into a straight line (because a log-log grid plots a constant rate of change as a straight line). The straight line is easier to read, and it simplifies forecasting since a constant learning rate always appears as a straight line on log-log coordinates. To verify the fact that both graphs represent the same thing, look at the number of hours needed to produce 100 units in Figures 14.4 and 14.5; both figures indicate about 50 hours per unit.

In addition to determining the direct labor component of price, the labor hour data also have the following purchasing applications. See Appendix A for additional applications of learning curves.

**Direct Materials**   Experience indicates that organizations "learn" how to purchase materials more efficiently as quantities increase and time progresses. It is the authors' experience that a 95 percent rate of learning applies to the purchase of the same material over time.

**Estimating Delivery Times**   Since the learning curve can be used to forecast labor time required, it is possible to estimate how many units a supplier can produce over a specified time with a given labor force. This information can be extremely helpful to a buyer in scheduling deliveries, planning his or her firm's production, and identifying suppliers that obviously cannot meet desired delivery schedules.

---

[7]Different types of labor generate different percentages of learning. Assembly-type labor generates the most rapid improvement, and fabrication-type labor the least. Fabrication labor has a lower learning rate because the speed of jobs dependent on this type of labor is governed more by the capability of the equipment than by the skill of the operator. The operator's learning in this case is confined to setup and maintenance times. In some situations, therefore, when a precise analysis is desired, a learning curve should be developed for each category of labor. Also, it should be noted that different firms in the same industry experience different rates of learning.

**Supplier Progress Payments**   Since the learning curve reflects changing labor costs, it provides a basis for figuring a supplier's financial commitment on any specific number of units. This information is important because suppliers often operate in the red during the initial part of a production run, until learning reduces costs below the average price. Supply managers can minimize supplier hardship by using the learning curve to break down an order into two or more production lots—each with successively lower average prices—and then set up progress payments that are based on the supplier's costs.

# Indirect Costs

Indirect costs represent 30 to 40 percent of many suppliers' total costs of production. Five of the most common indirect cost pools are engineering overhead, materials overhead, manufacturing overhead, general and administrative expense, and selling expense.

## Engineering Overhead

Engineering overhead is the cost of directing and supporting the engineering department and its direct labor staff. Costs include supervisory and support labor, fringe benefits, indirect supplies, and fixed charges such as depreciation.

## Material Overhead

This category of overhead usually includes the indirect costs of purchasing, transporting incoming materials, receiving, inspection, handling, and storage of materials.

## Manufacturing Overhead

Manufacturing overhead includes all production costs except direct materials, direct labor, and similar costs that can be assigned directly to the production of an item.

Manufacturing overhead includes the following:

- The cost of supervision, inspection (some firms charge quality assurance or inspection as a direct cost), maintenance, custodial, and related personnel costs.
- Fringe benefits such as Social Security and unemployment taxes, allowances for vacation pay, and group insurance.
- Indirect supplies such as lubricating oils, grinding wheels, and janitorial supplies.
- Fixed charges, including depreciation, rent, insurance, and property taxes.
- Utilities.

## General and Administrative

General and administrative (G&A) expenses include the company's general and executive offices, staff services, and miscellaneous activities.

## Selling

Selling expenses include sales salaries, bonuses and commissions, and the normal costs of running the department.

## Recovering Indirect Costs

A supplier allocates overhead costs to specific operations. Normally, this allocation is based on a product's age in terms of its life cycle. For instance, mature products generally incur lower G&A expenses than do new products, which require more development and marketing effort. This allocation results in the use of an overhead rate for each indirect cost pool. The rate is determined by management personnel, who select an appropriate base (or cost driver that causes the incurrence of the overhead costs) and then develop the ratio of the indirect cost pool dollars to that base. For example, the following allocation formula might be used for manufacturing overhead:

$$\frac{\text{Manufacturing overhead pool dollars}}{\text{Manufacturing direct labor hours}} = \frac{\$5,000,000}{\$1,000,000} = \begin{array}{l}\$5 \text{ per direct} \\ \text{manufacturing} \\ \text{labor hour}\end{array}$$

Overhead rates generally are established annually, typically before the start of the accounting period.

When determining the reasonableness of overhead rates, a buyer should not look only at the rate. He or she must consider the reasonableness of the indirect costs in the overhead pool and the appropriateness of the overhead allocation base. Since rates typically are established annually, the supply manager also should ensure that the allocation rate used by a supplier is applied consistently.

## Activity Based Costing

Activity costing can be traced back to the late 1700s. During the intervening 200 years, management focused on labor costs, since they represented over 50 percent of total costs. The allocation of overhead costs on the basis of the number of hours required to produce a product was relatively realistic and certainly easy.

However, as direct labor costs have shrunk to 10 percent or so of total costs, they have become a less logical and realistic basis on which to allocate indirect costs. During the 1980s, a band of accounting academics, led by Professors Robert Kaplan and Robin Cooper of the Harvard Business School and Claremont McKenna College, respectively, developed what has become known as activity based costing (ABC), a tool which more accurately identifies and allocates indirect costs to the products they support. In the 1990s, ABC evolved into activity based management (ABM). Activity based management essentially integrated ABC, continuous improvement, and business process analysis.

ABC or ABM can be used to identify opportunities to reduce the supplier's indirect costs. ABC goes beyond identifying and allocating those indirect costs to products by identifying the drivers of those costs.[8] Some examples of cost drivers are the number of orders, the length of setups, specifications, engineering changes, and liaison trips required. This identification allows management to identify and implement cost saving opportunities. Obviously, if the supplier's management does not implement the required changes, an alert supply manager can "encourage" such action.

In analyzing a supplier's cost breakdown, it is imperative that a supply management professional understand how the supplier estimates and applies overhead to the product being purchased; it is also important to be aware of how well the supplier understands his or her own overhead cost structure. (A supply professional should develop the expertise to understand and motivate a selling firm with poor cost control to

---

[8]The OSD Comptroller iCenter is a comprehensive online site related to the U.S. Department of Defense budget process, financial management, and best practices. Visit this site for educational information on the use of ABCosting, 2002. http://www.dod.mil/comptroller/icenter/learn/abcosting.htm.

improve its system of collecting and applying costs to products.) As overhead becomes a greater proportion of product cost and as supply managers continue to seek ways to reduce acquisition cost, a small error in estimating and applying overhead can affect the final cost significantly. A note regarding accuracy: Greater accuracy not only may allow for a lower purchase price but also may lead to a higher price because true costs are now known.

## Target Costing

A number of years ago the late management guru Peter F. Drucker wrote about five deadly business sins—avoidable mistakes that will harm and in many cases have harmed a business. Drucker's third deadly sin is cost-driven pricing. He argued, "The only thing that works is price-driven costing. . . . The only sound way to price is to start out with what the market is willing to pay . . . and design to that price specification."[9] Drucker's comments are as applicable to procurement today as they were then.

Some 40 years ago, the Ford Motor Company employed price-based costing in the development of its highly successful Mustang. The car was designed to retail at $1,995. That pricing objective drove design engineering to focus on cost as well as performance and aesthetics. In turn, that drove engineers and purchasing and supply management to identify target prices for items to be purchased from suppliers. Members of those two functions then worked with their potential suppliers to develop processes and procedures to produce the required materials and components at those target prices. Curiously, American management largely reverted to cost-based pricing during the next 40 years, while its Japanese competition adopted price-based costing. Dr. Drucker pointed out that "cost-based pricing is the reason there is no American consumer-electronics industry anymore."[10]

It is heartening to see a growing number of organizations replace their "adversarial bidding system with one in which the company designates suppliers for a component and then uses target pricing . . . to determine with suppliers the component prices and how to achieve them."[11]

## Profit

There are no precise formulas that can be used to help form a positive judgment about the right price, of which profit is one component (Price = Cost + Profit). There are, however, certain basic concepts of pricing on which scholars and practitioners agree. One objective of sound purchasing is to achieve good supplier relations. This objective implies that the price must be high enough to keep the supplier in business. The price also must include a profit sufficiently high to encourage the supplier to accept the business in the first place and to motivate that firm to deliver the materials or services on time. What profit does it take to get these two desired results? On what basis should it be calculated?

If profit were calculated on a percentage-of-cost basis, a high-cost inefficient producer would receive the higher profit (in absolute terms). To make matters even worse, under the cost concept of pricing, producers that succeeded in lowering their costs by attaining greater efficiency would be "rewarded" by a reduction in total profit. For example, if an efficient producer has costs of $1,000 and a fair profit is agreed to be 10 percent of cost, its profit will be $100. If an inefficient producer has costs of $1,500, its profit on

---

[9]Peter F. Drucker, "The Five Deadly Business Sins," *Wall Street Journal*, October 21, 1993, p. 14.

[10]Ibid.

[11]James P. Womack and Daniel T. Jones, "From Lean Production to the Lean Enterprise," *Harvard Business Review*, March–April 1994, p. 97.

the same basis will be $150. If the efficient producer lowered its costs to $800 by using better techniques, the reward would be a $20 loss in profit—from $100 to $80. Obviously, the concept of determining a fair profit as a fixed percentage of cost is unrealistic.

Another concept on which profit might be determined is the amount of capital investment required to produce the profit. Profit might be calculated as a percentage of capital investment. However, under this system, it still would be possible for an inefficient producer to receive a greater reward. For example, suppose firm A makes a capital investment of $2 million to produce product X. Firm B, in comparison, invests only $1 million in its plant to produce product X successfully. From the buyer's point of view, there is no reason why firm A, simply because of its greater investment, should receive a higher profit on product X than firm B receives. Firm B, in fact, is utilizing its investment more efficiently. Thus, profit calculated as a fixed percentage of a firm's capital investment is not a satisfactory method for a buyer to use in determining a fair profit.

In a competitive economy, the major incentive for more efficient production is greater profit and repeat orders. A fair profit in our society cannot be determined as a fixed percentage figure. Rather, it is a flexible figure that should be higher for a more efficient producer than it is for a less efficient one. Low-cost producers can price lower than their competitors while simultaneously enjoying a higher profit. Consequently, one of a buyer's greatest challenges is constantly to seek out efficient, low-cost producers.

Considerations other than production efficiency also rightly influence the relative size of a firm's profit. Six of the most common considerations are discussed briefly below.

**1.** Profit is the basic reward for risk taking as well as the reward for efficiency; therefore, higher profits justifiably accompany extraordinary risks, whatever form they take. For example, great financial risk usually accompanies the production of new products. For this reason, a higher profit for new products is often necessary to induce a seller to take the risk of producing them.

**2.** A higher dollar profit per unit of product purchased on small special orders is generally justified over that allowed on larger orders. The justification stems from the fact that the producer incurs a fixed amount of setup and administrative expense regardless of the size of the order. Consequently, the cost of production for each unit is greater on small orders than on large orders. Since producers incur this cost at the request of the buyer, they usually demand a proportionately higher absolute profit before accepting an order that forces them to use their facilities in a less efficient manner than they otherwise might use them.

**3.** Rapid technological advancement creates a continuing nationwide shortage of technical talent. The cost in dollars and time of training highly technical personnel frequently makes it necessary to pay a higher profit on jobs that require highly skilled people.

**4.** In the space age, technical reliability can be a factor of overriding importance. A higher profit generally is conceded to be justified for a firm that repeatedly turns out superbly reliable technical products than for one that produces less reliable products. Good quality control, efficiency in controlling costs, on-time delivery, and technical assistance that has resulted in better production or design simplification all merit profit consideration.

**5.** On occasion, because of various temporary unfavorable supply-demand factors (e.g., excessive inventories, a shortage of capital, a cancellation of large orders), a firm may be forced to sell its products at a loss to recover a portion of its invested capital quickly or to keep its production facilities in operation.

**6.** A firm that manufactures a product according to the design and specifications of another firm is not entitled to the same percentage of profit as a firm that incurs the risk of manufacturing to its own design. In the first instance, the manufacturing firm is assured of a sale without marketing expense or risk of any kind, provided only that it fulfills the terms of the contract. In the second instance, the manufacturing firm is without assurance that its product can be sold profitably, if at all, in a competitive market.

In summary there is no single answer to the question: What is a fair profit? In a capitalistic society, profit generally is implied to mean the reward over costs that a firm receives for *the measure of efficiency it attains* and the *degree of risk it assumes.* From a purchasing viewpoint, profit provides two basic incentives. First, it induces the seller to take the order. Second, it induces the seller to perform as efficiently as possible, deliver on time, and provide all reasonable services associated with the order. Except in temporary cases in which a firm is willing to sell at a loss, the profit is too low if it does not create these two incentives for the seller.

## Concluding Remarks

Obtaining the *right price* is one of supply management's most important responsibilities. When one is focusing on price, insight into the current economic environment and knowledge of the cost elements that underlie a selling price will support the most favorable procurement. In addition, a supply management professional should be aware of the various means available to locate potential suppliers, make price comparisons, and utilize competitive bidding and/or negotiation.

When price analysis is not possible, cost analysis becomes the basis of obtaining a *fair and reasonable* price. Armed with an understanding of cost principles, the buyer now is in a position to conduct an analysis of a potential supplier's proposal. Many costs are known and understood, but all companies have hidden costs that often reside in overhead. A supply professional needs an understanding of costs, cost systems, and overhead composition and allocation. Other key elements of cost analysis—labor efficiency, subcontracting, plant capacity, experience, cost modeling, and profit—should be permanent concepts in the minds of all supply management professionals.

The purchase or acquisition price should be evaluated in the context of the total cost of ownership.

## Discussion Questions

1. Describe the three fundamental ways in which suppliers compete.
2. Discuss the pricing strategy of oligopolistic industries.
3. Which classical market structure provides the best environment for price negotiations? Explain.
4. What is variable-margin pricing?
5. List and briefly describe the six categories of cost. Which ones are used in making an incremental cost analysis?
6. What are the five tools a supply manager can use to conduct a price analysis?
7. How has the Internet improved the ability of a supply manager to conduct a price analysis?
8. What are some of the issues involved in historical price considerations?
9. What are the four principal elements that affect cost? Describe the effects of each element on cost.
10. What are the three sources of cost data?
11. In what circumstances should cost models be used?
12. How can a reduction in direct cost generate more of a price savings for a supply manager than a similar percentage reduction in the seller's profit?
13. Discuss the two basic types of learning curves and their applications.
14. Why might a person working on a punch press exhibit a lower rate of learning than one working in a complex assembly operation?

15. How might the supply management department apply learning curves?
16. List some factors that contribute to a supplier's "learning."
17. What is the objective of activity based costing? Why is it considered a more logical and realistic approach to cost allocations?
18. Explain target costing. What important role does supply management play in implementing target costing?
19. Why might it be discouraging for an efficient producer to have its profit for a job based solely on its costs?
20. Discuss some of the considerations, other than production efficiency, that can influence the relative size of profits.

## Internet Exercise

### Defining the New Opligopolies

Visit the "Defining the New Oligopolies" website. Once you've read the home page, click on "more" at the bottom or any number of sites to the right under NAVIGATION to learn more about the changing face of oligopolies in this new economy.

(http://www.oligopolywatch.com/stories/2003/04/17/definingTheNewOligopoly.html)

## Suggested Reading

Brimson, James A. *Activity Accounting: An Activity Based Approach* (New York: John Wiley & Sons, 1991).

Burt, David N., and Richard L. Pinkerton. "Special Secondary Source Techniques for Estimating Cost Components," in *A Purchasing Manager's Guide to Strategic Proactive Purchasing* (New York: AMACOM. 1996), pp. 282–89.

Ellram, L. M. "Total Cost Modeling in Purchasing," Center for Advanced Purchasing Studies (CAPS), Tempe, AZ, 1994.

Ellram, Lisa M. "Implementation of Target Costing in the United States: Theory versus Practice," *Journal of Supply Chain Management* 42, no. 1 (Winter 2006), pp. 13–26.

Graw, Leroy H. *Cost/Price Analysis: Tools to Improve Profit Margins* (New York, N.Y.: Van Nostrand Reinhold Company, 1994).

Lopoukhine, Serge R., Kathy English, and Patricia A. Cox. "Cost/Price (Plus) Analysis = Opportunity," *Purchasing Today* 8, no. 9 (September 1997), p. 43.

Newman, Richard G. "Monitoring Prices Increases with Economic Data: A Practical Approach," *International Journal of Purchasing and Materials Management,* Fall 1997, pp. 35–40.

Newman, Richard G. *Supplier Price Analysis: A Guide for Purchasing Accounting and Financial Analysis* (Westport, Conn.: Quorum Books, 1992).

Newman, Richard G., and John M. McKeller. "Target Pricing—A Challenge for Purchasing," *International Journal of Purchasing and Materials Management*, Summer 1995, pp. 12–20.

Smith, Michael E., Lee Buddress, and Alan Raedels. "The Strategic Use of Supplier Price and Cost Analysis," abstract from the 91st Annual International Supply Management Conference, Minneapolis, MN, May 2006.

Stueland, Valerie J. "The Lowest Price Is Not Always The Best," *Inside Supply Management,* February 2006, pp. 12–14.

Whittington, Elaine. "Anatomy of a Price," abstract from the 86th Annual International Supply Management Conference, 2001, Tempe, AZ.

Yuva, John. "Achieving Sustainable Cost Savings," *Inside Supply Management* 15, no. 2 (February 2004), p. 22.

# Appendix A: Application of Learning Curves

Before applying a learning curve to a particular item, a supply manager must be certain that learning in fact occurs at a reasonably constant rate. Many production operations do not have those properties. Gross errors can be made if a learning curve is misapplied; therefore, buyers must be alert to the following problems.

## Nonuniform Learning Rates

Learning curve analysis is predicated on the assumption that the process in question exhibits learning at a reasonably constant rate. Direct labor data from such a process should plot in a straight line on a log-log grid. If a straight line cannot be fitted to the data reasonably well, the learning rate is not uniform and the technique should not be used.

## Low-Labor-Content Items

Continued learning occurs principally in the production of products that entail a high percentage of labor. The learning opportunity is particularly high in complex assembly work. In contrast, if most work on a new item involves machine time, in which output tends to be determined by machine capacity, there is little opportunity for continued learning.

## Small Payoffs

Obtaining historical cost data to construct a learning curve entails much time and effort, particularly when a supplier uses a standard cost accounting system. Therefore, learning curve analysis is worthwhile only if the amount of money that can be saved is substantial.

## Incorrect Learning Rates

Learning varies from industry to industry, plant to plant, product to product, and part to part. Applying one rate just because someone in the industry has used it can be misleading. Intelligent use of learning curves demands that learning rates be determined as accurately as possible from comparable past experience.

## Established Items

If a supplier previously made the item for someone else, a supply manager should not use the learning curve even if the product is nonstandard and new to the buying firm. Since most of the learning already has been done on previous work, any additional cost reduction may be negligible.

## Misleading Data

Not all cost savings stem from learning. The economies of large-scale production spread fixed costs over a larger number of output units, reducing the unit cost of the item. However, this phenomenon has nothing to do with the learning curve.

## An Example of Learning Curve Application: The Cumulative Average Curve

The following simplified example shows a basic application of the cumulative average learning curve concept in labor cost analysis and contract pricing.

**Figure 14.6** | Estimating Labor Cost for the New Contract

The ABC Corporation has purchased 50 pieces of a specially designed electronic component at $2,000 per unit. In the $2,000 selling price, $1,000 represents direct labor. An audit of product costs for the first 50 units established that the operation is subject to an 80 percent cumulative average learning curve. What should ABC pay for the purchase of 350 more units?

Solution:

1. Using log-log paper, plot 50 units on the horizontal axis against $1,000 direct labor cost on the vertical axis (see Figure 14.6).
2. Double the number of units to 100 on the horizontal axis and plot against a labor cost of $800 (80 percent as high as the original $1,000 cost).
3. Draw a straight line through the two cost points. The line represents an 80 percent learning curve constructed on the basis of labor cost data for the first 50 units of production.
4. Locate 400 units on the horizontal axis (the total expected production of 50 original units plus 350 new ones). Read from the curve the labor cost of approximately $510. This is the *average* expected labor cost per unit for the total production of 400 units.
5. To find the labor cost for 400 units, multiply 400 by $510, the direct labor cost per unit. The total is $204,000.
6. Subtract the labor paid in the original order to determine the labor cost of the new order of 350 units. Hence, subtract $50,000 (50 × $1,000) from $204,000. The answer is $154,000, the labor cost which should be paid for the new order of 350 units: $154,000 ÷ 350 units = $440 per unit labor cost, compared with the original $1,000 per unit.
7. Now determine the cost for materials, overhead, and profit on the 350 units. Add this figure to the labor cost determined in step 6 to obtain the total price ABC should pay for the additional 350 units.

## An Example of Learning Curve Application: The Unit Curve

The preceding application dealt with the use of a *cumulative average* learning curve. To illustrate the application of a *unit* learning curve, consider the following hypothetical situation.

**Table 14.5** | The Manufacturer's Production Data

| Column 1 Unit Produced | Column 2 Labor Hours Required to Produce the Corresponding Unit in Col. 1 | Column 3 Labor Hours Required as a Percentage of Those Required for the Preceding Unit |
|---|---|---|
| 1 | 60 | — |
| 2 | 51 | 85.0% |
| 4 | 43 | 84.3 |
| 8 | 37 | 86.0 |
| 16 | 31 | 83.8 |
| 32 | 26 | 83.9 |

Assume that a manufacturer receives an order to produce 515 units of a new product. After the necessary production and tooling design work has been completed, the manufacturer begins production. Prior experience with moderately similar products leads the manufacturing manager to believe that a *unit* learning curve phenomenon probably will be experienced as production operations proceed.

To investigate this possibility, for the first 32 units produced, the manager records the production data shown in Table 14.5, columns 1 and 2. Then she makes the calculations shown in column 3. As production doubled (1 to 2, 2 to 4, 4 to 8, etc.), in each case it is clear that a significant learning effect was experienced. (The 2nd unit took 85 percent of the time required by the 1st unit, the 4th unit required 84.3 percent of the time required by the 2nd unit, and so on, as indicated in column 3.) Although the rate varies slightly, the manager concludes that a unit learning curve of approximately 85 percent is a good indicator of the manner in which the process will behave during the production of the remainder of the order. (That is, that the 64th unit will require 85 percent of the time required by the 32nd unit, the 128th unit will require 85 percent of the time required by the 64th unit, and so on.)

Consequently, the supply professional constructs the curve on a log-log grid and reads directly from the graph that the 512th unit will require approximately 13.6 direct labor hours for its production. Similar determinations for all units produced permit her to calculate the total number of labor hours for the complete job. Using this information, she can schedule production efficiently as well as estimate the total labor cost the job will incur.

# Appendix B: Discounts

Discounts frequently are considered a routine, prosaic part of pricing. Perceptive supply professionals recognize that this is not always the case. As will be illustrated in the discussion that follows, discounts sometimes can be used as a technique for reducing prices after all other techniques have failed. The four most commonly used kinds of discounts are *trade discounts, quantity discounts, seasonal discounts,* and *cash discounts.*

## Trade Discounts

Trade discounts are reductions from list price given to various classes of buyers and distributors to compensate them for performing certain marketing functions for the original seller (usually the manufacturer) of the product. Trade discounts frequently are structured as a sequence of individual discounts (e.g., 25,

10, and 5 percent), and in such cases they are called series discounts. Those who perform only part of the distribution functions get only one or two of the discounts in the series. If the retail price of an item with such discounts is $100, the full discounted price is calculated as follows: 25 percent of $100 = $25; 10 percent of ($100 − $25) = $7.50; 5 percent of ($100 − $25 − $7.50) = $3.38. The manufacturer's selling price then is $100 − $25 − $7.50 − $3.38 = $64.12.

An industrial supply professional who purchases through distributors must, as a result of the nature of series trade discounts, be certain that the buy is from the right distributor (i.e., the distributor obtaining the most discounts). The general guideline is to get as close to the manufacturer as is practical. For example, a large buyer normally should not purchase paper requirements from a janitorial supply house which usually does not obtain all the discounts in the series for paper. If an account is sufficiently large, the buying firm should purchase from a paper distributor that normally does obtain all discounts in the series. That kind of supplier can, at the same profit margin as the janitorial supply house, offer buyers lower prices. Buyers with very large accounts should purchase directly from paper manufacturers.

## Quantity Discounts

These price reductions are given to a buyer for purchasing increasingly larger quantities of materials. They normally are offered under one of three purchasing arrangements:

1.   For purchasing a specific quantity of items at one time.
2.   For purchasing a specified dollar total of any number of different items at one time.
3.   For purchasing a specified dollar total of any number of items over an agreed-upon time period.

The third type of quantity discount noted above is called a cumulative discount. The period of accumulation can be a month, a quarter, or, more commonly, a year. For large-dollar-value repetitive purchases, buyers always should seek this type of discount. Also, because unplanned increases in business occur with regular frequency, supply professionals should include in all quantity discount contracts a provision that if the total purchases made under the contract exceed the estimated quantities, an additional discount will be allowed for all such excesses.

The quantity discount concept originally stemmed from the unit cost reductions inherent in large-volume manufacturing operations. In a traditional mass or batch production operation, a large production run of a single product spreads the fixed costs over the number of items produced and results in a lower production cost per item. With the continuing improvement of flexible manufacturing systems, however, the dilution of fixed setup costs becomes rather small compared with other product-specific cost elements. Consequently, if a quantity discount is based solely on the distribution of setup and order processing costs over the volume of production, there is clearly a declining incentive for such a supplier to offer this form of quantity discount.

## Seasonal Discounts

Because of the seasonal nature of some products (primarily consumer products), producers commonly offer discounts for purchases made in the off-season. For example, room air conditioners usually can be purchased at a discount during the fall and winter seasons.

## Cash Discounts

In many industries, sellers traditionally offer price reductions for the prompt payment of bills. When such discounts are given, they are offered as a percentage of the net invoice price. When suppliers extend credit, they cannot avoid certain attendant costs, including the cost of tied-up capital, the cost of operating a credit department, and the cost of some bad-debt losses. Most sellers can reduce these costs by dealing on a short-term payment basis. Therefore, they are willing to pass on part of the savings to buyers in the form of a cash discount.

Supply professionals should be aware of the importance of negotiating the highest possible cash discount. The most commonly used discount in practice is 2 percent 10 days, net 30 days. In industries in which prompt payment is particularly important, cash discounts as high as 8 percent have been allowed. A cash discount of 2/10, net 30 means that a discount of 2 percent can be taken if the invoice is paid within 10 days, while the full amount should be remitted if payment is made between 10 and 30 days after receipt of the invoice.

A 2 percent discount, viewed casually, does not appear to represent much money. In one sense, however, it is the equivalent of a 36.5 percent annual interest rate. Because the bill must be paid in 30 days and the discount can be taken up to the tenth day, a buyer that does not take the discount is paying 2 percent of the dollar amount of the invoice to use the cash involved for 20 days. In a 365-day year, there are 18.25 twenty-day periods (365/20 = 18.25). A 2/10 discount translates into an *annual* discount rate of 36.5 percent (2 percent times 18.25).[12] If a firm does not have sufficient cash on hand to take cash discounts, the possibility of borrowing the needed money should be investigated. Under normal conditions, paying 10 to 15 percent for capital that returns 36.5 percent is good business. Capable buyers understand the time value of money. In some situations, generous cash discounts can be obtained either for prepayment or for 48-hour payment.

Various other types of cash discounts are in use. One common type is the *end-of-month (EOM)* dating system. This system of cash discounting permits the buying firm to take a designated percentage discount if payment is made within a specified number of days after the end of the month in which the order is shipped. If materials are shipped on October 16 under 2/10 EOM terms, a 2 percent discount can be taken at any time until November 10.

Lower prices, in the form of higher cash discounts, are an ever-present source of price reduction that supply professionals always should explore. Frequently, sellers that will not consider reducing the prices of their products will consider allowing higher cash discounts. That action accomplishes the identical result for the purchasing firm. For example, a major petroleum company recently was able to gain a 6 percent price reduction on the purchase of a complex testing machine the manufacturer had never before sold below its listed $92,000 selling price. The $5,520 price reduction was achieved by the supply manager's offering to pay one-half of the purchase price one week in advance of the machine's delivery to his company's testing laboratory.

---

[12] A complete analysis of this situation must include the opportunity cost of early payment. If a firm's internal cost of capital is 15 percent/year, the net saving generated by the 2/10, net 30 discount is 36.5 percent −15 percent, or 21.5 percent on an annualized basis.

# 15 CHAPTER

# Methods of Compensation

## CHAPTER OBJECTIVES

*After reading this chapter, you should be able to:*

1. Understand the difference between a price arrangement and a cost arrangement.

2. Select the appropriate method of compensation for a particular procurement.

## VIGNETTE: R&D CONTRACT DEVELOPMENT AT PNS

Personal Network Systems (PNS) was in the process of developing a new smart network computer for home use. The first working prototype was planned for release in seven months. The design-to-cost objective was $600 for the 5,000th unit, with a planned production run of 1 million units.

A thorough make-or-buy analysis had been conducted. One of the more costly items studied in the make-or-buy analysis was a new wireless networking device. The design-to-cost analysis allocated $100 per unit for the device. The make-or-buy analysis concluded that PNS should outsource the device. On the basis of limited experience with similar but less sophisticated devices, it was estimated that contractual development costs would be in the range of a half million dollars.

Because of staffing problems, June Oster, a newly promoted supply manager at PNS, was handling the procurement of the R&D work. She had contacted five firms that had the capability to develop the device. Two firms declined to participate in the project. The third indicated that it would be delighted to proceed with the development on a no-cost basis provided that PNS would purchase a minimum of 500,000 devices. Production costs for those units would be based on a fixed price redeterminable contract, with the ceiling price to be negotiated on completion of the R&D portion of the work.

Oster received proposals for the R&D work from the remaining two firms. One appeared to be either a get-rich-quick proposal or a courtesy bid (she was not sure which—and did not care) of $2 million. The other proposal was from the Tigertronix Corporation of Skunk Hollow, Arkansas. Tigertronix had been founded five years before by four engineers who had worked together at a large electronics firm in Beaverton,

Oregon. The new company had expanded to 450 employees, had sales of $500 million, and had an excellent reputation in the wireless networking industry.

Oster met with Freddie Ready, vice president of marketing at Tigertronix, to discuss development of the new device. She indicated PNS's desire to pay for the development so that it would own any patents and data rights, including procurement specifications. Oster also indicated her desire to enter into an R&D contract which included a fixed price incentive option for production. PNS would retain the right to complete the production work. Obviously, the R&D supplier would have good insight into the costs and nuances of production.

On April 1, Tigertronix submitted a proposal (see Exhibit 15.1).

**Exhibit 15.1**

TIGERTRONIX CORPORATION
Skunk Hollow, Arkansas

April 2, 2008

Ms. June Oster
Supply Manager
Personal Network Systems
62 Technology Drive
Sunnyvale, CA 92116

Dear Ms. Oster:

We are pleased to submit our proposal for development of a smart network device. If we are able to begin work by April 15, we will be able to provide two prototype models by November 1, 2008.

We understand the confidential nature of the work and agree not to release any data to individuals not employed by your company.

We have submitted the cost breakdown data you requested. The total of our projected costs and profit is $1,242,000. We will be pleased to answer any questions you may have, while being sensitive to the time constraint under which we both are working.

In the interest of time, we are willing to enter into a cost reimbursement production option with a target cost of $100 per unit for the first 10,000 units of production. With this cost history, we then would be in a position to enter into a firm fixed unit price contract based on our production experience with these first 10,000 units.

Very sincerely,

Ron Cox
President

Attachment: Proposal

ATTACHMENT ESTIMATED R&D COSTS

| | |
|---|---|
| **Engineering** | |
| 4,000 hours @ $60/hour | $  240,000 |
| **Supervisory** | |
| 600 hours @ $100/hour | 60,000 |
| SUBTOTAL | $  300,000 |
| Overhead 250% | 750,000 |
| G&A 10% | 30,000 |
| SUBTOTAL | $1,080,000 |
| Profit | 162,000 |
| TOTAL | $1,242,000 |

**CRITICAL THINKING QUESTION**

1.  If you were June Oster, what action would you take? Why?

## Introduction to Compensation Arrangements

A wide selection of contract compensation arrangements is necessary to provide the flexibility needed for the procurement of a large variety of materials and services. The compensation arrangement determines (1) the degree and timing of the cost responsibility assumed by the supplier, (2) the amount of profit or fee available to the supplier, and (3) the motivational implications of the fee portion of the compensation arrangements. The following examples are introduced in an effort to portray visually the seller's problem and in turn the buyer's problem of dealing with uncertainty.

**Example 1: Low Level of Uncertainty**   In this example the seller's likely cost for a project is $1,000,000. The seller is confident that the lowest possible cost will be $950,000 and the highest cost will be $1,050,000. This information is portrayed in Figure 15.1. One can see that the seller is virtually certain that costs will be within the range of $950,000 to $1,050,000, with the most likely outcome near $1,000,000.

If the seller adds 10 percent for profit to the most likely cost outcome, it may be willing to agree to a firm fixed price of $1,100,000. Note that the supplier's actual profit will be in the range of $150,000 (if actual costs are $950,000) to $50,000 (if actual costs are $1,050,000). The most likely profit is $100,000 [$1,100,000 (the price) – $1,000,000 (the most likely cost outcome)]. In this example, the use of a firm fixed price contract (as discussed below) seems appropriate.

**Example 2: High Level of Uncertainty**   In this example, assume that the range of likely cost outcomes is much wider, say, $500,000 to $1,500,000. (A range of cost outcomes this extreme is highly unlikely but is used here to introduce the concept that the type of compensation agreement should be appropriate for the amount of uncertainty present.) Again, the most likely cost outcome is $1,000,000. This example is portrayed in Figure 15.2.

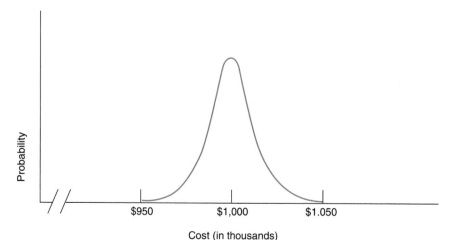

**Figure 15.1** | Probability of Cost Outcome: Low Level of Uncertainty

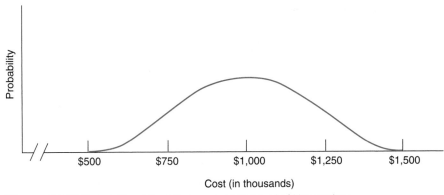

**Figure 15.2 I** Probability of Cost Outcome: High Level of Uncertainty

Most sellers are very risk averse; that is, they are unwilling to accept large amounts of uncertainty unless they are able to transfer the uncertainty to the buyer in the form of higher prices. In this case, the seller studies the distribution of likely cost outcomes and concludes that 9 times out of 10, the actual cost will be $1,400,000 or less. Accordingly, if the buyer is unwise enough to insist on using a firm fixed method of compensation, the seller may demand a firm fixed price of $1,540,000 [$1,400,000 plus $140,000 (10 percent profit on this cost)].

Table 15.1 portrays the supplier's profit under various cost outcomes for this example. It is fairly obvious that if the buyer could assume the risk inherent in this procurement, a lower price would be possible—except in the extreme case in which actual costs exceeded approximately $1,540,000.

Let us assume that the buyer and the supplier agreed to a cost plus fixed fee contract with a target cost of $1,000,000 and a fixed fee of $50,000. Note that the fee is relatively low: 5 percent of the target cost. This is the case because the supplier will not incur any risk. Table 15.2 portrays the price to be paid by the buyer under different cost outcomes.

**Table 15.1 I** Supplier's Profit Using FFP under Various Cost Outcomes

| Actual Cost | Actual Profit | Fixed Price |
|---|---|---|
| $ 500,000 | $1,040,000 | $1,540,000 |
| 1,000,000 | 540,000 | $1,540,000 |
| 1,400,000 | 140,000 | $1,540,000 |
| 1,500,000 | 40,000 | $1,540,000 |

**Table 15.2 I** Buyer's Profit Using CFFP under Various Actual Cost Outcomes

| Actual Cost | Fixed Fee or Profit | Price Paid |
|---|---|---|
| $ 500,000 | $ 50,000 | $ 550,000 |
| 1,000,000 | 50,000 | $1,050,000 |
| 1,400,000 | 50,000 | $1,450,000 |
| 1,500,000 | 50,000 | $1,550,000 |

**Table 15.3** | Fee and Price Outcomes at Various Cost Outcomes with Profit as a Fixed Percentage of Cost

| Actual Cost | Fee (10% of Actual Cost) | Price Paid |
|---|---|---|
| $ 500,000 | $ 50,000 | $ 550,000 |
| 1,000,000 | 100,000 | $1,100,000 |
| 1,400,000 | 140,000 | $1,540,000 |
| 1,500,000 | 150,000 | $1,650,000 |

The sophisticated reader may say: "Interesting. But a fee or profit of $50,000 on a cost of $500,000 [see row 1, Table 15.2] is 10 percent. That's too high considering that there's no cost risk! Why not apply a fixed percent fee to costs?" That approach is shown in Table 15.3. One does not have to be a rocket scientist to see that such an approach motivates the supplier to increase costs since the higher the cost, the higher the fee!

## Observation

Without going into further detail at this point, it should be apparent that selection of the right type of compensation arrangement can save money. Insightful readers may be asking themselves: "What would happen if instead of paying a fixed fee or a fixed percent of cost, we were able to incentivize the supplier to control costs?"

The supply manager has a range of compensation arrangements designed to meet the needs of a particular procurement. At one end of that range is the firm fixed price contract in which the supplier assumes all cost responsibility and profit and loss potentials therefore are high. At the other end is the cost plus fixed fee contract in which the supplier has no cost risk and the fee (profit) is fixed, usually at a relatively low level. Between these two extremes are numerous incentive arrangements that reflect a sharing of the cost responsibility.

# Contract Cost Risk Appraisal

The degree of cost responsibility a supplier reasonably can be expected to assume is determined primarily by the cost risk involved. It is to the supply manager's advantage to estimate this risk before negotiations. Since the majority of contracts are "forward priced," that is, priced before completion of the work, some cost risk is involved in each of them. The degree of cost risk involved depends on how accurately the cost of the contract can be estimated before performance. The accuracy of the cost estimate and the degree of cost risk usually are a function of both technical and contract schedule risk.

A supply manager should insist on a fixed price contract unless (1) the risks will result in a contract price containing large reserves for contingencies that may not occur, (2) the risks result in reliable suppliers refusing to agree to a fixed price contract because a significant loss might be incurred, or (3) the use of a fixed price contract could result in the supplier "cutting corners" to avoid taking a loss.

## Technical Risk

Technical risk is the risk associated with the nature of the item being purchased. Appraisal of technical risk includes analysis of the type and complexity of the item or service being purchased, stability of design specifications or statement of work, availability of historical pricing data, and prior production experience.

Analysis of technical risk in a complex system may include appraisals by a team with members from the user group, the engineering staff, and the purchasing and supply management group. Think, for example, of the technical risk involved in the Apollo mission to put a human on the moon: leaving the earth's gravity, sustaining life in a gravityless environment, landing on an unknown surface structure of the moon's crust, and reentering the earth's stratosphere without burning up.

Technical risk is reduced as the job requirements, production methods, and pricing data become better defined and the design specifications or statement of work becomes more stable. Research and development contracts in particular have a rather high technical risk associated with them. This is due to the ill-defined requirements that arise from the necessity to deal beyond, or at least very near, the limits of the current technology.

### Contract Schedule Risk

In addition to technical risk, schedule risk must be assessed in determining the supplier's cost risk. Preferred procurement practice calls for forward pricing of contract efforts. This practice is used in an attempt to anticipate material and labor cost increases during performance of the contract. These estimates, along with possible schedule slippage, are always subject to error.

## General Types of Contract Compensation Arrangements

Compensation arrangements can be classified into three broad categories: (1) fixed price contracts, (2) incentive contracts, and (3) cost reimbursement contracts.

### Fixed Price Contracts

Under a fixed price arrangement, the supplier is obligated to deliver the product called for by the contract for a fixed price. If, before completion of the product, the supplier finds that the effort is more difficult or costly than anticipated, the supplier still is obligated to deliver the product. Further, the supplier will receive no more than the previously agreed-on amount. The amount of profit the supplier receives will depend on the actual cost outcome. There is no maximum or minimum profit limitation in fixed price contracts. A fixed price arrangement normally is used in situations in which specifications are well defined and cost risk is relatively low.

### Incentive Contracts

Incentive contracts are employed in an effort to motivate the supplier to improve cost and possibly other stated requirements, such as schedule performance. In an incentive contract, the cost responsibility is shared by the buyer and the seller. This sharing addresses two issues: (1) the desire to motivate the supplier to control cost and (2) an awareness that if the supplier assumes all or most of the risk when significant uncertainty is present, a contingency allowance will be required, inflating the contract price.

Incentive contracts are of two types: (1) fixed price incentive and (2) cost plus incentive fee. With a fixed price incentive contract, the ceiling price is agreed to (or fixed) during negotiations. Under the cost plus incentive fee arrangement, the supplier is reimbursed for all allowable costs incurred, up to any prescribed ceiling. Obviously, the supplier's cost accounting system must meet commonly accepted standards and be open to the customer for review when incentives based on costs incurred are employed.

## Cost-Type Contracts

Under a cost-type arrangement, the buyer's obligation is to reimburse the supplier for all allowable, reasonable, and allocable costs incurred and to pay a fixed fee. Again, the supplier's cost accounting practices must meet commonly accepted standards and be open to the customer. Most cost arrangements include a cost limitation clause that sets an administrative limitation on the reimbursement of costs. Generally, under a cost-type arrangement, the supplier is obligated only to provide its "best effort." Usually, neither performance nor delivery is guaranteed. Cost-type arrangements normally are used when:

- Procurement of research and development involves high technical risk.
- Some doubt exists that the project can be completed successfully.
- Product specifications are incomplete.
- High-dollar, highly uncertain procurements such as software development are involved.

# Specific Types of Compensation Arrangements

There are a number of specific types of compensation arrangements under each of the categories listed above.

1. Fixed price compensation arrangements:
   - Firm fixed price
   - Fixed price with economic price adjustment
   - Fixed price redetermination
2. Incentive arrangements:
   - Fixed price incentive
   - Cost plus incentive fee
3. Cost-type arrangements:
   - Cost reimbursement
   - Cost sharing
   - Time and materials
   - Cost plus fixed fee
   - Cost plus award fee

The applicability, elements, structure, and final price computation for the various compensation arrangements are discussed in the following paragraphs.

## Firm Fixed Price Contracts

The most preferred contract type, if appropriate for the procurement, is the firm fixed price contract. A firm fixed price (FFP) contract is an agreement to pay a specified price when the items (services) specified by the contract have been delivered (completed) and accepted. The contracting parties establish a firm price through either competitive bidding or negotiation. Since there is no adjustment in the contract price after the work is completed and actual costs are known, the cost risk to the supplier can be high.

An FFP contract is appropriate in competitive bidding when the specifications are definite, there is little schedule risk, and competition has established the existence of a fair and reasonable price. An FFP contract also can be appropriate for negotiated procurements if a review reveals adequate specifications and if price and cost analysis establish the reasonableness of the price.

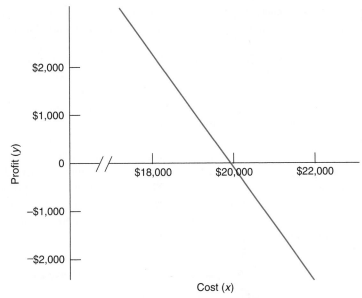

**Figure 15.3** | Firm Fixed Price Contract—$20,000

As was stated previously, under an FFP contract there is no price adjustment caused by the supplier's cost experience. Because the supplier has all cost responsibility, the actual outcome will show up in the form of profit or losses. Therefore, the supplier has maximum incentive to control costs under an FFP contract. If the supplier incurs expenses beyond the buyer's obligation, the seller must find the required funds elsewhere. Conversely, if the supplier reduces costs, all savings contribute to the supplier's profit. This dollar-for-dollar relationship between expenditures and profit is the greatest motivator of efficiency available. An FFP contract has only one contract compensation arrangement element: total price. Although negotiations may involve the discussion of costs and profit, the contractual document reflects only total price. This structure can be seen in Figure 15.3, which depicts an FFP contract for $20,000.

In this example, cost is shown as the independent variable (*x*-axis), and profit, since it is a function of cost, as the dependent variable (*y*-axis). The graph depicts the one-to-one relationship between costs and profit by showing that as costs increase by $1, profit decreases by $1.

Computing the final price in an FFP-type contract is a simple matter. If a $20,000 firm fixed price contract is awarded, on contract completion the supplier will receive $20,000 whether costs were $15,000 or $25,000 or any other amount.

It should be noted that a fixed price does not always stay fixed. A supplier who is losing money *may* request and get some relief if any of the following apply:

1. The customer in some way has contributed to the loss.
2. The customer badly needs the items and other suppliers are not willing to provide them at the established price.
3. The supplier has unique facilities and time is too short to do anything but get the product at an increased cost from the initial supplier.
4. The customer's representatives do not employ sound supply management practices.

As was discussed previously, early supplier involvement (ESI) with a decision to rely on one supplier during and after development results in many benefits that are based on the early matching of process and product. But ESI may result in cost overruns and higher costs if the supplier can't perform at the fixed price because of unforeseen (usually technical) reasons. It should be recognized that when a supplier fails to perform under a fixed price contract and the buying firm is forced to turn the business into a cost plus type of contract, the supplier has damaged its chance for future business with the customer and other potential customers. The supply manager, in contrast, can use the prospect of continued future business to keep the price well below what the supplier's leverage of the moment might suggest.

Variations of the FFP contract have been developed to meet special circumstances. One such variation is the FFP level-of-effort contract. This arrangement calls for a set number of labor hours to be expended over a period of time. The contract is considered complete when the hours are expended, although normally a report of findings also is required. The FFP level-of-effort contract is used appropriately when the specification is general in nature and when no specific end item (other than a report) is required. This arrangement is used most frequently for research and development efforts under $100,000 and for "get our foot in the door" consulting contracts.

## Fixed Price with Economic Price Adjustment Contracts

Fixed price with economic price adjustment (FPEPA) contracts are used to recognize economic contingencies, such as unstable labor or market conditions, which would prevent the establishment of a firm fixed price contract without a large contingency for possible cost increases or decreases in the unit cost of labor and/or materials. An FPEPA contract is simply an FFP contract that includes economic price adjustment clauses. Such provisions are common when items containing precious metals and items for construction services are purchased.

Economic price adjustments (EPA) or escalator/de-escalator clauses provide for both price increases and price decreases to protect the buyer and the supplier from the effects of economic changes. If such clauses were not used, suppliers would include contingency allowances in their bids or proposals to eliminate or reduce the risk of loss. With a fixed contingency allowance in the contract price, the supplier is hurt if the changes exceed its estimate, and the buyer will overpay if the input unit cost increases do not materialize.

An economic price adjustment clause may be used for fixed price–type arrangements resulting from both competitively bid and negotiated contracts. Price adjustments normally should be restricted to contingencies beyond the control of the supplier. Under an FPEPA contract, specific contingencies are left open subject to an EPA clause, and the final contract price is adjusted, depending on what happens to those contingencies. When cost pass-through or escalator clauses cover specific materials and/or labor, the buyer should be sure that the price increase does not occur until the higher-cost material is used or until the labor contract increase takes effect.

The use of economic price adjustment clauses varies with the probability of significant price fluctuations. Their use also increases when purchasing strategy favors early supplier involvement, longer-term contracts, fewer supplies, and more single-source suppliers. An economic price adjustment clause should recognize the possibility of both inflation and deflation in determining price adjustments. Further, labor and material costs that are subject to economic adjustment must reflect the effects of learning on both labor and material costs. It takes considerable purchasing skill to use economic price adjustment clauses well. Decisions must be made on what items to include and which price/cost index or benchmark is best for each item.

The cost elements to adjust are high-value raw materials, specific high-value components, and direct labor. A professional buyer generally should oppose including costs within the supplier's control, such as development, depreciation, fixed expenses, other overhead items, and profit, in the base subject to escalation.

In selecting indexes for price adjustment clauses, the following rules are suggested:

■ Select from the appropriate Bureau of Labor Statistics category.

■ Avoid broad indexes; use the lowest-level classification which includes the item.

■ Develop a weighted index for the materials in a product.

■ Select labor rate indexes by type and location.

■ Define energy indexes by fuel type and location.

■ Analyze the past history of each proposed index versus the actual price change of the item being indexed.

Using a broad index can produce strange results. One marketing executive used the producer price index (PPI) to adjust the purchase price of electronic apparatus, not recognizing that the PPI consists of about 40 percent food and fuel components with only 3 percent electronics input.

The details of the economic price adjustment clause must be thought through with various scenarios in mind. When will adjustments be made? Under what conditions can the contract be renegotiated? How will it be audited? By whom?

## Fixed Price Redetermination Contracts

These contracts provide for a firm fixed price for an initial contract period with a redetermination (upward or downward) provision at a stated time during contract performance [FPR (prospective)] or after contract completion [FPR (retroactive)]. The FPR (prospective) usually is used only in circumstances that call for quantity production or services where a fair and reasonable price can be negotiated for initial periods but not for subsequent periods. The FPR (retroactive) is used in circumstances where, at the time of negotiation, a fair and reasonable price cannot be established and the amount involved is so small and the performance period so short that the use of any other contract type would be impractical.

The data shown in Table 15.3 are also applicable to an FPR contract. As was observed, the supplier is motivated to increase costs, since the higher the cost, the higher the fee!

## Incentive Arrangements

Firm fixed price (FFP) and cost plus fixed fee (CPFF) contracts are extremes of the range of contract compensation arrangements since in either case, all of the cost responsibility falls on only one party. Between these two extremes are a number of contract arrangements in which the cost responsibility is shared between the customer and the supplier. These are called incentive-type contracts.

Incentives are applied to contracts in an attempt to motivate the supplier to improve performance in cost, schedule, or other stated parameters. By far the most frequent application of incentives is in the area of cost control. However, this is not the only type of incentive. The specific type of incentive applied depends on the desired outcome. For example, if the primary interest is in developing a high-performance read head, it would be logical to reward the supplier for the development and production of a read head which exceeds the minimum specifications. If the same read head were needed to meet a crash development effort, the schedule might be the appropriate basis of an incentive. For the same read head, funds may be a real constraint because of budgetary limitations, and a production unit cost incentive would be appropriate. If a combination of performance and cost objectives were of concern, a multiple-incentive contract could be developed.

In this book, the discussion of incentive arrangements is limited to cost incentives. The focus will be on the two most frequently applied cost incentive compensation arrangements: the fixed price incentive (FPI) contract and the cost plus incentive fee (CPIF) contract. A general discussion of how a simplified incentive contract is structured precedes analysis of the specific elements and structure of these two compensation arrangements. The elements of a simplified incentive contract include (1) the target cost, (2) the target profit, and (3) the sharing arrangement.

**Target Cost**   The target cost for an incentive contract is that cost outcome which both the buyer and the supplier feel is the most likely outcome for the effort involved. The target cost should be based on costs that would result under "normal business conditions." Although the target cost is thought to be the most likely, it is recognized that the probability that the supplier's final costs will be very close to the target cost is low. After all, if there were a high probability that the target cost would be close to the final cost, a firm fixed price contract would be appropriate. The target should be that cost point where both parties agree that there is an equal chance of cost going above or below the target.

**Target Profit**   In addition to a target cost, a target profit is developed. The target profit in an incentive contract is a profit amount that is considered fair and reasonable, based on all relevant facts, as discussed in Chapter 14.

**Allocating Costs above or below Target**   Since an incentive contract recognizes that the target most likely will *not* be met, a method of allocating cost increases above or decreases below the target is necessary. That method is an arrangement that reflects the sharing of the cost responsibility between the buyer and the supplier. This arrangement should reflect the cost risk involved as evidenced by the magnitude of potential increases and decreases for the specific effort. In addition, the sharing arrangement must address two questions: "What percent of the savings below target will be required to motivate the supplier to perform as efficiently as possible?" and "What percent of the cost overrun—cost above target—charged to the supplier (in the form of lower profit) will cause the supplier to perform as efficiently as possible?"

How is the magnitude of a potential cost increase or decrease established? It is developed through an assessment of possible cost outcomes, based on varying circumstances a supplier might face during contract performance. In addition to developing a target cost and profit outcome, the parties establish cost outcomes and associated profits for a "best-case" situation and a "worst-case" situation. The best-case cost outcome is referred to as the most optimistic cost (MOC) point, and its related profit is referred to as the most optimistic profit (MOPr) point. The worst-case cost outcome is referred to as the most pessimistic cost (MPC) point, and its profit is referred to as the most pessimistic profit (MPPr) point.

The difference between the target point and the most optimistic point provides the supply manager with the magnitude of a potential cost decrease. The difference between the target point and the most pessimistic point provides the supply manager with the magnitude of a potential cost increase. One normally would not expect these magnitudes to be equal, since the potential for things to go wrong is usually higher than the potential for things to go better than expected. Another way of looking at the magnitude of a potential cost increase is that it provides an estimate of the cost risk a supplier faces if the target cost is not met. This cost risk and the supplier's assumption of this risk are reflected in the sharing arrangement.

**Table 15.4 I** Fixed Price Incentive Fee

| | Estimated Dollars (in thousands) | Price (in thousands) |
|---|---|---|
| Target cost (TC) | $1,000 | |
| Target profit (TPr) | 80 | $1,080 |
| Most optimistic cost (MOC) | 800 | |
| Most optimistic profit (MOPr) | 120 | 920 |
| Most pessimistic cost (MPC) | 1,200 | |
| Most pessimistic profit (MPPr) | 0 | 1,200 |
| Ceiling price | 1,200 | 1,200 |

## Fixed Price Incentive Fee

Table 15.4 shows how a fixed price incentive fee contract is structured. The cost and profit outcomes shown in Table 15.4 were agreed on by the buying and selling firms. These data are portrayed in Figure 15.4.

Computing of the final payment under an incentive arrangement is more complex than it is under either an FFP or CPFF contract. Under an incentive arrangement, the supplier's profit is adjusted to reflect performance in the cost area. If the supplier has incurred costs above target, the profit is decreased by the supplier's share of the cost above target cost up to the ceiling price. Conversely, if the supplier's costs are below target, its profit is increased. The final price outcome is the supplier's cost plus profit.

**Figure 15.4 I** Fixed Price Incentive Fee

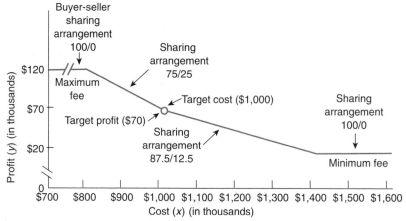

**Figure 15.5** I CPIF Arrangement

The supplier's profit equals the sum of the target profit plus or minus the supplier's share of the cost savings or cost increase.

## Cost Plus Incentive Fee Arrangements

CPIF contracts combine the incentive arrangement and the cost plus fixed fee arrangement. Under a CPIF arrangement, an incentive applies over part of the range of cost outcomes. The fee structure resembles a cost plus fixed fee contract at both the low-cost and high-cost ends of the range, as shown in Figure 15.5. This information also is depicted in Table 15.5. Thus, if cost were $800,000 or less, the fee would be $120,000. If cost were $1,400,000 or more, the fee would be $20,000.

A cost plus incentive fee arrangement is used in circumstances in which the cost risk warrants a cost-type arrangement but an incentive can be established to provide the supplier with positive motivation to manage costs. CPIF arrangements are most suitable for advanced development efforts and initial production runs. In these circumstances, risk may be too high to warrant the use of a fixed price arrangement or an FPI arrangement but not high enough to require a CPFF arrangement to get a reliable supplier.

The CPIF contract is structured in a manner very similar to the structuring of an FPI compensation arrangement. Cost and fee outcomes are established for the target, most optimistic, and most pessimistic points. These cost and fee outcomes are used to establish the sharing arrangement for cost decrease and increase situations. The difference between the structures of the FPI and CPIF arrangements is that under

**Table 15.5** I Cost Plus Incentive Fees

| | |
|---|---|
| Target cost | $1,000,000 |
| Target profit | 70,000 |
| Optimistic cost | 800,000 |
| Optimistic and maximum profit | 120,000 |
| Pessimistic cost | 1,400,000 |
| Pessimistic and minimum profit | 20,000 |
| Sharing below target (customer/supplier) | 75/25 |
| Sharing above target (customer/supplier) | 87.5/12.5 |

the CPIF arrangement the contract converts to a CPFF contract at both the most optimistic and the most pessimistic fee points.

The computation of the final price to be paid to the supplier on contract completion follows the same steps as in the fixed price incentive arrangement. However, in a CPIF contract a comparison is made between computed fees and minimum and maximum fees before the calculation of the final price. For example, using the CPIF contract structured in Figure 15.5, the supply manager would compute the final price, based on a final cost of $700,000, as follows:

Target cost—$1,000,000
Target profit—$70,000
Maximum fee—$120,000
Minimum fee—$20,000

1. Cost savings = Target cost − Final cost
$300,000 = $1,000,000 − $700,000
2. Supplier's share of cost savings = Cost savings × Supplier share
$75,000 = $300,000 × 0.25
3. Computed fee = Savings fee + Target fee
$145,000 = $75,000 + $70,000

Since there is a maximum limitation on fee, a comparison is made between the computed fee and the maximum fee. In this case, the supplier receives only the maximum fee, $120,000.

4. Final price = Final cost + Maximum fee
$820,000 = $700,000 + $120,000

The CPIF contract is an incentive arrangement that converts to a CPFF contract at both the maximum and minimum fee points. This type of contract gives the supplier some incentive to control cost outcomes in the area over which the sharing arrangements apply; that area is called the range of incentive effectiveness.

## Cost Plus Fixed Fee Arrangements

Under a CPFF contract, the buyer agrees to reimburse the supplier for all allowable, reasonable, and allocable costs that may be incurred during the performance of the contract. Moreover, the buyer agrees to pay the supplier a fixed number of dollars above the cost as the fee for doing the work. The fee changes only when the scope of work changes. Under the CPFF, the supplier has no incentive to reduce or control costs.

The contractual elements of this arrangement include an estimated cost and a fixed fee. The estimated cost represents the best estimate of the customer and the supplier for the work involved. The fixed fee is the amount of fee the supplier will receive regardless of cost outcome. Because the supplier has no cost risk under a CPFF contract, the profit potential is relatively low. Normally there is a limit on the customer's total liability.

A supply professional should remember that the final cost should be audited. Supply management departments spend hours negotiating the right to inspect the actual invoices for material and the hours worked. Many, however, don't conduct an appropriate audit. It is a good use of time to look at the details even though one might not expect to find any inappropriate charges. The knowledge gained often proves helpful in future negotiations.

**Table 15.6 |** Cost Plus Fixed Fee: Sample Price Outcomes

|  | Possible Outcomes (in thousands) | | | |
|---|---|---|---|---|
| Final cost | $800 | $900 | $1,000 | $1,200 |
| Fixed fee | 50 | 50 | 50 | 50 |
| Price to be paid to supplier | $850 | $950 | $1,050 | $1,250 |

Computing the final payment due the supplier under a CPFF contract is simply a matter of adding the incurred costs (assuming that an audit has found them to be reasonable, allowable, and allocable) to the fixed fee. In the case of a CPFF contract with an estimated cost of $1,000,000 and a fixed fee of $50,000, some possible final contract price outcomes are shown in Table 15.6.

A supply manager must remember that in a cost-type contract, the limit is on the fee, not on total customer obligation. Obviously, the CPFF-type contract should be used only when one cannot get a more favorable arrangement or when the presence of great uncertainty and risk would result in the inclusion of a large contingency in a firm fixed price contract. A CPFF contract also is appropriate in circumstances in which the technical and schedule risks are so high that the cost risk is too large for the supplier to assume. This type of contract is designed chiefly for use in research or exploratory development when the uncertainty of performance is so great that a firm price or an incentive arrangement cannot be set up at any time during the life of the contract. Costs normally are audited by the buyer before final payment.

## Cost Plus Award Fee

The cost plus award fee (CPAF) was pioneered by NASA when that agency was purchasing highly complex hardware and professional services to support the space program. The award fee is applicable to the procurement of software developed for the buying company and for janitorial, landscaping, and similar services when the ability to reward the supplier for nonquantitative aspects of its performance on a subjective basis makes good business sense. The award fee is a pool of money established by the buyer to reward the supplier on a periodic basis for the *application of effort in meeting the buyer's stated needs.* The key difference between the award fee and other fees is that the supplier's receipt of the fee is based on the buying firm's *subjective evaluation* of how well the supplier has applied its *efforts* in meeting the buyer's needs. The subjective aspect provides flexibility to contracting situations in an uncertain environment. When properly used, an award fee benefits both the buyer and the supplier. Superior performance receives superior rewards in the form of a superior fee. The award fee also introduces an element of flexibility since the buyer can change the areas receiving supplier attention by providing advance guidance for any performance period. The award fee gives the buying firm's management a flexible tool with which to influence performance.

## Cost without Fee

Nonprofit institutions such as universities frequently do research work for both government and industry without the objective of making a profit. That research is done under cost-type contracts without a fee. Because universities do much of the nation's pure research, as distinguished from the applied research done by industry, a growing number of contracts of this type are being used. Naturally, the universities recover all overhead costs, which generally include facilities costs and remuneration for personnel who work on the contracts. In recent years, high-technology firms have increased their use of this contract type.

## Cost Sharing

In some situations, a firm doing research under a cost type of contract stands to benefit if the product that is developed can be used in its own product line. In those circumstances, the buyer and the seller agree on what they consider a fair basis for sharing the costs (most often it is 50-50). The electronics industry has found this type of contract especially useful.

## Time and Materials

In certain types of contracts, such as those calling for repairs to machinery, the precise work to be done cannot be predicted in advance. For instance, it cannot be known exactly what must be done to a large malfunctioning pump aboard a ship until it is opened and examined. Perhaps only a new gasket is required to put it in good working order. However, its impeller could require a major job of balancing and realignment. A time and materials contract is one method of pricing this type of work. With this type of contract, the parties agree on a fixed rate per labor hour that includes overhead and profit, with materials supplied at cost.

Suppose a mechanic working on the ship's pump is paid $30 per hour. Assume also that overhead is calculated as 100 percent of the labor cost and profit is set at 10 percent of total cost. A billing rate for this mechanic for one hour would be calculated as shown in Table 15.7.

If it took the mechanic two days (16 hours) to repair the pump, using $320 worth of material, the job price would be $1,376 (16 × $66 + $320).[1] Profit should be paid only on labor and overhead costs. Note that the supplier is motivated to increase the number of hours for two reasons: (1) The $30 of overhead commonly is a fixed cost. Thus, every additional hour contributes $30 to an overhead which probably has been amortized. In effect, this $30 becomes a gift of $30 of additional profit. (2) The stated profit of $6 increases with each additional half hour.

A variation of the time and materials type of contract is called a labor-hour contract. In this type of contract, materials are not supplied by the seller; however, other costs are agreed to as in time and materials contracts.

## Letter Contracts and Letters of Intent

Letter contracts are used in those rare situations in which it is imperative that work start on a complex project immediately. Letter contracts are *preliminary contractual authorizations* under which the seller can commence work immediately. The seller can prepare drawings, obtain required materials, and start actual

**Table 15.7** | Time and Materials: Billing Rate

| | |
|---|---|
| Direct labor cost, per hour | $30 |
| Overhead at 100 percent of labor | 30 |
| Total cost | $60 |
| Profit at 10 percent of total cost | 6 |
| Billing rate, per hour | $66 |

---

[1]An alert reader will observe that this is really a cost plus percentage of cost contract. If the mechanic is a good worker, he might complete the job in 10 hours ($60 profit to his employer). If he is a poor worker, he could take 20 hours, and his employer would receive $120 in profit. Obviously, supply managers must exercise close control over this type of contract to make sure inefficient or wasteful methods are not used.

production. Under letter contracts, the seller is guaranteed reimbursement for costs up to a specified amount. Letter contracts should be converted to definitive contracts at the earliest possible date.[2]

## Considerations in Selecting the Method of Compensation

With such a wide variety of compensation methods available, a supply professional must exercise considerable care in selecting the best one for a particular use. If a bid or a quoted price is reasonable, this will help the supply manager decide to use a firm fixed price contract. In contrast, if the fairness of the price is in doubt, a fixed price contract could entail excessive expense to the buying firm and would be a poor choice. If price uncertainty stems from unstable labor or market conditions, fixed price with escalation may be a solution. If the uncertainty is due to a potential improvement in production effort, an incentive contract may be the best answer. Plainly, the many factors that affect procurement costs can guide a supply professional in his or her selection of the best type of contract for a specific purchasing situation.

The specific nature of the materials, equipment, or services to be purchased also can point to advantages of one contract type over another. The more complex or developmental the purchased item, the greater the risks and difficulties in using a fixed price contract. Any uncertainty in design affects a seller's ability to estimate costs, as does a lack of cost experience with a new item. The details of any purchase will indicate the magnitude of the price uncertainties involved. A full understanding of these uncertainties permits supply managers to allocate the risks more equitably between their firm and the supplier's firm through the proper choice of a compensation method.

Timing of the procurement quite frequently is a controlling factor in the selection of the compensation method. Allowing potential suppliers only a short time to prepare their bids can reduce the reliability of the cost estimates and increase prices. A short delivery period usually rules out the effective use of incentive contracts. In contrast, a long contract period provides time to generate and apply cost-reducing efficiencies, an ideal situation for an incentive contract. The facts of each procurement must be considered individually in determining which compensation method the supply manager should use.

Business practices in specific industries frequently can provide additional clues to the best choice of a compensation method. The construction industry, for example, traditionally accepts a wider range of competitive fixed price jobs than does the aerospace industry. The lumber industry accepts prices established in open auctions. Architects and engineers frequently will not enter into price competition with one another for architectural or engineering services, and some management consulting firms will not compete with one another on price. Business factors such as these help determine the best compensation method in a great many purchasing situations.

The scope and intensity of competition definitely can influence the method of compensation to use. If competition is intense and the prices bid are close, the buyer justifiably can feel that the prices are fair and reasonable and use a firm fixed price contract. However, if competition is not adequate and the supply manager has doubts about the reasonableness of prices, an incentive or cost contract may be appropriate.

In short, a supply professional's basic preference for a firm fixed price contract is just the starting point for an analysis of alternative compensation choices. As a supply manager considers all available compensation methods, he or she must weigh the preference for fixed prices against the risks involved, the time

---

[2]For more on this topic, see "Using Letters of Intent to Provide a Framework for Relationships with Suppliers," William A. Hancock, in *The Purchaser's Legal Adviser,* January 1994, published by Business Laws, Chesterland, OH (800-759-0920). Also see Judi. Coover, Esq.," Letter of Intent," *Inside Supply Management*, November 2006, pp. 32–33.

available, the degree of competition involved, experience with the industry involved, the apparent soundness of the offered price, the technical and developmental state of the item being purchased, and all the other technical and economic information that affects the purchase transaction. Determination of the best compensation agreement for a specific situation requires a careful analysis of all the factors relevant to that situation.

## Concluding Remarks

In most instances, a supply manager can enter into a firm fixed price contract even when significant cost risk is present. But if risk is high, there is a likelihood of either of two equally unsatisfactory results: The contract price will include a large contingency, or the supplier could incur a loss. The possibility of a loss may result in (1) reduced quality in an effort to minimize the loss, (2) a request to renegotiate, (3) refusal to complete the work, (4) insolvency, resulting in the loss of a good supplier, or (5) a "grin and bear it" approach.

The selection of the contract compensation arrangement to be used for a specific contract is an important determination. The selection must be based on the uncertainties and risks involved and the circumstances surrounding the procurement. The compensation agreement selected must result in a reasonable allocation of the cost risk and should provide adequate motivation to the supplier to assure effective performance. In addition, the compensation arrangement selected must be compatible with the supplier's accounting system. Sound application of these compensation methods will reduce expenditures significantly when cost risk is present.

## Discussion Questions

1. What three issues are addressed by a compensation arrangement? Explain what is meant by the "motivational implications" of a compensation arrangement.
2. A supply professional has a range of compensation arrangements designed to meet the needs of a particular procurement. What two types of contracts are at the extremes of this range?
3. What is meant by "cost risk"? What two elements contribute to the calculation of cost risk?
4. Identify and define the three categories of compensation arrangements. Give examples of specific arrangements in each category.
5. Explain why firm fixed price contracts are the greatest motivators of efficiency.
6. When one is using an economic price adjustment clause, which cost elements should be included? Which costs should be excluded?
7. What is the potential danger of using a fixed price redetermination contract?
8. What objective does the use of an incentive arrangement satisfy? What are the elements of an incentive contract?
9. Discuss the irony involved in setting cost targets.
10. Explain how the final price outcome is derived under an incentive contract. How does this motivate the supplier to perform as efficiently as possible?
11. Explain the comparison that is made in a cost plus incentive fee arrangement before the calculation of the final price. Why is this necessary?
12. Explain the structure of a cost plus fixed fee contract. What should a supply professional do to ensure the legitimacy of the final cost?
13. What is the difference between an award fee and other contractual fees? Discuss the advantages of award fees from the perspectives of the supplier and the buyer.

14. Under what situation might both the buying firm and the selling firm agree to engage in cost sharing?
15. Discuss some of the considerations that must be employed in selecting a particular contract type.

## Internet Exercise

### NASA Procurement: Use of Award Fees for Achieving Program Outcomes Should Be Improved.

Visit the government website below. Read about the use of CPAF compensation arrangements by NASA.

(http://www.gao.gov/new.items/d0758.pdf)

1. Why is the Government Accountability Office looking into the use of this type of compensation by NASA?
2. What is NASA procurement failing to do which is rendering the use of CPAF ineffective?
3. What are the recommendations of the GAO for improving the use of this method of compensating suppliers?

## Suggested Reading

Michels, William L., and George E. Cantrell. "An Ongoing Plan for Volatile-Priced Commodities," *Inside Supply Management,* August 2004, p. 22.

Ore, Norbert J. "Making the Most of the ROB," *Inside Supply Management,* May 2002, p. 36.

Whittington, Elaine M. "Types of Contracts," abstract from a presentation at the 79th Annual ISM International Conference Proceedings, Atlanta, GA, 1994, ISM, Tempe AZ.

## Websites

www.bls.gov/cpi/: Consumer price index

www.bls.gov/ppi/: Producer price index

http://www.bls.gov/ppi/ppifaq.htm: Information on how to use the producer price index for contract escalation/de-escalation.

# Negotiation

## CHAPTER OBJECTIVES

*After reading this chapter, you should be able to:*

1. Understand why you negotiate: What do you hope to attain?
2. Understand when to negotiate
3. Explain the negotiation process.
4. Identify various techniques used in negotiating.
5. Identify the characteristics that make a successful negotiator.
6. Become a successful negotiator.

## VIGNETTE: NEGOTIATING FOR GOLD

The Faustus Company is in the process of developing an alchemist's dream: a machine which will convert lead to gold. The team responsible for the project has developed a successful prototype. Because of the need for total secrecy, no suppliers have been involved in the new product development process. Faustus has developed specifications for the key items which must be purchased. The most critical one is a bipolar catalyst with an estimated cost of $250,000 each. Four firms which can make the catalysts have been identified. An RFP has been issued. The team has selected Metals 'R' Us as the most attractive potential supplier.

Angus McFee, the project engineer (and 10 percent owner of the company), is very excited. He sees an endless stream of reverenue for the firm and himself. "Let's bring Metals 'R' Us in and get a contract," says Angus. Most of his teammates concur.

Traci Hunt, a recent graduate of State University's supply management program, says, "Gentlemen, we've got many hours of work preparing to meet with Metals 'R' Us. The key to a successful negotiation is in its preparation. A good rule of thumb is 10 hours of preparation for every hour of face-to-face discussions." Traci doesn't enhance her popularity but slows the project down to allow for the necessary preparations for face-to-face negotiations with Metals 'R' Us. ■

## CRITICAL THINKING QUESTIONS

1.  What are some issues that should be investigated?

2.  What might be some of the objectives Faustus Company hopes to achieve through negotiating with Metals 'R' Us?

Negotiation is one of the most important as well as one of the most interesting and challenging aspects of supply management. In industry and at most levels of government, the term "negotiation" frequently causes misunderstandings. In industry, negotiation sometimes is confused with "haggling" and "price chiseling." In government, negotiation frequently is visualized as a nefarious means of avoiding competitive bidding and of awarding large contracts surreptitiously to favored suppliers.

Webster's dictionary defines negotiation broadly as "conferring, discussing, or bargaining to reach agreement in business transactions."[1] Herb Cohen describes negotiation as a pervasive process in which people ultimately attempt to reach a joint decision on matters of common concern in situations in which there is initial disagreement. Thus, a negotiation always requires both shared interests and issues of conflict. Obviously, without commonality there is no reason to achieve resolution.[2] To be fully effective in purchasing situations, negotiation must be utilized in its broadest context—as a part of a decision-making process. In this context, negotiation is a process of planning, reviewing, and analyzing that is used by a buyer and a seller to reach acceptable agreements or compromises. These agreements and compromises include all aspects of the business agreement, not just price.

Negotiations differ from a ball game or a war. In those activities, only one side can win; the other side must lose. In most successful business negotiations, both sides win something. In popular usage this approach is called "win-win negotiation." The "winnings," however, seldom are divided equally; invariably, one side wins more than the other. This is as it should be in business: Superior business skills merit superior rewards.

Increasingly, negotiations are conducted by cross-functional teams. These teams must be well coordinated to function as an integrated entity. Accordingly, we will use the term "negotiator" to refer to an individual supply management professional and also to a cross-functional negotiating team. Truly professional negotiators constantly search for opportunities to "enlarge the pie." Instead of focusing on finding a way to "share a fixed pie," they focus first on enlarging the pie.

---

[1]Leigh Thompson in the second edition of her insightful book *The Mind and Heart of the Negotiator* provides the following definition: "an interpersonal decision-making process by which two or more people agree how to allocate scarce resources." Leigh Thompson, *The Mind and Heart of the Negotiator* (Upper Saddle River, NJ: Prentice Hall, 2001), p. 2.

[2]*Herb Cohen, presentation at the Learning Annex, San Diego, CA, May 22, 2001.

# Objectives of Negotiation

Several objectives are common to all procurement/sales negotiations:

- To obtain the quality specified.
- To obtain a fair and reasonable price.
- To get the supplier to perform the contract on time.

  In addition, the following objectives frequently must be met:

- To exert some control over the manner in which the contract is performed.
- To persuade the supplier to give maximum cooperation to the purchasing company.
- To develop a sound and continuing relationship with competent suppliers.
- To create a long-term relationship with a highly qualified supplier.

## Quality

In most cases, the negotiator's objectives require obtaining the quality specified by design engineering or by the user group. In some cases, however, quality itself may be a variable. For example, assume that the cost per unit for a critical item of material, with a guarantee of no more than 1,000 defective parts per million incoming parts, is $5. Further, assume that the cost per unit with a guarantee of no more than 100 defective parts per million is $10. Does the higher unit price result in higher or lower *total* costs? Obviously, a highly advanced and accurate management information system must be available to provide the data a negotiator needs to make an optimal decision.

## Fair and Reasonable Price

In many cases, the establishment of a fair and reasonable price for the desired level of quality becomes the principal focus of the negotiation process. This aspect of negotiation ranges in complexity from the use of price analysis to the more complex analysis of the potential supplier's cost elements. While the negotiator may focus on obtaining a fair price, this must be done in the context of obtaining the lowest *total* cost, as was discussed previously.

## On-Time Performance

Inability to meet delivery schedules for the quality and quantity specified is the single greatest supplier failure encountered in supply management operations. It results primarily from (1) failure of requisitioners to submit their purchase requests early enough to allow for necessary supply and manufacturing lead times and (2) failure of supply management personnel or the negotiating team to plan the delivery phase of negotiations properly. Because unrealistic delivery schedules reduce competition, increase prices, and jeopardize quality, it is important that supply management personnel or the negotiating team obtain realistic delivery schedules which suppliers can meet without endangering the other requirements of the purchase.

## Control

Deficiencies in supplier performance can seriously affect, and in some cases completely disrupt, the operations of the buying firm. For this reason, on important contracts negotiators should obtain controls which will assure compliance with the quality, quantity, delivery, and service terms of the contract. Traditionally, controls have been found to be useful in areas such as labor-hours of effort, levels of scientific talent, special test equipment requirements, the amounts and types of work to be subcontracted, and progress reports.

## Cooperation

Cooperation is best obtained by rewarding suppliers that perform well with future orders. In addition to subsequent orders, however, good suppliers expect courtesy, pleasant working relations, timely payment, and cooperation from their customers. Cooperation begets cooperation.

### Supplier Relationship Management

Negotiators should recognize that current actions usually constitute only part of a continuing relationship. Conditions which permit a negotiator to take unfair advantage of sellers invariably, with time, change to conditions which allow sellers to "hold up" the purchasing firm. For this reason, a negotiator must realize that any advantage *not honestly won* will, in all likelihood, be recovered by the supplier at a later date—probably with interest. Thus, as a matter of self-interest, negotiators must maintain a proper balance between their concern for a supplier's immediate performance on the one hand and their interest in the supplier's long-run performance on the other hand. This balancing is an important aspect of supplier relationship management.

In summary, the objectives of negotiation require investigation, with the supplier, of every area of negotiable concern—considering both short-term and, normally, long-term performance. Negotiation not only is used to reach an agreement on price but also is a process employed throughout the procurement cycle. The negotiator's major analytical tools for negotiating prices were discussed in the preceding chapters: things such as price and cost analysis and learning curves. Additional negotiating tools, as well as the development of strategy and tactics for negotiation, are discussed throughout this chapter.

# When to Negotiate

Negotiation is the appropriate method for determining the reasonableness of a price when competitive bidding or reverse auctions are impractical. Some of the most common circumstances dictating the use of negotiation are noted below:

- *When any of the five prerequisite criteria for competitive bidding are absent.* Those criteria were discussed in Chapter 11.
- *When many variable factors bear not only on price but also on quality and service.* Many high-dollar-value industrial and governmental contracts fall into this category.
- *When early supplier involvement* (as described in Chapter 5) *is employed.*
- *When the business risks and costs involved cannot be predetermined accurately.* When supply management seeks competitive bids in such circumstances, excessively high prices inevitably result. For self-protection, most suppliers factor every conceivable contingency into their bids. In practice, many of these contingencies do not occur. Hence, the customer firm unnecessarily pays for something not received.
- *When a customer firm is contracting for a portion of the seller's production capacity rather than for a product the seller has designed and manufactured.* In such cases, the customer firm has designed the product to be manufactured and, as an entrepreneur, assumes all risks related to the product's specifications and salability. In buying production capacity, the objective is not only to

attain production capability but also to acquire as much control over it as may be needed to improve the product and the production process. This type of control can be achieved only through negotiation and the voluntary cooperation of the supplier.

- *When tooling and setup costs represent a large percentage of the supplier's total costs.* For many contracts, the supplier must either make or buy many costly jigs, dies, fixtures, molds, special test equipment, gauges, and so on. Because of their special nature, these jigs and fixtures are limited in use primarily to the customer firm's contract. The division of special tooling costs between those firms and a customer is subject to negotiation. This negotiation includes a thorough analysis of future buyer or seller use of the tools, the length and dollar amount of the contract, the type of compensation that is appropriate, and so on.

- *When a long period of time is required to produce the items purchased.* In these circumstances, suitable economic price adjustment clauses must be negotiated. Also, opportunities for various improvements may develop, for example, new manufacturing methods, new packaging possibilities, substitute materials, new plant layouts, and new tools. Negotiation permits an examination and evaluation of all these potential improvements. Competitive bidding does not. What supplier, for example, would modify its plant layout to achieve increased efficiency to produce the buying firm's unique material without assurance of sufficient long-term business to cover the cost involved and a reasonable profit for the effort?

- *When production is interrupted frequently because of numerous change orders.* This is a common situation in fields with fast-changing technology. Contracts in those fields must provide for frequent change orders; otherwise, the product being purchased could become obsolete before the completion of production. The ways in which expensive changes in drawings, designs, and specifications are to be handled and paid for are subjects for mutual agreement arrived at through negotiation.

- *When a thorough analysis is required to solve a difficult make-or-buy decision.* Precisely what a seller is going to make and what it is going to subcontract should be decided by means of negotiation. When free to make its own decision, the seller often makes the easiest decision in terms of production scheduling. This may well be the most costly decision for the customer in terms of price.

- *When the products of a specific supplier are desired to the exclusion of others.* This can be either a single or a sole sourcing situation. In this case, competition is minimal or totally lacking. Terms and prices therefore must be negotiated to minimize unreasonable dictation of such terms by the seller.

In all these situations, negotiation is essential, and in each case, quality and service are as important as price.

## Supply Management's Role in Negotiation

Depending on the type of purchase, a supply management professional plays one of two distinct roles in negotiation. In the first role, he or she is the company's sole negotiator. In the second, the supply professional leads a cross-functional team of specialists which collectively negotiates on behalf of its company.

### The Supply Management Professional Acting Alone

For low-dollar-value noncritical items, a supply management professional normally acts alone. Typically, for this type of purchase, a negotiation conference is held in the supply management professional's office with the supplier's sales manager (the seller's sole negotiator). These two persons alone negotiate all the important terms and conditions of the contract.

A supply manager's "solo negotiation" is not limited to periodic formal negotiating sessions; such negotiations continue on a daily basis with both current suppliers and visiting salespersons who wish to become suppliers. Consider several typical examples. A supplier calls on the telephone and informs the supply manager that prices are to be raised 20 percent within 60 days. The supply manager responds with the thought that production in her company's plant is slack and that a price rise as high as 20 percent could well trigger a "make" decision instead of what is now a "buy" decision. The supply manager is negotiating!

A seller's value analyst discovers a substantially less expensive method of manufacturing one of the purchasing firm's products. However, there is one drawback: An expensive new machine is required for the job. The supplier's sales representative informs the supply manager of the discovery. The supply manager and an engineer study the concept and determine that it is a good one. The two thank the sales representative for introducing the new idea. At the same time, the supply manager explains that his or her company is financially unable, at this time, to invest in the required new machine. Further, the supply manager conjectures that if the seller's company purchased the machine, the supply manager could get his company to reconsider the rejected long-term contract the seller proposed last year. Informal negotiations are being conducted.

A salesperson calls, and the supply manager says, "I have been thinking about your contract with us. Under the contract, our purchases now total roughly $60,000 per year, primarily for valves. But your company also manufactures a number of fittings that we use. If these fittings were combined with the purchase of the valves, what benefits would your company be able to grant us?" Another informal negotiation is under way.

The preceding year a supply manager purchased $300,000 worth of liquid oxygen in individual cylinders from a single supplier. Because of its high dollar value, the supply manager began to analyze oxygen usage requirements thoroughly. In this analysis, an interesting fact was discovered. If a bulk storage tank was installed at the purchasing firm's plant (at a cost of $160,000) and the suppliers personnel delivered the required liquid oxygen to the tanks, $70,000 could be saved per year. When the supplier's salesperson called, she was informed of the supply manager's study and was given the supply manager's worksheets to review and study. Negotiations were under way, and the total cost of liquid oxygen soon would be reduced.

## The Supply Management Professional as the Negotiating Team Leader

The complexity of a purchasing contract frequently correlates directly with the complexity of the item being purchased. For high-value, technically oriented contracts (such as those developed for the purchase of high-technology products, capital equipment, and research and development projects) and for the development of long-term relationships in which the supplier's production flows into the buying firm's operation, the supply manager typically is no longer qualified to act as a sole negotiator. His or her role therefore shifts from that of sole negotiator to that of negotiating team leader. A typical team consists of two to eight members, depending on the complexity and importance of the purchase to be made. Team members are selected for their expertise in the technical or business fields needed to optimize the team's negotiating strength. Customarily, members are from fields such as design engineering, manufacturing engineering, cost analysis, estimating, finance, production, traffic, supply management, and legal affairs.

Frequently, those team members have limited knowledge and skill in *professional* negotiations. Perhaps the largest challenge faced by the negotiation team leader is the belief by many of his or her teammates that they "know" how to negotiate. The truth of the matter is that most people have had experience in "haggling" but not in professional negotiation. Thus, the team leader must coach his or her teammates in the use of professional practices.

In the team approach to negotiation, the supply manager frequently serves as the leader of the team (and is called the negotiator). In this capacity, he or she functions as the coordinator of a heterogeneous group of specialists from several functional areas who can be expected to view similar matters differently. As the leader of the team, the negotiator must weld the team members into an integrated whole. The team leader must draw on the specialized knowledge of each team member and combine that expertise with his or her own. To accomplish this, it is very important that an overall strategy be developed by the team and that each team member be assigned a specific role. Additionally, mock negotiations should be included as one of the final steps in team preparation. Mock negotiations normally constitute the best possible insurance to preclude the team's committing the most costly error in negotiation—that of the members speaking out of turn and thus revealing their firm's position to the seller's team. In this way, the negotiating team develops a sound, unified approach to uncover, analyze, and resolve (from a companywide point of view) all the important issues applicable to the contract under negotiation.

# The Negotiation Process

In the broadest sense, negotiation begins with a firm's requirements for specific materials or services. The ultimate in purchasing value is possible only if design, production or operations, supply management, and marketing are able to reconcile their differing views with respect to specifications or the statement of work (SOW). The more open the specifications, the greater the leverage of the negotiating team. Negotiators must always think in terms of total cost and total value, not in terms of price alone.

The prelude to a negotiation normally begins with supply management's request for proposals from potential suppliers. The formal negotiation process consists of three major phases: (1) preparation, (2) face-to-face discussions which result in agreement on all the items in and conditions of a contract or a decision not to enter into an agreement with the potential supplier, and (3) the debriefing in which the negotiating team members review both the preparation and the face-to-face discussions for lessons learned.

## Preparation

*Ninety percent or more of the time involved in a successful negotiation is invested in preparation for the actual face-to-face discussions.* The negotiator must (1) possess or gain a technical understanding of the item or service to be purchased, (2) analyze the relative bargaining positions of both parties, (3) have conducted a price or cost analysis (as appropriate), (4) know the seller, (5) be aware of cultural nuances, and (6) be thoroughly prepared.

**Know the Item or Service**    The negotiator does not need to understand all the technical ramifications of the item being purchased. However, it is essential that he, she, or they have a general understanding of what is being purchased, the production or services process involved, and any other issues that will affect quality, timeliness of performance, and cost of production. The negotiator should understand the item's intended use, any limitations, and the existence of potential substitutes. The buyer should be aware of any prospective engineering problems which may arise. The negotiator should be aware of the item's procurement history and likely future requirements. Ideally, the negotiator will be familiar with any phraseology or customs relevant to the industry. A similar level of knowledge is appropriate in purchasing equipment and services.

**The Seller's Bargaining Strength**   The seller's bargaining strength usually depends on three basic factors: (1) how badly the seller wants the contract, (2) how certain he or she feels of getting it, and (3) how much time is available to reach agreement on suitable terms.

The negotiator should encounter no difficulty in determining how urgently a seller wants a contract. The frequency with which the salesperson calls and general market conditions are positive indicators of seller interest. The sellers' annual profit and loss statements, as well as miscellaneous reports concerning backlog, volume of operations, and trends, are valuable sources of information about individual sellers. Publications such as the Department of Commerce's "Economic Indicators," *The Federal Reserve Bulletin,* industrial trade papers, the Institute for Supply Management™ (formerly NAPM) *Report on Business*, and local newspapers provide a wealth of basic information about potential suppliers and their industries in general.

The less a seller needs or wants a contract, the more powerful its bargaining position becomes. The presence of an industry boom, for example, places it in a strong position. In contrast, when a seller finds itself in a general recession or in an industry plagued with excess capacity, its bargaining position is decidedly weakened.

If a seller learns that its prices are lower than the competition's or learns from engineering, production, or services personnel that it is a preferred or sole source of supply, it naturally concludes that its chances of getting the contract are next to certain. In these circumstances, a supplier may become very difficult to deal with during negotiations. In extreme situations, it may be unwilling to make any concessions whatever. When this happens, the negotiator sometimes has only one alternative—to accept the supplier's terms.

When trapped by such circumstances, a negotiator can threaten to search for other sources. Such threats are likely to be ineffective unless the seller knows that alternative sources are actually available and interested in the business. An alternative source of possible power which may be effective when patents are not involved is the threat to manufacture the needed item in the buyer's plant. When made realistically—when the supplier believes the buyer has the technical capability, the determination, and the capacity to make the product or service—such a threat frequently gains concessions.

A buying firm's negotiating position is always strengthened when the company has a clear policy that permits only members of its supply management department to discuss pricing, timing, and other commercial terms with sellers. Most prenegotiation information leaks that give sellers a feeling of confidence about getting a contract occur in the technical departments of a firm. Those leaks can be extremely costly, and because they often are not detected by general management, they can be a continuing source of unnecessarily high costs.

Short lead times drastically reduce one's negotiating strength. Conversely, they significantly increase the seller's bargaining strength. Once a supplier knows that a negotiator has a tight deadline, it becomes easy for the supplier to drag its feet and then negotiate favorable terms at the last minute, when the negotiator is under severe pressure to consummate the contract.

**The Buyer's Bargaining Strength**   The buyer's bargaining strength usually depends on four basic factors: the extent of competition among potential suppliers, the adequacy of cost or price analysis, the logic and reasoning behind the challenged cost, and the thoroughness with which the supply manager and all other members of the buying team have prepared for the negotiation.

Intense supplier competition always strengthens a buyer's position. Competition is always keenest when a number of competent sellers eagerly want an order. General economic conditions can bear heavily on the extent to which a firm really wants to compete. A firm's shop load, inventory position, and back-order position or the demand for its services are typical factors that also bear heavily on the ever-changing competitive climate.

When necessary, a supply manager can increase competition by developing new suppliers; making items in-house rather than buying them; buying suppliers' companies; providing tools, money, and management to competent but financially weak suppliers; and, above all, hiring highly skilled supply managers.

**The Adequacy of Cost or Price Analysis**    A comprehensive knowledge of cost analysis and price analysis is one of the basic responsibilities of all supply managers who are involved in negotiations. When an initial contract is awarded for a portion of a supplier's production capacity rather than for a finished product, cost analysis becomes vital. In this situation, the negotiators are not prepared to explore with the supplier the reasonableness of its proposals until after a comprehensive analysis of all applicable costs has been completed. Cost analysis in such purchases, in a very real sense, is a substitute for direct competition. Price analysis is usually sufficient to assure that prices are reasonable in contracts for common commercial items. In the aggregate, the greater the amount of available cost, price, and financial data, the greater the chances for a successful negotiation.

Caution must be exercised not to overfocus on price. If a collaborative long-term relationship is desired, price must be placed in the proper context: It is only one aspect of the negotiation!

**Know the Seller**    Professional negotiators should endeavor to know and understand both the prospective supplier firm and its representatives. World-class supply managers prepare for critical negotiations by reviewing financial data and articles dealing with prospective suppliers. The supply managers and all negotiating team members know how the supplier's business is faring, are aware of key personnel changes, and so on. One of the keys to successful negotiations is to put oneself in the other person's shoes, to understand his or her wants and needs. This level of preparation pays dividends when one is conducting face-to-face negotiations!

**Cultural Nuances**    A clear understanding of the effects and nuances of cultural similarities and differences is an essential skill for a contemporary business manager. Effective global executives are those with the ability to develop and use global strategic skills; manage change and transition; [and] manage cultural diversity and function within flexible organizational structures; work with others and in teams; communicate; and learn and transfer knowledge in an organization.[3]

**The Thoroughness of Preparation**    Knowledge is power. The more knowledge a negotiator acquires about the theory and practice of negotiation, the seller's negotiating position, and the product or service being purchased, the stronger his or her negotiating stance will be. A negotiator without thorough knowledge of the product being purchased is greatly handicapped. A negotiator is similarly handicapped if he or she has not studied and analyzed every detail of the supplier's proposal. Whenever feasible, before requesting proposals, a negotiator should develop an estimate of the price and value levels for the items or services being purchased. Knowledge of current economic conditions in the market for the product or service in question is also an essential element of preparation.

---

[3]Gerry, Darlington, "Culture: A Theoretical Review," in *Managing across Cultures: Issues and Perspectives*, ed. Pat Joynt and Malcom Warner. (London: International Thompson Business Press, 1996). Cited in a paper by James D. Reeds, "Understanding Cultural Diversity: The Influence of National Culture in Global Purchasing," 1998 International Conference of the Australian Institute of Purchasing and Materials Management, Paramatta, New South Wales, Australia, October 19, 1998.

Before the face-to-face negotiating session, all members of the negotiating team must evaluate all relevant data and carefully assess their own and the supplier's strengths and weaknesses. From this assessment, they develop not only a basic strategy of operation but also specific negotiating tactics. Alert suppliers readily recognize negotiators who are not prepared. They gladly accept the real and psychological bargaining advantage that comes to them from lack of preparation by members of the buying firm's negotiating team.

## Establishing Objectives

The outcome of contract negotiations hinges on relative buyer-seller power, information, negotiating skills, and the way both sides perceive the logic of the impending negotiations. Each of these controlling factors can be influenced by adroit advanced planning. This is why proper planning and preparation is, without question, the most important step in successful negotiations.

As part of the preparation process, the negotiating team should establish objectives. Negotiation objectives must be specific. General objectives such as "lower than previous prices," "good delivery," and "satisfactory technical assistance" are inadequate. For each term and condition to be negotiated, the negotiating team should develop three specific positions: (1) an objective position (or target), (2) a minimum position, and (3) a maximum position. Using the cost objective as an example, the minimum position is developed on the premise that every required seller action will turn out satisfactorily and be done with minimum cost. The maximum position is developed on the premise that a large number of required seller actions will turn out unsatisfactorily and be done with maximum cost. The objective position is the best estimate of what he, she, or they expect the seller's actual costs plus a fair profit to be.

In developing concrete objectives, desired or required dates are established for delivery schedules, desired or required numerical ranges for quality acceptance, and dollar levels for applicable elements of cost. The major elements of cost which traditionally are negotiated—and for which objective, maximum, and minimum positions are developed—include quantity of labor, wage rates, quantity of materials, prices of materials, factory overhead, engineering expense, tooling expense, general and administrative expense, and profit. In addition to determining a position for each major element of cost, the supply manager and the negotiating team members must estimate the objective, maximum, and minimum positions of the seller. Determining the seller's maximum position is easy; it is the offer made in the seller's proposal.

In addition to costs and prices, delivery schedules, and acceptable quality levels, specific objectives should be established for all items that will be discussed during the negotiation, including the following:

- All technical aspects of the purchase.
- Types of materials and substitutes.
- Buyer-furnished material and equipment.
- The mode of transportation.
- Warranty terms and conditions.
- Payment terms (including discount provisions).
- Liability for claims and damage.
- F.O.B. point.
- General terms and conditions.
- Details on how a service is to be performed.

Other objectives may include:

- Progress reports.

- Production control plans.
- Escalation/de-escalation provisions.
- Incentive arrangements.
- Patents and infringement protection.
- Packaging.
- Title to special tools and equipment.
- Disposition of damaged goods and off-spec (nonconforming) materials.

Simulations and role-playing negotiation exercises conducted at the University of San Diego over a 10-year period demonstrate that negotiators who establish a demanding objective *which is within the realm of reasonableness* normally achieve a more favorable outcome than do those who enter the negotiation with a less demanding objective.

### Identify the Desired Type of Relationship

We find it extremely desirable to determine the type of relationship which we hope to establish and/or maintain during and after the face-to-face discussions. The three primary approaches are transactional, collaborative, and alliance. These relationships were described in detail in Chapter 4. As we shall see shortly, the type of relationship desired affects the tactics employed.

## Five Powerful Preparation Activities

**The BATNA** Perhaps the most important aspect of preparation is the development of the firm's BATNA, an acronym for the "best alternative to a negotiated agreement," a term coined years ago by Roger Fisher and Bill Ury in their book *Getting to Yes*. The firm's BATNA describes what it would do if the negotiation were unsuccessful. The BATNA may be an alternative supplier (at a most likely price), a decision to "make," or incorporation of a substitute material (at a most likely total cost of ownership).

Insight into or an accurate estimate of the supplier's BATNA on each issue is of equal importance. A Fortune 500 company invests considerable resources (including the use of consulting services) in developing its suppliers' BATNAs on key procurements.

**The Agenda** Successful negotiators spend considerable time and effort developing their agendas before face-to-face discussions. They place major emphasis on the sequence in which they plan to address issues during all phases of the face-to-face discussions. Experience indicates that issues that are easier to agree on should be addressed early. Seasoned professionals sprinkle "throwaways" throughout their agendas but never "give" something for "nothing"; that is, they expect something in return!

All negotiations center on specific issues. One of the difficult tasks of negotiation is to define fully the important issues which are to be included on the agenda and then make sure the discussion is confined to those issues. Most authorities believe that the issues should be discussed in the order of their probable ease of solution. With this priority system, an atmosphere of cooperation and momentum can develop that may facilitate solving the more difficult issues.

**"Murder Boards" and Mock Negotiations** Experienced negotiators frequently finalize their preparation through the use of "murder boards" and mock negotiations. A murder board consists of senior supply management, finance, manufacturing, quality, engineering, operations, marketing, and general management personnel. The negotiating team presents its agenda, objectives, and tactics for the forthcoming negotiations. Members of the murder board dissect the negotiating plan in an effort to identify avoidable problems.

Mock negotiations allow the members of a negotiating team to prepare for the negotiation through a simulation of what is likely to occur during the face-to-face discussions. Other members of the organization (preferably from general management) play the roles of the supplier's negotiating team members during the simulated negotiation. Suppliers generally do a good job of preparing for critical negotiations through the use of murder boards or mock negotiations. It is essential that the buying team be equally well prepared.

Murder boards and mock negotiations enhance the negotiating team's level of preparation. Further, the processes result in general management's being aware of the negotiating team's agenda, objectives, and tactics. If the subsequent negotiations deadlock, management is in a position to step in and revitalize critical negotiations.

**Crib Sheets**   Experience gained through 10 years of directing negotiation courses demonstrates that the development and use of a "crib sheet" is an extraordinarily powerful preparation tool. The process of developing the crib sheet reinforces and upgrades the preparation process. Of equal importance, the negotiating team members function much more professionally when they have a single document to which they can refer. (Obviously, this sheet must be protected from "the other side"!)

**Draft Agreements**   The development of one or more "ideal" agreements also is a powerful preparation tool. The process of developing such agreements helps hone the negotiating team, and possessing such a document(s) has been shown to expedite closure of the face-to-face process.

# Face-to-Face Discussions

Establishing trust is a key ingredient in effective negotiations. Leigh Thompson lists several activities which can facilitate the development of a reasonable level of trust: agree on a common goal or shared vision, expand the pie, use fairness criteria that everyone can buy into, capitalize on network connections, find a shared problem or shared enemy (perhaps another supply chain), focus on the future (instead of the past), and use shared procedures.[4]

## Fact Finding

During the initial phase of a meeting with the potential supplier, professional negotiators limit the discussion to fact finding. Any inconsistencies between the supplier's proposal and the negotiator's information are investigated. Fact finding should continue until the negotiator has a complete understanding of the supplier's proposal. Questions of a how, what, when, who, and why nature are used by the negotiator. Experience has shown that when the negotiator limits this initial phase to fact finding, a satisfactory agreement normally results with a minimum of hassle and disagreement. During the fact-finding process, the negotiator should gain a better understanding of both the supplier's interests and the supplier's strengths and weaknesses.

The buying and selling representatives should disclose their interests, not their objectives. Altogether too much time is wasted in haggling over positions. Professional negotiators quickly learn their opposite's

---

[4]Leigh Thompson, *The Mind and Heart of the Negotiator* (Upper Saddle River, NJ: Prentice-Hall, 2001), p. 136.

interests. It is much easier to satisfy interests than it is to move one's opposites off their positions. On completion of the fact-finding process, the negotiator should call for a recess or caucus.

## Recess

During the recess, the negotiating team should reassess its relative strengths and weaknesses as well as those of the supplier. It also may want to review and refine its cost estimate and any other estimates or assumptions. The team then should review and revise its objectives and their acceptable ranges. Next, the team should reorganize the agenda it desires to pursue when the two teams return to the negotiating table.

## Narrowing the Differences

When the formal negotiations reconvene, the negotiator defines each issue, states the facts (and any underlying assumptions), and attempts to convince the supplier's representative(s) that the negotiator's position is reasonable. If agreement cannot be reached on an issue, the negotiator moves on to the next issue. Frequently, discussions on a subsequent issue will unblock an earlier deadlock.

During this phase of the negotiating process, problem solving and compromise are used to find creative solutions in which both parties win. For example, the buying team's manufacturing engineers may identify a more cost-effective process than the supplier had planned to use. Small acceptable changes in packaging, schedule, or tolerances; offers by the customer to furnish a material or an item of equipment; and payment terms (including possible advance payments) can unblock negotiations to the benefit of both parties.

The package approach lends itself to situations in which several issues are on the table. Let us assume there are five issues: A, B, C, D, and E. The two parties address issue A and reach tentative agreement. They then address B—no agreement. One party then says, "Let's put B on hold." On to C—agreement. On to D—no agreement. And no agreement on E. Then one party constructs and proposes a package (addressing all five points) which it feels is fair and appropriate for consideration. Further, the proposing party suggests that the package approach be looked at as a full bucket of water. If something flows into the bucket (e.g., a higher price, longer lead time), something flows out (improved warranty, better service, etc.). Experience has shown that the combination of the package approach and the full bucket of water is a most attractive way of avoiding deadlocks!

In most instances, it is possible to reach a satisfactory agreement through the use of these procedures. If a satisfactory agreement cannot be reached, the negotiating team has the choice of adjourning (an attractive alternative for the buyer if another supplier is waiting in the wings) or moving on to hard bargaining.

## Hard Bargaining

Hard bargaining, the last resort, involves the use of take-it-or-leave-it tactics. Its use is limited to one-time or adversarial situations in which long-term collaborative relationships are not an objective. The negotiating team should review and revise its objectives carefully and professionally and, if absolutely necessary, give the supplier the option of accepting or rejecting its final proposal. Possession of a BATNA (best alternative to a negotiated agreement) protects the buying firm from entering into an unwise agreement. An experienced negotiator does not bluff unless he or she is willing to have the bluff called. Unless a one-time purchase of an item already produced (e.g., an automobile on a dealer's lot) is involved, a wise negotiator avoids having the seller feel that it has been abused or treated unfairly Such feelings set the stage for future confrontations, arguments, unsatisfactory performance, and possible claims.

# Techniques

Negotiation techniques (tactics) are a negotiator's working tools. A negotiator uses them to achieve his or her goals. In the hands of a skillful negotiator, these tools are powerful weapons. In the hands of a novice, they can be dangerous booby traps. Competent negotiators therefore spend a great deal of time studying and perfecting the use of these techniques. There are so many negotiating techniques that not all can be discussed here. Those selected for discussion represent some of the techniques that have proved to be most important and most effective for the authors, their colleagues and students, and the working professionals entrusted to their guidance.

The objective of negotiation is agreement. Even though agreement is the fundamental goal of negotiation, sometimes negotiations end without agreement. In the short run, not reaching an agreement is better than reaching an unsatisfactory agreement. However, experienced negotiators seldom let negotiations break down completely. They do not intentionally maneuver or let their opponents maneuver themselves into take-it-or-leave-it or walkout situations unless they are involved in a one-time or adversarial relationship.

Negotiating techniques can be divided into three categories: (1) those which are universally applicable, (2) those which are applicable to transactional (and frequently adversarial) dealings, and (3) those which are applicable to collaborative and alliance relationships.

## Universally Applicable Techniques

These are techniques which are applicable to all negotiations, whether in transactional dealings or in collaborative relationships.

**Getting to Know You** Not only is this the title of an old hit tune, it is a powerful and effective negotiation technique! The negotiator is not dealing with abstract representatives but with human beings. If possible, he or she should get to know the individuals representing the seller before the face-to-face phase of the negotiation begins. Americans tend to be too eager to rush into negotiations without getting to know and understand the other side's representatives. We have much to learn from members of other cultures who spend a good amount of time becoming acquainted with those with whom they are to negotiate before entering into the formal face-to-face phase of negotiations. Those negotiators find ways to meet the seller's representatives informally. If possible, they arrive before the face-to-face negotiation is scheduled to begin and stay after it ends.

**Use Diversions** On the human side of negotiations, a negotiator who knows the seller personally or has carefully studied his or her personal behavior patterns (as should be the case) has an advantage. When tempers start to get out of hand, as they occasionally do, the experienced negotiator quickly diverts attention from the issue at hand. At such times a joke, an anecdote, or a coffee (or tea) break can be an effective means of easing tensions. This type of diversion is usually more easily accomplished when the participants know which situations are most irritating to their opposites.

**Use Questions Effectively** The wise use of questions is one of the most important techniques available in negotiation. By properly timing and phrasing questions, the negotiator can control the progress and direction of the negotiation. A perceptive question can forcefully yet tactfully attack the supplier's position.

Similarly, the negotiator can effectively defend his or her own position by asking the seller to evaluate certain carefully chosen data the negotiator has developed.

The technique of answering questions properly sometimes is as important as the technique of asking them properly. A successful negotiator knows when to answer, when not to answer, when to answer clearly, and when to answer vaguely. Not all questions require an answer. Many questions are asked for which the seller knows there is no answer; therefore, a reply is not really expected.

The correct answer to questions in negotiation is not governed by the criteria that govern the correct answer to questions in most other situations. For negotiation questions, the correct answer is the answer that furthers the negotiator's short-term tactics or long-range strategy. Labor leaders and politicians are experts at asking and answering questions. Their questions and answers are made to correlate with their strategic plans (strike platforms, party platforms, and so on). To an uninformed observer, it often appears that the answers given by politicians and labor leaders do not relate to the questions they are asked, but that observation is only partially correct. When answering questions, politicians and labor leaders tell their listeners what they want them to know about their platforms whether or not the responses fully answer the questions asked.

Successful negotiators realize that negotiation sessions are not like the classroom, where precise answers earn high marks. In negotiation, the purpose of questions and answers is not to illustrate to the seller how smart the negotiator is. Rather, it is to ferret out the seller's objectives and learn as much as possible about how the seller's representatives intend to maneuver to achieve them. For this purpose, precise answers are sometimes the wrong answers. The correct degree of precision is dictated by the particular circumstances of each negotiation.

**Use Positive Statements**    As with sophisticated questions, perceptively used positive statements can have a favorable influence on the course of negotiations. For example, assume a negotiator knows that certain questions will evoke an emotional reaction from the seller. The questions are asked, and an opportunity is created for the proper use of a positive statement. A competent negotiator will say something like this: "I see your point, and I understand how you feel about this matter. Your point is well taken." Contrast the effect of this type of positive response with that of an emotional, negative response in which the negotiator tells the seller that he or she is "dead wrong." When a negotiator tells a seller that the seller's viewpoint is understood and considered reasonable even though the negotiator does not agree with it, the seller is more likely to consider the negotiator's viewpoint objectively.

Machiavelli, in *The Prince,* gave the world some unusually sage advice about the use and misuse of positive statements: "I hold it to be proof of great prudence for men to abstain from threats and insulting words toward anyone, for neither . . . diminishes the strength of the enemy; but the one makes him more cautious, and the other increases his hatred of you, and makes him more persevering in his efforts to injure you."[5]

**Be a Good Listener**    Generally, salespeople thoroughly enjoy talking. Consequently, negotiators should let them talk. While talking, they very often talk themselves into concessions that a negotiator never could gain through negotiation. Listening, per se, recognizes a basic need of a seller. Additionally, listening carefully to a seller's choice of words, phrases, and tone of voice, while at the same time observing his or her gestures and other uses of body language, can be rewarding. By observing such actions, a negotiator can gain many clues about a seller's negotiating position.

---

[5]Niccolo Machiavelli, *The Prince*, Great Books of the Western World, *Encyclopedia Britannica*, 1982, vol. 23.

**Be Considerate of Sellers**   A small number of negotiation experts contend that negotiations are best won by negotiators who are as brutal and arbitrary as possible. This is definitely a minority opinion. Unquestionably, there are some purchasing situations in which a merciless frontal assault can be a proper and successful negotiating technique. However, for the vast majority of firms—those which seek profitable, continuing relationships with the seller—a more considerate and reasoned technique is recommended. Professionals lose no negotiating advantages whatsoever by being fully considerate of sellers personally, letting them save face, and reasonably satisfying their emotional needs.

## Transactional Techniques

Much negotiating literature is based on traditional, even adversarial (win-lose) approaches. Two effective books addressing this approach are Gerald Nierenberg's *The Complete Negotiator*[6] and Herb Cohen's *You Can Negotiate Anything*.[7] Two of the traditional tactics which deserve special emphasis are (1) keep the initiative and (2) never giving anything away.

**Keep the Initiative**   A negotiator should strive never to lose the initiative automatically obtained when the supplier's proposal is received and reviewed. There is a good deal of truth in the old saying that a good offense is the best defense. The negotiator should constantly "carry the game" to the supplier and keep the supplier on the defensive by confronting its representatives with point after point, making the supplier continually justify its position. For example, if the supplier states the cost of materials in dollars, the negotiator should ask the seller's representative to justify the figures with a bill of materials, appropriate scrap rates, and a full explanation of the manufacturing processes to be used. The more the negotiator bores in and the more pressure he or she maintains, the better his or her bargaining position will be. If the supplier's position seems sound, the negotiator can offer a counterproposal. In either case, the negotiator starts with the initiative and should work hard to retain it.

**Never Give Anything Away**   As a matter of strategy, a successful negotiator periodically lets the seller maneuver him or her into accepting one of the seller's proposals. This does not mean that the negotiator gives something away. He or she never "gives anything away." Professional negotiators always expect to get a concession in exchange. However, the negotiator does not feel obligated to match every concession made by the seller. Consequently, in the exchange process, a successful negotiator makes fewer concessions than does his or her less successful adversary. Through a continuation of this exchange process, a position close to the objectives of both parties usually is reached. Mutual concessions benefit both parties and a contract so negotiated is *mutually* advantageous, but it is not *equally* advantageous.

**Frame the Question**   Negotiating authority Herb Cohen points out that too many people allow "the other side" to frame the issue, in effect doing business on their terms. For example, the seller says, "Do you want alternative A or B?" The professional negotiator responds, "Those certainly may be viable options, but let's develop some others."[8]

**The Dynamics of a Transactional Negotiation**   Typically, the two parties' positions appear as shown in Figure 16.1. The seller's positions are generally all higher than the corresponding positions of the buying firm. The closer the two objectives are initially, the easier the negotiations. As negotiations proceed, the

---

[6]Gerald Nierenberg, *The Complete Negotiator* (New York: Nierenberg & Zeif, 1986).

[7]Herb Cohen, *You Can Negotiate Anything*, 2d ed. (New York: Bantam Books, 1982).

[8]Ibid.

**Figure 16.1** | Dynamics of Transactional Negotiation

seller tends to make concessions from its maximum position toward its objective. Simultaneously, the buying firm's negotiators reduce their demands, moving from the minimum position toward their objective.[9] Usually, little difficulty arises during this preliminary skirmish. That is not to say that this part of the negotiation process is easy or does not take time. Normally, vigorous testing is required to convince each party that the other is actually at his or her objective. Each party attempts to convince the other that the objective has been reached before this has in fact occurred. As each party approaches its objective, negotiation becomes difficult. The distance between the buying firm's objective and the supplier's objective can well be called the "essence" or "heart" of the negotiation. (See Figure 16.1.) Any concession made by either party from its objective position will appear unreasonable to the other party, based on the previous analysis of the facts. Changes in position, therefore, must now be the result of either logical persuasion and negotiating skills (entailing further investigation, analysis, and reassessment of the facts) or the pressure of brute economic strength.

A skillful negotiator stands out in the area of objective persuasion. He or she makes progress by uncovering new facts and additional areas of negotiation that permit the supplier to reduce its demands.

For example, an analysis of the supplier's manufacturing or services operations might reveal that if lead time were increased by only one week, the job could be done with fewer machines or human resources. This change could reduce the supplier's setup and scheduling costs substantially, thus permitting a price reduction. Additional lead time might be made available by making a slight modification in the buyer's production schedule. The cost of making this change could well be much less than the seller's savings from the longer production runs. Thus, both parties would profit from the change. It is this type of situation that competent negotiators constantly seek to discover and exploit in their attempt to close the gap between the seller's objective and their own. Such situations have the highly desirable effect of benefiting each party at no expense to the other party.

In some sole-source negotiations, the seller's objective is to maximize its position at the expense of the buying firm. In these situations, a continuing relationship is of secondary interest to the seller; therefore, it uses its bargaining strength to maximize price rather than to achieve a mutually advantageous contract that will lead to continued business. A negotiator who senses such a situation should start the negotiations by attacking the reasonableness of the seller's cost breakdown, using his or her own prepared cost estimates as the basis for those challenges. In the absence of competition, this is a negotiator's most logical and effective plan

---

[9]If the negotiator believes there is a possibility of actually achieving the minimum position, he, she, or they should open with a position below this point—*provided that such a position can be logically supported.*

of action. If the supplier refuses to divulge its cost data, the negotiator has only three available courses of action. He or she can appeal to the seller's sense of reason, pointing out the potential negative long-run implications of such actions. A second approach is to fight force with force by threatening to use substitutes or to redesign and manufacture the product or service. A third alternative is to develop and refine the firm's cost-estimating models and utilize them more forcefully in pursuing the original course of negotiating action.

When faced with this type of problem, the negotiator must attempt to bring the supplier's price as close to the objective as possible. In the short run, the negotiator usually pays the seller's price. In the long run, the negotiator works toward the development of competing sources, substitute products, and compromises with the supplier.

If a seller's negotiation objective is to resolve issues as quickly as possible by employing logical analysis rather than economic bargaining power, it is sometimes reasonable for the negotiator to start the negotiations by proposing his or her actual objective as the counteroffer to the seller's proposal. In fact, in industrial situations in which continuing relationships are the rule, each successive negotiation brings the objectives of both parties ever closer together. Under these conditions, representatives of the buying and selling firms need develop only their objective positions; there is no need for maximum and minimum positions.

## Collaborative and Alliance Negotiating Techniques

*Getting to Yes* by Roger Fisher and William Ury[10] is the most widely read book written on collaborative negotiations. The authors introduce what they call "the principled negotiation method of focusing on basic interests, mutually satisfying options, and fair standards, resulting in a wise agreement."

Fisher and Ury's method calls for the use of four powerful techniques:

- Separate the people (negotiators) from the problem (quality, price, etc.).
- Focus on interests, not positions.
- Invent options for mutual gain.
- Insist on using objective criteria.

Experience demonstrates that applying these techniques to collaborative (or win-win) negotiations will result in wise agreements and provide the basis of success for long-term relationships. Many of these relationships blossom into preferred partnerships and even into strategic supply alliances.

**Separate the People from the Problem**    Successful negotiators divide the negotiation into two components: the people issue and the technical issues such as quality, time, and price. People issues require negotiators to understand where the other party is coming from. In effect, the negotiators must walk in the shoes of the seller's representatives. Professional negotiators work at ensuring that they understand the other party, frequently rephrasing what they have heard to ensure understanding. In addition, they frequently ask the seller's representatives to describe in their own words what the negotiator has said.

Emotions frequently get in the way of successful negotiations. Both parties to a negotiation have a right to get upset or angry and to express those emotions. Wise negotiators allow their opposites to let steam off without taking offense or allowing the negotiation to be disrupted. The perception or belief that the "other side" is stubborn or irrational is likely to manifest itself in exactly such behavior. Stop and walk in their shoes! The most constructive negotiations occur when the representatives of the buying and selling organizations work together in a search for a fair agreement in which both sides are better off than they would be if there were no agreement.

---

[10]Roger Fisher and William Ury, *Getting to Yes* (Boston: Houghton Mifflin, 1981; New York: Penguin Books, 1991).

**Focus on Interests**    During the fact-finding phase of face-to-face negotiations, a professional negotiator learns the seller's interests while disclosing his or her own interests (but not objectives!). During the third phase (narrowing the differences), both parties work at reconciling and satisfying interests, not positions. Since both buyer and seller normally have multiple interests, it is wise to identify all of them and then work at developing a solution (agreement) which satisfies most or all of those interests. This approach calls on creativity and frequently results in increasing the size of the pie: the package of benefits to be shared by the two parties.

James K. Sebenius of the Harvard Business School said that "interest-driven bargainers see the process primarily as a reconciliation of underlying interest: you have one set of interests, I have another and through joint problem solving we should be better able to meet both sets of interest and thus create new value."[11]

**Invent Options for Mutual Gain**    Fisher and Ury's third principle flows from the use of creativity to develop many options. When both parties become involved in creativity or brainstorming, they generate creative solutions in which both parties benefit. Two rules of thumb are to (1) develop many options and (2) remain in option generation past the point of comfort. Many of the most creative ideas require time and even discomfort to develop. Only after a list including one or more truly creative ideas has been developed should the negotiators attempt to select from the list.

**Use Objective Criteria**    When a long-term relationship is an objective of both parties, the use of objective criteria will prevent much positional negotiation—and the possibility of disrupting or destroying the relationship. For example, if price is the issue under discussion, possible objective criteria could include (1) the supplier's agreed-to allowable costs plus a reasonable profit, (2) development of a cost model to be used as the basis of the price, (3) a market-based pricing methodology, or (4) target (design-to-cost) pricing (these issues were all discussed in Chapter 14.) After the identification of four possible objective criteria, the issue now becomes a discussion of which criterion, or combination of them, should be applied.

**Benefits Are Not Divided Equally**    In some supply management circles, there is a common misunderstanding that successful negotiation means an equal distribution of the benefits. While both buyer and seller should benefit from a well-negotiated contract, the benefits seldom are divided 50–50. On the basis of years of observation, 60 to 70 percent of the benefits of a typical negotiated contract go to the more skillful negotiator, leaving 30 to 40 percent for the less skilled negotiator. But both parties are better off than they would be if there were no agreement. (This is the meaning of a "win-win" outcome.)

## The Debriefing: An Incredible Learning Opportunity

Thompson points out, "Most people have little opportunity to learn how to negotiate effectively. The problem is not lack of experience but a shortage of accurate and timely feedback."[12]

Experience gained in academia demonstrates that a 15-minute debriefing conducted by the negotiating team provides an incredible opportunity for learning and improvement in future negotiations. After the completion of each negotiation, the negotiating teams are required to conduct a debriefing of their preparation process. They must identify both what was done well during their preparation process and the lessons they learned (e.g., what could/should have been done more professionally).

---

[11]James K. Sebenius, "Six Habits of Merely Effective Negotiators," *Harvard Business Review,* April 2001, pp. 87–95.

[12]Thompson, *The Mind and Heart of the Negotiator, op cit*, p. 5.

The team members then are required to analyze their "face-to-face" activities. They identify (reinforce) what went well, and then they identify weaknesses in their processes. (Feedback is at both an individual and a team level.) Undergraduates and graduates alike maintain that debriefing is a marvelous tool which they plan to implement in the "real world."

# Documentation

Personnel turnover and the frailties of the human memory make accurate documentation of a negotiation essential. The documentation must permit a rapid reconstruction of all significant considerations and agreements.

Documentation begins in the supply management office with the receipt of a purchase requisition and continues with the selection of potential suppliers and their proposals. Documentation of the actual negotiation must be adequate to allow someone other than the buyer to understand what was agreed to, how, and why. Burt, Norquist, and Anklesaria suggest the following format for the documentation of negotiations:[13]

**Subject**   This is a memorandum designed for readers with many different orientations. This section, together with the introductory summary, should give the reader a complete overview of the negotiation, including information such as the supplier's name and location, the contract number, and a brief description of what is being purchased.

**Introductory Summary**   The introductory summary describes the type of contract and the type of negotiation action involved, together with comparative figures from the supplier's proposal, the buyer's negotiation objective, and the negotiated results.

**Particulars**   The purpose of this section is to cover the details of what is being bought and who is involved in the procurement. This should be done without duplicating information that was included in the subject section.

**Procurement Situation**   The purpose of this section is to discuss factors in the procurement situation which affect the reasonableness of the final price.

**Negotiation Summary**   This section shows the supplier's contract pricing proposal, the buying firm's negotiation objective, and the negotiation results, tabulated in parallel form and broken down by major elements of cost and profit. Whether these are shown as summary figures for total contract value, summary for the total price of the major item, unit price for the major items, or some other form of presentation depends on how the negotiations were conducted. The general rule is to portray the negotiation as it actually took place.

# Online Negotiation[14]

Studies have compared the establishment and maintenance of business relationships based on forms of communication. Relationships founded solely on written communication tend to founder. Those which include written and telephone communication are sustainable, but the best relationships are those which go beyond other forms of communication to involve face-to-face meetings.

---

[13]David N. Burt, Warren E. Norquist, and J. Anklesaria, *Zero Base Pricing™: Achieving World Class Competitiveness through Reduced All-in-Cost* (Chicago: Probus Publishing, 1990), Chapter 13.

[14]Appreciation is expressed to Professors Lee Buddress and Alan Raedels of Portland State University and Professor Michael Smith of Western Carolina University for much of the material included in this section.

In face-to-face communication, one party can easily discern from facial expressions and shifts in body positioning the reaction of the other party to a stated position or even a misinterpretation. Immediate steps can be taken to remedy any misunderstandings or provide further explanation or support for a negotiation position. When communication takes place in written form, these remedies may not be available.

A carelessly drafted e-mail may damage a buyer-supplier relationship without the sender being aware of the impact on the receiver. One such situation involved a buyer who needed a prompt response to an e-mail message, and so he drafted the entire message in capital letters to signify urgency. The foreign supplier interpreted the message as insulting and an attempt at intimidation, the equivalent of shouting. Needless to say, the transaction did not proceed smoothly. The list of examples is nearly endless. Everyone has received e-mail messages containing spelling and grammatical errors. The unfavorable impression elicited by such messages extends not only to the sender but to the organization as well and may be virtually irreparable.

Examples abound of the different interpretations that a receiver may generate of communications delivered face to face versus the same communications delivered in written form. To some extent, this can be attributed to the fact that not all of the content is contained in the words; it is also in *how* we say those words. Our tone of voice may be hard or flat, soft, cheerful, loud or strident, and insistent. In response to a statement, we might say, "Oh, right," but while the words are the same in each case, if our tone signals enthusiastic agreement, the message received is considerably different from the message delivered with a tone of sarcasm.

A partial remedy exists in resorting to oral communication, but we have a device for accomplishing this on the telephone and do not need to resort to the Internet (except, perhaps, as a means to avoid long-distance telephone charges). Even this solution is only partial, and its inadequacy is well displayed in the frequency of business travel.

Beyond the presentation of our message, we also tend to convey substantially different content in what we write and what we might say. For example, think about the difference between writing a letter to a friend and telling that person the same information over the phone. In written communication, there is no sense of timing, as in delivering the punch line to a joke. It is easy to sense the urgency in someone's voice but more difficult to convey that in writing. How do all the jargon and slang words we routinely use in conversation look in print? Run-on sentences are hardly noticeable when spoken but are painfully obvious in writing.

Further, even if we advance to videoconferencing over the Internet, many of these concerns persist. Perhaps timing and presentation will begin to approximate that of face-to-face delivery when the technology has advanced enough. However, as pointed out by Lanier,[15] we have not yet reached that point. Further, even with the advancement of technology to provide similar capacity, it is likely that the use of the technology will continue to change the way we communicate; only some of that change may be coming into investigative focus at this juncture.

**Advantages to Online Negotiation**    Experience indicates that electronic communication can separate issues from personalities. There is some evidence that groups using electronic communication tools may be more productive at brainstorming. Online communication can free the buyer and supplier from location dependency and perhaps even the requirement to find a common time for conducting the negotiations.

**An Example of a Successful Application of Negotiating Online**    A *Wall Street Journal* article on thriving B2B software companies cited the following successful application:

> A South San Francisco–based company began marketing software this year to help automate dealings among close business partners. One of its biggest installations is Provision X, a Chicago-based meat-trading exchange unveiled this spring by five U.S. poultry, pork, and beef suppliers.

---

[15]J. Lanier, "Virtually There: Three-Dimensional Tele-Immersion May Eventually Bring the World to Your Desk," *Scientific American*, 2001, p. 14.

Before the exchange, a buyer for a supermarket chain might call up sales managers at one or two meat suppliers and request price quotes. Those sales managers, in turn, might call up pricing managers inside their own companies who are plugged into a range of factors that shape the quantity, quality, and price of their products. Armed with data from the pricing experts, the sales staff goes back and negotiates with the buyers.

Provision X transfers those processes online, creating an automated way of negotiating. Instead of trading phone and fax messages, buyers and sellers log on to create and solicit orders and price quotes, look up price lists, check sales performance against purchase contracts and quickly generate reports summarizing the results of recent activities. Throughout these activities the relationships and hierarchies are maintained, right down to specifying the names of people who have rights to see certain data or make certain transactions.

"We're not trying to take away the people-centric focus of this business," says Kevin Nemetz, Provision X's chief executive officer. "We are just trying to take those relationships online."[16]

**Drawbacks to Online Negotiation**   It is far easier to say no in writing than face to face. The psychological separation that goes with the lack of personal contact makes the termination of the relationship much easier. This can be a distinct advantage, because it curtails problems that may be associated with negotiating with people we know and like, including reluctance to disagree for fear of damaging the relationship.

Online negotiators are likely to feel a need to be more persuasives, more convincing. However, we must take care to avoid excessive stridency in our persuasive efforts, or our labors can easily turn counterproductive. Because of a lack of other cues, our use of language takes on particular importance, and we carefully consider the impact of each word. How might connotations or interpretations differ? Often, the same word can be taken in a number of different ways, and the limitations of online communication as currently realized make it difficult to evaluate the perception of the receiver.

Buddress, Raedels, and Smith propose the following hypotheses:

- The more important the issue is, the more likely it is that it will be negotiated face to face.
- The more politically sensitive the issue is, the more likely it is that it will be negotiated face to face.
- If either negotiator will be personally affected by the outcome, that person may want to conduct the negotiation in person.
- If the topic involves issues of firm sensitivity, such as trade secrets or core competencies, the negotiation is more likely to take place face to face.
- Buyer-supplier relationships will be perceived as more distant, the more online communication and negotiation are used.
- Less formal planning will occur before online negotiations than for those conducted face to face.

# Negotiating for Price

Historically, price has been the most difficult of all contract terms to be negotiated. Because of its high relative importance and its complexity, negotiation for price will be used as an example to illustrate what is involved in negotiating many other terms of the contract. If the reader understands what is involved in negotiating price, he or she can easily visualize what is involved in negotiating other issues.

When negotiating price, the negotiator must concurrently consider the method of compensation to be used. The compensation method and the negotiation of price are directly related; hence, they must be considered together.

---

[16]Don Clark, "Perception, Reality," *Wall Street Journal,* May 21, 2001, p. R16.

To assure buying at favorable prices, negotiators strive to develop the greatest practical amount of competition or enter into fact-finding discussions with representatives of preferred suppliers or "partners" about their costs and cost drivers. Therefore, whenever possible, the initial step for a negotiator seeking successful negotiation(s) based on competition is to get an adequate number of proposals from among the potential suppliers who are genuinely interested in competing for the contract. When cost negotiations are likely, requests for proposals usually ask for not only the total price but also a complete breakdown of all supporting costs.

For every negotiated purchase, either price analysis or cost analysis, or both, is required. Which analysis is best to use and the extent of the analysis required are determined by the facts bearing on each specific purchase being negotiated. Generally, price analysis is used for lower-dollar-value contracts and cost analysis is used for higher-dollar-value contracts. A discussion of the applicable uses of both price analysis negotiation and cost analysis negotiation follows.

## Price Analysis Negotiation

Price analysis negotiation (often referred to simply as "price negotiation") is the most commonly used approach when one is negotiating only for price. Some proponents of cost negotiation disparage price negotiation, referring to it as "unsophisticated" and "emotional." In the many cases in which price negotiations are undertaken in an unprofessional manner, that criticism is fully justified. Banging on the table and shouting "I want lower prices" or "I can get it cheaper from another supplier" is certainly not professional price negotiation.

However, in many specific cases in which pricing data are developed and utilized with professional skill, price negotiation can be just as advantageous as cost negotiation or more advantageous. Compared with cost negotiation, price negotiation has three distinct advantages: (1) Negotiation time is shorter, (2) support from technical specialists is seldom needed, and (3) pricing data are relatively easy to acquire.

The traditional sources from which supply management professionals get pricing data are federal government publications, purchasing trade publications, newspapers, and business journals. Competing suppliers are excellent sources of pricing data. They can provide the buyer with price lists, catalogs, numerous special pricing data, and formal price quotations. From these competing suppliers' data, a supply management professional can readily determine two very important facts: the nature of the market (competitive or noncompetitive) and the extent of supplier interest in this particular purchase. Historical pricing data and engineering estimates also provide a sound basis for price analysis.

**Price Comparison**    The negotiator's first step in price analysis is to determine the extent of market competitiveness and supplier interest. The second step is to examine in detail the absolute and relative differences among the various prices quoted by the competing suppliers. From this examination, a buyer detects that there are differences in prices among suppliers but does not learn the causes of those differences. The search for causes begins in the supply management department's supplier information file.

The price proposals of the competing suppliers are compared with past prices of similar purchases from the supplier information file. The causes of all significant variations are pinpointed and analyzed. Adjustments are made for changes in factors such as specifications, quantities ordered, times of deliveries, variations which have taken place in the general levels of business activity and prices, and differences which may have resulted from learning experience. After these adjustments are made, the negotiator, sometimes with the help of an engineering estimator or a price analyst, determines whether the prices offered are reasonable. From this determination, the negotiator decides on the target objective to use for his or her negotiating position.

**Trend Comparisons**    Historical prices paid for purchases of similar quantities can be analyzed to disclose helpful price trend information. For example, if prices have been increasing, it is reasonable to expect that the seller will attempt to maintain a similar pattern of increase. Hence, by carefully analyzing the reasons for all price increases, a negotiator can structure a bargaining position on the basis of any invalidities uncovered.

Similarly, a negotiator can analyze decreasing prices to determine whether the price decrease is too little or too much. If the negotiator determines that the decrease is too large, he or she must determine whether the trend is creating, or is likely to create, quality or service problems in contract performance. If the decrease is too little, the negotiator must determine whether the benefits of improved production processes are being reflected proportionally in lower prices.

Even a level price trend offers opportunities for price analysis. For example, the negotiator may ask whether level prices are justified, considering the many manufacturing improvements which have been made. Did the supplier charge too much initially? Has the supplier's competitive position in the industry changed? If the negotiator's analysis indicates that costs have fallen because of reductions in the supplier's cost for materials or because of improvements in the production processes, his or her negotiating position is clear. The professional negotiator obtains reductions that reflect those changes. (It must be noted that under collaborative or alliance relationships, these savings should be shared.)

## Cost Analysis Negotiation

As was stated previously, price analysis negotiation is more commonly used than cost analysis negotiation. In cost negotiations, each applicable cost element is negotiated individually, that is, design engineering cost, tooling cost, direct materials cost, labor hours, labor rates, subcontracting, overhead cost, other direct costs, profit, and so on. Cost analysis negotiation (commonly referred to as "cost negotiation") is steadily growing in use. It has been used successfully for decades by large firms such as General Electric, Ford, and Honda, and in recent years it has been employed increasingly by small and medium-size firms.

When sophisticated collaborative or alliance supply relationships are utilized by a firm, careful detailed analysis of the supplier's costs (both present and projected) replaces competition in the marketplace. Both the buying and selling firms' representatives must see themselves as members of a supply chain competing with other supply chains for the customer's purchasing dollar. Thus, discussions about costs, cost allocations, cost drivers, cost reductions, possible cost avoidance, and profits must be seen in context: if our supply chain becomes noncompetitive, we will fail to attract the customer's purchase dollars and we both will lose! Discussions can and often do get heated—conflict can be healthy—but the discussions should be conducted in the context of what is in the joint best interests of the two parties. In reality, the parties should see themselves as members of the same supply chain team.

# Characteristics of a Successful Negotiator

The characteristics of successful negotiators should now be clear. These people are skillful individuals with broad business experience. They have a good working knowledge of all the primary functions of business, and they know how to use the tools of management: accounting, human relations, economics, business law, and quantitative analysis. They are knowledgeable about the techniques of negotiation and the products and services their firms buy. They are able to lead meetings and conferences and integrate specialists into smoothly functioning teams. In addition to being well educated and experienced, successful negotiators excel in good judgment. It is good judgment that causes them to attach the correct degree of importance to each of the factors bearing on the major issues. Combining their skills, knowledge, and judgment, they develop superior plans. Additionally, they consider problems from the viewpoint of the firm as a whole, not from the viewpoint of a functional manager. A successful negotiator is pragmatic in the use of negotiating techniques. Always searching for a collaborative or "win-win" experience, a pragmatic negotiator can adapt when the other party uses hardball or win-lose techniques. A successful negotiator has high self-esteem and is always most interested in professionalism and the best interests of the enterprise. A successful negotiator is ethical and honest and is not influenced by friendship or gratuities.

Successful negotiators share five attributes:

1. All realize that specialized training and practice are required for an individual to become an effective negotiator. Although some people have stronger verbal aptitudes than others, no one is born with negotiating knowledge and skills.
2. All habitually enter into negotiations with more demanding negotiating objectives than their counterparts, and generally they achieve them.
3. All are pragmatic and flexible in their ability to deal with different negotiation techniques from "hardball" to "collaborative."
4. All are included, or are destined to become included, among an organization's most highly valued professionals.
5. All are good listeners.

## Concluding Remarks

Negotiation is free enterprise at its very best! When traditional negotiations (win-lose) are appropriate, negotiation pits the skills of determined buyers against those of equally determined sellers. Both explore ways to achieve objectives that tend to maximize the self-interest of their organizations. In short, in such circumstances negotiation is a powerful supply management tool which competent professionals use to achieve maximum value at minimum cost. By rewarding efficiency and penalizing inefficiency, the negotiation process not only benefits the negotiating firms but also benefits the nation's economy as a whole.

The increasingly common collaborative approach to negotiations that is required with collaborative and alliance supply relationships substitutes a win-win approach for the more traditional transactional one. With this approach, both parties are better off entering into the negotiated deal than they would be if they did not reach agreement. This approach substitutes the expertise of the buying and selling firms' representatives for the forces of marketplace competition. Thus, costs must be driven to their lowest possible levels (without adversely affecting quality or service) to ensure the survival and success of the buyer and seller's supply chain in the marketplace.

## Discussion Questions

1. What does "negotiation" mean in supply management? Why is it often confused with "hassling," "haggling," and "price chiseling"?
2. What are the six objectives common to most negotiations? Should a negotiation team pursue all of its objectives while negotiating?
3. In what circumstances should negotiation be used instead of competitive bidding?
4. Compare and contrast the terms "informal negotiation" and "mock negotiation."
5. What can a buyer do to prepare for a face-to-face negotiation? Why is preparation so important?
6. Discuss three factors that influence a selling firm's negotiating strengths and weaknesses.
7. Discuss three factors that influence a buying firm's negotiating strengths and weaknesses.
8. Why does a negotiation become more difficult as it progresses? How can buyers reduce or overcome these difficulties?
9. What are the four phases of a face-to-face negotiation?
10. What is the objective of the fact-finding phase?

11. What are the three categories of negotiating techniques? Give examples of techniques in each category.
12. Identify the difference between cost negotiation and price negotiation. When should you use cost negotiation?
13. Why is price the most difficult of all contract terms to negotiate?
14. Describe how the documentation for a negotiation is typically organized. What purpose does the documentation serve?
15. What are the advantages of online negotiation? What are the disadvantages?
16. What are the characteristics of a successful negotiator?

## Internet Exercise

### Reverse Auction Sites

Visit the "Reverse Auction Sites" website below. Read about one use of information technology in the supply management function.

(http://www.brajeshwar.com/finance/auctions/reverse_auction_sites.html)

1. Why are these auctions referred to as "reverse"?
2. Give a brief description of how these auctions work.
3. What does the site caution sellers to guard against?

## Suggested Reading

Bohan, Michael L. *Power Negotiations: Unlock Your Powers of Influence and Persuasion: A Self-Study Workbook.* The Institute for Supply Management, Tempe AZ, 2006.

Brett, Jeanne M. *Negotiating Globally: How to Negotiate Deals, Resolve Disputes, and Make Decisions across Cultural Boundaries* (San Francisco: John Wiley & Sons, 2007).

Dawson, Roger. *Secrets of Power Negotiating* (Franklin Lakes, NJ: Book-Mart Press, the Career Press, 2001).

Fisher, Roger, Bruce M. Patton, and William L. Ury. *Getting to Yes: Negotiating Agreement without Giving In* (New York: Houghton Mifflin Company, 1991).

Focus on Negotiations, 2nd ed. Tempe AZ, The Institute for Supply Management, 2003.

Ghauri, Pervez N., and Jean-Claude Usunier. *International Business Negotiations* (Bingley, U.K.: Emerald Group Publishing, 2003).

Lewicki, Roy J., Bruce Barry, David M. Saunders, and John W. Minton. *Essentials of Negotiation,* 4th ed. (Burr Ridge, IL: McGraw-Hill, 2007).

Lewicki, Roy J., and Alexander Hiam. *Mastering Business Negotiation: A Working Guide to Making Deals and Resolving Conflict* (San Francisco: Jossey-Bass, a Wiley Imprint, 2006).

Lewicki, Roy J., David M. Saunders, and Bruce Barry. *Negotiation,* 5th ed. (Burr Ridge, IL: McGraw-Hill/Irwin, 2006).

Nussle, Ron, and Jim Morgan. *Integrated Cost Reduction* (New York: Reed Press, 2004).

Payne, Stanley L. *The Art of Asking Questions*, Princeton University Press, Princeton, N.J. 1951 (The classic work on the subject).

Stark, Peter B., and Jane S. Flaherty. *The Only Negotiating Guide You'll Ever Need: 101 Ways to Win Every Time in Any Situation* (New York: Random House, 2003).

Ury, William. *Getting Past No.* (New York: Bantam Books, 1993).

Watkins, Michael. *Breakthrough Business Negotiation: A Toolbox for Managers* (San Francisco: Jossey-Bass, 2002).

# Managing Contracts
# and Relationships

Supply relationships start with contracts-agreements. These "relationships" must be managed in an ethical manner while respecting our social responsibilities.

Collaborative relationships are the most essential ingredient of successful supply chain management. Although relationships and ethics are addressed throughout the book, this section focuses on important relationship issues which are essential foundations of successful supply and supply chain management.

Chapter 17 addresses legal issues in supply management. While legal issues are addressed throughout the book, we believe that the importance of these issues requires a chapter focusing on legal considerations. The explosive growth of the Internet and global sourcing has forced supply managers to address these important topics in more detail.

The balancing of relationship management and contract management is addressed in Chapter 18. While many practitioners are tempted to focus on either relationship management *or* contract management, we believe that it is necessary to address these issues in a tightly integrated fashion. It is our observation that contract and relationship management—or what many call "post-award activities"—is the weakest of the key phases of supply management. As a supply manager told one of us a few years ago, "If the stuff is late, we'll expedite!" We believe in and advocate a more proactive approach which ensures that "the stuff is never late."

Although ethical issues are addressed throughout this book, we believe that the importance of ethics in the field of supply management necessitates a chapter dedicated to ethics. Chapter 19 addresses the many issues encompassing ethics and social responsibilities as they relate to supply management. ∎

# Contract Formation and Legal Issues

## CHAPTER OBJECTIVES

*After reading this chapter, you should be able to:*

1. Understand the importance of preventing legal issues from arising.

2. Understand the options for resolving contract disputes.

3. Know how the Uniform Commercial Code affects procurement contracts.

4. Define the status of an agent.

5. Know the four basic elements of a contract.

6. Explain the two types of warranties identified under the UCC.

7. Explain the concept of breach in regard to contracts.

8. Identify issues to consider in international contracts.

## VIGNETTE: CHRYSLER, LLC, VERSUS PLASTECH ENGINEERED PRODUCTS INC.

On February 4, 2008, the major U.S. automaker Chrysler, LLC, was forced to shut down production at four of its assembly plants. A fifth plant lost a full shift of production; all of those events were caused by lack of delivery on the part of a major supplier, Plastech Engineered Products Inc. A Chrysler supplier for the previous 10 years, Plastech supplies about 360 different parts that are used in nearly every vehicle the struggling number three U.S. automaker makes, including the Jeep Wrangler and the Dodge Ram pickup truck.[1,2] The cost to Chrysler of the shutdown was around $250 million, and continued interruption of supply threatened to affect all 14 Chrysler assembly plants. In an attempt to prevent further losses, Chrysler has been seeking to take equipment and business from Plastech and resource the work to other suppliers. To gain protection against having to surrender assets, Plastech has filed for Chapter 11 bankruptcy.

How does a relationship that has lasted a decade come to litigation in a U.S. bankruptcy court? Chrysler claims that Plastech no longer could meet its production demands. Chrysler wants to retrieve tooling to give it to a new supplier. Plastech felt that continued price pressures, in spite of rising material costs and declining production volumes, created financial instability that resulted in its inability to meet customer requirements.

U.S. bankruptcy Judge Phillip Shefferly feels that "allowing Chrysler to repossess its tooling so early in Plastech's bankruptcy proceedings 'will likely destroy the possibilities for an effective reorganization.' Chrysler will suffer some economic harm, Shefferly said, but has numerous options, including procuring more tooling for alternate suppliers or going back to the bargaining table with Plastech."[3] No matter how it ends, additional costs will be incurred to ensure uninterrupted supply and continued production. Also, it is likely that Plastech will be one of the first but certainly not the last auto industry supplier forced into bankruptcy by rising material costs, declining vehicle production volumes, and pressure for price cuts from the troubled Detroit-based automakers.[4] ■

## CRITICAL THINKING QUESTIONS

1. Who is really at fault?
2. Could the legal issues between Chrysler and Plastech have been resolved in a more constructive manner without litigation?
3. How could this situation have been prevented?

# Litigation Prevention

It can be argued persuasively that the best way to deal with legal disputes is to make sure to do one's best to avoid them in the first place! The maxim that an ounce of prevention is worth a pound of cure certainly comes to mind in this context. In professional life, most supply management professionals seldom—if they're fortunate—become involved in litigation. Yet their daily activities are subject to two major areas of the law: the law of agency and the law of contracts.

A supply manager or a buyer acts as an agent for his or her firm. Legally, that relationship is defined and governed by the law of agency. When a firm buys materials and services from other firms, each

---

[1]The authors of this textbook give thanks to Eric Drattell, Vice President and General Counsel of Risk Management Solutions, Inc., for his contribution in updating this chapter.

[2]http://www.cnbc.com/id/23192763/for/cnbc. "Chrysler, Plastech Reach Short-Term Supply Deal." Updated February 15, 2008.

[3]http://www.iht.com/articles/ap/2008/02/19/business/NA-FIN-US-Chrysler-Plastech.php. *International Herald Tribune*–Business with Reuters, "Judge Rules Chrysler Cannot Take Tools from Plastech for Now," Associated Press, February 20, 2008.

[4]http://www.cnbc.com/id/23192763/for/cnbc. "Chrysler, Plastech Reach Short-Term Supply Deal."

purchase involves the formation of a purchase contract. In fact, the courts assume that buyer agents are familiar with the applicable laws pursuant to their particular buying situation, industry, trade custom, and practice. If a serious disagreement arises between the purchaser and the supplier, the conflict becomes subject to the dispute resolution process, which ranges from negotiation, to mediation, to litigation, whether in front of an arbitration panel or before a court. In any event, the dispute will be resolved by applying the law of contracts.

A supply manager's basic responsibility is to conduct the firm's procurement business as efficiently and expeditiously as possible. Buying policies and practices therefore are predicated primarily on business requirements and business judgment rather than on legal considerations. From a business standpoint, contractual disputes normally can be resolved much more effectively and with less cost by negotiation. A lawsuit almost always alienates a good supplier. Additionally, the outcome of any court case is uncertain. Litigation is also costly even in the event of a favorable decision. The total cost of legal fees and expenses, executive time diverted to the dispute, and disrupted business operations seldom is recovered from damage awards. For these reasons, in resolving disputes, most business firms utilize litigation only as a last resort.

The fact that a supply management executive tries to avoid litigation, however, does not mean that he or she can overlook the legal dimensions of his or her role. On the contrary, a basic knowledge of relevant legal principles is essential to success. Unless a supply manager understands the legal implications of his or her job and the actions undertaken while doing it, legal entanglements are almost certain to crop up from time to time.

The purpose of this chapter is to review briefly some of the principal legal concepts as they relate to a supply management professional's responsibilities. The chapter does not attempt to provide a complete discussion of those concepts. Most supply professionals should acquire some depth in the field through selected studies in commercial law.

## Dispute Resolution

Serious contract disputes are a rarity in the lives of most supply managers, but in a complex business operation they arise from time to time. When a dispute does arise, after the appropriate "homework" has been done, the first step in the resolution process is to discuss the problem with the supplier. When one is attempting to resolve a dispute, it pays to keep in mind six considerations: (1) time, (2) money, (3) the complexity and/or formality of the method of dispute resolution, (4) stress, (5) visibility, and (6) damage to the relationship.

### Negotiation

Most disputes are best resolved through negotiation and compromise. In most cases, the executives involved want to avoid further confrontation simply because it may be too time-consuming, costly, messy and complicated, stressful, embarrassing, and damaging to the parties' relationship to do otherwise. If a satisfactory solution cannot be worked out by the two parties, however, limited alternatives remain. The parties can mediate or litigate.

### Mediation

If negotiation fails, the parties can consider mediation, which involves introducing a third party into the discussion. The mediator's role is to listen, sympathize, empathize, coax, cajole, and persuade. Depending on the level of trust and credibility the mediator has with the parties, he or she may even propose, suggest, or encourage possible solutions. For that reason, the more trusted and respected a mediator is, the more likely it is that he or she will be able to help resolve the dispute. One thing the mediator may not do, however, is decide anything.

## Litigation

Litigation may be brought before an arbitrator or before a court. There are plusses and minuses to each approach, and it is fair to say that one size does not fit all.

## Arbitration

Arbitration may take many forms, but its basic feature is that the outcome of a dispute is no longer in the hands of the parties but in the hands of a third party. Unlike negotiation or mediation, in which the parties attain resolution by agreeing on the outcome, arbitration vests the decision-making authority with the arbitral panel, which typically consists of one or three arbitrators. In those circumstances, a professional or agreed on arbitrator will hear testimony and study evidence from both sides, then make a decision on the basis of the facts and the law. If the contract contains a mandatory arbitration provision, the parties are *obligated* to arbitrate all disputes within the scope of that provision. However, as with mediation, the parties can agree, even after entering into a contract without an arbitration clause, to arbitrate any dispute which may arise.

## Courts

Litigation also may be brought in an appropriate state or federal court, depending on the location of the parties and the amount in dispute. Lawsuits may be heard by a judge or by a jury. In either case, relevant court rules of procedure will prescribe how the litigation will proceed, and the relevant rules of evidence will prescribe what evidence may and may not be presented to the trier of fact.

How can one avoid ending up in litigation? As was suggested at the beginning of this chapter, the best approach is avoidance and prevention of destructive legal disputes. Just how does one avoid and prevent destructive legal disputes? This is where a fundamental understanding of certain basic legal principles can prove invaluable. One benefits most from knowing the law well enough to avoid and prevent the destructive legal disputes that may ensue from ignorance of the law. After all, how many times has one heard the admonition that "ignorance of the law is no defense"?

# Development of Commercial Law

Historically, each state developed its own body of statutes and common law to deal with the problems prevalent in its particular spheres of activity. Individual state development ultimately led to the creation of a series of commercial laws that varied widely from state to state, a situation that produced difficulties for businesses involved in interstate commerce.

In an attempt to promote uniformity among the laws applicable to business transactions, the American Bar Association created a committee known as the National Conference of Commissioners on Uniform State Laws (NCCUSL) that worked with the American Law Institute (ALI) on the development of a model act for a uniform set of laws governing all aspects of commercial transactions.

The resulting code, called the Uniform Commercial Code (UCC), was published in 1952; revised versions of the code followed, with the most recent being published in 2001. Although the UCC deals with a wide range of commercial transactions, Article 2 deals specifically with the sale and purchase of goods.

The UCC does not apply to the purchase of services, but a judge may elect to use it as a guide, and when purchases include both goods and services, the UCC may apply. The language in the UCC does not prevent the code from being used to rule on services even though the UCC was written for the sale of goods. However, buyers must remember that ordinarily, services are not governed by the Uniform Commercial Code or the particular state version of it. This means a state's common law of contracting will apply and each state will have variations regarding warranties, damages, and other performance issues. Therefore, the statement of work (S.O.W.) must detail all the provisions normally covered in the UCC, plus unique conditions such as behavior rules, security, substance abuse, personal conduct, and attire.[5] In addition, the supply manager must reserve the right to approve all subcontractors. Issues of dispute resolution such as arbitration, mediation, and cancellation rights all must be spelled out in the S.O.W. In some cases, the contract will include both goods and services such as an installation, a situation often called a "hybrid contract"; equipment contracts are often hybrid. In case of conflict, most courts will use the "predominant purpose" guideline to determine which laws prevail.

Each state could determine how much or little of the UCC it wished to adopt. Article 2 has been adopted by the District of Columbia and all the states with the exception of Louisiana. The UCC has effectively eliminated a majority of the important differences between the commercial laws of the various states and also has provided new statutory provisions to fill many of the gaps in the prior laws. It should be noted, however, that the code is silent on some matters covered by earlier laws. Consequently, unless superseded by provisions of the UCC, laws dealing with matters such as principal and agent, fraud, mistakes, coercion, and misrepresentation continue to be in effect.

## Electronic Contract Considerations: Cyberlaw

The UCC was drafted before widespread use of software and the advent of e-commerce. As a result, Article 2 has been applied in many states by analogy to govern disputes concerning software licensing and e-commerce.

Many have argued that e-commerce has spawned the need for a new or expanded set of laws to cover cybertransactions. Accordingly, in 1995, the NCCUSL and the ALI set about drafting a proposed Article 2B to the UCC. The purpose of 2B was to govern licenses, including computer software. The completed draft, however, resulted in a split between the NCCUSL and the ALI. While the NCCUSL was satisfied with the draft, the ALI regarded many of the provisions as being too favorable to software licensors, at the expense of consumers.

After that split of opinion, the NCCUSL unilaterally decided to publish its draft separate and apart from the UCC. That model code became known as the Uniform Computer Information Transactions Act (UCITA), and beginning in 1999, the NCCUSL encouraged states to enact it. Soon afterward, however, a majority of state attorneys general asked the NCCUSL to revise the UCITA because they believed that it undermined consumer protection by classifying consumer software as nongoods. Only two states have adopted UCITA: Maryland and Virginia. Another major problem caused by E-Commerce (Internet and e-mail transactions) is the issue of electronic records and signatures as they pertain to the Statute of Frauds requirements for written records. Consequently in 1999, the NCCUSL published its proposed Uniform Electronic Transactions Act (UETA) which almost all the states have adopted.

If the contracting parties have agreed to honor electronic signatures, section 7 of UETA recognizes this deviation from the Statute of Frauds requirements for hard copy personal signatures, i.e., "a record or signature

---

[5]Ernest G., Gabbard, J. D., CPM., CPCM, "Contracting for Services: What Are the Differences?" *Inside Supply Management*, July 2005, pp. 14–15

may not be denied legal effect or enforceability solely because it is in electronic form,"[6] Section 14 of UETA also recognizes contracts "formed by machines functioning as electronic agents for parties to a transaction."[7] It is important to remember that there are certain legal instruments such as wills that are exempted from UETA. In addition, many business lawyers and supply professionals believe that major contracts should have the traditional formal signing ceremony to reinforce the significance of the agreement.

In 2000, the U.S. Congress enacted The Electronic Signatures In Global and National Commerce (E-Sign) ACT which incorporates much of the UETA language. E-Sign also allows states who have adopted UETA to preempt or substitute the act for the relevant UETA provisions.[8] It appears that E-Sign is also based on the rational developed in the United Nations Model Law on Electronic Signatures of The United Nations Commission on International Trade Law as amended and distributed, 12 December, 2001.[9]

Finally, most firms use some form of cryptographic (code) signature methods such as public key infrastructure (PKI) to secure, protect and authenticate on-line signatures.

### Attempts to Revise the UCC

Early in this decade, the NCCUSL and the ALI proposed revising significantly the provisions of Article 2 to make it current with contemporary practices. The proposed changes would radically alter a number of provisions, including (1) the minimum amount required for an agreement to be in writing (from $500 to $5,000); (2) revising the "battle of the forms" so that additional or conflicting terms in an acceptance or acknowledgment do not become part of the contract unless the parties otherwise have agreed to such terms; (3) delivery terms (e.g., F.O.B.) are deleted in favor of a reference to the International Chamber of Commerce's Incoterms; (4) revising the provision allowing for a seller to cure a nonconforming delivery; and (5) revising the statute of limitations from four years to five years in certain circumstances. To date, no state legislature has adopted any of the proposed revisions. This probably has resulted from the view that the current version, though flawed in some ways, is more or less consistent across the United States and that enactment of the proposed revisions once again would throw sand in the gears of interstate commerce.[10]

Topics treated throughout the rest of this chapter therefore reflect the provisions of the UCC where applicable, as well as the provisions of earlier laws that have not been displaced by the code.

# Basic Legal Considerations

### Status of an Agent

In the legal sense, an agent is a person who, by express or implied agreement, is authorized to act for someone else in business dealings with a third party. Regardless of the job title, this is precisely what supply managers and buyers do. A "supply manager" is not a legal party to his or her business transactions but acts as a representative of the company. In this capacity, the agent is required by law to be loyal to the employer (the principal) and use reasonable care, skill, and judgment in the performance of his or her duties.

---

[6]Richard A. Mann and Barry S. Roberts, *Smith & Roberson's Business Law*. 13th ed. Mason, OH. West Legal Studies in Business, an imprint of Thomson/South-Western, Thomson Higher Education, 2006. pp. 254, 983.

[7]Ibid. p. 983 and see http://www.law.upenn.edu/bll/ulc_frame.htm

[8]Ibid. p. 983 and see http:/www.cybersign.com

[9]http:/www.uncitral.org/uncitral/zh/publications/.html

[10]See, generally, Dr. John Murray, Jr., "What's New in UCC Article 2," http://www.purchasing.com/article/CA337305.html.

The agent owes the principal a fiduciary duty; therefore, the employer may hold a purchasing agent or supply manager personally liable for any secret advantages gained for himself or herself.

The authority under which a buyer, purchasing agent, or supply manager functions is granted by the employer. Since the law requires him or her to operate within the bounds of that authority, it behooves such individuals to know as precisely as possible the types of transactions in which they can and cannot legally represent the firm. In practice, the degree of authority delegated to buyers, purchasing agents, and supply managers varies significantly among companies. Hence, it is difficult for sales representatives to know the exact limits of a particular buyer's authority. Consequently, under the law, such individuals operate under three types of authority: actual or express authority, apparent authority, and implied authority. A third party dealing with an agent is entitled to rely on the buyer's actual or express authority. Issues arise, however, when the buyer does not have actual or express authority but holds himself or herself out as having the requisite authority to make an agreement (known as apparent authority) or when the third party reasonably believes that the buyer has authority comparable with that of similar agents in similar companies (known as implied authority).

If the third party reasonably relied on the buyer's apparent or implied authority, the buyer's principal probably will be held to the terms of the contract entered into by the buyer even if the buyer lacked the requisite authority. However, the buyer's principal can bring suit against the agent for acting beyond the limit of his or her actual authority.

Just as supply professionals occupy the legal status of buying agents for their firms, sales representatives hold the status of selling agents for their firms. Buyers, purchasing agents, and supply managers, however, usually are classified as general agents, whereas salespeople typically are classified as special agents, having somewhat more restricted authority. Consequently, in most cases a salesman or saleswoman does not have the authority to bind a company to a sales contract or a warranty. The courts usually hold that unless otherwise stated, as special agents sales representatives have authority only to solicit orders. It is important that buyers recognize this fact. On important jobs, to ensure that a legally binding contract does in fact exist, a buyer should require acceptance of the order by an authorized company officer, normally one of the supplier's sales managers who customarily serve as the company's general agents for this purpose.

## The Purchase Contract

Although a legalistic approach to purchasing is in most cases unnecessary, every buyer, purchasing agent, and supply manager must protect his or her company against potential legal problems. The buyer's major responsibility in this regard is to ensure that each purchase contract is satisfactorily drawn and legally binding on both parties. To be valid and enforceable, a contract must contain four basic elements: (1) an agreement ("meeting of the minds") resulting from an offer and an acceptance; (2) consideration, or mutual obligation; (3) competent parties; and (4) a lawful purpose.

Offer and Acceptance   When a buyer, purchasing agent, or supply manager sends a purchase order to a supplier, that act usually constitutes a legal offer to buy in accordance with the terms stated in the order. Agreement does not exist, however, until the supplier accepts the offer; when that occurs, the law deems that a "meeting of the minds" exists regarding the proposed contract. If a buyer requests a quotation or a bid from a supplier, the supplier's quotation usually constitutes an offer. Agreement exists when the buyer accepts the quotations (often by subsequently sending a purchase order to the supplier).

Under the Uniform Sales Act, the law required acceptance of an offer in terms that were identical with the terms of the offer—the mirror image concept. The UCC, however, eliminated that stringent requirement. The code states that "conduct by both parties which recognizes the existence of a contract is sufficient to establish a contract or sale although the writings of the parties do not otherwise establish a contract." The code also recognizes suppliers' standard confirmation forms and acknowledgment forms as a valid acceptance even if the terms stated in them are different from the terms of the offer.

In the case of a contract for the sale of goods, when the terms of an acceptance differ from the terms of the offer—the so-called battle of the forms—the terms of the acceptance automatically will be incorporated in the contract unless one of three conditions exists: (1) They materially alter the intent of the offer, (2) the offeror objects in writing, or (3) the offer explicitly states that no different terms will be accepted. What happens when an offer and an acceptance contain conflicting terms but none of the preceding conditions exist? All terms except the conflicting terms become part of the contract, and the conflicting terms simply are omitted from the contract. In that case, the UCC's "gap-filler" provisions (covering price, time and place of delivery, and time of payment) may apply to replace any conflicting provisions which have been knocked out. In the case of a contract not covered by the UCC, the so-called 'mirror image' rule may apply, in which case any contrary or additional terms in an acceptance will not operate as an acceptance but will be a counteroffer which the buyer may accept expressly or by performance.

The UCC contains another important provision relating to the acceptance of an offer to buy. The code recognizes as valid the communication of an acceptance in "any manner and by any medium reasonable to the circumstances." Consequently, when a supplier receives an order for the purchase of material for immediate delivery, it can accept the offer either by prompt acknowledgment of the order or by prompt shipment of the material. The code thus permits prompt supplier performance of such proposed contracts to constitute acceptance of the offer. The contract becomes effective when the supplier ships the material.

A long-standing principle of commercial law stated that an offer could be revoked by the offeror at any time before it was accepted, regardless of the time period stipulated in the offer. The UCC changed that principle with respect to the purchase or sale of goods. The code states that an offeror may offer to buy or sell material in a signed writing and expressly state therein that the offer remains valid for a stipulated time period; if no time period is stipulated, the offer remains valid for a "reasonable" period of time not to exceed three months. In either case, the offeror may not revoke the offer during the validity period.

This provision of the code has significant implications for industrial purchasers and their potential suppliers. Purchasers can use suppliers' firm quotations in making precise manufacturing cost calculations and rely on the fact that the quotations cannot be revoked before a certain date. Without the code, no such assurance existed. However, this provision limits a buyer's ability to cancel a firm order, without legal obligation, before acceptance. To maintain firm control, it is now doubly important that the buyer state in the order the length of time for which the offer is valid (or the date by which acceptance of the order is required).

**Consideration**   In addition to a meeting of minds, a valid contract must contain the element of obligation. Most purchase contracts are bilateral; that is, both parties agree to do something they otherwise would not be required to do. The buyer promises to buy from the supplier certain material at a stated price; the supplier promises to deliver the material in accordance with stated contract conditions. The important point is the mutuality of obligation. The contract must be drawn so that each party (or promisor) is bound. If both are not bound, in the eyes of the law neither is bound, and hence, no contract exists.

A buyer is confronted with the practical significance of the "mutual obligation" concept when he or she formulates the terms of purchase. The statements regarding material quantity, price, delivery, and so on, must be specific enough to bind both the buyer's firm and the supplier to definable levels of performance. In writing a blanket purchase order for pipe fittings, for example, it is not sufficient to state the quantity as "all company X desires." That statement is too indefinite to bind company X to any specific purchase. However, if the requirement is stated as "the quantity company X uses during the month of

March," most courts will consider it sufficient to define X's purchase obligation. It is also prudent to qualify the statement by indicating approximate minimum and maximum levels of consumption.

Similar situations arise in specifying prices and delivery dates. Some companies, for example, occasionally issue unpriced purchase orders. Aside from the questionable wisdom of that business practice, there is a legal question about the definiteness of the offer. From a legal standpoint, the question which must be answered is: Under existing conditions, can the price be determined precisely enough to define the obligations of both parties? The UCC provides more latitude in answering this question than did the Uniform Sales Act. The UCC specifically says that a buyer and a supplier can make a binding contract without agreeing on an exact price until a later date. If at the time of shipment a price cannot be agreed on, the code includes provisions by which a fair price will be determined. On such orders, however, a buyer should protect his or her firm by noting a precise price range or stating how the price is to be determined.

The issue of predatory purchasing involves an interesting situation in which predatory bidding can harm competition. The recent Ross-Simmons Weyerhaeuser court case has provided new case law on the subject. "The key message of Weyerhaeuser for supply management professionals is that aggressive bidding for scarce supplies is lawful in the vast majority of cases. Only when a buyer intentionally bids up the cost of supplies to a point that leads to below-cost pricing in the output market, and it is probable that the loss can be recovered after competitors are eliminated, is an anti-trust claim against the buyer likely to succeed."[11]

**Competent Parties**   A valid contract must be made by persons who have full contractual capacity. A contract made by a minor or by an insane or intoxicated person is usually entirely void or voidable at the option of the incompetent party.

**Legality of Purpose**   A contract whose purpose is illegal is automatically illegal and void. A contract whose primary purpose is legal but one of whose ancillary terms is illegal may be either void or valid, depending on the seriousness of the illegality and the extent to which the illegal part can be separated from the legal part of the contract. This situation occasionally may have relevance for buyers, for example, if a material was purchased at a price which violated restraint of trade or price discrimination laws.

**The Written and the Spoken Word**   Buyers should be aware of several basic concepts concerning the construction of a contract. Contrary to common belief, a contract is not a physical thing. A contract is actually a relationship which exists between the parties making the contract. When a contract is reduced to writing, the written document is not in fact the contract; it is simply evidence of the contract. Hence, a contract may be supported by either written or oral evidence. In most cases, courts hold an oral contract to be just as binding as a written one, although it may be substantially more difficult to prove the facts on which an oral contract is based. However, the law currently requires some types of agreements to be in writing. In the case of sales transactions between qualified "merchants,"[12] for example, the UCC specifically states that when a selling price of $500 or more is involved, the contract must be reduced to writing to be enforceable.[13]

---

[11] Anthony A. Dean, "Predatory Purchasing: Part 2," *Inside Supply Management,* May 2007, pp. 48–49.

[12] Section 2-104 of the UCC defines a "merchant" as one who deals in goods; one who holds himself out as having particular skill in the subject matter; or one who uses a person who holds himself out as having such knowledge or skill. Hence, it generally is held under this broad definition that almost every person in business, including a purchasing officer, is a 'merchant'. Even a person not in business may be classified as a 'merchant' if he or she employs a purchasing officer or broker.

[13] Before the enactment of the UCC, the Statute of Frauds required contracts relating to personal property, for which neither delivery nor payment had been made, to be in writing if the value of the sale exceeded a specified amount; the specified amount varied widely among states.

If an oral contract between a supplier and a buyer later is confirmed in writing, the written confirmation is binding on both parties if no objection is raised within 10 days. Hence, it is important to note that when a contract is reduced to writing, the written evidence supersedes all prior oral evidence. The courts generally hold that a contract expressed in writing embodies all preceding oral discussion pertinent to the agreement. Generally, this means that a buyer cannot legally rely on a supplier's oral statements concerning a material's performance or warranty unless the statements have been included in the written agreement. Consequently, from a legal standpoint, a buyer should carefully consider the content of his or her oral negotiations with a supplier and ensure that all relevant data to be included in the contract have been reduced to writing. The buyer also should be aware that courts have ruled that written or typed statements take precedence over printed statements on the contract form if conflicting statements appear in the document.

**Actions versus Words**   Under common law and the UCC, the ultimate test of whether a contract exists is the answer to the question, "Do the parties act as if they have a contract?" Previously discussed actions such as performance, use, acceptance, and other implied conformance can create a legally binding contract with or without a written or verbal agreement. Perhaps this is another aspect of the old adage "actions speak louder than words."

**Letters of Intent**   Letters of intent (LOI) and memorandums of understanding (MOUs) are a form of precontracting that essentially say, "We do not have a formal agreement, but here is what we have agreed on so far." Many parties to a contract use an LOI as a planning document to order material with long lead times, special tooling, or unique design work. Think of an LOI as a preliminary agreement with general open issues to be resolved. Both parties must be extremely careful about the wording in LOIs and MOUs lest the language unintentionally create a legally binding contract. Understandably, the legal profession does not favor these instruments, making the logical argument that you either have a contract or you do not.[14] However, there are situations in which their use is appropriate.

# Special Legal Considerations

## Inspection Rights

If a purchaser has not inspected the purchased material to ensure that it conforms to the terms of the contract, the law gives him or her a reasonable period of time to inspect the material after it is received. If the purchaser raises no objection to the material within a reasonable period of time, he or she is deemed to have accepted it. In court decisions on this matter, it has been largely industry practice which has set the standard for a "reasonable" amount of time.

## Rights of Rejection

A purchaser has the right to reject material that does not conform to the terms of the contract. If an overshipment is received, the purchaser can either reject the complete shipment or reject the quantity in excess of the amount stated in the contract. When a buyer does not wish to accept defectively delivered material, he or she is required only to notify the supplier of that fact, describing specifically the nature of the defect or default. The buyer is not legally bound to return the rejected material. However, the buying firm is

---

[14]Judi Coover, Esq., "Letter of Intent," *Inside Supply Management,* November 2006, pp. 32–33.

obligated to protect and care for the material in a reasonable manner. If the buyer neither returns the material nor notifies the supplier of rejection within a reasonable period, however, the buying firm is obligated to pay for the material.

## Title and Risk of Loss

From a legal point of view, the question of which party has title to purchased materials normally is answered by defining the F.O.B. point of purchase. In the case of an F.O.B. origin shipment, the buying firm becomes the owner when the material is loaded into the carrier's vehicle. When material is shipped F.O.B. destination, the supplier owns the material until it is off-loaded at the buyer's receiving dock.

Title is to be distinguished from the risk of loss of the goods. Put differently, risk of loss concerns which party assumes liability for goods that are damaged or destroyed before acceptance. It is a common misconception that risk of loss passes when title passes. The UCC, however, draws a distinction, and lack of knowledge of that distinction can be a trap for the unwary.

Risk of loss for *conforming* goods passes at the F.O.B. point unless the contract specifies otherwise. Risk of loss for *nonconforming* goods, however, does not pass until the seller delivers conforming goods or the buyer accepts the nonconforming tender. A savvy buyer will include in the contract language to the effect that risk of loss does not pass until it accepts the goods, including conforming goods.

## Warranties

The UCC identifies two specific types of warranties:

1. Implied warranty.
2. Express warranty.

An implied warranty is one which is read into the contract as a matter of law unless the parties agree to exclude one or more of the implied warranties. The warranties implied by the UCC are as follows:

*Implied Warranty of Good Title:* When a supplier agrees to sell a particular item, the firm implies that it (or its principal) has title to the item and hence has legal authority to sell it.

*Implied Warranty of Noninfringement:* A merchant seller warrants that the goods do not infringe a third party's intellectual property rights.

*Implied Warranty of Merchantability:* The supplier also implies that the item is free from defects in material and workmanship, that it is at least of "fair average quality." This means that the item meets the standards of the trade and that its quality is appropriate for ordinary use.

*Implied Warranty of Fitness for a Particular Purpose:* Another implied warranty a buyer may receive in certain circumstances is an implied warranty of fitness for a particular purpose. If a buyer communicates to a supplier which requirements the purchased material must satisfy and subsequently relies on the skill or judgment of the supplier in selecting a specific material for the job, the material usually carries an implied warranty of fitness for the stated need. This assumes that the supplier is fully aware of the buyer's need and knows that the buyer is relying on guidance from the supplier's personnel. Hence, it should be amply clear why buyers, purchasing agents, and supply managers must insist that purchase orders and related material specifications be written clearly and completely.

An express warranty is a promise or representation that the goods, services, or subject matter of the contract will have certain characteristics or qualities. It is not necessary that an express warranty be labeled as such. If a supplier accepts a purchase order without qualification, descriptions of the material included on the order form—model number, size, capacity, chemical composition, technical specifications, and so on—become an express warranty. The supplier warrants that the material delivered will conform to those descriptions. Additionally, suppliers frequently make express warranties for their products in sales and technical literature. Those warranties typically refer to the material's performance characteristics, physical composition, appearance, and so on. If a buyer has no way of determining the facts of the matter and consequently relies on such warranties, the supplier normally is held liable for them. The buyer also should recognize that an express warranty nullifies an implied warranty to the extent that it conflicts with the implied warranty (with the exception of an implied warranty of fitness for a particular purpose).

Numerous factors influence the extent to which a buyer can rely on an implied warranty in a specific situation. The knowledge and conduct of the buyer and the seller, as well as the specific conditions surrounding a transaction, are taken into consideration by the court in resolving a dispute over warranty. Generally, if a buyer acts in good faith and has no knowledge of conditions contrary to an implied warranty, the law holds a supplier liable for such implied warranties, unless otherwise stated in the contract.

Recent legislation has tended to increase warranty protection for buyers by strengthening and expanding the liability of manufacturers and sellers with respect to warranty performance.[15] A buyer should recognize, however, that the UCC permits a seller to exclude or modify the implied warranties for a product.

A supplier can disclaim or exclude the implied warranties in one of four ways: First, in the case of an implied warranty of merchantability, the seller must use the word "merchantability" in the disclaimer, and the disclaimer must be conspicuous. No magic words are required to disclaim an implied warranty of fitness for a particular purpose or other implied warranties. Second, the seller may disclaim implied warranties by using a statement such as "This item is offered for sale 'as is'" or "There are no warranties which extend beyond the description on the face hereof." Interestingly, in several states such warranty disclaimers have been declared to be contrary to public policy and, hence, invalid. Third, the buyer cannot rely on the implied warranties if it has either inspected the goods or refused to inspect the goods if the inspection would have revealed a condition breaching an implied warranty. Fourth, the implied warranty may be excluded by industry custom or practice or the parties' course of dealing or performance. As a general rule, however, a prudent buyer adopts a caveat emptor attitude in verifying the warranty protection he or she actually has in any specific purchase.

**Performance Bonds**   When contract compliance is critical, such as the completion date for hotels, hospitals, and other major construction products, buyers often negotiate the inclusion of a performance bond issued by a bond company (a type of insurance) paid for by the seller. Legally called "surety" or a guarantee of compliance, these bonds are expensive and usually are included only in contracts of significant magnitude. Buyers must remember that losses have to be documented to prove economic loss.[16]

## Evergreen Contracts

Many firms issue blanket orders in which the exact quantities are not fixed and/or there are no termination dates. There are many different terms for such contracts, such as corporatewide agreements, requirements

---

[15]The Consumer Product Safety Act and the Federal Warranties Act, as well as the UCC.

[16]Richard A. Mann and Barry S. Roberts, *Business Law and the Regulation of Business*, 6th ed. (Cincinnati, OH: West Educational Publishing Co—ITP, South-Western College Publishing, 1999), pp. 784–87.

contracts, and evergreen contracts.[17] Such contracts have become more common as electronic transactions have become more popular with the use of computer reorder systems. One problem with these contracts is how and when they can be amended as there are no fixed terms. In July 2007, the Ninth District Court of Appeals ruled that "one party to a contract is not required to continuously monitor the terms posted on the other party's website to make sure the other party hasn't surreptitiously changed the terms of the contract." This ruling reaffirmed a rather long-standing legal principle that a party to a contract must be given direct notice of any proposed changes and be given a reasonable amount of time to respond.[18]

## Order Cancellation and Breach of Contract

If a supplier fails to deliver an order by the delivery date agreed on in the contract or fails to perform in accordance with contract provisions, legally, the supplier has breached the contract. Not all breaches entitle a party to declare the other party in default. Only if the effect of the breach is to deny the nonbreaching party the "benefit of the bargain" can the nonbreaching party terminate the contract for breach and, if appropriate, seek damages.

Damages are measured on the basis of which party breached and when the breach occurred. If the seller has breached before acceptance, the buyer is entitled to either (1) purchase the goods from a third party and charge the breaching seller with the difference between the contract price and the price paid to the replacement contractor or (2) if the buyer does not replace the goods the seller contracted to supply, the buyer is entitled to the difference between the contract price and the market price of conforming goods as of the date of the breach. The first remedy commonly is known as "cover." If the buyer has accepted the goods, the buyer is entitled to recover the difference between the actual value of the goods accepted and their value if they had been delivered in conformance with the contract.

If the buyer has breached before acceptance, for example, by repudiating the contract or wrongfully refusing to accept conforming goods, the seller has an action for difference between the contract price and the market price if the seller hasn't resold the goods. If the seller has resold the goods, the seller is entitled to the difference between the contract price and the price at which the seller resold the goods. If the buyer has breached after acceptance, the seller is entitled to be paid the contract price.

**Anticipatory Breach**   "Anticipatory breach" is a legal term often used in situations in which one or both parties notify the other party of intent to breach before actual default. In the most common case of the buyer notifying the supplier (seller) of his or her intention to cancel the order before delivery, the buyer is responsible for all costs incurred by the seller to that date in addition to a reasonable profit on those costs, including labor, material, tooling, and overhead expenses.

**Liquidated Damages Provision**   If it is evident at the time a major contract is drawn up that breach of the contract would injure one or both parties severely and damages would be difficult to determine, it is wise to include a liquidated damages provision in the contract. Those provisions stipulate in advance the procedures to be used in determining costs and damages. In some cases, specific damage payments are stated. For example, if the contract is for the purchase of power-generating equipment to be used on a large construction project, the date of delivery may be critical for the purchaser. Perhaps installation of the equipment must precede other important phases of the construction work. If the project is delayed by late delivery of the generating equipment, the purchaser may incur heavy financial losses. It is sound

---

[17]Jane K. Winn, "Evergreen Customer Contracts," *Inside Supply Management,* February 2008, pp. 38–39.
[18]Ibid.

practice on such a contract to include a liquidated damages clause that requires the supplier to pay the purchaser damages of a set amount per day for late delivery. It is essential, however, that the specified damage figure be a reasonable estimate of the probable loss to the buyer and not be calculated simply to impose a penalty on the supplier. Courts generally refuse to enforce a penalty provision even if the parties have agreed to it in their contract.

## JIT Contracts

Because just-in-time purchasing and manufacturing operations are unique, they occasionally generate unexpected legal difficulties. The most common problems are reviewed briefly in the following paragraphs.

The major factor a buyer should keep in mind is that in most cases a JIT purchasing agreement requires levels of supplier performance different from those the supplier has been used to. Consequently, it is important that communications be clear and complete. This includes oral discussions before the purchase as well as the final written documents. Requirements for quality, delivery scheduling, inventory levels, and any other key factors should be spelled out in unequivocal terms so that there is little opportunity for misunderstanding that might lead to litigation.

Consider the following illustration. Assume that a buyer and a supplier have been doing business satisfactorily for several years. During the last year, approximately one-third of the shipments from the supplier arrived a week or so late, but the buyer accepted them without serious complaints. In the eyes of the law, these acceptances by the buyer may have set a precedent which waives the buyer's rights to timely delivery on future contracts—not good for a new JIT contract. What must the buyer do to regain his or her rights? The two legal requirements are as follows:

1. Give explicit written notice to the supplier.
2. Give the supplier a reasonable amount of time to gear up to meet the new delivery requirements.

With respect to the timing of design or configuration changes, the contract always should specify the minimal lead time, in terms of days or weeks of material usage, that the supplier will accept before supplying the modified material. Both parties should know what the supplier's planned inventory levels are so that the firm is not likely to be left with unusable stock built to the buyer's specifications. By the same token, the two also must agree on the minimum practical lead-time requirements for a delivery lot size increase or an accelerated delivery schedule.

The point is that JIT systems must be able to respond quickly to demand changes because of their tight scheduling and low inventory characteristics on the buyer's side. These requirements for flexibility must be built into the purchase contract to the extent possible. Although meshing the buyer's needs with the supplier's capabilities may be difficult, it is these issues which should be discussed ahead of time, agreed on, and stated in the contract.

Inspection and acceptance is another area that can pose problems. Many JIT shipments are delivered directly to the point of use without going through incoming inspection. In many cases, detection of nonconforming items does not occur until some time later, after the item has entered the production process. If no provision for this situation is made in the contract, legally the material may be considered to have been accepted when delivered. Consequently, this modified operating procedure should be detailed clearly in the contract. A satisfactory time frame for acceptance and the responsibility for subsequent rework costs should be stipulated.

In structuring JIT purchase orders and contracts, common sense tells the buyer to be conservative and to include ample detail about these unique issues in the contractual documents.

## Honest Mistakes

When an honest mistake is made in drawing up a purchase contract, the conditions surrounding each specific case weigh heavily in determining whether the contract is enforceable as written. As a general rule, a mistake made by only one party does not render a contract unenforceable unless the other party is aware of or should have been aware of the mistake at the time of contract formation. The mistake must concern a basic assumption on which the contract was made and must affect the agreed exchange of performance materially. To affect a contract, a mistake usually must be made by both parties in regard to some basic assumption of the contract or its subject matter. Even then, not every mutual mistake invalidates the contract.

Assume, for example, that a supplier intends to submit a quotation with a price of $260. Through an error, the price is typed on the quotation as $250 and is transmitted that way to the buyer. In such cases, courts have held that if the buyer accepts the offer, without knowledge of the error, a valid contract exists. The magnitude of the error is deemed insufficient to affect the agreement materially. However, if the $260 price were incorrectly typed as $26, the court probably would hold that a competent buyer should have recognized the error and sought clarification before accepting it.

Contrast the foregoing example with the following scenario, in which the contract would not be enforceable as written because of the failure of a basic assumption: If the buyer and a supplier agree on the sale of specific machinery and, unknown to either, the machinery has been destroyed or for some other reason is not available for sale, a mutual mistake exists and the contract will not be enforced.

Generally, a buyer should not assume that a mistake, however innocent, will release his or her firm from a contractual obligation. In the majority of cases, it will not do that. A prudent buyer employs all reasonable means to minimize the possibility of committing contractual mistakes.

## Patent Infringement

The law does not give a patent holder the exclusive right to manufacture, sell, and use a patented device for a specified number of years. Rather, the law gives a patent holder the right to *preclude* others from manufacturing, using, or selling the patented device for the term of the patent. A supplier who engages in any of these activities during the term of the patent without permission from the patent holder may be liable to the patent holder for patent infringement.

Buyers frequently have no way of knowing whether their suppliers are selling infringing materials with or without authorization from the patent holder. If a purchaser unknowingly buys an item from a supplier who has infringed the patent holder's rights, the purchaser also may be liable for infringement. To protect against such unintentional violations, most companies include protective clauses in their purchase contracts in which the supplier warrants that its materials do not infringe a third party's intellectual property rights[19] and that the supplier will indemnify the purchaser for all expenses and damages resulting from patent infringement. Clauses of this type do not prevent the patent holder from suing the customer. However, if properly stated, they can require the supplier to defend the customer in such legal proceedings and give the customer legal recourse to recover any resulting losses from the supplier.

---

[19]Note that in a contract for the sale of goods it is not necessary to have an express warranty of noninfringement. As was discussed on p. 409, under the UCC the supplier gives an implied warranty of noninfringement unless it is disclaimed

## Restraint of Trade Laws

The Robinson-Patman Act, a 1936 amendment to the Clayton Act, was designed to prevent price discrimination that reduces competition in interstate commerce. Generally, the act prevents a supplier from offering the same quantity of a specific material to similarly situated *distributors* at different prices unless (1) one distributor is offered a lower price because his or her purchases entail lower manufacturing or distribution costs for the supplier or (2) one distributor is offered a lower price to meet the legitimate bid of a competing supplier.[20]

As Pinkerton and Kemp state, while the law was designed primarily to protect small retail food businesses from large chain stores such as A&P, "the act could apply to typical industrial purchasing situations. Even though there have been very few cases involving industrial buyers purchasing materials, equipment, and components for their own use."[21] However, there have been several major cases, including Jacobs Manufacturing Company (manufacturer of industrial chucks used in portable machine tools) and the famous Minneapolis-Honeywell Regulator Company case of 1948.[22] While litigation is dormant at the present time, one must remember that the Robison-Patman Act is "still on the books" and future federal administrations may pursue its enforcement aggressively.[23] In addition, some suppliers will use the Robinson-Patman Act as a scare tactic to avoid granting legitimate volume discounts; that can be legal under the various defenses listed in this section and in the article by Pinkerton and Kemp.

# International Considerations

When a supply manager sources outside the United States, the chances are very good that a different set of laws will govern the related purchasing transactions. If it is stipulated and agreed on in the contract, the governing law could be U.S. law, or it could be the law of the supplier's country. Whether or not U.S. law is selected as the governing law, the United Nations' Convention on Contracts for the International Sale of Goods (CISG)—an international analog to the UCC but with several provisions which materially differ from the UCC—could be read into the contract unless expressly waived.

In any case, in international or global procurement, it is particularly important to stipulate in the purchase order or contract which body of law is acceptable to both the buyer and the seller and subsequently will govern the transaction. Similarly, it is important also to stipulate a mutually acceptable "choice of forum," that is, the location in which disputes will be heard if a legal dispute arises.

Many firms today select arbitration for dispute resolution under cross-border contracts. There are several factors which favor this approach over litigating a dispute in a foreign court. First, the parties can stipulate, among other things, who will supervise the arbitration (the London Court of International Arbitration or the International Chamber of Commerce, among many others), the venue for the arbitration, the language the arbitration will be conducted in, and the qualifications of the arbitrators. Second, countries which have signed the Convention on the Recognition and Enforcement of Foreign Arbitral Awards

---

[20]A third condition also permits the offering of a discriminatory price, namely, one in which the marketability of goods is affected. Seasonal goods or those approaching obsolescence or deterioration fall into this category.

[21]Richard L. Pinkerton, and Deborah J. Kemp, "The Industrial Buyer and the Robinson-Patman Act," *International Journal of Purchasing and Materials Management*, Winter 1996, pp. 29–36. Also see, W. C. Benton, Jr., *Purchasing and Supply Management*, Burr Ridge, IL: McGraw-Hill/Irwin 2007, pp. 250–257.

[22]Ibid.

[23]Ibid.

(known as the New York Convention) agree to enforce arbitral awards wherever obtained.[24] Third, the parties can avoid the situation in which one party is favored over the other by virtue of having the dispute litigated in its hometown.

The following sections provide an overview of two key topics for international purchasers: the CISG and the Foreign Corrupt Practices Act.

## Contracts for the International Sale of Goods

During the early 1980s, the United Nations facilitated the development of a uniform body of law to govern contracts for international sales of commercial goods. As was noted above, the title given to that body of law is the United Nations' Convention on Contracts for the International Sale of Goods, commonly known as the CISG. The CISG's objective is much like the objective of the Uniform Commercial Code projected to the international level. The CISG does not apply to the purchase of services or to personal purchases of consumer goods.

Generally, the CISG and the UCC have more similarities than differences. However, there are four significant differences that purchasing and supply professionals should know about:

- *Acceptance of an offer.* The CISG requires that an offer be accepted in identical terms—the mirror image concept. If an acceptance contains terms that conflict with those in the offer, no contract exists and the acceptance is treated as a counteroffer.

- *Revocation of an offer.* The CISG permits an offer to be revoked any time before an acceptance is received. One exception is that "if it was reasonable for the offeree to rely on the offer as being irrevocable and the offeree acted in reliance on the offer," the offer cannot be revoked. This revocation provision is less stringent than its counterpart in the UCC.

- *Formation of a contract.* Under the CISG, a contract is created at the time the acceptance is received by the offeror. Under the UCC, the contract is created when the acceptance is mailed or transmitted to the offeror.

- *Oral contracts.* The CISG recognizes oral contracts as being valid and enforceable. In contrast with the UCC, contracts exceeding $500 in value do not require written evidence.

CISG use by American purchasers is placed in focus by the following statement by an internationally known legal authority:

> The similarities between the CISG and the UCC are sufficient enough so business executives do not have to make an issue out of which set of rules applies. On the other hand, one should always be aware that there are these two sets of rules, and in specific cases one may be preferable to the other. In any event, the CISG would appear to be preferable (from the U.S. standpoint) to agreeing to (the use of) another country's law.[25]

## Foreign Corrupt Practices Act[26]

In the early 1970s Congress and the American public learned about a number of questionable payments made by U.S. multinational corporations to foreign government officials to gain an advantage in bidding

---

[24]As of the date of publication, 142 countries had signed on to the New York Convention.

[25]W. A. Hancock, "The UN Convention on the International Sale of Goods," *Executive Legal Summary*, May 1993, p. 100.004.

[26]This discussion is based on material presented by Glenn A. Pitman and James P. Sanford, "The Foreign Corrupt Practices Act Revisited: Attempting to Regulate Ethical Bribes in Global Business," *International Journal of Purchasing and Materials Management*, Summer 1994, pp. 15–20.

for business contracts awarded by those governments. As a result of the strong negative public reaction to those shady business dealings, the appropriate federal agencies investigated the international activities of U.S. firms that appeared to involve the possibility of commercial bribery. The investigation identified several hundred major firms that had been involved in such questionable dealings with potential international customers.

As a result of those findings, in 1977 Congress passed the Foreign Corrupt Practices Act (FCPA) as an amendment to the Securities Exchange Act of 1934. The objective of the new act was to curtail U.S. corporate involvement in foreign commercial bribery activities and, more generally, to enhance the image of the United States throughout the world.

The FCPA contains three major sections focusing on (1) antibribery issues, (2) record-keeping requirements, and (3) penalty provisions. The antibribery section makes it a crime for a U.S. firm to offer or make payments or gifts of substantial value to foreign officials. The intent is to prohibit payments in any form that would influence a major decision of a foreign government official.

Somewhat to the contrary, however, is the fact that the act does allow forms of bribery that are considered minor and inconsequential in influencing important government decisions. It is permissible to make payments (known as "grease money") to operating officials with ministerial or clerical duties. Although the FCPA is vague with respect to the details of application, the Omnibus Trade Act of 1988 specifies which types of payments are acceptable and who may receive them. Such payments are termed "transaction bribes" and are intended to accelerate the performance of a routine function such as loading and unloading cargo, processing goods through customs promptly, moving goods across country, or processing papers. It is expected that these types of payments may speed up governmental actions by lower-level officials that in time would have occurred anyway.

All other types of bribes are considered illegal. As the law now stands, the Omnibus Trade Act holds a firm criminally liable if evidence indicates that one of its representatives had actual knowledge that an illegal payment was made to a foreign government official to secure a favorable decision on a major issue.

Clearly, the FCPA and the related Omnibus Trade Act were designed primarily to curb unacceptable international sales practices. At the same time, however, they apply to international procurement practices. Purchasing professionals engaged in international buying should understand the provisions of these acts and must know the difference between acceptable transaction bribes and bribes whose intent and motivation are illegal.

## Concluding Remarks

The purpose of this chapter is to alert buyers and supply management professionals to the most basic legal considerations that relate to the purchasing and supply function, yet there is a danger in doing this: No author can accomplish this objective briefly without simplifying the issues. Such simplification at times may leave the reader with an incomplete understanding which lulls him or her into a false feeling of security.

Even though adoption of the UCC by all but one of the states has created greater uniformity among state commercial laws than ever before, it is unreasonable to assume that interpretations of the laws by the states will not vary. Only time can reveal how significant such variations will be. Moreover, the interpretation of the circumstances surrounding each specific case weighs heavily in the analysis of that case. These factors virtually defy a definite and unqualified analysis of a legal controversy by anyone who is not a highly skilled professional in the legal field. Heinritz, Farrell, Guinipero, and Kolchin state the matter cogently in saying that "the person who tries to be his or her own lawyer has a fool for a client."[27]

---

[27]Stuart Heinritz, Paul Farrell, Larry Guinipero, and Michael Kolchin, *Purchasing Principles and Applications* (Englewood Cliffs, NJ: Prentice-Hall, 1991), p. 241.

Perhaps the most important function of this chapter is to underscore the fact that supply professionals should seek sound legal counsel whenever potential legal problems arise.

Just as a lawyer is expected to exhibit skill in extricating his or her client from legal entanglements, a purchasing and supply executive is expected to exhibit skill in avoiding legal controversies. A supply manager must understand basic legal concepts well enough to detect potential problems before they become realities. At the same time, the most powerful tool he or she can utilize to avoid legal problems is skill in selecting sound, cooperative, and reliable suppliers. Vigilance in this area of responsibility minimizes the need for legal assistance.

## Discussion Questions

1. Why must a supply manager understand the legal implications of his or her job?
2. In the order of preference from most preferred to least preferred, identify and describe the four principal approaches to resolving disputes.
3. What are the implications of the terms "actual authority," "apparent authority," and "implied authority"?
4. Describe the four basic elements of a contract.
5. Describe the issue of "offer and acceptance" as it relates to purchase orders.
6. What are the implications of "the battle of the forms"?
7. Define the term "liquidated damages." When is the use of liquidated damages appropriate?
8. What are the implications of a supply manager unknowingly purchasing an item from a supplier who has infringed the patent holder's rights?
9. What additional legal issues should be addressed in global procurements?
10. What are the implications for supply managers of the Foreign Corrupt Practices Act?
11. How has e-commerce affected the UCC?
12. Are services *ever* covered under UCC provisions?

## Internet Exercise

### U.S. Bankruptcy Courts
Visit the U.S. Bankruptcy Courts website below. Read about the three main chapters of the Bankruptcy Code which protect troubled businesses.

(http://www.uscourts.gov/bankruptcycourts.html)

1. How is each of these chapters defined?
2. Describe how each chapter works.
3. Why do businesses often opt for Chapter 11 initially?

## Suggested Reading

Bouchoux, Deborah. *Protecting Your Company's Intellectual Property: A Practical Guide to Trademarks, Copyrights, Patents & Trade Secrets* (New York: AMACOM, 2002).

ISM. *Focus on the Legal Aspects of Supply Management: A Collection of ISM Legal Articles*, (Tempe, AZ: ISM, 2003), www.ism.ws.

ISM. *ISM Technotes: Contract Terms and Conditions for Purchase Orders and Other Contractual Agreements* (Tempe, AZ: ISM, 2001), www.ism.ws.

Mann, Richard A., and Barry S. Roberts. *Business Law and the Regulation of Business,* 9th ed. (Cincinnati, OH: Cengage Learning, 2007).

Pohlig, Helen M. *Legal Aspects of Supply Management,* 3rd ed. (Tempe, AZ: ISM, 2008).

## Uniform Commercial Code

American Law Institute, 4025 Chestnut Street, Philadelphia, PA 19104, and National Conference of Commissioners on Uniform State Laws, 211 E. Ontario St. Suite 1300, Chicago, IL 60611. Official Text, West Group, Box 61799, 620 Operman Drive, St. Paul MN 55164-0779.

## Uniform Commercial Code—ABCS of the UCC, Article 2: Sales

Gabriel, Henry D., and Linda J. Rusch, 1997, American Bar Association.

## Potential Changes to the UCC

http://www.law.upenn.edu/bll/ulc/ulc.htm

## Uniform Commercial Code and Commercial Law

http://lawschool.lexis.com/emanuel/contracts
http://www.megalaw.com
http://www.law.cornell.edu/uniform/ucc.html
http://lawcrawler.findlaw.com

# Contract and Relationship Management

*After reading this chapter, you should be able to:*

1. Understand the importance of contract management.

2. Develop a Gantt chart to manage a contract or project.

3. Develop a PERT chart and identify the critical path.

4. Develop a basic plan for monitoring suppliers' contract performance.

## VIGNETTE: MANAGING CONTRACT PERFORMANCE

Carol Gibbons, Hathway Technologies' expediter, is on her way to Sheffield, England, to visit CyberCirc Corporation, commonly referred to as 3C. Hathway's project manager, John Brown, has just learned that the printed circuit boards (PCBs) for his project will be eight weeks late because of problems 3C is having with its South Korean supplier of integrated circuits.

This project is Hathway's first in the British market. Thus, timely completion and high quality are essential to Hathway's future sales in that market. Hathway had awarded the PCBs to 3C because of its reputation as a quality manufacturer.

Carol's mission on this trip is to get 3C's delivery back on schedule. The delay will disrupt Hathway's ability to meet its scheduled completion date.

The resulting reputation for late completion will not help Hathway's efforts to obtain additional work in Europe. John's words are clear: "Make sure 3C understands that I will do anything in my power to ensure that they will not receive any more business if they cause problems on my project." ∎

## CRITICAL THINKING QUESTION

1. What should Hathway have done to avoid this situation?

# Need for Better Contract Management

Historically, the post-award phase of supply management has been a weak one at many organizations. Before the mid-1980s, large inventories were available to accommodate quality problems and late deliveries. Multiple sources of supply often allowed a buyer to get by with little supplier management. However, that mentality cost the buying firm dearly. Shorter production runs under a multiple-sourcing policy frequently resulted in higher prices, lower quality, and the receipt of items which were not identical. Late deliveries resulted in production disruptions, higher production costs, and broken delivery commitments to the firm's customers.

Today, most firms have reduced inventories as embodied in the just-in-time (JIT) philosophy. JIT creates an even greater need for professional post-award management. Under JIT, large inventories are no longer available to cushion the results of weak management at this stage in the process. JIT requires buyers and suppliers to work together to reduce the need for inventories. Tight schedule integration between supplier and customer must be maintained. Processes must be balanced. Waste must be reduced or eliminated. Communication must be in real time. These requirements combine to make buyer-supplier collaboration essential. That collaboration requires supply managers to take a proactive approach to managing both the contract and the supplier relationship. Professional supply relations management is a vital ingredient in several other settings: defense subcontracts, construction contracts, and the purchase of essential services.

The foremost prerequisite to successful contract and relationship management is a sound understanding by both parties of all the aspects of the program. Early supplier involvement, as described throughout this text, greatly facilitates the development of that understanding.

This chapter discusses the many activities a supply manager must perform to ensure that the quality specified in the contract is received on time and that relations with key suppliers are managed carefully in an effort to ensure satisfaction with the supplier's performance now and in the future.

# Pre-Award Conference: The Stage Has Been Set

When the dollar magnitude, complexity, or criticality of the work to be performed dictates, professional supply managers hold a conference with the prospective supplier immediately before the award of the contract. The supply management team—consisting of the supply manager, subcontract administrator or expediter, design engineer, manufacturing engineer, internal customer, quality engineer, and inspector(s), as appropriate—should have met with the supplier's team to discuss the supplier's plans for satisfying the customer's needs. The issues, presented in technical terms, will have been addressed in the request for proposal and the proposed contract. It is important that supply professionals be aware of the transformation of responsibility taking place within the supplying organization. *The supplier's employees responsible for consummating the sale normally are not responsible for performance under the contract. Thus, a new team consisting of operations, demand planning and management, quality, and the supplier's supply management assumes responsibility for performance under the terms of the contract. The pre-award conference is the vehicle the supply management professional and his or her team use to ensure that the contract provisions are fully understood and implemented.* The following items, as appropriate, should be addressed:

■ All terms and conditions.

■ Delivery or operations schedule.

■ Staffing and supervision.

■ Site conditions, work rules, safety (if appropriate).

■ Invoicing procedures and documentation (for incentive and cost contracts).

■ Materials purchase procedures (for incentive, cost, and time and materials contracts).

■ Background checks and security clearances.

■ Insurance certificates.

■ Permits.

■ Possible conflicts with other work.

■ Submission of time sheets (for incentive, cost, and time and materials contracts).

■ Buyer responsibilities. This includes buyer-supplied items such as customer-furnished purchased materials, tools, equipment, and facilities. Timeliness of buyer reviews and approvals for studies, reports, plans and specifications, and so on, must be established and accepted by both parties.

■ Collaboration milestones. Potential points of collaboration which improve designs, processes, communications, quality, and delivery should be identified as early as possible rather than after award of the contract.

■ Key contact people to communicate all of the above with progress reports.

Major one-time projects, such as large construction or site development jobs, have their own unique reporting requirements. Those requirements are described in Appendix A in this chapter.

## Monitoring and Controlling Project Progress

Suppliers are responsible for the timely and satisfactory performance of their contracts. Unfortunately, a supply manager cannot rely entirely on the supplier to ensure that work is progressing as scheduled and that delivery will be as specified. Poor performance or late deliveries disrupt production operations and result in lost sales. Accordingly, supply management must monitor supplier progress to ensure that the desired material is delivered on time. The method of monitoring depends on the lead time, complexity, and urgency of the order or contract. The level of monitoring depends on the criticality of the supplied material or service and the demonstrated ability of the supplier to meet the buying firm's requirements.

At the time a purchase order or contract is awarded, the supply manager should decide whether routine or special attention is appropriate. On many orders for noncritical items, simply monitoring the receipt of receiving and inspection reports may be adequate. On others, telephone confirmation that delivery will be as specified may be sufficient. However, on orders for items critical to the scheduling of operations, more detailed procedures are in order.

When evaluating a supplier's progress, a supply manager is interested in *actual* progress toward completing the work. Data about progress may be obtained from a variety of sources: progress conferences over the phone or face to face, faxes, e-mails, field visits to the supplier's facility, and periodic operations progress reports by the supplier.

## Operations Progress Reports

In some instances, the supplier is required by the terms of the contract to submit a phased production schedule for review and approval. A phased operations schedule shows the time required to perform the production cycle: planning, designing, purchasing, tooling, plant rearrangements, component manufacture, subassembly, final assembly, testing, and shipping.

In many cases, the supply manager may include a requirement for information on production progress in the request for proposal (RFP) and the resulting contract. The ensuing reports frequently show the supplier's actual and forecast deliveries compared with the contract schedule; delay factors, if any; and the status of incomplete preproduction work such as design and engineering, tooling, and the construction of prototypes. The reports also should contain narrative sections in which the supplier explains any difficulties and the actions proposed or taken to overcome those difficulties. In designing the system, the supply manager should ask himself or herself, "What is really essential information?" in an effort to prevent the system from becoming a burden instead of a tool for good management.

Operations progress reports do not alleviate the requirement to conduct visits to the supplier's work site on crucial contracts. The right to conduct those visits must be established in the RFP and the resulting contract. On critical contracts, in which the cost of such visits is justified, it may be desirable to establish a resident facility monitor to ensure the quality and timeliness of the work being performed at the supplier's facility.

When it is determined that an active system of monitoring the supplier's progress is appropriate, the first step in ensuring timely delivery is to evaluate the supplier's proposed delivery schedule for attainability. In their planning and control activities, most suppliers utilize a variety of graphic methods for portraying the proposed schedule and then for monitoring progress against it. These are useful management tools that also can be reviewed and evaluated by the buying team. These visual presentations are forceful and usually can be updated economically. Two progress planning and control techniques commonly used for important projects and jobs are discussed briefly below.

## Gantt Charts

Gantt charts are the simplest charting technique for planning and controlling major projects and the materials deliveries that flow from them. Gantt charting requires that (1) first, a project must be broken into its elements; (2) next, the time required to complete each element must be estimated and plotted on a time scale; (3) the elements then must be listed vertically in time sequence, determining which elements must be performed sequentially and which concurrently; and (4) finally, actual progress is charted against the plan on the time scale.

In addition to the detailed charts maintained by the supplier, the supply manager can construct a master chart to use in controlling the job. In this case, the supplier is asked to submit weekly or monthly progress data that are posted to the buying firm's master chart. Figure 18.1 illustrates a typical Gantt chart of this type.

A Gantt chart portrays the plan, schedule, and progress together in one easy-to-use chart. It shows the status of project elements, or activities, and identifies which are behind or ahead of schedule. Unfortunately, Gantt charts fail to provide the full impact of an activity's being behind or ahead of schedule and do not provide sufficient detail to detect some schedule slippages in a timely manner.

As long as the project is not too large or complex, Gantt charts work fine. As the number of *interdependent* activities increases, however, a Gantt chart fails to tell the supply manager one important fact he or she needs to know to manage the project efficiently. If slowdowns occur as work progresses on the various parts of the project, is the timing of some activities more critical than that of others? The answer is yes—and the Gantt chart does not indicate which ones! For every project, at least one group of interrelated

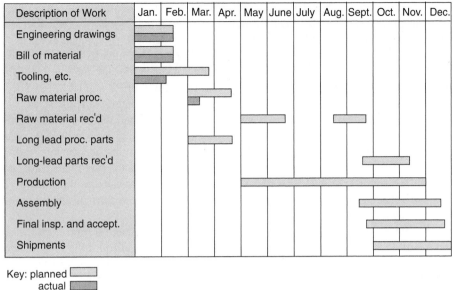

| Description of Work | Jan. | Feb. | Mar. | Apr. | May | June | July | Aug. | Sept. | Oct. | Nov. | Dec. |
|---|---|---|---|---|---|---|---|---|---|---|---|---|
| Engineering drawings | | | | | | | | | | | | |
| Bill of material | | | | | | | | | | | | |
| Tooling, etc. | | | | | | | | | | | | |
| Raw material proc. | | | | | | | | | | | | |
| Raw material rec'd | | | | | | | | | | | | |
| Long lead proc. parts | | | | | | | | | | | | |
| Long-lead parts rec'd | | | | | | | | | | | | |
| Production | | | | | | | | | | | | |
| Assembly | | | | | | | | | | | | |
| Final insp. and accept. | | | | | | | | | | | | |
| Shipments | | | | | | | | | | | | |

Key: planned
actual

**Figure 18.1** | Production Schedule and Progress Chart (Gantt Chart)

activities makes up what is called the *critical path.* If any of these activities fall behind schedule, the total project will not be completed on time. The supply manager must monitor these potential bottleneck activities very carefully. To overcome this Gantt chart deficiency, a computer-based technique called critical path scheduling has been developed to provide the required management capability.

## CPM and PERT

*Critical path scheduling* is a tool that can be used to manage project buying activities, construction projects, and research and development projects, to name just a few. The technique can be used for these and other complex projects of a one-time nature. The project's magnitude must justify the relatively high cost of this approach to management compared with more conventional methods such as the Gantt chart. Critical path scheduling is useful for planning, monitoring, and controlling complex projects composed of a large number of *interrelated* and *interdependent* activities.

The critical path approach quantifies information about uncertainties faced by the activities responsible for meeting a predetermined time schedule. The very process of analyzing these uncertainties focuses the manager's attention on the most critical series of activities in the total project from a timing perspective—those which constitute the "critical path." The critical path activities must be accomplished sequentially, thus representing the chain of activities that require the most time from start to finish of the project. When those activities are pinpointed, the manager can develop an appropriate control strategy to optimize the operating results.

When it is used for controlling contract performance, the posting of progress data permits the supply manager to compare actual accomplishments with those which were planned. He or she then can determine the likely implications of slippages with respect to critical path time requirements. The supply manager then works with the supplier to correct or minimize the resulting problems.

A variety of specific techniques have been derived from the basic critical path scheduling concept. The best known are the *critical path method* (CPM) and *program evaluation and review technique* (PERT). CPM was developed in 1955 by the Du Pont and Remington Rand companies for use in coping with complex plant maintenance problems. PERT emerged in 1958 through the joint efforts of the U.S. Navy; the Booz, Allen & Hamilton consulting firm; and the Lockheed Missile and Space Division in connection with the Polaris weapons program. With the passage of time, PERT and CPM have become very similar in concept. Currently, they differ only with respect to various details of application.

In practice, the application of CPM/PERT generally is accomplished with a computer program that uses network diagrams to show time and dependency relationships among the activities that make up the total project. The purpose of the technique is to keep all the "parts" arriving on schedule so that the total project can be completed as planned. By using CPM/PERT data outputs, the supply manager can evaluate possible trade-offs if supplier resources were reallocated in alternative ways to improve the chances of meeting the time schedule. This technique quickly can determine the results of alternative courses of action, thus allowing the best choice of the alternatives available.

Most important, the CPM/PERT technique is both a planning tool and a control tool. The fact that the individual activities of a project are structured into a network requiring time and sequence determination is critically important; it is the basis for all subsequent monitoring and control activity. Use of the technique forces a supply manager to conduct this step-by-step planning in advance and to reexamine the logic of the decisions periodically as the dynamics of the operation unfold. The mechanics of critical path scheduling are described briefly with an example in Appendix B at the end of this chapter.

### Closed Loop MRP Systems

Many manufacturers use a closed loop MRP system to schedule and control production, inventory levels, and deliveries from outside suppliers. Supplier-furnished data can be used by the individuals controlling the firm's incoming materials schedules as they monitor their system reports. Daily or weekly status reports flow from the supplier to the scheduler, who then inputs the data for the next MRP run. See Chapter 20 for a full discussion of MRP systems.

A growing number of firms link their suppliers' computer-based systems into their own computer system so that real-time data are available to both parties. If supplier-furnished data indicate that the supplier's delivery dates will result in a disruption of the buying firm's schedule, the appropriate scheduler or supply manager can take action to modify the supplier's schedule or adjust the buying firm's production schedule, as appropriate.

# Monitoring and Controlling Total Supplier Performance

The use of supplier performance evaluation systems is on the rise. A majority of major manufacturing firms, as well as an increasing number of service firms, either have established formal supplier-evaluation programs or are in the process of doing so.

Many progressive buying organizations monitor their critical suppliers' performance at both a contract level and an aggregate level. That information is used to control a supplier's contract performance and also is used during source selection for follow-on procurements to ensure that only satisfactory performers are considered.

## Supplier Performance Evaluation

After a major supplier has been selected and the buyer-supplier relationship has begun to develop, it is important to monitor and assess the supplier's overall performance. The purpose is to enhance the relationship and thus control performance.

Many evaluation teams use a three- to six-month moving average for the aggregate evaluation of a supplier's performance. For example, with a six-month window, a supplier's rating in June is an average of all the ratings accumulated between January and June. The moving average allows suppliers to start over at some point. The suppliers' misdeeds don't haunt them forever; they're motivated to improve. The length of the window is important and should be case-specific. A shorter window may be ineffective because it lets suppliers off the hook too easily. A longer window may be punitive and self-defeating.

Three types of evaluation plans are common: the *categorical plan,* the *weighted point plan*, and the *cost ratio plan.* Each of these plans is reviewed briefly in the following pages.

**Categorical Plan**   Under the categorical plan, personnel from various departments of the buying firm maintain informal evaluation records. The individuals involved traditionally include personnel from supply management, engineering, quality, accounting, and receiving. Each evaluator prepares a list of performance factors that are important to him or her for each major supplier. Each major supplier is evaluated against each evaluator's list of factors at a monthly or bimonthly meeting. After the factors are weighted for relative importance, each supplier is assigned an overall group evaluation, usually expressed in simple categorical terms such as "preferred," "neutral," or "unsatisfactory." This simple qualitative plan is easy to administer and has been reported by many firms to be very effective.

**The Weighted Point Plan**   Under this plan, the performance factors to be evaluated (often various aspects of quality, service, price, technology, and management skills) are given "weights." For example, in one circumstance, quality might be weighted 25 percent, service 25 percent, and price 50 percent. In another, quality could be raised to 50 percent and price would be reduced to 25 percent. The weights selected in any specific situation represent supply manager or supply team judgments concerning the relative importance of the respective factors.

After performance factors have been selected and weighted, a specific procedure is developed to measure actual supplier performance on each factor. Supplier performance on each factor must be expressed in quantitative terms. To determine a supplier's overall rating, each factor weight is multiplied by the supplier's corresponding performance number; the results for each factor then are totaled to get the supplier's final rating for the time period in question.

The following hypothetical case illustrates the procedure. Assume that a supply management department has decided to weight and measure the three basic performance factors as follows:

| Weight | Factors | Measurement Formula |
|--------|---------|---------------------|
| 50% | Quality performance = 100% − percentage of rejects | |
| 25% | Service performance = 100% − 7% for each failure | |
| 25% | Price performance  = | $\dfrac{\text{lowest price offered}}{\text{price actually paid}}$ |

Assume further that supplier A performed as follows during the last month. Five percent of its items were rejected for quality reasons; three unsatisfactory split shipments were received; and A's price was $100/unit, compared with the lowest offer of $90/unit. Table 18.1 summarizes the total performance evaluation calculation for supplier A.

**Table 18.1** I Illustrative Application of the Weighted Point Plan

*Supplier A Monthly Performance Evaluation*

| Factor | Weight | Actual Performance | Performance Evaluation |
|--------|--------|--------------------|------------------------|
| Quality | 50 | 5% rejects | $50 \times (1.00 - 0.05) = 47.50$ |
| Service | 25 | 3 failures | $25 \times [1.00 - (0.07 \times 3)] = 19.75$ |
| Price | 25 | $100 | $25 \times \frac{\$90}{\$100} = 22.50$ |

**Overall evaluation: = 89.75**

This procedure can be used to evaluate any number of different suppliers whose performance is particularly important during a particular operating period. The performance of competing suppliers can be compared quantitatively, and subsequent negotiating strategies can be developed accordingly. The user always should remember that valid performance comparisons of two or more suppliers require that the same factors, weights, and measurement formulas be used *consistently* for all suppliers.

In contrast to the categorical plan, which is largely subjective, the weighted point plan has the advantage of being somewhat more objective. The exercise of subjective judgment is constrained more tightly in the assignment of factor weights and the development of the formulas for factor measurement. The plan is extremely flexible, since it can accommodate any number of evaluation factors that are important in any specific case. Also, the plan can be used in conjunction with the categorical plan if buyers wish to include important subjective matters in the final evaluation of their suppliers.

Various research studies have noted, however, that a weighted point plan must be developed with care. The estimates of factor importance must be consistent from one situation to the next and must be consistent with the performance measurement formulas used because of the obvious interaction between them.

**Cost Ratio Plan**    This plan evaluates supplier performance by using the tools of *standard cost* analysis that businesspeople traditionally employ to evaluate a wide variety of business operations. When using this plan, the buying firm identifies the *additional* costs it incurs in doing business with a particular supplier; those costs are separated as costs associated with the quality, service, and price elements of supplier performance. Each of the costs then is converted to a "cost ratio" which expresses the additional cost as a percentage of the buying firm's total dollar purchase from that supplier. These three individual cost ratios then are totaled, producing the supplier's overall additional cost ratio. For purposes of analysis, the supplier's price is adjusted by applying its overall cost ratio. The adjusted price for each supplier then is compared with the adjusted price for other competitive suppliers in the final evaluation process.

For example, assume that for one supplier the quality cost ratio is 2 percent, the delivery cost ratio is 2 percent, the service cost ratio is −1 percent, and the price is $72.25. The sum of all cost ratios is 3 percent; hence, the adjusted price for this supplier is $[72.25 + (0.03 \times 72.25)] = \$74.42$. This is the price used for evaluation purposes vis-à-vis other suppliers.

Although the cost ratio plan is used by a number of large progressive firms, overall it is not used widely in industry. Operationally, it is a complex plan. It requires a specially designed, companywide computerized cost accounting system to generate the precise cost data needed for effective operation. Consequently, the majority of supply management departments that employ a quantitative type of evaluation rely on the simpler but effective weighted point plan, typically modified specifically to meet their unique circumstances. The use of activity based cost accounting (ABC) systems is essential to provide data for cost ratio plans.[1]

For these reasons, the cost ratio plan is not discussed in detail in this book. Nevertheless, it is an excellent concept that has the ability to provide the most precise evaluation data among the three plans discussed. For firms using sophisticated information systems, the cost of designing and implementing the cost ratio plan typically is repaid many times by savings resulting from more precise analysis of supplier performance.

All three of the plans discussed—categorical, weighted point, and cost ratio—involve varying degrees of subjectivity and guesswork. The mathematical treatment of data in two of the plans often tends to obscure the fact that the results are no more accurate than the assumptions on which the quantitative data are based. In the final analysis, therefore, supplier evaluation must represent a combined appraisal of facts, quantitative computations, and value judgments. It simply cannot be achieved effectively by the use of mechanical formulas alone.

Since the late 1980s, "scorecarding" has become a trendy but confusing term used to describe variations of these three methods. The confusion is due to misinterpretation of the balanced scorecard, a tool developed by Kaplan and Norton that focuses on four corporate goals: financial, customer, internal business processes, and learning and growth.

**Cost-Based Supplier Performance Evaluation**    A number of firms are experimenting with various types of cost-based evaluation plans similar to the cost ratio plan. Those plans address the issue of finding ways to measure overall supplier performance on a total cost basis. In addition to rationalizing lowest total cost performance suppliers, such plans demonstrate that supplier nonperformance costs can be measured. Recognizing the supplier as an integral member of the organization, competitive strategy requires the development of a system that provides supplier accountability and control while maintaining dependable, competitive suppliers. As organizations continue to secure longer-term supplier relationships, the ability to quantify performance becomes increasingly important. Companies can use the methodology as a contract monitoring tool when it is incorporated into long-term agreements. Again, the use of ABC accounting systems greatly facilitates this kind of evaluation.

# Motivation

Two common approaches are used to motivate suppliers to perform satisfactorily: punishment and reward. Many progressive supply managers use a combination of both approaches.

## Punishment

Obviously, the greatest punishment for unsatisfactory performance (if the area of litigation and punitive damages is ignored) is *not* to award contracts for future requirements. This is a powerful motivator, especially during periods when supply professionals are reducing the number of suppliers with which they do business.

---

[1]Mary Lu Harding, "The ABC's of Activities and Drivers," *NAPM Insights,* November 1994, p. 6. For further information on ABC, the OSD comptroller icenter is a comprehensive online site related to the U.S. Department of Defense budget process, financial management, and best practices. Visit this site for educational information on the use ABC costing. http://www.dod.mil/comptroller/icenter/learn/abcosting.htm.

Another method is to downgrade a supplier. Applied Materials, for example, grades suppliers into categories, the highest of which is preferred. A preferred supplier will have business increased over time and be included in Applied Materials' strategic plans. A poorly performing supplier can be downgraded, reducing its future business opportunities.

A less drastic approach called the "bill back" is especially appropriate in dealing with a "collaborative" supplier or a defense contractor. Under the bill back, incremental costs resulting from quality problems or late deliveries are identified and then billed back to the appropriate supplier. Some progressive supply managers have increased the motivational effect of the bill back by sending the bill to the supplier's chief operating officer so that he or she is aware of problems within his or her organization.

## Rewards

The biggest reward for satisfactory performance is follow-on business. Referring back to the example above, Applied Materials rewards superior performers with follow-on business as well as a greater opportunity for future business.

Additionally, as with raising children or dealing with "significant others," recognition is a powerful stimulant for future successful performance. Several years ago, an Arizona supply manager divided her suppliers into three categories: outstanding, acceptable, and marginal. She wrote an appropriate letter to the CEO of each supplier firm. The results of her efforts were rewarding. The outstanding group performed even better! Most of the CEOs from the second and third groups requested meetings to discuss what they could do better to earn *an outstanding ranking!*

A major appliance manufacturer publicly recognizes its most successful suppliers. Those suppliers are encouraged to share their recognition with their employees. The employees are encouraged to continue their efforts to improve quality and productivity. Many suppliers reward their outstanding employees with a trip to the buying firm to see how their products are used.

Each year, the appliance manufacturer selects its 100 "best" suppliers. This selection is based on a combination of service, responsiveness, value analysis suggestions, cost, and related factors. Each representative and CEO attends the Supplier Appreciation Group's Day. Over 50 senior managers from the buying firm also attend. Each of the 100 outstanding suppliers receives a plaque acknowledging its status and contribution. The buying firm publicizes this list in appliance and supply magazines, to the delight of those listed.

# Assistance

Progressive firms have discovered that several types of assistance to suppliers pay big dividends.

## Transformational Training

Many firms have learned the benefits of providing training to their suppliers in approaches such as statistical process control (SPC), just-in-time (JIT) manufacturing, and Six Sigma. Progressive firms recognize that their ability to procure quality products and services on time requires suppliers with competence in these tools and philosophies.

## Quality Audits and Supply System Reviews

As organizations realize their interdependence with their suppliers, they are becoming more proactive in ensuring that their suppliers' quality systems and procurement systems operate effectively. Such assurance often is provided by quality audits and supply system reviews given by the buying firm. These reviews should not be focused on punishment but on identifying opportunities for improvement.

A supplier's procurement system affects its quality, cost, technology, and dependability. In theory, competition rewards suppliers that have efficient procurement systems with *survival* and *profit* and penalizes suppliers with inefficient systems. However, the theory may take years to show results. Further, as firms move from reliance on market competition to collaborative and alliance relationships, the implications of inefficient supplier procurement systems become even more frightening. The supply system review provides a framework that a buying firm may follow in reviewing its key suppliers and helping them upgrade their supply systems. The review is conducted in a constructive, cooperative atmosphere.

## Problem Solving

Most progressive firms provide technical and managerial assistance to their suppliers when quality and related problems are encountered. Progressive supply managers have replaced the attitude "it's their contract and it's their problem" with the knowledge that the buying firm's success is dependent on its suppliers' success. Many problem-solving tools and techniques used in aiding suppliers are presented in Chapter 10. Honda has a rather elaborate troubleshooting team to visit a supplier to offer technical assistance.

# Collaboration

Experience in recent years has demonstrated that the most successful supplier management results are generated when the buyer and the supplier view their relationship as one of collaboration. Those relationships are based on mutual interdependency and respect. Collaborative relationships begin or are renewed with careful source selection during the product and/or service design and development process. At this point, the buying firm needs a dependable supplier to provide the required process, design, and technological input if a marketable, profitable product or a satisfactory service is to result. In turn, the supplier needs a responsible customer for its products and services. Supply professionals need the supplier as much as or more than the supplier needs them. This interdependence grows as a project moves from design into operations. Unexpected problems arise which require a "We shall overcome" attitude in the partners. During production, the buyers and suppliers must mesh their schedules, requiring another phase of cooperation.

The *ultimate* in collaborative relationships is a virtual integration of buyer and supplier in which two independently owned entities integrate their energies for as long as the relationship benefits both parties. One- or two-page memoranda of agreement replace lengthy contracts, change orders, and other legalistic and defensive procedures. As was discussed in Chapter 4, we reserve the term "alliances" for such relationships. Finally, many firms are asking suppliers to rate their (buying firm) purchasing practices; see Appendix C.

## Managing the Relationship

As was discussed previously, any supply management department normally will have a continuum of supplier relationships from arm's-length through collaborative to strategic alliances. The second and third types of relationships are increasing in number. Developing and managing such relationships are both challenging and fulfilling.

Several actions must be taken to ensure the success of each supply alliance relationship. (Supply managers should select and tailor appropriate actions when they are planning the management of collaborative relationships.) For example:

■ Ideally, an interfirm cross-functional team should be established to develop and manage plans, facilitate integration, and develop and manage appropriate metrics.

■ Appropriate cross-functional team members at both the buying firm and the selling firm should receive training in being constructive team players.

■ An interfirm team composed of representatives of both firms should be formed. Members should jointly receive training in cross-functional team skills.

■ The two firms must develop an integrated communication system that is responsive to the needs of both parties in their area of cooperation.

■ Plans to increase and measure trust between the two organizations should be developed and implemented.

■ Arrangements for colocation of key technical personnel and periodic visits to each other's facilities should be developed and implemented.

■ Plans should be developed and implemented for training on issues, including the designing of variance out of products and processes, quality, supply management, value analysis and engineering, strategic cost analysis, and activity based cost management.

■ Measurable quantifiable objectives must be established in areas such as quality, cost, time, and technology.

■ The results of such improvement efforts must be monitored and reported to appropriate management.

■ Ethics should win over expediency.

■ Interfirm team members and others who are closely involved must recognize the need to change their orientation from adversarial to collaborative.

■ Interfirm team members should become champions who ensure that their organizations understand and support the alliance's goals.

■ Transparency of cost and other critical data is vital.

It is in the interest of both the buying and supplying firms for the buying firm's personnel to support the supplier's operations.

## Concluding Remarks

Without question, management of supply contracts is a critical and challenging activity. Perhaps the most challenging aspect is the evolution from managing or controlling the supplier to managing the relationship. New attitudes and skills are required. Supplier relationships require the same amount of attention as a good marriage, but the many benefits of successful relationships make the efforts worthwhile.

## Discusion Questions

1. What are the possible results of late deliveries of critical materials?
2. Does JIT manufacturing call for more or less emphasis on supplier management? Why?
3. What is the foremost prerequisite to successful supplier management?
4. Describe and discuss the objectives of and potential topics for a pre-award conference.
5. What are logical sources of data on the supplier's actual progress?
6. What is the simplest progress charting technique? Describe it.
7. Describe critical path scheduling. When is it applicable?
8. How can closed loop MRP systems aid in controlling a firm's incoming materials?

9. Identify and describe three supplier performance evaluation plans.
10. How can a buyer motivate suppliers to perform satisfactorily?
11. Should industrial firms facilitate the training of their suppliers? If so, in what areas? Why?
12. What is a procurement system review? How can it help the buying firm?
13. What kinds of rewards seem to work the best?
14. Describe a supplier partnership.
15. Discuss the responsibilities of a supply relationship manager.

## Internet Exercise

### Reforming Project Management

Visit the website on project management below. Click on and read several of the articles in the series "Using Gantt Charts."

(http://www.reformingprojectmanagement.com/2007/01/28/748/)

1. Describe a project you believe would be better managed through the use of a Gantt chart.

## Suggested Reading

Anderson, Ruth, and Maytee Aspuro. "Managing the Contract," *NAPM InfoEdge* 2, no. 10 (June 1997).

Crowder, Mark A. "Project Organization and Management," *NAPM InfoEdge* 4, no. 2 (October 1998).

Giannakis, Mihalis, and Simon R. Croom. "Toward the Development of a Supply Chain Management Paradigm: A Conceptual Framework," *Journal of Supply Chain Management,* Spring 2004, pp. 27–37.

Greico, Peter, Jr., Michael W. Gozzo, and Jerry W. Claunch. *Supplier Certification II: A Handbook for Achieving Excellence through Continuous Improvement*, 3d ed. (Plantsville, CT: PT Publications, 1992).

Harding, Mary Lu. "The ABC's of Activities and Drivers," *NAPM Insights,* November 1994, p. 6.

Parker, Geoffrey G., and Edward G. Anderson, Jr. "From Buyer to Integrator: The Transformation of the Supply Chain Manager in the Vertically Disintegrating Firm," *Production and Operations Management* 11, no. 1 (Spring 2002), pp. 75–91.

Rollman, Mary. "Mind the Gap: Collaborative Sourcing and Supplier Relationship Software," *Inside Supply Management,* November 2006, pp. 12–13.

## Appendix A: Supplier Reporting Requirements for Unique Major Projects

During the pre-award conference, arrangements are made for the timely receipt of the following data, as appropriate:

■ *A program organization chart.* For a large job, the supplier designates its program manager and lists the key members of the organization by name and function. The program manager's functional authority should be defined clearly.

■ *Milestone plan.* For a complex project, a milestone plan identifies all major milestones on a time-phased basis, including those of the supplier's major subcontractors.

- *Funds commitment plan* (incentive and cost reimbursement contracts only). This plan shows estimated commitments on a dollar versus month basis and on a cumulative dollar versus month basis.
- *Labor commitment plan.* This plan shows estimated labor loading on a labor-hour versus labor-month basis.
- *Monthly progress information.* This report should be submitted 10 days after the close of each month. The report should contain the following as a minimum:
  - *A narrative summary of work accomplished* during the reporting period, including a technical progress update, a summary of work planned for the next reporting period, problems encountered or anticipated, corrective action taken or to be taken, and a summary of buyer-seller discussions.
  - *A list of all action items,* if any, required of the buying firm during the forthcoming performance period.
  - *An update of the milestone plan* showing actual progress against planned progress.
  - *An update of the funds commitment plan* showing actual funds committed against the planned funds by time (incentive and cost reimbursement contracts only).
  - *A report on any significant changes* in the supplier's program personnel or in the financial or general management structure or any other factors that might affect performance.
  - *A missed milestone notification and recovery plan.* The supplier should notify the supply manager by phone, fax, or e-mail within 24 hours after the discovery of a missed major milestone or an anticipated major milestone slip. The supplier should provide the supply manager with a missed milestone recovery plan within seven working days.

Such data can be costly to compile and should be required only when it has been determined that their cost and the cost associated with using them to manage an order will result in a net saving or the likely avoidance of a schedule slippage. The supply manager, on a case-by-case basis, must determine what level of detail is necessary.

## Appendix B: How Critical Path Scheduling Works

Critical path scheduling begins with the identification and listing of all significant activities involved in the project to be planned and controlled. When the list of activities is complete, the sequential relationship among all activities is determined and shown graphically by constructing an activity network (see Figure 18.2). The network shows the time required to complete each activity and explicitly indicates the relationship of each activity to all other activities. Finally, it establishes the sequence in which activities should be scheduled for efficient completion of the total project. Some activities can be paralleled, allowing many different jobs to be carried on simultaneously; other activities must be placed in series to allow step-by-step completion of inter-related tasks. The complete interrelationship of all project activities is the important feature that distinguishes critical path analysis from Gantt and other bar chart planning techniques.

Construction of the network permits determination of a project's *critical path:* the sequentially linked chain (or chains) of activities requiring the most time for completion from start to finish of the project. Once the critical path is determined, the planner can identify precisely and completely the activities that require close control. He or she also can determine which activities permit the greatest latitude in scheduling and can, if necessary, most easily relinquish resources to more urgent jobs. An activity network also highlights the activities that can be expedited most effectively in case a stepped-up pace becomes necessary.

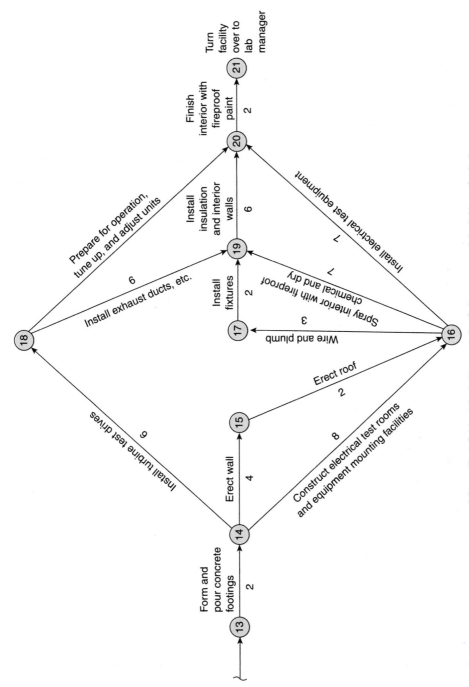

**Figure 18.2 |** Simplified Critical Path Network for Subcontracted Activities of a Laboratory Construction Job

**Figure 18.3 |** Data for Figure 18.2

| Activity (1) | Earliest (2) | | Latest (3) | | Slack (4) |
|---|---|---|---|---|---|
| | Start | Complete | Start | Complete | |
| 13–14 Form and pour concrete footings | 0 | 2 | 0 | 2 | 0 |
| 14–16 Construct electrical test rooms and equipment mounting facilities | 2 | 10 | 2 | 10 | 0 |
| 16–19 Spray interior with fireproof chemical and let dry | 10 | 17 | 10 | 17 | 0 |
| 19–20 Install insulatior and interior walls | 17 | 23 | 17 | 23 | 0 |
| 20–21 Finish interior with fireproof paint | 23 | 25 | 23 | 25 | 0 |
| 14–15 Erect walls | 2 | 6 | 4 | 8 | 2 |
| 15–16 Erect roof | 6 | 8 | 8 | 10 | 2 |
| 16–17 Install electrical wiring and plumbing | 10 | 13 | 12 | 15 | 2 |
| 17–19 Install fixtures | 13 | 15 | 15 | 17 | 2 |
| 14–18 Install turbine test drives | 2 | 8 | 5 | 11 | 3 |
| 18–19 Install exhaust ducts. etc. | 8 | 14 | 11 | 17 | 3 |
| 16–20 Install electrical test equipment | 10 | 17 | 16 | 23 | 6 |
| 18–20 Prepare for operation, tune up, and adjust drive units | 8 | 16 | 15 | 23 | 7 |

Figure 18.2 illustrates the mechanics of network development. This simplified example shows a partial network of the major subcontracted activities involved in the construction of a new laboratory. Engineering and purchasing activities done before site preparation have been omitted for reasons of simplification. The example shows only the major activities to be completed after the site has been excavated and prepared for the concrete subcontractor.

1. Column 1 in Figure 18.3 lists the major activities to be completed.
2. Figure 18.2 shows the activities in network form. The required interdependencies and sequencing of operations have been determined and reviewed with the project engineer and the various subcontractors. Each arrow in the diagram represents an *activity* that will be conducted during a period of time. Each circle represents an *event* that will occur at a specific point in time (e.g., the start of an activity and the completion of an activity).
3. Careful estimates of the time required to complete each activity have been made by the respective contractors and are noted next to the appropriate arrows.[2]
4. The critical path (longest chain of activities) consists of the activities 13-14-16-19-20-21; it will take 25 weeks to finish the project. The critical path is determined by totaling the time requirements for individual activities put together in every conceivable path from start to finish of the project. The critical path is the one requiring the longest time. Using the given time estimates, it is impossible to complete the project in less time.

---

[2]The PERT technique often is used for jobs whose time requirements cannot be estimated accurately. For this reason, PERT requires three time estimates for each activity: (1) $t_l$ = longest time required under the most difficult conditions (expect once in 100 times), (2) $t_s$ = shortest time required under the best conditions (expect once in 100 times), (3) $t_m$ = most likely time requirement. The expected time $t_e$, the figure actually used on the network, is a weighted average computed as

$$t_e = \frac{t_l + t_s + 4t_m}{6}$$

5. At this point, the objective is to determine the amount of "slack time" (extra time, or leeway) in each of the noncritical paths. This is done by developing the figures in column 2 (the earliest start and completion dates for each activity) and then those in column 3 (the latest possible start and completion dates for each activity) of Figure 18-3.

    The earliest start and completion dates for each activity are determined by starting with the first activity and totaling the time requirements of the various paths through the network. If we say that the earliest start date for 13–14 (the concrete work) is today (the 0 point in time), the earliest completion date for 13–14 is the end of week 2 (0 + 2 = 2). Therefore, the earliest start date for both 14–15 and 14–16, which cannot begin before 13–14 is completed, is the end of week 2. The earliest completion date for 14–16 is the end of week 10 (2 + 8 = 10), and for 14–15 it is the end of week 6 (2 + 4 = 6). The earliest start date for 15–16 is the end of week 6, and the earliest completion date is the end of week 8 (6 + 2 = 8). What is the earliest start date for the electrical wiring and plumbing activity 16–17? Is it the end of week 8 or week 10? Clearly, it is the end of week 10, because the wiring cannot be started until the electrical test rooms and mounting facilities are completed. The analysis continues in this manner through the entire network until column 2 is complete.

    The latest possible start and completion date for each activity (column 3) is determined in exactly the reverse manner. Begin with the completion date for the final activity and work backward through the network, determining the latest completion and start dates that can be used for each activity without delaying the completion of the project. All activities on the critical path will have identical "earliest" and "latest" dates. This is not true, however, for the noncritical path activities.

    The latest completion date for the final painting activity (20–21) is the end of week 25, and the latest start date is the end of week 23 (25 – 2 = 23). Therefore, the latest completion date for 18–20 is the end of week 23, and the latest start date is the end of week 15. Notice, however, that the latest completion date for 14–18 is not the end of week 15. Activity 14–18 must be completed by the latest start date for activity 18–19, which is the end of week 11 (23 – 6 – 6 = 11). This procedure, then, is followed back through the network to complete column 3.

6. The purpose in developing columns 2 and 3 is to determine the amount of *slack time* in each noncritical, or slack, path (column 4). The slack time for a particular activity is simply the difference between the earliest start date and the latest start date (or between the earliest completion date and the latest completion date). This important factor represents leeway which can be used in scheduling the slack path activity most efficiently in light of other demands for facilities and manpower.[3]

The preceding discussion has dealt only with the rudiments of the critical path planning concept. In practice, performance is monitored, and progress data are compared periodically with the original plan. The technique is therefore an effective control device as well as an aid in making future planning decisions as changes in plans occur. The projects to which the technique is applied in practice often are made up of several thousand activities. After the initial network is constructed for such projects, a computer program such as Microsoft Project typically is used.

    Its current popularity indicates that a large number of users find critical path analysis profitable primarily because it forces suppliers to do more planning than they otherwise would do. Numerous governmental and industrial buyers require subcontractors to submit a critical path network (for major events, or "milestones") with their bids on subcontract and construction jobs.

---

[3]Column 4 indicates that both activities 14–15 and 15–16 have two weeks' slack. Notice that this is an either-or situation. Two weeks' slack cannot be utilized in both activities; two weeks represents the total combined slack for both activities.

# Appendix C: Supplier Questionnaire

The Supply Management and Internal Audit Departments at——have developed a short questionnaire to determine the weaknesses and strengths of our procurement and payable functions. To ensure creditability, all suppliers being requested to complete this form were selected by Internal Audit. We would appreciate your taking a few minutes and completing the form. While you need not identify yourself, we would appreciate a generic description of the product or service you provide—see question #7. A self-addressed postage-paid envelope is enclosed for your convenience.

1. Do you find that the supply managers you interact with at _____ possess the necessary expertise to evaluate your products or services fairly?

    _____ Yes _____ No

2. Are you accorded a prompt and courteous interview in the Supply Management Department?

    _____ Yes _____ No

3. When requested to respond to written bids, is your firm allowed sufficient time?

    _____ Yes _____ No

4. On a scale of 1 to 5, 5 being the highest, how would you rate the ethics (honesty, willingness to listen to both sides of an issue, impartiality, etc.) of members of the Supply Management Department?

    Circle one:   1     2     3     4     5

5. Are invoices paid on time? _____ Yes _____ No

6. Do you receive a prompt response when calling about a delinquent payment?

    _____ Yes _____ No

7. Please identify the product or service you provide—examples: laboratory equipment/supplies, agriculture-related products, computer equipment/supplies, etc.

    _____

    _____

    _____

8. Are there any additional comments you have relative to the operation of the purchasing and accounts payable functions at _____ ?

Please return the completed questionnaire to: _____. We would appreciate a return date by _____. Your comments will be appreciated. Thank you!

# CHAPTER 19

## Ethics and Social Responsibilities[1]

### CHAPTER OBJECTIVES

*After reading this chapter, you should be able to:*

1. Understand the basics on which organizational ethics are judged.

2. Define the most important ethical principle for supply managers.

3. Understand how global supply management tempers ethical considerations.

4. Describe confidential supplier information and the responsibility of the supply manager toward that information.

5. Define a supply manager's responsibility to suppliers.

6. Describe the "sharp practices" supply managers can fall into using.

7. Define a supply manager's responsibility in the area of ethics.

8. Understand social responsibilities.

### VIGNETTE: A QUESTION OF ETHICS?

Stacy Nakamura, director of Supply Management at Fremont Equipment Company (FEC), while scanning his e-mail, discovered an invitation from a supplier. The invitation was from Mandy Smith, sales representative of Coastal Lubricants. Every year FEC purchases approximately $1,000,000 worth of

---

[1]The authors of this text give thanks to Eric Drattell, Vice President and General Counsel of Risk Management Solutions, Inc., for his contribution in updating this chapter.

lubricants from one supplier who is selected on the basis of competitive bids each January. Coastal Lubricants is the current supplier. Stacy has been impressed by the persistent efforts of Mandy to keep her company in his thoughts and decision making. Every month she either calls him on the phone or sends an e-mail to discuss existing contracts and new products. This time the e-mail was a draft of an invitation, pending Stacy's approval, to 21 of FEC's executives and supervisors to attend a party. Those invited from FEC are:

- The supply manager, her assistant, and three buyers.
- The plant manager and his assistant.
- The chief design engineer and four engineering section heads.
- The maintenance superintendent and his three foremen.
- The production manager and his staff assistant.
- The controller and her assistant.
- The sales manager.
- The industrial relations manager.

The personnel from Coastal Lubricants attending are:

- Two corporate sales managers and the district manager.
- Several sales representatives.
- A representative from the corporate research department.
- Two representatives from the corporate technical applications department.

The party is planned for a Friday evening in the private dining room of a local hotel and includes the following program:

| | |
|---|---|
| 6:30–7:30 | Cocktail hour |
| 7:30–8:30 | Dinner |
| 8:30–9:00 | Informal discussion and a video of the supplier's technical research activities and achievements |
| 9:00–9:30 | Video of the Olympic Games |
| 9:30–10:00 | Video of "New Dimensions in Musical Entertainment" |
| 10:00 | Adjourn for continuation of the cocktail hour |

Stacy looked over the draft of the invitation and wondered what he should do. He thought, "Should I accept the invitation outright? Should I place some stipulations on the party? Should I reject the invitation? Does FEC have any policies on this issue? If not, should FEC have policies on this issue? Should I really be the one to make the decision to accept the invitation?" ■

## CRITICAL THINKING QUESTION

1. How would you respond to Stacy's questions?

# Ethics in the Supply Management Context

Corporate and academic interest in business ethics has blossomed in recent years. It is, however, well beyond the scope and purpose of this chapter to undertake a review of the extensive literature pertaining to business ethics. This is particularly true when one considers how ethics varies from one culture to another. Instead, most of this chapter focuses on ethical issues and guidelines frequently encountered in the context of supply management.

For the purposes of this chapter, our operational definition of ethics can be stated as the guidelines or rules of conduct by which we aim to live. Organizations, like individuals, have ethical standards and, frequently, ethics codes and policies. The ethical standards of an organization are judged by its actions and the actions of its employees, not by pious statements of intent put out in the company's name. The *character* of an organization is a matter of importance to its employees and managers, those who do business with it as customers and suppliers, and those who are considering joining it in those capacities.

Whether the market rewards good corporate behavior with respect to social responsibility and ethics is open to debate. Nevertheless, a review of the literature shows that increased social responsibility most likely will result in favorable financial performance. The review found 33 studies showing a positive relationship, 5 showing a negative relationship, and 14 showing no effect or inconclusive results.[2]

Procter & Gamble (P&G) understands the connection between ethical corporate behavior and financial performance. P&G takes the issue of ethics to a higher level by linking it to trust. In a visit to the University of San Diego, Stephen Rogers, former director of Technology Purchases at P&G, said the following:

> We believe buyers and suppliers optimize the results of the working relationship when there is a foundation of trust. By treating suppliers honestly, ethically, and fairly, we do our part in building that foundation, just as the supplier must do its part. We honor the confidentiality of proprietary supplier information regarding technology, cost, or other sensitive information unless given written permission to share it. We do this not only because we believe it to be right, but also because it makes working with P&G and supplying our requirements attractive to current and future suppliers. We strive to give a clear understanding of the "rules of the game" to suppliers before and after commercial interactions.[3]

There is little doubt that in the minds of most people, including responsible businessmen and businesswomen, ethical conduct is a more substantive and relevant issue today than it was several decades ago. Unfortunately, however, this is not a unanimous view. One of the classic dilemmas facing management at all levels of any organization is the issue of "time focus": Do we focus on the short run or the long haul? There are still a fairly significant number of individuals who are willing to "operate on the margin," or sacrifice long-term values for short-term gains acquired through unethical activities. A survey of 4,035 employees at all levels across a variety of industries[4] is quite revealing on this point:

> Ninety-seven percent of the employees surveyed said good ethics are good business. But responses to other questions indicated that many employees don't think that their companies agree. Two-thirds of the respondents said that ethical conduct isn't rewarded in American business. Eighty-two percent believe that managers generally choose bigger profits over "doing what's right." One-fourth said that their companies ignore

---

[2]Tony McAdams with contributing authors James Freeman and Laura P. Hartman, *Law, Business, and Society*, 6th ed. (New York: Irwin/McGraw-Hill, 2001), p. 95.

[3]Stephen Rogers, presentation at the University of San Diego. Reprinted with the permission of Procter & Gamble Company, November 2001.

[4]McAdams, *Law, Business, and Society*, p. 42.

ethics to achieve business goals. One-third reported that their superiors had pressured them to violate company rules.[5]

This research may appear dated, yet a 2007 National Business Ethics Survey found that the "ethics and corporate social responsibility picture for American business really hasn't changed since the intense period of business scandals early in this decade."[6]

# Professional Supply Management Ethics

We live and work in a highly competitive market economy with an emphasis on results. There is pressure on margins, pressure to compromise, pressure to succeed in an environment of both internal and external competition, and pressure resulting from government regulations. The *pressures* that the marketplace exerts indirectly on supply management departments and individual buyers make it essential that top management and supply management recognize and understand both the professional and the ethical standards required in the performance of their duties.

# Principles and Standards of Ethical Supply Management Conduct[7]

The Institute for Supply Management, whose membership primarily consists of U.S. supply managers, has addressed the issue of ethics since its inception over 80 years ago. ISM published *Principles and Standards of Ethical Supply Management Conduct* in 1992 and updated the principles in 2008.* The principles given in the 2008 ethical standards are:

- *Integrity in your decisions and actions*
- *Value for your employer*
- *Loyalty to your profession*

From these principles are derived standards of supply management practice, as presented in the following sections, with minor editing.

## 1. Perceived Impropriety

*Prevent the intent and appearance of unethical or compromising practice in relationships, actions, and communications.*

The results of a perceived impropriety may become, over time, more disruptive or damaging than an actual transgression. It is essential that any activity or involvement between a supply management professional and active or potential suppliers that in any way diminishes, or even appears to diminish, open and fair treatment of suppliers be strictly avoided. Those who do not know us will judge us on appearances. We must consider this—and act accordingly. If a situation is perceived as real, it is in fact real in its consequences.

---

[5]Shaun O'Malley, "Ethical Cultures—Corporate and Personal," *Ethics Journal*, Winter 1995, p. 9.

[6]"National Business Ethics Survey® Shows Observations of Unethical Behavior In American Business Back to Pre-Enron Levels," *Business Wire*, November, 26, 2007, http://findarticles.com/p/articles/mi_mOEIN/is_2007_Nov_26/ai_n21121151.

[7]Based on the content of the Institute for Supply Management's 2004 publication titled *Principles and Standards of Ethical Supply Management Conduct.* http://www.ism.ws/tools/content.cfm?ItemNumber=4740&navItemNumber=15959.

*Principles and Standards of Ethical Supply Management Conduct: With Guidelines*, Tempe AZ, Institute for Supply Management (ISM), 2008.

## 2. Conflict of Interest

*Ensure that any personal, business or other activity does not conflict with the lawful interests of your employer.*

Supply management professionals have the right to engage in activities that are of a private nature outside of their employment. They must not, however, use their positions in any way to induce another person to provide any benefit to themselves or to persons with whom they have a family, business, personal, or financial relationship. Even though a conflict technically may not exist, supply management professionals must avoid the *appearance* of such a conflict. Whenever a potential conflict of interest arises, a supply management professional should notify his or her supervisor for guidance or resolution.

## 3. Issues of Influence

*Avoid behaviors or actions that may negatively influence, or appear to influence, supply management decisions.*

This principle concerns what commonly are known as "gratuities." Gratuities include any material goods or services offered with the intent of, or providing the potential for, influencing a buying decision. Unfortunately, gratuities may, from time to time, be offered inappropriately to a buyer or to other persons involved in supply management decisions (or members of their immediate families). Having any influence on the supply management process constitutes involvement. Those in a position to influence the supply management process must be dedicated to the best interests of their employer. It is essential to avoid any activity which may diminish, or even appear to diminish, the objectivity of the supply management decision-making process.

Gratuities may be offered in various forms. Common examples are money, credits, discounts, supplier contests, sales promotion items, product test samples, seasonal or personal gifts, food, drinks, household appliances and furnishings, clothing, loans of goods or money, tickets to sporting or other events, dinners, parties, transportation, vacations, cabins, travel and hotel expenses, and various forms of entertainment. Extreme caution must be used in evaluating the acceptance of any gratuities (even if of nominal value), and the frequency of such actions, to ensure that one is abiding by the spirit of these guidelines.

The following site has selected guidelines for dealing with gratuities: http://www.ism.ws/tools/content.cfm?ItemNumber=4740&navItemNumber=15959.

**Business Meals**    Occasionally, during the course of business, it may be appropriate to conduct business during meals.

- Such meals shall be for a specific business purpose.
- Frequent meals with the same supplier should be avoided.
- A supply management professional should be in a position to pay for meals as frequently as the supplier does. Supply management professionals are encouraged to budget for this business activity.

**Personal Relationships**    Personal relationships are an inherent aspect of supply management. Supply management professionals interact extensively with suppliers' representatives. Individuals in many other functional areas in both the buying and supplying organizations also interact extensively with one another. The development of personal relationships from such interactions is both expected and desirable because this can lead to relationships based on understanding and trust. It also must be recognized that the purchasing decision must not be influenced by anything other than what is in the best interest of the organization and that personal relationships that develop beyond what is necessary to ensure understanding and trust may be inappropriate. It is important, therefore, for supply management professionals to monitor closely the nature of relationships with suppliers' representatives to ensure that personal friendships do not develop that would result in decisions that are not in the organization's best interest.

**International Practices**   In some cultures, *business* gifts, meals, and entertainment are considered part of the development of the business relationship, as are close personal relationships. It is important, therefore, for supply management professionals to understand such practices and establish policies and procedures to deal effectively with suppliers from different cultures to ensure that they make supply management decisions that are in the best interest of the organization. This requires that suppliers be informed of the organization's policies with respect to business gifts, meals, entertainment, and the nature of personal relationships. It also requires that supply management professionals act courteously to suppliers' representatives who inadvertently may act in ways contrary to the organization's policies.

■   In many foreign cultures, business frequently is conducted in the evenings and over weekends, which may be the only time key executives are available. In these circumstances, it is understood that the supply management professional would be expected to accept or provide for meals and entertainment when business matters are conducted. This is typically a more sensitive issue during the initial phase of the business relationship and may be tempered as the relationship progresses.

■   Reciprocal giving of gifts of nominal value is often an acceptable part of the international buying and selling process. When you are confronted with this—when company policy does not exist—an appropriate guide would be to ensure that actions are in the best interest of your employer, *never for personal gain.*

■   The definition of nominal value may be higher or lower than nominal value in your country as a result of custom, currency, and cost-of-living considerations and often is guided by the duration and scope of the relationship. A supply management professional must evaluate nominal value carefully in terms of what is reasonable and customary. When in doubt, consult company managers, professional colleagues, and your conscience.

**Political Considerations**   All organizations are subject to internal and external forces and pressures. Internal forces and pressures result from an organization's culture. External forces and pressures may include economic conditions, laws, regulations, public opinion, special interest groups, and political entities. The negative influence of internal and external forces and pressures on supply management can be minimized when the organization adopts practices that are based on ethical principles and standards.

**Advertising**   Care should be exercised in accepting promotional items or participating in activities that tend to promote one supplier over another or that could be perceived as preferential supplier advertising by a supply management professional.

**Market Power**   Supply management professionals must be aware of their organization's position (economic size, power, etc.) in the marketplace and ensure that that position is used within the scope of ethical behavior by the supply management professional and the organization.

**Specifications and Standards**   Supply management professionals must ensure that specifications and standards are written objectively to encourage appropriate competition.

## 4. Responsibilities to your Employer

*Uphold fiduciary and other responsibilities using reasonable care and granted authority to deliver value to your employer.*

A supply management professional's foremost responsibility is to achieve the legitimate goals established by the employer. It is his or her duty to ensure that actions taken as an agent for the employer will be in the best interests of the employer, *to the exclusion of personal gain*. This requires application of sound judgment and consideration of both the legal and the ethical implications of one's actions.

## 5. Supplier and Customer Relationships

*Promote positive supplier and customer relationships through courtesy and impartiality.*

It is the responsibility of a supply management professional to promote mutually acceptable business relationships with all suppliers and customers. Affording all supplier representatives the same courtesy and impartiality in all phases of business transactions will enhance the reputation and good standing of the employer, the supply management profession, and the person involved. Rudeness, discourteousness, or disrespectful treatment of a supplier may result in barriers to free and open communications between buyer and seller and ultimately in a breakdown of the business relationship.

A supply management professional should extend the same fairness and impartiality to all legitimate business concerns. It is natural and even desirable to build long-term relationships with suppliers on the basis of a history of trust and respect, but those relationships should not prevent the establishment of similar working relationships with other suppliers.

## 6. Sustainability and Social Responsibility

*Champion social responsibility and sustainability practices in supply management.*

It is generally recognized that all business concerns, large or small, majority- or minority-owned, should be afforded an equal opportunity to compete. Within existing legal constraints, many government entities and corporations have developed specific procedures and policies designed to support and stimulate the growth of socially diverse firms.

## 7. Confidential and Proprietary Information

*Protect confidential or proprietary information with due care and proper consideration of ethical and legal ramifications and governmental regulations.*

Supply management professionals and others in positions that influence buying decisions deal with confidential or proprietary information of both the employer and the supplier. Proprietary and confidential information should be released to other parties (internal and external) only on a need-to-know basis. It is the responsibility of a supply management professional sharing confidential or proprietary information to ensure that the recipient understands his or her obligation to protect that information.

The ISM recommends several practices to ensure that confidential or proprietary information is managed properly. Those recommendations include the following:

1. Developing and communicating a policy covering proprietary and confidential information.
2. Requiring that confidential and proprietary information be identified as such, whether disclosed in tangible form or orally.
3. Using confidential information agreements.
4. Not accepting another's confidential or proprietary information unless there's a need for such information.
5. When dealing with any information, whether or not it is confidential or proprietary, exercising care in determining the effects of its use.

A supply management professional should avoid releasing information to other parties, including those within the supply management professional's own company, until assured that they understand and accept the responsibility for maintaining the confidentiality of the material. Extreme care and good judgment should be used if confidential information is communicated orally. All confidential or proprietary information should be shared only on a need-to-know basis.

Information of one supplier must never be shared with another supplier unless laws or government regulations require that such information be disclosed. If one is unclear about disclosure requirements, legal counsel should be consulted. When a supply management professional is privy to cost or profit data or other supplier information not generally known, it is his or her responsibility to maintain the confidentiality of that information.

Examples of information that may be considered confidential or proprietary are:

1. Pricing.
2. Bid or quotation information.
3. Cost sheets.
4. Formulas and/or process information.
5. Design information (drawings, blueprints, etc.).
6. Organizational plans, goals, and strategies.
7. Financial information.
8. Information that may influence stock prices.
9. Profit information.
10. Asset information.
11. Wage and salary scales.
12. Personal information about employees, officers, and directors.
13. Supply sources or supplier information.
14. Computer software programs.

## 8. Reciprocity

*Avoid improper reciprocal agreements.*

Transactions that favor a specific customer as a supplier or influence a supplier to become a customer constitute a practice known as reciprocity, as does a specific commitment to buy in exchange for a specific commitment to sell. The true test for reciprocity, however, is in the motive, since the process may be less vague than a written or formal commitment. In any such transactions, reciprocity may be illegal if it tends to restrain competition or trade and if the transactions are coerced. In organization structures in which the supply management and marketing functions report directly to the same individual, the potential for reciprocity may be greater.

Supply management professionals must be especially careful when dealing with suppliers who are customers. Cross-dealings between suppliers and customers are not antitrust violations per se. Nevertheless, giving preference to a supplier who is also a customer should occur only when all other factors are equal. Dealing with a supplier who is also a customer may not constitute a problem if, in fact, that supplier is the best source. A company is engaging in reciprocity, however, when it deals with a supplier solely because of the customer relationship. A professional supply manager must be able to recognize reciprocity and its ethical and legal implications.

## 9. Applicable Laws, Regulations and Trade Agreements

*Know and obey the letter and spirit of laws, regulations and trade agreements applicable to supply management.*

Supply management professionals should pursue and maintain an understanding of the essential legal concepts governing their activities as agents of their employers. For example, key laws and regulations a supply management professional should be aware of when conducting business in the United States of America are:

- Uniform Commercial Code (UCC) and the Uniform Computer Information Transactions Act (UCITA)
- Uniform Electronic Transactions Act (UETA) and the Federal Electronic Signatures in Global and National Commerce Act (E-Sign)
- The Sherman Act
- The Clayton Act and the Robinson-Patman Act
- The Federal Trade Commission Act
- The Federal Acquisition Regulations (FAR) and Defense Federal Acquisition Regulation Supplement (DFARS)
- Environmental Protection Agency (EPA) laws
- Equal Employment Opportunity Commission (EEOC) laws
- Occupational Safety and Health Administration (OSHA) laws
- The Foreign Corrupt Practices Act
- The Public Company Accounting Reform and Investor Protection Act of 2002 (Sarbanes-Oxley Act of 2002)

Knowledge of international laws also may be relevant to a supply management professional.

The ISM provides several recommendations to supply management professionals for understanding and complying with applicable laws:

- Supply management professionals should obtain training in the legal aspects of supply management to understand the laws that govern their conduct and so that they know when to seek legal counsel.

- Supply management professionals involved in a cross-border transaction must understand the laws which govern the transaction, including laws specific to the country within which they are doing business and laws of the country in which the seller resides, especially if they conflict with or supplement the laws of the country in which they are doing business.

- Interpretation of the laws should be left to legal counsel. It is often beneficial to involve legal counsel early in analysis and planning to identify and avoid potential legal pitfalls rather than involve legal counsel only after problems arise.

- Supply management professionals involved in government procurement must understand and apply laws that are specific to their particular agency.

## 10. Professional Competence

*Develop skills, expand knowledge and conduct business that demonstrates competence and promotes the supply management profession.*

Professional competence is expected of supply management professionals by their employers, their supply management peers, others in their organizations, suppliers, and society at large.

A distinguishing characteristic of a profession is that its practitioners combine ethical standards with technical skills. Because of the impact that the conduct of supply management professionals has on the stature of the profession, it is important for all those in the profession to consider what is meant by professional competence and the way it is perceived by others.

Professional competence can be defined in many ways. Most definitions include the concept of mastery of a body of knowledge, continued efforts to increase one's ability and knowledge of the profession, communications skills, willingness to share knowledge with others, and conformance to the highest standards of ethical behavior.

The ISM recommends that supply management professionals:

■ Ensure a basic understanding of all the requirements to be recognized as a competent supply management professional.

■ Monitor trends and developments in the profession.

■ Conduct a self-assessment of talents and skills.

■ Establish a development plan to meet the needs of immediate and future employment.

■ Seek out mentors and role models.

■ Serve as a mentor.

■ Earn and maintain the CPM or other credentials such as the certified professional in supply management (CPSM).

■ Become actively involved in one or more professional associations.

The stature of the profession is enhanced through ethical actions and behavior of supply management professionals. When individuals combine in professional groups or associations, their actions and behavior become highly visible and enhance the stature of the profession. This has a direct impact on the profession and on the professional's organization, peers, and suppliers.

The ISM recommends that supply management professionals:

■ Support professional development and interchange of ideas through membership in professional and service organizations.

■ Actively seek and support change in ethical standards and practice when appropriate (e.g., changes in the environment or technology).

■ Be aware that supply professionals are obligated to support only those actions and activities which uphold the highest ethical standards of the profession.

■ Support the ethical principles and standards of each organization with which a supply management professional is affiliated.

■ Encourage, support, and participate in ongoing ethical training and review within business and professional organizations.

■ Strive to achieve acceptance of and adherence to these principles and standards by all those who influence the supply management process.

## National and International Supply Management Conduct

A supply management professional should conduct supply management in accordance with national and international laws, customs, and practices; his or her organization's policies; and the ISM ethical principles and standards of conduct.

Legal systems vary throughout the world, as do business customs and practices. Supply management professionals therefore must be knowledgeable about these variations and the potential conflicts inherent in them when doing business across borders.

The ISM recommends that supply management professionals:

- Be especially sensitive to customs and cultural differences with respect to social and business behavior and issues of influence.

- Recognize that suppliers may not be familiar with laws, customs, and practices of various countries or with the company's policies. Consequently, it is important to ensure that appropriate information is communicated effectively to each supplier.

- Recognize which national laws may apply and which do not apply in other countries.

- Utilize organization management, legal counsel, and other available resources for guidance whenever there is uncertainty about which actions to take.

- Maintain an awareness of national and international standards (ISO 9000, ISO 14000, Ethical Trade Initiative, etc.).

# Important Areas Requiring Amplification

## Avoid Sharp Practices

In business, the term "sharp practices" has been used for years, and this topic is particularly relevant for supply management professionals. One of the standards in an earlier version of ISM's *Standards of Conduct* reads, "Avoid sharp practices." The term "sharp practices" typically is defined as evasion and indirect misrepresentation that is just short of actual fraud. These unscrupulous practices focus on short-term gains and ignore the long-term implications for a business relationship.

Some examples of sharp practices are:

- A supply manager talks in terms of large quantities to encourage a price quote on that basis. The forthcoming order, however, is substantially smaller than the amount on which the price was based. The smaller order does not legitimately deserve the low price thus developed.

- A large number of bids are solicited in hopes that the buyer will be able to take advantage of a quotation error.

- Bids are obtained from unqualified suppliers that the supply manager would not patronize in any case. Those bids then are played against the bids of responsible suppliers to gain a price or other advantage. The preparation of bids is a costly undertaking that deserves buyer sincerity in the solicitation stage.

- A supply manager who places in competition the prices of seconds, odd lots, or distressed merchandise misrepresents a market.

- An attempt is made to influence a seller by leaving copies of bids or other confidential correspondence where that supplier can see them.

- A concession may be forced by dealing only with "hungry" suppliers. The *current* philosophy is that a purchase order should create a mutual advantage with a price that is fair and reasonable.

- Obscure contract terms of benefit to the supply manager's firm are buried in the small type of contract articles.

■ Taking advantage of a supplier who is short of cash and who may seek only to cover its out-of-pocket costs. Such a situation poses a dilemma, since the supplier may be saved from borrowing at a disadvantage and may look upon such an order as a blessing![8]

Acurex Corporation adds the following items to the preceding list of practices to be avoided:[9]

■ Allowing one or more suppliers to have information about their competitors' quotations and *allowing such suppliers to requite*.

■ Making statements to an existing supplier that exaggerate the seriousness of a problem to obtain better prices or other concessions.

■ Giving preferential treatment to suppliers that higher levels of the firm's own management prefer to recommend.

■ Canceling a purchase order for parts already in process while also seeking to avoid cancellation charges.

■ Getting together with other supply professionals to take united action against another group of people or a company.

■ Lying to or grossly misleading a salesperson in a negotiation.

■ Allowing a supplier to become dependent on the supply management organization for most of its business.

While many of these practices were once commonplace, Dr. Felch notes that they have been replaced by a philosophy that holds that mutual confidence and integrity are far more desirable ends than the short-term gains obtained through willful misrepresentation.

## Competitive Bidding[10]

Supply management professionals respect and maintain the integrity of the competitive bidding process. They:

■ Invite only firms to submit bids to which they are willing to award a contract.

■ Normally award the contract to the lowest *responsive*, responsible bidder. If the buyer anticipates the possibility of awarding to someone other than the low bidder, he or she notifies prospective bidders that other factors will be considered. (Ideally, these factors will be listed.)

■ Keep competitive price information confidential.

■ Notify unsuccessful bidders promptly so that they can reallocate reserved production capacity.

■ Treat all bidders alike. Clarifying information is given to *all* potential bidders.

■ Do not accept bids after the announced bid closing date and time.

---

[8]Robert I. Felch, "Proprieties and Ethics in Purchasing Management," *Guide to Purchasing* (Oradell, NJ: ISM, 1986), pp. 4.7–3 and 4.7–4.

[9]Richard E. Trevisan, "Developing a Statement of Ethics: A Case Study," *Journal of Purchasing and Materials Management*, Fall 1986, p. 13.

[10]Much of the discussion included in this section is based on material in ISM's *Guide to Purchasing*, section 4.7: "Proprieties and Ethics in Purchasing Management," by Dr. Robert I. Felch. Specific footnotes are utilized where appropriate.

- Do not take advantage of apparent mistakes in the supplier's bid.
- If the buyer needs to reopen the bidding, send the request for new bids to all who initially submitted bids.

However, it *is* ethical for a buyer to work with the low bidder in an effort to identify possible areas of savings. Those identified savings allow the potential supplier to reduce its *costs* and its price.

## Negotiation

Supply professionals maintain high ethical standards during all negotiated supply management activities.

- Competitors are informed of the factors that will be involved in source selection.
- All potential suppliers are given equal access to information and are afforded the same treatment.
- Supply professionals strive to negotiate terms that are fair to both parties. They do not take advantage of mistakes in the supplier's proposal.[11]

## Samples

Many potential suppliers offer, even push, the acceptance of samples: "Just try it and see if it doesn't do a superior job for you." When a sample is accepted, supply professionals ensure that appropriate tests are conducted in a timely manner. The potential supplier then should be informed of the test results and suitability of the item in meeting the buyer's needs. In some instances, it may be wise to pay for the actual production cost of the sample.

## Treating Salespeople with Respect

As was noted earlier, the use of courtesy and consideration by supply management personnel can influence the effectiveness of supplier relationships. The treatment of salespeople clearly produces overtones in the area of professional standards of conduct.[12]

- Salespeople should not be kept waiting for protracted periods; appointments should be kept meticulously. The power that is attached to the patronage position of a supply professional must not be abused so that the long-run interests of the buying company will be advanced.
- A mutually effective policy is for supply management personnel to see every salesperson on his or her first call. The appropriateness of follow-up visits should be determined by the potential strength of the buying firm's need for the supplying firm's product.

## Substandard Materials and Services

When substandard materials or services are received, two proprieties should be observed:[13]

1. The supplier should be given prompt notice.
2. The appropriate supply manager should conduct negotiations for adjustments with the appropriate sales personnel in the supplier's organization.

---

[11]Felch, *Guide to Purchasing*, pp. 4–5.

[12]Ibid, p. 7.

[13]Ibid.

## Gifts and Gratuities

Nothing can undermine respect for the supply management profession more than improper action on the part of its members with regard to gifts, gratuities, favors, and so forth. People engaged in supply management should not accept from any supplier or prospective supplier any substantive gifts or favors. All members of the supply management system must decline to accept or must return any such items offered to them or members of their immediate families. The refusal of gifts and favors should be done discreetly and courteously. When the return of a gift is impractical for some reason, disposition should be made to a charitable institution, and the donor should be informed of the disposition.

Personal business transactions with suppliers or prospective suppliers should be avoided scrupulously. Offers of hospitality, business courtesies, or favors, no matter how innocent in appearance, can be a source of embarrassment to all parties concerned.

The buying firm's representatives should not allow themselves to become involved in situations in which unnecessary embarrassment results from refusal of hospitality or a business courtesy from suppliers. Generally, the best policy is to decline any sort of favor, hospitality, or entertainment to *ensure that all relationships are above reproach at all times.*

Clearly, all situations require the use of common sense and good judgment. For example, acceptance of company-provided luncheons during the course of a visit to a supplier's plant in a remote area is certainly reasonable. Similarly, the acceptance of supplier-provided automobile transportation on a temporary basis when other means are not readily available is a reasonable course of action for a supply professional to take.

Supply management personnel may ethically attend periodic meetings or dinners of trade associations, professional and technical societies, or other industrial organizations as the guest of a supplier when the meetings are of an educational and informative nature and attendance is considered to be in the professional interest of the buyer-seller relationship. Even so, the repeated appearance of an individual at such regularly scheduled meetings as the guest of the same company is the type of situation that should be avoided tactfully.

A simple casual lunch or cocktail with a supplier's representative typically is a normal expression of a friendly business relationship or frequently a timesaving expediency. It would be prudish to raise any serious questions on this score. The individual himself or herself is in the best position to judge when this point has been passed. Any breach of ethics can be rationalized, but members of the supply management system can avoid embarrassment or possible unethical behavior by asking, *"How would this look if reported in the company newsletter?"* The desire to continue to talk shop or resolve a business issue accounts for most buyer-supplier lunches. Because the buying firm's prestige also is involved, *there is good reason why an adequate expense account should be available to the supply professional.* This permits him or her to pick up the bill for lunch! It is a small price to pay for maintaining a position free from any taint of obligation.

**"There's No Such Thing as a Free Lunch"**   Several years ago, Mike Darby of the ISM–Silicon Valley organization addressed the issue of free lunches. His comments were so appropriate that they are included below for the benefit of our readers.

> The person who came up with this quote many years ago was probably a materials manager. There are many pros and cons about buyers going to lunch with their suppliers. I don't propose to advocate one or the other, but I would like to point out some ideas that may help you to make up your own mind.
>
> First and foremost in my mind is *why* would a company want to spend some of its dollars that would normally flow directly to the bottom line to have me join them for lunch? I've asked this question of many suppliers. Some of

the answers I've received include: "I have to take somebody to lunch every day, and it might as well be somebody I like"; "If I take you to lunch, then my lunch is free also"; "It will give us an opportunity to get to know each other better." These are all good answers, some of them more honest than I expected.

When I asked the same question of the buyers, the answer changed slightly. "We may need this supplier in the future, and I want to develop a close relationship with him"; "We have some serious problems to discuss"; "This will give me a good opportunity to negotiate a better deal with them."

Whatever the justification, the bottom line to me gets down to this. The supplier is willing to commit some of his profit dollars to this form of entertainment in *the belief that it will help him generate more profit in the future*. He may be in hope that the relationship he is building will help sustain him in your company through rough times, such as poor delivery performance or bad quality. He may be expecting to increase his prices, and a friend will never complain about a small change in price. He may ask you to lunch expecting that the slight social obligation he has just obtained from you may be paid back by getting another crack at a quote, first look at a new drawing, etc. Or he may join you for lunch hoping to obtain some information that will be useful to him in future negotiations.

All the above tend to add up to a one-sided deal, favoring the supplier and putting the buyer in the position of having to be very careful. Let's face it, the sales force of the supplier is being paid to perform a service to the supplier, and this is a good tool for him to use. He gets your undivided attention for a good hour or so, to use as he sees fit. Remember, it's impolite in our society to refuse to answer a question. A question as simple as "How's business?" provides the supplier with important information as to its market share within your company, business trends, and helps to set his expectations in future negotiations. It's also very difficult as a supply professional not to show a slight amount of favoritism toward the supplier that you had lunch with last Friday. Should he ask, "Where do I stand on that quote, and what do I need to do to get the job?" It gets difficult to be firm and say no to such a request.

Now before I get blasted out of the water for being one-sided, let me say that there are times when a business meal is appropriate. If you have a supplier in from out of town, and your business discussions extend through lunch or past business hours, a meal is probably appropriate. In this circumstance, I like to use the Host rule—If the meeting is in your territory, then you should be the host. If you are visiting the supplier's territory, then he can be the host. Make it fair and equitable, and the supplier loses any advantage he might have held from an obligation point of view. Remember, an obligation is in the mind of the person who received the favor. If, because of the manner in which you handle your conduct, there was no potential for a favor, then there can also be no obligation.

As a supply professional, picking up the check can quickly change a supplier's expectations, and as such is a very useful negotiation tactic. If he thought he had a contract in the bag, he suddenly begins to think that he may not be as secure as he thought. It also sends the message that you too are a professional and certainly not an easy target.[14]

Mature supply managers know that they are classified among the sales fraternity by the amount of entertainment they expect or will accept. Salespeople usually speak with real respect of the supply manager who pays his or her share of entertainment expenses. The supply management expense account is the most effective answer to this ethical problem.

**Traditional Sales Techniques**    Many supply management personnel feel that any form of gratuity constitutes a conflict with ethical standards. Others—in fact the majority, according to ISM studies—consider many of these items to be traditional sales tools. They therefore do not believe that such gratuities are offered with the expectation of favorable consideration.[15]

---

[14]*Pacific Purchaser*, November–December 1988, p. 11.

[15]Michael H. Thomas, "Know Where You Stand on Ethics," *Purchasing World*, October 1984, p. 90.

There are two common ways to control the acceptance of these kinds of gifts. The first is by placing a dollar limit on what can be accepted. In this case, a supply management department may have a stated policy of refusing any gratuity with a value in excess of, say, $10 or $15. Such policies provide a very simple, measurable guideline for how a buyer should decide about acceptance.

The other common policy is to forbid acceptance of any gratuity *the buying firm is not in a position to reciprocate*. Thus, if a firm's supply professionals accept sales promotion items such as pens or planning calendars, they should be in a position to reciprocate with similar items from their own firm.

**Cultural Ramifications**    Executives of many foreign suppliers expect that supply professionals will exchange gifts with them. That action is an accepted part of many foreign cultures. Some supply professionals encounter situations in which refusing a gift would interfere with the development of relations prerequisite to consummating a transaction. In such cases, supply professionals *report* the situation to their superiors and arrive at a solution that may include acceptance *and* a reciprocal gift.[16] If a supply manager hides his or her action, he or she automatically knows that the action is unethical.

# Management Responsibilities

## Written Standards

Management's first responsibility is to develop a set of written ethical and professional standards that are applicable to all members of the organization's supply management system. Supply management supervisors, buyers, expediters, design engineers, manufacturing engineers, quality assurance personnel, maintenance supervisors, receivers, and accounts payable personnel all must accept and observe those standards. The standards should address the topics discussed in this chapter. Research has shown clearly that *written* policies dealing with ethical issues have a strong positive influence on the behavior of a firm's supply management professionals.[17]

## Ethics Training and Education

Professional supply managers, with the *assistance of top management* and their colleagues in other functional areas, must ensure that appropriate personnel receive periodic training or education with respect to the organization's ethical and professional standards. That training cannot address all issues. It can, however, increase the sensitivity of those who receive it. All members of the supply management system must respect their roles as agents of their employer and must represent the best interest of their organization. Subsequent to such training, many organizations require the attendees to sign *a statement to the effect that they have taken the training and understand and will honor the standards*.

Supply managers also should ensure that their personnel receive training in current thinking and techniques in the areas of requirements planning, source selection, pricing, cost analysis, negotiation, and supplier management, as well as ethical and professional standards.

The vast majority of supply managers are dedicated and conscientious people. Accordingly, it is almost shocking to see how little high-quality training many of these individuals have received. Supply management

---

[16]Somerby Dowst, "Taking the Mystery Out of Conflict of Interest," *Purchasing*, September 11, 1986, p. 70A1.

[17]G. B. Turner, G. S. Taylor, and M. F. Hartley, "Ethics Policies and Gratuity Acceptance by Purchasers," *International Journal of Purchasing and Materials Management*, Summer 1994, p. 46.

system reviews conducted by the authors indicate that a substantial number of buyers are being asked to perform tasks for which they have received little current training, including training in the area of ethical and professional conduct.

## Departmental Environment

Department policy should make it clear that buying personnel engage in any unethical activity at the risk of losing their jobs. It is a generally accepted view that a small percentage of Americans are dishonest, that an equally small percentage are completely honest, and that most people are honest *or* dishonest, *depending on the circumstances*. Consequently, after the basic policy and training frameworks have been established, it appears that the surest way to encourage ethical conduct is to create a working environment in which unethical temptations seldom become realities.

The foundation for that environment consists of the people themselves. Management will be repaid many times for the effort put into thorough, careful investigation and selection of buying personnel. Habits and attitudes are "catching" in the close working environment of a supply department. If most of the personnel are basically honest, departmental management has the major part of the ethics battle won.

The age-old adage "monkey see, monkey do" is certainly applicable in the matter of ethical conduct. Departmental management and supervisory people must *live*, to the letter, the department's policies and ideals. Numerous studies have confirmed beyond doubt that the actions and attitudes of supervisors are the most influential single factor in determining the attitudes of a work group.

## Miscellaneous Factors

Two concluding thoughts are worthy of consideration. First, some progressive organizations have established an internal or external ombudsman who can be contacted with impunity about ethical issues. Once accepted, the practice seems to work well.

Second, the president of Seldon Associates suggests greater utilization of post-purchase audits as desirable safeguards. He writes, "When every buyer knows that his or her purchases may be audited, there is a built-in safeguard tending to assure ethical purchasing."[18]

# Dealing with Gray Areas

All supply professionals have ethical obligations to three groups of people: *employers, suppliers, and colleagues*:

- *Employer.* Guidance should focus on the characteristics of loyalty, analytical objectivity, and a drive to achieve results that are in the very best interest of the employing organization.
- *Suppliers.* The essence of the guiding spirit in dealing with the supplier community is honesty and fair play.
- *Colleagues.* All individuals engaged in supply management work are regarded by outside observers as members of an emerging profession. As such, they have an obligation to protect and enhance the reputation of that body of professionals.

---

[18]Doyle Seldon, "Ethics, an Additional Look," *Purchasing Management*, December 1988. p. 41.

When supply management professionals must take action in a "gray area" not clearly covered by policy, they may find guidance by seeking answers to the following questions:

1. Is this action acceptable to everyone in my organization?
2. Is the action compatible with the firm's responsibilities to its customers, suppliers, and stockholders?
3. What would happen if *all* buyers and salespeople behaved this way?
4. If I were in the other person's shoes, how would I feel about this action if it were directed toward me?
5. Would it be comfortable to have this act or action reported on a newscast to the general public?

### The Four Way Test

The businessmen and businesswomen of the Rotary International organization provide a follow-up of four questions. They apply the Four Way Test to the things they think, say, and do:[19]

- Is it the TRUTH?
- Is it FAIR to all concerned?
- Will it build GOODWILL and BETTER FRIENDSHIPS?
- Will it be BENEFICIAL to all concerned?

In making the final decision, a few moments' thought may well be devoted to the following lines, entitled "What Makes a Profession."[20]

If there is such a thing as a profession as a concept distinct from a vocation, it must consist in the ideals that its members maintain, the dignity of character that they bring to the performance of their duties, and the austerity of the self-imposed ethical standards. To constitute a true profession, there must be ethical tradition so potent as to bring into conformity members whose personal standards of conduct are at a lower level, and to have an elevating and ennobling effect on those members. A profession cannot be created by resolution, or become such overnight. It requires many years for its development, and they must be years of self-denial, years when success by base means is scorned, years when no results bring honor except those free from the taint of unworthy methods.

## Social Responsibilities

Aside from proper, ethical, and legal conduct and, whenever possible, using qualified minority suppliers, supply chain managers have a major role in protecting the physical environment. In addition to issues previously discussed in this and other chapters, supply managers must understand statutes such as the Clean Air Act of 1970 (1990) and the Comprehensive Environmental Response Compensation Act (CLERCA, the Super Fund law). In addition, the current focus on the "Green Movement" has serious implications for all members of the supply chain.

For example, various state and federal agencies are mandating minimum mileage standards on vehicles to reduce carbon emissions as part of the effort to control global warming. This mandate has triggered the need for new product designs in vehicles and, in particular, engines. Cross-functional design teams and

[19]*Manual of Procedures*, Rotary International, Evanston, IL., 2007, p. 80.

[20]*NAPM Standards of Conduct*, 1959.

early supplier involvement (ESI), as described in many chapters in this text, will be even more important to accomplish the proper response to these new regulations.

In addition, specifications and contract provisions must consider the mandate from the U.S. Environmental Protection Agency (EPA) to reduce waste, stimulate reuse, reallocate, and recycle (the 4 Rs).[21] Supply Chain Pollution Avoidance (SCPA) is a good term to remind supply chain managers always to think from Mother Earth to disposal or back to Mother Earth."[22, 23]

The Institute for Supply Management (ISM) has defined Seven Principles of Social Responsibility as follows:[24]

- *Community initiatives.* This includes providing cash, equipment, people, and other resources to nonprofits and educational or other community groups.
- *Diversity in supply management.* This has been discussed in many parts of this text, in particular increased sourcing with minority and disadvantaged firms and individuals.
- *Environmental impact or change.*
- *Ethics.*
- *Financial responsibility,* which includes full and accurate disclosure beyond what is required by law, such as risk assessment.
- *Human rights.* Having respect for individual differences of race, religion, age, and sexual orientation.
- *Safety* for employers, customers, and suppliers. This obviously includes OSHA compliance but goes beyond the stated requirements.

Organizations should embody these principles in a written document distributed to all employees and suppliers. Studies have revealed that organizations that have high ethical and social standards tend to be more profitable in the long run as opposed to the Enrons of the world.

## Concluding Remarks

As you finish reading this chapter about ethics and social responsibilities, consider an event that occurred at a career planning workshop for students who soon would be entering the job market. The workshop facilitator instructed the participants to write their own obituaries. Morbid? Maybe. Useful? Absolutely!

The purpose of the exercise was to force the students to project to the end of their lives and then summarize how their lives had been lived. This exercise of coerced self-reflection was designed to examine each student's values. What kind of career unfolded? How did this person treat other people? Did this person touch the lives of others in such a way that he or she was missed?

All of us, of course, write our own obituaries each day of our lives by the way we choose to live our lives. If your obituary discussed your ethics, what would you want it to say? Finally, what did you do to help protect our physical and social environment?

---

[21]R. Jerry Baker, "The Environment: Playing Our Part," *NAPM Insights*, April 1994. p. 2. Also see Jeff Marcus "Trends, Purchasing and the Environment," ibid, p. 28.

[22]David N. Burt, and Michael F. Doyle, *The American Keiretsu* (Homewood, IL: Business One Irwin, 1993), p. 109.

[23]Steve V. Walton, Robert B. Handfield, and Steven A. Melnyk, "The Green Supply Chain: Integrating Suppliers into Environmental Management Process," *International Journal of Purchasing and Materials Management* 34, no. 2 (Spring 1998), p. 2.

[24]Lisa Cooling, "Social Responsibility in the Real Business World," *Inside Supply Management*, March 2008, pp. 26–29.

# Discussion Questions

1. On what basis are the ethical standards of an organization judged?
2. To whom is the character of an organization important?
3. What is the most important ethical principle for supply managers?
4. How does global supply management temper ethical considerations?
5. Describe two examples of confidential supplier information. What responsibility does the supply manager have for such information?
6. How must professional supply managers treat suppliers?
7. What is the supply manager's responsibility to diversity suppliers?
8. Describe four "sharp practices."
9. How do professional supply managers respect the integrity of the competitive bidding process?
10. Is it ethical for a supply manager to work with the low bidder after the close of bidding? What is the likely outcome of that practice?
11. Is there such a thing as a "free lunch" for a supply manager?
12. What is management's first responsibility in the area of ethics?
13. What role should ethics training and education play?
14. What is the role of a post-purchase audit in ensuring ethical conduct?
15. If your obituary discussed your ethics, what would you want it to say?
16. What role does the issue of social responsibility play during the negotiation process?

# Internet Exercise

## Corporate Ethics

Visit the website below. Read one of the recent stories on ethical issues in corporate America. (http://www.pbs.org/newshour/bb/business/ethics/)

1. Describe the situation you have just read about. How could it have been avoided?

# Suggested Reading

Carter, Craig R. *Ethical Issues in Global Buyer-Supplier Relationships*, Tempe AZ. Center for Advanced Purchasing Studies, 1998.

Cooling, Lisa. "Spread the Carbon-Neutral News: James Martin Plays a Key Role as News Corporation Commits to Reducing its Environmental Impact throughout the World," *Inside Supply Management*, October 2007, pp. 30–32.

Cooper, Robert W., Garry L. Frank, and Robert A. Kemp. "The Ethical Environment Facing the Profession of Purchasing and Materials Management," *International Journal of Purchasing and Materials Management* 33, no. 2 (May 1997), p. 2.

Cooper, Robert W., Garry L. Frank, and Robert A. Kemp. "The Ethical Environment Facing the Profession of Purchasing and Materials Management," *International Journal of Purchasing and Materials Management* 33, no 2 (Spring 1997), pp. 2–11.

Hartley, M. F., G. B. Turner, and W. C. Ferguson. "Purchasing's Role in the Development of Corporate Ethics Statements," Ethics Policy Statements for Purchasing, Supply, and Materials Management, 137–141, Tempe, AZ: National Association of Purchasing Management, 1995.

Lindsay, R. M., L. M. Lindsay, and V. B. Irvine. "Instilling Ethical Behavior in Organizations: A Survey of Canadian Companies," *Journal of Business Ethics*, 15(1996), pp. 393–407.

Marchetti, Anne M. *Beyond Sarbanes-Oxley Compliance: Effective Enterprise Risk Management* (Hoboken, NJ: John Wiley & Sons, 2005).

Roberts, Julie S. "Navigating the Ethics of E-commerce," *Purchasing Today* 12, no. 12 (December 2001), p. 28.

Robertson, D. C., and B. B. Schlegelmilch. "Corporate Institutionalization of Ethics in the United States and Great Britain," *Journal of Business Ethics* 12 (1993), 301–12.

Schildhouse, Jill. "Corporate Ethics: Taking the High Road," *Inside Supply Management* 16, no. 3 (March 2005), p. 30.

Shaw, B. "Business Ethics Today: A Survey," *Journal of Business Ethics* 15(1996), pp. 489–500.

Trevino, Linda K., and Katherine A . Nelson. *Managing Business Ethics: Straight Talk about How to Do It Right*, 4th ed. (Hoboken, NJ: Wiley & Sons, 2007).

Turner, G. B., M. F., Hartley, and S. Taylor. "Ethics, Gratuities, and Professionalization of the Purchasing Function," *Journal of Business Ethics* 14(1995), pp. 751–760.

Zsidisin, George A., and Sue P. Siferd. "Environmental Purchasing: A Framework for Theory Development," *European Jounal of Purchasing and Supply Management*, July 2000, pp. 61–73.

# Materials Management

Scheduling incoming materials and internal flow to work stations is another critical task of supply management. Thus, production and inventory control are subjects all supply personnel must understand including the fundamentals of incoming transportation.

Purchasing and supply management personnel at all levels are deeply involved in materials management. Chapter 20 describes production planning and control systems, including scheduling, order release, master scheduling, material requirements planning (MRPI and MRP II), capacity requirements planning (CRP), control techniques and their impact on purchasing and supply, buyer-planner and supplier scheduler concepts, just-in-time (JIT) production planning and its impact on purchasing and supply, and ERP systems. The chapter continues with the functions of inventories, the different types of inventories, ABC analysis, dependent and independent demand distinctions, inventory costs, the economic order quantity (EOQ) concept, and various types of inventory control systems. The fundamentals of inbound transportation are explained in the Appendix to Chapter 20.

Chapter 21 describes the relationship between supply, demand, and logistics management, including strategic demand management, the bullwhip effect, forecasting techniques and methods, the concept of time fencing in demand management, and the basics of logistics. ∎

# CHAPTER 20

# Production and Inventory Control

## CHAPTER OBJECTIVES

*After reading this chapter, you should be able to:*

1. Understand the components of production planning and scheduling.

2. Design an aggregate planning and master scheduling system.

3. Explain to others the elements of material requirements planning (MRP) techniques and programs and the logic format.

4. Know the differences between dependent demand and independent demand.

5. Know how capacity requirements planning (CRP) and MRP systems interact.

6. Evaluate the accuracy of critical inputs to MRP, bill of materials, on-hand inventory, encumbered inventory, and the master schedule.

7. Explain the evolution of MRP to MRP II systems

8. Understand buyer-planner and supplier scheduler concepts.

9. Understand the fundamentals of just-in-time production planning and its impact on purchasing and supply.

10. Explain the functions of inventories and the different types of inventories and their functions.

11. Conduct inventory analysis.

12. Work with ABC analysis and the 80-20 concept.

13. Know the cost breakdown associated with inventories: carrying acquisition.

14. Perform economic order quantity (EOQ) analysis, including understanding its weakness.

15. Know and work with the various types of inventory control systems, such as cyclical, flow control, JIT, MRP, fixed order point, two-bin and the role of safety stocks, and supplier managed inventory.

16. Understand the importance of inbound transportation planning (Appendix).

### VIGNETTE: SALES FORECASTS: FACT OR FICTION?

The Materials Planning Committee for Advanced Technology Corp., a global manufacturer of precision metal parts for medical analytical devices, is holding its weekly planning and control meeting on Monday at 8 A.M. in the quality control conference room.

Sandy, the Chief Production Scheduler; Tim, the Inventory Manager; Dick Jones, the senior buyer; and Joe, one of their key suppliers, are meeting to discuss some recent late shipment problems. Joe leads off with, "The reason we are often late shipping you part 707A is that we are constantly receiving change orders, which louses up our MRP system." Sandy says, "Joe, I know you are right, as I have a problem getting an accurate sales forecast from the marketing guys." Tim interrupts with, "You think your MRP program is inaccurate? You should check our on-hand inventory status reports with your shipping records on part 707A; they seldom match." All three agree that both organizations are at fault. ■

### CRITICAL THINKING QUESTIONS

1. How critical is the sales forecast in this situation? How does this set of numbers affect MRP systems?
2. What are some reasons for changes in the sales forecast?
3. What factors might account for inaccurate inventory files?
4. What action steps and/or plans should these three managers take to solve this problem?
5. Is the concept of demand management relevant in this situation?

## PART I: THE FUNDAMENTALS OF PRODUCTION PLANNING

The objective of the production planning and control function is to coordinate the use of a firm's resources and synchronize the work of all individuals concerned with production to meet required completion dates, at the lowest total cost, consistent with desired quality.

Historically, all firms conducted their production planning and control activities manually with the use of a variety of Gantt charts and specialized visual scheduling/control boards. Today, most firms utilize some type of computer-based system to perform essentially the same types of activities in a more comprehensive, semiautomatic manner. Regardless of the specific operating system used, an effective production planning and control operation involves five general activities:

1. Preliminary planning.
2. Aggregate scheduling.
3. Detailed production scheduling.

4. Release and dispatching of orders.
5. Progress surveillance and correction.

**Preliminary Planning**   After the initial product design and process design work have been completed by the appropriate engineering groups, the preliminary planning work begins. The product's engineering bill of materials is restructured for compatibility with the firm's planning system. *For the specific product (or special job),* analysts then determine the specific material requirements, standard labor and machine requirements, and tooling requirements. In most intermittent manufacturing operations, one or more work-flow routings through the shop are determined.

**Aggregate Scheduling**   The next step in the process is scheduling: first aggregate scheduling and then detailed production scheduling. As orders and forecasts are generated, they are matched against and coordinated with the facility's overall capability. Aggregate scheduling is simply a first-pass, broad-brush determination that shop capacity—equipment and people—and required materials probably can be made available through careful, detailed scheduling work.

**Detailed Production Scheduling**   The ensuing step consists of the detailed production scheduling work. The aggregate planning work is broken down into specific product models and configurations, and for each one the detailed manufacturing steps are scheduled into specific work centers or on specific machines. Start and completion dates for each operation or set of related operations are assigned, indicating the desired production priorities. Specific material and tooling requirements for the job are determined, as is the specific shop routing for the job.

**Release and Dispatching of Orders**   The work completed up to this point in the process has led to the development of an operating plan. When the order is released to the shop, the plan becomes operational and the order is dispatched from one operating unit to the next until it is complete. One of the key functions in this activity is to review the production priorities established in the prior scheduling activity. Any desired changes can be made at this point.

When the order is released, it is accompanied by a packet of paperwork and instructions. The packet typically contains things such as the engineering drawings and perhaps the bill of materials, tooling and material requisitions or computer entry instructions, a routing sheet, and detailed operations instructions for the production people. It also may contain instructions for charging labor and moving the job from one operation to the next.

**Progress Surveillance and Correction**   The last step in the process is the control function. Progress at each stage of the operation is monitored and fed back to the shop dispatcher and the production scheduler, who compare actual performance with the plan. Significant deviations from the schedule typically require some type of corrective action: rerouting, rescheduling, the use of overtime work, and so on. Those decisions, if fairly routine in nature, typically are made by production planning and control personnel. If a serious trade-off of resources or priorities is involved, marketing and manufacturing personnel may enter the decision-making process.

## Modern Production Planning Systems

The preceding discussion sketched the fundamental activities that must be accomplished in planning and controlling production operations effectively. In practice, manufacturing firms conduct those activities in a variety of ways, some with great detail and precision and others with less sophistication. As competition in the marketplace has become increasingly keen, however, firms have been forced to meet higher performance standards and do that cost-effectively. This economic reality, coupled with the availability of relatively inexpensive computing capability, has spawned a new era in production planning. Within a few

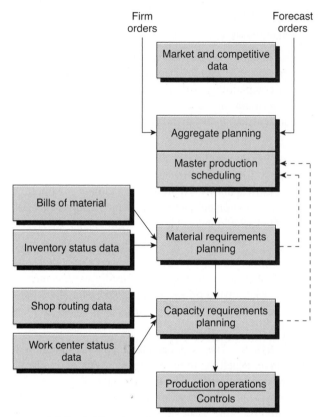

**Figure 20.1 |** A Basic Flowchart for a Modern Production Planning System

years, a progressive firm without a sophisticated, computer-based production planning and control system will be a rarity.

Although numerous different systems are evolving, both as custom-designed and as standard commercial software packages, most utilize essentially the same basic elements. Figure 20.1 portrays, in flowchart form, the basic operating elements in most current computer-based production planning systems.

## Aggregate Planning and Master Scheduling

The development of a viable aggregate plan and a coordinated master production schedule is the starting point for the use of a detailed computer-based planning system.

The *aggregate plan* is based on the expected receipt of a certain number of orders for a specific family of products during the planning period. For the near term, a number of firm orders typically are in hand. As the planners peer farther into the future, they use various forecasting techniques to determine an approximate aggregate demand for the product family. The most commonly used forecasting approaches are the following:

- Bottom-up analysis, utilizing the opinion, judgment, and market surveys of field sales personnel.
- Time series analysis.

- Exponential smoothing techniques.
- Regression and correlation analysis.

Forecasting activities typically are conducted or coordinated by a specialized staff group and generally are handled as a responsibility separate from the computerized planning system activities. In a majority of firms, forecasting demand is the responsibility of the marketing/sales department.

Development of the aggregate plan is usually a top management responsibility. General management, sales management, and manufacturing management personnel jointly develop the initial version of the plan on the basis of the known and expected order data.

With the assistance of senior production planning personnel, in most firms the plan is developed for a period of 6 to 12 months. To be effective, the schedule must cover a time span that exceeds the cumulative lead time of the finished product. The plan must be firmed up for a reasonable period because overall production volume cannot be changed abruptly without incurring significant unplanned costs. Every production volume utilizes a particular mix of labor, materials, and equipment. When the output rate is changed, a new optimal mix must be achieved by readjusting the usage rate of the various resources. In the longer term this can be done by replanning the variables: the employment level, the use of overtime, the use of subcontracting, and the variation of inventory levels. In the short run it usually is difficult to do efficiently.

The *master production schedule (MPS)* is developed directly from the aggregate plan and is the instrument that drives the firm's entire production system. The aggregate plan establishes an overall level of operations that balances the plant's capability with external sales demand. The master schedule translates the aggregate plan into specific numbers of specific products to be produced in identified time periods.

The relationship between the master schedule and the aggregate plan is shown in Figure 20.2. In this hypothetical illustration, an appliance manufacturer's aggregate plan for refrigerator production is shown at the top of the figure. (When this plan is added to the firm's aggregate plans for ranges, washing machines, and dryers, the firm's total production capacity will have been utilized for the year.) Note that

**Figure 20.2** Illustrative Relationship of the Aggregate Plan and the Master Production Schedule

**Aggregate Plan for Refrigerators**

| Month | Jan. | Feb. | March | April | May | June | July | Aug. | Sept. | Oct. | Nov. | Dec. |
|---|---|---|---|---|---|---|---|---|---|---|---|---|
| Number of refrigerators | 500 | 500 | 600 | 700 | 700 | 800 | 800 | 700 | 600 | 500 | 400 | 400 |

**Master Production Schedule for Refrigerators**

| Month | Jan. | Feb. | March | April | May | June | July | Aug. | Sept. | Oct. | Nov. | Dec. |
|---|---|---|---|---|---|---|---|---|---|---|---|---|
| Business Model | | | | | | | | | | | | |
| • Standard | — | 100 | — | 200 | — | 200 | — | 150 | — | 100 | — | 100 |
| • Heavy Duty | — | 100 | — | 100 | — | 100 | — | 100 | — | 50 | — | 50 |
| Model A | | | | | | | | | | | | |
| • Standard | 200 | 100 | 300 | 150 | 300 | 200 | 350 | 200 | 250 | 150 | 150 | 100 |
| • Deluxe | 50 | — | 50 | — | 100 | — | 100 | — | 50 | — | 50 | — |
| • Executive | — | 100 | — | 150 | — | 200 | — | 150 | — | 100 | — | 100 |
| Model B | | | | | | | | | | | | |
| • Standard | 200 | 100 | 200 | 100 | 200 | 100 | 250 | 100 | 250 | 100 | 150 | 50 |
| • Deluxe | 50 | — | 50 | — | 100 | — | 100 | — | 50 | — | 50 | — |

the master production schedule breaks down the aggregate production of refrigerators into the production of seven specific models, time-phased by quantity per month for the planning period of a year. For example, the 500 units planned in January consist of 200 Model A Standards, 50 Model A Deluxe units, 200 Model B Standards, and 50 Model B Deluxe units. The master schedule for the rest of the year is constructed in the same manner.

The next step in the development of the master schedule is to evaluate its feasibility by means of simulation, checking the availability and balance of required materials and capacity resources. If bottlenecks or imbalances are encountered, the schedule is modified by trial and error until an acceptable arrangement is found. Many computerized planning systems have this simulation capability built in, as will be discussed shortly.

Once an acceptable schedule has been determined, its outputs—the volume and timing of the production of specific products—become the inputs required for the subsequent detailed computer planning work that drives the production, inventory, and purchasing operations.

Before moving on to this part of the discussion, however, it is necessary to say a word about timing and modification of the original plan. The time interval used in master scheduling obviously varies from firm to firm; it depends on the types of products produced, the volume of production, and the lead times of the materials used. However, weekly periods probably are used most commonly, followed by biweekly and monthly intervals. Thus, within the time frame of a 6- to 12-month aggregate plan, the master schedule typically is updated weekly to reflect changing sales demands and perhaps internal problems that require rescheduling. If the system is to work effectively, it is essential that the schedule be updated regularly. After each update, many firms follow the policy of holding the next four weeks' schedule *firm,* providing only modest flexibility for adjustment in the schedule for weeks 5 through 8, and providing considerable flexibility for change in the schedule for weeks 9 through 12.[1]

## Material Requirements Planning

*Material requirements planning (MRP)* is a technique used to determine the quantity and timing requirements of dependent demand materials used in a manufacturing operation. The materials can be purchased externally or produced in-house. The important characteristic is that their use be directly dependent on the scheduled production of a larger component or finished product, hence the term "dependent demand." For example, a refrigerator door is a dependent demand item in the production of a refrigerator.

The material requirements planning and the capacity requirements planning (CRP) segments of the production planning system are the responsibility of the production planning and control group. In practice, the actual number crunching and paperwork generation usually are accomplished by computer.

Production planning personnel are responsible for structuring and formatting the product bills of material that eventually are contained in computer memory. The same group is responsible for setting up the part and component inventory status records (perpetual inventory records), which also are computerized. In addition to the current inventory balance, an inventory status record typically contains the timing and size of all open (scheduled) orders for the item, the lead time, safety stock levels, and any other information used for planning purposes. When this preliminary planning work is completed, material requirements for a specific time period can be generated.

Although details of the software operation may vary, generally, the MRP segment works as follows. It takes the master production schedule output for a particular product and calculates precisely the specific

---

[1]Some firms use time frames of five or six weeks rather than four weeks.

part and component requirements for that product during the particular period of operation. This is done by "exploding" the product bill of material (listing separately the quantity of each part required to make the product) and extending those requirements for the number of units to be produced. Since a part often is used in more than one finished product, the process is repeated for all products. Then all products' requirements for a given part can be summed to obtain the total requirement for that part during the stated period of operation.

For illustrative purposes, let us return to the refrigerator example in Figure 20.2. Assume that all the refrigerator models produced except the Model B Deluxe use one standard 1-horsepower electric motor. Because of an additional freezing compartment, the Model B Deluxe uses two standard 1-horsepower motors. For the month of January, the MRP system would determine that the manufacturing operation requires 550 standard 1-horsepower electric motors.

Returning to our general discussion of the MRP processing activity, after a part's requirements for the operating period are calculated, the computer compares those requirements with the inventory balance, considering open orders scheduled for receipt, to determine whether a new order has to be placed.

The output of the MRP system, then, can be the following items:

1. Current order releases to purchasing (or to previously selected suppliers), with due date requirements.
2. Planned order releases to purchasing for ensuing periods (considering inventory balance, scheduled requirements, and lead-time requirements).
3. Current and planned order releases for in-house production, with completion date requirements.
4. Feedback to the master production scheduler in case operating changes or supplier performance has produced problems of material availability.
5. With revised output from the master production schedule, the MRP system will replan and schedule the material requirements.

A more detailed illustration of an MRP system's operating logic is provided in the following section.

**MRP Logic and Format**[2]     As they are utilized today, most versions of MRP act as information processing systems which seek to develop and maintain a set of orders that support the production plan while simultaneously maintaining inventories within the production system at reasonably low levels. Orders within an MRP system fall into two categories: (1) open orders which have been released but have not arrived yet and (2) planned orders which are developed in anticipation of future releases. As was noted previously, each category can contain both purchase orders and shop orders.

The processing logic of MRP centers on the development of a materials planning record for each item. Figure 20.3 illustrates a typical planning record based on the data contained in the master production schedule, bill of materials, and inventory record file shown at the top. The top row of each record shows the "gross requirements," or anticipated usage of the item projected into the future. The second row shows all current "open orders (scheduled receipts)," with each order assigned to the time period in which it is expected to arrive. The "on hand" row projects the inventory balance into the future. This is calculated by determining the impact of gross requirements (planned withdrawals) and open orders (planned receipts) on the inventory balance. The current inventory balance is shown to the left of period 1. The bottom row shows the "planned order releases" for the item, with each order assigned to the period in which it should be released.

---

[2]Based on Daniel J. Bragg and Chan K. Hahn, "Material Requirements Planning and Purchasing," *Journal of Purchasing and Materials Management,* Summer 1982, pp. 18–20. Used with permission of the authors. This article is considered a classic.

**Figure 20.3 |** A Typical MRP Planning Record

The development of the planning record is based on three fundamental concepts which form the essence of the MRP-based approach to materials planning and control:

- Dependent demand.
- Inventory/open order netting.
- Time phasing.

*Dependent demand* takes the multistage product into account in the planning for individual items. Clearly, decisions to acquire purchased materials should be based on anticipated production plans. Those decisions include both quantity and timing considerations. Dependent demand logic is used to calculate the gross requirements for each planning record. This projected usage includes the planned production of all other products which require the item being planned.

*The inventory/open order netting* concept is used to develop the "on hand" balance row of the planning record. Efficient use of inventory implies that current stocks should be largely depleted before the acquisition of additional inventory. The netting process accomplishes this by allocating current inventory and open orders to the earliest requirements. When the on-hand balance falls below zero, additional stock must be ordered. This process not only signals the need to plan an order but also determines when the order should arrive. This "need date" becomes the due date for the order.

*Time phasing* utilizes lead-time information and need dates. The "planned order releases" row of the planning record shows time-phased orders whose placement dates are offset from the need dates of the orders by the lead time of the item. Each order, if released in the period designated by the planned order row, should arrive exactly when it is needed by a following production stage.

Utilization of the three basic concepts can be observed in the simplified illustration in Figure 20.3. The bill of materials diagram shows that item B is a fabricated part that is manufactured using D as a raw material and that B is used as a component of A. The dependent demand concept is seen in the gross requirements data; the planned usage of B matches the planned production of A in both quantity and timing.

The netting process calculations determine the need for additional orders to be planned. For item B, in week 2, 150 units are needed. Since the on-hand quantity of 100 is used to meet week 1 requirements, an order release for 150 units is shown in week 1. Time phasing maintains the timing difference between the planned order and its need date; this is the item's lead time. In this case the lead time is one week. A similar process is used to develop the remaining orders in the "planned order releases" row. For item D, for example, the process is repeated, with the only difference being that D is dependent on B.

MRP not only plans for each order but also allows the replanning of orders. Replanning is generally necessary when the status of an item is changed as a result of new information. An example of a status-changing event would be notice of a late delivery. Using item D as an illustration, an open order currently is planned to arrive in week 2. If this order is known to have an altered delivery date of week 3, the current plan should be adjusted (replanned) to reflect the new information. The impact of this change can be traced to every other item by reversing the processing logic and working from bottom to top rather than from top to bottom.

The impact of the shortage also can be reduced by adjusting the orders for the other items. Take item B, for example. The planned order release in week 2 is no longer feasible and should be shifted into week 3. The requirement that was to be covered by this planned order no longer can be supported. It also should be shifted into the next week, thus affecting the master production schedule.

Thus, the MRP system generates a complete set of planned orders for all manufactured parts and purchased materials that is based on the information inputs. Clearly, the validity of the plan produced by the system is dependent on both accurate and timely lead-time information from purchasing personnel. At the same time, if system planning is done far enough in advance (and rescheduling activity is kept to a minimum), the advance knowledge about specific material requirements certainly can facilitate the planning and conducting of the buying activities.

It is important to understand that all MRP systems rely on the following:

1. *A very accurate master schedule,* which is based on the sales forecast. This means that production planners must interact constantly with the marketing department, scheduling starts with the organization's customers, not in the operations department.

2. *Absolute accuracy of all inventory counts,* including on hand, on order, and encumbered (earmarked). For example, sloppy inventory counting, including failure to adjust for shrinkage, will result in inaccurate records being "read" by the computer.

3. *Up-to-date bills of materials* which reflect all engineering and quantity changes. Many MRP systems have failed because specification revisions failed to reach all members of the supply chain.

## Capacity Requirements Planning

The next step in the production planning process is capacity requirements planning (CRP). The function of the CRP segment of the process is to convert the shop orders produced by the MRP system into scheduled workloads for the various factory work centers. In addition to the MRP system output, two other sets of data inputs are required to do this: (1) shop routing data and (2) work center status data. These inputs for CRP operation are analogous to the bill of materials and inventory status inputs for MRP operation.

In an intermittent production operation, the manufacture of each product or component requires that a series of specific machine or human operations be performed on the item as it progresses toward completion. Those required operations define the "route" the item must travel through the manufacturing facility. Sometimes more than one routing sequence is possible. In any case, one of the required preliminary planning activities is to develop one or more shop routing plans for each product and component produced in-house. In addition to the physical routing plans, standard processing time requirements must be determined for each operation in the sequence and included in the shop routing data file. In a continuous manufacturing operation, these activities usually are simplified by the design and layout of the production facility.

The work center status data file maintains a perpetual record of the capacity—equipment and human—that is available (and committed) in each of the factory's work centers. Capacity typically is measured in standard labor or machine hours per time period.

With shop routing data and work center status data files loaded in computer memory, the CRP system is ready for operation. Recall that during the development of the master production schedule, a preliminary analysis of work center capacity was done before the schedule was firmed up. While this "rough cut" produced approximate data accurate enough for overall scheduling purposes, it is not precise enough for the detailed work-loading job at hand. Therefore, with the MRP-generated current and planned shop order releases now known with certainty for a specific period, a second pass is made. The CRP program first obtains the necessary routing and timing data for each scheduled order and then checks the appropriate work center status files to determine whether the required capacity is available. Frequently the proposed plan does not mesh satisfactorily with the availability and timing of capacity in the required work centers. In this case, the CRP activity becomes an iterative process, and replanning continues until realistic work center loads are developed. The variables that can be manipulated by the system and the planner to achieve a reasonable balance typically include the following:

- Alternative routings.
- Personnel reallocation.
- Use of overtime.
- Inventory-level variations.
- Use of alternative tooling.
- Use of subcontracting—outsourcing.

Occasionally an impossible scheduling situation is encountered. In this case the system communicates to the scheduler the need for selected capacity modification or for a revision of the master schedule. Most of the time, however, a reasonable fit can be achieved. The normal output of the system in these cases is:

1. Verification of the planned orders from the MRP system.
2. Work center load reports that reflect the priorities established by the MRP system.

This information subsequently is used in the final stage of the planning and control process.

## Control of Production Activities

According to a time-honored adage, "the proof of the pudding is in the eating." The validity and usefulness of the detailed planning done to this point in the process will now be seen as it is applied to production operations in the shop.

The output of the MRP and CRP systems is transmitted to the manufacturing organization in the form of order releases and a dispatch list. Referring again to Figure 20.3, the planned order releases shown on line 4 of the planning record, when released as the date moves into the current period, officially become the open orders (scheduled receipts) shown on line 2 of the planning record. Before releasing an order, the planner must make a final check to ensure that the priority sequencing of the order is still valid, capacity is still available, and materials are available. If all factors are not "go," release may be delayed rather than having the order held up after it is started in the shop.

When an order is released, typically it is accompanied by a packet of materials and instructions required to complete the job. Included are things such as engineering drawings, bills of materials, route sheets, move tickets, materials requisitions, and labor charge forms. Depending on the extent to which the entire system is computerized, some of these functions may be handled through the use of online terminals.

The dispatch list, containing a series of order releases, is prepared by the planner and may cover a period ranging from a day to a week. It goes to the appropriate work center foreman, who schedules his or her machines and people in accordance with the due dates specified for each order on the list.

If daily dispatch lists are used, the foreman generally has little discretion in scheduling the jobs in the work center. In contrast, if the list covers several days of work or more, the foreman has an increasing amount of latitude in his or her detailed scheduling activities. This provides a better opportunity to maximize the operating efficiency of the work center. Perceptive planning and scheduling by the foreman usually can minimize setup and material move costs and maximize the utilization of equipment and labor. Consequently, it is important that planners coordinate the development of their dispatch lists closely with the appropriate foremen in an effort to optimize both planning control and shop efficiency. Team-type spirit and effort usually produce the best results.

As was noted earlier, control is an essential element if the entire process is to work effectively. In most operations this is accomplished at two levels. First, as a job progresses, status and related information are fed back to the planner from either the operator or the foreman on the job. The information reported typically includes order status, anticipated delays, materials shortages, and rework and scrap data. As appropriate, such feedback occurs either daily or when a job is started and completed. Some firms report only on an exception basis. In continuous manufacturing operations, the reporting typically is done less frequently at predetermined checkpoints in the process. In any case, that information is used by the planner to determine whether replanning or other corrective action is necessary to meet the firm's sales commitments.

In addition to order status types of control reports, most systems require one or more types of capacity control reports. The most commonly used one is an input/output report, typically developed weekly. This type of report usually shows the hours of work planned for a particular work center, the number of hours actually worked on the planned jobs, and the difference between the two. Significant deviations from the plan can produce obvious problems in the CRP and subsequent scheduling activities. Hence, in most operations, this type of control is essential.

Reporting and monitoring methodology varies among firms. Some firms are totally computerized, with computer graphics output, while others use a combination of computer and manual communication and charting techniques. The use of Gantt charts and schedule/control boards is still fairly common.

In most organizations, control also is exercised at a second level: personal control right on the shop floor. One or more dispatcher/expediters, usually assigned to the production planning and control group, spend most of their time on the floor visually following jobs through the manufacturing operation. This individual's job is threefold: (1) to ensure the integrity of the job priority plan, that is, make sure the routing and scheduling instructions for jobs are implemented reasonably; (2) to ensure reasonable capacity control, that is, ensure that the hours scheduled in the various work centers actually are being worked; and (3) to help the operating people solve unexpected planning and scheduling difficulties. As problems arise, the dispatcher/expediter works with the various foremen to resolve them. This person is the planning group's representative on the shop floor. Within reason, he or she has the authority to suggest certain micro planning and scheduling changes that may be able to resolve a problem directly and expeditiously.

To summarize, the production planning activities all come together on the shop floor to initiate and control the production operations. Overall responsibility for *control* of operations usually is vested with the production planning and control manager or the materials manager. In firms without a materials management department, the manufacturing manager is sometimes responsible. The control function usually has both a centralized component and a decentralized component. Order release, dispatching, and formal status control are the responsibility of the centralized production planning and control group. Decentralized informal control on the shop floor is the joint responsibility of dispatcher/expediter personnel and the line foremen responsible for the actual production operations. Viewed in another sense, it is the responsibility of the foremen to do the micro work center scheduling and to run each production operation so that planned completion dates are met. It is the responsibility of production planning and control to keep work flowing through the shop at a steady rate, focusing always on order priority control and capacity control.

## Two Management Considerations

It is appropriate at this point to reiterate two important concepts that may have gotten buried in the details of the discussion of the total planning system.

The first concept concerns the *multilevel nature of the operation of the production planning system.* A review of Figure 20.1 will reveal that for the most part, the aggregate planning and the master scheduling activities are top management and staff responsibilities. In comparison, most activities associated with the MRP and CRP activities are primarily the responsibility of production planning and control personnel. Finally, the control of the production operations themselves is a joint responsibility of production planning and control personnel and supervisory operating personnel. For a system to function effectively, the coordinated efforts of all three groups are required.

The second concept focuses on the *dynamic nature of the total production planning system.* Although time periods vary for different organizations, a majority of firms that use a comprehensive computer-based planning system work from an aggregate plan structured for the coming year. The master schedule subsequently covers the same year's period, but typically it is delineated further by month and by week. Material and capacity requirements also are structured in weekly "time buckets." To maintain a current plan that correctly reflects changing sales demands and internal scheduling and capacity constraints, the entire operation typically is replanned on a weekly basis. Therefore, the firm, semifirm, and flexible portions of the total operating schedule simply drop the week just past and encompass one new week as replanning occurs each week. Some systems utilize a technique in which only selected portions of the operation that are influenced by changing conditions are replanned; this approach has some obvious logistical advantages. Regardless of the specific technique used, however, the important point is that the dynamic nature of the planning system keeps it current on at least a weekly basis. From a practical point of view, this is the feature that makes such a system so valuable to a large complex firm operating in a competitive environment.

## Evolution of MRP and MRP II Systems

As innovations are accepted and refined in the business world, inconsistencies in the use of terminology and variations of the concept inevitably emerge with the passage of time. This has been the case with MRP and its subsequent derivatives. The following paragraphs describe briefly the evolution of MRP and its progeny, MRP II.

The computer-based material requirements planning technique had its first significant industrial use in the early 1970s. Though it became known as MRP, for a number of years it was used primarily to generate orders for parts and materials that related to a specific demand schedule. Later, users found that with some refinement it could be used as a scheduling technique. It could be employed to feed back schedule change data and subsequently reschedule existing orders to maintain valid material and shop order dates. Hence, it became a much more valuable tool.

However, from a production planning point of view, MRP still left something to be desired because it was unable to deal with the capacity variable. Before long, though, necessity proved to be the mother of invention, because soon a capacity requirements planning module was developed and linked to the original MRP module. With further development of the master production schedule concept, in many firms the bulk of the planning activities shown in Figure 20.1 were integrated into a single planning and scheduling package. Today, with the exception of the aggregate planning and the production operation controls segments, this entire integrated package is identified as a *closed loop MRP system.* Thus, both the concept and the terminology have changed with time.

The last step to date in this evolutionary process is an expanded system known as *MRP II— manufacturing resource planning.* This system simply adds two new capabilities to a closed loop MRP system. The most significant addition is the financial interface. This module provides the ability to convert operating production plans into financial terms so that the data can be used for financial planning and control purposes of a more general management nature. Related to this feature, the second addition provides a simulation capability that makes it possible for management to do more extensive alternative planning work in developing the marketing and business plans. This can be done by asking "what if" types of questions, that is, by modifying an operating variable and receiving a systemwide response to the proposed operating change.

As MRP and MRP II systems developed in different firms, they often included somewhat different levels of capability. For example, some MRP systems originally did not include comprehensive CRP capability and did not function fully as closed loop systems. When MRP II capability subsequently was developed, it included the features which previously were missing. As a result of this situation, along with the fact that MRP II is more comprehensive in nature, many users see MRP II as the "umbrella" system, with MRP as a major component of that system.[3]

## Impact on Purchasing and Supply Management

Sooner or later, most manufacturing firms will use some type of MRP-based system as a central component of their production planning systems. If present experience is a reasonable indicator of the future, purchasing operations will be affected in the following important ways:[4]

1. Expanded use of the buyer-planner or the supplier scheduler concept.
2. Expanded use of contract buying.
3. Necessity for greater supplier flexibility and reliability.
4. Development of closer relationships with suppliers, including more partnering arrangements.
5. Increased accuracy and timeliness of materials records.
6. Direct interface between the buyer's and supplier's MRP system.

**Buyer-Planner and Supplier Scheduler Concepts**   The nature of an MRP operation places the planner in close, continuing contact with material requirements and their frequently changing schedules. Typically, the planner has a more sensitive feel than does the buyer for the probable usage pattern of most materials. Consequently, to improve the efficiency of the planning-buying activity as well as communications with suppliers, many firms have used one of several organizational schemes that utilize the planner as the supplier contact person for day-to-day material flow activities.

*The buyer-planner concept* is a commonly used approach. In essence, the buyer's job and the planner's job are combined into a single job done by one individual. This person obviously handles a smaller number of items than originally were handled by either the buyer or the planner. The buyer-planner is responsible for determining material requirements, developing material schedules, making order quantity determinations, issuing all material releases to suppliers, and handling all the activities associated with the buying function. Thus, in this integrated role, the buyer-planner maintains close contact with various supplier personnel.

Another popular approach is to assign to the planner the responsibility for dealing directly with suppliers in releasing and following upon materials orders. In this arrangement, the buyer handles all the normal purchasing responsibilities except requirements releases against existing contracts. The planner handles the latter function and becomes the buying firm's supplier contact on all day-to-day material scheduling matters. Most firms refer to this arrangement as the *supplier scheduler concept.*

---

[3]For an interesting discussion of MRP II development, see Troy Juliar, "Completing the Mix: Materials Management and MRP II," *Purchasing Management,* February 1987, pp. 6–11.

[4]An MRP-type system also generates output that can be utilized easily and effectively as input for an electronic data interchange (EDI) system. Consequently, as EDI operations are used more widely, MRP systems will tend to facilitate their use.

In a recent survey of MRP users, researchers found that approximately 55 percent of the firms use the supplier scheduler concept and 30 percent use the buyer-planner organizational arrangement. Only 15 percent of the firms surveyed utilize the traditional pattern of operation.[5] It seems clear that continued expansion of the use of these two concepts will accompany MRP development in the future.

**Contract Buying**   Because an MRP system requires the placement of frequent orders for relatively small quantities of materials, it obviously would be inefficient, if not impossible, to make a new buy for every weekly requirement. The alternative, of course, is to place annual or longer-term contracts with suppliers for the required materials and then simply issue a telephone or an MRP schedule release against the contract as the production operation requires.

Not only is this buying approach required in an MRP-scheduled operation, as a general rule it is excellent buying practice. It permits more careful purchasing planning and more thorough market and supplier research, and it needs to be done only once every year or two for each material. In addition, such contracts usually produce attractive pricing arrangements and improved supplier relations.

**Supplier Flexibility and Reliability**   Because of the weekly updating of most MRP systems, coupled with the frequent rescheduling that sometimes occurs, a supplier has to be more than reasonably flexible. Even if a supplier has the buyer's MRP schedule with weekly or biweekly requirements for the next two months, the irregularity of demand and the short notice given on schedule changes present a difficult operating situation for most suppliers. Resolution of the potential problems requires careful cooperative planning and usually some compromises by both parties.

It is obvious that supplier reliability is a must. The buying firm typically carries some inventory, but not as much as in the traditional operating situation since one of the objectives of the system is to reduce inventory levels. Hence, there is much less of a cushion in the system to handle the problems of late deliveries and off-spec materials.

The bottom line for these two stringent operating requirements is that supplier selection is a critical yet a more difficult task.

**Closer Relationships with Suppliers**   The use of contract buying and the need for unusual supplier flexibility and reliability create an operating situation in which the buyer-supplier relationship must be closer and more cooperative than it normally might be. As discussed in the chapters on sourcing in this book, this type of operating situation requires the ultimate in coordination, cooperation, and teamwork. A mutual understanding of each other's operations and problems is essential for achieving this type of effectiveness. It literally is an informal partnership operation, and it must turn out to be a win-win deal.

The buyer-planner or the supplier scheduler must stay in close touch with the supplier's counterpart on a week-to-week basis as far as scheduling and delivery matters are concerned. Also, the buyer (or buyer-planner) must handle the broader issues of the relationship with appropriate supplier sales and technical personnel on a regular and timely basis.

As one reviews the MRP segment of the production planning system, it is readily apparent that the accuracy of the system can be no better than the accuracy of the data used in its calculations. If the system is to work effectively, records such as specifications, bills of materials, supplier lead times, receiving reports, and inventory balances must be as close to 100 percent accurate as possible.

---

[5]J. E. Schorr and T. F. Wallace, *High Performance Purchasing: Manufacturing Resource Planning for the Purchasing Professional,* Wight Publications Inc., Essex Junction VT, 1986, p. 150.

# Just-in-Time Production Planning

Although originally pioneered by Henry Ford, the just-in-time manufacturing concept has been refined and developed over the last several decades in Japanese industry. The purpose of this recent concerted effort was to improve quality and reduce costs to help Japanese business become more competitive in world markets for selected product lines. The resounding success of the Japanese effort prompted a growing number of U.S. firms to develop and implement modified versions of the system in this country.

The just-in-time concept is considered by many to be a technique used for reducing inventories, but in reality, it is much more. The complete JIT concept is an operations management philosophy whose dual objectives are to reduce waste and increase productivity. However, operationally, the basic theme of the JIT concept is that *inventory is evil*. Inventory is considered undesirable for three reasons:

■ It hides quality problems.

■ It hides production inefficiencies and productivity problems.

■ It adds unnecessary costs to the production operation: carrying costs of approximately 25 to 35 percent of the inventory value per year.

Inventories of production materials permit suppliers' quality deficiencies to be covered up, and in-process inventories permit off-spec work in-house to be given less attention than it should. This occurs because the unacceptable items can be replaced with good items from inventory while those which are unacceptable are being reworked. The same rationale applies to schedule slippages caused by inefficiencies in the workplace and in the system itself. The end result, claim JIT proponents, has been a tendency among U.S. managers and their employees to accept mediocre, second-rate work as the norm.

Hence, in an effective JIT application, the operating policy is to minimize production inventories and work-in-process inventories by providing each work center with just the quantity of materials and components needed to do a specific job at the exact time they are needed. In an ideal situation, each unit of output would be produced just as it was needed at the succeeding work station. In reality, this ideal is not achieved, but within reason, it is a viable objective in many organizations. Practically speaking, the result is a reasonably continuous flow of small-lot production. At the supply end of the operation, materials that are procured in a JIT mode are delivered frequently by suppliers in fairly small quantities. Deliveries may range from twice a day to once a week.

Consequently, throughout the system, with only minimal inventories on hand to cover for poor-quality materials and workmanship, the focus is on consistently high-quality material and in-process work. Without that, the system breaks down.

To summarize, the basic operating plan is to gear production and final assembly as closely to sales demand as possible. Individual production operations also are geared more closely together. This is accomplished either by means of a product-type layout of equipment and work centers[6] or by means of a material-pull, "kanban" type of material movement system[7] in a process-oriented layout. Finally, the firm's total

---

[6]*A product-type layout* is one in which the various types of equipment required to make a product are arranged adjacent to each other so that operations occur sequentially, in line, from one end of the manufacturing process to the other. An automobile assembly plant is a good example of product layout. A *process-type layout* groups similar types of equipment together without regard for the flow of the product being manufactured; for example, all lathes are grouped together, all boring machines are grouped together, and so on. A traditional job shop exemplifies this type of layout.

[7]A *kanban material production and movement system* is one in which no more than approximately an hour's supply of material is produced in one run in each work center, and the next production run does not occur until the material is called for by the succeeding operation. It is this feature of the operation that produces the *small batch* and *pull-flow* characteristics of the system.

**Figure 20.4** | How JIT Was Implemented in One U.S. Firm

production operation, through its purchasing activities, is geared as closely as practical to key suppliers' production operations. Thus, the characteristic of small-lot flow can be traced through the entire system from a supplier's plant, through the buyer's plant, and out into the finished goods distribution system. The actuating element is sales demand, which *pulls* the various stages of in-process work and materials through the complete system.

## A JIT Illustration

Figure 20.4 provides a flow diagram of the major production operations in an electronic instrument manufacturing plant both before and after the firm implemented a JIT system.

The top portion of the figure shows the original operation. After incoming material was received, counted, and logged into the system, it went through a standard visual receiving inspection operation where potential quality problems were detected and perhaps was submitted to quality assurance for further detailed inspection. The next step was to prepackage the materials, parts, and components that subsequently would be used in putting together a particular subassembly. This was done for each subassembly produced to facilitate stock picking for the later assembly work. Most production inventories thus were stored in this subassembly kit form. After subassembly operations occurred, subassembly units were inventoried until they were used in a product's final assembly operation. Approximately a week's finished goods inventory for most products was maintained at the plant.

The lower portion of Figure 20.4 shows the dramatic change that occurred as a result of JIT implementation. The receiving inspection and quality control technical inspection operations for purchased materials were eliminated completely. *The responsibility for incoming quality was placed with the purchasing department and delegated to each supplier organization.* This required a reasonable amount of supplier education. In most cases purchasing and quality control (QC) worked with suppliers to develop and install statistical process control (SPC) systems in their manufacturing operations. SPC control charts then were required to be submitted with each shipment of delivered material.

The next major change occurred on the shop floor. The facility originally utilized a specialized process-type layout, similar to a large job shop. That was revised to achieve a modified product-type layout. Although the firm produced approximately half a dozen different product lines, there was enough similarity between products to permit the use of several product-flow types of facilities arrangements. This layout permitted the use of an open-type storage system adjacent to the production operations so that incoming materials were delivered directly to the point of use in the shop.

Production scheduling subsequently was based completely on units of finished product rather than on the production of subassemblies. This made it practical to eliminate the subassembly prepackaging and storage activities as well as the subassembly operations themselves. The firm's closed loop MRP system still was used to generate requirements and overall schedules, but it was necessary to "smooth" the master schedule to facilitate the reasonably continuous small-lot production. Consequently, the total shop now resembles a continuous manufacturing operation in contrast to its previous job shop character.

As shown underneath each of the two flow diagrams, inventory levels were reduced greatly. Production inventory was decreased approximately 70 percent, and in-process inventories were reduced from about a 15-day supply to a 1-day supply. Finished goods inventory was reduced by about 40 percent. Hence, the total float figure declined from approximately 50 days to 12 days, and the firm reports that quality problems have declined noticeably.

In summary, the following elements tend to characterize most successful JIT operations[8]:

1. The JIT concept is most applicable to manufacturing operations that produce a relatively small number of different products in at least a quasi-continuous environment.

2. Product demand must be reasonably predictable, and requirements must be generated accurately. A closed loop MRP system can be used to do this, but typically the master production schedule must be smoothed on a daily basis.

3. Statistical process control typically is used in both the buyer's and the suppliers' organizations to ensure tight control of material and production quality. This is vital to the functioning of the low-float, small-volume, relatively smooth-flowing operation.

4. Production operation setup requirements must be able to be reduced to relatively short times. Most firms target for tool changes and equipment setups of less than 10 minutes. Without this capability, small-batch and smooth-flow production of different models or different products cannot be accomplished efficiently.

---

[8]The following articles provide good in-depth analyses of JIT applications: Chan K. Hahn, Peter A. Pinto, and Daniel J. Bragg, "Just-in-Time Production and Purchasing," *Journal of Purchasing and Materials Management,* Fall 1983, pp. 2–15; C. H. St. John and K. C. Heriot, "Small Suppliers and JIT Purchasing," *International Journal of Purchasing and Materials Management,* Winter 1993, pp. 11–16; P. A. Dion, P. M. Banting, S. Picard, and D. L. Blenkhorn, "JIT Implementation: A Growth Opportunity for Purchasing," *International Journal of Purchasing and Materials Management,* Fall 1992, pp. 32–38.

5. Purchasing must be able to reduce material replenishment lead times. This usually is accomplished by reducing the four major elements of lead time: internal paperwork and ordering time, supplier queue and manufacturing time, transportation time requirements, and incoming receiving and inspection requirements.

6. Successful JIT operation suppliers must be able to be flexible to meet the buying firm's stringent, short-fused material requirements, and they must be reliable to the nth degree.

These considerations lead logically to a discussion of the impact of a JIT system on the purchasing operation.

## The Impact of JIT on Purchasing and the Supply Chain

Purchasing and supply plays a key role in any JIT operation. *Whether a JIT production system works depends on how well purchasing does its job in selecting and managing suppliers.*

Obviously, it is not practical to procure all materials on a JIT basis. Most successful JIT firms buy from 5 to 10 percent of their individual materials—those which account for 60 to 75 percent of the firm's materials expenditures and those which are space-intensive—in a JIT mode. This keeps the administrative part of the job manageable.

Finding reliable suppliers that are willing to comply with a JIT buyer's stringent requirements typically is not an easy task. Consequently, purchasing usually utilizes two basic strategies:

■ A specific plan to reduce the number of suppliers utilized, using single and dual sources in many cases.

■ Extensive use of long-term contracting.

Evaluation and qualification of JIT suppliers clearly is a critical and time-consuming activity.

The nature of a JIT purchasing operation requires, and in fact usually creates, a closer, more cooperative relationship between the buying and supplying firms. Hence, from a practical point of view a reduced supplier base is a necessity, and a longer-term contract is the primary incentive that attracts a supplier to consider that arrangement. Only with knowledge of the buyer's long-term requirements schedule can a supplier schedule production and size inventories so that replenishment lead time can be reduced while simultaneously providing both flexible and reliable service.

As was noted earlier, the basic objective of the "partnering" relationship is to reduce costs, improve efficiency, and increase profitability for *both* organizations. The development of scheduling guidelines and parameters, the implementation of SPC quality systems, and the conduct of value analysis work on the purchased items must be done jointly in a team-type environment. To assist in all these activities, the buyer often makes greater use of *performance specifications* to encourage the supplier to exercise as much creativity as possible.[9]

Reducing the delivering carrier's transportation time is also an important objective. Consequently, suppliers situated near the buyer's operation may offer a distinct advantage. The most important strategy in this element of the equation, however, is to work out a longer-term contractual JIT arrangement with a small number of selected carriers. This type of transportation service can be purchased in the same manner that material is purchased from a JIT supplier. This topic is discussed further in the appendix to this chapter.

---

[9]For a detailed discussion of the buyer-seller relationship, see C. R. O'Neal, "The Buyer-Seller Linkage in a Just-in-Time Environment," *Journal of Purchasing and Materials Management,* Spring 1989, pp. 34–40.

Another impact of JIT is seen in the form of a shift in the workload within the purchasing and supply department. The buyer's job now involves more responsibility for contract administration and supplier management than it did previously. The tight delivery schedules, the emphasis on control of quality and performance, and the joint resolution of problems with suppliers require this. At the same time, the nature of the JIT buying operation now requires less routine, nitty-gritty buying work. In effect, the JIT buyer's job tends to require a broader range of professional and managerial skills than typically was the case previously.

## ERP Systems

One must remember that enterprise resource planning (ERP) systems are macro data input software programs for all of a firm's information. ERP systems include production planning and inventory control programs but go well beyond their scope.

The benefits of ERP systems include cycle time reduction of key business processes, better financial management, and facility linkage to e-commerce systems; they also help make knowledge and information systems explicit. When an ERP system is well designed, there is complete transparency throughout the enterprise and across the supply chain. However, critics of ERP cite many negatives, including long implementation periods, inflexibility, excessively hierachical organizations, obsolete technology, and high cost.[10] However, there are many successful ERP implementations, and all the major ERP packages now support XML.[11]

In addition, ERP software firms obviously are dominated by information technology personnel who often write unrealistic rules such as "no back orders" and "no partial shipments." There must be professional purchasing input to avoid such mistakes.

## Conclusion

The interface between procurement and production planning is an extremely important one. Production planning decisions influence the parameters within which purchasing does its work. At the same time, the effectiveness with which purchasing does its job directly influences the success of the production planning system.

In recent years, with the aid of computerized systems, production planning has evolved into a highly specialized and sophisticated activity. Closed loop MRP systems, MRP II systems, and JIT systems all significantly affect the design and implementation of a firm's purchasing and supply systems. To a great extent, the purchasing strategies used in prior years must be modified and in some cases replaced with new approaches to create the supply environment required to support and sustain these evolving planning systems.

In this dynamic environment it is imperative that the procurement and production planning functions be developed in close coordination because of their interdependencies and that operationally they be coordinated effectively on a day-to-day basis.

# PART II: THE FUNCTIONS OF INVENTORIES

The preceding discussion of the JIT concept highlighted the disadvantages inventories can bring to a manufacturing operation. In many circumstances, however, inventories have some redeeming values—they are not all bad. The trick is to obtain the best of both worlds at a reasonable cost.

---

[10]Thomas H. Davenport, *Mission Critical—Realizing the Promise of Enterprise Systems* (Boston: Harvard Business School Press, 2000), pp. 6–7.

[11]*Ihid.*, pp. 16–19. Also see Matthew Friedman and Marlene Blanshay, *Understanding B2B* (Chicago: Dearborn Trade, 2001).

Generally, inventories make possible the smooth and efficient operation of a manufacturing organization by *decoupling individual segments* of the total operation. *Purchased-part* inventories permit the activities of purchasing and supply personnel to be planned and conducted somewhat independently of shop production operations. By the same token, those inventories allow additional flexibility for suppliers in planning, producing, and delivering an order for a specific part.

Inventories of *parts and components produced in-house* in an intermittent operation decouple the many individual machines and production processes from various subassembly and assembly activities. This typically enables management to plan production runs in individual production areas in a manner which utilizes manpower and equipment considerably more efficiently than would be the case if all were tied directly to the final assembly line. In addition, *finished goods* inventories perform the function of decoupling the total production process from distribution demands, allowing the development of similar efficiencies of production on a broader scale. These inventories also help *balance the firm's supply with the market forces of demand.*

Thus, well-planned and effectively controlled inventories can contribute to the effective operation of a firm and to a firm's profit. The basic challenge is to determine the inventory level that works most effectively with the operating system or systems existing within the organization and that realistically is the most feasible in dealing with specific suppliers and material markets.[12]

If the inventory issue is viewed through the eyes of various operating department managers, an interesting situation appears. The *marketing manager* tends to favor larger inventory stocks to assure rapid assembly and delivery of a wide range of finished product models. This capability obviously can be used as an effective sales tool. The *production manager* is inclined to go along with the marketing manager, but for a very different reason. He or she argues for higher inventory levels because they allow more flexibility in daily planning; unforeseen problems in producing a component can be mitigated if productive efforts can be transferred easily to another component for which the required raw materials are on hand. Likewise, a reasonable inventory of the required items *ensures against production shutdowns* caused by delivery problems, supplier problems, and stockouts, thus avoiding the incurrence of high production downtime costs. These arguments reveal the flip side of the arguments favoring a JIT system.

The *financial officers* of the firm, in contrast, argue convincingly in favor of very low inventory levels. They point out that the company's need for funds usually exceeds availability and that reduced inventories free sorely needed working capital for other uses. They also note that total indirect inventory carrying costs drop proportionately with the inventory level. The *purchasing and supply manager* is the final participant; he or she is concerned with the size and frequency of individual orders. Purchasing often favors a policy of placing fewer and larger orders. Unless contractual arrangements with routine delivery-release systems can be worked out with suppliers, fewer and larger orders usually increase the total inventory level. At the same time, however, they tend to minimize operating problems with suppliers, and in some cases they may reduce unit material prices. Large-volume buying also permits more *efficient utilization of buying personnel* and more effective advance planning for major activities such as market studies and supplier investigations. Thus, it is clear that each departmental executive supports his or her position with legitimate justification.

Concepts and techniques useful in analyzing the inventory issue to arrive at sound policy decisions are the focal point of the investigation in this chapter.

---

[12]For an interesting discussion of the JIT system and the value of inventories, see George Newman, "As Just-in-Time Goes By," *Across the Board*, October 1993, pp. 7–8.

# Definition of Inventories

Although inventories are classified in many ways, the following classification is convenient for use in further discussion of the topic:

1. *Production inventories:* raw materials, parts, and components which enter the firm's product in the production process. There are two general types: (1) special items manufactured to company specifications and (2) standard industrial items purchased "off the shelf."
2. *MRO inventories:* maintenance, repair, and operating supplies which are consumed in the production process but do not become part of the product (e.g., lubricating oil, soap, machine repair parts).
3. *In-process inventories:* semifinished products found at various stages of the production operation.
4. *Finished goods inventories:* completed products ready for shipment.

In most manufacturing companies, production and MRO inventories together represent the major segment of total inventory investment.

Let us now place the discussion in perspective. Inventory planning occurs at several levels in an organization and covers various time spans. The concern in this chapter is the planning and control of production and MRO inventories in a short-run situation, involving weekly, monthly, and in some cases quarterly or yearly decisions. Hence, the discussion assumes that the longer-range activities of sales forecasting, product modification, aggregate planning, and master scheduling have been completed. The investigation begins at this point in the planning cycle.

# Inventory Analysis

The inventory of a typical industrial firm includes as many as 5,000 to 50,000 different items. Initial planning and subsequent control of such an inventory is accomplished on the basis of knowledge about *each* of the individual items and the finished products of which each one is a part. Consequently, the starting point for sound inventory management is the development of a complete inventory catalog, followed by a thorough ABC analysis.

## Inventory Catalog

After all inventory items have been completely described, identified by the manufacturer's part number, cross-indexed by user's identification number if necessary, and classified generically for indexing purposes, some form of inventory catalog, usually computerized, should be prepared for use by all personnel.[13] Careful preparation and maintenance of such a catalog pays two important dividends.

An inventory catalog serves first as a medium of communication. It enables personnel in many different departments to perform their jobs more effectively. A design engineer, for example, may have a choice between two standard parts in an experimental design; an inventory catalog quickly indicates whether either part is carried in inventory and may be available immediately for use in the experimental work. Suppose the item in question is to be used in large quantities on the production line. If one of the alternative parts is a stock item and the other is not, the engineer knows immediately that procurement

---

[13]Most firms have a companywide materials standardization program. The materials included in the inventory catalog all should have been accepted as company "standards." This topic is discussed further in Chapter 6.

time and cost probably will be lower for the part which already is being purchased and used elsewhere in the plant.

As a further example, envision a mechanic who has just removed a faulty bearing from a major production machine that has broken down. Upon examination, the mechanic finds the manufacturer's name and part number stamped on the edge of the bearing. Unfortunately, though, the storeroom clerk cannot help, because that particular bearing is not carried in stock. If the mechanic or a supervisor consults the inventory catalog, however, he or she may well find that a satisfactory substitute bearing, carried under another manufacturer's part number, is in stock. Proper cross-indexing in the inventory catalog can inform users about common interchangeable parts, a typical situation with many MRO supplies.

A second significant benefit produced by an inventory catalog accrues to the inventory control operation itself. This benefit takes the form of more complete and correct records through the reduction of duplicate records for identical parts. A purchasing department often buys the same part from several different suppliers under various manufacturers' part numbers. Unless control requirements dictate otherwise, identical parts from all suppliers should be consolidated on one inventory record. A simple situation? Perhaps, but one is amazed to find in highly reputable companies many similar cases in which two or more inventory records have different numbers for the same part. A carefully constructed catalog significantly reduces the possibility of such problems.

## ABC Analysis: The 80-20 Concept

As soon as an inventory is identified and described, the manager must determine the importance and dollar value of each individual inventory item. This calls for a study of each item in terms of its price or cost, usage (demand), and lead time, as well as specific procurement or technical problems. Without the data provided by such a study, an inventory manager normally does not have enough information to determine the best allocation of departmental effort and expense to the tasks of controlling thousands of inventory items.

A study of several hundred medium-size West Coast manufacturing firms conducted by the authors revealed the data shown in Figure 20.5. This figure shows that in the typical firm a small percentage of the total number of items carried in inventory constitute the bulk of the total dollars invested in inventory. In the study cited, 10 percent of the inventory items account for approximately 75 percent of the investment, and only a quarter of the items make up approximately 90 percent of the total investment. The remaining 75 percent of the items constitute roughly only 10 percent of the inventory investment. While these figures vary somewhat from one firm to another, the magnitude of variation usually is not great. Several similar studies in large corporations have produced strikingly similar results, leading to what some firms call the *80-20 phenomenon* (20 percent of the items account for 80 percent of total inventory investment). Historically, some firms have termed this phenomenon the *Pareto principle,* based on the law of "the vital few and the trivial many" developed by the Italian economist Vilfredo Pareto around the turn of the twentieth century.

In different companies this type of analysis is known by several different names, with *ABC analysis* and *Pareto analysis* being the most common. In practice, such an analysis can be made on the basis of either the average inventory investment in each item or the annual dollar usage of each item. The analysis is easy to conduct once inventory has been identified properly and usage records have been maintained for a complete operating cycle. First, *all items are ranked in order of their average inventory investment* (or dollar usage). The total of those values (average inventory investment or annual usage) for all inventory items then is computed. Then the value of each item is expressed as a percentage of the total. By going down the list and successively cumulating the individual percentages for each item, one can determine which items

**Figure 20.5** I Graphic Analysis of Production and MRO Inventories

make up the first 75 percent of inventory investment, the first 90 percent, and so on. If it is convenient to use the three arbitrary classifications noted above, they can be labeled A, B, and C, respectively, and each inventory item becomes an A, B, or C item.

The value of such an analysis to management is clear. It provides a sound basis on which to allocate funds and time of personnel with respect to procurement management and the refinement of control over the individual inventory items. Obviously, no supply manager wants to spend as much time and effort managing the items that make up 20 percent of the investment as is spent on those making up the remaining 80 percent. In this sense, management may take several forms. It may involve minimizing acquisition cost, maximizing service and reliability, minimizing inventory investment, minimizing indirect costs associated with inventory, or utilizing personnel effectively. The concept clearly permeates a number of departmental operations: purchasing, production control, stores, and accounting, for example.

In practice, a never-ending problem is that of adequately planning for handling the thousands of low-value C items. In many cases, availability and reliability for these items are just as important as they are for the A and B items. Even with good purchasing planning, because of the sheer number of C items, low-value nuisance purchases frequently require more time than should be allotted to them. Consequently, they reduce the amount of time available to purchasing and supply personnel for supplier studies, value analysis, and other creative work involving high-value A and B items.

A problem that has grown out of the discussion in the preceding paragraph focuses on another potential dimension of the ABC classification. Some firms have observed that in addition to the varying dollar magnitude (or turnover) represented by each material in the three categories, the *criticalness* of each material to the firm's operation also varies and is important from the standpoint of managerial control.

To provide additional guidance for supply managers, James A. G. Krupp, director of corporate materials for Echlin Inc., suggests that each material also might be classified according to its service or operating importance on a three-point scale: 1—critical, 2—medium, and 3—noncritical. Thus, a less important A material would be designated an A-3 item, and a critical C material would be identified as a C-1 item.

Depending on the circumstances in a specific situation, the C-1 item might require more stringent management attention than the A-3 item. In any case, some firms have adopted this two-digit classification system to provide additional managerial guidance.[14]

An effective inventory management system must help resolve the problems identified in the preceding paragraphs.

## Dependent Demand and Independent Demand

As discussed in the MRP section in this chapter, to do the job well, an inventory manager needs one additional bit of information about each of the items in inventory: Is the demand (usage) for the item "dependent" or "independent"?

An item is said to exhibit *dependent demand* characteristics when its use is directly dependent on the scheduled production of a larger component or parent product of which that item is a part. Hence, in a plant producing automobile engines, the demand for engine block castings is a dependent demand; once the production schedule for a group of engines is established, the planner knows with certainty that one block will be required for each engine. Conversely, the demand for cutting oil used in the machines on the line cannot be calculated accurately from the production schedule and bills of materials; thus, cutting oil is said to have an *independent demand*. Generally, in an assembly or fabrication-type operation, most production inventory items have a dependent demand while MRO and similarly used items have an independent demand.

Although the distinction seems relatively simple, it is important for an inventory manager to know whether an item exhibits dependent or independent demand. Certain inventory control systems function more effectively with one type of item than with the other.

# Costs Associated with Inventories

From a managerial point of view, two basic categories of costs are associated with inventories: (1) inventory carrying costs and (2) inventory acquisition costs. These costs plus a related variable cost are discussed in the following subsections.

## Carrying Costs

Carrying material in inventory is expensive. Before the relatively recent periods of higher interest rates, a number of studies determined that the *annual cost* of carrying a production inventory averaged approximately 25 percent of the value of the inventory. The escalating and volatile cost of money in recent years, however, has increased the typical firm's annual inventory carrying cost to a figure between 25 percent and 35 percent of the value of the inventory. Five major elements make up these costs in the following manner:

| | | |
|---|---|---|
| 1. | Opportunity cost of invested funds | 12–20% |
| 2. | Insurance costs | 2–4% |
| 3. | Property taxes | 1–3% |
| 4. | Storage costs | 1–3% |
| 5. | Obsolescence and deterioration | 4–10% |
| | Total carrying costs | 20–40% |

[14]For a complete discussion of this interesting approach, see James A. G. Krupp, "Are ABC Codes an Obsolete Technology?" *APICS—The Performance Advantage,* April 1994, pp. 34–35.

Let us briefly examine these carrying costs.

1. *Opportunity cost of invested funds.* When a firm purchases $50,000 worth of a production material and keeps it in inventory, it has that much less cash to spend for other purposes. Money invested in productive equipment or in external securities earns a return for the company. Conceptually, then, it is logical for the firm to charge all money invested in inventory an amount equal to what it could earn if invested elsewhere in the company. This is the "opportunity cost" associated with inventory investment.

2. *Insurance costs.* Most firms insure their assets against possible loss from fire and other forms of damage. An extra $50,000 worth of inventory represents an additional asset on which insurance premiums must be paid.

3. *Property taxes.* As with insurance, property taxes are levied on the assessed value of a firm's assets; the greater the inventory value, the greater the asset value, and consequently the higher the firm's tax bill.

4. *Storage costs.* The warehouse in which a firm stores its inventory is depreciated a certain number of dollars per year over the length of its life. One may say, then, that the cost of warehouse space is a certain number of dollars per cubic foot per year. This cost conceptually can be charged against the inventory occupying the space.

5. *Obsolescence and deterioration.* In most inventory operations, a certain percentage of the stock spoils, is damaged, is pilfered, or eventually becomes obsolete, a situation often called inventory shrinkage. No matter how diligently warehouse managers guard against these occurrences, a certain number always take place. With new products being introduced at an increasing rate, the probability of obsolescence is increasing accordingly. Consequently, the larger the inventory, typically the greater the absolute loss from this source.

Generally, this group of carrying costs rises and falls nearly proportionately with the rise and fall of the inventory level. Further, the inventory level is directly related to the quantity in which the ordered material is delivered. When the complete order is shipped at one time, the larger the order quantity, the higher the *average* inventory level during the period covered by the order. Hence, the costs of carrying inventory vary nearly directly with the size of the delivery. This relationship is illustrated by the *CC* curve in Figure 20.6.

**Figure 20.6** | Relationship of Inventory-Related Costs to Inventory Level (*AC* = Acquisition Costs; *CC* = Carrying Costs)

If a firm has estimated its approximate inventory carrying cost as a percentage of inventory value, the *annual* inventory carrying costs that would be generated by delivery quantities of various sizes can be calculated as follows:

(Carrying cost per year) = (Average inventory value) × (Inventory carrying cost as a percentage of inventory value)

(Carrying cost per year) = (Average inventory in units) × (Material unit cost) × (Inventory carrying cost as a percentage of inventory value)

$$CC = \frac{Q}{2} \times C \times I$$

where

$CC$ = carrying cost per year for the material in question

$Q$ = order or delivery quantity for the material, in units[15]

$C$ = delivered unit cost of the material

$I$ = inventory carrying cost for the material, expressed as a percentage of inventory value

## Acquisition Costs

When one looks at inventory costs in another light, a different set of indirect materials cost factors emerges. These factors all contribute to the cost of generating, processing, and handling an order, along with its related paperwork. Examples of these costs are listed below and can be thought of as inventory acquisition costs.

1. A *certain portion of wages and operating expenses* of departments such as purchasing and supply, production control, receiving, inspection, stores, and accounts payable—those departments whose personnel devote time to the generation and handling of the order.

2. *The cost of supplies* such as engineering drawings, envelopes, stationery, and forms for purchasing, production control, receiving, accounting, and so forth.

3. *The cost of services* such as computer time, telephones, fax machines, telegraphs, and postage expended in procuring material.

When considering this group of acquisition costs, observe that they behave quite differently from carrying costs. Acquisition costs are not related to inventory size per se; rather, they are a function of the number of orders placed or deliveries received during a particular period of time.

One simplified example will illustrate this point. Suppose a buyer in the purchasing and supply department receives a requisition for a special fabricated part used in the manufacture of one of the firm's products. Assume further that that part has been purchased before and that price quotations from three or four shops are on file. The buyer first reviews the current inventory situation and probably checks with production control to see if any significant changes are anticipated in future production. Drawings and specifications of the part are reviewed to refresh his or her memory about required tooling and other technical details of the purchase. Next, the buyer reviews the quotations to determine why the order was placed with supplier A last time. Before deciding if supplier A should receive the order again, the buyer must review supplier performance data. Finally, the buyer decides which supplier should receive the order and subsequently inquires about the firm's current shop loads and any other matters that have arisen during the investigation. It is entirely possible that a negotiation session also may be required.

In total, the buyer's investigation may require anywhere from an hour to several days. The total cost of the buyer's time to the company will be the same whether the purchase order is written for 20 parts or

---

[15]When the entire order is delivered in one shipment, $Q$ for the order and $Q$ for the delivery are the same number. When the order is delivered in several shipments, $Q$ per delivery is smaller than $Q$ for the order. In this case, $Q$ for the delivery should be used in the formulas to calculate the carrying cost.

200 parts. This process may result in the development of a term contract with the supplier, in which case the buyer's effort is spread over all deliveries of the item during the life of the contract. If this is not the case, however, the next time the buyer receives another requisition for this part, he or she will go through somewhat the same process, generating almost the same indirect cost for the company.

The largest segment of the acquisition cost element is made up of these types of indirect labor and overhead costs, which are generated in purchasing and in the other departments that subsequently become involved in handling some activity associated with the purchase. The cost of supplies and services consumed in the placement and handling of an order typically varies directly with the number of orders placed. While these costs are significant, they are considerably less significant than the human and related overhead cost figures just discussed. The variable acquisition cost per order varies widely among firms, depending on the specific cost inclusions and the type of material. Today the range appears to run from approximately $50 to $125 per order.

If a firm experiences a certain annual usage of an item, the number of orders placed during the year will decline as the individual order quantity increases, thus generating lower *annual* acquisition costs. The experience of numerous firms over the years reveals that this relationship is not linear but follows the approximate contour of the *AC* curve shown in Figure 20.6.

If a firm's cost accounting department can estimate its approximate acquisition cost *per order,* the *annual* acquisition cost that will be generated by order quantities of various sizes can be calculated as follows:

(Acquisition cost per year) = (Number of orders placed per year) $\times$ (Acquisition cost per order)

$$AC = \frac{U}{Q} \times A$$

where

$AC$ = acquisition cost per year for the material in question
$U$ = expected annual usage of the material, in units
$Q$ = order or delivery quantity for the material, in units[16]
$A$ = acquisition cost per order or per delivery for the material

## Economic Order Quantity Concept

If one has to make decisions about managing an inventory, it is useful to understand the behavior of the inventory-related cost factors discussed above. These factors often help a manager determine which items should or should not be carried in inventory, what inventory levels should be carried for specific items, and what order quantities are appropriate for particular items.

The latter part of this chapter discusses several types of systems that can be used in managing an inventory. In each case one of the short-term operating questions that must be answered is: How much of the item should be ordered? Among the factors that often enter this decision process is a concept known as EOQ—the notion of an economic order quantity. As its name suggests, this concept holds that the appropriate quantity to order may be the one that tends to minimize all the costs associated with the order: carrying costs, acquisition costs, and the cost of the material itself.

---

[16]When the entire order is delivered in one shipment, the $Q$ value and the $A$ value for the order are the same as they are for the delivery. However, in the case of a term contract, $Q$ and $A$ values should be calculated on the basis of each delivery. Thus, purchasing expenses incurred in generating the order and administering the contract should be spread over the deliveries so that $A$ = the acquisition cost per delivery and $Q$ = the delivery quantity. This approach produces the most useful $A$ value and is also consistent with the approach used in calculating inventory carrying costs.

**Figure 20.7** | Graphic Representation of the EOQ Concept
*(AC=* incremental acquisition costs; *CC* = incremental carrying costs; *TC* = total
incremental costs).

Concentrating for the moment on the first two costs, Figure 20.6 shows clearly that as the order or delivery quantity increases, carrying costs rise—and at the same time acquisition costs decrease. To see the total picture more clearly, if carrying costs and acquisition costs are added together over the order quantity range shown on the graph, the total indirect materials cost curve, *TC,* is produced. This transformation is shown in Figure 20.7. The economic order quantity concept simply says that the sum of all the indirect costs associated with inventory will be minimized on an annual basis if the material for which the graph is drawn is ordered (or delivered) consistently in the quantity that corresponds with the low point on the *TC* curve. This is the *economic order quantity.*

Note that the low point on the total cost curve coincides with the point at which the carrying cost curve intersects the acquisition cost curve. This makes it easy to develop the basic formula that can always be used to calculate a material's *basic* EOQ. Recall the two simple cost formulas developed for annual carrying costs and annual acquisition costs. Those formulas can be used to develop the EOQ formula.[17]

The EOQ occurs when

$$\text{Annual carrying cost} = \text{Annual acquisition cost}^{18}$$
$$CC = AC$$
$$\frac{QCI}{2} = \frac{UA}{Q}$$

Solving for *Q*:

$$Q^2 CI = 2UA$$
$$Q = \sqrt{\frac{2UA}{CI}}$$

---

[17]A more straightforward mathematical solution can be obtained using differential calculus: (1) Write the equation for the total cost curve, (2) differentiate the equation, (3) find the minimum value of the function by setting the derivative equal to 0 and solving for *Q*.

[18]See footnotes 15 and 16 for the use of the EOQ formula in term contracts with multiple deliveries.

This formula is the fundamental mathematical representation of the EOQ concept. It can be modified to accommodate numerous special conditions, but in practice it probably finds its most effective application in this form.

Professor Daniel Jones, who has researched various lot sizing concepts, says that the EOQ concept can be used in conjunction with a variety of inventory management systems, including JIT. He writes: "When the EOQ model is properly employed, there is little difference between lot sizes based on the JIT model and the EOQ model." He points out that all relevant incremental costs must be included when one is using the EOQ model. This is perhaps an obvious observation, but it is one that he finds is violated frequently in practice.[19]

Thus, despite some criticisms, the EOQ concept continues to be a versatile and useful tool when it is applied properly.

**Incremental Costs and Stability**   Note that the vertical axis in Figure 20.7 is labeled "annual *incremental* costs." It is appropriate at this point to emphasize the fact that the costs which are relevant in making an EOQ analysis are incremental costs. *Incremental costs are those costs which actually change as a result of a particular operating decision.* For example, if the decision to issue more purchase orders during the year actually increases supply and service costs, these are incremental costs. If it requires the addition of a buyer or a clerical person to handle the load, the additional payroll costs are incremental costs. *Incremental costs are either variable costs or opportunity costs* that represent a forgone opportunity to utilize an asset in some other productive way.

By their nature, most of the inventory carrying costs discussed here are incremental costs and are reasonably stable. The distinction is less clear when one is dealing with inventory acquisition costs. Judgment usually is required in estimating the portion of the human effort that represents a legitimate opportunity cost. In any case, EOQ produces valid results only when the $I$ and $A$ cost factors are largely incremental and when the usage and unit cost elements, as well as $I$ and $A$, are reasonably stable over the operating period.

**Material Prices and Quantity Discounts**   In the discussion of EOQ analysis to this point, it has been assumed that material prices and transportation costs are constant factors for the range of order quantities considered. In practice, some situations occur in which the delivered unit cost of a material decreases significantly if a slightly larger quantity than the originally computed EOQ is purchased. Quantity discounts, freight rate schedules, and perhaps anticipated price increases may create such situations. These additional variables can be included in the basic formula, but from a practical point of view they usually can be handled more easily with a separate simple calculation.

If one uses $Q$ computed with the basic formula, such alternative quantity decisions can be made quickly and accurately. If one simply compares annual material cost savings resulting from the purchase of the additional quantity with the additional inventory carrying costs occasioned by the increased purchase the most economical decision quickly becomes evident. With a limited amount of practice, a buyer can determine in a matter of seconds whether material cost savings exceed carrying costs for the additional inventory.

## Other Uses of the EOQ Concept

A final word should be said about *general* usage of the EOQ concept. Even though this discussion has been set entirely in the purchasing environment, the EOQ concept logically has broader application as well.

A very common situation in which the concept is used is the determination of economic production lot sizes in a manufacturing operation. Consider the formula for a moment and look at the individual factors in

---

[19]Daniel Jones, "Don't Let JIT Overrule EOQ," *Supplier Selection and Management Report,* June 1991, p. 10.

light of both the purchasing operations and the production operations. When the formula is converted for production use, the annual usage and carrying cost factors are the same as they were in the purchasing application. The unit cost factor, however, is no longer delivered price; instead, it consists of direct labor and materials and production overhead costs. Production acquisition cost is similar to purchasing acquisition cost except that production setup cost replaces most of the purchasing and related departmental wage and operating costs.

Buyers also should consider (from a supplier's point of view) the formula in this form when determining lot sizes on term contract purchase orders going to various types of job shop suppliers. A supplier's costs and subsequent product price obviously are influenced by the size and frequency of such orders.

## The Weaknesses of the EOQ Formula

The EOQ formula has been explained in detail more for its philosophical merit than for its actual use. In other words, the logic, themes, and concepts are all proper elements to consider. In practice, many experts have questioned the use and accuracy of the formula for the following reasons[20]:

- It is *not* fully compatible with MRP and JIT despite the case presented by Professor Jones.
- All demand inputs are yearly *estimates*, and so the output is just an estimate.
- Only incremental costs are appropriate, that is, the cost of the *next* setup, the cost of the *next* purchase order preparation, and the cost of the *next* stored unit (warehouse cost).
- Most users of this technique erroneously use "average costs," which destroys the logic. Until one needs to build a new warehouse, there is no increase in "sunk" warehouse cost as inventory increases.
- For inventory that moves from location to location, one set of costs does not apply.
- The carrying costs usually are overstated badly, based on broad "industry averages" and often on pure estimates just short of guesses.
- Purchase ordering costs for long-term contracts are one-shot expenses. Release costs, especially by computer, would be or are fractions of a cent or, for a fax, perhaps $1.00. Repeat purchase orders for the same material would be nominal.
- Few firms have accurate studies of carrying cost to hold inventory other than the cost of capital of the material. This cost could never be much more than the going commercial loan rates and the average rate of return of the firm. Thus, figures of 25 to 35 percent are suspect.
- The opportunity cost aspect of EOQ rests on gigantic assumptions such as storage costs. Most warehouses are on the books as sunk costs with zero alternative use in the short term.
- EOQ assumes constant demand for the next year, which hardly ever is the case.

We agree with James Gardner, a leading author and consultant in materials management, when he says, "In the same vein, suppose there is excess storage capacity from time to time. The accounting department will tell you to include all available space into carrying costs because if you are not using the space, it could be rolled out. They are dealing in pure fantasy. Whom are you going to rent it to? How would you go about finding someone who would inconvenience himself by renting out a few feet of your floor space

---

[20]David N. Burt and Richard L. Pinkerton, *A Purchasing Manager's Guide to Strategic Proactive Procurement* (New York: AMACOM, 1996), pp. 90–91.

on a temporary basis at your stated rate when he could get all the space he needs at a public warehouse and probably save money in the bargain."[21]

# Types of Inventory Control Systems

To this point in the discussion, we have considered background concepts that are useful in formulating fundamental aspects of plans to manage inventories. The discussion now turns to the specific operating systems that can be used. Generally, four types of inventory control systems are in use: (1) the cyclical or fixed order interval system, (2) the JIT approach, (3) the MRP-type system, and (4) the order point or fixed order quantity system. Each system is used to monitor and control inventory levels, and each system, on the basis of its unique characteristics, provides an inventory manager with information that helps answer the two basic questions of *when* to order and *how much* to order.

## Cyclical or Fixed Order Interval System

The cyclical system, or fixed order interval system as it sometimes is called, is the oldest and simplest system now in use. Years ago, when most businesses were small and uncomplicated, this control system was used in all types of operations: manufacturing, service, wholesale, and retail. With the exception of one variation called flow control, the cyclical system is not used widely today except in smaller and medium-size operations.

Operationally, the system works like this: It is *a time-based* operation which involves *scheduled periodic reviews* of the stock level of all inventory items. Looking at it in a manufacturing setting, when the stock level of a specific item is not sufficient to sustain the production operation until the next scheduled review, an order is placed to replenish the supply. The frequency of reviews is determined by judgment and varies with the degree of control desired by management; A items might be reviewed weekly (or more often), B items monthly or bimonthly, and C items quarterly or semiannually.

Stock levels can be monitored by physical inspection, visual review of perpetual inventory record cards, or automatic computer surveillance. In most operations, a perpetual inventory record is maintained[22] either by computer or manually except in simple flow-controlled shops (which will be examined shortly). Physical stock counts are required once or twice a year to reconcile actual values with book values in all systems that use perpetual inventory records.

The first operating question—when to order—is answered or controlled by the review dates established by the inventory manager. If material usage has remained reasonably stable, an order (or a release against an order) usually is placed each time the item is reviewed.

The order date decision also is affected by the quantity previously ordered, so let us consider the second question also: How much should be ordered? The quantity to be ordered generally is determined by three factors: the number of days between reviews, the anticipated daily usage during the cycle period, and the quantity actually on hand and on order at the time of the review. One of the primary reasons this system is used is to control high-value items closely and maintain a relatively low investment in inventory. Hence, the order quantity typically is the quantity required to cover only the ensuing period, with allowance for order lead time. Occasionally a two- or three-period supply is ordered, but not as a rule.

---

[21]James A. Gardner, *Common Sense Manufacturing: Becoming a Top Value Competitor* (Burr Ridge, IL: Business One Irwin, 1992), p. 24.

[22]A perpetual inventory record for a material that is controlled in a closed stores system is maintained simply by posting receipts from invoices or receiving reports and disbursements from stores material requisitions or similar withdrawal authorizations. In most firms today, perpetual records are computer-based.

Consequently, as its name implies, the system works in a cyclical fashion, with an order typically placed at each review date for a quantity large enough to cover the ensuing cycle plus the order lead time. A small safety stock generally is carried, based on the observed lead-time variability. Inventory levels and tightness of control thus are determined by the establishment of the period of the cycle. High-value A and B items typically are placed on short cycles, and C items on longer cycles.

This system can be used with both dependent demand and independent demand materials. It works most effectively in an organization that has a continuous operations function, manufacturing or service, in which demand is fairly stable and can be predicted with reasonable accuracy. Additionally, it is probably the most efficient system to use for independent demand items that experience irregular or seasonal demand and for any items whose purchases must be planned months in advance because of infrequent supplier production schedules. In these cases, it tends to keep inventory levels lower than would be possible with the other applicable systems. When used for materials with these characteristics, however, the system must be augmented with a minimum balance figure which signals the need for an early reorder when there is a sharp usage increase.

To conclude, the cyclical system finds its greatest usage in organizations that have large numbers of independent demand items to control and in relatively simple process operations in which dependent item demand can be projected easily from the production schedule. When it is used for dependent demand items in an intermittent manufacturing operation, it becomes difficult to determine cycle period demands if many products are involved or if individual items are used in several different products. The bill of materials explosion and time-phasing capabilities of an MRP system must be handled manually in the cyclical system. As product complexity increases, this becomes a virtual impossibility, and so historical demand data tend to become the basis for order quantity determination; this soon leads to unreasonably high inventory levels because of the uncertainties associated with near-term demand. For these reasons, MRP *systems have replaced most cyclical systems in intermittent manufacturing operations.*

**Flow Control System**     The flow control method of managing inventories is a special variation of the cyclical system. This method is applicable in continuous manufacturing operations that produce the same basic product in large quantities day after day. Most materials used in that kind of operation are purchased on term contracts and scheduled for daily or weekly delivery throughout the term. The production cycle is often a day or less in duration, and in effect material flows through the plant in continuous streams. Inventory floats consequently can be kept quite low, thus requiring only a minimum investment in production inventory.

In this type of operation, an open stores system is used for most production materials, and the individual items are stored on the line near the point of use. Stores personnel visually review the level of all material stocks daily and report any imbalances to the purchasing or production control department. Changes in production schedules must be relayed immediately to buyers so that delivery schedules can be revised accordingly.

## The Just-in-Time Approach

The just-in-time concept was explored in detail earlier in this chapter. It was pointed out that in total, JIT is an operating management philosophy. With reference to that philosophy, a number of specific operating techniques have been developed for manufacturing operations, production planning, and inventory management. Those dealing with inventory management are the products of the JIT decisions made in the manufacturing and planning areas.

The operating concept of the system is to gear factory output tightly to distribution demand for finished goods, gear individual feeder production units tightly together, and gear the supply of production inventories tightly to the manufacturing demand schedule. This means that all inventories in the system, including production inventories, are maintained at absolutely minimal levels.

It should be emphasized at the outset, however, that as a practical matter, most firms utilize the JIT concept for no more than 5 to 10 percent of the materials handled by the purchasing and supply activity regardless of the extent of the commitment in the manufacturing operation. This means that the production inventory items handled in the JIT inventory system are primarily high-value A items. All these items are purchased on a long-term contractual basis, with small-volume deliveries scheduled as frequently as once or twice a day or as infrequently as once or twice a week.

If one observed a JIT operation strictly from an inventory point of view, it would look very much like a flow control operation, with material flowing into and through the plant operation in continuous streams. In fact, it functions much as a flow control operation does, only more tightly and more stringently controlled. From strictly an inventory point of view, the systems have almost identical objectives. Many JIT materials are delivered directly to the production operation and are stored close to the point of use; others are handled in a conventional closed stores operation.

From a practical point of view, a JIT inventory system in its purest sense is workable only in continuous manufacturing and processing operations or in intermittent operations that produce a small number of standard products and, because of that, are similar to continuous operations. Most, if not all, of the materials handled are dependent demand items.

How are the "when" and "how much" questions answered? As was discussed in the preceding section, the buyer and the supplier work together closely on the matters of delivery volumes and scheduling. The buying firm's production schedule drives the entire process. The detailed production schedule typically is firmed up for one or two weeks at a time and, in more general terms, for a month or so ahead. Specific daily requirements for JIT materials can be determined from this schedule and are relayed directly to the contracting supplier. The exact size and frequency of each delivery are worked out jointly in an attempt to minimize the buyer's incremental inventory-related costs and, at the same time, maintain an efficient and practical operation for the supplier. As a general rule, the buyer does not identify a specific safety stock component in the firm's inventory figure. Depending on the material, the buying firm typically works on an inventory of several days' to a week's supply. As is the case in a flow control system, stores personnel on the shop floor visually monitor stock levels at least daily and communicate potential overage or shortage problems to the appropriate buyer.

To this point, the discussion has covered only the 5 to 10 percent of a firm's production materials that typically are handled by its JIT purchasing and inventory management system. What about the remaining 90 to 95 percent of the items? As a rule, they are handled in the more conventional manner with one of the other standard systems: an MRP system or an order point system.

## Material Requirements Planning System

The section on production planning in this chapter detailed how closed loop MRP systems function as complete production planning and control systems. The material requirements planning module is an integral part of such a system. Through its bill of materials explosion and aggregation process, this element of the system generates on a weekly basis the projected materials requirements for all the finished products included in a firm's updated master production schedule for the coming two- to three-month period.

After taking the projected gross requirements for a specific material during the planning period, the MRP module calculates the net requirements by subtracting on-hand inventory and any scheduled receipts of the item as production is scheduled to progress through the planning period. This produces a "time-phased" purchase order requirement that will be released at a calculated future date. The reader can review this logic by referring to Figure 20.3.

The inventory that is carried in the system is a function of three factors: (1) the quantity purchased when each order is placed, (2) the purchase lead time specified by the buyer, and (3) any safety stock that is carried routinely. The objective of time-phasing the order point is to keep the inventory as close to zero as practical until the material actually is needed for production. Consequently, using an MRP system, the average inventory levels of most materials are relatively low over the long term.

In the case of some materials, no safety stock is carried. In other cases a one- to two-week supply may be carried as a hedge against uncertainties such as possible fluctuations in demand, variations in supplier lead-time requirements, and anticipated scrap or reject rates. Variations in supplier lead-time requirements may be covered simply by extending the lead-time figure used in calculating the order release date; in this case, safety stock is reduced correspondingly. These safety stock and lead-time hedge values typically are determined by judgment on the basis of past experience with specific materials and suppliers.

The *"when to order"* question, then, is answered by the logic of the system. Deciding *how much to order* is in part a judgmental issue. The most common approach, as is the case in the cyclical system, is to order the quantity required during the planning period: the "lot for lot" approach. This method typically tends to minimize the inventory in the system. At times, however, the lot-for-lot approach may produce an order quantity that is too small to be economical. Because of high acquisition costs or production setup costs, order size may have to be larger. In this case, the EOQ or a related least-cost calculation frequently is used to obtain a more appropriate order quantity figure. A number of other decision rules sometimes are used, but those just mentioned appear to be the most common.

The MRP system is designed for use with dependent demand items, that is, production materials. The only way it can handle an independent demand item is by tying that item's use into a product bill of materials. For production tools and certain other MRO supplies, it is sometimes possible to do this in an approximate way by estimation. However, the system's most important use by far is with dependent demand materials in an intermittent manufacturing operation. An MRP system can be adapted for use in a continuous operation or a processing-type operation, but it does not fit such operations well and usually offers few significant advantages over the other types of systems.

## Order Point or Fixed Order Quantity System

The order point system, historically known as the fixed order quantity system, is another inventory control system that has been used for years in this country by both manufacturing and nonmanufacturing organizations. The system recognizes the fact that each item has its own unique optimum order quantity, and it therefore is based on *order point* and *order quantity* factors rather than on the time factor.

Operation of an order point system requires two things for each inventory item:

1. The *predetermination of an order point* so that when the stock level on hand drops to the order point, the item automatically is "flagged" for reorder purposes. The order point is computed so that estimated use of the item during the order lead-time period will cause the actual stock level to fall to a planned minimum level by the time the new order is received. Receipt of the new order then increases the stock level to a preplanned maximum figure.

2. The *predetermination of a fixed quantity to be ordered* each time the supply of the item is replenished. This determination typically is based on considerations of price, rate of usage, and other pertinent production and administrative factors.

The automatic feature of the system is achieved by maintaining a perpetual inventory record for each item. The computer, or an inventory clerk in the case of a manual system, continues to post all material issues until the balance of an item falls to its order point. At this point the system notifies the appropriate buyer, who replenishes the stock in a quantity that takes the inventory to its planned maximum level. During the course of operation, the ongoing inventory level thus is maintained between the planned minimum and maximum values.

The predetermined order point, then, tells the buyer *when* to order. In most organizations the order point is determined in the following manner: First, basic operating data about demand and lead time must be obtained. Next, a decision must be made about the desired service level. For most materials, most firms target for 100 percent; that is, they don't want to run out of stock before the new order arrives. At this point in the discussion, the process can be described most easily with the use of a simple illustration. Suppose the following data have been determined for a given inventory item:

Purchasing lead time = 1 week (very stable; little chance of variation)

Material usage = 50 units per week, with ±10 percent variation over the long run

Thus,

Maximum usage during lead time = 55 units

Average usage during lead time = 50 units

Minimum usage during lead time = 45 units

Figure 20.8 shows a simplified, or ideal, inventory movement pattern for the material in question, with the usage rate constant at the maximum level of 55 units per week. If the buyer does not want to run out of stock, at what inventory level should the new order be placed? If lead time is known to be one week and the *maximum* usage has been determined to be 55 units per week, the new order clearly should be placed when the stock level falls to 55 units. Under these conditions, the new order will arrive just when the stock level reaches zero. Thus, the order point is 55 units.

What happens when the usage rate runs around 50 units per week, as it does much of the time? The inventory movement pattern shown in Figure 20.8 then becomes the dashed sawtooth pattern shown in Figure 20.9. With an order point of 55 units, as long as the *average* usage rate of 50 units per week prevails, the new order will arrive when 5 units (55 − 50 = 5) are still left in stock. This brings us to the definition of safety stock. In an order point system set up as was described above, *safety stock* normally is

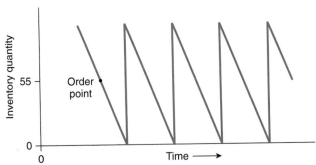

**Figure 20.8** | Illustrative Simplified Inventory Movement Pattern for a Given Material, with a Maximum Usage Rate

**Figure 20.9** I Movement Pattern in Figure 20.8 with an Average Usage Rate, Showing Safety Stock Determination

defined as *the maximum lead-time usage minus the average lead-time usage.* In this case, then, the order point is 55 units and the basic safety stock is 5 units.

In operation, over a period of time, this means that the low point of the inventory sawtooth pattern occasionally will fall to 0 as the new order arrives (55 − 55 = 0), and when usage is at its lightest, the low point of the sawtooth will be as high as 10 units when the new order arrives (55 − 45 = 10). Most of the time, the low point of the sawtooth will fluctuate between these two extremes, with occurrences concentrated around the safety stock value of 5, which also is defined as the *theoretical* planned minimum. Figure 20.10 depicts this situation hypothetically.

Now that the question of when to order has been answered, how does the buyer determine how much to order? Any number of decision rules can be used, but the most common approach is to determine the EOQ value. A fixed order quantity system is a natural for EOQ application. The EOQ value can be calculated automatically almost instantaneously with a computer-based order point program. In a manual system, tables of EOQ values can be precalculated and prepared for the nearly-instantaneous use of inventory clerks. Nomographs and preprogrammed handheld calculators also can be used easily and quickly. More general decision rules sometimes used by experienced managers are to order a one- to four-week supply of A items, a one- to two-month supply of B items, and a four- to six-month supply of C items.

The major advantages of an order point system are the following: (1) Unlike the cyclical and JIT approaches, the EOQ concept (if the data inputs are accurate) can be applied easily in this system, and so each material can be procured in the most economical quantity; (2) this preplanned approach utilizes the time and

**Figure 20.10** I Typical Inventory Movement Pattern for a Reasonably Stable Material, with a Fixed Order Quantity

efforts of people efficiently—purchasing and inventory control personnel automatically devote attention to an item *only when that item requires attention;* and (3) within limits, control can be exerted easily to maintain inventory investment at a target level simply by varying the planned maximum and minimum values.

On the other side of the coin, the system has some serious limitations:

■ The most serious problem in using an order point system stems from the fact that it works on the basis of historical rather than actual demand data. Therefore, the order point cannot be time-phased to correspond with actual demand requirements. This means that over the long term, an order point system almost always produces a higher average inventory level than would a comparable MRP system.

■ The system functions correctly only if each of the materials exhibits reasonably stable usage and lead-time characteristics. When these factors change significantly, a new order point and a new order quantity must be determined if the system is to fulfill its objectives. Consequently, although it can be adapted, the system becomes costly and cumbersome to operate effectively when applied to materials with highly unstable demand and lead-time patterns.

Bearing in mind the advantages and disadvantages discussed above, it is appropriate to note that an order point system can be used equally well with both independent demand and dependent demand items. In a *dependent demand* manufacturing environment, a time-phased MRP system is far superior to an order point system because of its use of actual demand data and its ability to maintain average inventories at significantly lower levels. However, if it is not practical to use MRP for low-value C items, an order point system can be used very effectively, and the increased inventory levels will affect total costs very little. In managing *independent demand* inventories, as in a retail operation, a well-designed order point system has no peer; it works extremely well.

As was pointed out earlier, an order point system is versatile: It can be used in any type of operation from manufacturing to service. For school districts, hospitals, banks, retail firms, and numerous other service-oriented institutions, virtually all inventory items exhibit independent demand characteristics. As one would suspect, order point systems are used in the vast majority of these types of operations.

**Two-Bin System**   A variation of the basic order point system can be seen in the operation of the simple two-bin system. The distinguishing feature of this system is the absence of a perpetual inventory record. In practice, the stock is separated physically into two bins, or containers. The lower bin contains a quantity of stock equal to the order point figure. This typically is just enough stock (or slightly more) to last from the date a new order is placed until the incoming material is received in inventory. The upper bin contains a quantity of stock equal to the difference between the maximum and order point figures. At the outset, stock is used from the upper bin; when that supply is depleted, it signals the clerk that the order point has been reached. At this point an order is placed, and material from the lower bin is used until the new stock is received. Upon receipt of the new order, the proper quantities of material are placed in the two bins. This method demonstrates very simply the fundamental concept which underlies the basic order point system.

The two-bin method is used widely in all types of operations for handling low-value hardware and supplies whose usage is not recorded on a perpetual record. The major advantage of the method is the reduction of clerical work. Issues do not have to be posted to determine the proper reorder time. Receipts, however, usually are posted to reveal significant changes in usage or lead time. A possible disadvantage of the system in some cases is the requirement of additional storage facilities and perhaps some practical difficulty in keeping the two stocks properly separated.

To generalize, it should be pointed out that none of the systems or their adaptations discussed in this chapter are mutually exclusive. *Several or all of them may be used advantageously for different materials in a single firm.*

**Supplier Managed Inventories**   Many firms have "outsourced" some of their inventory management. For example, one of the authors, in his role as a consultant to a high-tech firm in Silicon Valley, California, negotiated a contract with Granger, a large industrial distribution company, to restock the MRO supplies under a long-term contract. Granger issued a monthly inventory usage report and, using reorder points, restocked as necessary; this resulted in significant savings. Other applications of this concept include tools, office supplies, and other support materials.

# Concluding Remarks

For the last five years or so, production planning and inventory management activities have been in a state of change. New and evolving systems have spawned new and increasingly sophisticated planning and control capabilities. In some cases, the more traditional inventory control systems have been replaced for certain types of applications; in other cases they have not. Table 20.1 draws together in summary form the most significant applications features of the systems in use today.

**Table 20.1 |** Comparison of Characteristics and Applications of Inventory Control Systems

| Type of System/characteristics | Order Point | Cyclical | MRP | Flow Control | JIT |
|---|---|---|---|---|---|
| Maintains low inventory levels | Fair | Fair/good | Good/excellent | Excellent | Excellent |
| Application to items, type of demand | • All types<br>• Particularly good for independent demand | All types | Primarily dependent demand | Primarily dependent demand | Dependent demand |
| Application to type of operations | • All types of manufacturing operations<br>• Particularly good for service operations | • All manufacturing operations<br>• Service operations | Primarily intermittent manufacturing operations, with great product variety | Continuous manufacturing operations, with little product variety | Continuous manufacturing, with moderate product variety |
| Demand data used | Historical | • Actual in simple operations<br>• Historical in complex operations | Actual | Actual | Actual |
| Time-phased order point | No | • Yes in simple operations<br>• No in complex operations | Yes | Yes | Yes |
| Computer required? | Optional | Optional | Yes | Optional | Optional |
| Bill of materials explosion/ aggregation capability | No | No | Yes | Yes | Yes |
| Administrative effort required | Minimal | Moderate | Moderate | Heavy | Heavy |

It is becoming increasingly difficult for most firms to control inventories effectively. One major reason for this is the expansion of product lines and models. A second key reason is that more and more components going into the typical firm's products are being *purchased* as fabricated parts rather than being produced from basic materials in the firm's own shops. In many firms, this means that the number of inventory items to be managed is constantly growing. Because of the increasingly technical nature of materials today, the number of dollars that may be invested in inventory is growing at an even faster rate than is the number of items.

In its daily operation, inventory control should be largely a series of clerical or computerized activities carried on within a carefully defined and controlled framework. The routinization of the daily operation, however, often camouflages the importance of sound management in this area.

At this point in the discussion, there should be little doubt that the basic responsibility for inventory control should lie with top management. The effects of poor inventory management, unfortunately, are not directly visible on the operating statement as a composite cost of inventory management. Nevertheless, in most organizations these indirect costs, which are dispersed and hidden throughout the operating statement, can have a significant impact on profit. For this reason, top management should carefully formulate and periodically review the basic policies and operating plans that constitute the framework within which the daily inventory control operation functions.

## Discussion Questions

1. "An effective production planning and control operation must accomplish five general activities." Identify these activities and discuss each one briefly.
2. What is aggregate planning? Discuss its significance in the production planning process.
3. How is the information used in the aggregate planning process developed? Discuss briefly.
4. What is the relationship between the aggregate plan and the master schedule?
5. Describe how the material requirements planning module works and what it does in a modern production planning system,
6. What does the capacity requirements planning module accomplish in a production planning system? Discuss.
7. Frequently, the proposed production plan does not mesh satisfactorily with the availability and timing of the capacity in required work centers. What variables may be manipulated by the planner to achieve a reasonable balance between the proposed requirements and available capacity? Discuss.
8. What is meant by "the multilevel nature of the operation of the production planning system"? Discuss.
9. What is the difference between a regular MRP system and an MRP II system? Discuss.
10. Identify and discuss the impacts of an MRP system on a purchasing and supply department's operation.
11. Describe how the buyer-planner concept works.
12. Describe how a just-in-time production system works.
13. According to JIT proponents, why are inventories undesirable?
14. Identify and discuss the key characteristics of a JIT production operation.
15. How does a firm's purchasing operation contribute to the success of its JIT production operation? Discuss in some detail.

16. "The interface between procurement and production planning is an extremely important one." What is your reaction to this statement? Discuss in depth.

17. What function do inventories serve in a manufacturing concern? Discuss both the advantages and the disadvantages.

18. Managers and firms that promote the use of the JIT concept state in no uncertain terms that inventories are evil. What is your view of this statement? How does the statement relate to your answer to the preceding question?

19. Detail in step-by-step form how you would conduct an ABC analysis of an inventory. As a materials manager in an organization, how would you utilize the results of the ABC analysis?

20. How can an ABC classification system be modified to recognize the service and operational importance of some C items?

21. Explain what is meant by the terms "inventory carrying costs" and "inventory acquisition costs."

22. In making an EOQ calculation, the text states that all costs included should be "incremental costs." Why? Discuss. Define an incremental cost.

23. What is opportunity cost, and why should it be included as an inventory carrying cost?

24. Can the economic order quantity approach be used just as easily with all four basic control systems (cyclical, JIT, MRP, and order point)? Explain.

25. What is the difference between a dependent demand and an independent demand inventory item?

26. In determining a firm's incremental acquisition cost per purchase order, should the salaries of the purchasing manager and the senior buyers be included? Explain.

27. Discuss briefly the major features of the cyclical ordering system. What are the primary advantages and disadvantages of that system?

28. What is a flow control system? Under what conditions might you consider the use of a flow control inventory management system? What are the advantages and disadvantages of using such a system?

29. Explain briefly how the order point system operates. From an operating point of view, what are the major advantages and disadvantages of using an order point system?

30. Explain how an MRP system operates. How is an MRP system able to keep inventory levels relatively low?

31. Under what operating conditions can an MRP system be utilized most effectively?

32. What is the economic order quantity concept? Explain the theory underlying the concept. What are the weaknesses of EOQ?

33. What is meant by a time-phased order point? Explain.

34. Assume that you have just been hired to develop an inventory system for a company which in the past paid little attention to the management of inventories. Prepare an outline of the approach you would use to carry out this assignment. Discuss each point on your outline in some detail, indicating the information you would need, the problems you would expect to encounter, and any other pertinent factors management would be interested in when evaluating your approach to the problem.

35. In an order point system, how is safety stock determined?

36. Referring to the example on page 496, what would the order point and safety stock values be if the lead-time figure were 1 week ±20 percent?

37. List and discuss the chief limitations of EOQ theory.

# Suggested Reading

American Production and Inventory Control Society (APICS) newsletters and other material: www.apics.org.

Bragg, Steven M. *Inventory Best Practices* (Hoboken, NJ: John Wiley & Sons, 2004).

Burton, Terrence, and Steven Boeder. *Lean Extended Enterprise: Moving Beyond the Four Walls to Value Stream Excellence* (Fort Lauderdale, FL: J. Ross Publishing, 2003).

Esty, Daniel C., and Andrew S. Winston. *Green to Gold: How Smart Companies Use Environmental Strategy to Innovate, Create Value, and Build Competitive Advantage* (New Haven, CT, and London: Yale University Press, 2006).

Gross, John M., and Kenneth R. McInnis. *Kanban Made Simple: Demystifying and Applying Toyota's Legendary Manufacturing Process* (New York: AMACOM, 2003).

Hanna, Mark D., and W. Rocky Newman. *Integrated Operations Management: A Supply Chain Perspective,* 2d ed. (Mason, OH: Thomson Advantage Books, SouthWestern/Thomson Learning, 2007.)

Jacobs, F. Robert, Richard B. Chase, and Nicholas J. Aquilano, *Operations and Supply Management* 12th ed, (Burr Ridge, IL: McGraw-Hill/Irwin, 2009).

Krajewski, Lee J., and Larry P. Ritzman. *Operations Management, 6th ed.* (Upper Saddle River, NJ: Prentice Hall, 2002).

Muller, Max. *Essentials of Inventory Management* (New York: AMACOM, 2003).

Oliver Wight International. *The Oliver Wight Class A Checklist for Business Excellence,* 6th ed. Hoboken, NJ: (John Wiley & Sons, 2005).

Seifert, Richard. *Collaborative Planning, Forecasting, and Replenishment: How to Create a Supply Chain Advantage* (New York: AMACOM, 2003).

Vollmann, Thomas, William L. Berry, D. Clay Whybark, and Jacobs F. Roberts, *Manufacturing Planning and Control for Supply Chain Management,* 5th ed. (Burr Ridge, IL: McGraw-Hill/Irwin, 2005).

Wincel, Jeffrey P. *Lean Supply Chain Management: A Handbook for Strategic Procurement* (New York: Productivity Press, 2003).

# Appendix : The Fundamentals of Inbound Transportation[23]

Buyers and other supply personnel are deeply involved in determining how materials are delivered to internal customers. This appendix gives detailed checklists to help them achieve the lowest possible freight costs and show them how to work with the transportation department. It also defines the multitude of shipping terms. Attention to details is very important. For example, incorrect classifications of freight can double transportation costs.

---

[23]By Richard L. Pinkwerton, Ph.D., CPM and Edward J Marien, Ph.D. Published as the April 1997 issue of *Info Edge,* National Association of Purchasing Management (NAPM), now the Institute for Supply Management (ISM), Tempe, AZ. © Institute for Supply Management™. All rights reserved. Reprinted, with minor editing, with permission from the publisher, the Institute for Supply Management. The textbook authors want to thank Joseph V. Shannon, President of PO$E, a transportation consulting firm in Cleveland, Ohio. Mr. Shannon verified on March 27, 2008, that this appendix is "still current, useful and educational today, 11 years later.

# Appendix Objectives

*After reading this appendix, you should be able to:*

1. Understand transportation as a strategic objective.
2. Select the proper mode and carriers.
3. Understand deregulation and tariffs.
4. Effectively use proper selection criteria to establish an effective transportation program.

Traditional materials functions such as warehouse and stores management and investment recovery as well as the management of surplus materials are best covered in logistics and related courses. While these topics are extremely important, their treatment is beyond the scope of this text. Environmental and other "green" issues are covered in Chapter 19.

# Critical Thinking Questions

1. Buyers and supply managers are very busy individuals. Why should they take on one more task: transportation planning?
2. Why are freight terms so important? What do they control?
3. Is deregulation in the transportation industry good for both buyers and sellers or just for the buyers?
4. Is a good transportation plan more important for a JIT system or an MRP system?

# Transportation as a Strategic Objective

Many purchasing and supply managers are responsible for buying inbound transportation services for their organizations. Yet many practitioners may not feel fully "at home" in this complex field, especially with recent deregulation and reregulation.

Mastering this area can add value to the organization and to the purchasing and supply management functions (see the following box) because transportation, which can be very costly, can have a significant impact on the bottom line. For one thing, if the supplier makes transportation decisions, there is no guarantee that the choices made will be the most cost-effective for the organization. Profits can be improved by:

- Improving carrier services.
- Reducing inventory.
- Advancing the use of just-in-time.
- Reducing delivery costs.
- Cutting lead times.

It is purchasing and supply management's responsibility to team with other functions in the organization to plan and negotiate the most cost-effective transportation method and align it with the organization's service requirements. This goal can be a challenge. It can be met with a thorough analysis and assessment of material requirements and by knowing how to negotiate and partner with, when appropriate, selected carriers.

## Benefits of a Transportation Program

When purchasing/supply management takes control of or contributes to transportation decision making, this should develop into a program that is managed as carefully as any other within the function. The benefits of such a program can add value to the organization through the following:

- Lower delivered costs coupled with improved delivery service.
- Identifying key areas of opportunity for improving the delivery of goods and services at the lowest total costs.
- Control of the business terms of sale to best determine the routing, cash flow, and risk management associated with delivering goods to end users.
- Recognizing strategic opportunities to interface with other functional units within and between the organizations of the purchasers, suppliers, and transportation carriers to achieve inbound supply chain management initiatives.
- Identifying options to manage and control the inbound routing of freight, including the outsourcing of third-party logistics services.

## Understand the Impact of Transportation on Inventory

The time it takes to manufacture and deliver a product is frequently the basis of supplier performance measurement. Freight carriers that most often supply consistent, timely service can help reduce manufacturing/delivery time, which helps an organization reduce its inventory and plan production by using tighter schedules. Carriers that provide effective service also can contribute to just-in-time efforts provided that they can work reliably within the precise schedules required.

## Checklist: How to Evaluate a Carrier

Selecting a carrier is actually a standard sourcing issue which includes a thorough investigation of specific factors. The following points should enter into the evaluation of a carrier to help determine reliability, flexibility, consistency, and financial stability and strength:

- Assets and debts.
- Revenues and expense categories.
- Operating ratio: operating expenses divided by revenues.
- Method of financing capital improvements and new equipment.
- Billing process/methods.
- Billing accuracy.
- Pricing and contract terms.
- On-time delivery, including JIT capability.
- Use of electronic data interchange (EDI) and/or other information technologies.
- Damage and claims record (including time to correct).
- Length of time in business.

- Number of employees in the organization.
- Equipment: type, variety, condition, age.
- Availability of additional/backup equipment.
- Tracing and tracking abilities.
- Terminals and warehouse services.
- Safety program(s).
- Training and management of drivers.
- Insurance for bodily injury, property damage, cargo, and catastrophic risks.
- General reputation with other shippers.
- Intermodal capability.
- Hazardous materials program(s).
- Accident/safety record.
- Citations record.
- Reputation with other shippers.
- Services such as in-transit options and auditing.
- Routes and geographic area served.
- Outsourcing logistics services capability.
- Freight forwarding services.
- State and federal registrations.

## Know How to Select the Best Carriers

When purchasing/supply management manages or works with the transportation function, the selection of a carrier is in its hands and is specified on the purchase order (called the routing). The routing also is provided via a routing letter or in a routing guide to the supplier and to all parties who have a need to know this information, such as the receiving and traffic departments.

Carrier selection involves determining, the appropriate method and the specific carrier that can provide the best service to meet delivery requirements. The following factors should be considered:

- Door-to-door or door-to–point of use (such as the shop floor) costs.
- Door-to–point use of transit time.
- Financial stability of the carrier.
- Willingness to negotiate rate changes.
- Carrier reliability and/or consistency.
- Frequency of service.
- Scheduling flexibility.
- Capabilities of operating personnel.
- Shipment expediting and tracing.
- Claims processing and prevention.
- Special equipment or services available.

In the current deregulated environment, customer service has become an important attribute of carrier selection. Nonetheless, there must be complete understanding between purchasing and the carrier regarding the service level required and the criteria for measuring performance as defined by the factors listed above. Carrier billing charges are often not what actually is paid because factors in pricing structures, such as discounts, and negotiated terms can alter such charges significantly.

Most commercial transportation is via rail, pipeline, motor carriage, air, or water. About 75 percent of the agricultural products and manufactured goods tonnage is transported by truck, which is usually faster, more flexible, and more versatile than rail.

*Note:* Suppliers should be asked for their recommendations, since they may have other customers in your area with whom you can combine loads. There also may be opportunities for backhauling, where trucks carrying your product to your customers can then carry material from your suppliers back to your facility.

The following are guidelines for choosing the mode of transportation, which is the first step in the traffic-transportation decision.

## Motor Carriers

Motor carriers transport goods Less Than Truckload (LTL) or Truckload (TL). To determine which is appropriate, purchasers should consider the weight and volume (cube density) of the shipment. Rates are significantly lower for TL and among TL carriers can vary as much as 10 to 20 percent. Freight forwarders take advantage of long-haul TL rates by consolidating small shipments from LTL shippers into TL shipments.

## Rail Carriers

Rail is generally used for bulky and heavy goods shipped in large volumes, such as chemicals, coal, petroleum, and lumber, and for goods that have low per-unit value. Rail shipments generally encompass goods traveling long distances, usually beyond a one-day truck trip (about 450 to 500 miles). There are fewer rail carriers today than there were in the past, and they generally operate on contract rates (indicating a long-term need for rail services), although tariff rates have not been abandoned completely. Rail rates tend to be cheaper than those of motor carriers, but compared with motor carriers, rail does have disadvantages, including the following:

- Less flexible routes.
- More time-consuming.
- Diverting freight from one destination to another is not as easy.
- Obtaining goods in transit may be inconvenient.
- Requires more secure blocking and bracing to help prevent damage.

## Water Carriers

Except for pipeline, the cheapest way of moving freight is generally water-inland: inland barge carriers, Great Lakes carriers, and coastal/intercoastal and ocean carriers. Water is best for shipping high-bulk, low-value commodities; basic raw materials, including coal, iron ore, and petroleum; and agricultural products such as grains. Water carriers charge on the basis of weight or volume, depending on which one gives the carrier greater revenue. The disadvantage of shipping by water is that transport is slow. This is due to infrequent sailing schedules, the lack of water routes in many commercial areas, and the limited speed of marine vessels, although ships are getting faster.

## Air Carriers

Air, while the most expensive, is the fastest transportation service. It is generally used for high-value, low-density items. Frequency and reliability are high, but disadvantages include the following:

- Time lost to terminal delays.
- Lack of direct, door-to-door capability.
- High transport charges.

Yet air transport offers trade-off possibilities for the purchaser. Aside from the common use of special small package services such as UPS, RPS, and FedEx, air can be cheaper than truck or other modes if one looks at total landed costs as opposed to freight charges alone. Packaging and handling costs can be much lower than truck and rail. In addition, many organizations have discovered they can reduce inventories substantially by shipping via air.

## Intermodal Carriers

As the name implies, intermodal carriers combine modes of shipping goods, such as trailer or container on a flatcar (motor-rail), and landbridge (rail-ocean). Intermodal transportation is common for shipments arriving from foreign destinations. It also should be considered as an alternative to motor carriage. Service can be very cost-effective, especially when rail carriers have a heavy volume of traffic to keep costs low.

---

## Dealing with Hazardous Materials

Hazardous materials are defined as those dangerous goods which pose a risk to health, safety, and property. They include:

- Explosives.
- Flammables.
- Poisons.
- Corrosives.
- Radioactive and nuclear materials.

Hazardous materials must be packaged, labeled, handled, and transported according to stringent regulation from several agencies. Current U.S. regulations appear in the Code of Federal Regulations, Title 49, Parts 171–178. However, the Hazardous Materials Transportation Uniform Safety Act of 1990 is the primary law covering the transportation of hazardous materials. International shipments must comply with docket HM-191, where the term "dangerous goods" is used interchangeably with "hazardous materials."

Make sure you, the shipper, and the carrier comply with all rules as they apply to hazardous materials. Never assume your shipment is exempt and make sure the carrier you select is not only competent to move these goods but has a record of doing so safely.

---

## Know Carrier Classifications

There are four types of general transportation carriers.

## General Purpose

These carriers handle goods, as the name implies, without specificity. However, some will provide a unique service designed to meet the purchasing organization's specific requirements. This can include common carrier or contract carrier services. A common carrier holds itself out to service the general public, but only for the types of freight for which it has the capability and capacity to transport, such as food, chemicals, or machinery. A contract carrier operates only under negotiated contractual agreements, which generally are reviewed every one to two years.

## Carriers of High-Risk, Dangerous Bulk Commodities

Dangerous cargos that are transported in bulk include flammable liquids, certain wastes, nuclear materials, and other hazardous materials (see box on page 507). Because of the sensitive nature of transporting these items, rates are not a priority in selecting a carrier. Purchasers should focus instead on building a fixed-price relationship based on mutual trust, shared risk, and reward.

## Specialized Carriers

Specialized carriers are those which have developed services based on certain requirements. Examples include refrigerated trucks for carrying food items, cooled and air-ride trucks for electronic equipment, and trucks to carry oversized items such as rigging equipment. Selection of this type of carrier depends on the basis of competitive advantage balanced against other costs.

## Commodity-Type Carriers

This category includes carriers that offer less specialized services and includes most LTL common carriers. Since these suppliers are generally interchangeable, rates are important in the selection process.

---

## Common Shipping Terms

The following terms are the most commonly used, but note that there are several variations.

■ Free on Board (FOB) Purchaser's Plant Freight Prepaid, also called a "destination" sale. Title is with seller until delivery. The seller must:

1. Place goods on or in transport vehicles.
2. Secure receipted bill of lading.
3. Pay all transportation charges to destination.
4. Be responsible for filing cargo loss-claims with carrier.

   The purchaser must:

1. Move the goods after arrival.
2. Be responsible for loss or damage after arrival.
3. Pay any detention or demurrage charges and storage fees.

■ FOB Seller's Plant, Freight Collect, also called an "origin" contract. Title passes to the purchaser when the shipment is turned over to the carrier. FOB seller's plant is generally the preferred method because it allows the purchaser to control the transportation. The seller must:

1. Place goods on or in transport vehicles.
2. Secure receipted bill of lading.
3. Be responsible for cargo loss or damage until goods have been placed in or on transport vehicle at point of origin and a clean bill of lading has been furnished.

   The purchaser must:

1. Provide for movement after goods are on board.
2. Pay all transportation charges to destination.
3. Be responsible for filing loss or damage claims.
4. Pay any detention or demurrage charges and storage fees.

■ FOB Named Point of Origin Freight Allowed. This is the same as FOB seller's plant except the shipper agrees to reimburse the purchaser for the freight charges for a selected mode, such as rail. Buyers often prefer truck transport and opt to pay for truck service. Title passes to purchaser when the shipment is turned over to carrier. The seller must:

1. Place goods on or in cars or trucks.
2. Secure receipted bill of lading.
3. Be responsible for loss or damage until goods have been placed in or on transport vehicles at point of origin and clean bill of lading has been furnished by the carrier.

   The purchaser must:

1. Provide for the movement of goods after they are on board.
2. Be responsible for loss/damage-claims while in transit.
3. Pay all transportation charges to destination.
4. Pay any detention or demurrage charges and storage fees.

For international terms, see the INCOTERMS box on page 513.

## Be Familiar with Shipping Terms

To simply indicate "ship the cheapest or best way" on a purchase order is an abdication of any freight analysis. It is critical to know shipping terms (see Glossary, page 521), especially since they indicate who owns what and when they own it. The point at which a purchaser takes title determines who selects the carrier, who pays the carrier, who negotiates with the carrier, and who files any necessary claims. Freight costs are part of the product costs, and ultimately, the purchaser will pay all costs unless the freight costs are negotiated to include a discount. Under a delivered, freight prepaid by seller, FOB purchaser's plant, or warehouse agreement, the freight costs are "hidden" or averaged somewhere in the price.

## Transportation Documentation: Domestic and International

The most common documentation used in transportation is as follows:

■ *Bill of Lading or Air Bill*—certifies the transfer of goods from shipper to carrier and carrier to recipient. It is the basis for proof of delivery as well as the shipment contract for transportation (contract for cartage). The bill of lading may be incorporated in a master contract.

- *Manifest*—consolidates multiple shipments from the shipper to the carrier for single or multiple recipients and lists the contents of all orders on one document.
- *Delivery Receipt*—a document signed by the recipient showing the shipment has arrived in good order and is not damaged. The bill of lading also can be used for this purpose.

International shipments can require the following:

- *Letter of Credit (LC)*—letter from purchaser's bank saying funds have been set aside to pay for the shipment. The LC specifies exact terms and conditions for shipment and must coincide with the terms and conditions of the purchase order.
- *Commercial Invoice*—standard invoice indicating all charges and the value of the shipment; used for customs purposes.
- *Shipper's Letter of Instruction (SLI)*—letter to a freight forwarder with a confirmation to all parties, including the purchaser, of the terms of purchase and responsibilities for risks of transport.
- *Export Declaration*—content and value of the shipment prepared for the U.S. Department of Commerce.
- *Certificate of Origin*—document states the country of origin of the goods shipped.
- *Packing List*—contains a list of contents of all cartons in shipment. Domestic bills of lading usually are included to cover motor transport to and from ports.
- *Airway or Ocean Bill of Lading*—same as packing list, but for air and sea shipments.
- *Dock Receipt*—proof of delivery to dockside outbound freight terminal.
- *Independent Inspection Certificate*—in those cases in which an independent inspection takes place (quality control or calibration check at the shipper's facility before crating) a certificate of inspection is provided. This must be stated in terms of the letter of credit.
- *Import License*—many countries require a basic license or special permit to bring specific goods in.
- *Arrival Notice*—arrival of the vessel; identifies shipment, number of packages, weight, and when free time transpires.
- *Consumption Entry Form*—U.S. Customs form showing origin, value, description of goods, and duty estimated.
- *Immediate Delivery Entry Form*—expedites clearance, allows up to 10 days to pay duty and processing consumption entry ID.
- *Immediate Transportation Entry Form*—allows goods to be moved from dockside to inland destination on a bonded carrier without payment of duties and finalization of entry forms.
- *Carriers Certificate and Release Order*—advises customs of the details of the shipment, its ownership, port of lading; carrier certifies ownership.
- *Delivery Order*—consignee or customs broker order (authority) to release shipment to inland carrier.

## Understand Freight Rates

The common freight rates are:

1. Contract rates, such as point-to-point specific rates for a given material shipped in large quantities, for example, TL on a continuing basis.
2. Common carrier tariffs rates, which are offered by the carrier in a price list and are usually lower than common carrier rates.

The actual freight rate paid by the shipper requires analysis; use a spreadsheet application for comparison and options. As a rule, negotiated rates should be based on cost, value, and competitive factors.

Freight equalization sometimes is allowed for uniform or like commodities and raw materials such as steel. For example, basing point systems charge all freight from one mill shipping point to foster competition. For example, if the actual CWT is $0.75 per hundred pounds for a distant supplier compared with the close supplier rate of $0.50 per hundred pounds, the shipper can pay the freight bill at $0.75 and subtract the $0.25 from the total commercial invoice.

## Consider a Third-Party Provider

Freight forwarders provide transportation service to organizations purchasing goods in LTL, airplane load, ship load, or carload lots. Forwarders consolidate small shipments from several clients into unit loads and schedule the shipment as a large load at lower rates. Freight forwarders have carrier responsibility, move freight on their master bills of lading or waybills, and generally do not own line-haul transportation equipment.

Long-haul and pickup and delivery owner/operators service many of these forms of carriers as independent contractors but are not themselves registered carriers providing services at a price comparable to that of a carrier.

Other third-party arrangements include:

- Transportation property brokers which arrange freight for motor carriers but are not themselves a carrier with cargo liability.
- Private logistics service providers that may partner with your organization.
- Small package/courier service carriers which simplify and reduce costs for small shipment service.
- All-service logistical organizations with which a purchaser-shipper can outsource the entire transportation function.

The practice of outsourcing the transportation function is becoming more popular as purchasers look at the total landed cost versus a single freight rate. These providers offer a wide range of integrated services, including transportation, and warehousing and distribution functions. They can perform trade-off analyses, conduct commodity rate investigations, perform auditing, handle intermodal needs, provide pool car arrangements, and tender and track shipments.

---

### Forging a Long-Term Contract

Services defined in a long-term contract go beyond the common carrier services offered to the general public. The driving force in such contracts is to identify the distinctive needs and then document those performance agreements with the attendant legal charges. The principles apply for all physical modes of carriage. The following is a review of types of services that lend themselves to long-term agreements between shippers and carriers.

1. Volume of services over a period of time. Contracts for a volume of shipments during a specified term. This factor offsets the services strictly on a transactional, shipment-by-shipment basis.
2. Continuous move or round-robin rates between two points. The trip includes two or more shipments for which even trip billing may occur.
3. Monthly agreements as to average weight agreements per shipment. Most often, shipment charges are assessed on scaled weights or on a metered basis. If the shipper and the carrier agree

with the weights determined on a computed basis, then actual assessment of shipment charges can be computed on an agreed-upon billing cycle, such as weekly or monthly, and weights can be monitored or checked on a sample basis for average weight. Individual freight bills do not need to be generated, only batched in a summary form on a weekly or monthly basis.

4. Debit/credit loading and unloading detention demurrage charges on a periodic basis. Instead of assessing detention/demurrage charges on a per shipment basis, an average amount of time can be agreed on, such as two hours for truckload traffic, and then debits and credits can be accumulated over a periodic basis, such as a month. Specifically, if a shipper or receiver loads or unloads in 45 minutes versus the two-hour standard, the shipper gets a debit in its account. If the shipper or receiver takes four hours to load or unload, it gets a credit in its account—a liability to pay. At the end of the month, the shipper and the carrier tally up to see who pays.

5. Performance-based contracts with perks and penalties for on-time delivery. If a carrier delivers service above the agreed upon standard, such as 95 percent on-time pickup and/or delivery, the carrier is entitled to a perk—a bonus. However, if the carrier does not meet the standard, the carrier can be penalized for the poorer service. Monthly billing is conducive to this type of arrangement.

6. Performance of value-added services, including light duty assembly, and just-in-time delivery with the possible use of returnable containers to a receiver for a supplier. With so many carriers developing contract logistics services beyond carriage, contracts make sense in defining the business and legal responsibilities of the parties involved. Specifically, legal party responsibilities include that of a supplier, a carrier, a warehouser, and possibly a light assembly supplier agent. This situation exemplifies the need for a contract or contracts among the supplier, the third-party agent, the carrier, and the receiver for providing defined duties, the nature of the involved legal parties, the charges for performing the duties, and how billing and payment procedures are to be performed.

7. Performance of services involving high degrees of information technology. Many evolving relationships among shippers, carriers, receivers, and third parties involve information technologies such as bar coding, EDI, radio frequency transponders, image processing systems, GPS/GIS positioning systems, and radio frequency tracking systems that go beyond offered common carrier services. These services relate to shipment tracking and diversion services, billing and invoicing, and payment processes.

## Be Savvy about Contracting

Many carriers and shippers adopt carrier rules tariffs into long-term contracts. Unless a review process with formal notice and addendum procedure is incorporated into the contracts, shippers may be subjecting themselves to rules, additional charges, and rate increases of which they are not aware. Carefully review contracts as to how rules, tariffs, and classification systems are referenced.

Other clauses to include are damaged freight provisions, salvage rights, a statement that the carrier is subject to common carrier liability, and any unique needs such as dedicated equipment for the shipper.

*Note:* The statute of limitations for overcharge claims for common carriers is now six months; this is a compelling reason to use contract carriage and to pre-audit freight bills (see the next two sections).

Finally, make sure freight discounts are part of your contract or purchase order and that the purchasing organization receives this discount if paying assessed freight charges on commercial invoices. Also, include an arbitration or dispute resolution procedure requirement in the event of disputes.

# A GUIDE TO INCOTERMS

International shipping terms and rules are called "INCOTERMS." Here is a listing of the most important INCOTERMS.

|  | **General Definition** | **Specific Incoterm** |
|---|---|---|
| Group E | Goods are made available at the supplier's named site. Buyer assumes all responsibility for transportation, cost, and risk beyond this point. | **EXW** Ex works (supplier's site). |
| Group F | Supplier delivers goods to specified carrier location. Buyer assumes all costs and risks associated with the main carriage and beyond. | **FCA** Free carrier at a named place. Supplier clears goods for export.<br>**FAS** Free alongside ship (on dock). Buyer clears goods for export.<br>**FOB** Free on board (on ship). Supplier clears goods for export. |
| Group C | Supplier contracts for main carriage and assumes all costs to the destination country. Buyer assumes all risks during main carriage, plus cost of delivery from destination dock to buyer's site. | **CFR** Cost and freight to the port of destination. Supplier clears goods for export.<br>**CIF** Cost, insurance, and freight to the port of destination. Same responsibilities as CFR, except supplier is responsible for insurance during main carriage.<br>**CPT** Carriage paid to the named destination. Supplier clears goods to export.<br>**CIP** Carriage and insurance paid to the named destination. Same responsibilities as CPT, except supplier covers insurance during main carriage. |
| Group D | Supplier assumes all risks and costs to the specified destination. | **DAF** Delivered at frontier (country border) at a specified location, but before the customs border of the adjoining country. Supplier clears goods for export.<br>**DES** Delivered ex ship at specified port of destination. Goods are available aboard ship, uncleared for export.<br>**DEQ** Delivered ex quay (dock) at the named port of destination. The duty can be paid or unpaid, depending on the agreement.<br>**DDU** Delivered duty unpaid at the specified place of destination.<br>**DDP** Delivered duty paid at the specified place of destination. Supplier bears all risks and costs, including duties, taxes, and other charges of delivering the goods, cleared for import. |

The first wave of transportation deregulation came with the Air Cargo Act of 1977, followed by the Staggers Rail Act of 1980, the Motor Carrier Act of 1980, and the Shipping Act of 1984. Those acts substantially reduced the rules of entry, price discounting, route offerings, service offerings, and the role of the Interstate Commerce Commission (ICC—which became defunct) in regulating the air, truck, rail, and water carriers involved in interstate commerce. Those acts provided freedom and ease to negotiate rates, expand private contracting, and offer other services.

However, those acts also brought problems and instability. For example, the ensuing increased competition in motor trucking brought about discounting practices, which in turn led to bankruptcy. After several Supreme Court cases (in particular the Maislin and Transcon cases), Congress passed the following amendments:

1.  *The Negotiated Rates Act of 1993 (NRA).*   Effective December 3, 1993, this act prohibits motor common and contract carriers from providing a tariff rate reduction to the nonpayer of freight charges except under certain rules of disclosure to the party responsible for paying (or his or her agent), when indicated on the freight document and for performance of a particular service.

2.  *The Transportation Industry Regulatory Reform Act of 1994 (TIRRA).*   Requires motor carriers to provide, on request of the shipper, a written or electronic copy of the rate, classification, rules, practices, and any other information affecting the rate. This requirement also is known as "verified pricing documentation." This act also eliminated the (then) ICC rules for motor carrier contracting.

3.  *The Federal Aviation Administration Act of 1994.*   An aviation bill rider, this act takes the states out of intrastate economic regulation of motor carriers. It carries the provisions of the Motor Carrier Act of 1980 down to the state level; that is, states cannot regulate intrastate motor carriers unless the motor carriers in the state petition the state to exercise regulation.

The latest legislation is the ICC Termination Act (ICCTA) of 1995 (see box on page 515).

## Understand "Common Law" Price Lists and Rules Tariffs

Carriers (motor and rail) still can include rules tariffs in their "common law" price lists, which allow for amendments without the knowledge or consent of the shipper. For example, references to classification tariffs mean that the *shipper* is subject to the rules related to uniform bill of lading forms, liability limits, package specifications, released rates, and other rules and charges in the National Motor Freight Classification (NMFC) for trucks, the Uniform Freight Classification (UFC) for rail, and loading rules published in the Association of American Railroads (AAR) loading pamphlets.

These rules tariffs include provisions for surcharges, various value-added ancillary services for which the carrier assesses additional charges. Many carriers, instead of relying on the NMFC, are publishing their own rules tariffs. The new law also enables carriers and shippers to develop their own unique bills of lading rather than using the uniform bills of lading incorporated in the NMFC or in the Uniform Commercial Code of states.

## Know Where Contract Carriage Fits in the ICCTA

Two precepts of the ICC Termination Act (ICCTA) are that the federal government has jurisdiction to oversee (as opposed to regulate) U.S. transportation policy and that carriers provide *nondiscriminatory* service at reasonable charges. Some attorneys and practitioners believe that under the policies of ICCTA, all carriers are now common carriers with the right to develop long-term contracts (contract carriage). However, under deregulation these carriers aren't required to file tariffs with any agency.

The question arises as to how shippers, receivers, and third parties will know if they are being discriminated against by other service/price offerings. How can one use contract carriage to discriminate among shippers legally? Contracts are a legal means as long as distinctive services are identified in the contracts. The answers to these questions may lie in the courts. Parties who claim to be injured by discriminatory services and prices may be able to know only if and when court cases force discovery. If this is the case, further legislation may be needed.

---

## The ICC Termination Act of 1995 (ICCTA)

Effective January 1, 1996, the Interstate Commerce Commission (ICC) was abolished, and limited functions were transferred to the newly created Surface Transportation Board (the Board), within the Department of Transportation (DOT). ICCTA is a massive revision of the Interstate Commerce act. The major changes relevant to purchasing include:

- Elimination of railroad tariff filings (but rail carriers must publish rates, including a 20-day notice of rate increases, even though the act does not specify where the rates are to be published).
- Limitation of the authority of the Board to set minimum rail rates and investigate and suspend new rail rates except to prevent irreparable harm. The Board also cannot initiate rail rate investigations but can respond to complaints.
- Use of stand-alone cost (SAC) methods to determine rail rate reasonableness (and other methods when SAC preparation is too costly).
- Repeal of the Elkins Act against rail rebates, along with the commodities clause and special regulations for transportation of recyclable or recycled materials.
- Retention of the motor carrier, water carrier, freight forwarder, and broker provisions of TIRRA of 1994 which eliminated much of the tariff filing and rate regulation for interstate transportation.
- Retention and some expansion of the provisions of the Federal Aviation Administration Reauthorization Act of 1994 and the Negotiated Rates Act of 1993 (NRA).
- Inclusion of domestic port-to-port water and intermodal motor-water carriage regulations under the Board from the Federal Maritime Commission.
- Requirement that collective rate-making agreements be reviewed every three years and tested for public interest.
- Modification of the 180-day time limit to file claims to include 180 days from the start of rebillings by carriers.
- Substitution of market determined rates to prevail instead of "rate reasonableness" and "tariff requirements," which now apply only to household goods.
- Simplified licensing procedure for new carriers, freight forwarders, and brokers, who register with the Federal Highway Administration (FHWA).
- Eliminates the distinctions between common and contract carriers.
- Authority for transportation carriers to offer line-haul and various accessorial, value-added services either under common carriage for the general public or under contracts for specific services.
- Broadens the term "transportation" to include packing and unpacking activities.
- Removes the states from any obligation to determine and regulate tariffs.

The following are the basic steps needed to establish and maintain an effective transportation program.

### Step One: Take Control

The importance of gaining control of inbound transportation is twofold:

1. If the supplier determines these costs, it may not be to the purchaser's benefit.
2. Within the organization, purchasing/supply management has the best opportunity to work with suppliers to reduce transportation costs.

Purchase orders must state that the buying organization is paying for inbound transportation as this forces purchasing personnel to determine the shipping method. This is necessary if purchasing/supply management is to take control of transportation, which otherwise would be determined by the supplier. In most cases, it is a benefit to the purchaser to specify on the purchase order *free on board (FOB) origin, freight collect, or FOB shipping point, freight collect* (see glossary).

### Step Two: Coordinate Efforts with Suppliers

Even though your supplier no longer will determine the specifics of inbound transportation, supplier cooperation is vital to a successful program. Your supplier may have contacts that can prove valuable to you and also will be required to help coordinate the movement of goods from its facility to yours.

### Step Three: Form a Team

In large organizations as well as small ones, the team approach is the most effective in establishing a capable transportation program. This is the case because cooperation and coordination are necessary from several functions within the organization, including:

- Transportation/traffic.
- Manufacturing/operations.
- Production planning and inventory management.
- Warehousing and receiving.
- Product and supply quality assurance.
- Accounting.

Purchasing/supply management should assume team leadership, especially since the success of the program depends on the ability of purchasing/supply management to gain the cooperation of suppliers whose commitment must be long-term.

### Step Four: Analyze Requirements

Several factors should be considered preparatory to selecting a carrier. They include:

- Types of goods to be transported—size, weight, density, packaging, and specific physical characteristics.
- Mode of transportation—motor, rail, air, water, or combinations of these.
- Shipping point(s) and volume "traffic lanes."
- Delivery requirements—time needed or required.

- Organizational requirements.
- Carrier capabilities.

### Step Five: Outsource If Appropriate

Analyzing requirements may lead to a decision to outsource one or more of the inbound transportation functions. This may be especially true if purchasing/supply management wishes to control inbound transportation but doesn't have the time or necessary staff to support the program.

### Step Six: Analyze Opportunities

Any number of creative methods can be used to maximize inbound transportation. Here are some ways to manage the process proactively:

- Switch from FOB Delivered, Freight Prepaid to FOB Origin, or Freight Collect (see glossary), which can be a cost saving if actual freight is less than the average freight charges built into the delivered price of the goods.
- Use customer pickups to build leverage from outbound freight delivery; backhauled inbound freight can be negotiated to your advantage.
- Negotiate the right of routing for better control over loading and unloading schedules.
- Check shipment weights; always determine the correct weight for shipments.
- Review supplier source locations.
- Consolidate where possible.
- Make sure the correct freight classifications are used to avoid over payment.

### Step Seven: Investigate Tariffs

Under deregulation, the transportation industry has become very competitive. Carriers of the same mode now may compete with one another as well as with carriers in a different mode.

Understand the rate structures of each mode of transportation and the rates offered by carriers in each mode. Don't assume that the rate/tariff quoted is valid until you are presented with a copy of the actual tariff showing the date stamp and effective date of the tariff. If a lower negotiated rate is used before the effective date, the carrier may later file an undercharge claim, and the purchasing organization will be legally obliged to pay it. Tariffs are available in electronic format on floppy disks or through computer transfer.

Purchasers and supply managers should always keep a printed copy of any tariff transactions on file.

---

### Transportation Contract Checklist

The following items should be included when one is contracting transportation services: Be sure to check the glossary on pages 521–524 for any unfamiliar terms.

- Responsibility for cargo loss and damage—defines the basis of liability and the rule of mitigating damages and claims filing.
- Disclosure of goods—determines the value of goods shipped (without this notice, the carrier can avoid paying for any damages claimed).
- Routing mode.

- Method of transportation—eliminates any possibility of inappropriate methods or equipment.
- Responsibility for equipment specification—designates which party is responsible for all equipment.
- Volume requirements—defines the minimum amount of goods required of the shipper and the minimum of equipment to be provided by the carrier.
- Rate escalation/de-escalation—specifies changes in rates, including escalation and de-escalation; defines what indexes the rates are tied to, how rates can or will change, when, under what circumstances, and with what notice.
- Terms of transportation charges—includes all descriptive detail, including who pays for what services.
- Billing and payment—specifies documents to be used, what constitutes a bill, billing error rectification, credit extended, rights of lien, and all other such matters.
- Force majeure.
- Title of goods—defines when title passes and who is entitled to make a claim.
- Applicable law—specifies which court system will have jurisdiction over dispute resolution.
- Assignability—specifically, will it be allowed?

### Step Eight: Evaluate and Select a Carrier

Selecting a carrier encompasses standard sourcing methods. A thorough investigation of candidates should focus on items such as financial strength, billing procedures, pricing and contract terms, equipment upkeep, personnel training, delivery record, damage and claims record, safety programs and safety record, insurance, reputation among other shippers, service capabilities, geographic area served, and routing. The selection process also should take into account the use of a third-party provider such as a freight forwarder or transportation broker.

### Step Nine: Negotiate Price

Purchasing and supply management's task is to negotiate with the carrier for the lowest class of rates available for the purchased goods. Transportation consultants sometimes are employed for this purpose, especially if an organization is small or does not have a transportation or traffic manager on staff. Class rate negotiation is important because it lays the platform for all further negotiations about price.

Once class rates have been established, negotiate for the best discount you can obtain. It's the combination of the class rate and the discount that eventually determines the charge that will appear on the invoice. This is calculated once the goods have been delivered and the weight or volume of the order has been established. Charges are ultimately based on:

- Origin and destination points.
- Volume or weight.
- Packaging.
- Specific characteristics such as perishability.
- Handling.

### Step Ten: Negotiate a Contract

For other than one-time deliveries, contracts are essential for carriers that will provide long-term services to your organization.

*Note:* Contracts are also necessary for one-time deliveries in which a special service will be provided, such as the use of oversized equipment.

As with any other supplier, it's important to develop and partner with carriers with which a relationship of mutual trust can be built. Contracts ultimately should aim for the best service at the most competitive price. A transportation consultant can also be helpful when you are negotiating such a contract.

*Caveat:* A carrier sometimes will try to insert its rules tariffs into a contract. Do not allow this to happen. Rules tariffs should be incorporated into the carrier's bill of lading. Rules tariffs contain items such as late payment penalties and liability limitations which, if cited in the contract, require the shipper to surrender certain rights. When rules tariffs are part of the bill of lading, the purchasing organization retains its right to challenge any claims made by the carrier.

### Step Eleven: Expediting and Tracing Shipments

Expediting means the shipper wants or needs faster than normal service-delivery time. This request must be made before shipment and may incur extra charges. Expediting should be used only when necessary, not only because of the cost but because the requests will be ignored if they become habitual. Expediting should never be a substitute for production planning.

Tracing systems are used to locate a shipment while it is in the possession of the carrier and can take place even while the shipment is in transit. To trace a shipment, the following information is needed:

- Date tendered to the carrier.
- Shipper/origin.
- Destination.
- Freight bill or pro number.
- Description of the goods.
- Recipient of the goods.
- Date shipped.
- Appropriate documents.
- Truck or car number.

Most tracing systems are automated and utilize electronic/satellite tracking, which literally follows the shipment at any point in the route.

### Step Twelve: Pre-Audit Freight Invoices

Shippers have the right to pre- and post-audit their freight bills within a six-month period. Pre-auditing is the prudent course of action, for it can save a great deal of money. Pre-auditing is particularly important in international shipping (export or import) as tariff and custom duties are based on how the goods are classified. Many independent rate consultants figure that the average shipper overpays by 15 to 20 percent in areas that include:

- Incorrect classifications.
- Duplicate payments.

- Mistakes in rate-invoice calculations, such as incorrect mileage or weights.
- Incorrect FOB terms.
- Incomplete documentation.
- Wrong routing.
- Inclusion of carrier rules tariff for late payment penalties, falsely claimed liability limitations, exemption from special damages, and other such "hidden charges."
- Poor delivery and missed arrival deadlines.
- Wrong mode.
- Incorrect packaging.
- Wrong source.
- Miscellaneous extra charges (such as demurrage) not justifiable and any other deviation from the intended contract.

If your organization does not have in-house resources, a special auditing firm will provide pre-auditing services on a 50 percent commission on savings on net recoverable overcharges.

*Caveat:* Freight bills should never be paid without first being audited.

### Step Thirteen: File Claims When Necessary

Inevitably, even with the best carriers, claims will be filed for over, short, or wrong goods shipped by the supplier or goods damaged while in transit. Claims are filed when either the supplier or the carrier fails in its efforts to correct the situation.

Sometimes it is difficult to assign culpability. For example, material delivered short can be the result of a mistake by either party. The receiving function, which should be part of your team, is vital in this phase of the transportation program. Receiving must verify that all shipments arrive as specified.

The rules governing the filing of claims are founded in law and must be followed strictly. Certain government and international rules also apply. In addition, claims rules are found in the carrier's tariffs and/or in the bill of lading.

### Step Fourteen: Evaluate Carrier Performance

Standard performance measures should be applied to carrier performance. Specific parameters to be measured include:

- Transit time between facilities.
- Equipment utilized.
- Billing accuracy.
- Claims occurrence.
- Pickup and delivery performance.
- Rate negotiation service.
- Sales representative information.
- Technology or innovations offered.
- Follow-up performance.

Many carriers supply a monthly service report to customers containing shipment and delivery date information. If such a report is not normally issued by a carrier, ask for one. Measuring carrier performance not only should serve as a means of monitoring performance but also should be part of continuous improvement operations.

## Glossary

The following are common transportation terms. Not all will have been discussed in the text because of space limitations. These definitions are from the NAPM Glossary of Key Purchasing Terms.

**AIR WAYBILL**—The document used for the shipment of air freight providing information such as commodities shipped, shipping instructions, and shipping costs.

**ASSIGNMENT**—A transference of a property right or title to another party. In shipping, it is commonly used with a bill of lading, transferring rights, title, and interest to a named party.

**BILL OF LADING (B/L)**—A carrier's contract and receipt for goods transported from one place to another, delivered to a designated person. Types of bills of lading include:

- A *Certified Bill of Lading*, provided when a consular officer endorses an ocean bill of lading, specifying that the shipment meets the requirements of the country of importation.
- A *Clean (Clear) Bill of Lading*, or a carrier-receipted bill of lading, provided when a shipment is deemed in good condition with no apparent loss or damage. This means the bill of lading contains no exceptions and is a readily negotiable instrument.
- An *Export Bill of Lading*, issued by an inland carrier to contract the movement of goods from an interior point of origin to a foreign destination.
- A *Government Bill of Lading*, supplied by the U.S. government for shipment of government-owned property or goods within the government.
- A *Negotiable (Order) Bill of Lading*, consigned directly to the order of a party, usually a shipper or a bank, whose endorsement is required to transfer the title of the goods. The bill of lading must be surrendered to the carrier before the goods are released.
- A *Nonnegotiable (Straight) Bill of Lading*, consigned directly to the consignee and not negotiable. The goods usually are delivered without surrender of the bill of lading.
- An *Ocean Bill of Lading*, issued by an ocean carrier for marine transport of goods.
- An *Order-Notify Bill of Lading*, similar to a negotiable bill of lading, except that it contains an additional clause directing that a specified third party, usually at the port of destination, be notified upon arrival of the goods. However, this party does not take title.
- A *Short-Form Bill of Lading*, unlike the straight bill of lading, only refers to the contract terms but does not include them.
- A *Through Bill of Lading*, issued by a shipping company or its agent, covering more than one mode of transportation.

**CARLOAD (C/L)**—The weight and/or volume necessary to qualify for a rail carload rate, or a rail car loaded to its capacity. The carload quantity referred to on a carload rate has nothing to do with the actual quantity required to fill the rail car, but is the minimum weight specified to qualify for a lower-class rate.

**CARTAGE**—A charge made for the hauling and transferring of goods, usually on a short haul basis; drayage. Also, the physical movement of the goods.

**CLASS FREIGHT RATE**—A rate resulting from a classification rating of the freight. While commodity rates are available only on selected commodities, a class rate can be found for almost all commodities.

**COMMODITY FREIGHT RATE**—A rate for a specific commodity, moving between specified points, sometimes in a certain direction, and typically for a specific minimum quantity.

**COMMON CARRIER**—A common law carrier holds itself out to serve all customers, but carries only the types of freight for which it is registered. The most accepted characteristic of a common transportation carrier is the availability of nondiscriminatory service to anyone seeking such transportation.

**CONSIGNEE**—The person or organization to whom a shipper directs the carrier to deliver goods, generally the purchaser of the goods.

**CONSIGNOR**—The shipper of a transportation movement.

**CONSOLIDATION**—Combining less-than-truckload or less-than-carload shipments from various facilities for transport as one larger shipment, typically at a lower freight rate.

**CONTAINERIZATION**—Using large, sealed, standard-size containers primarily for intermodal and international shipping. The containers can be transloaded between rail, motor, and water carriers to reduce transit time, theft, packaging requirements, damage, and costs. "Piggyback" often is used to designate containers on flat cars (COFC) and trailers on flat cars (TOFC), with "fishyback" used for water transfer. Roll on-Roll off (RoRo) is used when equipment or containers can be driven directly onto the water carrier.

**CONTRACT CARRIER**—A contract carrier, regardless of mode, provides transportation and/or related services according to a contractual agreement. Tariff rates do not apply; contract rates are generally lower than regular common carrier rates.

**COST AND FREIGHT (CFR)**—The supplier quotes a price for the goods being sold, including the cost of transportation to a specified destination; it is used most commonly in international shipping.

**COST, INSURANCE, AND FREIGHT (CIF)**—A sales practice in international trade whereby the supplier quotes a price that includes the cost of the material, freight charges to a destination point, and marine insurance en route.

**DECLARED VALUE**—The practice of stating the value of goods being transported on the shipping document, often to achieve a lower freight rate or to obtain insurance.

**DEMURRAGE**—A fee charged by a carrier against a consignee, consignor, or other responsible party to compensate for the detention of the carrier's equipment in excess of allowable free time for loading, unloading, reconsigning, or stopping in transit. The term is also used by suppliers of material delivered in a variety of returnable containers, such as gas cylinders.

**DOOR-TO-DOOR**—The through transportation of a shipment from the consignor directly to the consignee.

**EXPEDITE**—To contact a supplier or carrier to speed up delivery of an inbound shipment.

**FREE ALONG SIDE (FAS) VESSEL**—The supplier agrees to deliver the goods in proper condition along side the vessel, with the buyer assuming all subsequent risks and expenses after delivery to the pier.

**FREE ON BOARD (FOB)**—In domestic trade (when the term is used with no further explanation), FOB means delivery of the goods with all charges paid aboard the carrier's equipment without cost to the buyer. Modified FOB terms include:

- *FOB Destination, Freight Collect* means that title passes from the supplier to the buyer at the destination point, and that the freight charges are the responsibility of the purchaser. (The supplier owns the goods in transit and is responsible for filing loss and damage claims against the carrier, but the purchaser pays and bears the freight charges and files any overcharge claims.)
- *FOB Destination, Freight Prepaid* means that title passes from the supplier to the buyer at the destination point, and that the freight charges are paid by the supplier. (The supplier pays and bears the freight charges, owns the goods in transit, and may file claims for overcharges, loss, and damage.)

- *FOB Destination, Freight Prepaid and Charged* means that the title passes at the destination point, and that the freight charges are paid by the supplier and added to the invoice. (The supplier pays the freight charges, owns the goods in transit, and files all claims for overcharges, loss, and damages. The purchaser bears the freight charges.)
- *FOB Origin, Freight Allowed* means that the purchaser obtains title where the shipment originates and is responsible for all claims against the carrier, but that the supplier pays the freight charges.
- *FOB Origin, Freight Collect* means that title passes to the buyer at the point of origin; the buyer pays the freight charges. (The buyer owns the goods in transit, and files all claims against the carrier.)
- *FOB Origin, Freight Prepaid and Charged* means that title passes to the buyer at the point of origin, and that the freight charges are paid by the supplier and then collected from the purchaser by adding the amount of the freight charges to the invoice. (The supplier pays the freight charges and files claims for overcharges. The purchaser bears the freight charges, owns the goods in transit, and files claims for loss and damage with the carrier.)

**FREIGHT BILL**—The carrier's invoice for transportation charges applicable to a shipment.

**FREIGHT BILL AUDIT**—A critical review of freight bills to determine classification, rating, or extension either by a third party or an inside auditor.

**FREIGHT CLAIM**—A claim against a carrier due to loss or damage to goods transported by that carrier; or for erroneous rates and weights in assessment of freight charges.

**FREIGHT FORWARDER (Domestic)**—A carrier that collects small shipments and consolidates them into larger shipments for delivery to the consignee.

**INTERMODAL FREIGHT SHIPMENTS**—Transportation shipments involving more than one mode, e.g., rail-motor, motor-air, or rail-water.

**IN-TRANSIT PRIVILEGES**—Special privileges which give rail shippers (buyers and sellers) the right to stop a shipment en route, unload it, perform certain processing operations on the material, reload the processed material, and continue the shipment at the original rate plus a modest additional charge.

**INVENTORY IN TRANSIT**—Physical inventory en route aboard a carrier. The term also indicates the capital costs of materials, parts, and finished goods en route aboard a carrier. This cost is commonly computed by multiplying the opportunity cost rate by the value of the inventory, then by the percentage of time (annualized) the goods are en route, plus the cost of the material itself.

**KNOCKED DOWN (KD)**—Disassembled goods for the purpose of reducing the cube space of the shipment for transportation and storage.

**LESS THAN CARLOAD (LTC)**—A shipment which is less than the amount required to be eligible for carload rates.

**LESS THAN TRUCKLOAD (LTL)**—A shipment which is less than the amount required to be eligible for truckload rates.

**LOADING ALLOWANCE**—A reduced rate or refund offered to shippers and/or consignees who load and/or unload the shipment.

**MANIFEST**—A list of items shipped, plus related details (often a copy of the freight bill).

**OVER, SHORT, AND DAMAGE REPORT**—Issued by a freight agent indicating any discrepancies between the bill of lading and freight on hand.

**PACKAGING LIST**—An itemization of package contents prepared by the shipper.

**PICKUP AND DELIVERY (PU & D)**—Transport from the shipper's dock to the consignee's dock.

**POINT OF ORIGIN**—The location where a transportation company receives the shipment.

**PREPAID FREIGHT**—Transportation charges which are paid by the shipper at the point of shipment.

**PRIVATE CARRIER**—A carrier that owns or leases vehicles and provides transportation services for the firm which owns it.

**RELEASED VALUE RATE**—A transportation rate based on a reduced value of the shipment which, in turn, limits the carrier's liability to a lesser amount.

**ROUTING**—Determination of how a shipment will move from the point of origin to the destination, including selection of carriers and geographic routes.

**SHIPPING RELEASE**—A form used by the purchaser to specify shipping instructions for goods purchased for delivery at a future date.

**STOPOVER PRIVILEGE**—An arrangement whereby a shipment can be stopped at stations en route to take advantage of transit privileges, such as complete loading or partial unloading.

**STORE DOOR DELIVERY**—Delivery to the consignee's receiving platform by motor vehicle or rail car.

**TRANSSHIPPING**—Transferring goods from one transportation line to another.

**UNIFORM FREIGHT CLASSIFICATION**—A listing of commodities showing the assigned class rate for determining rail freight rates, together with governing rules and regulations.

**WAYBILL**—A document prepared at a shipment's point of origin showing point of origin, destination, route, consignor, consignee, description of the shipment, and the amount charged for transportation.

**WEIGHT, GROSS**—Total combined weight of the article, container, and packing material.

**WEIGHT, NET**—Weight of the contents of a container or the cargo of a vehicle.

**WEIGHT, TARE**—Combined weight of an empty container and packing materials.

## Facing the Future

Taking control of transportation represents a challenge and an opportunity for the purchaser or supply manager to add significant value to the organization. With deregulation there is intense competition for the movement of goods, with truck, rail, and water carriers competing for tonnage and with carriers in the same mode vying for business. It behooves purchasers of transportation not only to become familiar with the fundamentals of transportation but to look for ways to creatively use price and service options to advantage.

Practitioners should also keep abreast of developments in the oversight of the transportation industry. Degregulation and reregulation may not be over. Expect cases to come to court which may challenge the ICC Termination Act. Any decisions handed down may prompt new legislation and regulations.

## Discussion Questions

1. What criteria would you use to select the best carrier?
2. What are the advantages of shipping by air versus by truck?
3. How would a buyer "control" the shipping decisions?
4. What is the difference between a general-purpose carrier and a contract carrier?
5. Who owns the material under the terms "FOB seller's plant, freight collect"?
6. What is meant by the term "intermodal"?

7. How would you plan to negotiate a long-term contract?
8. What is the difference between "common law" price lists and rules tariffs?
9. Do rate bureaus still exist? If so, what is their current function under deregulation?
10. What did the ICC Termination Act of 1995 (ICCTA) accomplish?
11. "Transportation services should be purchased much as any material or service is purchased." Analyze and discuss this view.
12. Some firms prefer to buy F.O.B. supplier's plant. What do you see as the major arguments for and against this policy? Discuss
13. What are Incoterms? Why are they important?
14. When a buyer specifies the method of transportation to be used in shipping an order, he or she has at least a dozen different choices in some cases. List and discuss the significant factors the buyer should consider when viewing the possibility of shipping by each of the following methods:

    **a.** Parcel Post
    **b.** Intercity bus service
    **c.** Air cargo

15. Answer question 4 with respect to the following methods of transportation:

    **a.** Freight forwarder
    **b.** Intercoastal or inland water freight
    **c.** Piggyback and fishyback
    **d.** Pipeline

16. Recognizing that there may be many specific exceptions, if you were to state a general rule, under what conditions is it usually most advantageous to use rail freight, and under what conditions is it usually most advantageous to use truck freight?
17. Is intermodal carriage increasing or decreasing in volume? Why do you think this is occurring?
18. What is the significance of the Staggers Rail Act of 1980? Of the Motor Carrier Act of 1980? Of the Shipping Act of 1984?
19. What is the difference between a class rate and a commodity rate?
20. **a.** Define the term "expedite."

    **b.** Define the term "trace."

    **c.** Under what conditions might a shipper or a purchaser engage in either of these activities?

21. **a.** Define the term "demurrage."

    **b.** Explain the different types of demurrage agreements under which a firm may operate.

22. Discuss in detail the various things a firm might do to reduce its transportation costs.
23. Why do some purchasers attempt to develop strategic alliances with carriers? Why do so few buying firms do this?

## References

■ *Armstrong's Guide To Third Party Logistics Providers and Dedicated Contract Carriers* (Stoughton, WI: Transportation Education Specialists 1995).
■ *NAPM Insights*, April 1995, "Supreme Court Rules for Shipper in Undercharge Case" (by Helen M. Pohlig).

- *NAPM Insights,* February 1995, "Negotiating with Cariers in Light of New Laws" (by W. J. Augello).
- *Purchasing Today™,* April 1996, "Logistics: The Road Less Traveled?" (by Thomas P. Hommrich).
- *Purchasing Today™,* March 1996, "Are You a Victim of Off-Bill Discounting?" (by M. Theodore Farris II).
- *Transportation & Distribution,* November 1996, "Making Logistics Count in Your Company" (by Edward J. Marien).
- *Transportation & Distribution,* September 1996, "Making Sense of Freight Terms of Sale" (by Edward J. Marien).
- *Transportation & Distribution*, July 1996, "Contract Carriage with Less Regulation" (by Edward J. Marien).
- *Transportation & Distribution,* May 1996, "Overcoming Claims as Losing Propositions" (by Edward J. Marien).

## Suggested Reading

Ballou, Ronald H. *Business Logistics/Supply Chain Management.* 5th ed. (Upper Saddle River, NJ: Prentice Hall, 2004).

Bowersox, D. J., D. J. Closs, and M. B. Cooper. *Supply Chain Logistics Management* (New York: McGraw-Hill/Irwin, 2002).

Coyle, John J., Edward J. Bardi, and Robert A. Novack. *Transportation,* 6th ed. (Mason, OH: South-Western College Publication, 2006).

Frazelle, Edward H. *World-Class Warehousing and Material Handling* (New York: McGraw-Hill, 2001).

*Incoterms, 2000* (New York: International Chamber of Commerce (Publishing, 2000).

Langley, C. J., G. R. Allen, and G. R. Tyndall. *Third-Party Logistics Study: Results and Findings of the 2001 Sixth Annual Study* (Tempe, AZ: Cap Gemini Ernst & Young, Institute for Supply Management, 2001).

Stewart, Emmett. *Excellence in Warehouse Management: How to Minimise Costs and Maximise Value* (West Sussex, England: John Wiley & Sons, 2005), http://www.wiley.com.

Stock, James R., and Douglas M. Lambert. *Strategic Logistics Management,* 4th ed. (New York: McGraw-Hill, 2001).

# Demand Management and Logistics

## CHAPTER OBJECTIVES

*After reading this chapter, you should be able to:*

1. Understand the empirical relationship between supply, demand, and logistics management.

2. Define the characteristics of supply, demand, and logistics management.

3. Understand the importance of an accurate forecast in managing supply.

4. Describe the impact of the bullwhip effect on the supply chain.

5. Explain the use of time fences in demand management.

## VIGNETTE: CIRCUS TENTS FOR MCC LOGISTICS

Steve Lilly, VP of Supply Chain Management for Monster Communications Corporation (MCC), watched as another large "circus-style" tent was raised outside one of the warehouses he managed. The tent was needed to handle the inventory that had accumulated over the last month as a result of late deliveries from Texas Digital Systems (TDS). TDS had been a reliable supplier in the past, but recent increases in orders from MCC clearly had exceeded TDS's capability and capacity.[1]

TDS supplied one specially designed rapid communications device (RCD) component that was kitted with 13 other parts at MCC's regional warehouses. The suppliers that provided the other 13 components were delivering their parts on time, and as a result, parts were being stockpiled in the warehouses. Since demand was roughly 90,000 kits per month and TDS was about a month behind on its deliveries, MCC was storing in excess of 1,170,000 parts. That volume exceeded MCC's total warehouse space across the

---

[1]This vignette is based on a real-world scenario witnessed by one of the authors at one of the world's largest telecommunications companies.

United States by over 770,000 parts. Tents were required to store the excesses at every regional warehouse across the United States except in Dallas, where the warehouse had large amounts of excess capacity.

At the last meeting with Steve's team of regional logistics managers, a discussion took place on TDS's responsibility for the inventory problems. Steve and his team also wanted to avoid similar problems in the future. The discussion quickly became heated when it was suggested that TDS send the appropriate managers to address both issues.

Bob Hoskins, Logistics manager of the California region, started the barrage: "Yeah, let's invite them! We can crucify their management right on the wall over there!" Bob pointed to the largest empty wall in the room.

Janet Baker, manager of Operations in Michigan, chimed in: "I agree. TDS has caused me to exceed my budget. It is making us look bad. I say we find a new supplier—pronto!"

Steve replied, "I don't think replacing TDS is an option. We committed to them for the long term in our last contract negotiation. Let's call Procurement and resolve whether canceling the contract is even an option." Steve called Rhonda Stevens, MCC's chief procurement officer, on the speaker phone to answer a couple of the group's questions. Steve asked the first question: "Rhonda, can we find another supplier to replace TDS?"

Rhonda replied, "Not an option, Steve. It would take at least six months to bid a new contract and get the new supplier tooled and trained to produce the products."

Bob chimed in: "Rhonda, how the heck did we get into a contract with a supplier that could not meet our demand?"

Rhonda replied, "Bob, TDS offered the lowest price and always delivered on time in the past, so we awarded the contract to them."

Getting a bit angry, Bob said, "Tell me something I don't know, Rhonda! Let me rephrase the question. What type of investigation of TDS did your Procurement group do to ensure that they could meet our demand? Did any of your people even visit their production facilities?"

After some hesitation Rhonda replied, "Well, no, we didn't visit their facilities. We have far too many suppliers to investigate each one thoroughly. Besides, no one ever consulted Procurement about any potential issues. And the only time we ever hear from Logistics is when a problem arises with a supplier."

This story is essentially true, including the highly negative comments from the logistics managers. They were angry. ∎

## CRITICAL THINKING QUESTIONS

1. How do companies get into these expensive supply chain problems?
2. How can such problems be avoided in the future?

(The answers are probably more obvious than you might think.)

# The Key to Supply Chain Management

Supply management is the key to supply chain management (SCM). While many functional areas lay claim to the emerging field of SCM, supply management has the strongest claim. The argument is simple: Since supply professionals are responsible for developing and managing the contractual, behavioral interrelationships between supply chain members, supply management is the critical function responsible for managing the supply chain.

The issue of how to harness the power of SCM is creating debate in upper management boardrooms and academic classrooms across the world. Firms need to come to terms with how they are going to improve their competitiveness in the future through SCM. Competition is not just firm versus firm but chain versus chain (or network versus network.)

## The SCM Triangle

As companies gear up for this chain versus chain struggle, the need to manage the supply chain effectively is becoming increasingly critical. We believe that successful Strategic Supply Chain Management consists of three critical components: world-class supply management, demand management, and logistics management.

## Evolution to Strategic SCM

Currently, at least three stages of SCM exist: (1) SCM is the management of the internal supply chain, (2) SCM is supplier-focused, and (3) SCM is the management of a network of enterprises which includes the customer as well as suppliers. Most firms invest their resources sequentially. Generally, firms evolve from the first stage through to the last over the course of several years of effort to improve SCM. World-class SCM encompasses all three stages operating in parallel.

**Internal Supply Chain Focus**   In this stage, the first priority of a business enterprise is to integrate and optimize its own operations before making any attempt to extend supply chain rationalization to external organizations. The internal customers need to acknowledge the presence of the supply management organization when they are implementing the product development and planning process.[2] Therefore, SCM may be defined as the integration of previously separate operations such as marketing, engineering, and operations within a business enterprise.

Historically, initial attempts at internal functional integration followed the materials management concept. Materials management was used to integrate activities such as purchasing, inventory management, material control, stores, warehousing, materials handling, inspection, receiving, and shipping. Further internal integration was achieved by linking information systems between sales order entry, production planning and control, and distribution. The focus on MRP/MRP II planning and control systems, along with the alignment of customer demand and supplier response, led to further functional integration.[3] In the 1990s, enterprise resource planning (ERP) systems were developed to complete internal information system integration and automate many activities.

A majority of firms attempting to engage in SCM are still preoccupied with the internal integration of functional activities and material and information flows. The real potential of SCM can be realized only after external integration of customers, key suppliers, and information flows has been attained.[4]

---

[2]Peter E. O'Reilly, "Attaining a World Class Supply Management Organization through Strategic Initiatives," presented at the 89th Annual International Supply Management Conference, Philadelphia, PA, April 2004, Tempe, AZ, ISM.

[3]Martin Christopher, *Logistics and Supply Chain Management: Strategies for Reducing Cost and Improving Service* (London: Financial Times/Pitman, 1998), pp. 18–19.

[4]Christine Harland, "Supply Chain Management," *Blackwell Encyclopedic Dictionary of Operations Management*, ed. Nigel Slack (Oxford, England: Blackwell Publishers, 1997), pp. 213–15.

**Supplier Focus**   The supplier focus stage of SCM emphasizes the importance of fostering long-term collaborative relationships with key suppliers. Collaboration with suppliers has been the focus of much of the supply management and contract management literature in recent years.[5] The thrust of this thinking is based on a belief in the elimination of adversarial relations between buyer and seller and the formation of long-term relationships with fewer suppliers to gain the benefits of economy of scale, reliability, and quality.

Often overlooked in the supplier-focused stage of SCM are the potential benefits derived from expanding the role of key suppliers in the supply chain. The expertise of key suppliers can provide technical and supportive assistance at a nominal cost when it is secured through purchased services.[6]

**Network Management Focus**   The network management focus stage of SCM recognizes the complex nature of business relationships. The drivers of this perspective emphasize outsourcing of nonstrategic functions and processes. The high level of outsourcing often results in greater physical separation of operations and functional areas. In such an environment, information technology becomes critical to maintain communications.

A network view helps one visualize accurately the true relationships between supply chain entities. The network view aids in developing an appreciation of the range of significantly different products, processes, markets, geographic markets, and time that are concurrently present in any supply chain.[7] The network perspective properly focuses on a reality in which multiple supply chains exist within the same network.

# Strategic Demand Management

A major driver of the recession of 2001–2002 was the proliferation of errors in forecasts which were not identified, analyzed, and acted on until billions of dollars worth of inventories had accumulated in some supply chains. The primary reason for inaction on the part of the supply chains that were caught with excessive inventory levels was the absence of demand management. Demand management is used to estimate, control, smooth, coordinate, balance, and influence the demand and supply for a firm's products and services in an effort to reduce total costs for the firm and its supply chain. Demand management recognizes that forecasts are developed at several points throughout an organization. Demand management does not develop forecasts. Rather, it accepts forecasts from other functions and updates them on the basis of actual, real-time demand. Demand management's need to reconcile forecast errors with the actual order rate of an enterprise is one of the most overlooked potentials in the successful management of inventory levels, customer satisfaction, staffing strategies, and facility expansion or contraction.

In addition, demand management works with the supply side to adjust the inflow of materials and products. Demand management is "a collaborative process that involves accurately determining how much product needs to be produced (the demand) at each level of the supply chain through the end customer."[8] It is responsible for creating a smooth master production schedule and for smoothing production after

---

[5]Richard L. Pinkerton, "The Evolution of Purchasing to Supply Chain Management,"; Business Briefing: European Purchasing and Logistics Strategies."; World Markets Research Centre, London, July 1999, pp. 16–28. Reprinted in *The Purchasing and Supply Yearbook, 2000 Editorial,* ed. John Q. Woods, and National Association of Purchasing Management (New York: McGraw-Hill).

[6]O'Reilly, "Attaining a World Class Supply Management Organization through Strategic Initiatives."

[7]Harland, "Supply Chain Management."

[8]Steve Miller, "21st Century Logistics: Harnessing the Demand Chain," presented at the 86th Annual International Conference Proceedings, Orlando, FL, 2001, Tempe AZ, ISM.

**Figure 21.1 |** Demand Management Information Flows

schedules have been released to internal production and external suppliers. Smoothing requires that demand managers recognize that demand management is a process that requires the utmost in coordination and communication between the responsible parties. Demand can change daily, weekly, and monthly. Demand managers must develop contingency plans with supply chain members to allow modification of short-term schedules when necessary. Demand management also balances the total costs of not meeting demand against the total costs of adding the additional resources required to meet demand.

Figure 21.1 shows the primary information flows required for demand management. No single figure can completely capture the full complexity of demand management activities and information flows between a single buying firm and a single supplying firm. The complexity increases exponentially as the "real-world" situation of multiple suppliers and buyers is included.

Figure 21.1 assumes that all firms have dedicated demand managers who are actively involved in demand decisions throughout the life cycle of the product and/or service. Demand managers are involved with product and service design teams in the early stages of design. Early involvement in design provides a critical opportunity for demand management to convey the "voice of the customer" on need issues and provide proactive contributions on strategic product mix decisions. Subsequent to design, demand managers must work tightly with internal marketing and production and supply managers to ensure that production planning at the strategic capacity and aggregate planning levels is communicated to and reconciled with suppliers.

At the demand planning level, demand management works with production and supply managers to reconcile the many problems inherent in the master schedule, which is based on the forecast and actual orders. The basic objectives of demand management are to create close collaboration among all trading partners and unify the demand and supply requirements of the business.[9] Effective demand management takes tactical and strategic corrective actions as required to bring forecast demand in line with actual demand from the marketplace. Tactical-level corrective actions require adjustment to the master schedule. At a strategic level, integrated operational planning "links three or more supply chains working together to determine the end-users' needs and then taking action up and down the chain to optimize operations."[10] If these adjustments to the schedule are not managed effectively, they can result in drastic fluctuations, producing a bullwhip effect throughout the supply chain.

## The Bullwhip Effect

Failure to estimate demand accurately and share information among supply chain entities can result in bloated inventory levels caused by a cumulative effect of poor information cascading up through a supply chain. Poor demand data force the supplying firm to carry additional inventory or increase lead times to account for the uncertainty. Either way, inventory levels in the supply chain are increased. If lead times are increased, the buyer (based on conventional reorder point calculations) will increase order quantities. The supplier will interpret the increase in the order quantity as increased customer demand. The supplier then will need to take action to increase capacity to meet the fictional trend. To add more irony, just as the supplier has added capacity to meet the increase in demand, demand falls off because the buying firm has excessive stock available. The supplier then will need to reduce its capacity through firing, selling assets, or some other approach. The problem of fictional or "phantom" demand has been termed the bullwhip effect in SCM. The following example presents another way in which the bullwhip effect can occur.

**Bullwhip Effect Example[11]**   An extreme example of this is the behavior of an individual employed as a sales representative at a large tobacco firm in Richmond, Virginia. Every evening he would telephone 10 tobacco retailers out of several hundred to obtain reports on the day's sales of his firm's cigarettes. Each of the retailers believed that the frequency of those queries was an indication of likely increased demand for cigarette products, and they all increased their orders with the tobacco firm. The sales representative noted the increase in retail orders and modified his own sales forecast input to the factory.

The manufacturing manager at the cigarette factory observed the upsurge in retail demand in the form of actual orders as well as his sales representative's modification (upward) of the forecast. He planned the addition of a third shift operation for the next month, informed supply management to order more materials, and asked human resources to hire additional workers for the next month. To meet the immediate upturn in demand, he authorized the use of overtime and expedited raw tobacco deliveries to fill the increased orders from the retailers. The cigarette firm had increased its capacity and its orders with its tobacco producers. The firm's tobacco growers concluded that the increase in orders from the factory

---

[9]John Yuva, "Demand Management: Creating Balance through Collaboration," *Inside Supply Management* 15, no. 3 (March 2004), p. 20.

[10]Miller, "21st Century Logistics: Harnessing the Demand Chain."

[11]The problems identified with the "Bullwhip effect" and false demand were first identified as "the Phoney Backlog" by the late Oliver Wight in the late 1970s. See Oliver W. Wight, *MRP II: Unlocking America's Productivity Potential* (Williston, VT: Oliver Wight Publications, 1981), pp. 33–38.

reflected an increased market demand for cigarettes. Accordingly, they made plans to expand planting acreage for the next season and purchase additional harvesting equipment and hire additional casual labor.

However, toward the middle of the following month, tobacco retailers noticed that their stocks of cigarettes were not moving from the shelves as they had expected. In fact, sales were declining as the result of ongoing antismoking campaigns and the increase in the cost of tobacco products resulting from increases in tobacco product taxes. Swamped with unsold inventories of cigarettes, the retailers called the sales representative and canceled virtually all outstanding orders. They maintained that they now had many weeks of inventory on the shelves and that they had to work off the inventory before placing additional orders. The tobacco firm's sales manager reacted quickly by slashing the sales forecast. The manufacturing manager reacted to the change in the sales forecast and the cancellation of retail orders by eliminating the third and second shifts and furloughing all the newly hired workers as well as eliminating all overtime. Supply management canceled its orders for raw tobacco with the growers, who in turn canceled their orders for new harvesters, labor, and so on. Everyone involved in this scenario wondered, "What went wrong?"

## Evolution of Strategic Demand

Forecasting often has been viewed as being minimally more accurate than a glance into a crystal ball. Historically, many organizations have employed manual and/or visual systems of order replenishment. Such approaches generally fall under the category of reorder point replenishment techniques (ROP). Later, calculations on the effects of setup, holding, and carrying costs in addition to purchased and manufactured lot size quantities were considered and resulted in replenishment calculations known as statistical reorder point techniques. With the introduction of the computer into the manufacturing and distribution environment, material requirements planning and distribution requirements planning (MRP and DRP) were used to schedule orders for products against lead times and bills of materials. The resultant effect was a drastic decrease in inventory at all levels (finished goods, work-in-process, components, and raw materials) held in the production system. It is important to remember that wise forecasters combine many different forecasts by using multiple quantitative and judgment methods and keep adjusting for new developments.[12]

Further integrative refinements (known familiarly as manufacturing resources planning and distribution resources planning—MRP II and DRP II) of computer-based information systems provided capabilities to manage production capacity as well as the demand for materials. These planning and information systems enabled business enterprises to gauge the financial impact of various inventory-customer service-capacity decisions effectively and run "what-if" simulations of various material and capacity scenarios without the risk of inventory, labor, equipment, or facilities commitment.

Later, the many influences of planning techniques such as just-in-time (JIT) manufacturing and its requirements for lean operations, total quality, continuous process improvement, and the elimination of waste in all forms further defined the need for many functional disciplines to communicate and collaborate in ways never before envisioned.

Most recently, many businesses have purchased and installed enterprise information systems. The potential of those systems lies in the seamless integration of the many databases typically found in any firm. Thus equipped, the prototypical planning and control information systems applied to production and distribution have become known as the step beyond MRP II: enterprise resource planning (ERP).

---

[12]Philip Kotler, *Marketing Management, Analysis, Planning, Implementation, and Control*, 10th ed. (Upper Saddle River, NJ: Prentice Hall, 2000).

While the advent of highly integrated enterprise planning systems and the application of e-commerce, e-procurement, and B2B capabilities have manifested themselves in recent years, by themselves they do not address the fundamental questions posed by effective demand management. For instance, thorny issues often arise when trade-off issues are considered. When the following questions arise as a firm examines the levels of customer service in terms of inventory on hand, there is often no clear solution:

■ What is enough inventory?

■ What is too much inventory?

■ What are the cost implications?

■ What are the effects on customer service levels?

■ What short- and long-range capacity management decisions must be made to address demand (i.e., overtime for line workers or outsourcing to contract manufacturers)?

With traditional manual replenishment techniques and later disaggregated legacy information systems, the answers to these vital questions most often were not available. There were simply not enough resources on hand (both workers and machines) to answer such questions easily or quickly. With the advent of enterprise information systems and the emergence of the transparent and electronic seamless transfer of planning information between businesses, the true potential of sharing planning information throughout the supply chain finally may be realized.

## Forecasting Demand

The most important output of demand management for a particular product or service is an accurate forecast of customer demand. What is a forecast? In terms of SCM, a forecast is an estimate of future demand. In other words, it is a calculated guess or estimate about the future demand for a firm's products and services under conditions of uncertainty. Forecasts fall into two categories: quantitative and qualitative.

Quantitative methods require mathematical analysis of historical data. Common mathematical approaches based on historical data are regression analysis, moving averages, and exponential smoothing. A frequently favored forecasting method among managers who have little knowledge of forecasting techniques is the naïve method, in which the last period's historical value becomes the forecast for the next period. However, historical data may not be complete or available.

Qualitative forecasts are created subjectively, using estimates from sources such as market surveys, in-depth interviews, and experts. When historical data are available, qualitative forecasting usually is employed to verify or adjust quantitative forecasting methods. In some cases, when historical data are not available, qualitative forecasting is the only alternative.

In most organizations, forecasting starts in the marketing department and/or with an economic forecasting staff. In other words, we take our cue from the sales forecast. For example, this forecast is the source for the master schedule in MRP and ERP programs.

Why are forecasts necessary in SCM? The primary reason is that lead times exist for production, distribution, and services. If lead times were zero, demand could be met as it arose. Since lead times do exist, supply chains must operate on the basis of forecasts.

Most managers today do not trust forecasts because they are fraught with error. Comments often heard from supply managers in industry are:

■ "Forecasts are always inaccurate—why try to improve them?"

■ "Forecasts are always wrong—they cannot be made right!"

■ "Forecasts constantly change!"

■ "Someone must be to blame for an inaccurate forecast!"

■ "If only we had a good computerized forecasting software module."

■ "You cannot believe the numbers!"

■ "Using statistical forecasting tools takes too much time."

## Planning with Time Fences

Many companies reduce uncertainty in demand by establishing time fences. A time fence reflects management decisions regarding production and supplier commitments about changes allowed to the scheduling of materials and capacity elements. Figure 21.2 presents three typical approaches to time fences: frozen, slushy, and fluid.

Typically, the demand time fence is for a short period, such as the current production month. The demand time fence establishes planning rules which, if broken, may prove very disruptive and/or costly to a firm. The most common rule is that production schedules that are within the demand time fence cannot be changed even if the demand forecast is changed. Thus, schedules in the demand time fence often are said to be "frozen," that is, made very difficult or even impossible to change without top management approval.

Within the "slushy" time fence, many commitments for a firm's material, capacity, capital equipment, and related financial resources can be made on an advisory basis. The intermediate period is usually two to six months into the future. Some actions cannot be delayed until the frozen period. For example, materials with a long lead time may need to be ordered.

"Fluid" time fences acknowledge that greater uncertainty exists as forecasts are extended farther out in the planning horizon. Commitments for materials, capacity, capital equipment, and related financial resources are highly subject to change. The chief advantage of planning during the "fluid" time fence for

**Figure 21.2 |** The Concept of Time Fencing in Demand Management

Source: Thomas E. Vollmann, William L. Berry, and D. Clay Whybark, *Manufacturing Planning and Control Systems,* 4th ed. (New York: McGraw-Hill, 1997), p. 246.

materials, capacity, capital equipment, and finances is to provide as much forward visibility as possible. In SCM, that forward visibility about the changing nature of demand is of critical importance for suppliers so that they can manage their own resources effectively. Buying firms that communicate planned orders on a continuous basis with their supply chain members will achieve a distinct advantage over firms that do not share their plans.

### Implications for Supply Management

Since a primary role of demand management is to coordinate demand between the buying firm and supplying firm, demand management must work effectively with supply management and supply chain management. Demand management requires open, honest, trusting, and collaborative relationships between customers and suppliers throughout the supply chain. This point underscores the critical importance of trust and relationship management in effective SCM.

The greatest potential—and challenge—for effective supply and demand management is to achieve collaborative planning, forecasting, and replenishment driven by actual customer demand. Changes in demand patterns suggest that the formal planning evolutions that once were confined largely to processes and functions within a firm must be shared with all supply chain members, particularly downstream customers.

Demand management requires a shift from a focus on component- and commodity-level planning to a focus on strategic product– and subassembly-level planning. Demand and supply managers must become involved in strategic planning if they are to be relevant in the management of the supply chain.

The use of interfirm supply chain contracts can help achieve optimization of inventory levels for entire channels of distribution. The use of mathematical approaches such as buyback contracts can be useful tools to reduce risk in demand management.[13]

# Strategic Logistics Management

Logistics management forms the third side of the SCM triangle. Logistics professionals play an important role in the success of supply chain management in the management of transportation, storage, and warehousing activities. Unfortunately, many companies define logistics as synonymous with SCM, ignoring the contributions and roles of supply management and demand management.

### Logistics Defined

Logistics management deals with the handling, movement, and storage activities within the supply chain, beginning with suppliers and ending with the customer. One of the best-selling books in logistics states: "Logistics is the part of the supply chain process that plans, implements, and controls the efficient, effective flow and storage of raw materials, in-process inventory, finished goods, services, and related information from point of origin to point of consumption (including inbound, outbound, internal and external movements) for the purpose of conforming to customer requirements."[14]

### The Role of Logistics in Supply Chain Management

As the competitive context of business continues to change, logistics activities and processes must be integrated into strategic-level thinking and planning. "From procurement, to inventory management, inbound supplies and materials, and outbound distribution, logistics is the performance that links them

---

[13]Wallace J. Hopp, *Supply Chain Science*, Burr Ridge, IL, McGraw-Hill/Irwin, 2008, pp. 195–201.

[14]J. J. Coyle, E. J. Bardi, and R. A. Novak, *Transportation*, 6th ed. (Mason, OH: Thomson South-Western, 2006).

together physically."[15] Because of the critical role of logistics, much of the focus on logistics has been on the reduction of cycle times in logistics activities. Cycle time reduction and the elimination of waste in logistics processes have had a direct correlation with the enhancement of customer satisfaction. Customer needs vary, and firms can tailor logistics systems to serve them better—and more profitably.

Logistics and supply management will realize their greatest gains in efficiency and effectiveness through collaboration. Only then can both traditionally separate disciplines achieve a world-class supply chain. The major professional organization in logistics is the Council of Supply Chain Management Professionals in Chicago, IL.[16]

## Eliminate the Warehouse, If Possible

Sun Microsystems in Santa Clara, California, has developed what it calls a "one-touch supply chain" which eliminates the distribution warehouse component of its supply chain.[17] Under the old system, the supplier (in Asia) built and boxed the server board and shipped it to an external manufacturing hub and then to a third-party integration-box configuration center, which sent the product to a distribution hub, which sent it to a channel and reseller for shipment to the final customer. Under the new system the board and box go directly to the customer for standard products and to a geographic configuration center for custom orders. Sun now ships more than 50 percent of the orders directly to customers from suppliers, and that has reduced logistics costs by 20 percent and finished goods inventory by as much as 40 percent and increased customer predictability performance by more than 10 percent. Interestingly, Sun had to fool the ERP system into believing the material was on-site in order to ship and invoice the order. The lesson here is never to be a slave to an ERP system.

# Concluding Remarks

For many in the field of SCM, the future holds substantive and far-reaching changes. These changes are largely driven by the following trends:

- Institutionalization of the SCM perspective.
- Increasing emphasis on supply chain relationships.
- Increasing emphasis on the long-term view.
- Use of information technology to enhance supply chain communications.
- Use of information technology to foster rapid decision making.
- An increasing focus which looks "outward" toward the intricacies of supplier and customer relations.
- Learning to manage demand as opposed to only reacting to it.
- The emergence of the supply management professional as a "manager and facilitator of relationships" versus an information broker whose attention is defined by commodity knowledge.

A thorough grasp of the continually evolving perspectives of SCM is a necessary component of the skill set of any proactive supply management professional. Such perspectives recognize the continuing

---

[15]Roberta J., Duffy, "Logistics: A Custom Link," *Purchasing Today* 10, no. 3 (March 1999), p. 22.

[16]Founded in 1963 as the National Council of Physical Distribution Management, the council changed its name in 1985 to the Council of Logistics Management, and again in 2005 to the Council of Supply Chain Management Professionals. http://cscmp.org.

[17]John, Yuva, "A One-Touch Supply Chain: How Sun Microsystems Steamlined Its Inventory Process," *Inside Supply Management*, December 2007, pp. 25–27.

need to integrate the many competencies traditionally resident in other functional disciplines, particularly demand management and logistics. Further, successful supply chain optimization depends on the coordination of cross-functional competencies in cross-enterprise teams. The supply management professional is the logical "team leader" for such initiatives.

## Discussion Questions

1. Describe the links between supply management, production planning and control, and logistics in a supply chain management environment.
2. What characteristics define supply management?
3. What characteristics define demand management?
4. What characteristics define logistics management?
5. Why is it so difficult to prepare an accurate forecast for planning production?
6. What are some typical approaches (tools and techniques) used in deriving a forecast?
7. What are the sources of demand in a typical manufacturing firm?
8. Where do forecasts come from?
9. What is meant by the bullwhip effect?
10. Explain the use of time fences in demand management.
11. What are the roles and responsibilities of a firm in communicating demand throughout the supply chain?
12. What are some ways to reduce the logistics cycle time?

## Internet Exercise

### Infor SCM: Transportation and Logistics

Visit the "Transportation and Logistics" website below. Read about one software supplier's solutions to navigating the complexities of global transportation.

(http://www.infor.com/solutions/scm/transportation/)

1. Why is it essential to "manage orders from inception to delivery"?
2. Click on "Transportation Planning" and explain how Infor SCM software helps reduce transportation costs and improve service levels.
3. Click on "Route Planning" and identify some issues of route optimization.
4. Click on "Transportation Management" and explain how this software can improve supply chain efficiency.

## Suggested Reading

Ballou, Ronald H. *Business Logistics/Supply Chain Management,* 5th ed. (Upper Saddle River, NJ: Pearson/Prentice Hall, 2004).

Bechtel, Christian, and Jayaram Jayanth. "Supply Chain Management: A Strategic Perspective," *International Journal of Logistics Management* 8, no. 1 (1997), pp. 15–34.

Bender, Paul. "Going around the World Makes the (Business) World Go 'Round," *Inside Supply Management* 17, no. 2 (February 2006), p. 34.

Bowersox, Donald, David Loss, and M. Bixby Cooper. *Supply Chain Logistics Management* (Burr Ridge, IL: McGraw-Hill/Irwin, 2005).

Bruning, Bob, and Rich Hoole. "Adding Value through Demand Management," *Inside Supply Management* 16, no. 6 (June 2005), p. 8.

Cavinato, Joseph L. "The Latest Trends in Logistics," *Purchasing Today* 11, no. 5 (May 2000), p. 76.

Chopra, Sunil, and Peter Meindl. *Supply Chain Management: Strategy, Planning, and Operation* (Upper Saddle River, NJ: Prentice Hall, 2004).

Cohen, Shoshanah. "Forging the Chain," *American Executive,* May 2005, pp. 28–30.

Cohen, Shoshanah, and Joseph Roussel. *Strategic Supply Chain Management: The Five Disciplines for Top Performance* (Burr Ridge, IL: McGraw-Hill/Irwin, 2005).

Cook, Thomas A. *Global Sourcing Logistics: How to Manage Risk and Gain Competitive Advantage in a Worldwide Marketplace* (New York: AMACOM, 2007).

Cooper, M. C., and M. Ellram. "Characteristics of Supply Chain Management and the Implications for Purchasing and Logistics Strategy," *International Journal of Logistics Management* 4, no. 2 (1993), pp. 13–24.

Coyle, J. J., E. J. Bardi, and R. A. Novak. *Transportation*, 6th ed. (Mason, OH: Thomson South-Western, 2006).

Emmett, Stuart. *Supply Chain in 90 Minutes (Integrating the Flow of Goods and Information from Supply to Demand).* (Gloucestershire, UK: Management Books, 2005).

Hoole, Rick. "Demand Management: Optimizing the Demand-Side Drivers of Total Cost of Ownership," presented at the 89th Annual International Supply Management Conference, Philadelphia, PA, April 2004, Tempe, AZ, ISM.

Jacobs F. Robert, Robert B. Chase, and Nicholas J. Aquilano. *Operations Management for Competitive Advantage,* 12th ed. (Burr Ridge, IL: McGraw-Hill, 2009).

Krajewski, Lee J., Larry P. Ritzman, and Manoj K. Malhotra. *Operations Management: Process and Value Chains,* 8th ed. (Upper Saddle River, NJ: Prentice Hall, 2007).

Lambert, D. M., and R. Burduroglo. "Measuring and Selling the Value of Logistics," *International Journal of Logistics Management* 11, no. 1 (2000), pp. 1–17.

Lambert, Douglas, M. *Supply Chain Management: Processes, Partnerships, Performance,* 2d ed. (Sarasota, FL: Supply Chain Management Institute, 2006).

Seifert, Dirk. *Collaborative Planning, Forecasting, and Replenishment: How to Create a Supply Chain* (New York: AMACOM, 2003).

Tracy, John J., Jr. "You Can See Eye to Eye," *Purchasing Today* 10, no. 3 (March 1999), p. 12.

Van Hoek, Remko I. "The Purchasing and Control of Supplementary Third-Party Logistics," *Journal of Supply Chain Management* 36, no. 4 (Fall 2000), p. 14.

Wight, Oliver. *The Executive's Guide to Successful MRP II. (Oliver Wight Manufacturing)* (New York, NY: John Wiley & Sons, 1993).

Wisner, Joel D., Keah-Choon Tan, and G. Keong Leong. *Principles of Supply Chain Management: A Balanced Approach,* 2nd ed., Mason, OH, South-Western Cengage Learning. See the Demand Forecasting, pp. 137–172 and Resource Planning-Systems, pp. 172–214.

Yuva, John. "Collaborative Logistics: Building a United Network," *Inside Supply Management* 13, no. 5 (May 2002), p. 42.

Yuva, John. "Demand Management: Creating Balance through Collaboration," *Inside Supply Management,* March 2004, pp. 20–27.

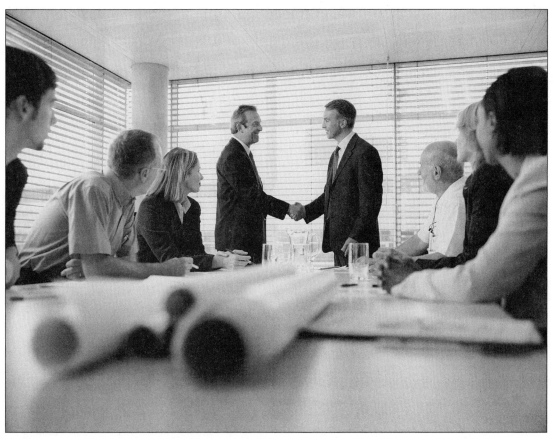

# Implementing Value
# Network Management

Implementation of Value Network Management requires planning to accomplish all the concepts, methods, procedures, techniques and philosophies contained in Chapters 1–21.

Relationships are the key to both successful supply management and successful supply chain management. Relationships are where companies can realize the greatest impact on the bottom line.

Chapter 22 describes a path to implementing not only relationships but all the concepts that have been set forth in this textbook. This chapter demonstrates Dr. Robert Kemp's belief that leadership is the key to successful supply management implementation. We hope you enjoy the change from the necessarily prescriptive writing in this book to a more narrative style in the concluding chapter. ∎

# Implementing Value Network Management

*After reading this chapter, you should be able to:*

1. Describe the power of Value Network Management (VNM).

2. Understand why Value Network Management is the future of supply management, logistics, and marketing.

3. Understand the various stages of implementation of Supply Chain Management as it evolves to VNM.

4. Understand the role of leadership in effecting change to VNM.

5. Recognize the characteristics that make role models effective.

6. Distinguish between inconsequential training and training to improve organizational performance.

7. Realize how the concepts presented in the previous chapters of this text are used to achieve VNM.

## Overview

Value Network Management addresses the fact that business in the modern world is conducted in a network fashion. It is far easier to visualize chains, whether supply chains or value chains, but truth be known, we live and operate in a world of networks! Networks are flexible virtual systems linked by communication systems and collaborative relationships. Within any network, many things are happening simultaneously. Cooperative relationships must be established with suppliers and their suppliers back to Mother Earth and the marketing and distribution systems which bring the goods and services to the ultimate customer. Networks are designed and managed to drive cost out while ensuring that one member does not benefit at the expense of another. World-class value networks are highly adaptive: They focus on value and speed, they are innovative, and they are tightly integrated.

Obviously, the implementation of Value Network Management requires many changes throughout the firm, especially in marketing. However, this is a book on supply management. Accordingly, this chapter will focus on the supply aspects of Value Network Management.

# Megatronics: Background

Two months ago, you were selected to become the new Vice President of Supply Management at Megatronics,[1] a global manufacturer of test and measurement equipment with $10 billion in annual sales revenue. The position of Vice President of Supply Management is a new one which has replaced the previous position, Director of Purchasing. The Vice President of Supply Management will report to the President. Megatronics' average pretax profit is 3 percent, or $300 million. Megatronics' current spend is $5.25 billion. The firm has over 800 employees in supply management worldwide. The supply management departments at corporate headquarters and the four operating divisions manage a total annual operating budget of $75 million. There is one division in the United States, one in Europe, and two in Asia.

Megatronics recently completed a strategic planning session focusing on surviving and thriving during the coming years. The following vision statement and value proposition were agreed to at the meeting:

## Vision Statement

Megatronics combines forces with its customers and suppliers to create world-class value networks which anticipate and meet its customers' needs in a timely and cost-effective manner. It embraces customer research; cost-effective, reliable, customer-friendly products which are profitable for the company; a global perspective; and innovation. It addresses and balances the needs of all stakeholders in a highly ethical manner. Each person who comes in contact with Megatronics—customer, employee or supplier—should enjoy the experience.

## Value Proposition

Megatronics, together with its customer and supplier networks, will:

- Reduce Megatronics' new product development time by 50 percent.
- Cut time to market by 30 percent.
- Reduce post-introduction revisions (upgrades and changes, etc.) by 70 percent.
- Increase customer satisfaction from 85 percent to 98 percent.
- Increase the impact of the firm's test and measurement equipment on customer profitability by 15 percent.

Recognizing the increasing role of supply management, CEO Art Hughes decided to create a new operating and executive committee position: Vice President of Supply Management. A worldwide search of potential supply executives led to your selection. President Frank Lazarus was assigned the task of agreeing

---

[1]The name Megatronics was coined for this chapter. It is not intended to bear any similarity to an actual firm.

to the specifics of your employment. During the negotiation leading to your employment, you and President Lazarus agreed to the following terms:

- *Compensation:* Your base salary will be $450,000 per year plus a potential $450,000 per year bonus, based on meeting target goals, which will be awarded as stock grants; there is also an award fee provision.

- *Hiring authority:* You may hire a maximum of 16 new supplier development professionals. You can decide where each will be assigned: to corporate supply management or to one of Megatronics' four divisions.

- *Career development:* You are authorized to invest $3.25 million to retain a consulting firm which will work with you and your colleagues to (1) develop position descriptions (P.D.'s) for your headquarters staff and the U.S. operating division. (Once established, these P.D.'s will be adapted to the overseas operating divisions.) These P.D.'s will be based on the skills required to deal successfully with the challenging world of Value Network Management. The positions will be established with career development in mind so that all personnel can understand the opportunities for career advancement, will identify gaps between assigned personnel and their position descriptions, and will be used to develop a training program providing the opportunity to learn the skills necessary to meet the demands of the appropriate position descriptions and the skills required for consideration for promotion. All members of Megatronics' supply management system are to receive appropriate training, not only members of the supply management departments.

- *Executive status:* You will become Vice President of Supply Management and a member of the executive committee. You will become a member of the corporate strategic planning group that is composed of the CEO (Art Hughes) and the president (Frank Lazarus) and the vice presidents of Marketing (Andy Allen), Operations (Barbara Withers), Engineering (Mike Hall), and Finance (Dianne Pattison).

- *Obligations:* Simply stated, your obligations are in the following four areas:

1. Reduce the cost of purchased goods and services by an average of 5 percent per year, or $1.575 billion over the next six years, based on this year's expenditures. (A detailed measurement system was agreed to.) The reduction assumes a steady state of purchased goods and services over the next six years.

2. Reduce incoming material defects from a current average of 1,000 ppm[2] to 10 ppm over the next five years.

3. Improve cutting-edge technology inflow by 10 percent per year. (When Megatronics develops a new or modified design, cutting-edge technology from suppliers will be integrated where appropriate. Measurement will be based on an increase in the percentage of new technology components in designs.)

4. Reduce the average product development cycle by 20 percent per year by your third year as the Chief Supply Officer.

Success will be based on a combination of action plans and documented success implementing these goals.

---

[2]PPM is a common term in modern-day business. It means defects per million.

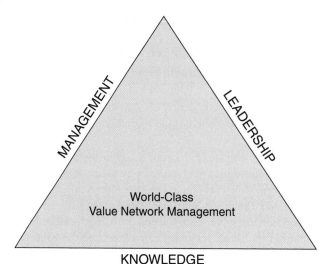

**Figure 22.1 |** Three Critical Skills

## Leadership

Shortly after accepting this offer, you met with your mentor and former instructor, Professor George W. Zinke of the University of San Luis Obispo (USLO), to discuss the opportunities and possible dangers of this challenge. True to form, Professor Zinke could not help but profess, in this case not the glories of supply management but the crucial role of leadership in making the desired transformation in Megatronics' supply management system. He pointed out that your job requires you to demonstrate three critical skills. Professor Zinke jumped to his white board and drew Figure 22.1.

He stated, "You've demonstrated excellence in the areas of knowledge and management." (You guess that he forgot about the A– he gave you in Strategic Cost Management.) "But leadership is the key. I've watched too many of our graduates become superstar supply managers and then plateau. They appear to have the knowledge and management skills but, I suspect, not the leadership skills."

Captured by Professor Zinke's aura of excitement, you asked, "Professor, how do you define leadership?"

The good professor responded, "Let's look at what really successful leaders do. They help members of their organizations establish a vision of what they want to contribute to the larger organization, their stakeholders, and society."[3] The resulting vision statement must tell people what's expected of them in the broadest sense, provide a sense of direction, energize them, and stretch them—but not to the point of breaking— and should serve as the basis of the organization's strategies.

"The leader then helps all members of the organization prepare for necessary change and helps them cope with the change as they struggle through it. He or she must motivate and facilitate necessary adaptive work by all members of the organization. Highly successful leaders energize people, maintain focus in facing adversity, listen actively, communicate clearly and convincingly, know how and when to disarm conflicts, function as empathetic mentors and process-oriented facilitators, and adapt to change quickly. One of the challenges you face is that Value Network Management (VNM) requires more than thinking

---

[3]Mary Siegfried, "Filling the Leadership Void," *Inside Supply Management*, April 2007, pp. 22–25.

### Burt-Lynch Supply Chain Evolution Model*

#### Building to World Class

| STAGE OF DEVELOPMENT AND THINKING / VARIABLE | 1. Purchasing Clerical-Tactical Buying | 2. Procurement Bid-Based Transactional Buying | 3. Supply Chain Management Process Based | 4. Value Chain Management Strategic | 5. Value Network Management Systemic |
|---|---|---|---|---|---|
| | | | Quality, Just In Time, Total Cost of Ownership | Innovation, Top and Bottom Line, Internal Integration; Revenue and Bottom Line Impacts, Increase Share Holder Value, Transform Innovation into Value | Total Value Impact, Innovation, Costs, Revenue, Speed; Present and Future Revenue, Bottom Line Impacts, Supplier and Stakeholder Impact |
| Value Driver | Timely Availability, Convenience | Purchase Price | Improve Bottom Line, Some Consideration of Revenue Impacts | Moderate Integration Internal and External Integration: Supply, R&D, Logistics, Operations, Engineering, Marketing, Customer Service | Full Internal and External Integration: Supply, Procurement, Logistics, Operations, Engineering, R&D, Sales, Marketing, Service, Customer's Strategy |
| Financial Impact | Overhead Cost Center | Improve Bottom Line No Consideration of Revenue Impacts | Partial Internal Integration Procurement, Logistics, Operations, Engineering | | |
| Integration Level and Functional Elements | No Internal Integration Purchasing | Low Internal Integration Procurement and Logistics | Through put, Global Impact | Coordination and Synchronicity, Interconnectedness, Relationships and Trust | Hyper-Competition, Technology Hybridization, Speed, Innovation, and Customization |
| Basis of Competitive Advantage | Do the Job | Leverage Size of Buyer, Power Dynamics between Buyer and Seller | Coordination and Cost, Develop Suppliers | Speed, Effectiveness, Monitor Supply Environment | Innovation, Synchronicity, Synergy, Monitor Customer Environment |
| Performance Metrics | Timeliness and Efficiency | Low Component/Unit Cost, On-Time Delivery | Process Innovation, Develop Requirements, Near Defect-Free Supply | Speed and Integration, Design Supply Base, Integrated Supply Strategy | New Processes, Systems Solutions, Leverage Supplier Technology |
| Innovation Metrics | Nothing | Squeeze the Vendor, Internet Auctions | | | Customer's Future Needs, Industry Trends, Connectivity |
| Knowledge | Thomas Directory, Phone Book, Rolodex | e-Commerce, "Should Cost" Analysis | Understand Suppliers | Understand Industries, Supply Base | Multi-Dimensional, Collaborative, Networked |
| Supplier Relationships | Personal, Suppliers are an Expense | Adversarial and Transactional, Suppliers are an Expense | Transactional and Collaborative, Suppliers are an Expense | Transactional, Collaborative, and Alliance, Suppliers are an Asset | Vision and Values Based, Suppliers are an Asset |
| Time Focus | Isolated from Customer | Reactive to Customer | Responsive to Customer | Proactive to Customer | Pre-Active with Customer |
| Environmental | Not Considered | Added Cost Factor | Considered As Part of TCO | Proactive as Market Differentiator for Customer | Pre-Active with Customer to Reengineer as Added Value |
| | Note: Some elements of an earlier stage are carried as a foundation into the next stage, while other elements may be discarded. | | | | |
| Rating | 1.0   1.5 | 2.0   2.5 | 3.0   3.5 | 4.0   4.5 | 5.0  World Class |

**Figure 22.2 |** The Burt-Lynch Supply Chain Evolution Model

*Copyright D.N. Burt & R.P. Lynch. Evolved from* The American Keiretsu *by David N. Burt and Michael F. Doxle. Business One-Irwin, Homewood, IL, 1993, p. 21.*

outside the supply management box. The old supply management box was a set of artificially imposed constraints that limited proactive, strategic, and synergistic efforts. Recently, I attended a workshop in which Professor David Burt and his colleague Robert Porter Lynch introduced what they call a supply chain evolution map (see Figure 22.2). This model should allow you to benchmark where you are and develop plans to help you get where you want to go!

"VNM calls for destroying the old box that was reactive and clerical and creating a new vision where these constraints are removed and the leadership capabilities and capacities are enabled and unleashed. VNM also addresses the fact that business in the modern world is conducted in a network fashion. It is far easier to visualize chains, whether supply chains or value chains. Networks are flexible virtual systems linked together by communication systems and alliances.

"Within any network, many things are happening simultaneously. Value networks focus on the ultimate customer. They are designed and managed to drive cost out while ensuring that one member does not benefit at the expense of another. World-class value networks are highly adaptive: they focus on value and speed: They are innovative, and they are tightly integrated."

You responded, "I'm not so sure, Professor Zinke. Many people in our field may not be capable of doing what you are describing. Must a person be born with these skills, or can they be learned?"

"Fortunately, they can be learned. One of our most successful programs at USLO is a Master's in Executive Leadership. It's taught in a user-friendly, nontraditional format. I encourage you to enroll yourself and a cross-functional team of supply professionals at the earliest possible time. In the meantime, there are five literary pieces that I would encourage you to read. Relax. Three of them are only two or three pages each. I have asked several highly respected colleagues to commit to writing their observations on three of the great leaders of supply management." (At this point Professor Zinke hands you Exhibits 22.1, 22.2, and 22.3. The three write-ups are on Dave Nelson; Thomas Stallkamp, formerly of Chrysler; and the late Gene Richter.) "There is much to learn from these leaders! The fourth reading, in my mind, is a world-class article on leadership: 'The Work of Leadership.' The article appeared in the December 2001 issue of the *Harvard Business Review*, and I also encourage you to obtain and read an outstanding book: *Becoming A Master Manager*. One additional thought: As soon as possible, it would be great if you could arrange for action-oriented training on effective leadership for all managers."

"As we discussed, the leader helps all the members of the organization prepare for necessary change. The transformation to Value Network Management is an incredible shift in both thinking and action."

---

## EXHIBIT 22.1 | THE STRATEGIC LEADERSHIP SKILLS OF R. DAVID NELSON

*By Dr. Robert Kemp*[4]

Strategic Leadership inspires others to greatness and empowers them to reach world-class goals. Strategic *supply management* leaders involve their teams in creating a vision for excellence and a road map for achieving efficiencies, effectiveness, and growth, both internally and within the supply base. For more than 50 years, R. David Nelson has epitomized this kind of leader. At TRW, he rose through the ranks from a worker in the metallurgical laboratories in 1957 to Director of Purchasing Worldwide in 1985. In 1987 he became Vice President–Purchasing at Honda of America Manufacturing, where he served from 1987 to 1997. During his four and one-half years at Deere & Co., Nelson created a hunger for world-class excellence and fostered the organizational cooperation required to reach it. In 2002, Nelson joined Delphi Corporation as Vice President–Global Supply Management, where he led its worldwide supply management operations until 2007. David is now CEO and Chief Supply Chain Officer at Best Window Company.

[4]Robert A. Kemp, Ph.D., CPM, President, Kemp Enterprises, Professor Emeritus, Drake University. Dr. Kemp served as the President of the National Association of Purchasing Management (NAPM) in 1997–1998 and was the 2005 winner of the J. Shipman Gold Medal Award, the profession's highest honor.

One of Nelson's lasting achievements at Honda of America was the increased use of domestic suppliers. As Vice President–Purchasing, Nelson and his team added more than 250 domestic suppliers to the supply base. Local content in American-made products increased from 40 to 90 percent, and domestic purchases rose from $600 million to $6 billion. Under his leadership, one of Purchasing's most dramatic accomplishments was the use of best practices to reduce the cost of the new model 1998 Honda Accord by more than 20 percent, compared to the previous model. In 1992, McKinsey & Co. recognized the company as a leader in procurement practices. In 1995 *Purchasing Magazine* presented Honda of America with its Medal of Excellence—purchasing's highest award. In 1996, Honda of America rewarded Nelson by naming him Senior Vice President of Purchasing and Corporate Affairs and, in 1997, promoting him to the Honda of America Board of Directors. He also served on the Corporate Executive Committee and the Global Purchasing Council.

Nelson joined Deere & Co. in December 1997 as Vice President, Worldwide Supply Management. His directive: Make John Deere's supply base the most competitive in the world. With the support of top Deere leadership, Nelson established ambitious goals, recruited a strong leadership team from inside and outside the company, and married the best of his ideas with those of the divisions and factories. The result was standardized, cross-divisional supply management processes that now are paying off.

One of Nelson's first priorities was to enhance John Deere's supplier development process. John Deere immediately added 94 supplier development engineers, 4 of whom had Ph.D.s, and increased its involvement with key Deere suppliers. Results were profound. Deere's $7 million investment in supplier development in 2000 brought $22 million in cost savings. At the same time, he worked tirelessly to bring parties with diverse divisional needs together to pursue common enterprise goals in supplier development, e-business, cost management, workforce development, and strategic sourcing. John Deere's benchmark strategic sourcing process promises long-term cost savings on Deere's $7.1 billion annual buy. Initial successes have resulted from the empowerment of sourcing teams at the factory, division, and enterprise levels and coordination and cooperation across divisions.

World-class results require the right people, and Nelson stresses careful recruiting, rotational job assignments, mentoring, involvement in annual leadership conferences, and education and development activities. Under Nelson, Deere has established close relationships with 12 college supply management programs. These relationships include scholarships, faculty support, research fellowships, and a unique online MBA program in supply management at Arizona State University for selected Deere employees worldwide.

Nelson's leadership at John Deere has not gone unnoticed by others. In 2001, John Deere won *Purchasing Magazine*'s Medal for Professional Excellence, and in 2006 he was honored with the highest honor in Supply Management, the J. Shipman Gold Medal Award. He continues to contribute to the Institute of Supply Management and as a consultant to industry.

R. David Nelson leads through communication, dedication to purpose, vision, persistence, humility, support for associates, involvement in processes, benchmarking to world-class standards, honesty, and loyalty. This includes his relentless efforts to advance the supply management profession. He has served as chairman of the board and former president of the Institute of Supply Management (formerly the National Association of Purchasing Management) and serves on the Board of Trustees of CAPS Research. Dave Nelson has been a member of the University of San Diego's Supply Chain Management Institute and its predecessor since their establishment in 1984. Wherever he goes, Nelson's success in leading those around him reflects his ability to facilitate discussion, help people focus on organizational objectives, and reach a balance between competing viewpoints.[5]

---

[5]Jim Collins, *Good to Great* (New York: Harper Business, 2001).

# EXHIBIT 22.2 | THE STRATEGIC LEADERSHIP SKILLS OF THOMAS T. STALLKAMP

*By Robert Porter Lynch*[6]

In the automotive industry, because of the high levels of supplier content, long lead times, integration of components, inventory control, and rapid response needed to changes in technologies and customer preferences, supply management is one of the most important and challenging management functions.

### Addressing a Crisis

In the early 1990s, Chrysler Corporation was faced with mounting losses, an aging line of cars, and uncompetitive cost structures. Japanese rivals were continuing to take large chunks of market share. Eighty percent of a Chrysler's vehicle content was sourced from suppliers, making cost issues essential to Chrysler's very survival.

However, years of intense cost-cutting negotiations had only produced a frustrated relationship between procurement and its suppliers. Chrysler was losing money, and the suppliers were running on razor-thin margins while seeing their receivables stretched inordinately. Chrysler was confronted with a crucial decision: find a new way to get its costs in line or face eventual bankruptcy.

Contrary to his peers at Ford and General Motors, Tom Stallkamp, then senior vice president of procurement, embarked on a bold strategy: rather than continue to squeeze his vendors with ever-increasing adversarial negotiation tactics, he took the opposite course—collaborate with suppliers as if they were members of his team, engage them in early involvement in car design, utilize their research and design capabilities, provide long-term contracts in return for their commitment to continuous improvement, and share the rewards for joint cost reduction. His SCORE (*Supplier Cost Reduction Effort*) program saved Chrysler over $5 billion during the 1990s, thus making a major contribution to saving the company and serving as a model for what collaboration can do.

Under Tom Stallkamp's leadership, suppliers were brought into the new car design cycle far earlier. The result was dramatic; the cycle time to bring a new car into production was reduced by more than half, enabling Chrysler to beat its rivals to market with new exciting designs. Through collaborating with suppliers and sharing the rewards, a continuous stream of new design innovations was brought to Chrysler far in advance of those ideas being provided to competitors. But there was more: Because Tom Stallkamp was willing to break with tradition by sharing both risks and rewards, Chrysler suppliers were willing to make substantial investments in much-needed research and development, resulting in tremendous savings for Chrysler. For example, a typical new car introduction would traditionally require a capital investment of $1–2 billion. But under Tom Stallkamp's collaborative strategy, Chrysler's cost for the Sebring convertible's introduction was only $200 million, with the remainder being borne by the suppliers.

One might think that the suppliers would be reluctant to absorb such steep costs. To the contrary, the suppliers actually became more profitable during Stallkamp's regime because the suppliers' financial coffers had been drained by the hidden costs of adversarial relationships between buyers and sellers. Everyone benefited under the new SCORE program.

### Leadership Principles

Stallkamp went beyond procurement's short-term perspective that typically limited many of his competitors' ability to produce real value. He believed that supply chain management mandated a greater strategic imperative to

---

[6]Robert Porter Lynch is CEO of the Warren Company, Providence, RI, www.warrenco.com. He is the founder of the Association of Strategic Alliance Professionals (ASAP). Also see: "How Chrysler Created an American Keiretsu" by Jeffry H. Dyer, *Harvard Business Review on Managing the Value Chain*, Boston, MA, Harvard Business School Press, 2000, pp. 61–90.

address the core issue of how suppliers could create competitive advantage at Chrysler. He employed five key supply *leadership principles* that helped achieve this success:

1. *Challenge conventional thinking.* Too often, managers revert to their "proven" playbook to solve current problems. While experience is extremely valuable, sometimes the old ways need to be scrapped and new thinking introduced into the process. New approaches and methods make the work more interesting and engaging for the team. We cannot always revert back to how things were done in the past to solve new problems of the future. Be willing to innovate with new ideas if you need to be a leader in the field.

2. *Coach, don't command.* If you order people to do things, they will eventually abdicate their decisions upward. Modern managers need to establish an environment that builds a team, not a bunch of highly talented, unrelated individuals. The leader guides, plants the seed of ideas, and challenges a team with questions. A leader who is always telling people what to do will siphon the energy out of people—they will stop thinking innovatively.

3. *Encourage debate, but make firm decisions promptly.* Leaders need to encourage subordinates to develop their own solutions while at the same time guiding the process toward conclusion. The objective is to obtain their buy-in to your own decisions and see them as their own. Time is precious in our fast-moving business world. Therefore, you must make the decision rather than taking a vote, for this is not about democracy but leadership. But the debate can highlight alternatives that you might not have considered.

4. *Avoid the micro details; concentrate on the macro.* Executives must not get absorbed in so much detail that they miss the larger picture and solution. Leave the analysis of the micro details to the management team so that they can become engaged and contribute to the solution. Leadership means rising above the details to see the broader objective and guiding the team to that goal; let the middle managers dive down into the details. Narrow financial analysis can be deceiving. Be careful about listening to MBAs who translate everything into financial impacts but cannot see the larger, integrated picture and miss how one issue can impact another.

5. *Know what you are talking about.* Leaders don't have to be experts, but it helps to take the time to undertake the major issues and factors affecting the decisions before launching opinions or answers. This is what cross-functional teams with real-world operating experience do best.

Tom also was deeply aware that there were critical supply chain management factors that would enable this leadership approach to produce dramatic results. Because he saw that supply management was such a vital function for Chrysler, he was insistent that it report directly to the president of the firm. These he referred to as his "key factors for success."

## Key Factors for Success

Tom Stallkamp was emphatic about how he focused his team on the few critical elements that would produce great results.

1. *Develop a "supply" approach instead of just "purchasing."* The concept of actively *managing the supply chain* is larger that just the smaller segment that Purchasing represents. Supply is responsible for more than just the initial buy; it is responsible for managing the total relationship with the supplier. Functions to be incorporated include production, control, logistics, program scheduling, and quality. A supply manager should be looking not just at the first-tier supplier relationship but also at how that supplier is managing the flow of materials, quality, and ideas several tiers below.

2. *Utilize strategic procurement.* Define what is really critical to the firm and what commodities and items are just routine. Use cross-functional input to develop formal written strategies that detail the objectives of the strategy. This is particularly important when innovation flows are vital to the future of your company. A supplier's investment in R&D can provide a major competitive advantage.

*(continued)*

*(continued from page 551)*

3. *Treat suppliers as equals, not second-class citizens.* Each link in the supply chain is just as important as every other and must be managed with respect and clear direction. Manage (but don't control) the supply chain by making strategic suppliers core members of your team.

4. *Establish clear requirements and measure progress.* Measurement and reporting the progress toward achieving the goals are critical to modern supply chain management. Most firms have not clearly defined what they expect of their suppliers and treat them as remote and separate. Establishing clear and simple requirements for quality, cost, delivery, and technology is essential in managing suppliers.

5. *Be proactive rather than reactive.* Leaders in Supply Chain management must think forward and plan for possible future events rather than being reactive to situations that come up. This requires strategic visionary skills, as well as operational competencies to foresee problems, opportunities, and interactions between competitive and tactical forces. Supply chain management is like a chess game where you should be thinking many moves in advance, anticipating the strategies of your competitors, the forces in the marketplace, and the needs of customers and suppliers.

As a result of Tom Stallkamp's visionary leadership in Supply Chain Management, not only was he largely responsible not only for saving billions of dollars which helped return Chrysler to health, he also was at the center of bringing many innovative products and new, faster, more streamlined processes into Chrysler. In recognition of his insights, Tom then became President and Vice Chairman of Chrysler until its acquisition by Daimler in 1998. Unfortunately, Daimler's leadership did not concur with Stallkamp's insights and dismantled his programs, which soon led to a long series of financial difficulties, an erosion of value, and ultimately the sale of the company by Daimler to Cerberus. See: *Taken for a Ride* by Bill Vlasic, N.Y., N.Y. Harper Collins, June, 2001.

Tom Stallkamp's legacy is clear: He broke new ground in enabling people in procurement to see their role in a new, more dynamic and strategic way; he demonstrated unequivocally that collaboration with suppliers is better than adversarial conflict and that companies can have relationships just as people do. He has contributed in more than a small way to changing the traditional way American businesses manage and maintain their place in the global economy.

# EXHIBIT 22.3 | THE STRATEGIC LEADERSHIP SKILLS OF GENE RICHTER (1937–2003)

*By Theresa Metty[7]*

Gene Richter, Chief Procurement Officer at IBM from 1994 until 2000, began developing his unique leadership style when he was a junior buyer at Ford Motor Company nearly 40 years ago. His solid grounding in procurement fundamentals is just one reason he earned immediate respect and credibility with any procurement team he led. Having performed nearly every job in procurement, from junior buyer to chief procurement officer, Gene could relate at all levels, on any commodity, with buyers and suppliers anywhere in the world. This made him

[7]Theresa Metty is the former Corporate Vice President and Director of Worldwide Supply Chain Operations for Motorola's Personal Communications Sector. Before working at Motorola, she held key supply chain management positions at IBM, including Vice President of Global Procurement.

very "approachable" and therefore more in touch with issues and opportunities. He liked to get to know buyers on a personal level, and used lunch as a time to catch up on his people. Gene took chances on people. He promoted people to positions of great responsibility. He knew that they were ready even before they realized it.

Gene had a very participative management style. He surrounded himself with strong procurement professionals with diverse backgrounds, then engaged them in every key decision on policy, strategy, practices, structure, initiatives, and objectives. He really listened to his staff, and he welcomed dissenting views. He was big on "group think," convinced that two heads are better than one, four are better than two, particularly when those "heads" came from different backgrounds with different experiences and views. Decisions were made swiftly, but only after his key staff members were consulted. He also involved suppliers in group think. He didn't just "listen" to suppliers; he actively involved them in key decisions received invaluable input from suppliers.

Gene was amazingly consistent in his messages and his expectations. He constantly reminded everyone of procurement's core values, its mission, its goal, and its objectives. He ensured that everyone knew where they were going, how to get there, and what to expect when they got there. Gene was always very results-oriented. Unmeasurable objectives (improve relationships with clients, reduce inventory, improve savings, etc.) were replaced with three or four very clear, very measurable objectives (achieve 85 percent client satisfaction, achieve 24 inventory turns, save $1.2B over the next 12 months using October as the baseline). He believed in measuring progress against IBM's objectives and sharing those results with all buyers every month. It was astonishing to see thousands of buyers all over the world energized to achieve a common set of consistent objectives with results better than the year before.

Gene is the only individual to lead a procurement organization who has won the Purchasing Medal of Professional Excellence three times: IBM, HP, and Black & Decker.

The accomplishments at IBM under Mr. Richter's leadership were astounding:

- Cumulative savings on direct and indirect materials exceeded $9B.
- The procurement "rulebook" was reduced from 100 pages of brain-numbing rules to 12 pages of guidelines based on sound procurement practices.
- Supplier contracts were reduced from 40+ pages of legalese to simple six-page agreements, and the contract cycle time was cut from 6 to 12 months to less than 30 days.
- The move to an e-procurement environment reduced Purchase Order cycle time from an average of 30 days to less than 1 day.
- He moved the procurement function from failing most business controls audits to passing 100 percent of all audits for the second year in a row.
- Internal customer surveys showed that customer satisfaction was moved from a shocking 47 percent to consistent satisfaction ratings in excess of 80 percent. Similarly supplier surveys showed that IBM moved from dead last to first place in nearly every category.
- For the only time in history, the procurement function at IBM received the coveted "Chairman's Award" for its leadership in e-procurement. Never before had this award been given to an internal function. CEO Lou Gerstner was so impressed by the sweeping movement within procurement to create an "e-business" within IBM that he broke with tradition to recognize the procurement function for its leadership.

Gene Richter created a culture of constant benchmarking with other companies. IBM held benchmarking sessions monthly with dozens of other companies, learning and sharing best practices. He encouraged active involvement of suppliers on many occasions. Gene and his people never assumed that they could represent their suppliers adequately in key decisions on policy and practices.

Gene was always very interested in knowing what was on his suppliers' minds. He created an Ombudsman office to give suppliers a penalty-free path of escalation on any issue. He hosted an annual Supplier Appreciation

*(continued)*

*(continued from page 553)*

Day for the CEOs and presidents of IBM's most critical suppliers and select IBM corporate officers. He hosted numerous roundtables with suppliers to hear their views on specific topics. Gene's staff always learned and improved every time they involved their suppliers in "group think" on procurement policies, procedures, and practices.

Richter was also a fierce defender of procurement people and their values. There were times a buyer would be pressured to award business to a supplier without following IBM's procurement process. Without exception, Gene defended Procurement's decision and almost always won the day. This set the tone for all buyers in IBM. They knew that Gene would defend their decisions. This gave the buyers confidence and boosted morale to all-time highs.

Gene also believed in supporting the procurement profession by his direct active involvement in professional organizations such as the Purchasing Council of Manufacturing Alliance for Productivity and Innovation (MAPI) and the Conference Board. He taught us that we could always learn from others. He taught us: There is a better way—find it. Even after we won the Medal of Professional Excellence, he led the procurement force with passion, constancy, ethics, candor, edge, vision, and a great sense of humor. What more could you want from a leader?

Gene refused to take credit for these many accomplishments; instead he gave credit to his strong procurement leadership team. This is just one of Gene's many outstanding leadership skills and one more reason he was held in the highest regard by his employees, his peers, his customers, and his suppliers—all over the world. In honor of Gene Richter's contribution to SCM, in 2006, ISM instituted the R. Gene Richter Awards for Leadership and Innovation in SM. (See Appendix A in this chapter.)

# Transformational Training

You then observed, "Professor Zinke, I've discovered the paradox of training. During boom times, firms don't have time for training. During bad times, when they should be getting ready for the next upside of the cycle, they claim that they can't afford it. But I've seen that after firms finally bite the bullet and invest in training, they all say, 'Why did we wait so long?' I'm committed to training as a vehicle of transformation. Do you have any thoughts on the subject?"

Professor Zinke commented, "I emphatically agree! I understand that you have funds to invest in the development of an appropriate and comprehensive training program. Be careful when developing your training program. Based on nearly 40 years in the procurement and supply management business, I believe that all training must be transformative; that is, it must lead to an improved state of operations. Exposing people to theory and best practices may be a waste of time unless it leads to transformation. I could spend days on this belief, but I'm running late for a meeting with my dean.

"Before I leave, here's a draft list of 12 Golden Rules for World Class Supply Management$^{SM}$ my friend and colleague David Burt has developed." [Professor Zinke located a copy (see Exhibit 22.4) and presented it to you.]

As you prepared to depart from this fountain of insight, you extracted a commitment that he would support you in any way he could.

On October 1, you joined Megatronics. Together with your Director of Supply Engineering, Mike Doyle, and a former direct report from your previous employer, Troy Garrow, you conducted a quick evaluation of Megatronics' supply management system. For over 60 years, Megatronics operated in a decentralized

---

## EXHIBIT 22.4 | BURT'S 12 GOLDEN RULES OF WORLD CLASS SUPPLY MANAGEMENT<sup>SM</sup>

1. Operate Supply Management as an integrated system including customers, operations, quality, demand management, supply management, logistics, and suppliers.
2. Implement continuous improvement in all activities internally and externally.
3. Apply strategic sourcing in the selection, maintenance, and development of the supply base.
4. Focus on the total cost of ownership, not purchase price.
5. Train and educate supply personnel in world-class processes, leadership, and change management.
6. Work in a cross-functional mode with internal functions and with key suppliers.
7. Recognize and reward excellence, both internally and externally.
8. Study and understand supply management's business environment.
9. Involve supply management and external suppliers in the earliest stages of new product development.
10. Develop and manage appropriate supply alliances.
11. Identify, verify, track, and control savings.
12. Foster an environment of collaboration.

---

mode, as shown in Figure 22.3. Reflecting this orientation, the corporate procurement staff you are inheriting currently numbers only five. There are between 180 and 225 procurement personnel at each of the four operating divisions. You have met with a representative sample of personnel from each division to gain a better understanding of the existing organizational structure and the culture at each division. You also have visited with the chief executive officers and account managers of 10 of Megatronics' major suppliers. As a result of those meetings, you have gained information and insight which will be useful in developing your plans for greatly improved relations with your supply base.

After studying the Burt-Lynch Supply Chain Evolution Model, the four of you have agreed that Megatronics employs a combination of mechanical and proactive activities and actions. You and your three colleagues have agreed that Megatronics' supply management system deserves an overall rating of 2.5 on a scale of 5.

## Transformational Planning

At this point, you thought it essential that the purchasing managers at Megatronics' four divisions be involved in the strategic planning process. Discussions with your predecessor, the departing Director of Purchasing, had painted a picture of a group of individuals who preferred to maintain their autonomy. Two of the individuals resented you before they met you since each felt that he or she 'deserved' your position. You met with each of Megatronics' four divisional purchasing managers. You concluded that you could work with three but that the director of the Medical Division, John Adams, had to go. Discussions with Human Resources resulted in a retirement package that John could not refuse.

Again working with Human Resources, you brought Susan Reese on board to replace John. You had hired Susan out of Arizona State's outstanding supply management program eight years ago. Last year Susan completed her M.S. in Supply Chain Management through the University of San Diego's hybrid

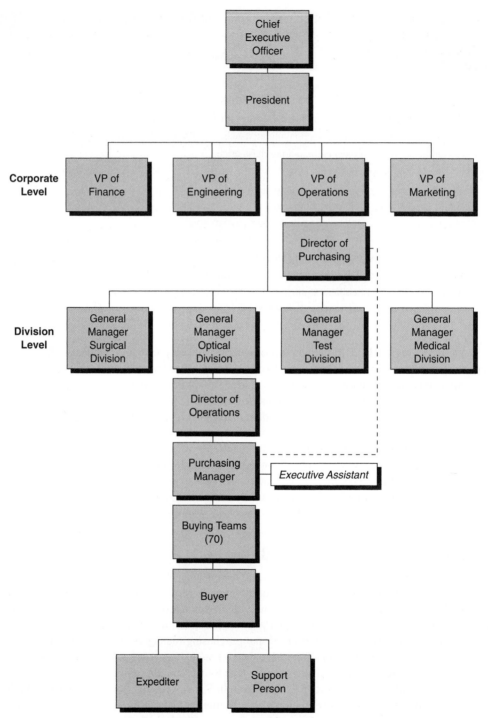

**Figure 22.3 l** Megatronics Corporation Organization Chart, 2008

campus/distant learning program. Susan was your Director of Operations at your last employer, ProAktive. She shares your vision, could charm a lioness into giving you her cub, and is a gifted agent of change. Your plan is to have Susan lead change at her division and set the standard for her colleagues at the three other divisions.

On November 1, you scheduled an all-day, off-site planning meeting with your enhanced team of Mike Doyle, Troy Garrow, Professor Zinke, and the four divisional supply managers. The meeting was held at the Silverado Conference Center in Napa Valley, California. Your objective was to reach consensus on a vision statement, a mission statement, and strategic plans with measurable goals in the following areas: costs of purchased goods and services, incoming quality, technology inflow, product development cycle time, supplier diversity, and supplier ratings of Megatronics as a customer. You plan to input these goals and the supporting initiatives in both corporate and supply management's strategic plans next January.

You opened the meeting by pointing out that supply management must develop and manage the firm's supply strategy as an integrated whole instead of a series of unrelated strategies. The corporation's strategy is the key driver of the supply strategy. The technology, marketing, finance, and production strategies are all inputs to the supply strategy. Conversely, the supply strategy is an input to the corporation's strategies for technology, marketing, finance, and production.

You addressed your belief in the importance of a name or title and indicated that your title, effective January 2, is "Vice President of Supply Management." You hope to become known as Megatronics' CSO (Chief Supply Officer).

Paul Wilson, Purchasing Manager of the Surgical Division, asked, "How does the term 'supply manager' differ from 'purchasing manager'?"

You responded, "Thanks, Paul. Let's start with the term 'supply management.' Supply management involves purchasing but is far more strategic. Supply management here at Megatronics will have as much or more impact on our bottom line than will any other function. It will contribute to increases in profitable sales by improving the quality and reliability of our products, reducing time to market, and enabling the inflow of technologies which are the basis of successful new products. Toyota obtains over 60 percent of its innovations from its supply base. Procter & Gamble recently placed major emphasis on the role its suppliers must play in providing technology leading to successful new products. As Megatronics advances to World Class Value Network Management, we must work with our suppliers to increase the inflow of innovative suggestions from them!

"In addition, supply management gives our marketing colleagues the freedom to maximize our net revenue through the application of pricing elasticity. At the same time, our supply management activities also will focus on the total cost of ownership of the materials, equipment, supplies, and services we purchase.

"You, your supply managers, and our expanded group of supply professionals at corporate will be the agents of change who will make all of this happen. Supply managers are far broader than traditional buyers. They must combine knowledge of best in class supply management processes and practices with skills in both management and leadership. Supply managers must be blessed with, or acquire, people skills. They must be proactive. They must be visionaries. They must be leaders and champions. In short, our supply managers will become recognized as keys to Megatronics' success and survival!

"The supply manager is neither departmentally nor internally focused but concentrates on proactively improving processes with the long-term goal of upgrading the competitive capability of our firm and its supply chain. I'm making arrangements with H. R. at each of your divisions to change your titles to "Director of Supply Management" in January. The transformational training program we are developing will help your subordinates and colleagues understand this key difference between 'purchasing' and 'supply

---

## EXHIBIT 22.5 | MEGATRONICS' SUPPLY MANAGEMENT VISION AND MISSION STATEMENTS

**The Vision Statement**

Supply management at Megatronics will perfect its worldwide process, resulting in totally delighted customers and shareholders.

**The Mission Statement**

We will design and implement necessary process and cultural changes to create a fully integrated customer-driven supply management system. We will integrate suppliers into our business plans and processes in an environment of respect and trust, establish full cooperation throughout the enterprise, and establish supply management as a core competency. We will improve the bottom line by facilitating increased profitable sales while minimizing the total cost of ownership of all materials, equipment, supplies, and services. We will ensure that diversity suppliers have opportunities to play vital roles in our supply base.

---

management.' Hopefully, this transformational training will help all of our present-day buyers grow into their new roles as supply managers. If not, we will attempt to reassign them to other departments, clearing the way for the hiring of 'supply managers.'"

Next, two hours of time were well-invested in reaching agreement on your team's vision and mission statements (see Exhibit 22.5).

You then addressed the nine areas in which you desired to establish stretch goals for the next year to lay the foundation for measurable accomplishments in the following years: cost, quality, technology, the new product development cycle, supplier feedback, social responsibilities, standardization, value engineering and value analysis, and organization and staffing.

## Cost

On the basis of your belief that there was much low-lying fruit, you proposed an overall savings goal for the first year of 10 percent on the costs of purchased materials, equipment, supplies, and services. After half an hour of hearing why that goal was totally unreasonable, you proposed, "During the next hour, let's assume for the sake of discussion that 10 percent *is* our goal. *What do we have to do to achieve it?*" The discussion ranged from suggestions on supplier bashing to examining with key suppliers the drivers of cost and deciding what action must be taken jointly to drive wasteful costs out. You observed, "Value Network Management requires high connectivity with suppliers. This is not an option. It is essential to building the relationship with suppliers which will allow us to reach that 10 percent goal." The group accepted the fact that in a perfect world it might be feasible to reduce purchase prices an average of 10 percent in the first year. The group then agreed to put the cost reduction issue on hold for the moment.

You then addressed a challenging issue: total cost of ownership. The group expressed skeptical interest. An hour was spent discussing the issue. The biggest concern expressed was that employment of a TCO basis of source selection might increase the price paid in some instances. You pointed out that the TCO analysis was in the company's best interest, and you said, "I believe that we can implement a TCO approach while moderating our *price* savings objective so that we have any necessary cushion resulting from the occasional higher purchased price. Our focus must be TCO. If we pay a price premium that is offset with a greater reduction in the total cost of ownership, we will document our analysis. For example, I have been shocked to learn of our incredibly high number of warranty claims on our test equipment due to defects in purchased materials. If we can reduce incoming defects significantly, we can reduce our total cost of ownership. Eventually, after we've gained creditability, we may be able to transform to a TCO basis of awards. Let's hold implementation off until everyone has had the appropriate training in TCO say, Q3 next year." The group then tentatively agreed on the following.

**Strategic Sourcing**   "During Q1 of next year, all commodity classes, equipment, and service expenditures representing a total of 80 percent of Megatronics' spend will be identified. ABC analysis will help start this benchmarking process. Some supply executives refer to this stage of planning as the 'audit' or 'diagnostic phase,' i.e., What is the current situation? The supply base employed to satisfy this spend will be identified. Based on my experience, less than 10 percent of our suppliers are responsible for 80 percent of our spend. These will be the ones we focus on. The appropriate supply manager and the division supply manager will rate each supplier on the following criteria (using a scale of 1 to 10):

- Cost minimization.
- Willingness to share cost data.
- Incoming quality levels (ppm, if feasible).
- On-time delivery.
- Current technology status: leader/follower.
- Ability to meet Megatronics' technology needs in 3 years.
- Potential to become an alliance supplier.
- On time delivery.

"These two individuals then will categorize suppliers into one of four groups:

- World Class.
- Suppliers who are acceptable and have the potential to be developed to world-class status.
- Suppliers who are acceptable and provide products and services where a supply alliance is not needed.
- Suppliers to drop.

"Appropriate action will be taken as follows with suppliers in each group:

"Discussions will be held with our world-class suppliers. We will express appreciation for their continuing support. We will ask what *we* can do to improve the relationship. We will ensure that we are in collaborative relationships and on the road to alliance relationships. We will extol them to do 'even better.' We will publicize our recognition and appreciation of a job well done in appropriate trade literature. I guarantee that the best will get even better!

"The second group (ones with potential) is more challenging. We will prioritize them by spend. Simultaneously, we will look for opportunities to rationalize our supply base. I don't want to make downsizing an initiative, but it should be a 'guiding principle.' We probably can reduce our base by 50 percent as we match our needs with the desired supply base. By and large, I prefer a 70/30 guideline: 70 percent of an item or commodity class to our preferred supplier and 30 percent to our 'backup' supplier. When we start enjoying supply alliances, I prefer to have one alliance supplier for an item and another alliance supplier for a similar item. Ideally, each supplier will provide backup capability for the other supplier if an unforeseen situation arises. But those issues will have to be examined on a case-by-case basis.

"I understand that we do not provide supplier development assistance to our suppliers to help them learn how to become world class. We need to create supplier development teams immediately. I have obtained budgetary approval to hire four supplier development engineers at each operating division. At first, we will be able to address only the biggest dollar volume suppliers or those of critical or strategic importance. We will discuss our rating with them and ask if they desire to progress to world-class status. If the answer is 'No, we will survive without you,' we will consider sourcing with a more cooperative supplier. Normally, a key salvageable supplier will welcome our offer of supplier development assistance. Such suppliers are candidates for collaborative relationships and may become candidates for supplier alliances downstream.

"I propose that we field four teams of four professionals possessing the following expertise: supplier development, cost management, supply management, and quality management. In working with the chosen supplier, we will follow the steps laid out in the chapter on supplier development in the recently published textbook *Supply Management*. In parallel with this action, we will train and educate in-house resources in world-class supplier development. In time, I believe that we will be able to field 12 such teams, pulling additional resources from our supply departments at the divisions.

"The impact of the supplier development teams will be felt quickly. It is common to discover that 70 percent of a supplier's cycle time is non-value-added wasteful activity that can be easily reduced or, better yet, eliminated. A major benefit for Megatronics will be shorter lead times for orders, which translates into smaller order quantities and lower inventories."

"Wow," observed Ray Hummell, Director of Supply Management at the test division. "I think your cost reduction objective may be achievable!"

Susan observed, "We demonstrated that it was possible at ProAktive. We worked closely with key suppliers to drive costs out of the relationship. We shared savings with the suppliers in much the same manner as did Chrysler during the early 1990s. Not only did we drive cost down, we started eliminating incoming quality problems. Based on our experience, I believe that reducing our total spend by 10 percent may be possible—but it's going to be quite a reach in the first year. We may not have the resources to deploy the optimal number of supplier development teams for some time." After much discussion, the group agreed on a savings objective for the first year of 5 percent in constant year dollars rather than your proposed 10 percent. You pointed out: "This translates to a $260 million improvement in Megatronics' bottom line, or a 26 percent increase."[8]

## Quality

You continued by observing that the team had begun discussing the quality program both in the retention of Megatronics' best suppliers and in focusing on supplier development. The group agreed that it should be possible to reduce incoming defects by 10 percent the first year. But there was more. "I believe that we should have at least one quality engineer in supply management at each division. This individual will focus on the six components of a total quality management program at the division level:

- Development of clear and concise specifications by our internal customers. We will stress appropriate specifications to avoid overengineering issues.
- Quality considerations during sourcing.

---

[8]A 5 percent reduction on a spend of $5.25 billion = $262 million. This savings will increase Megatronics' pretax profit from $1 billion to $1.26 billion.

- Development of a clear understanding with suppliers on all aspects of quality—both prior to and subsequent to award of a contract.
- Identification of opportunities for supplier development.
- A comprehensive monitoring system; supplier certification.
- A motivational program addressing quality, cost, and service."

Susan asked, "What about a Six Sigma black belt program for our people? It sure helped at ProAktive." A short discussion ensued in which Susan described the program. It was agreed that such a program should be implemented after completion of the second round of training. The group agreed that the combination of those actions would lay the foundation for much more aggressive quality goals two years out.

## Technology

You continued, "The biggest challenge with the existing supply base appears to be with the issue of technology. The inflow of technology is a function of two variables: the supplier's investment in advancing its technological capabilities and the supplier's willingness to share its innovations with us. The first factor (willingness to invest) can be measured through a combination of financial analysis and an independent evaluation of the firm's technological prowess by an in-house expert or consultant. The second variable (its willingness to work with us and share appropriate technology) is a function of our relationship with the supplier. A collaborative supplier will be far more willing to share its technology than will an arm's-length one, and an alliance supplier will be much more inclined to share technology than will a collaborative one.

"I believe that over the next two years, we need an initiative to develop 12 individuals capable of developing and managing strategic supply alliances. If we are going to develop supply alliances, we first will need an initiative to identify supplier relationships that should progress to alliance status. These 12 professionals can handle both initiatives. Developing and managing alliances will improve our inflow of technology, enable continuous improvement, reduce costs, reduce defects, and compress new product development time. I doubt if we will have a measurable impact on technology inflow next year. Therefore, I recommend that we not establish a goal for next year but undertake appropriate initiatives. We should start seeing benefits the following year."

## The New Product Development Cycle

Jason Patel, Supply Manager of the Optics Division, asked, "How will these alliances reduce development time?" You answered, "Not only will these suppliers be the best of the best, but hopefully, they will be readily accepted as contributors to our new product teams.[9] I believe that we can take at least 50 percent out of the development cycle by involving carefully screened suppliers early in the process."

Jason responded, "What if we are developing a new product and we don't have an alliance partner?"

You observed, "Then the new product development team—which must include a supply professional with engineering knowledge—must select from two or three carefully prequalified suppliers. Under such circumstances, we must be careful about sharing any of our technology and our technology plans with a nonalliance supplier. Obviously, the sooner we develop appropriate alliances, the better.

---

[9]The concept of early supplier involvement entered the literature in 1987 in an article in *Purchasing* by the managing editor, Somerby Dowst: "Early Supplier Involvement Gives Design Team the Winning Edge," *Purchasing*, March 12, 1987, pp. 56–63.

"Early involvement of both supply management and suppliers will help us greatly in meeting our objective of reduced development time. Recently conducted research indicates that early supplier involvement (ESI) and early supply management involvement (referred to as EPI at most firms) can reduce new product development by 20 to 40 percent. Honda of America reduced its new product development cycle by over 60 percent one year during the 1990s! And in the long run, such action will help Megatronics reduce new product costs and increase reliability. Professor Zinke and many supply professionals estimate that 75 to 85 percent of a product's costs and virtually all of its reliability are designed in during the development stage. By working with carefully prequalified suppliers, we can reduce costs, time to market, and quality problems very significantly. Thus, it's imperative that qualified supply managers and suppliers be involved in this process!"

Jason said, "Most engineers and new product development managers talk to my people only when they want them to buy something. The idea of involving my people or our suppliers in the development process is ludicrous, at best!" Jason's two longtime colleagues concurred. Susan observed, "Sounds like another initiative to me!"

You responded, "Actually, it may be two or three—or even more—initiatives. The first is to upgrade some of our trainable staff so that they bring value to the new product development process. The second may be to promote and train four Megatronics design engineers to become supply engineers. I believe that this activity will be performed best at the division level by our new supply engineers. But I want Mike Doyle to monitor and facilitate the process at each division. Mike will provide any necessary help in convincing the divisional engineers that supply management has much to contribute and that supply engineers or engineering-knowledgeable supply managers must be involved early in all new product development programs. I'll talk to Human Resources about the feasibility of this one. The third initiative will be to bring some fresh talent in."

Susan said, "I recommend that with the impact early involvement of suppliers and supply management has on cost, time to market, and quality, we pursue all three initiatives!" Everyone agreed.

You observed, "The other initiative is to get these valuable new resources onto appropriate new development teams. Let's start moving on these three initiatives early next year. We should be able to begin upgrading our people by the end of the second quarter. With the economy the way it is, we should be able to bring in several supply engineers by next fall. Developing supply engineers from in-house engineers is more complex and may take longer, say, one and a half years. Once we have qualified resources, I have to secure engineering's acceptance of their involvement."

"Lots of luck!" Jason said.

You calmly commented, "I think I'll solicit Professor Zinke's help on this one. Doc, do you think you can convince engineering of the critical importance of such early involvement?" The professor responded, "Not a problem! I'll be happy to meet with you and the vice president of engineering as soon as you can schedule such a meeting."

Over a lunch of sand dabs, pommes frites, and Caesar salad, you raised another issue. "Let's assume that we could develop, promote, or hire a total of eight supply engineers by the end of June next year. What impact will our action have on achieving our objectives?"

Mike Doyle, who had been a process engineer at Megatronics for seven years, responded, "I don't see much impact next year or even the following one. Considering the typical development cycle and product life cycle, it will be three years before we see much impact; in fact, it will be four years before we begin to receive major benefits."

You responded, "Which means that we in supply management must carry the ball on cost, quality, and technology inflow for quite some time. Speaking about quality, while the largest impact we will have on quality is through early supplier and supply management involvement, we've got to get going on areas where we can have more immediate impact. We've outlined plans for driving cost down. Are there any other thoughts on cost before we address quality more fully?"

JoAnn Barber, your newly appointed Director of Measurements and Standards at the corporate level, responded, "What about Ariba Software?"

Susan commented, "This system may save a bit of money on purchase price, but the big savings are in human resources. We implemented Ariba at ProAktive three years ago. It took over a year to implement, and we were just beginning to see monetary savings after two years. It will probably take three to four years for a full payback at ProAktive, but we thought that we might save 18 MRO buyers and 12 A.P. clerks some time this year. For what it's worth, I recommend that with the number of initiatives on the table we hold this one for a year or two."

You countered, "I had a similar impression of these systems until talking with a colleague from the automotive industry earlier this year. He got payback after only four months! He indicated that much of the savings resulted from the virtual elimination of maverick spending. He estimated that 60 to 70 percent of MRO spending had been done outside of the formal supply management system. Based on his experience and that of another colleague in the pharmaceutical industry, I think that we should study this one before moving forward."

This recommendation received consensus almost immediately.

Susan then asked, "What about reverse auctions? I understand that they are saving 10 to 20 percent!"

Professor Zinke observed, "There are situations in which carefully designed and professionally run reverse auctions can achieve significant savings. I recommend that when you review your commodity class as we discussed this morning, you identify standard commodities for reverse auctions. Remember that unless the auction is handled very professionally, you may disrupt important collaborative relationships. A client of mine employs reverse auctions as a means of rationalizing his supply base. For example, he hoped to reduce the number of injection mold suppliers from 110 to 12 worldwide. Once he had rationalized this supply base, he planned to progress through collaboration to alliance status with each of the 12 suppliers. Based on my observations, you may want to apply this sourcing and pricing tool to about 20 percent of your spend; 20 percent of a spend of $5,250,000,000 is over $1 billion, which may lend itself to reverse auctioning. Assuming a 15 percent savings, that's $150,000,000. With a bit of luck, you're well on your way to achieving your savings goal. But remember, usually you're best off using reverse auctions only once or, at most, twice for a commodity or commodity class. Assuming that you've used the procedure correctly, you then should consider developing a collaborative relationship with the selected suppliers. Once you've developed a collaborative or alliance relationship, I recommend the use of other processes to ensure that you're paying a low but fair price."

You responded, "Thanks, Doc. Now let's return to the quality issue. You may remember that when we discussed supplier development this morning, we talked about having a quality engineer or manager on each supplier development team. For those of you who were not present, we plan to create a supplier development program along the lines of Chapter 11 of the textbook *Supply Management*. Very simply, we plan to work with our suppliers to become 'world class.' The program will be tailored to each supplier's needs. It will result in suppliers who are more productive and more efficient, whose quality is drastically improved, and whose products' costs are reduced. Additionally, these upgraded suppliers will be a source of innovation, much as Toyota's suppliers are. But this will be a relatively slow way of improving our overall incoming quality. Can anyone think of other initiatives which might be faster?"

Susan responded, "Yes, I can think of five:

■ We should consider a Six Sigma program.

■ We should improve our source selection process.

■ We must ensure that there is a complete understanding of all of our requirements both before and after award of a contract—before the supplier commences production.

■ We should transfer the responsibility for ensuring quality from incoming inspection to the supplier whenever appropriate. This will give suppliers a greater sense of 'owning' the quality issue. Additionally, we may be able to reallocate some inspectors to higher-value-added work.

■ We will work with our colleagues in quality and investigate the feasibility of certifying our major suppliers.

"And lastly, when we become aware of a problem, it's in our interest to work with the supplier to correct the root cause of the problem."

You indicated that the Six Sigma program should be a corporate initiative, not a supply management one. You planned to introduce it at the next corporate executive session. After a boisterous discussion and the promise of the afternoon break, the group reached quick agreement in support of each of Susan's other suggested initiatives. The group agreed that a 10 percent reduction from 1,000 ppm to an average of 900 was a realistic goal for year one. In succeeding years, Megatronics should gain the benefit of those initiatives and reduce incoming defects by 50 percent per year or more indefinitely.

When the group reconvened, you observed that there were only a few remaining issues: ratings from suppliers of your competence as a responsible customer, Megatronics' social responsibilities, and the issues of standardization, value engineering, and staffing.

## Supplier Feedback

Mike Doyle, Director of Supply Engineering, volunteered, "I'd like to assume responsibility to initiate a program in which suppliers give us semiannual ratings on how well we are doing as a customer. I have several ideas that I'd like to run past you, Professor Zinke." Everyone agreed that this was a "done deal . . . another initiative."

## Social Responsibilities

Paul Wilson, Supply Manager for the Surgical Division, offered, "As you might suspect, supplier diversity is important to me." (Paul is an African American who has worked his way up from the factory floor to his present position. He is respected by his colleagues and the suppliers with whom he comes in contact.) "Megatronics claims to support diversity, but I don't see it. How many women- or minority-owned businesses are even considered for anything other than MRO and services? I was reading about the programs at Agilent, Lucent, and Deere in the seventh edition of *World Class Supply Management*<sup>SM</sup>.[10] I volunteer to establish a program as good as the best!"

You then pointed out that a world-class value network plays a major role in protecting Mother Earth. You stated, "Within a very short time, I expect to see customer firms impose on their suppliers programs

---

[10]There are several articles on this topic in *Inside Supply Management*. See especially Craig Brown, "Supplier Diversity Goes Global," *Inside Supply Management*, September 2007, p. 44. Also see "Diversity Spend Escalates," a 2005 Center for Strategic Supply Research (CAPS) study cited in *Inside Supply Management*, March 2006, pp. 40–41.

to reduce the consumption of energy, dispose of waste in an environmentally friendly manner, recycle obsolete equipment, and adapt the use of recyclable materials whenever feasible."

JoAnn Barber added, "As a global player, we willl encounter some fascinating ethical, financial, and legal issues in the very near term."

You then asked Troy Garrow to assume responsibility for the development of programs for your suppliers which would result in reduced energy consumption, pollution avoidance, and the use of recyclable materials. You asked JoAnn Barber to accept responsibility for the development of a program addressing ethics in the workplace for your suppliers, whether domestic or global.[11]

## Standardization

"My initial discussions with several of our people and representatives of key suppliers led to the conclusion that a standardization program would help us in the areas of cost, quality, and compressing the development cycle. While there probably are many opportunities for standardization at the division level, I believe that standardization must be corporatewide. (During the short discussion which followed, there was agreement that standardization would provide benefits at both the division and corporate levels.) "With your concurrence, I propose hiring a standards engineer to propose a standardization program to use and then to manage the program." The new hire would work directly under JoAnn Barber in the measurement and standards group. Everyone agreed.

## Value Engineering and Value Analysis

"I've been fascinated to see that there are no value engineering or value analysis activities or even relevant training here at Megatronics." (A short discussion involving quite a bit of defensive behavior ensued.) "As we all know, VE/VA pays back an average of 10 to 30 times the investment in such programs. I propose that each division hire one or more value engineers. Based on experience, talk with your counterparts in operations and engineering to see if they may have candidates before going outside."

## Organization and Staffing

You continued, "Before taking a break, I'd like to share my vision of our evolving organization for supply management and where I see our staffing in four to six years. Many of the activities and functions we have been discussing can best be performed at corporate. Others are better at division. In time, I hope to have a direct reporting relationship with each of you who are at the division level. I believe that it is best for me, best for you, and best for Megatronics.

"Staffing is a very sensitive issue. I am confident that supply management will grow larger with the many new positions we have been discussing and then will decrease to about 40 percent of the present size. As we upgrade those of our existing workforce who are upgradeable—and this includes present-day buyers, expediters, and support staff—and as we take advantage of e-Commerce II, I see us downsizing to a workforce largely consisting of supply management professionals. Collaborative and alliance relationships will virtually eliminate the need for expediters. Ariba or a similar system will eliminate the need for MRO buyers. For better or worse, most support positions will be eliminated.

"Our focus will shift from tactical to strategic. Our work will become far more challenging, stimulating, and fulfilling."

---

[11]See Lisa Cooling, "Spread the Carbon-Neutral News," *Inside Supply Management*, October 2007, pp. 30–32.

You called the group to attention after a boisterous break. "It should be apparent that we desperately need high-quality training and education. While I was at a recent University of San Diego Strategic Supply Management Forum, I heard several excellent presentations. One speaker described a four-tier program consisting of (1) Boot Camp (basics for supply management personnel); (2) Advance Boot camp (more advanced training for selected personnel); (3) intermediate training and education for selected managers; and (4) a commitment to fund tuition for carefully selected personnel to pursue an M.S. in Supply Chain Management. The initial boot camp was conducted in a unique format that both trained and laid the foundation for the client's transformation to a world-class player. I propose that we adapt the program to meet our needs. I have the budget to hire a consulting firm to work with us to develop position descriptions and the necessary training in the skills our people will need as we progress to World Class Value Network Management status. It is my intention that we work with the consultant to develop an understandable career promotion path for our people. Any reactions or thoughts?"

After several minutes of discussion, the group indicated that basic boot camp should commence next February. Selected high-potential supply management personnel would be encouraged to enroll in the next available cohort of USD's hybrid classroom/Internet-based graduate program in supply management.

Troy Garrow observed that he'd heard about the use of metrics to improve supply management from his colleagues at the local chapter of the Institute for Supply Management$^{TM}$. He asked, "What role, if any, should metrics play in our program?"

You pointed out, "If you can't measure it, you can't manage it." You thanked Troy for raising the topic and proposed bringing Ted Ramsted, former senior procurement executive at Scott Paper, in to discuss metrics at your team's February meeting. Because of the meeting, Ted was retained under JoAnn Barber's leadership to facilitate the development of appropriate metrics and conduct metrics training. Within four months, Ted had completed his mission and Megatronics' supply management personnel had customized appropriate metrics for strategic and tactical issues and for appropriate contracts.

Susan then raised the issue of commodity teams. After a stimulating 20-minute discussion, it was agreed that more foundation building was required before moving on this initiative. It was tabled until next year's meeting.

"Lastly, I believe that we should invite all Megatronics' high-value suppliers to a suppliers' day sometime in February. Mike, will you handle this one?"

Paul Wilson, Director of Supply Management for the Surgical Devices Division, offered an observation: "I believe that we are developing a set of excellent plans and initiatives, but something puzzles me. For years, I've heard about benchmarking, but there's no benchmarking on our list of initiatives."

Professor Zinke responded, "Three of my colleagues have a wonderful book out on supply management. The book addresses countless world-class practices and reduces the need for conventional benchmarking since it is possible to benchmark against the world-class processes they advocate without investing in field trips. However, there may be occasions on which a benchmarking visit makes sense. Such benchmarking visits can provide insight on 'how to implement' or 'how to overcome' resistance to change."

It was 5 P.M. and nearly time for wine tasting at a nearby vineyard. You casually mentioned this before observing that it was essential to summarize the commitments agreed to during the day. You reminded the group that the goals, together with the supporting initiatives, would become supply management's portion of the next corporate strategic plan. You stated that there was agreement on both the vision statement and the mission statement and promised to provide the group with a summary list of the goals and initiatives agreed on for next year (see Exhibit 22.6).

# EXHIBIT 22.6 | GOALS AND INITIATIVES FOR YEAR ONE

## Goals

- Reduce average price on incoming goods and services by 5 percent
- Reduce average incoming defects by 10 percent to 900 ppm

## Initiatives

- Implement strategic sourcing, starting Q1 (first quarter)
- Document and obtain verification of savings, Q1
- Initiate supplier development program, starting Q2
- Implement a total cost of ownership program, Q3
- Develop and implement a training program, commencing Q1
- Initiate study of an operating resource management system, Q3
- Conduct "Supplier Day" in Q1 and annually thereafter
- Develop or hire 8 individuals capable of developing and managing supply alliances, Q4
- Identify supplier relationships which have the potential of progressing to alliance status, Q2
- Train alliance champions, Q2
- Enter into first supply alliance, Q4
- Train and upgrade all staff members so that they bring value to all processes, Q2
- Promote and train several Megatronics engineers for supply engineering billets, Q2
- Hire supply engineers by Q3
- Include supply engineers on appropriate new development teams, Q4
- Initiate reverse auctions where appropriate, Q4
- Increase emphasis on quality capabilities during source selection, Q1
- Ensure understanding with all suppliers of their quality, time, and service obligations, Q1
- Document all contract files on understanding issue, Q1
- Initiate supplier certification program, Q3
- Work with suppliers to correct root causes of quality problems, Q2
- Collect and analyze feedback from suppliers on how "we" perform as a customer, Q4
- Design, develop, and implement an aggressive social responsibilities program, Q2
- Hire a standards engineer to develop and manage a standardization program, Q2
- Add a value engineer to each division's staff, Q2
- Increase compensation of supply professionals to reflect the increased value they provide, Q4
- Study implications of purchasing Ariba Software, Q3

You observed, "I had planned to establish goals on technology infusion, reduced development cycle times, diversity, and a supplier scorecard. But as we were discussing our plans, it became apparent that finite objectives in these areas probably are premature.

"I plan to hire an executive assistant whose primary purpose will be to monitor these initiatives and help me utilize project management techniques to help manage the processes to ensure timely action. Ladies and gentlemen: It's Wine Time!"

Cathy Reyes, Director of Supply Management at the Test Division, sighed, "Oh, darn, I'd been looking forward to an eggnog latté."

## Bringing the Troops Onside

It's the second Monday in January of the following year. You have decided to honor Megatronics' decentralized divisional status and have chosen to meet with all the members of the supply management system, division by division. At 8 A.M. you step onto the stage of the 250-seat auditorium at the Holiday Inn, Redondo Beach, California. The room is nearly full. Your retired predecessor introduces you. You begin, "Ladies and gentlemen, I'm delighted to be here and honored to have been selected to lead you in the transformation of Megatronics purchasing to World Class Value Network Management status. We have the potential and the power to help Megatronics achieve greatness. To help you understand the road we must travel, I'm going to ask you to spend the next 10 minutes reviewing the step chart on page 2 of the brochure each of you received on entering the auditorium and rate our relative status on the chart. Please be honest and objective in your ratings." (See again Figure 22.2.)

After 10 minutes, your executive assistant, Karen Kukta, turns the projector on so that the step chart is legible to virtually everyone. You continue, "Okay, let's see where we are on the road to world-class status. Any 5s? (Silence and a bit of restlessness.) Any 4s? (One timid hand.) Any 3s? (Five more hands.) Okay, I'll assume that the rest of you feel that we're something less than a 3! Now, you might ask, 'So what?' How many of you think that your job is to push papers? (A few uncomfortable titters.) How many of you think that your job is to chase parts? (Several expediters raise their hands.) How many of you spend a significant amount of your time resolving discrepancies with accounts payable? (Thirty or more hands.) How many of you think that your job is to beat your suppliers' prices down? (Twenty-five half-raised arms.) How many of you visit your suppliers other than to expedite? (Ten hands.) How many of you think that your job is to increase sales? (No hands, but many puzzled looks.)

"Again, thanks for your honesty! Now, let's turn to page 3 in your brochure. (See Figure 22.4.) Ladies and gentlemen, our sole reason for existence is to improve Megatronics' bottom line. Let's look at our impact on sales. Some 75 percent of our field failures can be traced back to purchased materials. Our current incoming defect rate is over 1,000 defects per million. This is not surprising since purchased materials represent over 75 percent of all direct costs! Think of the impact on our sales of reducing this incoming defect rate to 50 ppm. Think of the cost savings to our colleagues in customer service. As we gain an image as the quality leader, our share of the market will grow and our bottom line will improve significantly through additional profitable sales.

"Now, let's look at our role in bringing new technology in to our design people. When Bill and Dave laid the foundation for this firm some 60 years ago, they were pretty well self-contained, technologically speaking. Today, industry analysts indicate that our competitors attribute an average of 35 percent of their new products to technology received from their suppliers. The same analysts estimate our technology infusion at less than 10 percent. As we change our focus during sourcing from price to total cost of ownership, quality, and technology and as we build trusting relations with our key suppliers, I expect to see

## Net Income

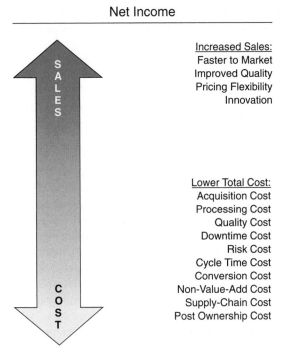

**Figure 22.4** | Contributions to Net Income

enormous growth in the number of successful, profitable new products based on supplier technology. As you probably know, the highest profit margins flow to the first firm to market a product meeting customer needs. We can and must become that firm!

"Next, let me turn to the issue of continuity of supply. Angel Mendez, your vice president of Operations at Corporate, has spoken of the problems, challenges, and frustrations she and her people at all divisions face because of the late arrival of materials. Not only do late shipments result in challenges for our operations department, they also lead to late deliveries to our customers. Dissatisfied customers soon take their business elsewhere! Better and more dependable suppliers, better-understanding suppliers, and more-trusting supplier relations are the keys to this one. Every late shipment should generate an action item identifying planned and completed corrective action. Both your department manager, Barbara, and I want to see these action items."

You had planned on discussing some of supply management's other impacts on sales but decided that that might be overkill at this time. Maybe in six months. You next address the bottom half of Figure 22.4, the cost component of supply management's impact on the bottom line. Recognizing the danger of information overload, you say, "You'll notice that page 3 identifies 10 cost drivers, ranging from purchase price to post-ownership costs. If you don't mind, we won't go into these components of the total cost of ownership today other than to say that we want you to start thinking and acting TCO, not purchase price, from this day on! Now, let's take a 20-minute break for a cup of coffee."

During the break, you and Susan Reese mingle and try to take the group's pulse. Comments range from "This guy's been eating too many nuts and berries" to "Wow! This really excites me!"

After the 20-minute break (which always takes longer), you reconvene the meeting. "Last month, the four divisional directors of supply, Mike Doyle from my staff, Professor Zinke of USLO, and I hammered out a vision statement of what supply management must become if Megatronics is to regain its position as number one in the industry. Let's take a look at our vision statement. (The screen comes to life, and everyone reads: "Supply management at Megatronics will perfect its worldwide process, resulting in totally delighted customers and shareholders.")

"Let's take this vision to the next stage and describe our mission statement and our value proposition." The screen then displays:

### Mission Statement: Megatronics Supply Management System

"We will design and implement necessary processes and cultural changes to create a fully integrated customer-driven supply management system. We will integrate suppliers into our business plans and processes in an environment of respect and trust, establish full cooperation throughout the enterprise, and establish supply management as a core competency. We will drive the bottom line by facilitating increased profitable sales while minimizing the total cost of ownership of all materials, equipment, supplies, and services. We will ensure that diversity suppliers have an opportunity to play vital roles in our supply base."

You continue: "Before we go any further, let me assure you that we have developed a world-class transformational training program to be conducted by USLO and the Strategic Supply Management Institute, Ltd. You will be given the tools to become world-class supply managers. A considerable part of your training will focus on cross-functional teams. Whenever possible, you will be trained in a cross-functional team mode with colleagues from engineering, operations, quality, legal, and others, as appropriate. This training also will be available to key suppliers on a no-cost basis. Sign-up sheets for seven sections of the first two-day workshop are outside. There will be five additional modules, one per month. The training program is both extensive and exhaustive. On completion of the basic and then advanced training, we hope to sponsor several of you to participate in USD's two-year Master of Science in Supply Chain Management program. After another 20-minute fruit and veggie break, I'd like to describe briefly our strategic initiatives for this year."

This time, the break takes only 25 minutes. "Last November, our supply management executive team met to establish the vision statement and mission statements which you've seen this morning. We committed to the following goals and initiatives shown on the screen. [See again Exhibit 22.6.]

"One last thing: We are attempting to develop a model 'rewards' system and sincerely solicit your thoughts. It probably will take several months to develop a refined system that HR and the corporate executive committee will bless, but we believe in recognizing and rewarding your contributions. I'm going to ask Troy Garrow to initiate a corporatewide monthly newsletter in which we can share our success stories.

"Thank you for your attention. Now, as we move to the banquet room for a bit of sustenance, you'll realize that there truly is no such thing as a 'free lunch'!"

You repeat similar programs in Germany and China over the next few months.

The following Monday, you meet with CEO Frank Lazarus and the executive committee. They seem to be awed by your plans and initiatives. There is unanimous support of both. You discuss the need for Six Sigma training at the corporate and divisional levels. After considerable discussion, you and Barbara Withers, vice president of Operations, are charged with the responsibility of implementing appropriate training. The program is to commence in March.

In June, you begin poking around Megatronics' outsourcing process. You quickly recognize that there are both immediate and strategic icebergs floating in the sea of outsourcing. Discussions, first with the vice presidents of operations and finance, confirm both the dangers and the opportunities present. You are appointed director of Outsourcing at the next meeting of the executive committee. You immediately hire your former colleague Lee Buddress to develop, institute, and manage a comprehensive outsourcing program.

In November, you, your executive team, and Professor Zinke meet for a two-day retreat in Dana Point. Although the final results will not be available until next January, it appears that your goals will be met or exceeded. With the dramatic improvements in the capabilities of the workforce, it has been easy to "ratchet" your goals up.

## More Initiatives

On Friday, the group moved on to the development of the goals and initiatives shown in Exhibit 22.7. The goals and the supporting initiatives will become supply management's strategic plan and will be input to Megatronics' corporate strategic plan.

Your group then focused on initiatives that will support your goals. You have been duly impressed with the initiatives undertaken by Megatronics' supply management personnel as a direct result of their transformational training. Over half of next year's initiatives already are being introduced at the team level by one or more teams.

The Executive Board reviewed supply management's accomplishments and updated plans at its January meeting. You felt acceptance and respect. It was time to propose a more cross-functional approach to change at Megatronics. You summarized Carlos Ghosen's 1999 and 2000 experience in turning Nissan around and the critical role played by cross-functional teams.[12] You pointed out that your supply management team was making great progress but that all too often progress was blocked or impeded by functional silos.[13] You proposed bringing Dr. David Lehmann, vice president of Operations, Solar (retired), in to address the topic at the next Executive Board meeting. There was agreement by all members.

The Board's next meeting focused on change and the possible role of cross-functional teams in the change process. Dr. Lehmann was retained to develop an appropriate program. He reported directly to the Chairman and the President. The program was a resounding success and resulted in positive changes that went beyond your wildest dreams. Resistance to necessary change down through middle management throughout Megatronics began to dissipate.

During the first half of the year, it became apparent that the functional silo mentality of the logistics and demand management personnel was blocking your efforts to integrate those functions with supply management. Several senior-level discussions resulted in supply management, logistics, and demand management being integrated into a new organization known as Supply Network Management under your leadership. The transformation and integration of those three activities were both challenging and satisfying. The board also agreed that your de facto reporting relationship with the operating divisions be ratified: You officially have line authority over all supply management personnel. The anticipated benefits started flowing almost immediately!

Lastly, you announced to the board that the total number of employees in supply chain management now was less than one-half of the over 800 you had inherited from purchasing in 2008 plus the 80 you recently acquired from demand management and logistics.

---

[12]Carlos Ghosen, "Saving the Business without Losing the Company," *Harvard Business Review*, January 2002, pp. 37–45.

[13]The term "functional silo" is used in industry to describe how functions, such as marketing, finance, and engineering, often do not work with other functional areas toward the greater good of the firm.

## EXHIBIT 22.7 | GOALS AND INITIATIVES FOR YEAR TWO

**Goals**

- Reduce average price of incoming goods and services by 5 percent
- Reduce average incoming defects by 50 percent to 450 ppm
- Reduce average time required to develop a new product by 10 percent
- Reduce production disruptions caused by late delivery of materials by 50 percent
- Increase the number of new products based on supplier-furnished technology by 10 percent
- Decrease the supply base by 15 percent
- Increase award of production contracts to diversity suppliers to 5 percent

**Initiatives**

- Develop a world-class information system, Q3
- Document, verify, and track cost savings, Q1
- Implement value engineering and value analysis programs, Q1
- Develop or hire a cadre of eight cost engineers, Q2–3
- Develop 14 corporatewide commodity teams, Q2–3
- Expand strategic sourcing to all commodity classes, Q4
- Initiate creation of a global supplier network, Q3
- Develop an internal Megatronics-wide education program for understanding and managing supplier diversity, Q2
- Develop a recognition program for suppliers that embrace Megatronics' pollution avoidance program, Q3
- Increase supplier development efforts, ongoing
- Develop four new supplier alliances, Q4
- Increase integration of suppliers into the development process, ongoing
- Develop Web-based applications to link suppliers with Megatronics, Q1
- Analyze supply management skills systematically
- Conduct training to upgrade personnel to required levels, ongoing
- Develop leadership from within, ongoing
- Implement a college recruiting leadership program, Q1
- Recruit best candidates to fill entry-level and midcareer openings, ongoing
- Ensure clear employee performance goals, Q2
- Provide career development opportunities, ongoing
- Implement rewards and incentive plan for members of supply management system, Q2
- Ensure retention of promising employees, ongoing
- Integrate supply management, logistics, and demand management, Q3
- Increase compensation of supply professionals, Q4

It's now November of the following year. The planning meeting is in Palm Springs. Your group has been enlarged to include a senior logistician from one of the divisions and a demand manager from another. Year-to-date results look great.

You introduce a topic about which you feel very strongly: the Toyota supplier family. "It is my belief that one of the fastest and best ways of driving Megatronics' supply management to the next level is to borrow from Toyota the idea of supplier families. These families are closely integrated networks. Best practices are shared and implemented. The impact on cost, quality, time to market, continuity of supply . . . heck, on everything, is awesome. I'd like to be personally involved in initiating this program with our first alliance partner, Diapole International." (There is enthusiastic endorsement of your idea!)

Knowing that the full benefits of early supplier and early supply management involvement are really kicking in, the group agrees on the goals shown in Exhibit 22.8. Once again, over half of next year's initiatives are a direct result of your investment in transformational training. Empowerment works!

It's November of the following year, and you are in Maui. Ah, the joys of success! But at what a price! Mike Doyle has taken the CSO position at HP. Troy has moved to Cisco as CSO. Susan has become your deputy and heir-apparent, having turned down several lucrative offers. JoAnn Barber has moved to Sommers,

---

## EXHIBIT 22.8 | GOALS AND INITIATIVES FOR YEAR THREE

**Goals**

- Reduce average price of incoming goods and services by 5 percent
- Reduce incoming defects by 50 percent to an average of 225 ppm
- Improve forecast accuracy to $\pm 5$ percent for 30 days and $\pm 10$ percent for 30 to 120 days

**Initiatives**

- Develop 10 new supplier alliances, Q4
- Document, verify, track, and control savings, Q1
- Increase purchases from diversity suppliers to 6 percent of production materials, Q2
- Initiate one supplier family (à la Toyota) by a key first-tier supplier, Q3
- Initiate 20 quality teams, four operating groups, Q4
- Develop 16 new commodity teams, Q2
- Integrate inbound and outbound traffic, Q3
- Upgrade order and fulfillment processes, Q1
- Go global on all aspects of supply chain management, Q1
- Introduce "lean" into Megatronics' supply chain, Q2
- Optimize use of the Internet, Q3
- Increase emphasis on contract and relationship management, ongoing
- Provide ethics training to all in-house members of supply chain management system, Q2
- Focus negotiation training on synergy with suppliers, Q2
- Conduct debriefings addressing "lessons learned" on all negotiations, Q1
- Study implications of employing other than firm fixed price compensation, Q2

New York, where she has become VP, Global Supply Management (her friend and colleague Rose Layo has moved to Raleigh, where she has become Director of Supply Chain Management). Paul Wilson has become a full-time minister. Jason Patel has become CSO for Freightlines. Ray Hummell is completing his Ph.D. at Claremont. Professor Zinke has retired to his wine estate in the Barossa Valley outside of Adelaide, South Australia. Fortunately, your training, education, and career progression programs have minimized the impact of the departure of those wonderful people. You have been able to fill every vacancy from your existing staff.

In preparation for this year's meeting, you have invited Professor Zinke's protégé, Professor Alan Goldstein, to join the group as "academic in residence." After a wonderful light breakfast on the lanai, you and your new team get down to business by addressing goals for the following year. You agree on the goals shown in Exhibit 22.9.

---

## EXHIBIT 22.9 | GOALS AND INITIATIVES FOR YEAR FOUR

### Goals

- Reduce total cost of ownership on incoming goods and services by 5 percent
- Reduce average incoming defects by over 50 percent to an average of 110 ppm
- Develop 17 new supplier alliances
- Increase purchases from diversity suppliers to 6.5 percent of production materials
- Increase the number of firms embracing Megatronics' pollution avoidance program to 53
- Globalize the pollution avoidance program
- Add two supplier families
- Improve forecast accuracy to $\pm 4$ percent for 30 days and $\pm 8$ percent for 120 days

### Initiatives

- Champion the firm's pursuit of the Malcolm Baldrige Award by developing a three-year plan, Q2
- Develop and deploy a new metric for measuring institutional trust, Q2
- Implement a program of integrated financial transaction work flows coupled with tax-effective supply chain management practices, Q3
- Develop and implement supply chain scorecards, Q3
- Implement an aggressive publicity program, both corporatewide and, network members, Q4
- Award 50 percent of savings documented from VE/VA programs to suppliers, Q1
- Replace long-winded contracts with short ones whose intent is to promote teamwork, ongoing
- Experiment with allowing suppliers to construct their own contracts on our website, Q2
- Establish supply management as a recognized competency corporate wide, ongoing
- Integrate supply chain management planning tightly with other systems at all levels, ongoing
- Align Strategic Sourcing strategies across the enterprise, ongoing
- Optimize global logistics operations (inbound and outbound), ongoing
- Develop a globally integrated order fulfillment process, Q1
- Set consistent performance standards, Q2

- Communicate expectations and feedback results to suppliers, Q2
- Expand Megatronics' supplier network around the globe, ongoing
- Enable suppliers to interact seamlessly within Megatronics, ongoing
- Support strategic sourcing, supplier integration, product delivery, and order fulfillment processes with timely and effective cost/financial information, Q3
- Utilize supplier development to transform the supply chain toward lean manufacturing, maximum flexibility, reduced cycle times, improved quality, and reduced overall total cost in the supply chain, ongoing
- Integrate the supply chain into the technology delivery process, ongoing
- Integrate e-Commerce II processes with all the key processes to enable better integration and strategic planning, Q3
- Develop worldwide purchase data gathering and sharing capabilities, ongoing
- Provide needed education and training, globally, across the enterprise and enable distance learning, ongoing
- Provide meaningful work, challenging assignments, and development opportunities, ongoing
- Develop individual development and succession plans, ongoing
- Identify common activities and roles where redundancies can be eliminated, ongoing
- Identify and optimize synergies across the supply chain, ongoing
- Identify and develop business marketplaces that enable supply chain leverage and synergy, ongoing

After lunch, the group tees off and plays a round at Maui's finest golf course. This is pure business, since you had charged the group to come up with 15 initiatives the next day. The evening's luau is somewhat disappointing, although the mai-tais are delightful and the entertainment is provocative.

You begin the next day's meeting by observing: "When we have completed development of a list of initiatives for next year, we're done with the formal part of our agenda."

Being highly motivated, the group agrees on the initiatives shown in Exhibit 22.9.

# January 2012

It's January 2012, four and a half years since you were hired as CSO. Megatronics' stock has increased fivefold during your tenure. You enter your new office. You get a thrill out of the sign on your new door: Office of the President and Chief Executive Officer. During a series of discussions in your first month with the new VP, Supply Network Management, and her managers in your former organization and then with your corporate board, you have taken advantage of your honeymoon and reorganized. Susan Reese has officially been given a new title and additional responsibilities. She is the Vice President of Supply Network Management. The new organization is depicted in Figure 22.5.

# Concluding Remarks

Implementing World Class Supply Management[SM] and World Class Value Network Management is as much about leadership and management as it is about supply management concepts and practices. Transformational-based training and education play essential roles. The pace of change must be based on the principle "Stretch, but don't break."

Based on its integrative, relationship, and boundary spanning nature, there is no question in our minds: "World-class supply managers have the essential skill set to become Chief Executive Officers!" Finally,

**Figure 22.5 |** Megatronics Corporation Supply Network Management Organization, 2012

Appendix B provides a good Example of the change in thinking so necessary to start the road to value network management, i.e., The Rolls-Royce North America story.

## Discussion Questions

1. How would you describe the distinction between Supply Chain Management and Value Network Management?
2. What is the difference between the vision statement and the mission statement?
3. Why is it important to have early supplier involvement (ESI) in new product development?
4. Where do technical procedures described earlier in the text such as ABC analysis and total cost of ownership (TCO) fit in with both tactical and strategic planning?
5. How can the preparation of an annual materials report listing all supply activities assist in selling VNM to senior management?
6. What are the characteristics of supply leaders such as David Nelson and Thomas Stallkamp that make them so effective?

## Suggested Reading

Banfield, E. *Harnessing Value in the Supply Chain* (New York: John Wiley & Sons, 1999).

Cohen, Shoshanah, and Joseph Roussel. *Strategic Supply Chain Management: The 5 Disciplines for Top Performance* (New York: McGraw-Hill, 2005).

Giannakis, Mihalis, and Simon R. Croom. "Toward the Development of a Supply Chain Management Paradigm," *Journal of Supply Chain Management,* Spring 2004, pp. 27–37.

*Harvard Business Review on Supply Chain Management,* Boston, MA: Harvard Business School Press, 2006.

Hunt, Shelby D., and Donna F. Davis. "Grounding Supply Chain Management in Resource Advantage Theory," *Journal of Supply Chain Management* 44, no. 1 (January 2008), pp. 10–21.

Long, C., and G. Meyer. *Sacred Cows Make the Best Barbecue: Supply Chain Management: A Revolutionary 26 Week Action Plan* (Seal Beach, CA, Vision Press, 1998).

Parker, Devlon B., George A. Zsidisin, and Gary L.Ragatz. "Timing and Extent of Supplier Integration in New Product Development: A Contingency Approach," *Journal of Supply Chain Management* 44, no. 1 (January 2008), pp. 71–83.

Siegfried, Mary. "Transforming Supplier Relationships: Supply Management Professional Profile: Rolls-Royce North America," *Inside Supply Management* 19, no. 1 (January 2008), pp. 32–34. See Appendix B in this chapter for a full version of this article.

Trent, Robert J. *Strategic Supply Management: Creating the Next Source of Competitive Advantage* (Fort Lauderdale, FL: J. Ross Publishing, 2007).

Wilson, J. Holton, and Barry Keating, John Galt Solutions, Inc. *Business Forecasting with ForecastX Software & Student CD,* 5th ed. (New York: McGraw-Hill, 2007).

# Appendix A: The Institute for Supply Management's R. Gene Richter Awards for Leadership and Innovation in Supply Management

Named after the late distinguished R. Gene Richter (1937–2003), a supply executive at Black & Decker Corp. and Hewlett-Packard Company and later a vice president at IBM, these awards are given to organizations that demonstrate excellence in leadership and innovation in supply management. There are four categories, with a winner or winners selected in each one: Process, Technology, People, and Organization/Structure.

The first awards were given in 2006 to the following recipients:

### Process

1. Johnson & Johnson, manufacturer of health care products, for unique and innovative partnership of the supply management organization and the law department for both in-house and outside counsel with savings/cost avoidance of $48.7 million in the first year. www.jnj.com

2. KLA-Tencor, a leading supplier of process control and yield management solutions for the semiconductor industry. For moving from a transaction-based procurement system to a strategic organization with a cross-functional focus, including sourcing in the company's well-established product life cycle (PLC) management. Before a product can exit the investigation phase, a strategic sourcing input is required. Product cost reductions 5 to 10 times that of former projects were achieved. www.kla-tencor.com

### Technology

1. Fluor Hanford manages several major activities for the U.S. Department of Energy at the Hanford site in southern Washington State. For development of its Web-based material sourcing "Wizard" search application. The goal was to develop a system that would allow workers in the field to order needed routine supplies through an easy-to-use, one-stop shopping system while the supply staff concentrated on strategic issues. Savings include about $300,000 in 12 months from redundant

buying, $2 million per year in reduced transaction costs, and reduced unit prices from 10 to 60 percent. www.Fluor.com/govenerment

2. Rockwell Collins, a leader in the design, production, and support of communication and aviation electronics for commercial and government customers. For taking its supply collins.com portal, a successful Web-based tool for suppliers, to the next level by adding applications that would automate three key purchases-to-pay processes, requests for quotes, quote receipts, total cost of ownership analysis, and automated purchase orders. The volume of transactions from quote release to final payment has increased from 46 to 70 percent. www.rockwell.com

### People

1. London-based BP, P.L.C., one of the world's largest energy companies, for developing eight core training modules that address most skill sets, including living strategy and program management, communication and engagement, internal performance, financial decision making, strategic sourcing, and supplier management. Compressed into six-month periods for 140 members of the global refining and marketing (downstream) and corporate and functions (indirect) procurement community. Nearly 50 percent of the program evaluations indicated a perceived significant improvement in the skills area. www.bp.com

### Organization/Structure

1. Daimler Chrysler, a major German automobile manufacturer, for consolidation of its global procurement. Its International Procurement Services (IPS) department focused on consolidation of global nonproduction material procurement responsibility in Germany and for the Chrysler Group in the United States and Canada. The results include an 80 percent increase in value added, increased internal customer satisfaction, and the implementation of one common information technology solution. www.daimlerchrysler.com

## 2007 Award Winners

### Process

1. Johnson & Johnson, a major health care product manufacturer, for launching a consulting sourcing initiative for North America. Using three teams, J&J increased the level of consulting procurement expertise and increased the value of and emphasis on master services agreements, including improved rating of consultant capabilities. www.jnj.com

### Technology

1. Alltel Communications, Inc., which operates the largest wireless network in the United States, for designing the Workflow Management Tool, which was created entirely in-house by the Procurement and Logistics Group (PLG) at Alltel Wireless. This system assigns works, tracks savings and project status, and provides visibility into the sourcing/savings funnel, allowing the organization to see "what tomorrow might look like" across the company. The benefits include project tracking and management, status updates, workflow management, single-source reporting for PLG savings and metrics reporting, visibility into all sourcing projects at a macro level, deal summaries and saving funnels by group, ability to forecast gross margin impacts, ability to recommend changes to the financial planning/budgeting process, and increased integrity in savings reporting. www.alltel.com

## People

1. BP, P.L.C. This London-based firm is one of the world's largest energy companies. For developing the rapid sourcing team, a program to develop and train new university recruits to improve the sourcing process, drive adoption of e-sourcing tools, and address low-value spend categories that often are overlooked. Results include savings of more than $550 million through the use of e-sourcing tools during 2005–2006. www.bp.com

## Organization/Structure

No award winners in 2007.

# 2008 Award Winners

## Process

1. Lockheed Martin (LM) Aeronautics Company, a leader in design, research and development, systems integration, and production and support of advanced military aircraft and related technologies. To prevent shortages of critical raw materials such as titanium, the LM Material Management and IS&T departments joined forces to launch a "preemptive strike" with their forecast raw material application (FORM), which generates a comprehensive, time-phased raw material forecast for the F-35 joint strike fighter program. This achieved a significant reduction in negotiated pricing for long-term raw material contracts and much better demand planning for raw materials for all program trading partners. www.lockheedmartin.com/aeronautics
2. Pfizer, Inc., a global leader in pharmaceuticals. Three years ago Pfizer World Wide Procurement was challenged to achieve $2 billion in savings in purchased goods and services by 2008. Using a new reverse auction system to source commodities considered core to the research and development organization items of a highly technical nature. Pfizer used cross functional/cross-disciplined teams to develop a unique collaborative model between World Wide Procurement and the development of medical organizations. This model facilitated the prequalification of suppliers to participate in reverse auctions with major cost savings. www.pfizer.com

## Technology

1. Masco Corporation, one of the world's largest manufacturers of brand name consumer products for the home improvement and new construction markets. Masco Global Purchasing and IT teams designed a supplier management tool (SMT) that allows Masco to leverage its spend, share supplier information, improve payment terms, track commodities, evaluate and rate suppliers, and track spending globally. This highly decentralized supply management organization uses SRM to unite disparate ERP systems into a robust spend analysis tool, integrating more than $10.8 billion in spend and 22 million transactions across 38 divisions representing 695 manufacturing and service locations. From October 2004 to September 2007, Masco divisions posted eight figures in savings, ranging from 4 percent to 67 percent. www.masco.com

## Process

1. Royal KPN telecom provides telephone, Internet, and television services to customers through its fixed network in the Netherlands and internationally. KPN had been experiencing an adverse relationship with its outsourced IT supplier, ATOS Origin. To restore trust and desired performance,

KPN formed a steering committee composed of senior KPN and ATOS Origin Executives that eventually produced what they called the collaborative KPI program, which revised the original outsourcing contracts to eliminate unrealistic revenue guarantees for ATOS Origin and focused on cost reduction. Thus, the new collaboration efforts created a value-based relationship rather than one based on cost-driven goals. This new contract established an escrow account for revenues, a set of performance measures for the supplier, and a two-way set of KPIs containing performance targets for both supplier and buyer. Complaints for poor service from KPN's customers dropped from 15 percent to 5 percent monthly. www.kpn.com

2.  HP supplies printing, personal computing, software, services, and other IT products and services worldwide. HP has distinguished itself as a promoter of social and environmentally responsible (SER) programs within its operations, supply chain, and industry. Indeed, in 2002, HP was the first electronics company to publish a social and environmental responsibility supplier code of conduct. The company conducts regular supplier assessments and audits for all suppliers but in particular for its 16 direct material suppliers with more than 300 factories in countries identified by HP as "higher risk countries." Those suppliers listed in audits with major deficiencies in the SER program have from 30 to 180 days to address the particular issues. HP also has several "zero-tolerance" areas such as using underage child and forced labor, serious safety issues, and other violations of environmental laws. Special projects are now going on in China and Central Europe. www.hp.com

*Note:* In 2008, there were four process, one technology, and no people or organization/structure awards. See the June 2008 issue of *Inside Supply Management* by Mary Siegfried.

What do all these winners have in common? In the opinion of the authors of this text, they are characterized by:

1.  Vision for the future.
2.  Proactive action.
3.  A focus on supply as a value-adding member of the chain versus a cost center.
4.  Being creative: How can we do it better?
5.  Use of cross-functional teams.
6.  "Best-in-class" practices.
7.  Use of the tools, methods, procedures, and philosophy contained in this and other leading texts, trade books, and ISM material.

With permission of ISM, Tempe, AZ. www.ism.ws

References: June 2006, June 2007 and June 2008 issues of *Inside Supply Management,* by Mary Siegfried, John Yuva, Lisa Cooling, RaeAnn Slaybaugh.

# Appendix B: At Rolls-Royce North America, an organizational shift is the driving force behind an innovative new journey to engage its supply chain.*

For two years, Kathi D. Bridgewater, purchasing process and business development executive for Rolls-Royce North America, lived and breathed supplier relationship strategy. That's because Bridgewater and a team of nine other senior-level Rolls-Royce executives were on a journey to radically change the way the

---

*By Mary Siegfried, "Transforming Supplier Relationships: The Rolls Royce Case Study." *Inside Supply Management*, Jan. 2008, pp. 32–34.

company works with its suppliers. The results of that journey not only brought about changes to the company's supplier strategy, it sparked an organizational transformation that continues to shape Rolls-Royce today.

The transformation began several years ago when the supply management organization took a close look at itself and its supply chain. The organization's focus at that time was on driving piece price down year after year. It realized, however, that such a focus was leading to adversarial behaviors in the supply chain, and failed to address the bigger issue of lower total costs. That initial examination prompted Rolls-Royce, which provides power systems and services for use on land, sea and air, to hire an outside consulting firm to conduct a comprehensive supplier survey, Bridgewater recalls. When the "dismal survey results" came back in early 2004, it was clear to Rolls-Royce's top-level executives that significant improvements needed to be made. The U.K.-based company, with 38,000 employees in offices and manufacturing and service facilities in 50 countries, also realized that to make significant improvements, an organization-wide commitment to change was needed.

At that point, a working relationship team was formed with the goal of changing and redefining the manner in which Rolls-Royce engages its supply chain. Bridgewater was chosen as a team member, representing Rolls-Royce North America's manufacturing facility in Indianapolis. She emphasizes that the senior-level team was cross-regional, cross-functional and cross-business because the challenge it was undertaking involved the entire company. "It was not a purchasing-related activity. This was about a transformation of how the company interfaces with our suppliers and the relationships we have with them," she says.

Team members signed a two-year commitment to the project, and it became their full-time job. For Bridgewater, that meant living in England for four months at the outset of the project, and then traveling back and forth regularly during the course of the two years.

She admits that the early days were tough, as the team worked to find common ground, common goals and to identify its vision. Because Rolls-Royce is a company that is "trusted to deliver excellence and is very driven in that area," Bridgewater says the team had to step out of its comfort zone at times and remind itself that its goal was to improve relationships.

"It was not just about processes, and documenting and fixing processes," she notes. "It's about how we work with suppliers. We had to ask ourselves what a good relationship with a supplier looks like. Then we had to draw that as our vision."

A visual management room was set up, and the team used it throughout the two years as it identified goals and made its business case for change.

## A Supplier Survey Reveals the Truth

Because the supplier survey results sparked the need to re-examine supplier relationships, Bridgewater says those results became the foundation from which the team worked to make improvements and changes. She admits that the results of the supplier surveys were not necessarily surprising, but they were sobering. "No one likes to hear that their scores are low, but those who worked in the supply chain area were aware of the issues brought out in the survey," she says. "By and large, I don't think there was a message in the survey that no one anticipated."

For example, the survey made it clear that Rolls-Royce "did not have one voice," Bridgewater says. One supplier company in the survey said that, on average, it interfaced with 44 different people at Rolls-Royce. Others pointed out that because of the focus on keeping piece price down, there seemed to be a lack of concern for suppliers' profitability.

Other key messages from the supplier survey were:

- A lack of trust;
- Good performance did not translate into more business;

- Functional silos, not integrated business;
- A short-term approach;
- Poor use of suppliers' capabilities.

Deciding what issues to focus on was one of the team's first challenges. "The toughest part was boiling the issues down to a workable number of topics, say 10 or 12," Bridgewater notes. When the team identified specific areas that it wanted to address, such as organizational interface, earlier engagement of suppliers in projects and technical interface with suppliers, then a team member became the "owner" of that workstream.

For example, the engineer on the team was responsible for the technical interface workstream. His responsibilities included taking the plans the team was working on back to the engineers to get their feedback and buy-in on proposals. Bridgewater says the team sought and received "constant feedback" from stakeholders to make sure it was on the right track.

Another key element in the process, Bridgewater emphasizes, was supplier participation. "We couldn't forget that this is all about suppliers. We had to test our thinking on the suppliers," she says. Supplier focus groups were formed within the first few months of the process, and were asked to participate in interactive workshops from time to time throughout the two years.

From the outset, the team understood that although it would disband, the process of improving supplier relationships would be continuous. The policies and plans developed by the team became part of Rolls-Royce's business plan. "It all fed back into the organization," she says. "For example, you can look at our deliverables and our business plan in the purchasing area and see a lot of the output from the team's activity feeding into the organization in terms of goals and objectives."

Some of the deliverables developed by the team are:

- A new supplier strategy process for developing, documenting and sharing strategies with suppliers;
- A "Relationship Profiling Tool" that provides a framework for Rolls-Royce and a supplier to assess their strengths and weaknesses as a supply chain team;

## FIRST-CLASS LESSONS FOR SUCCESS

Kathi D. Bridgewater, purchasing process and business development executive for Rolls-Royce North America, says she has learned many lessons from her two-year participation on a team that developed a comprehensive plan for improving Rolls-Royce's relationship with its supply chain. Some of those lessons include:

- Senior level support is crucial. "If you don't have top management's support, you will fail," Bridgewater says.
- In forming a team, take a holistic approach. Engage all businesses in the organization, because all businesses have relationships with suppliers.
- Team members should understand the organization, and be at a senior level in order to have access to resources and "know their way around the company."
- Get suppliers involved early in the process and seek their feedback throughout.
- Don't expect immediate results. "It took many years to get your organization in the shape it's in; it's not going to come in six months."
- Focus efforts on a workable number of topics. Set deliverables for each topic.
- When you see success, celebrate it.

## ROLLS-ROYCE: A SNAPSHOT

**Headquarters:** United Kingdom
**Founded:** 1904
**CEO:** Sir John Rose
**Annual Revenue For 2006:** $3.9 billion pounds
**Number of Supply Management Employees:** 1,620 as of October 2007
**Primary Products and Services:** Rolls-Royce, a world-leading provider of power systems and services for use on land, at sea and in the air, operates in four global markets—civil aerospace, defense aerospace, marine and energy. It continues to invest in core technologies, products, people and capabilities with the objective of broadening and strengthening its product portfolio, improving efficiency and enhancing the environmental performance of its products. These investments create high barriers to entry.
**Interesting Fact:** In 2007, Rolls-Royce was one of the sponsors of an expedition called Polar First, undertaken by two pilots who flew a Bell 407 helicopter around the world, from the North Pole to the South Pole. A Rolls-Royce Model 250 engine—produced at the company's Indianapolis facility—powered the helicopter that helped to set this record.

- A program for training and "up-skilling" employees;
- A supply chain technical interface methodology to cover joint technology development and a new product introduction process to better use suppliers' capabilities.

Bridgewater cautions that organizations seeking to improve their own supplier strategies should not expect overnight results. "When you are talking about cultural transformation and managing relationships, you are on a long journey," she says. "It's about sticking with it and about being consistent."

The proof of success is in sustainability, Bridgewater notes, stressing that strategies should be dynamic and ongoing. Suppliers are telling Roll-Royce that they are impressed by the company's commitment to improving relationships and engaging them in the process, Bridgewater adds, although some are taking a wait-and-see attitude. A follow-up survey will be done, although the timing has not yet been decided.

Despite the challenges the team faced, Bridgewater says the journey was worthwhile because it demonstrated Rolls-Royce's commitment to its customers. It also was clear from the start that the company had to invest in a supplier relationship strategy if it wanted to survive and compete in today's business environment.

"The strategies and plans we developed are now part of the way we work, a continuation of the journey. In all organizations, from engineering to supply management, they (plans and strategies) are part of our core business plans. It is embedded in the way we move forward," she says.

# NAME INDEX

Page numbers followed by n indicate notes.

## A

Adams, Cary W., 175
Agusti, Filiberto, 296
Ahmet, Satir, 236n
Akao, Yoji, 175
Allen, G. R., 526
Amdt, Michael, 239
Ammer, Dean S., 36n
Anderson, Edward G., Jr., 431
Anderson, Ruth, 431
Andraski, Joseph C., 20
Anklesaria, Jimmy, 195n, 296, 297n, 299n, 331n, 334n, 390n
Antill, Peter B., 47n
Aquilano, Nicholas J., 502, 539
Arnold, Uli, 95n
Aspuro, Maytee, 431
Assaf, Michael, 296
Augello, W. J., 526
Auguston Field, Karen, 193
Axelsson, Bjorn, 115, 213, 221n
Ayers, James B., 62

## B

Baker, R. Jerry, 455n
Baldwin, David G., 43, 44n
Ball, Donald, 296
Ballou, Ronald H., 526, 538
Banfield, Emiko, 45n, 576
Banting, P. M., 476n
Bardi, Edward J., 526, 536n, 539
Barkman, Sandra, 317
Barnes, Dan, 20
Barry, Bruce, 396
Basu, Ron, 175
Beall, S., 262
Bechtel, Christian, 538
Bender, Paul, 538
Bendorf, Robi, 279n
Bennet, James, 38
Bensaou, M., 77n
Benton, W. C., 262, 414n
Berggren, Christian, 116

Berry, John, 239, 296
Berry, William L., 502, 535
Bhote, Keki R., 70n, 154n
Birou, Laura M., 37n
Blanshay, Marlene, 480n
Blenkhorn, D. L., 476n
Boeder, Steven, 502
Bohan, Michael L., 396
Bonincontro, Cynthia, 296
Bouchoux, Deborah, 417
Bowersox, Donald J., 526, 539
Boyer, Kenneth, 20
Bragg, Daniel J., 467n, 476n
Bragg, Steven M., 502
Brealey, R. A., 188n, 190n
Brenner, F. Cecil, 140
Brett, Jeanne M., 396
Bretz, Bob, 255n
Bridgewater, Kathi D., 580–583
Brimson, James A., 346
Brown, Craig, 564n
Brown, Diane, 46n
Brue, Greg, 175
Bruning, Bob, 539
Brunsson, Nils, 140
Buddress, Lee, 346, 390n, 392
Budzki, Robert A., 20
Burt, David N., 12n, 42n, 46n, 52n, 54n, 97n, 99, 105, 107n, 111, 119n, 129n, 144n, 195n, 331n, 334n, 346, 390n, 455n, 491n, 513, 547
Burton, Terrence, 502
Butler, Linda, 258n
Butterfield, Bill, 254n
Buzzell, Robert D., 10n

## C

Calantone, Roger J., 134, 262
Cali, James F., 148n, 175
Campanella, Jack, 155n
Cantrell, George E., 370
Carbone, James, 254n
Carlisle, John A., 97n

Carr, Amelia S., 81
Carter, Craig R., 262, 456
Carter, Joseph R., 69n, 239, 246n, 247n, 275n, 276n, 277n, 299n
Carter, Philip L., 69n, 246n, 247n, 262, 275n, 277n
Casale, Frank, 235n
Casillas, Raul, 279n
Casper, Steven, 162n
Cavanagh, Roland R., 149n
Cavinato, Joseph L., 17, 18n, 20, 51n, 54n, 61n, 74n, 317, 539
Chase, Richard B., 502, 539
Chen, Injazz J., 68n
Chiazza, John, 235
Choi, T. Y., 262
Chopra, Sunil, 539
Christensen, Clayton M., 230n
Christopher, Martin, 529n
Clark, Don, 392n
Claunch, Jerry W., 176, 431
Clausing, Don, 100n, 156n
Clevenger, David B., 260n
Click, Rick L., 239
Closs, David J., 39, 526, 539
Cohen, Herb, 372n, 386n
Cohen, Linda, 239
Cohen, Shoshanah, 539, 576
Cole, Robert E., 164n
Collins, Jim, 549n
Conrad, Ginger, 258n
Constable, Gordon K., 170n
Contino, Richard, 193
Cook, Thomas A., 296, 539
Cooling, Lisa, 455n, 456, 565n
Cooper, M. Bixby, 526, 539
Cooper, Martha C., 39, 539
Cooper, Robert W., 456
Cooper, Robin, 342
Coover, Judi, 368n, 408n
Copeland, Michael, 296
Corbet, Michael F., 239
Cox, Andrew, 76n, 77n, 220

Cox, Patricia A., 346
Coyle, John J., 526, 536n, 539
Crawford, Merle, 116
Crews, Mary, 46n
Crocker, Barry, 81
Croom, Simon R., 20, 39, 115n, 431, 577
Crosby, Philip, 145, 149, 171, 172n, 175
Crowder, Mark A., 431
Culliton, J. W., 237n

**D**

Dairs, James, 254n
Darby, Mike, 450
Darlington, Gerry, 379n
Daugherty, Patricia J., 62
Davenport, Thomas H., 480n
Davis, Donna F., 577
Dawson, Roger, 396
De Boer, L., 262
Dean, Anthony A., 407n
Dean, James W., Jr., 42n
Degraeve, Z., 317
Dell, Michael, 79n
Deming, W. Edwards, 144, 165, 170, 176
DeRose, Louis J., 204n
DeWitt, William, 62, 315n
Di Benedetto, Anthony, 116
Dion, P. A., 476n
DiOrio, N. A., 280n
Dirsmith, N. W., 192
Dischinger, John, 39
D'Itri, Michael P., 299n
Dobler, Donald W., 107n, 513
Dodge, Harold F., 169n
Dowst, Somerby, 452n, 561n
Doyle, Michael F., 119n, 129n, 455n
Dratell, Eric, 400n
Drucker, Peter F., 98n, 343n
Duening, Thomas N., 239
Duffy, Roberta J., 74n, 213, 244n, 537n
Dunn, Steven C., 262
Durant, William, 98
Dyer, Jeffrey H., 17n, 65, 70n, 72n, 81n, 84n, 550n

**E**

Earle, Beverley, 296
Elderkin, Kenton W., 288n, 290n
Ellram, Lisa M., 39, 81, 101n, 219n, 228n, 229n, 262, 303n, 313n, 317, 346, 539

Emmett, Stuart, 81, 539
Engardio, Pete, 239
English, Kathy, 346
Ensign, Marc, 244n, 246n
Erb, Martin S., 109n
Erlicher, Harry, 106
Essig, Michael, 95n
Esty, Daniel C., 502
Ettlie, John E., 95n, 116
Ettorre, Barbara, 283, 284n
Evans, James R., 164n

**F**

Fallon, Carlos, 109n
Faltra, Robert M., 256n
Farney, Samuel D., 296
Farrell, Paul, 416n
Farris, M. Theodore, 526
Fawcett, Stanley E., 37n, 69n, 83n
Fearon, Harold E., 32n
Feigenbaum, A. V., 155n
Felch, Robert I., 448n, 449n
Ferguson, W. C., 456
Fernandez, Richard R., 176
Ferrara, William L., 192
Ferrin, Bruce G., 317
Field, Anne R., 100n
Fine, Charles H., 115n, 239
Finszer, Paul H., 203n
Fisher, Roger, 381, 388n, 396
Flaherty, Jane S., 396
Flanagan, Patrick, 255n
Flynn, Anna E., 20, 26n, 32n, 213
Ford, Henry, 476
Forker, Laura, 245n, 288n, 289n
Foster, Trevor, 211n
Foust, Dean, 239
Frank, Garry L., 456
Frantz, Paul, 296
Frazelle, Edward H., 526
Freeman, H. A., 169n
Friedman, Matthew, 480n
Friedman, Milton, 169n
Frohlich, Markham, 20

**G**

Gabbard, Ernest G., 403n
Gabriel, Henry D., 418
Gardner, James A., 491, 492n
Garrison, David H., 198, 199n, 213
Garvin, David A., 176
Gattorna, John, 39
Gaze, Bradley T., 10n

Geringer, Michael, 296
German, T., 262
Gettinger, Marilyn, 36n, 37, 56n
Ghauri, Pervez N., 396
Ghosen, Carlos, 571n
Giannakis, Mihalis, 20, 39, 431, 577
Gietzmann, M. B., 239
Gozzo, Michael W., 176, 431
Graw, Leroy H., 346
Greaver, Maurice F., 239
Greenspan, Alan, 292
Greico, Peter, 176, 431
Grenoble, William, 39
Gross, John M., 502
Guerra, Pat, 102n
Guertin, Ron, 48
Guinipero, Larry, 416n
Gupta, Praveen, 175

**H**

Hahn, Chan K., 467n, 476n
Hall, Edward T., 285n
Hall, Mildred, 285n
Haluch, Frank, 61n
Halvey, John K., 239
Hamel, Gary, 241n
Hamm, Gary, 131
Hammer, Michael, 20
Hampden-Turner, Charles, 285n
Hancke, Bob, 162n
Hancock, William A., 368n, 415n
Handfield, Robert, 12n, 20, 35n, 39, 61n, 81n, 98n, 115n, 117, 455n
Hanna, Mark D., 502
Harding, Mary Lu, 28n, 193, 317, 427n, 431
Harland, Christine, 529n, 530n
Harris, George L., 28n, 39
Harry, Mikel, 176
Hartley, Janet L., 252n, 262, 263
Hartley, M. F., 452n, 456, 457
Hartmann, Evi, 65n
Hatfield, Jo Ellen, 213
Hauser, John R., 100n
Hays, Robert B., 219n
Heinritz, Stuart, 416n
Hendrick, T., 262
Heriot, Kirk C., 246n, 262, 476n
Hershauer, J., 245n
Hiam, Alexander, 396
Hickman, Thomas K., 296
Hickman, William M., Jr., 296
Hill, C. W., 117

Hinkelman, Edward G., 296
Hitt, Michael A., 42n, 47n
Holldorsson, A., 39
Hommerich, Thomas P., 526
Hoole, Rick, 539
Hopp, Wallace J., 536n
Hoyle, David, 140
Hugos, Michael, 20
Hukt, Thomas, 20
Humphreys, Paul K., 62, 81, 239
Hunt, Shelby D., 577
Hurkens, Krisje, 317
Hurson, Kathleen, 47n
Hutchins, Greg, 147n, 163n

**I**

Imai, Masaaki, 145, 148
Irvine, V. B., 457

**J**

Jacobs, F. Robert, 502, 539
Jacobs, Heidi, 283, 284n
Jacobs, Mary, 50
Jacobsen, Sally, 290n
Jahns, Christopher, 65n
Janis, Richard, 305n
Janson, Robert J., 20
Jap, S., 262
Jayaram, Jayanth, 538
Jessop, David, 12n
Johnsen, Stephen, 296
Johnson, P. Fraser, 32n
Johnstone, James M., 260n
Jones, Daniel T., 12, 254n, 343n
Jones, Gwen, 252n
Jones, Ted., 49
Juliar, Troy, 474n
Juran, Joseph, 146, 149, 155n, 176

**K**

Kahn, Kenneth B., 116
Kamauff, John W., 20, 48, 62,
    247n, 253n
Kane, Jo-Anne, 138n
Kannan, Vijay R., 262
Kaplan, Robert, 342, 427
Karol, Robin, 116
Katzenbach, Jon R., 48
Katzorke, Michael, 20
Kauffman, Ralph C., 20, 61n, 74n
Kaufman, Lutz, 262
Keating, Barry, 577
Keebler, James S., 62, 315n

Keller, Paul A., 176
Keller, Scott B., 62
Kemp, Deborah J., 414n
Kemp, Robert A., 456, 548
Kerzner, Harold, 140
Khalil, Frediric, 198, 199n, 213
Killen, Kenneth H., 20, 48, 62
Knemeyer, A. M., 117
Kolchin, Michael, 416n
Kono, Toyohiro, 116
Kotler, Philip, 533
Krajewski, Lee J., 502, 539
Krause, Daniel R., 262
Krupp, James A. G., 484, 485n
Kulkarni, Subodh P., 262
Kumar, Nirmalya, 81n
Kwon, Ik-Whan G., 81

**L**

Labro, E., 262
Lacey, Steve, 109n
LaFasto, Frank M. J., 48
Lakemond, Nicolette, 116
Lambert, Douglas M., 20, 39, 62, 117,
    526, 539
Langley, C. J., 526
Lanier, J., 391n
Larson, Carl E., 48
Larsson, P. D., 39
Laseter, Timothy M., 46n
Leenders, Michiel R., 32n
LeFevre, Laurie, 196n
Leibs, Scott, 236n
Lewicki, Roy J., 396
Lindemann, Exkhard, 69n
Lindsay, Linda M., 457
Lindsay, R. Murray, 457
Lindsay, William M., 164n
Little, Nick, 16n, 20
Liukko, Timo, 193
Locke, Richard, 280n, 283n, 285n, 296,
    297n, 299n
Lockstrom, Martin, 65n
Logothetis, N., 144n, 145n, 149n,
    165n, 171n
Long, C., 577
Long, Gary, 109n
Lonsdale, Chris, 220n
Lopoukhine, Serge R., 346
Lorincz, J. A., 28n
Lousdale, Chris, 77n
Lugo, Dave A., 110n
Lummus, R. R., 39

Lynch, Robert Porter, 317n, 547, 550n
Lynn, Leonard, 116

**M**

Machiavelli, Niccolo, 385n
Maciejewski, D., 262
Magnan, Gregory M., 37n, 69n, 83n
Maier, Norman, 39n
Malhotra, Manoj K., 539
Maltz, Arnold, 219n, 228n, 229n
Mann, Richard A., 211n, 404n,
    410n, 417
Marchall, Donna, 39
Marchetti, Anne M., 457
Marcus, Jeff, 455n
Marien, Edward J., 502n, 526
Markham, William J., 239
Marks, Bryon S., 317
Marshall, S. L., 77n
Martin, James W., 176
Matthesen, Steve, 237n
May, Robert E., 123n
McAdams, Jerry, 42n
McCauly, John, 50
McCulloch, Eileen, 39
McCullock, Wendell, 296
McGinnis, Michael A., 95n, 113n, 116
McHugh, Marie, 81
McInnis, Kenneth R., 502
McIvor, Ronan T., 81, 239
McKeller, John M., 346
McKenna, Regis, 100n
Melby, Barbara Murphy, 239
Melnyk, Steven A., 134, 455n
Menezes, Sanjit, 193
Mentzer, John T., 62, 315n
Metty, Theresa, 552n
Meyer, G., 577
Michels, William L., 370
Miles, Lawrence D., 106n
Miller, Steve, 530n, 532n
Milligan, B., 317
Minor, Michael, 296
Mobley, Calvert G., 77n
Moffat, Paul, 147n
Monczka, Robert M., 20, 35n, 38n, 39,
    48, 61n, 69n, 81n, 115n, 239, 246n,
    247n, 262, 275n, 276n, 277n, 296
Montabon, Frank, 134n
Moody, Patricia E., 12n, 21, 262
Moore, David M., 47n
Moore, Kevin R., 62

Morehouse, James E., 308
Morgan, James P., 20
Morgan, Jim, 396
Morlacchi, P., 262
Moser, Roger, 65n
Mosteller, Frederick, 169n
Muller, Max, 502
Murray, John, Jr., 404n
Musselwhite, Ed, 47n
Myers, Matthew B., 62
Myers, S. C., 188n, 190n

**N**

Nair, Saresli, 100n
Nathan, Scott J., 235n
Nellore, Rajesh, 116
Nelson, Beebe, 116
Nelson, Katherine A., 457
Nelson, R. David, 12n, 21, 33, 253, 262,
    281, 306n, 548–549
Neuman, Robert P., 149n
Newman, Debbie, 258n
Newman, George, 481n
Newman, Richard G., 193, 346
Newman, W. Rocky, 502
Nichols, Ernest L., 20, 39
Nierenberg, Gerald, 386n
Nix, Nancy W., 62
Norquist, Warren E., 35, 55n, 58n, 61,
    195n, 196, 271n, 288n, 290n, 331n,
    334n, 390n
Norton, David, 427
Novack, Robert A., 526, 536n, 539
Nussle, Ron, 396

**O**

Ogden, Jeffrey A., 213
Ohno, Taiichi, 148–149, 171
O'Malley, Shaun, 440n
O'Neal, Charles R., 95n, 479n
Ore, Norbert J., 370
O'Reilly, Peter E., 198, 199n, 213,
    529n, 530n
O'Shea, David J., 44n, 45n
Ouchi, William, 168n
Overholt, William H., 296

**P**

Pacelli, Lonnie, 140
Pande, Peter S., 149n, 173n
Paquette, Larry, 263
Park, Seungwook, 263
Parker, David W., 239

Parker, Devlon B., 577
Parker, Geoffrey G., 431
Parker, Glenn M., 42n, 48
Parker, Robert C., 97n
Patton, Bruce M., 396
Paulraj, Antony, 68n
Pavlou, Paul A., 95n, 116
Payne, Stanley L., 396
Pearson, John N., 68n, 81
Perrin, Craig, 47n
Perrons, R. K., 239
Petcavage, S., 78n
Peters, T. J., 237n
Petersen, Kenneth J., 81n, 115n, 117,
    262, 275n, 296
Pfeffer, J., 76n
Picard, S., 476n
Pinkerton, Richard L., 13n, 21, 42n, 46n,
    52n, 54n, 81, 84n, 88, 97n, 99, 105,
    107n, 111, 144n, 154n, 260n, 261n,
    291n, 292n, 346, 414n, 491n,
    502n, 530n
Pinto, Peter A., 476n
Pisano, Gary, 219n
Pitman, Glenn A., 415n
Plank, Richard E., 317
Platts, K., 239
Pohlig, Helen M., 417, 525
Pooler, David J., 296
Pooler, Victor H., 296
Porter, Hal, 285n
Porter, Michael E., 220n
Prahalad, C. K., 219n, 241n

**Q**

Quinn, James Brian, 228n, 239

**R**

Raedels, Alan, 346, 390n, 392
Ragatz, Gary L., 78n, 81n, 98n, 115n,
    117, 249n, 577
Raia, Ernest, 97n
Raines, Tim, 50
Rainey, David L., 117
Ramberg, Jan, 296
Reeds, James D., 379n
Regan, Gordon, 26n
Reider, Richard G., 64n, 84n, 88
Richards, M. G., 239
Richards, Patricia, 258n
Richardson, William L., 290n
Richter, Gene, 96, 552–554, 577
Ritzman, Larry P., 502, 539

Roberts, Barry S., 211n, 404n, 410n, 417
Roberts, Jacobs F., 502
Roberts, Julie S., 213, 317, 457
Robertson, D. C., 457
Robinson, Bryan, 207n
Robinson, John F., 258n
Rogers, Ben, 131
Rogers, D. S., 117
Rollman, Mary, 431
Rometty, Ginni, 68n
Romig, Harry G., 169n
Roodhooft, F., 317
Roussel, Joseph, 539, 576
Ruamsook, Kusumal, 176
Ruch, W., 245n
Rusch, Linda J., 418
Russell, Dawn, 176
Russell, Katie A., 239

**S**

Sager, Ira, 96n
Sampson, Keith, 131
Sanderson, Joe, 77n
Sanford, James P., 415n
Sarkis, Joseph, 263
Saunders, David M., 396
Scacchitti, Vince, 48
Scannell, Thomas V., 262
Schaffer, Richard, 296
Schary, Philip B., 296
Schildhouse, Jill, 457
Schilling, M. A., 117
Schlegelmilch, B. B., 457
Schmitz, Jorge, 296
Schorr, J. E., 475n
Schroeder, Richard, 176
Schulte, Tom, 43n
Schuster, Camille, 296
Schwarzwalder, Robert, 132n, 140
Sebenius, James K., 389n
Seifert, Richard, 502, 539
Seldon, Doyle, 453n
Semanik, John, 21
Shainin, Dohan, 154
Shannon, Joseph V., 502
Shaw, B., 457
Shingo, Shigeo, 171
Sickinger, Janet, 197
Siegfried, Mary, 32n, 546n, 577, 580n
Siferd, Sue P., 317, 457
Simkins, Robert J., 193
Simonson, Steven W., 239
Singh, H., 65, 81

Sislian, Eric, 236n
Skjott-Larsen, Tage, 296
Slaight, T. H., 69n, 246n
Smeltzer, Larry A., 213
Smid, Dennis, 138n
Smith, Carlo D., 62
Smith, Douglas K., 48
Smith, Michael E., 346, 390n
Smith, Robert M., 168n
Smith, William C., 109n
Smith-Doerflein, Kimberly A., 77n
Smock, Douglas A., 20
Sollish, Fred, 21
Soonhoong, Min, 62
Spear, J., 247n, 253n
Speier, Cheri, 39
Spekman, R. E., 247n, 253n
Spivak, Steven M., 140
Sroufe, Robert, 134
St. John, Caron H., 246n, 476n
Stallkamp, Thomas T., 550–552
Stank, Theodore P., 62
Stanley, Linda L., 68n
Stark, Peter B., 396
Stegner, Jonathan R., 12n, 21, 262
Stewart, Emmett, 526
Stewart, Shelley, Jr., 20
Stock, James R., 203n, 526
Stone-Newton, Barbara, 203, 204n
Stueland, Valerie J., 346
Suh, Taewon, 81
Susman, Gerald I., 42n
Sutton, Stephen, 196
Swan, A. J., 69n, 246n
Swietlik, Dave, 97

**T**

Taguchi, Genechi, 145–146, 155, 156n
Talluri, Srinivas, 78n, 249n, 263
Tan, Chong Leng, 97n, 117
Tan, Keah Choon, 262
Tarasewich, Peter, 100n
Taylor, Frederick, 34

Taylor, G. S., 452n
Taylor, S., 457
Thies, James B., 192
Thomas, Michael H., 451n
Thomchick, Evelyn, 176
Thompson, Leigh, 372n, 382n, 389n
Thorelli, H. B., 76n
Tompkins, Bruce W., 239
Tompkins, James A., 239
Tracey, Michael, 77n, 97n, 117, 263
Tracy, John J., Jr., 539
Trent, Robert J., 21, 35n, 39, 47n, 48, 61n, 275n, 276n, 296, 577
Trevino, Linda K., 457
Trevisan, Richard E., 448n
Trompenaars, Fons, 285n
Turner, G. B., 452n, 456, 457
Tyndall, G. R., 526

**U**

Upchurch, Brian E., 239
Ury, William, 381, 388n, 396
Usunier, Jean-Claude, 396

**V**

Vallopra, R. M., 95n, 113, 116
Van Hoek, Remko I., 539
van Weele, Arjan, 115, 116, 221n
Vandervalk, Wendy, 317
Vickery, Shawnee, 299n
Vickrey, Donn W., 268n
Vlasic, Bill, 552
Vokurka, R. J., 39
Vollman, Thomas, 502, 535
Vonderembse, M., 263
Vuori, Risto, 193

**W**

Wagner, Stephan M., 69n
Walker, Danielle, 296
Walker, Forrest, Jr., 258n
Walker, Thomas, 296
Wallace, T. F., 475n

Wallis, W., 169n
Walton, Steve V., 455n
Walz, Gene, 96n
Waterman, R. H., 237n
Watkins, Michael, 396
Watson, Glyn, 77n
Wehrman, Jim, 243
Weinstein, Larry, 249n, 255n
Welch, Jack J., 151n
White, Cherish Karoway, 292n
Whitney, D. E., 239
Whitney, Eli, 132–133
Whittier, Roger A., 26n
Whittington, Elaine, 346, 370
Whybark, D. Clay, 502, 535
Wight, Oliver, 532n, 539
Williams, Alvin, 109n
Wilson, Bill, 49
Wilson, Charles E., 175
Wilson, J. Holton, 577
Wincel, Jeffrey P., 502
Winn, Jane K., 411n
Winston, Andrew S., 502
Womack, James P., 12, 254n, 343n
Woods, John A., 13n
Woodside, Arch G., 193
Wooten, Bob, 260n
Wright, J. Nevan, 175
Wynstra, Finn, 115, 213, 221n, 317

**Y**

Yacura, Joe, 200n
Young, Allie, 239
Young, Richard R., 61n, 262
Yuva, John, 58n, 308n, 346, 532n, 537n, 539

**Z**

Zacharia, Zach G., 62
Zenger, John H., 47n
Zielinski, David, 42n
Zimdars, Leroy, 114n, 308n
Zsidisin, George A., 457, 577

# SUBJECT INDEX

Page numbers followed by n indicate notes.

## A

ABC analysis, 483–485
Acceptance, 24, 405–406
Accounts payable, 58–59
Acknowledgment, 24
Acquisition costs, 11, 184, 186–187,
    304–306, 487–488
Activity based costing (ABC), 308, 314,
    342–343, 427
Activity based management (ABM),
    308, 342
Acurex Corporation, 448
Administrative costs, 35
Advertising and promotion, 55
Agency, law of, 400–401, 404–405
Aggregate planning, 464–466
Aggregate scheduling, 463
Air bill, 509
Air carriers, 507
All-in-cost, 95
Alliances, 63–64, 65, 70–76, 84–87, 334
Alltel Communications, Inc., 578
Alpha Corporation, 40
Alps Manufacturing, 279
Alternative development, 101–103
American Express, 200
American Institute of Electrical
    Engineers, 133
American Law Institute, 402
American Motors Company, 143
American National Standards Institute,
    133–134, 161
American Production and Inventory
    Control Society, 100
American Society for Quality, 133, 161
Andean Community, 293
Anticipatory breach, 411
A&P, 414
Apple Computer, 96
Applied Materials, 254, 255, 428
Appraisal costs, 155
Arbitration, 402, 414
Ariba, 57
Arm's-length relationships, 66

Artificial intelligence, 200
Asia Pacific Economic Cooperation, 294
Association of American Railroads, 514
Association of Southeast Asian
    Nations, 294
A. T. Kearney, 308
Auctions
    reverse, 62, 78, 249, 331, 396, 563
    for used equipment, 183–184
Audits
    of invoices, 25–26, 519–520
    quality, 428–429
Authority, 34–36, 405
Awards
    for leadership, 577–580
    for quality, 162, 164–165

## B

Balanced scorecard, 427
Bargaining, hard, 383–384
Bargaining strength, 378–379
Barter, 277, 288
BATNA, 381, 383
Battle of the forms, 404
Baxter Healthcare, 44, 58
B2B commerce, 2, 57, 78–79, 331
Benchmarking, 17, 553
Best alternative to a negotiated
    agreement (BATNA), 381, 383
Best-in-class, 17
Best Window Company, 548–549
Bid bonds, 210
Bidding
    competitive, 23, 247–250, 330, 374,
        448–449
    invitation for, 41, 250
    versus negotiation, 247–249
    prerequisites, 248
    two-step, 249–250
Bill back, 428
Bill of lading, 509
Bill of materials, 23, 463
Black & Decker, 553, 577
Blackbelt, 151, 561

Blanket orders, 27–28, 410
Blockbuster, 69
Boeing, 104, 288
Boilerplate, 24
Bonds, 210, 410
Booz Allen Hamilton, 46, 424
Boundaryless collaboration, 151
BP, 578, 579
Branding, 123–124
Breach of contract, 59, 411
Bribery, 284
British Standards Institute, 133, 161
British Steel, 290
Brokers, 183, 280, 282
Bullwhip effect, 532–533
Business process outsourcing,
    228–229, 237
Business relationships, 60
Buy-back/compensation, 288
Buyer-planner concept, 474–475
Buyer-supplier relationships, 63–88
    alliances, 63–64, 65, 70–76, 84–87, 334
    collaborative, 65, 68–70, 429–430
    future, 79–80
    portfolio approach, 77
    questions to ask, 72–73, 74
    role of power, 76–77
    skills and attitudes needed, 77
    success factors, 68–69
    supplier's perspective, 73
    transactional, 66–68
Buying exchanges, 259–260, 331

## C

CAD, 98
Cancellation, of orders, 411–412
Capabilities of management, 332–333
Capacity
    make-buy analysis, 224–226
    plant, 333–334
    supplier, 255–256
Capacity capability analysis, 246
Capacity requirements planning (CRP),
    466, 470–471

Capital equipment purchasing, 177–193
  identifying need, 179
  leasing, 187–191
  nature/size of expenditures, 178–179
  objective identification, 181
  post-award activities, 191
  project management, 179
  sourcing, 186
  spare parts, 184
  specification development, 184–186
  total cost of ownership, 184, 186–187
  used equipment, 181–184
  using a team, 179–181
Carrying costs, 485–487
Cash discounts, 350–351
Catalog
  of inventory, 482–483
  materials, 137–138
  supplier, 242
Catalog pricing, 330
Categorical plan, 425
Cause-and-effect diagrams, 153–154
Center for Advanced Purchasing Studies, 32, 275
Central limit theorem, 160n
Centralized authority, 34–36
Centralized stores, 26
Certificate of origin, 510
Certificates of insurance, 211
Certification, of suppliers, 70, 172–174
Certified Purchasing Manager (C.P.M.), 240
Change management, 233–234
Change order, 24
Chevrolet, 323
Chief Resource Officer (CRO), 235–236
Chrysler, 71–72, 97, 252, 253–254, 550–552
Cisco Systems, 220, 255
CISG, 282, 415
Claims, 520
Clayton Act, 414
Clean Air Act, 454
Closed loop MRP systems, 424, 473
Collaborative development, of specifications, 120–121
Collaborative negotiation, 388–389
Collaborative relationships, 65, 68–70, 429–430
Colocation, with suppliers, 72, 114
Commercial analysis, 285–286
Commercial invoice, 510
Commercial law, 402–404
Commercial standards, 126

Commission houses, 280
Common law, 514
Communication, 41
Company standards, 133
Compaq, 96
Compensation agreements; see Contracts
Competence, professional, 445–447
Competent parties, 407
Competition
  alliances and, 75–76
  conditions of, 322–324
  limiting of, 131
  pure, 322–323
  regulation by, 328–330
  time-based, 10, 224
Competitive bidding, 23, 247–250, 330, 374, 448–449
Complex specifications, 125–128
Comprehensive Environmental Response Compensation Act, 454
Computer-assisted design, 98
Computer simulation, 104, 153
Concept formation stage, 100–104
Concurrent engineering, 51, 95
Confidentiality, 235, 443–444
Conflict of interest, 259, 441
Conoco, 26
Consensus development, 129
Consideration, 406–407
Consignment, 29
Consolidation, 35
Consortium purchasing, 259–260
Construction services, 207–211
Consumption entry form, 510
Continuous improvement, 148–149
Contract buying, 475
Contract management, 419–436
  assistance, 428–429
  collaboration, 429–430
  CPM/PERT, 423–424
  evaluating supplier performance, 424–427
  monitoring progress, 421–424
  motivation, 427–428
  pre-award conference, 420–421, 431–432
  quality; see Quality management
  using Gantt charts, 422–423
Contract schedule risk, 357
Contracts; see also Legal issues
  administration of, 207
  breach of, 59, 411
  considerations for selection, 368–369
  construction, 207–211

cost plus award fee, 366
cost plus fixed fee, 365–366
cost-reimbursable, 209
cost sharing, 367
cost-type, 358
cost without fee, 366
design and build, 209–210
electronic, 403–404
evergreen, 410–411
extension of, 206
firm fixed price, 209, 358–360
fixed price, 357
fixed price redetermination, 361
fixed price with price adjustment, 360–361
forward, 298
incentive, 357, 361–365
JIT, 412
letter, 367–368
mistakes in, 413
oral, 407–408
performance based, 512
risk appraisal, 356–357
time and materials, 367
transportation, 511–512, 517–518
uncertainty, 354–356
Control charts, 154, 160–162
Convention on Contracts for the International Sale of Goods (CISG), 282, 415
Conversion costs, 12, 307
Core competencies, 219
Corporate credit cards, 29
Corporate United, Inc., 260
Cost analysis
  activity based, 308, 314, 342–343, 427
  defined, 332
  discounts, 349–351
  elements affecting, 332–334
  learning curves, 68, 337–341, 347–349
  negotiations and, 379, 394
  profit, 343–345
  should-cost, 334
  sources of data, 334
Cost-based supplier evaluation, 427
Cost plus award fee contracts, 366
Cost plus fixed fee (CPFF) contracts, 365–366
Cost plus incentive fee (CPIF) contracts, 364–365
Cost ratio plan, 426–427
Cost-reimbursable contracts, 209

Cost sharing contracts, 367
Cost type contracts, 358
Cost without fee contracts, 366
Costs
    acquisition, 11, 184, 186–187,
        304–306, 487–488
    administrative, 35
    appraisal, 155
    carrying, 485–487
    categories of, 326–328
    of changing suppliers, 68
    conversion, 12, 307
    customer dissatisfaction, 310
    cycle time, 12, 307
    data sources, 334
    direct, 328, 334–337
    downtime, 12, 306
    environmental, 309
    failure, 155
    financing, 306
    fixed, 326
    global sourcing, 276–277, 278
    indirect, 328, 341–342
    labor, 8
    leasing, 190
    liability, 309–310
    life-cycle, 178n
    materials, 8, 9
    non-value added, 12, 307–308
    outsourcing, 223–227
    overhead, 328, 341
    ownership, 306–309
    planning, 305
    post-ownership, 12, 309–310
    prevention, 155
    processing, 11
    quality, 11, 155, 305
    risk, 12, 306–307
    selling, 341
    semi-variable, 326
    service providers, 202
    supplier, 35
    supply chain, 12, 308–309
    switching, 75
    target, 101, 338–341, 343, 362–363
    tooling, 337
    variable manufacturing, 326
    warranty, 12, 309
Counterpurchase, 288
Countertrade, 277, 288–290
COVISINT, 260
Cp, 158–159
Cpk, 159
CPM, 423–424

Creator role, 18
Credit card purchasing, 29, 58–59
Crib sheets, 382
Critical dependencies, 220
Critical path scheduling, 423–424,
    432–435
Cross functional teams, 37–38, 39–47,
    97, 129–130
CRP, 466, 470–471
Cultural issues, in global sourcing, 277,
    284–285, 379
Cumulative curve, 337–338
Currency issues, 286–288, 296–299
Current ratio, 268
Customer dissatisfaction costs, 310
Customer satisfaction, 11
Customization, 134
Customs brokers, 282
Customs duties, 305
Cyberlaw, 403–404
Cycle time, 10, 11, 12, 307
Cyclical inventory control system,
    492–493

### D

Daimler Chrysler, 71–72, 552, 578
Damages, 411–412
Debit cards, purchasing using, 29
Debriefing, 389–390
Debt to equity, 270
Decentralized authority, 34–36
Decision-making authority, 34–36
Decoupling, 481
Deere & Co., 33, 70, 102, 281, 548–549
Defects
    causes of, 144
    detection of, 170–171
    zero, 145
Defects per million, 150, 545
Define, measure, analyze, improve and
    control, 150–152
Delayed differentiation, 135
Delivery times, 340
Dell, 15, 71, 133, 135
Delphi Corporation, 548–549
Demand
    dependent, 469, 485, 498
    forecasting, 534–535
    management of, 530–536
Demand time fence, 535–536
Demand volatility, 75
Deming Prize, 145, 161, 165
Dependent demand, 469, 485, 498
Depreciation tax shield, 310n

Deregulation, 514
Design analysis, 107–108
Design and build contracts, 209–210
Design of experiments, 70, 154,
    244, 245
Design reviews, 104, 106
Design secrecy, 229
Design S.O.W., 197
Design specifications, 51, 126–127
Differentiation, 135, 323, 325
Direct costs, 328, 334–337
Direct labor, 336–337
Direct materials, 337, 340
Direct offset, 288
Direct suppliers, 282–286
Discounted cash flow analysis, 190
Discounts, 34, 349–351, 490, 512
Dispatch lists, 471
Dispute resolution, 401–402, 414
Distribution function, 15
Distribution requirements planning
    (DRP II), 533
Distributors, buying from, 257–258
Diversion, used in negotiation, 384
Diversity, in the supply base, 564
DMAIC cycle, 150–152
Dock receipt, 510
Documentation, 390
Double outsourcing, 235
Downtime costs, 12, 306
DPM, 150
Drop shipment, 257
DRP II, 533
Du Pont, 424
Dun & Bradstreet, 245, 268, 283
Duties, 305

### E

E-commerce, 3, 36, 57, 78–79, 331
E-Sign Act, 404
Early supplier involvement (ESI)
    benefits of, 129, 253
    new product development, 95–97,
        102–103, 123, 561–562
    potential problems with, 360
Economic order quantity (EOQ),
    488–492, 497
Economic price adjustment contracts,
    360–361
EDI, 36, 57, 474n
80/20 concept, 483–485
Elasticity, of pricing, 10
Electronic data interchange, 36, 57, 474n
Electronic materials catalogs, 138

Electronic signatures, 403–404
Engineering bill of materials, 23
Engineering change management, 112–113
Engineering drawings, 127
Engineering function, 51–53
Engineering overhead, 341
Engineering tests, 167
Enterprise resource planning (ERP), 80, 138, 480
Environment
  costs, 309
  green sourcing, 258
  hazardous materials, 507
  social responsibility, 454–455
Environmental Protection Agency, 181, 455
EOQ, 488–492, 497
Equipment, purchase of; *see* Capital equipment purchasing
ERP, 80, 138, 480
Escalation clauses, 360–361
ESI; *see* Early supplier involvement (ESI)
Estimated costs, 310–312
Ethics, 437–457
  competitive bidding and, 448–449
  confidentiality, 253, 443–444
  conflict of interest, 259, 441
  defined, 439
  gratuities and gifts, 441, 450–452
  gray areas, 453–454
  importance of, 439–440
  influence and, 441–442
  international, 442
  legal issues and, 445
  management responsibilities, 452–453
  professional competence, 445–447
  reciprocity, 55, 259, 444
  sharp practices, 447–448
  social responsibility, 443, 564–565
  standards, 440–447, 452
  training, 452–453
Euro, 291–293
European Foundation for Quality Management, 162, 164
European Monetary Unit, 291
European Organization for Quality, 162
European Quality Award, 162, 164
European Union, 290–293
Evergreen contracts, 410–411
Exchange rates, 286–287
Exchanges, 259–260, 331
Executive sponsorship, 42

Expatriates, 281
Expediting, 33, 519
Exploded bill of materials, 467
Export brokers, 282
Export declaration, 510
Express warranty, 409–410
Extended enterprise, 17, 308

**F**
Face-to-face negotiation, 382–384
Fact finding, 382–383
Failure analysis, 104, 106
Failure costs, 155
Federal Acquisition Regulations, 107
Federal Aviation Administration Act, 514
Federal Bureau of Specifications, 133
Federal Express, 507
Finance function, 56, 180
Financial Accounting Standards Board, 189
Financial lease, 188–189
Financial statement analysis, 268–270
Financing costs, 306
Finished goods inventories, 482
Firm fixed price contracts, 209, 358–360
Fishbone diagram, 153
Five M's, 7–8
Five rights, 2, 6
Fixed asset turnover, 269
Fixed costs, 326
Fixed manufacturing costs, 326
Fixed order interval system, 492–493
Fixed order quantity system, 495–499
Fixed price contracts, 357
Fixed price incentive fee, 363–364
Fixed price redetermination contracts, 361
Fixed price with price adjustment contracts, 360–361
Flexibility, of suppliers, 475
Flexibility capability analysis, 246–247
Floating currency, 297
Florida Power and Light, 165
Flow control system, 493
Fluid time fence, 535
Fluor Hanford, 577–578
Follow-up, 24, 33
Ford, 258, 323, 394, 550
Forecasting, 55, 464–465, 534–535
Foreign Corrupt Practices Act, 284, 415–416
Forward contracts, 298
Free on board (FOB), 508–509
Freight bill auditing, 519–520

Freight discounts, 512
Freight forwarders, 282, 511
Freight rates, 510–511
Freight terms, 508–509
Frequency histograms, 154
Frozen time fence, 535
Full-service lessors, 189
Function and fit specifications, 123
Functional silos, 37, 571
Functional S.O.W., 197
Funds management ratios, 269–270

**G**
Gantt charts, 422–423
General and administrative costs, 341
General Electric, 28, 96, 102, 106, 151–152, 252, 309, 394
General Motors, 98, 143, 550
German Institute for Standards, 133
Getting to know you technique, 384
Gifts and gratuities, 441, 450–452
Global Opacity Index, 278
Global supply management, 273–299
  CISG, 282, 415
  countertrade, 277, 288–290
  cultural issues, 277, 284–285, 379
  direct suppliers, 282–286
  ethics, 442
  European Union, 290–293
  future of, 275
  INCOTERMS, 404, 513
  legal issues, 414–416
  payment/currency issues, 286–288, 296–299
  political/economic alliances, 290–294
  problems with, 277–278
  questions to ask, 279
  reasons for, 276–277
  stages of, 276
  supply channels, 279–281
  using IPOs, 281
Globalization, 37
Goalpost philosophy, 155–156
Goals, balancing of, 120–121
Government procurement, 60
Grading, 125
Graham Packaging, 64, 84–88
Granger, 499
Gratuities, 441, 450–452
Green supply management, 258
Greenbelt, 151
Gross profit margin, 269
Group buying, 259–260
GTE, 46

**H**

Hard bargaining, 383–384
Hazardous materials, 507
Hedging, 298–299
Hewlett-Packard, 102, 553, 577, 580
Histograms, 154
Hitachi, 165, 280
Honda of America, 20, 70, 243, 252, 253, 394, 548–549, 562
Honeywell, 244
Horizontal integration, 220–222
Human specialization, 70
Hybrid structure, 36

**I**

IBM, 68, 71, 96, 167, 254, 552–554, 577
ICC Termination Act, 514–515
Imperfect competition, 323
Implied warranties, 409–410
Import brokers, 280
Import license, 510
Import merchants, 280
Impropriety, perceived, 440
Improvement curve, 337
In-process inventory, 482
In-process testing, 112
Incentive contracts, 357, 361–365
Incentives, for team performance, 42
Income-base shifting, 305
Income tax issues, 189–190
INCOTERMS, 404, 513
Incremental costs, 490
Independent demand, 485, 498
Independent inspection certificate, 510
Indirect costs, 328, 341–342
Indirect offset, 288
Industry standards, 133
Influence, ethics and, 441–442
Informal approach, to specification development, 128
Information technology, 2, 56–58
Information technology capability analysis, 247
Innovation, 10–11
Insourcing, 233–234
Inspection, 25, 127, 168–172, 408
Institute for Supply Management, 8, 162, 243, 378, 440, 455
Institutional trust, 70, 81–84
Insurance, 210–211
Integration, 220–222
Intel Corporation, 26, 100
Interfirm teams, 46

Intermediaries, 280–281, 282
Intermodal carriers, 507
International Aero Engines, 191
International Chamber of Commerce, 404, 414
International Organization for Standardization (ISO), 133, 147, 152, 161, 163–164
International procurement offices, 281
International sourcing, 256–257, 276; *see also* Global supply management
International standards, 133
Internet
    B2B commerce, 2, 57, 78–79, 331
    e-commerce, 3, 36, 57, 78–79, 331
    electronic ordering systems, 28
    negotiation using, 390–392
    netsourcing, 232–233
    role in product development, 102
    services purchasing and, 207
    supplier selection and, 242
Interpreters, 285
Inventory catalog, 482–483
Inventory management
    analysis of, 482–485
    bullwhip effect, 532–533
    centralized stores, 26
    control systems, 492–499
    costs, 485–488
    definition, 482
    EOQ, 488–492, 497
    fixed order interval system, 492–493
    functions of, 480–481
    in global sourcing, 278
    JIT; *see* Just-in-time (JIT)
    order point system, 495–499
    supplier managed, 499
    supplier stores, 29
    turnover, 269
    two-bin system, 498
Investigation phase, of product development, 100–104
Invitation for bids, 41, 250
Invoices, audit of, 25–26, 519–520
Irrevocable letter of credit, 287
ISO standards, 134, 152, 163–164
ITT, 145

**J**

Jacobs Manufacturing Company, 414
Japanese Academy of Quality, 145
Jidohka, 170–171
John Deere, 252, 254
Johnson & Johnson, 577, 578

Just-in-time (JIT)
    contracts, 412
    flexibility capability analysis, 246–247
    inventory management and, 493–494
    kanban, 149, 476
    local buying and, 256
    production planning and, 476–480
    quality and waste management, 149
Justitia International Inc., 284

**K**

Kaiser Aluminum Chemical, 26
Kaizen, 145, 148
Kanban, 149, 476
Kawasaki, 98
Keiretsu, 98
KLA-Tencor, 577
Knowledge transfer, 110
Kodak, 236
KPMG LLP, 305

**L**

Labor
    costs of, 8
    direct, 336–337
    efficiency of, 333
    problems with, 278
Law of agency, 400–401, 404–405
Lead time, 11, 276, 277
Leadership
    awards for, 577–580
    defined, 546
    skill sets, 548–554
    of teams, 43–44, 47
Lean manufacturing, 221–222
Learning curves, 68, 337–341, 347–349
Learning organization, 77
Leasing, 187–191
Legal issues, 399–418; *see also* Contracts
    authority, 34–36, 405
    breach of contract, 59, 411
    cancellation of orders, 411–412
    commercial law, 402–404
    consideration, 406–407
    cyberlaw, 403–404
    damages, 411–412
    dispute resolution, 401–402, 414
    ethics, 445
    evergreen contracts, 410–411
    global sourcing, 414–416
    inspection rights, 408

law of agency, 400–401, 404–405
litigation prevention, 400–401, 402
offer and acceptance, 24, 405–406
patents, 413
restraint of trade, 414
rights of rejection, 408–409
title/risk of loss, 409
transportation, 512, 514
UCC, 199, 402–404, 418
warranties, 409–410
Less than truckload (LTL), 506
Letter contracts, 367–368
Letter of credit, 287–288, 510
Letter of intent, 367–368, 408
Level-of-effort S.O.W., 197
Leveraging, 10–11, 34
Liability
cost of, 309–310
environment and, 258
Life cycle
product, 101
technology, 229–230
Life cycle costing, 178n
Life tests, 106
Liquidated damages, 411–412
Liquidity, 268
Litigation prevention, 400–401, 402
Local sourcing, 256–257
Lockheed Martin, 424, 579
Logistics function, 58
Logistics management, 536–537
Loss function, 156
Loss to society, 155–156
Lot sizing, 488–492

**M**

Machine power, 7–8
Maintenance, repair and operating
(MRO), 11, 260, 482
Make-or-buy; *see also* Outsourcing
administration of activities,
235–237
factors influencing, 223–232
volatile nature of, 233–235
Malcolm Baldrige National Quality
Award, 162, 164
Management, role of, 17–18
Management capability analysis, 246
Manifest, 510
Manufacturers, buying from, 257–258
Manufacturing, lean, 221–222
Manufacturing operations, 53–54, 314
Manufacturing overhead, 341
Manufacturing plans, 110

Manufacturing resource planning
(MRP II), 473–475
Margin tests, 106
Market grades, 125
Market prices, 330–331
Marketing function, 13, 15, 55
Masco Corporation, 579
Mass production, 132–133
Master production schedule (MPS),
465–466
Master scheduling, 464–466
Material and method-of-manufacture,
127–128
Material costs, 8, 9
Material overhead, 341
Material requirements planning (MRP),
21, 23, 466–470, 494–495
Materials, 7, 21
Materials catalog, 137–138
Materials engineers, 114, 129
Materials management, 36–37
Mattel, 276
McKinsey & Co., 548
Mediation, 401–402
MERCOSUR, 293
Metric Conversion Act, 134
Minority-owned businesses, 258, 564
Mission statement, 558, 570
Mistakes, in contracts, 413
Mixed manufacturing costs, 326
Mock negotiation, 381–382
Modified rebuy, 23n
Monopolistic competition, 323
Monopoly, 323–324
Most optimistic cost (MOC), 362–363
Most optimistic profit (MOPr), 362–363
Most pessimistic profit (MPPr),
362–363
Motivation, 427–428
Motor Carrier Act, 514
Motor carriers, 506
Motorola, 147, 150, 154
MRO, 11, 260, 482
MRP, 21, 23, 466–470, 494–495
MRP II, 473–475
Multiple sourcing, 232, 254–255
Murder boards, 381–382
Mutual obligation, 406–407

**N**

NAFTA, 293
NAICS, 261
National Association of Educational
Buyers, 243

National Association of Purchasing
Agents, 8
National Bureau of Standards, 133–134
National Conference of Commissioners
on Uniform State Laws, 402
National Institute of Governmental
Purchasing, 243
National Lumber Manufacturers'
Association, 133
National Motor Freight
Classification, 514
National sourcing, 256–257
Natural tolerance range, 156
Need, 21–23, 101, 179
Negotiated Rates Act, 514
Negotiation, 371–396
activities to prepare for, 381–382
for alliance building, 86–87
versus bidding, 247–249
characteristics for successful,
394–395
cultural preparation, 284–285
debriefing, 389–390
defined, 372
for dispute resolution, 401
documentation, 390
establishing objectives, 380–381
ethics and, 449
face-to-face, 382–384
objectives of, 373–374
online, 390–392
preparation for, 377–380
for price, 392–394
process, 377–381
supply management's role, 375–377
techniques for, 384–389
of transportation contracts, 518–519
using a team, 41, 187, 376–377
when to use, 374–375
Net present value analysis, 310–312
Netsourcing, 232–233
Netting, 469
Network management, 530
Networks, supply, 15–16, 308–309, 315
New Directions Consulting
Group, 37, 56
New product development, 93–117
alternative development, 101–103
colocation with suppliers, 72, 114
concept formation, 100–104
cycle time and, 10, 11
design analysis, 107–108
design process, 97–99
development phase, 104–106

New product development—*Cont.*
early supplier involvement, 95–97, 102–103, 123, 561–562
engineering change management, 112–113
investigation phase, 100–104
outsourcing of, 103, 221
process, 99
production phase, 110–112
using teams, 39–47, 113, 561–564
value engineering, 68, 106–110, 565
Nippon Steel, 165
Nissan, 165
Non-value added costs, 12, 307–308
Noncompetitive markets, 75–76
Nonrandom variations, 159
North American Free Trade Agreement (NAFTA), 293
North American Industry Classification System (NAICS), 261
NPV, 310–312

**O**

Objectives
establishment of, 380–381
identification of, 181
of negotiation, 373–374
statement of, 101
Obsolescence, 189, 486
OEM, 15, 19
Offer and acceptance, 24, 405–406
Offsets, 277, 288
Offshoring, 8
Ok Tedi Mining Limited, 196
Oligopoly, 323–324
Omnibus Trade Act, 416
Online negotiation, 390–392
Opacity Index, 278
Open order netting, 469
Operating lease, 188
Operating services, 206
Operational responsibilities/activities, 33–34
Opportunity cost of capital, 310, 486
Or equal, 124
Oracle, 57
Oral contracts, 407–408
Order point system, 495–499
Orders
blanket, 27–28, 410
cancellation of, 411–412
completion of, 25–26
electronic system, 28
EOQ, 488–492, 497

fixed interval system, 492–493
fixed quantity, 495–499
follow-up of, 24, 33
purchase, 23–24
small, 26
Organizational structure
factors affecting, 33–36
hybrid, 36
materials management, 36–37
placement of supply management, 32
staffing, 565–568
supply chain management, 37
OSHA, 181, 258
Outsourcing, 217–239; *see also* Make-or-buy
administration of, 235–237
of business processes, 228–229, 237
cost analysis, 223–227
dangers of, 234–235
double, 235
framework, 236
horizontal integration, 220–222
increase in, 218–219
insourcing, 233–234
lean manufacturing, 221–222
netsourcing, 232–233
new product development and, 103, 221
of services, 7, 8, 195
strategic issues, 219–220
of supply management, 229
tactical decisions, 222–223
technology risk, 229–230
transportation, 511, 517
Overcharge claims, 512
Overhead costs, 328, 341
Owens On-Line, 284
Ownership costs, 306–309

**P**

P-D-C-A, 149
Pacific Bell, 200
Packing list, 510
Pareto analysis, 483
Pareto charts, 153–154
Partnerships; *see* Alliances
Patent infringement, 413
Payment bonds, 210
Payment issues, 25, 286–288, 296–299
Pegged currency, 298
Perceived impropriety, 440
Perfect competition, 322–323
Performance based contracts, 512
Performance bonds, 210, 410

Performance contracting, 211
Performance evaluation
benchmarking, 17, 553
of suppliers, 424–427, 520
of supply management, 17
Performance S.O.W., 197
Performance specifications, 98, 122–123, 184, 479
Personal relationships, 441–442
PERT, 423–424
Pfizer, Inc., 579
Physical asset specialization, 70
PIMS, 10
Plan, do, check, act, 149
Planned order release, 469
Planning costs, 305
Planning time fence, 535–536
Plant capacity, 333–334
Plant visits, 245, 263–268, 270–272, 286
Poka-yoke, 171
Polaroid, 35, 55, 61, 196
Portfolio approach, 77
Post-ownership costs, 12, 309–310
Power, role of, 76–77
Pre-award conference, 420–421, 431–432
Preferred supplier, 73
Prevention costs, 155
Price
analysis of, 330–332, 379
categories of cost, 326–328
conditions of competition, 322–324
historical, 331
impact of controlling, 10
independent cost estimates, 331–332
negotiation for, 392–394
product differentiation, 323, 325
purchase, 304–305
regulated/catalog/market, 330–331
regulation by competition, 328–330
of service contracts, 204
variable-margin, 324–325
volatility of, 74–75
Price adjustment contracts, 360–361
Price indexes, 361
Prime contractor, 333
Probability, 269–270
Problem resolution, 40
Problem solving, 429
Process capability analysis, 156–159
Process capability index, 158–159
Process control, 110, 112
Process engineering, 179
Process flow charts, 153
Process-oriented layout, 476

Processing costs, 11
Procter & Gamble, 15, 238, 439
Procurement, 6; *see also* Purchasing
Procurement cards, 29, 58–59
Producibility, 101
Producer price index (PPI), 361
Product differentiation, 323, 325
Product liability costs, 309–310
Product life cycle, 101
Product testing, 166–167
Product-type layout, 476
Production inventories, 482
Production phase, of product
    development, 110–112
Production planning, 462–480
    activities of, 462–463
    aggregate planning, 464–466
    control of activities, 227, 471–472
    CRP, 466, 470–471
    DRP II, 533
    ERP, 80, 138, 480
    flowchart of, 464
    JIT; *see* Just-in-time (JIT)
    management considerations, 472–473
    master scheduling, 464–466
    MRP, 21, 23, 466–470, 494–495
    MRP II, 473–475
    objectives of, 462
Professional competence, 445–447
Professional services, procurement of,
    205; *see also* Services,
    procurement of
Profit, 343–345
Profit Impact of Market Strategy
    approach, 10
Profit margin, 269, 329–330
Program evaluation and review
    technique (PERT), 423–424
Progress payments, 341
Project management, 179
Project teams, 113
Promissory Estoppel, 211
Promotion and advertising, 55
Prompt payment, 25
Proprietary information, 443–444
Prototypes, 104
Public key infrastructure, 404
Pull system, 149
Punishment, 427–428
Purchase description; *see*
    Specifications
Purchase order, 23–24
Purchase price, 304–305
Purchase requisition, 21, 23

Purchasing; *see also* Supply
    management
    careers in, 5–6
    defined, 2, 6
    five rights of, 2, 6
Purchasing cards, 29, 58–59
Purchasing cycle, 21, 22
Purchasing Management Association
    of Canada, 243
Pure competition, 322–323

**Q**

Quaker Oats, 63–64, 84–87
Qualification testing, 106
Qualified products list (QPL), 125
Qualitative forecasts, 534
Quality capability analysis, 245
Quality function deployment, 100
Quality management, 141–176
    audits, 428–429
    awards, 162, 164–165
    common tools, 153–154
    continuous improvement,
        148–149
    cost of, 11, 155, 305
    defects, 144, 145, 150, 170–171, 545
    defined, 165–166
    design of experiments, 70, 154,
        244, 245
    DMAIC, 150–152
    evolution of, 143–144
    inspection, 25, 127, 168–172, 408
    involvement with supply
        management, 54–55
    ISO, 134, 152, 163–164
    kaizen, 145, 148
    loss to society, 155–156
    management approaches to,
        146–147
    outsourcing and, 228
    philosophy of, 144–146
    process capability analysis, 156–159
    six sigma, 149–152
    standards, 134, 152, 162–164
    statistical process control,
        159–162, 478
    supplier certification, 70, 172–174
    of suppliers, 166–168
    supply management and, 10
    TQM, 147–148, 308
Quality Management System, 152
Quantity discounts, 350, 490
Quick ratio, 268
Quotation, request for, 23

**R**

R. Gene Richter Awards for Leadership
    and Innovation, 577–580
R chart, 160–161
Rail carriers, 506
Random variations, 156
Rebuys, 23n
Receiving reports, 27
Recess, during negotiation, 383
Reciprocity, 55, 259, 444
Regulated pricing, 330
Rejection, rights of, 408–409
Relationship management, 33
Request for proposals (RFP), 186,
    200, 250
Request for quotation (RFQ), 23
Requirements, 21, 90–91
Requisition, 21, 23
Research, 130
Responsibilities, classification of, 33
Restraint of trade, 414
Retail sector, 314
Return on assets, 270
Return on equity, 270
Return on investment (ROI), 13, 14,
    56, 57
Reverse auctions, 62, 78, 249, 331,
    396, 563
Rewards, for good performance, 428
Rework, 336
Rights of rejection, 408–409
Risk, technology, 229–230
Risk appraisal, 356–357
Risk costs, 12, 306–307
Risk of loss, 409
Robinson-Patman Act, 414
Rockwell Collins, 578
ROI, 13, 14, 56, 57
Role conflict, 41
Rolls-Royce, 580–583
Rotary International, 454
Royal KPN, 579–580
RPS, 507
Run plots, 154

**S**

Salaries, 6
Sales, increase in, 10
Samples, 124–125, 449
Scatter diagrams, 154
Scheduling, 463–466
Scorecard, balanced, 427
Scott Paper, 317–320
Scrap disposal, 12

Seasonal discounts, 350
Secrecy, of design, 229
Securities Exchange Act, 416
Selling costs, 341
Semi-variable costs, 326
Service capability analysis, 246
Service level agreement, 234
Service providers, 9, 313
Services, procurement of, 194–213
    construction, 207–211
    contract administration, 207
    contract extension, 206
    contractor selection, 201–204
    costs, 202
    importance of, 195
    Internet, 207
    operating services, 206
    outsourcing of, 7, 8, 195
    pricing, 204
    process, 25
    professional services, 205
    statement of work, 23, 25, 196–201
    technical services, 205–206
    transportation, 511–512
70/30 approach, 255
Sharp practices, 447–448
Shipper's letter of instruction, 510
Shipping terms, 508–509
Shortages, 3, 53
Should-cost models, 334
Simple specifications, 122–125
Simplification, 90, 108, 135–136
Simulation, 104, 153
Single sourcing, 254–255
Six sigma, 149–152
Slushy time fence, 535
Small-orders, 26
Small-volume requirements, 230–231
Social responsibility, 443, 454–455,
    564–565
Society of Automotive Engineers, 133
Society of Mechanical Engineers, 133
Solectron, 255
Solicitation, 250; *see also* Bidding
Sourcing, 240–272; *see also* Suppliers
    for capital equipment, 186
    early supplier involvement; *see* Early
        supplier involvement (ESI)
    ethics, 259
    evaluating potential suppliers,
        244–247
    green, 258
    group buying, 259–260
    internationally, 256–257, 276

    locally, 256–257
    manufacturer versus distributor,
        257–258
    minority/women-owned businesses,
        258, 564
    multiple, 232, 254–255
    nationally, 256–257
    single versus multiple, 254–255
    strategic, 7, 241, 559–560
Southern California Edison, 45
Spare parts, 184
SPC, 159–162
Specialization, 8, 35
Specifications, 118–140
    brand or trade name, 123–124
    categories of, 121–128
    commercial standards, 126
    complex, 125–128
    conformance to, 155
    design, 51, 126–127
    development of, 128–132
    engineering drawings, 127
    for equipment purchasing, 184–186
    function and fit, 123
    market grades, 125
    material and method-of-manufacture,
        127–128
    performance, 98, 122–123,
        184, 479
    problems with, 130–132
    purpose of, 120–121
    samples, 124–125, 449
    simple, 122–125
    simplification, 90, 108, 135–136
    standardization, 90, 119,
        132–138, 565
Spin City, 102
Sponsorship, of teams, 42
Staffing, 565–568
Staggers Rail Act, 514
Standard industrial classification
    system, 261
Standardization, 90, 119, 132–138, 565;
    *see also* Specifications
Standards
    commercial, 126
    company, 133
    for ethics, 440–447, 452
    industry, 133
    international, 133
    for quality, 134, 152, 162–164
    team development of, 137
    types and sources of, 133–134
Statement of objectives, 101

Statement of work (SOW), 23, 25,
    196–201
Statistical process control (SPC),
    159–162, 478
Stockless purchasing, 28
Stores, centralized, 26
Strategic demand management, 530–536
Strategic network, 17
Strategic outsourcing, 235
Strategic planning, 33, 555–568
Strategic responsibilities/activities,
    33–34
Strategic sourcing, 7, 241, 559–560
Strategic supply chain management,
    529–530
Stress testing, 104
Structured multilevel bill of
    materials, 23
Subcontracting, 333
Subsidiaries, 280–281
Substandard materials and services, 449
Suitability, 101
Sun Microsystems, 252, 254, 537
Supplier delivery system, 29
Supplier equality, 78
Supplier feedback, 564
Supplier managed inventory, 499
Supplier relationship management, 374
Supplier samples, 124–125, 449
Supplier scheduler, 474–475
Supplier stores, 29
Supplier surveys, 244, 263–268,
    581–582
Suppliers
    alliances with, 63–64, 65, 70–76,
        84–87, 334
    capacity, 255–256
    certification of, 70, 172–174
    collaborating with, 429–430
    colocation with, 72, 114
    cost to change, 68
    development/management of, 172,
        252–253
    direct, 282–286
    early involvement with; *see* Early
        supplier involvement (ESI)
    evaluating potential, 244–247
    financial analysis of, 245, 268–270
    locating, 241–244
    minority/women-owned, 258, 564
    monitoring progress, 421–424
    performance evaluation, 424–427, 520
    preferred, 73
    quality analysis, 166–168

questionnaires for, 436
reduction in number, 253–254
selection of, 23–24, 122–123,
      201–204, 242, 247–252
as a source of cost data, 334
specialized knowledge, 230
visits to, 245, 263–268, 270–272, 286
Supply base reduction, 253–254
Supply chain evolution map, 547
Supply chain management
    defined, 13–15
    evolution to, 529–530
    implementing, 17, 18
    key to, 528–529
    stages of, 529–530
    traditional approach, 16
Supply Chain Pollution Avoidance
      (SCPA), 455
Supply channels, 279–281
Supply management; *see also*
      Purchasing
    careers in, 5–6
    classification of responsibilities, 33
    evaluation of, 17
    external environment, 60–61
    in government, 60
    impact of, 2–3, 9–12, 32
    mechanics of, 21–29
    monitoring changes in supply, 60–61
    in nonmanufacturing, 59
    outsourcing of, 229
    placement with organization, 32
    progression to supply chain
        management, 13–17, 18
    relationship with other departments,
        51–59
    ROI, 13, 14, 56, 57
    role of professionals, 17–18
    stages of, 2, 6–7
Supply management research, 130
Supply networks, 15–16, 308–309, 315
Supply system review, 428–429
Surveys, suppliers, 244, 263–268,
      581–582
Sustainability, 443; *see also*
      Environment
Switching costs, 75
Systems contracting, 28

**T**

Target cost, 101, 338–341, 343, 362–363
Target profit, 362–363
Tariffs, 305, 514, 517
Tax Reform Act of 1986, 190

Taxes, 189–190, 305
Teams
    for capital equipment, 179–181
    cross functional, 37–38, 97, 129–130
    for development of standards, 137
    incentives for, 42
    interfirm, 46
    leadership of, 43–44, 47
    for negotiation, 41, 187, 376–377
    product development, 39–47, 561–564
    project, 113
    role conflict, 41
    skills needed, 44–45
    for transportation purchasing, 516
Technical analysis, 285–286
Technical inspection, 169–170
Technical risk, 356–357
Technical services, procurement of,
      205–206
Technology risk, 229–230
Terms and conditions, 24
Testing, 106, 166–167
Time and materials contracts, 367
Time-based competition, 10, 224
Time fences, 535–536
Time phasing, 469
Time to market, 70
Timex, 56
Title, to goods, 409
Tolerance stacking, 156
Tolerances, 131–132
Tooling costs, 337
Toshiba, 229
Total cost of ownership
    acquisition costs and, 11, 184,
        186–187, 304–306, 487–488
    components of, 304–310
    implementation example, 317–320
    importance of, 312–315
    net present value analysis, 310–312
    ownership costs, 306–309
    post-ownership costs, 309–310
    reducing, 11–12
Total production costs, 327
Total quality management (TQM),
      147–148, 308
Toyota, 15, 148, 149, 165
Tracing of shipments, 519
Trade agreements, 305
Trade discounts, 349–350
Trade names, 123–124
Trade shows, 243
Trading companies, 280
Trading Process Network (TPN), 28

Training
    ethics, 452–453
    for teams, 45
    transformational, 428, 554–555
Transactional negotiation techniques,
      386–388
Transactional relationships, 66–68
Transformational training, 428,
      554–555
Transportation, 502–526
    benefits of controlling, 504
    carrier classifications, 507–508
    carrier evaluation and selection,
        504–506
    contracts, 511–512, 517–518
    deregulation, 514
    documentation, 509–510
    expediting, 33, 519
    freight bill auditing, 519–520
    freight forwarders, 282, 511
    freight rates, 510–511
    freight terms, 508–509
    glossary of terms, 521–524
    of hazardous materials, 507
    impact of, 504
    legal issues, 512, 514
    modes of, 506–507
    outsourcing, 511, 517
    steps in controlling, 516–520
    tariffs, 305, 514, 517
Transportation Industry Regulatory
      Reform Act, 514
Transportation savings, 35
Truckload (TL), 506
Trust, 70, 73, 81–84
TRW, 548–549
Turnover, of inventory, 269
Two-bin system, 498
Two-step bidding, 249–250

**U**

Uncertainty, 354–356
Undifferentiated products, 325
Uniform Commercial Code (UCC), 199,
      402–404, 418; *see also* Legal issues
Uniform Computer Information
      Transactions Act, 403
Uniform Freight Classification, 514
Uniform Sales Act, 405
Unit curve, 337–338, 348–349
United Technologies, 38, 154
UPS, 507
Use tests, 167
Used equipment, 181–184

**V**

Value analysis/engineering, 68,
  106–110, 565
Value chain, 2, 13, 15–16
Value network management, 543–583
  leadership, 546–554
  new product development, 561–564
  organization and staffing, 565–568
  overview of, 543–544
  quality, 560–561
  R. Gene Richter Award, 577–580
  Rolls-Royce example, 580–583
  social responsibility, 564–565
  standardization, 565
  strategic planning, 555–568
  technology, 561
  transformational training, 554–555
  value proposition, 544–545

Variable manufacturing
  costs, 326
Variable-margin pricing,
  324–325
Variations, 156, 159
Verbal contracts, 407–408
Vertical integration, 220
Virtual corporation, 17, 220
Virtual integration, 429
Vision statements, 544, 558
Volume discounts, 34

**W**

Wal-Mart, 15
Warehousing, 537
Warranties, 409–410
Warranty costs, 12, 309
Waste, elimination of, 149

Water carriers, 506
Weighted-average cost of capital
  (WACC), 310n
Weighted-factor analysis, 250–251
Weighted point plan, 425–426
Weyerhaeuser, 407
Win-win negotiation, 394
Women-owned businesses, 258, 564
Workforce stability, 231–232
Working capital, 268
World Trade Organization, 293

**X**

X chart, 160–161
Xerox, 253

**Z**

Zero defects, 145